Dubrovnik (Ragusa)
A Classic City-state

Dubrovnik (Ragusa)
A Classic City-state

FRANCIS W. CARTER

*Department of Geography, University
College, and School of Slavonic
and East European Studies,
London, England*

1972

SEMINAR PRESS · London and New York

SEMINAR PRESS LTD.
24/28 Oval Road
London NW1

U.S. Edition published by
SEMINAR PRESS INC.
111 Fifth Avenue
New York, New York 10003
Copyright © 1972 By SEMINAR PRESS LTD.

Library of Congress Catalog Card Number: 78–183463
ISBN: 0–12–812950–6

Printed in Great Britain by
Willmer Brothers Limited, Birkenhead

To my parents

Svuda ga jes puna slava, svud on slove
hrvatskih ter kruna gradov se svih zove.

(Because it is known and praised everywhere
it is called the crown of all Croatian cities.)

IVAN VIDALI (fl. 1564)

Preface

Suggestions made by the Report of the Sub-Committee on Oriental, Slavonic, East European and African Studies of the University Grants Committee, (H.M.S.O. London, 1961) recommended that new centres of 'area studies' should be established. The idea was to 'bring together teachers and research students from different disciplines to specialize in studies related to the same area or region', and 'it is in the history, geography, law, economics and other social science departments and faculties that the new developments should take place'. It is with this idea in mind that the following chapters have been written.

The history of geographical research and writing in the lands comprising present-day Yugoslavia really began in the second-half of the nineteenth century when Petar Matković became Professor of Geography at Zagreb University. Matković, a student of Karl Ritter, specialized in historical geography and contributed to a better understanding of early developments along Balkan trade routes. My own interest in the historical geography of Dalmatia was first aroused as a student member of the Sheffield University excursion to Hvar Island in the summer of 1960, largely resulting from the enthusiasm imparted to us for this part of Europe by Professor Alice Garnett. This short sojourn was enough to stimulate further enquiry, which has lasted over the past decade. Following numerous visits to Yugoslavia, coupled with research in state libraries, archives and museums, I gradually focussed my attention on Dubrovnik and the former importance of its republic. I was attracted by the individualism, independence and character of this small republic which managed to survive through six centuries of European history. Its personality is best summed up by the motto over the main gate of Lovrjenac tower: *Non Bene Pro Toto Libertas Venditur Auro* – Freedom cannot be measured in gold.

This book is an attempt to present English readers with a concise account of the Dubrovnik Republic as an episode in the development of the Balkan lands. Yet it is impossible to understand the great problems it faced without some knowledge of Balkan history. The mutual jealousies of Bulgarian, Croatian and Serb, the struggle of various races for supremacy in Macedonia, the alternate friendship and enmity of the Russian and the Turk are all facts, which have their root deep down in the past annals of the Balkan Peninsula. It should not be forgotten that there was a time when the Serbian and Bulgarian Empires were great powers and their respective rulers, with the proud title 'Tsar', governed a vast realm, still remembered by ardent patriots. Even today many problems in south-eastern Europe still await solution, and are once more pressing themselves upon the attention of thoughtful men. Thus in the narrative the emphasis has been placed on those aspects of the past which it is hoped contribute to a better understanding of the present.

Although in size and wealth Dubrovnik was far inferior to the city republics of Italy, her close proximity to a world of barbarism and the vastly important events in which she played a part, make the republic a place worthy of further investigation. The book may be divided into three parts. First, some discussion is made of Dubrovnik's geographical situation and general development up to the present-day. The early history is reviewed and some attempt is made to analyse Dubrovnik's trading organization including information on trade routes, trading colonies and transport costs. The second part, Chapters 5-7, deals with the small republic during the later Middle Ages. Political relations influenced her commerce, particularly the Ottoman occupation of the Balkan peninsula, her friendship with the Turks, and persistent commercial rivalry with the Venetian Republic. Some attempt is then made to discern the main commodities in Dubrovnik's commerce and the distribution patterns of their origin and destination. The final section follows the fortunes of Dubrovnik after 1500. Again political effects on commerce are studied, especially her neutrality during several European wars. Likewise changes in the type of commodities traded and their distribution patterns are again reviewed leading up to the reasons for the decline in her commercial importance. The fall of the Ottoman Empire, shrinking markets in the Levant, Bulgaria and Serbia, meant greater concentration on local areas, but even these were uncertain. Even so the cultural life of the republic continued to flourish in architecture, painting and literature, but the occupation of 1806 by French forces led to the final disintegration of this small political unit.

Inevitably a book of this size has its imperfections, but I should greatly appreciate receiving further source material and items qualifying for inclusion in the text, for future reference.

June, 1972   F. W. Carter

Acknowledgements

I should like to acknowledge the receipt of a Yugoslav Government Scholarship organized through the British Council which allowed me to spend a year at Zagreb University, and a University of London Central Research Fund Grant which enabled me to analyse some of my data.

Further I wish to express my gratitude for the valuable help of all my colleagues in south-east Europe and this country, who advised me in the preparation of this book, some of whom should be mentioned specifically. In Yugoslavia, I am particularly indebted to Dr Zdravko Šundrica of the State Archives in Dubrovnik, whose help was essential during the collection of material, and who made several valuable suggestions on the history and organization of the Dubrovnik Republic; Professor J. C. Roglić and Dr V. Rogić from the department of Geography at Zagreb University, whose precious time I took up during the early stages of this work, and Dr S. Traljić, from the Historical Institute at Zadar for his advice on documentary material. In this country help was particularly forthcoming from Professor M. J. Wise, Dr A. Lambert, Dr F. E. I. Hamilton and Mr D. J. Sinclair all of the Department of Geography at London School of Economics, and is greatly appreciated.

The preparation of a manuscript for the press is a labour which often threatens to deprive an author of any pleasure which he may have had in writing the book. I have been fortunate in having the services of a most helpful and patient team of people; these include members of the Cartographic Unit at University College London, especially Mr Alick Newman, for the skilful preparation of the maps, Mrs Sheila Newland who typed the manuscript and Mrs Jane Duncan of Seminar Press for her patience and skilled guidance in seeing the book through the press. To all those who have helped to make this book possible I offer my grateful thanks.

June, 1972   F. W. Carter

Contents

3
Under Venetian Rule 1204–1358   84

4
The Trading Organization of the Dubrovnik Republic   135

List of Illustrations

Figure   page

Figure   **page**

Figure   page

Note on Pronunciation and Geographical Names

The majority of literature referred to in this book has been written in the Slavonic group of the Indo-European languages. The oldest of these languages were written in the Cyrillic script, and many (Russian, Bulgarian, Ukrainian, Serbian, Macedonian) are still. For the purposes of this text, however, they have been transliterated into the Latin script, as in modern Czech, Polish, Slovene and Croatian. In the spelling of Slavonic names I have adopted the Serbo-Croatian orthography as being the most convenient and the most accurate. The vowels are a, e, i, o, u and r, the first five being like father, fate, feet, fog and food, the sixth rather like the 'r' in such a word as 'myrtle' when the first syllable of this is pronounced in a purring way with light trilling of the 'r'. The consonants roughly correspond to those of English, except that:

c = ts in 'bits'. Thus Cavtat is pronounced Tsavtat.
č = ch in 'which'. Thus Bačka is pronounced Bachka.
ć is almost identical to the above, but is used only at the end of a word when preceded by an 'i'. Thus Roglić is pronounced Roglich.
g is always pronounced hard, as in 'gig'.
h is like the German 'ch' in 'Buch'.
j = y in 'yet'. Thus Jajce is pronounced Yaytse. When at the end of a word and preceded by the letters 'l' or 'n' it softens them into something like the French 'l' in 'mouillé' and the French 'gne' in 'signe'. Thus Sandalj and Sinj.
s = s in 'since' (never like 's' in 'nose').
š = sh in 'shave'. Thus Dušan is pronounced Dushan.
z = z in 'blaze'.
ž is like the French 'j' in 'jour'.

Some of the other Slavonic accents and diacritical marks involved in this transliteration are explained below; in addition the pronunciation of the special characteristics in Rumanian (a Romance language) and Hungarian, a language belonging to an entirely different family (Finno-Ugrian), are also noted.

Czech	Polish	Rumanian	Hungarian	English equivalent
c	c	ț	c	ts
t'	ć	—	—	tsh
č	cz	ce, ci	cs	tch
ch	h, ch	h	—	'ch' in 'loch' (translit. 'kh')
d'	dź, dzi	—	gy	'd' in 'dew'
j	j	i, ii, ie	j, ly	'y' in 'yet'
k	k	ca, co, cu, ch	k	'c' in 'cat'
ň	ń	—	ny	'n' in 'new'
ř	rz	—	—	simultaneous 'r' + French 'je'
s	s	s	sz	s
š	ś, sz	ş	s	sh
v	w	v	v	v
ž	ž, ź	j	zs	's' in 'pleasure'
('u' translit. from Bulgarian)		ă	ö	'er' in 'bigger' phonetic 'a'
ě	je	ie	je	ye
—	ą	—	—	French 'on'
—	ę	—	—	French 'in' in 'vin'
(translit. 'y' from Russian)		î	—	nearest equiv. is the 'i' in 'ill'
—	—	—	ö	'or' in 'word'
—	—	—	ü	cf. German ü

Many places in the Balkans are called by three or even four different names, as to whether the speaker is more familiar with Italian, Serbo-Croatian, Greek, Turkish or Albanian. Since it is often difficult to determine which one is best known internationally, I have adopted, where possible, the name under which the place is known at present in that country. In Serbo-Croat, but not in Macedonian or Slovene, the stress usually falls on the antepenultimate syllable. Words are, therefore, divided, as far as possible, in open syllables, i.e. ending in a vowel and beginning with a consonant; if a syllable ends closed, the tendency is still to begin it with a consonant. Some examples are as follows:

ORIGINAL	PRONUNCIATION	ORIGINAL	PRONUNCIATION
A		**J**	
Aleksinac	Al-ek-si-nats	Jablanica	Yab-la-ni-tsa
B		Jajce	Yay-tse
Banja Luka	Ban-ya Lu-ka	**K**	
Beograd	Be-og-rad	Karlovac	Kar-lo-vats
Bihác	Bi-hach	Kaštela	Kash-te-la
Biokovo	Bi-ok-o-vo	Kopaonik	Kop-a-on-ik
Bojana	Boy-a-na	Korčula	Kor-chu-la
C		Kosovo polje	Kos-o-vo pol-ye
Celje	Tsel-ye	Kosovska	Kos-ov-ska Mi-
Cetina	Tset-i-na	Mitrovica	tro-vi-tsa
Cetinje	Tset-in-ye	Kraljevo	Kral-yc-vo
Cincer	Tsin-tser	Kruševac	Kru-she-vats
Crna Gora	Tsŭr-na Gor-a	Kumanovo	Ku-ma-no-vo
Ć		**L**	
Ćićarija	Chi-cha-ri-ya	Lastovo	Las-to-vo
Č		Leskovac	Les-ko-vats
Čačak	Chach-ak	Ljubišnja	Lyu-bish-nya
Čiovo	Chi-ov-o	Lošinj	Losh-inj
D		Lovćen	Lov-chen
Dedinje	Ded-in-ye	**M**	
Donji grad	Don-yi grad	Mačva	Mach-va
Dubrovnik	Du-brov-nik	Makedonija	Mak-ed-on-i-ya
Đ		Metohija	Me-to-hi-ya
Đakovica	Dyak-o-vi-tsa	Mljet	Mŭl-yet
F		Morača	Mor-a-cha
Fruška Gora	Frush-ka Gor-a	Morava	Mor-a-va
G		**N**	
Gacka	Gats-ka	Neretva	Ne-ret-va
Glamoč	Glam-och	Nikšić	Nik-shich
Gorica	Gor-i-tsa	Niš	Nish
Gornjigrad	Gorn-yi grad	**O**	
H		Omiš	Om-ish
Hercegovina	Herts-eg-ov-i-na	Opatija	Op-at-i-ya
Hrvatska	Hŭr-vat-ska	**P**	
I		Peć	Pech
Idrija	I-dri-ya	Plačkovica	Plach-ko-vi-tsa
Ilijiaš	I-li-yash	Ploče	Ploch-e
		Podgorica	Pod-gor-i-tsa

Popovo polje	Pop-o-vo pol-ye	Šibenik	Shib-en-ik
Primorje	Pri-mor-ye	Šumadija	Shu-ma-di-ya
Priština	Prish-ti-na		
Ptuj	Pŭt-uy	**T**	
		Titograd	Ti-to-grad
R		Trebišnjica	Treb-ish-nyi-tsa
Raša	Rash-a	Trepča	Trep-cha
Raška	Rash-ka	Trogir	Trog-ir
Rijeka	Ri-ye-ka		
Rodopi	Rod-op-i	**V**	
		Valjevo	Val-ye-vo
S		Velebit	Vel-e-bit
Sarajevo	Sa-ra-ye-vo	Vršac	Vˇr-shats
Senovo	Sen-o-vo		
Skopje	Skop-ye	**Z**	
Smederevo	Smed-e-re-vo	Zadar	Zad-ar
Soča	Soch-a	Zagorje	Zag-or-ye (Slovenia)
Srbija	Sŭr-bi-ya		Zag-or-ye (Croatia)
Sremska	Srem-ska Mi-tro-vi-tsa	Zagreb	Zag-reb
Mitrovica		Zenica	Ze-ni-tsa
Strumica	Stru-mi-tsa	Zeta	Ze-ta
Sušak	Su-shak	**Ž**	
		Železnik	Zhel-ez-nik
Š			
Šar Planina	Shar Plan-i-na		

There follows a list of some principal geographical names occurring in this study, with their foreign equivalents,

PLACE	SERBO-CROATIAN	ITALIAN	TURKISH
Bar	*ibid.*	Antivari	Bar
Beograd (Belgrade)	Beograd	Belgrado	Belgrād
Bosna (Bosnia)	Bosna		Bōsna
Buda (Germ.: Ofen)	Budim		Büdūn
Dubrovnik	*ibid.*	Ragusa	Dubrovnīk or Dūbravnīk
Durrës	Drač	Durazzo	Drāç
Edirne (Adrianople)	Drinopolje		Edirne
Évvoia (Euboia)			Aġrībūz
Fársala			Cotlūca
Gabela	Gabela, or Neretva		Ġ.b.la or Ġ.bāla or Neretva
Hercegnovi	*ibid.*	Castel Nuovo	Nōva
Hercegovina	*ibid.*		Hersek
Klis	*ibid.*	Clissa	Klīs

Kotor	*ibid.*	Cattaro	
Lárisa			Yeñişehir
Lesh	Leš	Alessio	Leş
Návpaktos		Lepanto	İnebahti
Neretva (river)		Narenta	
Sarajevo	*ibid.*		Serāy
Shkodra	Skadar	Scutari	İskenderīye
			Üskūb (pron.: Üsküp)
Smederevo	*ibid.*	Semendria	Semendere
Ston	*ibid.*	Stagno	
Tríkkala			Terhala
Ulcinj	*ibid.*	Dulcigno	Ūlkūn (pron.: Ülkün)
Velestínon			Velesīn
Volos			Ġulūs or Ġülūz
Vlora		Valona	Avlōnya
Zadar	*ibid.*	Zara	Zādra

1
Introduction

Dubrovnik, formerly Ragusa, is situated on the southern coast of present-day Yugoslavia. It is mainly dependent on tourism for its existence and is somewhat isolated from the rest of the country, yet during the Middle Ages the town, with its small republic, grew and developed mainly through her function as a trade and political mediator between the underdeveloped regions of the Balkans and Levant, and the more developed regions of western Europe. Relying on the profits made from her entrepôt trade and the shrewdness of her diplomats in preserving a neutral policy during wartime, Dubrovnik managed to prosper making the best of 'purely local trade and the most profitable part of distant or international commerce'.[1]

Today the 'commune' of Dubrovnik is an administrative and territorial unit belonging to the district of Split (Dalmatia) which in turn is part of the Socialist Republic of Croatia. The commune occupies an area of 978·6 km², and lies between the Neretva River in the north and the entrance to the Bay of Kotor in the south, and includes the Pelješac peninsula and a group of offshore islands. These from north to south are, Mljet (106 km²), Šipan (16·5 km²), Lopud (4·4 km²), Koločep (2·3 km²) and the smallest one, Lokrum (0·72 km²) near the entrance to the old city. The city of Dubrovnik had 22,961 inhabitants at the time of the last official census (1961) of which about 6,000 lived within the old walled city, whilst the others were concentrated in the modern suburbs of Ploče in the south, Pile, Kono, Gruž (Dubrovnik's port) and the Lapad peninsula in the north. Total population for the whole commune was 53,597 in 1961.

The Physical Background to Southern Dalmatia

The southern coast of Dalmatia differs in two major respects from that immediately to the north. First, except for the chain of small

B

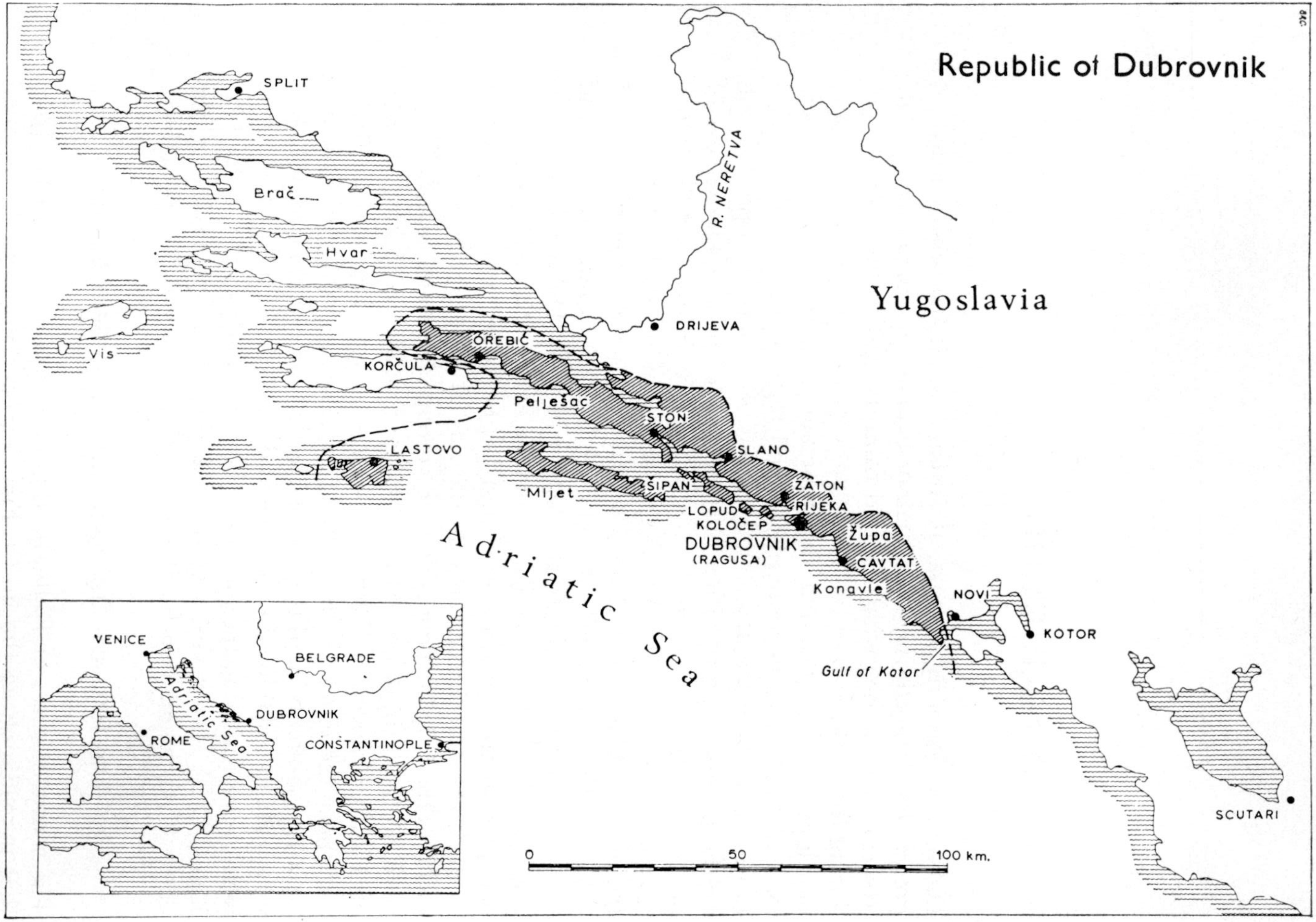
Republic of Dubrovnik
Yugoslavia
SPLIT
Brač
Hvar
Vis
R. NERETVA
DRIJEVA
OREBIĆ
KORČULA
Pelješac
STON
LASTOVO
SLANO
Mljet
ŠIPAN
ZATON
LOPUD
RIJEKA
KOLOČEP
DUBROVNIK
(RAGUSA)
Župa
CAVTAT
Konavle
Adriatic Sea
NOVI
KOTOR
Gulf of Kotor
SCUTARI
0
50
100 km.
VENICE
BELGRADE
Adriatic Sea
DUBROVNIK
ROME
CONSTANTINOPLE

FIG 1

islets and islands extending through Šipan, Lopud and Količep and terminating off Dubrovnik, there are no islands offshore in this region. South of the chain of small islets, the coast descends sharply to the deep central Adriatic basin, off which there are no islands. Secondly, although the general direction of the coast is from north-west to south-east, the coast in this region, rather more than in other sections of the littoral to the north, is embayed into some impressive inlets. The most pronounced and spectacular of these is the great cliff-bounded and landlocked inlet of Kotor which is one of the most outstanding landforms of the Adriatic basin. Almost everywhere the coastal relief is bold. From Ston, as far south as the Kotor inlet the shore line is backed immediately by the moderately elevated plateaux of the southern karst of Montenegro. Throughout this southern coastal region, the geological characteristics are somewhat complex, but in general three different geological zones are developed along this littoral, though not all three types are necessarily everywhere present.

i. The outermost zone consists of a very narrow belt of Cretaceous limestones which usually forms a moderately sharp coast range.

ii. Inland this is succeeded by a parallel narrow zone of Tertiary Flysch rocks, which are more easily dissected so that they either form a broad furrow parallel with the coast behind the coast range, and on which surface drainage may exist, or there is an embayment where they run out to the coast.

iii. Inland, again, there occur the massive Triassic and Jurassic limestones which form extremely bold mountain ranges and abrupt scarps overlooking the Flysch depressions.

North of Dubrovnik, the coastal Cretaceous limestone belt is separated from the mainland and partially submerged to form the chain of islands in front of the Količep Channel, tapering from the southern Pelješac peninsula to Dubrovnik. The mainland behind the islands is therefore composed of Tertiary rocks. From Dubrovnik to Bar, all three geological zones are present, grained one behind the other in the Dinaric direction (N.W.–S.E.). The coastal features are carved in the Cretaceous limestones and are backed by a longitudinal valley dissected along the Flysch beds, while the older limestones rise abruptly to the high plateaux behind the Flysch. The region is fairly well populated, with numerous villages situated especially on

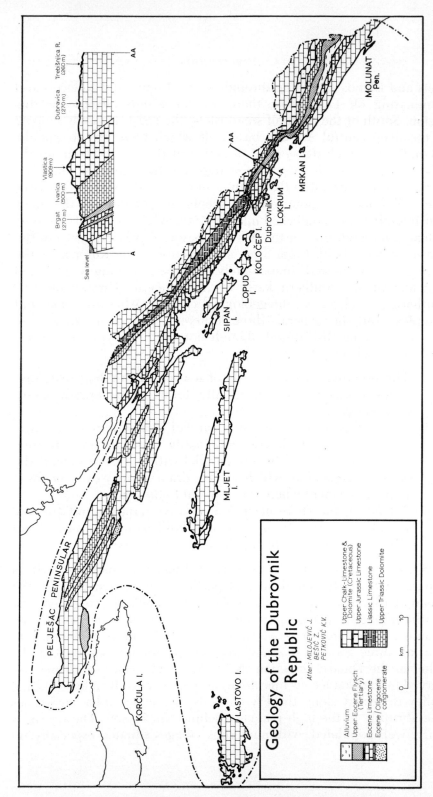

Geology of the Dubrovnik Republic

After: MILOJEVIĆ J.
BEŠIĆ Z.
PETKOVIĆ K.V.

Alluvium

Upper Eocene Flysch (Tertiary)

Eocene Limestone

Eocene/Oligocene conglomerate

Upper Chalk-Limestone & Dolomite (Cretaceous)

Upper Jurassic Limestone

Liassic Limestone

Upper Triassic Dolomite

0   km   10

PELJEŠAC PENINSULAR

KORČULA I.

LASTOVO I.

MLJET I.

ŠIPAN

LOPUD I.

KOLOČEP I.

Dubrovnik

LOKRUM I.

MRKAN I.

MOLUNAT Pen.

T.

A

AA

AA

Brgat (270 m)   Ivanica (500 m)   Vlastica (909 m)   Dubravica (270 m)   Trebišnjica R. (260 m)

Sea level

A

AA

Fig. 2.

the Flysch zone. There are, in addition, a number of small coastal settlements and small ports; outstanding among these is the city of Dubrovnik, with its modern port of Gruž. From the entrance of Ston Channel, southward to Dubrovnik the mainland coasts face Koločep Channel, which is comparatively narrow, though nowhere less than a mile in width, and is confined to the sea waters between the mainland coast and the chain of islands tapering southward from Pelješac. There are depths everywhere within it of 15–35 fm; it is easy to enter at all seasons, and its shores afford some of the best and most important anchorages in the Adriatic. East of Irbljava Point, the coast is embayed eastward as far as the inlet of Slano. The coast, generally, as far as the Ombla inlet (Rijeka Dubrovačke), is steep. North of Zaton inlet, it is cultivated, and in some places covered with a luxuriant vegetation, notably near the village of Trsteno. The land behind the coast rises to at least 300 m and in places to 600 m within a mile of the shore, and thence expands into the broad karst plateau, about 15·2 km wide, that separates Popovo Polje from the sea. The population of the coast is distributed among fairly numerous villages sited above the shore, while the coves below serve as small harbours for fishing boats. The two chief harbours of this section of the coast are associated, however, with the two short inlets which open towards the north-east, over a length of more than a mile, at Slano and Zaton respectively. Slano, the more northerly and the broader of the two inlets, is almost land-locked. It is better protected from the Bora than any other anchorage in the Koločep Channel with depths of 6–18 fm. The tiny village of Slano, at the head of the bay, is flanked by steeply-rising limestone hills culminating in the barren crests of Ogradenica (940 m) and Neprobić (970 m), but to the north-east of these the land rises to a pass only 300 m high, not 3 km from Slano and leading by easy gradients to Popovo Polje. Zaton inlet, 17 km to the south of Slano, has depths of 9–13 fm, but is much narrower than Slano Bay. The harbour lies on the west side of the inlet, which is not only less hilly, but also well cultivated, and bordered with houses. For nearly 3 km to the south of Zaton, the coast rises steeply in sterile hills, though there is excellent shelter offshore. At this point, the remarkably narrow inlet of Ombla enters the sea from the east over a length of roughly 5·5 km. This inlet is only 320 m wide at its seaward end, and though bordered on its more gentle lower slopes by houses, gardens and cultivation, it is overlooked on its northern side and at its head by limestone crests exceeding 600 m, less than a mile

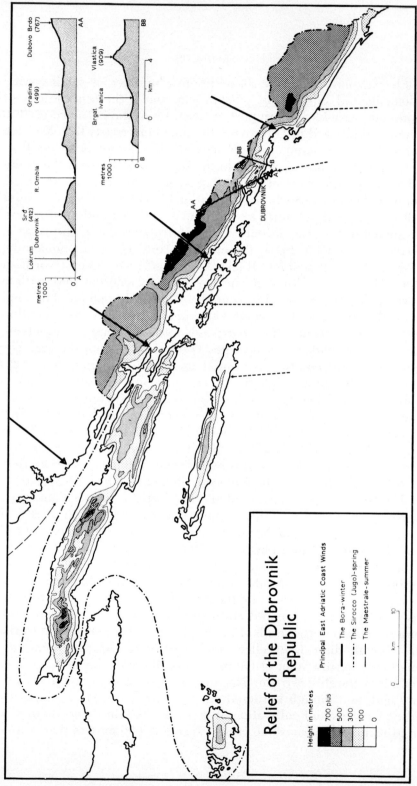

FIG. 3.

inland. The depths in this unusually narrow inlet vary from 17 fm to 4 fm; in fact, the inlet represents the valley of a river that has been drowned by the sea almost up to its source. The River Ombla rises in a spectacular manner. It gushes out of the mountain-side from underground caverns, less than a mile from the head of the inlet, as a clear, fully-grown river of great volume; this is the point of emergence of a considerably sized underground river which has collected a part of the underground drainage from Popovo Polje. Almost immediately this curious river enters the sea, at the head of the Ombla inlet. Unfortunately this inlet does not afford good anchorages because of the difficulties of navigating so narrow a passage.

To the south of the Ombla inlet, the land rises sharply to a small limestone upland exceeding 307 m, and sloping abruptly towards the sea. It is fronted, westward, first by the narrow, deep and very sheltered Gruž inlet, which trends at right angles to the Ombla, opening from south to north, and beyond this, by the low wooded promontory of Lapad and the dark, fir-covered slopes of Mount Retka (200 m), which finally descend to the sea in reddish-brown cliffs. Beside the inlet at Gruž and over the narrow isthmus south of this, the twin settlements of Dubrovnik and Gruž have developed.

South of Dubrovnik, as far as Pelegrin Point, coastal ranges of limestone hills rise abruptly, though not to very great altitudes. Between Pelegrin Point and Sustjepan Point, the shore-line recurves in the broad sweep of Župski Bay, and there the coastal limestone range is broken so that lowlands, coinciding with the Flysch rocks, run out to the sea on either side of the bay, forming a conspicuous broad plain, especially to the north, in the Postranje. The lowlands are well cultivated with vines and olive trees, and small streams drain their surfaces, in contrast to the adjacent sterile hills. The eastern side of Župski Bay is backed immediately by steep limestone hills rising to more than 523 m close to the sea. Amongst the many small towns and villages bordering the bay, Cavtat is the largest (pop. 871, 1961). It is situated on the most eastern of two small rocky promontories—Sv. Rok Point and Sustjepan Point—between which there is a small sheltered bay opening north-westward. This forms a natural harbour, but it can accommodate only a few small vessels. Good anchorage can be found for vessels in the eastern part of Župski Bay, either in a Bora or in south-easterly gales.

Over a distance of 29 km south-eastward of Cavtat, as far as the entrance to the Kotor inlet, the coast is immediately backed by a moderately elevated limestone range that is rugged and forbidding. Towards the south, the range exceeds an altitude of 300 m and even approaches 600 m close to the sea. These mountains are covered here and there with trees and thin brushwood. There is deep water near the coast and practically no shelter except in the small harbour of Molunat, off a small peninsula which projects from the coast, 9·6 km north of Oštri Point. Behind the forbidding coast range which is only 3 km wide, the land descends into a longitudinal valley not 61·5 m above sea level, trending parallel with the sea, as far as Hercegnovi. In the north, this depression is known as the Konavlje, and in the

FIG. 4.   Aerial view of Dubrovnik.

south as the Sutorina, and it continues the zone of Flysch rocks in Župski Bay. The vale is well cultivated, drained by surface streams, and behind the Konavle and Sutorina, the massive limestones rise inland as an abrupt scarp.

The Site and Situation of Dubrovnik

The site of Dubrovnik (42, 40 N., 18, 07 E.), is nearly on the same parallel of latitude as Barcelona (41, 25 N.) and Rome (41, 53 N.) and on the same meridian as Stockholm (18, 05 E.). The situation of the settlement is favourable both towards the sea and extensive hinterland and its geographical position is one of the keys to the city's success. It lies at the foot of Mount Srđ (412 m), a completely exposed limestone hill which rises steeply above Dubrovnik, and stretches beyond, towards the interior of Yugoslavia, the extensive, poor and karstic Dinaric mountains. It is therefore difficult to understand the site of Dubrovnik under contemporary conditions and one is tempted to ask what conditioned the founding, development and prosperity of the city during the Middle Ages. Much of this is answered in its subsequent history, but it is sufficient at present to grasp a thorough knowledge of its physical site and situation.[2]

The first point to notice is that Dubrovnik is situated in a straight valley trough below Mount Srđ, which was formed from the erosion of the weak resistant crumbly dolomite rock by water action. Secondly to the south-west of the dolomite valley there is a more elevated area of resistant limestone which has been formed into a small hill, or graben, called Lapad, together with a similar smaller formation on the westward side of Dubrovnik itself, which housed the original settlement. Thirdly, with the post-glacial rise of sea level, the lower parts of the dolomite valley were flooded and created the extensive Gruž Bay to the north, and Stari Porat in the south which in former times encircled the area of present-day Stradun, leaving the small limestone knoll of the city's original core isolated. It is difficult to confirm if this knoll, with its steep seaward cliffs (laus, from which Rausa, to Rausium the Roman name for Dubrovnik) was completely separated from the land, or whether the present day Stradun (palude) was a shallow stretch of swampy sandy deposits which was used as a routeway from the early settlement. Nevertheless it is safe to assume that this limestone hill, with both poor soil and water supplies, was not utilized for agricultural purposes. On the

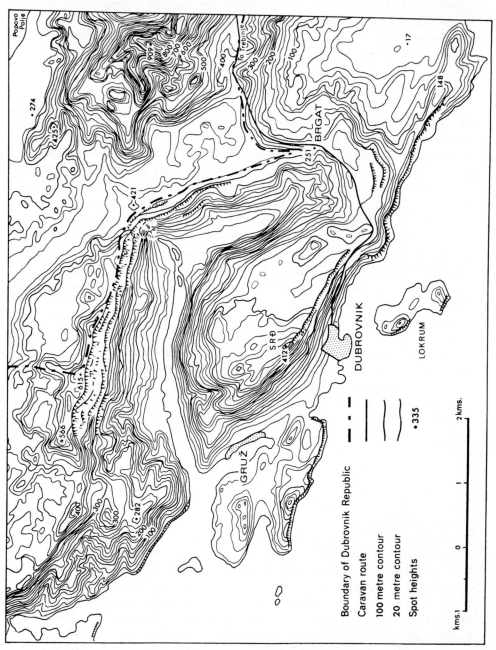

FIG. 5. Topographical position of Dubrovnik.

Popovo Polje

To Trebinje

BRGAT

SRĐ

DUBROVNIK

GRUŽ

LOKRUM

Boundary of Dubrovnik Republic

Caravan route

100 metre contour

20 metre contour

Spot heights   •335

0   1   2 kms.

kms.1

other hand the Dolomite valley, with deeper soil deposits, abundant water supply from wells and a rich vegetation cover was satisfactory for settlement, and was probably the main reason for enticing the early Slavic settlers. The area dividing the fortified Rausium/ Ragusium and the Slavic suburb of Dubrovnik was filled in and became Stradun, which connected the 'Platea' or 'Campus' containing the medieval wells, and has, since the eleventh century, become the main centre of the two unified settlements.

Tectonically, there is need to stress the importance of earthquakes, which have been frequently felt in Dubrovnik. The Greek writer, Pliny, referred to the problem of earthquakes in this area, but Dubrovnik first felt the full impact of such an occurrence in 1520. Such a calamity, the harbinger of worse visitations to come, befell the city on May 17, 1520. On that day an earthquake damaged many houses, the cathedral and several other public buildings, so that 100,000 zecchini covered only the cost of damage within the walls and 50,000 that in the remaining territory of the republic. (In the later days of the Venetian Republic the sequin, zecchino, or gold ducat was worth 47½p., and the silver ducat 18p. in English money.) For the next twenty months shocks continued to be felt, and recent work by Mihailović has distinguished fourteen separate periods of seismic activity in this area between 1430 and 1640.[3] It was, however, the catastrophy of 1667 which destroyed the main part of the city and killed two thirds of the population, that drew attention to the town and evoked sympathy throughout much of Europe at that time. Early on the morning of April 6, 1667, without any warning, an earthquake shock flattened most of the public buildings and many private houses. Afterwards the town caught fire and hordes of plunderers from the surrounding countryside, and possibly the city itself began to rifle and carry off anything they could find of value, including many church treasures. Order was at length restored by the presence of mind of some of the leading citizens and aid was forthcoming from several Italian and other European states for the rebuilding of the city. Various schemes were proposed for moving the city to a safer place (reminiscent of the more recent Skopje disaster), but the majority of the people were not to be persuaded to abandon the ancient centre, and Dubrovnik still stands on its original site. It is significant that as a result of this tragedy, Dubrovnik took several years to regain some of its former importance.

The two bays at either end of the town were also important for

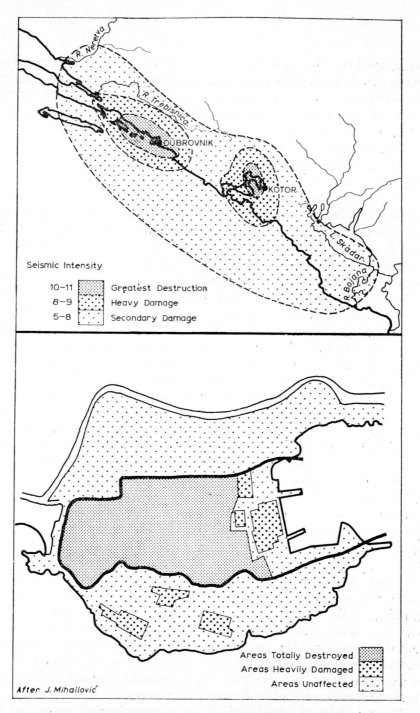

FIG. 6.   Upper: earthquake intensity in the south-east Adriatic, April 1667. Lower: limits of earthquake destruction in Dubrovnik, April 1667.

commercial growth. Stari Porat became the city's main harbour, and enabled boats to come right into the heart of the city. Unfortunately with the growth of ships' tonnage some of the more modern vessels could not be accommodated, so that an alternative, larger harbour was built in Gruž Bay. Therefore from the second half of the nineteenth century Gruž became the main port of Dubrovnik, with its large passenger and freight steamships, so that the small village of Gruž gradually grew into a suburb of the main city. During the first half of the twentieth century a new residential quarter was built between Gruž and Dubrovnik, and more recently with the development of tourism, new settlements have appeared over much of the Lapad peninsula, on the higher slopes of Mount Srđ, and outside the walls to the south at Župa.

Climate

The Mediterranean coastlands and islands of the east Adriatic are regions which experience a 'Mediterranean' climate; their climate is conspicuous for its mild winters and long, very hot summers, and for the sharp seasonal distribution of rainfall, associated with very dry summers and rainy winters. A special characteristic of this area is the particular stormy and rainy weather in autumn, dominated by the effects of such contrasting local winds as the Bora and the Scirocco. These bring alternating shorter or longer spells of bitingly cold winds, and of warm 'muggy' days, with low cloud and driving rain. Although so many days in winter may be rainy and overcast, the season as a whole is, nevertheless, notable for its long hours of sunshine and periods of bright, clear skies when visibility is at times extremely marked. Two to six days of unsettled weather, with rain and cloud and strong winds, may be taken as an average for autumn and winter. The mean temperatures for these seasons conceal the important fact that periods of cold weather, with temperatures falling even below freezing point or at least far below the mean, may persist either with, or without, strong winds perhaps for more than three weeks. In summer, weather remains continually sunny and rainless, often with long spells of light winds or of calm. Proximity to the sea brings a high atmospheric humidity, and as a result the seasonal and diurnal range of temperature is less here than over any other part of Yugoslavia. Where the coastal mountains rise abruptly from the sea, the boundary of the Mediterranean climatic region is sharply defined, and lies very near to the coast itself.

With this general synoptic situation in mind[4] it is now possible to examine more closely the local climate of Dubrovnik. The mean

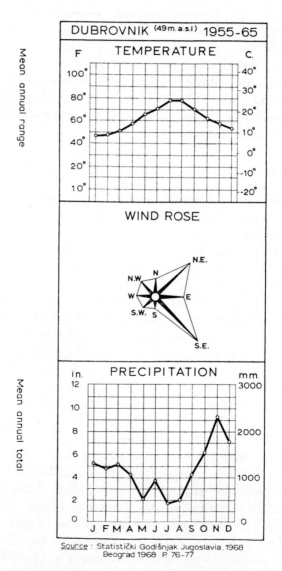

FIG. 7. Temperature, windrose and precipitation, Dubrovnik (49 m.a.s.i.) 1955–65.

temperature of the coldest month (February) is 4·6°C, and the warmest (August) 26·2°C. In winter the maritime influence of the sea prevents any great fall in temperature and in fact in January the town is on average 2·2°C warmer than Split and 0·6°C higher than Hvar. The steep elevation of Mount Srđ shelters the city from the cold Bora wind of the interior, but both Gruž and Rijeka Dubrovaćke are more exposed to its effects. The average annual cloud cover totals 4·3 hr/day (over a 33 year period of observations). Dubrovnik has 2,584 hours of sunshine annually (average over a five-year period of observations), with one of the highest rates of insolation in southern Europe. The winter total of sunshine hours lags behind that of some other centres (Dubrovnik 4·0 hours/day; Nice 4·9; Almera 6·5) but the summer values are the highest in Europe, with a daily average in July of 12·4 hours, the same as Alexandria in Egypt. Total annual precipitation is 1,361 mm of which 68% falls during the cold months of the year, with a maximum in October (181 mm). The total average of days with rain is 106, of which 29 are in spring, 14 in summer, 26 in autumn and 37 in winter. Snow is very rare. The resulting vegetation is of a subtropical character (almonds, olives, citrus fruits), rosemary, laurel, holm oak, black pine, Italian stone pine, cypress, which has been defined by Adamović as part of the 'evergreen zone' reaching up to 350 metres.[5]

Population

Until the nineteenth century there is no reliable statistical information on Dubrovnik's population, when the first census of 1807 showed that there were 4,175 people living inside the walls and a further 3,749 in the suburbs.[6] Exaggerated figures from chroniclers and writers exist who give the town's population as between 30,000 and 40,000 people, whilst during the sixteenth century the total area of the republic was 1,092 km², with, according to Roglić, a population of 80,000 inhabitants.[7] Despite their inaccuracies it is interesting to examine some of the earlier population estimates.

One early piece of information dates from 1348, when Dubrovnik suffered from an outbreak of the plague, or black death, which swept across Europe. The maritime trade of the republic had brought great riches to the citizens of Dubrovnik, but contact with the East also brought the plague in its train. In fact it was probably introduced into the west by the Tartars besieging Caffa in 1344, and although that town was saved, the relieving force caught the disease, which spread through Europe with lightning rapidity. The following document preserved in the book of wills (Testament) in Dubrovnik archives written by eye-witnesses, gives a vivid picture of the terror created by the disease:

'Our Lord God sent a terrible judgment, unheard of in the whole world, both on Christians and on pagans, a mortality of men and still more of women, through an awful and incurable disease, which caused the spitting of blood and swellings on various parts of the body, so contagious that sons fled from their fathers and still more often fathers from their sons; all the art of Apocrates, Galen, and Avizena proved useless, for no art or science availeth against Divine judgment. This disease commenced at Ragusa on the 15th day of December, in the year of our Lord 1348, and lasted for six months, during which 120 persons or more died each day; of the (Great) Council there died 110 nobles'.[8]

According to Gelcich, the total number of deaths in the town ranged from 7,000 to 10,000, including 160 nobles and 300 burghers; it is impossible to conjecture how many died in the territory. It made its appearance at the same time at Split, preceded, according to the legend, by an eclipse of the sun, so complete that the stars were visible by day, and by a drought so great that the dust remained suspended in huge clouds in mid air.[9] Ragnina, who wrote more than a century after the event, declares that the belief that the Jews had poisoned the wells was very prevalent while others believed that the cause of the disease was a conjunction of three planets under Jupiter and Mars.[10] At this time no sanitary precautions were taken against further visitations, but large sums were collected to build the votive church of San Biagio (Sv. Vlah). Between 1348 and 1691 the plague occurred eighteen times, and although the figures quoted by Dubrovnik chroniclers is excessive, there is no doubt there were losses, which needed some form of compensation. The greatest sufferers were the artisan classes particularly those working in close connection with the boats and in the warehouses where it was most easily caught.[11] Between 1348 and 1456 there were twelve plagues in Dubrovnik and its territory. If the first plague in 1348 killed about 7,500 people it was followed by others in 1363, 1374 (when 18,000 are said to have died) and again in 1381. In 1400–1401 one estimate stated that there were only 2,500 inhabitants remaining in the city and a further 4,000 in the rest of the republic. The plague of 1416 killed 3,800 people. As a result of all these losses the Great Council brought in laws to try and prevent the plague in 1397 (January 5; May 25; and June 28,) stating that all foreigners who came to the republic must remain outside the city and republic for a total of one month's quarantine and if they broke this rule they would be fined 100 ducats. Foreigners usually stayed on the small island of Mrkan, near Cavtat, or at the Benedictine monastery on Mljet Island. Later the period of quarantine for all foreigners was extended to two months. On the June 28, 1397 a law was passed forbidding the import of wheat, fruit or cloth from places which had the plague.[12] In 1438 there was another serious outbreak of the plague, which killed many of the ruling class. After this event many new positions of authority in the republic had to be created, and as late as 1546 the government ruled that only clean, purified merchandise could be stored in the quarantine house (Lazaret). Leprosy was also found in Dubrovnik in the thirteenth century, having come it is said from the East, during the time of the Crusades. All lepers were kept in a place near the Danče promontory not far from the city, and this was in use until the second half of the fifteenth century.

Various census records exist in the Dubrovnik Archives, but it is difficult to judge their validity and also some of them were taken with a specific purpose in mind and do not give an overall picture of the population density. Probably the oldest was taken on December 31, 1357 but how exact it was is open to conjecture. Another one was conducted on November 13, 1380 on a fairly wide basis in part of the republic, including both men and women resident on the islands and in Astarea.[13]

There were three main censuses in the fifteenth century. The first was on November 22, 1429 and records all people working on the digging of a moat in Konavle, between the ages of sixteen and sixty years. The moat was being built in case of enemy attack in the area.[14] A further census was held in Konavle in October 16, 1463 but this time included the islands and Astarea. The main purpose was for the supply of wheat (always in short supply) and the need to know the precise number of houses and people in the area.[15] Probably a more extensive survey was held on August 26, 1480 when a financial census was taken to find out each family that possessed more than one ducat. It recorded all houses and families in the whole territory of the republic.[16] Presumably on the basis of these various documents,

Tadić has estimated that the population of Dubrovnik at the beginning of the sixteenth century was 7,000 inhabitants.[17] The plague visited the city again in 1526, carried in goods from Ancona by a merchant whom the infuriated citizens carted through the city and tortured. The government was moved to Gruž and the city was only occupied by a small guard. The plague continued for six months, and is said to have carried off 2,000 victims.

One of the best sources of information on Dubrovnik's population is contained in the Dubrovnik Archives (in the series *Isprave i akti XVII stoljeća* No. 1809) and records the population census taken throughout the Dubrovnik Republic in 1673/74, a few years after the disastrous earthquake.[18] There appears to be some confusion about the actual date of the census, because the decision to hold one, and its actual completion, were carried out by different governments. For census purposes each župnik (parish priest) was responsible for his župa (parish) in which he had to record firstly the number of 'souls' and secondly to find out the number of houses belonging to men, women and children over 12 years of age. There were thirty-two parishes and the whole census was conducted between November 3, 1673 and March 31, 1674. Naturally the population after the earthquake was much smaller than previously, and the second largest town in the republic was Ston. The census had some faults for it was not universally the same; some places included the number of houses, others not, some recorded the age structure, others failed to etc. Nevertheless it is interesting to compare the population totals of the Dubrovnik Republic in 1673/4 with those of 1573, when one of the nobles, Frano Gundulić wrote to the Pope, maintaining that the territory contained 80,000 people. The latter census totalled 9,175 inhabitants. A further census was taken in April 17, 1764 of Dubrovnik and its suburbs[19] which tends to support the view that political importance and economic wealth did not influence any marked growth in population. The walled city with its limited space, the problem of hygiene and water supply meant that only a limited population density could be accommodated and refutes any claims of over-enthusiastic, chauvenistic chroniclers in the city. One of the books in the Dubrovnik Archives entitled *Maestrello di popolazione* estimates that at the end of the eighteenth century, Dubrovnik had 4,474 inhabitants. During the French occupation there was another census (1808) in which Dubrovnik had 6,536 inhabitants; Rijeka Dubrovačke, 1,669; Župa, 1,595; Lopud, 716; Šipan, 821; Mljet, 896;

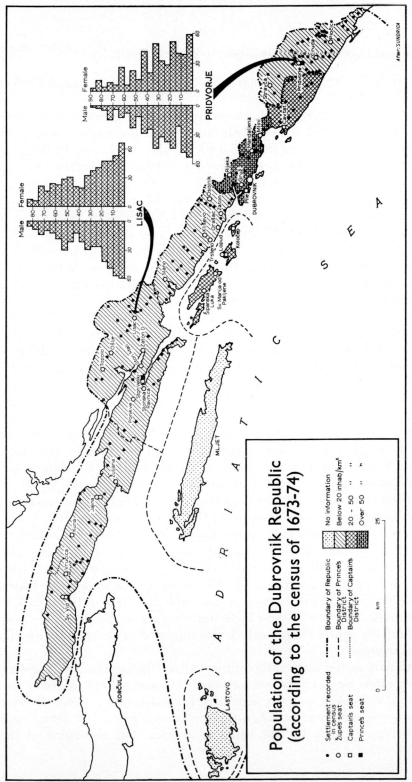

Population of the Dubrovnik Republic
(according to the census of 1673-74)

Settlement recorded
● in census
○ Župe's seat
□ Captain's seat
■ Prince's seat

—·—·— Boundary of Republic
— — — Boundary of Prince's District
············ Boundary of Captain's District

No information
Below 20 inhab/km²
20 – 50   "   "
Over 50   "   "

PRIDVORJE

Male   Female
90
80
70
60
50
40
30
20
10
0
60   30   0   30   60

LISAC

Male   Female
80
70
60
50
40
30
20
10
0
60   30   0   30   60

A   D   R   I   A   T   I   C   S   E   A

DUBROVNIK

MLJET

KORČULA

LASTOVO

km
0   25

After: SUNDRICA

FIG. 8.

Slano, 1,675; Imotica, 970 and Lisac, 1,200 – giving a grand total of 16,078 people.[20]

More reliable census data exists from the late nineteenth century. In 1880 there were 4,805 inhabitants inside the walls; 1900, 5,346 people; 1910, 5,590 and in 1953 a total of 5,181 citizens. In the light of these figures it appears that population growth was slow but continually growing right up to World War I. The suburbs, on the other hand, displayed a quicker growth. Dubrovnik parish (i.e. territory of the city and its suburb) totalled 10,936 inhabitants in 1880 rising to 13,194 by 1900, and 14,367 by 1910. Due to boundary changes within the parish the 1931 total was 18,765 which by 1948 had dropped to 16,735 people but this was partly a result of a decrease in the size of the parish compared with 1931. In 1953 population rose to 19,172 reaching 22,961 eight years later.

Two other interesting questions remain concerning Dubrovnik's population; the first is the role of migration in the city's growth, and the second the problem of the Latin-Slav symbiosis of the inhabitants. According to Sindik[21] most of the immigrants to Dubrovnik came from Hercegovina, particularly Popovo Polje, and those areas adjacent to the city's inland trade routes. The immigrants also came from other parts of the Balkan peninsula, for Jireček states that people came to live in Dubrovnik from the Neretva region, Konavle, the Drin valley and mining settlements in Bosnia such as Srebrnica, Rudnik and Novo Brdo.[22] Others, including ruffians, vagabonds and hired soldiers came from various parts of Croatia and Hungary, married and stayed in Dubrovnik. Besides the land route immigrants also came by sea; some came from the north-west Dalmatian towns, others from the south-east (Kotor, Budva, Bar, and Albania) and yet a third group came from Italy. The main reasons for the migration were diverse. In the Dalmatian towns the landed gentry often tried to marry off their daughters in Dubrovnik, whilst sometimes family disagreements meant that it was imposible for some of the gentry to remain in the place of their birth and thus emigrated to Dubrovnik. Besides the gentry the townsfolk also migrated to Dubrovnik, usually as craftsmen.

Already in the thirteenth century Albanians migrated to the city. They often came as traders, artisans, but particularly as friars and priests, because it was not necessary for consecrated priests to have alternative employment when there was such prosperity from trade and shipping. The Italians came as artisans, but also some of the professional classes such as doctors, teachers, lawyers, chancellors etc. They came from all over Italy[23] but particularly from the west Adriatic coast. Slavonic refugees during the fifteenth century also swelled the city's population. Dubrovnik became the refuge of many noble and wealthy families from the interior, who fled from the Turks at the fall of the Slavonic kingdoms. Gelcich gives a long list of the principal houses and all of them seem to have become Italianized, and most of them were engaged in commerce, many of them having brought considerable wealth to their new home. Philippson maintains that the main motive of all these people was the search for wealth.[24] This was the prime reason for all the migrations from the north and inland towards the Mediterranean Sea, and the richness of Dubrovnik was certainly well known in Hercegovina. It was possible for the people of the inland towns to see each day, along the Dubrovnik trade routes, the caravans loaded with goods either going to or coming from the city. Also hunger was often prevalent inland, but in Dubrovnik it was rare and only for short periods. State officials kept a careful watch over the state granaries, from where wheat was divided up amongst the poor people and children free of charge during periods of famine. Further, the inland peoples also knew that all sorts of privileges were granted to the Dubrovnik peasants (kmets), who were respected, sheltered and able to share some of the gains accrued from the republic's power, where 'the feet of an unfriendly people had not marched for four hundred years.'[25] Finally the feudalistic attitudes of the lords of Zahumlja and Travunja also encouraged the local people to flee from their bondage and take refuge in Dubrovnik's territory.

Nevertheless the Dubrovnik government had to take steps to control this immigration. There was a need for good administrative organization, usually by a small number of the population to control and account for each immigrant. In 1385 the government ordered that 'land owners in Župa and other lands received from Tsar Uroš, must build houses and huts for the new people there. If there are any Slavs amongst these foreign peasants who wish to settle there, they must build themselves a house within a year. Failure to do so would mean expulsion from the said land.' A less severe version of this law was introduced in 1413, because the former one had proved too difficult for the immigrants. The new law stated that 'in future the kmets had to inform the chancellor that they had dwelt for a year where their landlords had ordered them, and they were then free to live anywhere in the new land, providing they had their landlords' permission.' Unfortunately this law was not easily understood, because it did not say where the peasants must spend their year's residence. Also these orders only referred to the immigrant population in the villages. The minutes of the Great Council often mentioned that one or other of its 'habitor Ragusiji' had become 'civis'. This stress on the difference shows that the rest of the immigrants, regardless of their place of origin, had to spend some time in the city before they could get real citizenship. It was even more complicated if a Slav immigrant wished to achieve this distinction. Separate laws were issued in 1450 for those Slavs who wished to come directly to Dubrovnik city from the hinterland. The first of these laws prohibited the Small Council from giving Slav citizenship. If the Slavs wished to stay in Dubrovnik, then their requests must come before the Small Council in which all twelve members must be present. If eight of the council members grant the request, it must then go to the Great Council, where there must be at least 100 members present, of which two-thirds must give their consent to the request. Only then could a Slav become a Dubrovnik citizen.[26]

There appear to be two main reasons for Dubrovnik's attitude towards immigrants, one economic, the other political. Too large a population meant the threat of famine, and the money the republic had to spend on food could be better spent on strengthening the existing fortifications against attack. Politically, Dubrovnik's attitude is best explained by the motto of the republic's landlords 'keep homogeneous'. This was applicable as a principle, regardless of the class a citizen belonged to, and to some extent must have suppressed any chance of particular people developing their individuality. The main aim was to keep this homogeneity within the state so that the territory could not be broken up by political or religious differences. Laws concerning religious faith were strict, forbidding all but the Roman Catholic beliefs up to the fall of the republic in 1808. The Greek Orthodox Church could hold services in private houses during the eighteenth century, but this was only after political pressure from Russia. The Jews were tolerated but their faith was definitely suppressed. Most of these religious laws had their origin in the Middle Ages under the dictum 'cujus regio, ilius religio'.

This meant that a careful watch had to be kept on immigrants. Most of the immigrants were known and surveyed, particularly any who were likely to be politically dangerous. Even so Dubrovnik's government did show compassion towards its immigrants. In 1371 a large crowd of people came from the hinterland (Kratovo) with their families and possessions, maintaining they had been pursued by the Turks.[27] Jireček quotes further examples of Slavs from inland coming to Dubrovnik's territory in the fourteenth century,[28] whilst Truhelka gives examples of people coming daily and *en masse* to escape from the Turks in the fifteenth century, though most of these were only for temporary residence. Nevertheless there is one example dating from 1430, when 50–60 houses were occupied by immigrants following heavy fighting in Planina the northern part of Konavle.[29]

Finally there is the question of internal migration, within the republic. There appear to have been two main movements; firstly migrations towards the towns, and secondly from the upper to the lower villages or to the islands. The towns especially attracted the islanders. On the islands the kmet system was not so rigorous for the peasants, giving them more freedom, whilst the more prosperous islanders always made efforts to go and live in the towns, and develop their commercial interests. It was more difficult for would-be immigrants from the upper or lower villages to go to the towns for peasants often found it difficult to leave their landlords because on doing so they lost all privileges. Young peasants did come to the towns where they worked as apprentices, or assistants in shops. If they saved some of their money these young kmets (djetić) were allowed to open shops of their own, or given permission by the government to be posted to a ship, or on to a priest's estate. Sometimes peasant families were sent to work on property and possessions outside Dubrovnik, particularly in the Levant. They went there first as servants for Dubrovnik merchants and later as independent shopkeepers, some of whom became quite rich. When they returned to the republic they did not live in their former villages but resided in the city, often living with families who had formerly come from their village. Some internal migration occurred from the towns to the villages, usually by the sons of local rulers who gave up their dignified position for the quieter village life. Examples of this, however, were rare.

The Latin-Slav symbiosis in Dalmatia has long proved of interest.[30] In Dubrovnik, with its wealth of archival material, it is possible to get a closer insight into the rate and amount of assimilation that went on in the city. A census on Lokrum Island between 973 and 1025 AD mentions thirty names of which only two were Slavic. An-

other census there in 1044 had fifty-two names but only eight were
of Slavic origin. In 1190 one Dubrovnik list had sixty names on it
with only six which were definitely Slavonic, but it is safe to assume
that before the end of the twelfth century there were some Slavonic
families in the city. Later in 1253 of the 101 people mentioned in
Dubrovnik, only 8% were Slavonic. The following table gives some
idea of the difference between the two groups:

Table I

	10th–11thC.	12thC.	13thC.	14thC.
	Number of names			
Latin	39	67	236	209
Slav.	7	29	104	150

From Table I it can be seen that the number of Latin names between the tenth and fourteenth centuries, show a growth of 5·5
times; in comparison the Slav element has increased 21·5 times over
the same period.[31] Skok believes that some time during the fifteenth
or sixteenth centuries, the Latin-Slav city of Dubrovnik became completely Slav,[32] but even as late as 1472 a proposal was put forward to
the government to adopt the Slavic language in all walks of life, but
the proposal was rejected, due to a majority decision by the 'old
Ragusans' and pro-Italianists. Nevertheless according to Haumant
by 1482 the 'victory of the local tongue was complete' and in 1496
one Arnold von Honff stated that in Dubrovnik, Slav was the
universal language.[33]

Other factors indicate a change taking place in the fifteenth century. First, Latin was only still dominant amongst the governing
classes and the nobility; secondly many of the families appear to have
been bilingual by this time. Also a list of Dubrovnik's noblewomen
exists for this period, and each woman has given her name twice –
in Latin and Slav; thirdly, the practice of borrowing Latin words for
Slavic speech seems prevalent at this time particularly in fishing
where some Latin words are still used today. Skok has also noticed
the similarity between the dialects of Dubrovnik, southern Italy and
Sardinia. Like the Sardinians, people in Dubrovnik conserve their
vowel sounds, placing a 'c' and 'g' before 'e' and 'i', which Skok
further maintains can 'all be admirably explained by the geographical position of Dubrovnik'.[34] Further evidence of bilingual use can

be gleaned from historical evidence from the mid-fifteenth century. For example, wearing apparel of the noblewomen sometimes had bilingual names; earrings were referred to both by the Slav 'oboci' (singular 'obodac') and the local Dubrovnik dialect, 'kerkel' from the Latin 'circellus'. Similarly the head-dress of married women was called 'kličak' in Slav and 'reguletum' in Dubrovnik-Latin. Other bilingual designations are found, for example, for the mayor or head of the city – 'comes' in Latin and 'knez' in the Slavonic tongue, where the Slavic vocabulary has been adapted to the needs of the Latinized urban population. By the time of the Renaissance, Novak believes this urbanism was already completely Slav,[35] and that therefore by the sixteenth century the 'Romani' of Constantine Porphyrogentus had become the 'Slovinci'.

Economic Development up to 1939

The continuation of the commercial functions of the former Roman town of Epidauros (Cavtat) explains the successful and rapid development of the new settlement on the defensible but otherwise valueless rocky island of Ragusium. The commercial orientation and the close relationship with the hinterland explains the rapid coalescence of the refugee centre of Ragusium with the Slavic Dubrovnik. Consuls were placed at Venice and in the ports on both shores of the Adriatic, and colonies of Dubrovnik traders settled in the interior of the Balkans to open a way for commerce with Italy, taking with them into those countries the influences of a superior civilization. The principal exports from the interior were livestock, skins, cheeses, wax and silver in return for which salt, wine, oil and woven stuffs were imported from Italy.

In the fifteenth century Dubrovnik grew rapidly and prospered, and the trade of the small republic greatly increased. The city had trading stations in the main ports of the Mediterranean and made commercial treaties with Spain in 1494, France in 1508, and Egypt in 1510, which at last opened to her a way to the Indies. The harbour was enlarged, her ships were to be found in every commercial port and the republic entered upon a period when she was at peace with her neighbours and respected by her rivals. Twenty-one confraternities or guilds of different industries existed in the city, besides others outside the wall, and besides several trades not represented by a guild. Towards the end of the sixteenth century and beginning of the seventeenth, this idyllic situation began to change. Pestilence, earthquakes, and continual rivalry between the Turks and Venice disturbed the life of the city. By the time peace was restored and Dubrovnik had more leisure to attend to its commerce, it found that the commerce itself had begun to take on a fresh appearance. England and Holland had become maritime powers, the trade of the Mediterranean had passed almost entirely to the Venetians, and the traffic with Hercegovina was almost all that remained.

The terrible events of the seventeenth century seem to have disorganized the state and left disorder and faction behind them. The old nobility, and the new nobility (post-seventeenth century), were constantly in opposition, whilst their fellow citizens disapproved of their senseless feuds. Trade declined, and the Turk, now reduced to court favour of the Venetians whom he formerly defied, directed the stream of his commerce towards Venice rather than Dubrovnik. The fall of Venice in 1797 seemed to throw fresh opportunities for commercial activity into Dubrovnik's path, and the mercantile marine rapidly rose to 400 ships. Unfortunately, both France and Russia longed to control her and neutrality became impossible. The French ultimately occupied the city and on January 31, 1808, the republic as such ceased to exist. In 1814 the French were driven from the city and Dubrovnik, like the rest of Dalmatia, was to remain under Austrian rule for the next hundred years.

After 1808 Dubrovnik became a small town centre in a new political setting. Trade connections with the hinterland were reduced to a minimum, as a result of the building of a new railway network, which gradually drained off the main comercial traffic towards the north Adriatic ports. With the loss of trade in the hinterland Dubrovnik now made efforts to repair her maritime commerce. This new emphasis was based on her old traditions, but now much of her strength lay as a service port, carrying the goods and trade of other nations, not her own. The development of the steamship meant that the old harbour at Stari Porat was no longer suitable for ships of larger draught, and as yet Gruž had not been equipped with suitable conditions to accept them. Also Gruž did not have communication links with the interior. The building of a narrow-gauge railway inland, which connected Dubrovnik, via Gruž, with Sarajevo, was unfortunately not built with commercial interests in mind, but was for strategic reasons in which the Austrians could connect their various military harbours in the Bay of Kotor.

Despite the lack of commercial advantages, Dubrovnik did manage to expand its harbour and gradually affirmed its position once again as an important commercial port, with a total shipping traffic of 188,749 tons in 1913. In fact up to 1926 Dubrovnik had the highest tonnage total in Yugoslavia, whilst from 1926 to the outbreak of World War II, it continued to hold second place (except in 1935, when it lagged behind Šibenik, Sušak and Split). Thus between the wars Dubrovnik gradually became an important trade centre prolonging its old tradition into the twentieth century, as a significant domestic steamship centre. A measure of this importance is seen from the fact that in 1931, Dubrovnik citizens owned 194,750 or 53% of the country's total shipping tonnage. To this may be added the fact that 91% of Yugoslavia's total tonnage for passenger boats belonged to the port, together with being one of the country's leading boatbuilding centres. Any deficiencies found from the loss of commercial traffic at the beginning of the twentieth century was made up for by a growth in tourism. A large growth in tourist traffic took place long before World War II, and Dubrovnik in a very short time, affirmed herself as an international tourist centre. This is reflected in pre-war statistics, which show a continual increase in the number of visitors, from 23,260 guests in 1925 (of which 19,165 were Yugoslavs) to 58,050 visitors in 1938, of which 40,970 were foreigners as opposed to 17,080 domestic tourists.

Post-War Economic Development

Since the Second World War two main factors have influenced the economic life of Dubrovnik. First, there has been a decline in the importance of the port. This has been mainly due to the construction of an alternative modern harbour, at Ploče, on the shore of the Neretva Channel (Neretvanski kanal) 117 km to the north of Dubrovnik. The building of modern port installations began in 1937, a railway line inland to Sarajevo in 1940, and modern apartment blocks and offices in 1946 has meant that this place has gradually taken away much of Dubrovnik's former trade. Secondly, Dubrovnik has seen a phenomenal growth in tourism.[36] The number of guests in 1953 (65,087) exceeded the pre-war maximum of 1938; by 1959 the number of tourists had risen to 99,138 and ten years later (1969) had reached 242,000.[37] The relationship between the numbers of domestic and foreign tourists has also changed. There has been a distinct fall in the number of domestic visitors which in 1954 totalled 45,565 compared with 26,554 foreign guests; by 1969 there were only 70,000 domestic visitors as compared to 172,000 foreigners. Nevertheless the rapid development of tourism is not without its problems. Probably the major difficulty is guest capacity. In 1958 there were only 3,209 hotel beds available, but more recently new hotels have been built, particularly at Lapad, together with increased camping facilities. To the south-east of the old town lies Dubrovnik's main tourist district of Ploče, with its hotels and beaches, to the west at Lapad (sports facilities, beaches and parks) and to the north-west the port of Gruž, the main harbour and railway terminal. Further tourist development is dependent upon increasing secondary facilities including better road, rail, maritime and air connections. The Adriatic Highway ('Magistrala') runs along the slope of Mount Srđ above the town, and an important road (Put Maršala Tita) runs from Pile to Gruž railway station. In the opposite direction there is a road towards the suburb of Ploče (Put iza Grada, continued as Put Frana Supila), and a more recent road (Put Jugoslovenske narodne armije) leads through to the suburb of Kono, then passes through Ploče. The whole zone of the town (Pile-Put Frana Supila-Put Jugoslovenske narodne armija-Gruž harbour-Lapad-Put Maršala Tita) is connected by a circular bus route. Dubrovnik's airport is at Močići in Konavle, six kilometres from the city. It is used for both domestic and international air services, has a 2 km long runway, and is one of the most modern airports in south-east Europe, situated near Čilipi on a branch road of the Adriatic Highway. Finally, some attempt is being made to increase the cultural life of the city particularly since 1950 with the establishment of the Dubrovnik Summer Festival (Dubrovačke ljetne igre), a festival of music, drama, folk songs and dances. The festival is held during the tourist season on seventeen different stages throughout the city, most of them in the open air.

Industrially, Dubrovnik concentrates on two main branches, namely shipbuilding and light industry. Shipbuilding has an old tradition in the city, and despite a short post-war recession is now again being redeveloped. Today there are workshops for repairing boats and yards for building smaller wooden craft. Dubrovnik is also the seat of one of the country's main shipping companies – the 'Atlantska plovidba' with up to twenty vessels totalling over 110,000 tons gross. In addition to boatyards for small craft, Dubrovnik has several minor industrial plants. Many of these depend on local raw materials (olives, grape husks and stalks, tobacco and tomato seeds, juniper beans etc.) together with some imported materials such as oil seeds (ground-nut, sesame, flax). These industrial sites are mainly located in the Gruž area, and include factories producing industrial and edible oils, flour paste, liqueurs, paints and carbon-graphite products. The carbon-graphite factory (T.U.P.) is the only one of its kind in Yugoslavia and prepares brushes for dynamo engines, and carbon sticks for the cinematography industry. Even so the main industries of the city still remain namely the tourist trade and shipping. Other settlements near to Dubrovnik also have some specialist industrial production as for example salt from the coastal pans at Ston, a fish canning factory at Slano, and the large wine warehouses at Potomje and Gruda. Much of this is closely tied to local agriculture, which predominantly concentrates on wine-growing (about 40 million vines) and oil production (more than 100,000 olive-trees). Electrical energy used to depend on the old thermal power station at Gruž, but more recently the large hydro-electric power system based on the River Trebišnjica has been completed with an annual output of 2·91 milliard kwh. The new hydro-electric power station at Zavrelje, near Mlini, is connected to the long distance transmission lines via Trebinje and Bileč, giving Dubrovnik direct access to the Jablaničke hydro-electric power station.

In conclusion, it can be said that Dubrovnik benefits from certain obvious advantages. The beauty of its setting makes it one of the most attractive places on the Adriatic coast, and it has become a tourist resort and meeting place for international conferences and festivals. Unfortunately it tends to be somewhat isolated, for it lacks good rail connections with the rest of the country and is therefore dependent mainly on sea and air connections, both liable to interruption by bad weather. Also tourism, the main industry, is seasonal, which leaves Dubrovnik rather isolated in winter, but it is hoped that the climatic advantages of the city may gradually induce some growth in winter tourism. The city is also well placed for the development of new villas and hotels, but these must be supported by national funds as local economic resources are rather limited. Similarly, secondary factors must be considered, particularly the provision of a sufficient water supply to accommodate possible future demands. Indeed looking at the city and its immediate area under present conditions it is difficult to understand how Dubrovnik and its small republic had such an illustrious history, which survived for so long. One is tempted to ask what conditioned the founding, development and prosperity of the city during the Middle Ages and later, and from what source did Dubrovnik's livelihood come, and even more intriguing why was the city built on this particular inhospitable site? It is hoped to answer these questions in greater detail as the story of the Dubrovnik Republic unfolds.

1. Notes

1. C. G. Crump and E. F. Jacob, *The Legacy of the Middle Ages*, Oxford (1926), Ch. 8 'The economic activity of towns', N.S.B. Gras, p. 461.
2. I. Sindik, 'Dubrovnik i Okolica', *Srpski Etnografski Zbornik* Knj. XXXVIII, Belgrade (1926), pp. 1–228;
   L. Marčić, 'Dubrovnik i Okolina', *Geografski Pregled*, Belgrade (1937), pp. 1–24;
   B. Ž. Milojević, 'Dinarsko primorje i ostrova u našoj Kraljevini', *Srpska Kral. Akademija*, Belgrade (1933), p. 160;
   Ž. Bešić, 'Prilog ka poznavanja geologije Dinarida', *Glasnik prirodnjačkog muzeja srpske zemlje*, Serija A, Knj, 5, Belgrade (1952), 96 pp;
   'Dubrovnik', *Pomorska Enciklopdija*, Vol. 2, Zagreb (1955), pp. 544–546.
3. J. Mihailović, *Seizmički Karakter i trusne Katastrofe Našeg Južnog Primorija* (Od Stona do Ulcinj) *Srpska Akademija Nauka* Knj. CXL, Belgrade (1947), p. 33.
4. S. Škreb, *Klima Hrvatske*, Geofizički Zavod, Zagreb (1942), 139 pp.
5. L. Adamovič, 'Građa za floru dubrovačku', *Glasnik Hrvatskog prirodoslovnog društva*, Vol. I, Zagreb (1887), pp. 4–6; 161–216.
6. *Enciklopedja Jugoslavije*, Vol. III, Zagreb (1958), p. 124.
7. J. Roglić, 'The geographical setting of medieval Dubrovnik', *Geographical Essays on Eastern Europe* (N. J. G. Pounds, ed.) Vol. 24, The Hague (1961), p. 144.
8. G. Gelcich, *Istituzioni Maritime e Sanitarie della Republica di Ragusa*, Trieste (1892), p. 37.
9. *Ibid.*, p. 38.
10. N. Ragnina, *Annali di Ragusa*, South Slavonic Academy, Zagreb (1890), ad ann 1348.
11. I. Sindik, 'O. Naseljima i Migracijama u Dubrovniku i Okolini', *Glasnik Geografskog Društva*, Vol. 9, Belgrade (1923), p. 51.
12. K. Vojnović, 'Sudbeno Ustrojstvo Republike Dubrovačke', *Rad J.A.* Knj. CVIII, CVIV, Zagreb (1892, 1893), pp. 175–178, Dubrovnik Archives (28/VI/1397), *Liber Viridis* cap. 91.
13. Dubrovnik Archives, (13/XIII/1357) *Reformationes* 17, fol. 45, (13/XI/1380) *Reformationes* 24, fol. 135.
14. Dubrovnik Archives, *Consilium Rogatorium* 4, folder 126–127.
15. Dubrovnik Archives, *Consilium Rogatorium* 17, folder 281.

16. Dubrovnik Archives, *Consilium Maius* 14, folder 174–5.
17. J. Tadić, *Dubrovački portreti*, Belgrade (1948).
18. Z. Šundrica, 'Popis stanovništva Dubrovačke Republike iz 1673/74 godine', *Arhivske Vjesnik*, God. II, Sv. 2, Zagreb (1959).
19. Dubrovnik Archives, *Consilium Rogatorum*, 175, folder 156.
20. K. Kovać, 'Crtice o statistici i vojničkim ustanovama u Republici Dubrovačkoj', *Glasnik Zemalja Muzeja u Bosnia i Hercegovina*, Sarajevo (1916), pp. 303–310; *Enciklopedije Jugoslavija*, *op. cit.* p. 124.
21. I. Sindik, *op. cit.*
22. K. Jireček, 'Die Romanen in den Städten Dalmatiens während des Mittelalters' *Denkschriften der Akademie*, Bd, XLVIII and XLIX, Vienna (1900), Vol. I, pp. 43–44.
23. K. Jireček, 'Die mittelalterliche Kanzlei der Ragusaner', *Archiv für slavische Philologie*, Vol. XXV, Vienna (1904), p. 515.
24. A. Philippson, *Das Mittelmeergebiet*, Leipzig (1904), p. 1.
25. M. Medini, *O Postanku i razvitku kmetski i težačkih odnošaja u Dalmaciji*, Zadar (1920), p. 89.
26. Dubrovnik Archives, *Liber Viridis*, cap. 428.
27. St. Novaković, *Srbi i Turci XIV i XV veka*, Belgrade (1893), p. 185.
28. K. Jireček, 'Die Wlachen und Maurowlachen in der Denkmälern von Ragusa', *Sitzungsberichte der böhm, Gesellschaft der Wissenschaften*, Prague (1879), p. 117.
29. D. Truhelka, *Tursko-Slovenski spomenici dubrovačke arhive*, Sarajevo (1911), p. 189.
30. V. Novak, 'The Slavonic-Latin symbiosis in Dalmatia during the Middle Ages', *The Slavonic and East European Review*, Vol. XXXII (78), pp. 1–29.
31. I. Sindik, 'Dubrovnik i Okolica', *op. cit.* pp. 203–205.
32. P. Skok, 'Les Origines de Raguse', *Slavia, Časopis pro Slovanskou Filologii*, Vol. I, Prague (1931), pp. 495–500.
33. E. Haumant, 'La Slavisation de la Dalmatie', *Revue Historique*, Vol. CXXIV Paris (1917), p. 292.
34. P. Skok, 'L'Importance de Dubrovnik dans l'Histoire des Slaves', *Le Monde Slave*, Vol. VIII, (2), Paris (1931), pp. 165–170.
35. V. Novak, *op. cit.* p. 29.
36. A. Degl' Ivellio, 'Promet Turista na Području Komune Dubrovnik Nekad i Danas', *Geografske Horizont*, Broj 3–4, Zagreb (1967), God. XIII, p. 55–58.
37. *Statistički Godišnjak Jugoslavije*, Savezni Zavod za Statistiku, Belgrade, (for relevant years).

2
The Early Development of a Pre-industrial City

The city and civilization are inseparable: with the city's rise and spread man at last emerged from the primitive state. In turn, the city enabled him to construct an ever more complex way of life and some scholars regard the city as second only to agriculture among the significant inventions in human history. One such type of city is the pre-industrial, or non-industrial city.[1] Not only do pre-industrial cities survive today, but they have been the foci of civilization from the time of their first appearance in Mesopotamia in the fourth millenium BC. Even when Europe entered the Dark Ages and city life waned over much of the continent, the Eastern Roman Empire and Spain experienced a vibrant urban life. With the collapse of Roman rule only those portions of Europe under Byzantine or Muslim influence had a flourishing urban life; Byzantium (Constantinople), Preslav, Salonika (Thessaloniki) and along the eastern shore of the Adriatic Sea, particularly in Dalmatia.

The Dalmatian Littoral

Dalmatia has at all times been essentially a borderland. Geographically it belongs to the eastern peninsula of the Mediterranean, to the Balkan lands. But this narrow strip of coast as Freeman[2] states 'has not a little the air of a thread, a finger, a branch cast forth from the western peninsula'. In its history its character as a march land is still more noticeable, and this feature has always been manifested in a series of civilized communities in the towns, with a hinterland of barbarous or semi-civilized races. Here were the farthest Greek settlements in the Adriatic, settlements placed in the midst of a native uncivilized Illyrian population. Here the Romans came and conquered, but did not wholly absorb the native races. Then the land was disputed between the Eastern and Western Empires, later between Christianity and Islam,[3] later still between the Eastern and Western Churches. The Slav invasion, while almost obliterating the native Illyrian race, could not sweep away the Roman-Greek civilization of the coast.

The beginnings of Dalmatian history are purely legendary, and very little is known about the ethnographical character of its original inhabitants. Wanderers from pre-Homeric Greece are said to have settled along its shores, and repeated migrations had connected the islands and the littoral with the neighbouring mountainous regions, which gradually developed a unique cultural and economic region that today is broadly called the Mediterranean littoral region. The cultivation of choice fruit trees – olive, fig and grapes – led to the establishment of permanent settlements and a stabilized population along the coast, whilst inland the cattle-breeding nomads followed their seasonal migrations with their flocks of sheep and goats, between the sea coast and the high mountain pastures. In the seventh century BC a Celtic invasion took place by the Galli Senones, who founded Senogallia in Italy, Tedastum (Modrussa) and Senia (Senj) in present-day Croatia, and established a kingdom of Illyria, extending over Istria, Kvarner and the northern part of Macedonia, with Skoder (now in Albania) as its capital.[4] In the fifth and fourth centuries, the Greeks, ever seeking to establish new colonies on the shores of the Mediterranean, did not overlook the natural advantages of the east Adriatic coast with its sheltered islands and indented natural anchorages. A colony of Sicilian Greeks from Syracuse was settled by Dionysius on the island of Issa (Vis) in 385 BC, and from the island of Paros in the Aegean built a new Paros, or Pharos (meaning 'lighthouse') on the island of Hvar. These people were creditable sailors as shown not only by the establishment of settlements on the remotest of islands, but from the drawing of a ship, discovered in Grabak Cave on Hvar.[5] Other colonies included Dyrrhachium or Epidamnus (Dürres), Epidauros or Epidauron, where Cavtat now stands, and Tragyrion or Tragurium (Trogir) all Greek colonies on the mainland, the latter being peopled by Syracusans from Issa. Inscriptions found on Korčula prove that there were Greek settlements there also including Kerkyra Melaina (Corcyra Nigra).

Without raising the question whether the Illyrians had descended into the Mediterranean region together with the Greeks, or whether the Dorians had found them there during their migration, it is important to establish that the Illyrian tribes had occupied the whole of the western coast of the Adriatic. Thus, in the first millenium BC the Liburnii tribe were holding the whole area from Corfu to Istria and later crossed the Adriatic to the Appenine peninsula. In the third century BC Illyria was welded into a powerful kingdom by a native ruler Agron, son of Peuratus, and his widow Teuta, regent during the minority of her stepson Pineus. During this period there were clashes with the Romans, who now, for the first time, carried their

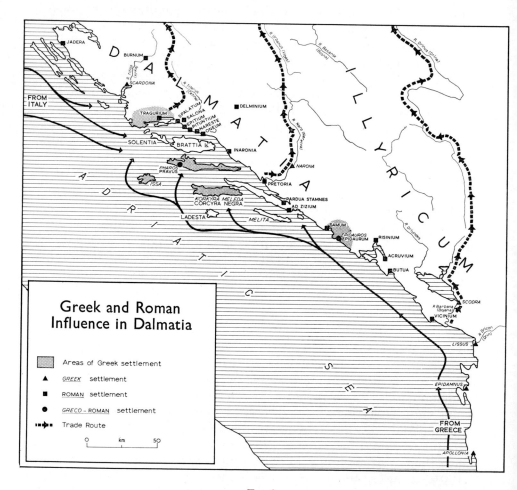

Fig. 9.

raids across the Adriatic. The islanders of Issa, unable to protect themselves against the Illyrian attacks, appealed to the Romans for protection in 232 BC. This in turn led to the First Illyrian War of 229 BC and Second in 219 BC in which the Illyrian threat was quelled. In the year 180 BC the Dalmatians, a people inhabiting the middle part of modern Dalmatia, revolted from the Illyrian kingdom and became independent. Their territory extended from the River Naro (Naretva) to the Titius (Krka), which divided Dalmatia from Liburnia. During the second and first centuries BC the Romans waged no less than ten wars in Illyria, which was not completely reduced until the year AD 9 when Dalmatia was finally subdued.

The Roman occupation led to the Illyrians finding a new source of subsistence in agriculture, as well as their former cattle-breeding activities. Under the Roman Empire the maritime district of Dalmatia seems to have had a 'propaetor' or 'legate' of its own, and the whole province was divided into 'dioceses', or 'conventus', each with a central city to which the inhabitants of the conventus resorted for public or private business. The well-planned colonization succeeded in transforming the whole of Dalmatia, especially the littoral belt, into another Italy. A number of Latin colonies were settled along the coast, supplanting those of the Greeks, and their splendour and importance may be gauged from the magnificent Roman remains, especially those of the great palace built by Diocletian, himself an Illyrian, at Split, and of Salona (called the 'Dalmatian Pompeii'), the ancient capital of the province. Roman Dalmatia included besides the modern region of that name, the whole of Bosnia, Hercegovina, Montenegro, and parts of Croatia and Albania. Diocletian divided Dalmatia into two provinces, 'Dalmatia proper' to the north, and 'Praevalis', or 'Praevalitana' to the south and in 305 AD abdicated and retired to his villa at Aspalathus (Split) where he died in 313.

At the time of the partition of the Roman Empire, Dalmatia was apportioned to the Western Division, the neighbouring provinces of Dardania Moesia Superior, and Praevalis to the Eastern. When the barbarian hordes began to make inroads into southern Europe, Dalmatia and Pannonia 'no longer exhibited the rich prospect of populous cities well cultivated fields and convenient highways; the reign of barbarism and desolation was restored', and the Latin or provincial subjects of Rome were displaced by hordes of Bulgarians, Gepidae Sarmatians and Slavonians. Much of the Eastern Province of the Roman Empire remained under Roman rule until early in the sixth century, but Dalmatia was conquered in 481 by Odovaker, and added it to the Gothic kingdom of Italy. Both these facts emphasize Dalmatia's character as an outpost of the West in the Eastern world, a constantly recurring theme throughout the history of this region. The Slavs, the last of the barbarians to march westwards and southwards, soon began to press ever more closely against the Roman settlements, and the colonists were driven from the interior to the coastal towns. From the letters of Pope Gregory I, it is seen that at this time (590–603), Epidauros, Salona, Doclea and a few other Roman cities still survived. Nevertheless in 600 AD Gregory noted in a letter to the Bishop of Salona his great sorrow that Dalmatia was hard pressed by the barbarians. 'De Sclavorum gente, quae vobis imminet, affligor vehementer et conturbor'. The whole province was becoming desolate. In 535 Dalmatia and Pannonia were overrun by Huns, Bulgarians, and Slavs who took the territory from the Goths, but was liberated by Narses in 552, and added to the Exarchate of Ravenna. Later it was made into a separate Exarchate, but after the death of the Emperor Maurice, the Slavs became masters of the greater part of the country.

When the Eastern Empire was divided into themes, the remaining fragments of the Roman colonies on the Illyrian shore were erected into the Themes of Dalmatia and Dyrrhachium. The former is described at length by Constantine Porphyrogenitus in his *De Administando Imperio* (Cap. XXIX to XXXVI) written in 949; it consisted of little more than a few cities and islands, all the rest of the land being peopled by barbarians. The capital of the Dalmatian theme was no longer Salona, which together with Epidauros had been destroyed by the Avars in the seventh century, but Jadera (Zadar). The other towns of the theme were: Veglia, Arbe and Opsara (comprising Cres and Lošinj) in the Kvarner; Tragurium, Spalatum or Aspalathum, and Rhagusium (Dubrovnik), Decatera (Kotor), Rosa (Risan), and Butova (Budva). The theme was governed by a Greek Statagos residing at Zadar (Jadertinus Prior) and by inferior officials (dukes) in the smaller centres, their authority hardly extending beyond the town walls. The inhabitants of these cities in the themes of Dalmatia and Dyrrachium were the remains of the Roman provincials from all parts of Illyria. Porphyrogenitus calls them Romans, as distinguished from the 'ρωματοι' or Byzantine Greeks. In spite of all the subsequent Slavonic incursions Latin, and later Italian, always remained the official language; it was also the common language of the people all down the coast, save at Dubrovnik, where Slavonic was also spoken at an early date. Other fragments of the Roman population were to be found perhaps among the shepherds in the mountains, who were either Latins or Latinized descendants of the native Illyrians. The Slavs speak of them together with the town-dwellers, as Vlachs, or Wallachians. The towns people described these shepherds as Maurovlachs, meaning 'Sea Vlachs' or 'Black Vlachs'.[6]

Outside the towns the main occupants were the Southern Slavs, of whom the two principal tribes were the Servians or Serbs, and the Chorvati or Croatians. The Croatians settled in the northern part of the country; their frontiers were the Rivers Sava, Kupa, Vrbas and Cetina. Their settlement seems to have preceded that of the Serbs. In 634 AD the Croats from Southern Poland and Gallica, drove the Avars out of Illyria and occupied their newly gained territory. Croatia was divided into fourteen župe or counties, each governed by a župan. The various župans owed a somewhat shadowy allegiance to a Grand Župan, whose title was afterwards changed to that of King. The Serbs, who also came from Galicia, settled in territory to the south and east of the Croatians, including present day Serbia, Montenegro, Northern Albania and Dalmatia, south of the River Cetina. For many centuries they recognized no central authority, but were divided into tribes, of which the most important were the Diocletiani or Docletiani, who occupied what is now Montenegro and part of Albania; the Terbuniotae, whose country, called Terbunia, Tribunia or Travunia, centred round the modern town of Trebinje, with the semi-independent southern district of Canale or Canali (Konavle);[7] the coast north of Dubrovnik up to the Naretva River was occupied by the Zachlumje, Zachumlia, Hlum or Chelmo, corresponding to present-day Hercegovina.[8] In the vicinity of the Neretva River lay the land of the Narentani (the $'A\rho\epsilon\upsilon\tau\acute{\alpha}\nuοι$ or $\Pi\alpha\gamma\acute{\alpha}\nuοι$ of Porphyrogenitus), notorious for their piratical exploits. The tribe was converted to Christianity much later than the other Serbs, hence their name of Pagani. Inland from here was the area of present-day Bosnia, inhabited by various tribes, whilst still deeper in the interior was the territory of the Serbs proper.[9]

Thus by the eighth century AD there were a series of coastal towns and a few islands peopled by Latins still under the rule of the Eastern Roman Empire set in the midst of a country whose inhabitants were all Slavs, with the exception of the Latin or Latinized Vlach shepherds. Imperial influence over these townships gradually declined, and at an early date they constituted themselves into city-states of the Italian type, for their municipal statutes present many analogies with those of Italy. As they grew rich and powerful they acquired territory, developed their trade, both seaborne and with the interior, until they were finally absorbed by the Venetian Republic. Their conditions are in many respects, therefore, similar to those prevailing in the maritime republics of Italy during this period. In Italy there was a Latin civilization, overwhelmed by hordes of pagan, or partly pagan, barbarians. Further comparison is difficult for in Italy the barbarian hordes never settled in such large numbers that they were able to absorb the Latins, whereas the Slavs in Dalmatia far outnumbered the Roman colonists, and save for the Latin fringe, the territory soon became a Slavonic land. Also whereas in Italy the Latins and barbarians soon amalgamated, in Dalmatia, the Latins and Slavs remained distinct and separate in language, character and ideals for a much longer time. Further the Latin cities, like islands in a Slavonic sea, had a different relationship with the hinterland than those in Italy. In Italy the feudal system arose among the Germanic peoples, and Germanic lords had Latin subjects and serfs, whereas the Slavonic chieftains of Dalmatia had few Latin dependents. The causes of this division of race and language, which exercised so deep an influence on the history and development of the Dalmatian municipia, are not very apparent. They are probably to be found in the different proportions of barbarians to Latins in the two countries. In Italy the number of invaders who settled permanently in the country was never very great compared with that of the Latin inhabitants. The conquered were therefore soon able to absorb the conquerors, but in Dalmatia the Slavs were far more numerous than the Latin burghers; the former could not absorb the coastal communities because they were more civilized, whilst the latter failed to absorb the Slavs because they were so few in number. It should also be remembered that even the Latins were originally colonists from another land, and that the native Illyrians (from whom present-day Albanians are said to be descended) may perhaps have been merged with the Slavs and helped to increase their numbers.[10]

The Dalmatian townships had many features in their development similar to those of the towns of Italy, especially of the maritime republics, for in the ninth and tenth centuries the increasing consolidation of kingdoms, with the ensuing upsurge of commerce, induced a growth of urban communities all over western Europe.

Among the first to achieve prominence in this renaissance were the Italian towns of Padua, Venice, Milan, Florence, Pisa and Genoa. Most of them became independent 'city-states' that functioned as intermediaries in the large scale trade that came to be pursued between Byzantium and the Near East and the Low Countries.[11] But the Dalmatian townships were always near to the advancing Slav tribes and this fact imparts to their history its peculiar character. They were essentially border fortresses, always aware of the possibilities of attack by the inland Balkan peoples. Of all these towns, that in which this feature was most marked is Dubrovnik.

The Foundation of Dubrovnik

The origin of Dubrovnik is very obscure. It is possible to imagine that even in the prehistoric period some form of fishing settlement may have existed on the site of the present city judging from the number of tumuli and other finds from the neighbouring region, especially in Konavle. From the Roman period there is little definite evidence for Dubrovnik, but an inscribed stele, with the signature CIL III, has been found, probably from the sarcophagus of a Roman officer, Annianus. Roman relics in the museum are mainly from nearby Cavtat, and even further down the coast from Risan. There is also little evidence of occupation of the site during the early Christian period, even before the seventh century AD, but Rubić suggests that a small Illyrian-Greek settlement may have existed there during the fourth or third centuries BC.[12]

The exact year of the foundation of Dubrovnik is uncertain, but it was probably between the years 639 and 656 AD, the first of these being marked by a partial destruction of the neighbouring Epidauros by the Avars and the second by the total ruin of this city by the Croats. Dubrovnik annals and chronicles from the twelfth and thirteenth centuries appear to give two different versions on the origin of the city. The first and probably more popular version is that the town was founded by refugees from towns destroyed by the Avars, especially Salona and Epidauros. Of Salona near Split extensive ruins remain, but with regard to the site of Epidauros there has been a division of opinion among archaeologists. It is generally held that the remains of Cavtat, 11 km to the south-east of Dubrovnik are those of the ancient Epidauros.[13] In the neighbouring Konavle valley, there are the ruins of a Roman aqueduct, whilst the former name for

Cavtat, Ragusavecchia corroborates the tradition that it was the original home of Dubrovnik's citizens; its Slavonic name, Cavtat, is probably derived from the Latin 'civitas'. Some archaeologists doubt this, particularly Gelcich, who is of the opinion that Epidauros must be sought for, somewhere on the Sutorin promontory in the Bay of Kotor. Fragments of Roman brickwork and mosaic pavement have been found there too, and according to Gelcich, the Konavle aqueduct is so built that it must have served a city farther south than Cavtat. On the other hand, the statements of classical writers, especially Pliny, seem to bear out the general opinion of the more northerly site.

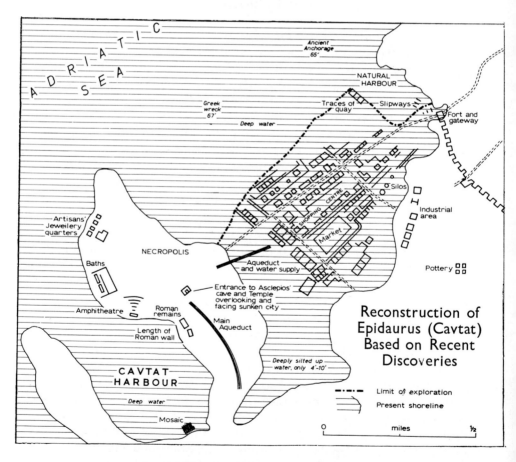

FIG. 10. (after Falcon-Barker)

The exact date of the incursion of the Avars and of the destruction of Epidauros has also been the subject of controversy. According to some writers the city was destroyed by the Goths in the third century AD[14] but documents written between the third and seventh centuries mention it as still existing. Pope Gregory I is the last writer who alludes to Epidauros, so that it was evidently not destroyed before 603. Nevertheless, accounts exist which put its destruction before this date.[15] The Avars made their first appearance in Dalmatia in the years 597–598.[16] They belonged to the same Tartar group as the Huns, and their path was marked with the same ruin and destruction. At one time they were in the service of Justinian, but under his successors particularly Chagan they became powerful and insolent against the Greek Emperors. In 597 they raided Dalmatia and destroyed over forty towns, whilst during the next thirty years they conquered the whole country with the exception of some of the coastal settlements, unimpeded by the Greeks, who were then occupied fighting the Saracens. In 619 they destroyed Salona some of whose inhabitants escaped and took refuge in Diocletian's palace at Split. It is thought that some wandered southwards and helped found Dubrovnik. About the year 656 AD the Avars swept down on Epidauros and razed it to the ground, the surviving inhabitants fleeing to Dubrovnik.[17] This year is generally accepted as the date of the city's foundation. In all probability, it was not founded at any definite period but arose gradually through the influx of refugees from all parts of southern Dalmatia, from a fishing village into a town. The original settlers consisted of six families[18] who were nearly all Latins, and it was not until later that a certain number of Slavs were admitted. Constantine Porphyrogenitus says that the Slavs, whom he mixed up with the Avars, had destroyed Epidauros (τὸ κάστρον πίταυρα), the inhabitants being mostly killed or captured. The survivors fled and on an inaccessible rock founded the new city of Ραούσιον. The full text of Porhpyrogenitus is seen in Fig. 11.[19] Freely translated this account is as follows:

'The castle of Ragusa is not called that in the Roman dialect, because it stands on the precipice, and the precipice is called by the Romans "Lagussei", that is those who live on the precipice. But the common habit which many times transforms the name by changing the letters, altered the word and called them "Ragussei". These same Ragussei held the old castle, the so called "Pitvara", because at the time the other castles were held by the Slavs, who were in the region, this castle was held by them. Others were killed or captured, and those who were able to escape and rescue themselves settled down on the precipitous place, where the castle now stands, which at first was small and later enlarged. After this they increased the castle wall, in order to satisfy their needs, because they increased in size and population. Among those who moved to Ragusa were the following: Gregorias Arsafios Victorinos, Vitalios, Valentine the archdeacon, Valentine the father of Stephanos the protospatharios (a dignitary of the Byzantine Empire). The period elapsing from their emigration to today (949 AD) is 500 years. In the same castle lies the body of Saint Parigratios, in the church of St. Stefanos, which is in the centre of the same castle'.

Thus Porphyrogenitus speaks of Dubrovnik as having been founded by refugees from Salona five hundred years before his own time, about 449. It has been suggested that the ϕ–500 of Porphyrogenitus may be an error in transcription for T–300, which would correspond better with the generally accepted date of the destruction of Epidauros.[20] All these confused accounts and inconsistent dates have led modern historians to the sensible conclusion that the colonization of Dubrovnik was gradual and extended over a long period, though no doubt she received a sudden increase in numbers when Epidauros and Salona were destroyed in the seventh century. Whatever may have been the date of their arrival the refugees brought with them the ancient Roman language and culture, and 'Rausium' is one of the towns mentioned by Porphyrogenitus as continuing in his day Roman in the midst of a country peopled by Slavs.[21] This version really reflects the Byzantine thesis which established the continuity of its rule over Dubrovnik's rulers in their effort to establish the succession of their laws and 'their heritage' over territory surrounding the town, particularly Dubrovačke Župe and Konavle (in the fourteenth century).

The second version is a native account of the foundation of Dubrovnik. The ancient Ragusa (Dubrovnik) it says stood 'ne Captate' (at Cavtat) and possessed the whole 'župa' of Konavle; when the city fell and was destroyed, 'the Lords of Chum and Rascia', occupied this župa, and the inhabitants of the city took refuge on a strategic place, where they founded the modern Dubrovnik. An alternative version of this is that a Slavic King, Pavlimir, grandson of King Radoslav, re-

Ὅτι τὸ κάστρον τοῦ Ῥαουσίου οὐ καλεῖται Ῥαούση τῇ
Ῥωμαίων διαλέκτῳ, ἀλλ' ἐπεὶ ἐπάνω τῶν κρημνῶν ἵσταται,
λέγεται δὲ Ῥωμαϊστὶ ὁ κρημνὸς λαῦ, ἐκλήθησαν ἐκ τούτου
Λαουσαῖοι ἤγουν οἱ καθεζόμενοι εἰς τὸν κρημνόν. ἡ δὲ κοινὴ
συνήθεια, ἡ πολλάκις μεταφθείρουσα τὰ ὀνόματα τῇ ἐναλλαγῇ
τῶν γραμμάτων, μεταβαλοῦσα τὴν κλῆσιν Ῥαουσαίους τούτους
ἐκάλεσεν. οἱ δὲ αὐτοὶ Ῥαουσαῖοι τὸ παλαιὸν ἐκράτουν τὸ κάστρον τὸ ἐπιλεγόμενον Πίταυρα. καὶ ἐπειδὴ ἡνίκα τὰ λοιπὰ
ἐκρατήθησαν κάστρα παρὰ τῶν Σκλάβων τῶν ὄντων ἐν τῷ
θέματι ἐκρατήθη καὶ τὸ τοιοῦτον κάστρον, καὶ οἱ μὲν ἐσφά-
γησαν οἱ δὲ ᾐχμαλωτίσθησαν, οἱ δὲ δυνηθέντες ἐκφυγεῖν καὶ
διασωθῆναι εἰς τοὺς ὑποκρήμνους τόπους κατῴκησαν, ἐν ᾧ
ἐστιν ἀρτίως τὸ κάστρον, οἰκοδομήσαντες αὐτὸ πρότερον μικρὸν
καὶ πάλιν μετὰ ταῦτα μεῖζον, καὶ μετὰ ταῦτα πάλιν τὸ τεῖχος
αὐτοῦ αὐξήσαντες μέχρι δ' ἔχειν τὸ κάστρον διὰ τὸ πλατύ-
νεσθαι αὐτοὺς κατ' ὀλίγον καὶ πληθύνεσθαι. ἐκ δὲ τῶν με-
τοικησάντων εἰς τὸ Ῥαούσιον εἰσὶν οὗτοι, Γρηγόριος, Ἀρσάφιος,
Βικτωρῖνος, Βιτάλιος, Βαλεντῖνος ὁ ἀρχιδιάκων, Βαλεντῖνος ὁ
πατὴρ τοῦ πρωτοσπαθαρίου Στεφάνου. ἀφ' οὗ δὲ ἀπὸ Σαλῶνα
μετῴκησαν εἰς Ῥαούσιον, εἰσὶν ἔτη φ' (500) μέχρι τῆς σήμερον,
ἥτις ἰνδικτιῶνος ἑβδόμης ἔτους ͵Ϛυνζ' (6457 = Christi 949).
ἐν δὲ τῷ αὐτῷ κάστρῳ κεῖται ὁ ἅγιος Παγκράτιος ἐν τῷ ναῷ
τοῦ ἁγίου Στεφάνου τῷ ὄντι μέσον τοῦ αὐτοῦ κάστρου.

Const. Porph. de Adm. Imp., ch. xxix.

FIG. 11. Text of Porphyrogenitus.

turned from exile in Italy to claim lands in the Balkan peninsula ruled by his ancestors. He arrived with his fleet at Gruž (6 km from the city-centre) and proceeded to found the city of Dubrovnik. This viewpoint has been supported by numerous Dubrovnik annalists and chroniclers, particularly by the notary and chronicler Priest Dukljanin.[23] The Slavic interpretation stresses the relatively early Slavicization of Dubrovnik, despite more than five centuries of Byzantine rule, and the continued connections the city had with the Slav hinterland, which later was one of the most important elements in the prosperity of Dubrovik's merchants.

The Name of Dubrovnik

The traditional origin of the name Dubrovnik is connected with the situation of the city on a precipitous ridge. According to Porphyrogenitus, it is derived from 'Λαῦ', meaning 'stone' or 'rock'[24] and was originally Lausa. The 'l' changed to 'r', and it became Rausa or Rhausion, which Skok maintains is derived from a transliteration of the Latin word 'lau' into Greek.[25] Conversely, Jireček[26] believes this derivation is quite inaccurate. The rocky seaward ridge, even in the thirteenth, fourteenth and fifteenth centuries, was called 'Labe' or 'Laue', from the Latin word 'labes', a precipice. The form 'Ragusa' is found in William of Tyre, and used by the Arabic writer Edrisi in 1153.[27] This remained the Italian name of the city, but later the form 'Rausa' was used, and in the fifteenth century 'Raugia', 'Ragugia', and occasionally 'Ragusium'; Ragusa was also used in Arabic sources.[28]

The Slavonic name 'Dubrovnik' is said to be derived from 'dubrava', which comes from the old Slavonic 'dobr'-'dubr' (dub-tree grove, wood, woodland; or daˌbrovъ from daˌbrъ=oak). This sounds quite probable entymologically, as there is a wood in close proximity to the town, a rarity in this part of the world. Turrill believes that much of the Balkans was naturally forested during prehistoric and classical times the deforestation occurring in later periods due to Man's activity.[29] Jireček states that from 'Dubrava' the original form should have been 'Dubravnik', but this does not appear anywhere. The Presbyter Dioclas writes: 'Dubrounich, id est silvester sive silvestris, quonium quando eam aedificaverunt, de silva venerunt'. Yet another theory derives the name from Epidauro Novo',[30] but the Slavonic name occurs for the first time in a privalege from 1189, written in Latin and Serbo-Croat. In the Turkish documents, the name Dubrovnik is used from the very beginning; written Dubrovnik, Dubravnik, Dubr.vnik, or Dupr.vnik. It is also vocalized[31] Dubrovunik, and has been mentioned as Raguza Nova (the city of Dubrovnik), with Raguza Vaga (Cavtat), whilst in seventeenth century sources, Dubrovnik also appears as Dubra Venedik.[32] Some authors also emphasize that for the Middle Ages, Dubrovnik should be called Ragusa,[33] either alone or with Dubrovnik maintaining that it is misleading to use only Dubrovnik, its modern Slavic name. To avoid too much confusion and to ensure a sense of continuity throughout, Dubrovnik alone is used in this book. Whatever may be the philological value of these various forms, they indicate the double character (both Latin and Slavonic) of Dubrovnik in the early if not earliest times.

Early Development

Dubrovnik's development shows in every way a stronger individuality than that of any other Dalmation coastal settlement. Three characteristics enabled it to attain and preserve such a peculiar position in the Adriatic. The first is its geographical situation. Dubrovnik was, as it were, the gate of the East, the meeting point of Latin and Slav, of the Eastern and Western Churches, of Christian and Mohamedan. One of the chief commercial highways from the coast to the interior had its terminus at Dubrovnik, while the sheltered position of its harbour, and of that of the neighbouring Gruž, favoured its development as a great commercial centre. Here the Slavs from the interior found their nearest market, and the nearest place where civilization and culture flourished.

The second characteristic of Dubrovnik is its natural position. It is built partly on a precipitous rocky ridge jutting out into the Adriatic, and partly on the mainland, ascending the steep slopes of the Mount Srđ (412 m). The original town was limited to the seaward ridge, which was formerly an island divided from the mainland by a marshy channel, and seemed indeed a suitable place on which to erect a city, in days when security was the first, almost the only consideration. There was also a settlement of Serbs on Mount Srđ opposite. The ridge slopes gradually up from the channel, but drops down with a sheer drop on the side facing the sea. The former island was geologically part of a group of islands that stretch from Cavtat as far as Dubrovnik, and include Mrkan, Bobova, Supetar, Superk and Lokrum, peaks of a mountain chain, before the sea level rose to make them into individual islands.

An old drawing (Fig. 12) in the library of the Franciscan monastery in Dubrovnik, shows the town as it was when it only occupied the ridge. It is surrounded by a wall, and divided into two parts by another wall. Three extensions of the walls are recorded prior to the twelfth century, rendered necessary by the ever increasing number of fugitives who took refuge within its walls. Gelcich maintains that

> 'The original city was limited to the centre of the northern slope now called Santa Maria (Sv. Marija), which was separated from Monte Sergio (Mt. Srđ), and stretched forth in an opposite direction to that of the neighbouring peninsula of Lapad; it comprised a quarter of the town between the diocesan seminary and the street leading from the Chiesa del Domino (Dominican church) to the summit of the ridge'.[34]

The earliest extensions were the suburbs of Garište and Pustijerna, the former on the western side, the latter to the east reaching as far as the harbour. Thus the whole rock of the seaward ridge was occupied and surmounted by a wall. The channel which divided it from the mainland soon became a marshy field, and finally dried up. As a protection against the Slavonic settlement on Mount Srđ a castle was built by the sea, guarding the bridge to the mainland. Later the Serbian colony was also absorbed, and the town walls were extended to their present circuit.

A third feature intimately connected with the last was Dubrovnik's character as a haven of refuge. During the troubled centuries following the fall of the Roman Empire no settlement however large, or influential, could feel entirely secure. The Byzantine Emperor Justinian failed to make his northern boundary safe during the sixth century, gradually changing the racial and social aspect of the Balkan peninsula. The Slavs, of Indo-European stock, first pushed towards the Danube from within the arc of the Carpathian mountains[35, 36] at the beginning of the sixth century and by the early seventh century were able to expel or assimilate the greater part of the existing native population over much of the Balkan lands. The coming of the Slavs profoundly affected the future of the whole Balkan peninsula, especially Dalmatia. Previously the Dinaric mountains had proved a defence against the relatively small bands of marauding Avar cavalry,

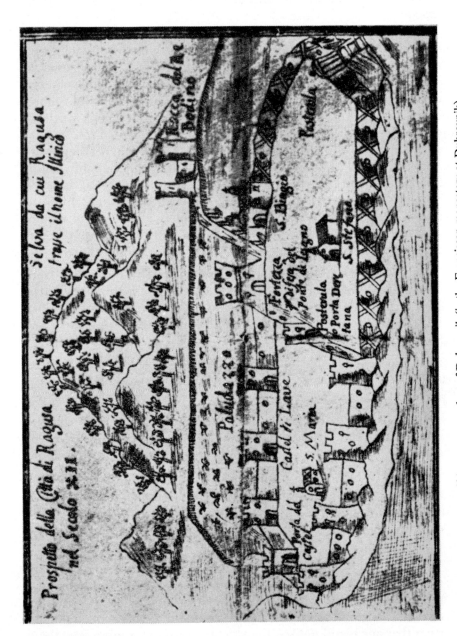

FIG. 12. Twelfth century woodcut of Dubrovnik (in the Franciscan monastery at Dubrovnik).

but the larger scale of the Slav invasion overcame this mountain obstacle.

It was in circumstances such as these that the site of Dubrovnik provided a haven for refuge. Of the various groups of refugees who settled within the hospitable walls of Dubrovnik fairly reliable accounts exist. Porphyrogenitus mentions the earliest of these immigrations, and also gives us the name of the most prominent among the newcomers: Arsaphios, Gregorios, Victorinos, Vitalios, Valentinos the archdeacon, and Valentinos the father of the Protospathar Stephen. All these have unquestionably a Latin sound; they were probably Roman provincials from the minor Dalmatian townships destroyed by the barbarians. Besides the Latin refugees, at an early date a certain number of Slavs, who preferred the quiet life and safety of Dubrovnik to the constant turmoils and disorders among their own people, added to the population. The Anonymous Chronicle of Ragusa describes several of these immigrations:

'690. Many people came to Ragusa with all their goods from Albania and the parts of Bosna, because many in Bosna were partisans of Duchagini (an Albanian tribe, Dukadjin, south of Skador), and wished to save themselves from being accused (punished)'.

This evidently refers to a civil war, but the date given is much too early: it is not likely that Dubrovnik's citizens would have admitted barbarians within their walls so soon after the destruction of Epidauros:

'691. There came to Dubrovnik the men of two castles on the mainland, from Chastel Spilan and Chastel Gradaz (not been identified), and they all made their dwellings on the coast for they were of the race of Epidauros destroyed by the Saracens'.

This obviously refers to the Latin colonists mentioned by the imperial historian:

'743. Many people came from Bosna with much wealth, for the King, Radoslav, was a tyrant, and lived according to his pleasure; Murlacchi from the Narenta also came, and Catunari, among whom there was a chief above all the others; they came with a great multitude of cattle of all sorts: to them was assigned the mountain of Saint Serge (Mt. Srđ) as a pasture, for it was so covered with trees that one could not see the sky, and so much timber was there that they made beams for their houses'.

Of the first two centuries of Dubrovnik's history little is known. The town, like the other Latin communities of Dalmatia, at first formed part of the Eastern Empire. They were the better defended maritime cities such as Kotor and Zadar, which like Dubrovnik, had been able to withstand the Slavic invaders and had formed places of refuge for the Romanized population. Heraclius, head of the Eastern Empire, had abandoned all the rest of the country to the Slavs, leaving Dalmatia as 'a Slavonic land with an Italian fringe'[37] but even in the coastal towns imperial authority was becoming ever more shadowy. Under Michael II Balbus they were granted what practically amounted to autonomy, and they constituted themselves into city-states of the Italian type.[38] These better-defended sites were ever desirous of maintaining their freedom but they were usually obliged to accept the protection of a powerful neighbour. In 806 AD the northern portion of Dalmatia was included within the realm of Charlemagne, the coastal towns (including Dubrovnik) were subject to Byzantine authority. Dubrovnik, although still small, was increasing in size. At that time, with a world of barbarism all round, with numerous wars between the various Slav tribes of the interior, there was indeed an opening for such a haven of refuge as this city offered.

Internal Structure

Of the internal constitution of the community in these early days, of its laws and customs, we have the meagrest information. The only account of them which is known is that given in the Anonymous Chronicle, a not very reliable document of a much later date than the events recorded. The chief passage on the subject is as follows:

> 'In Dubrovnik a division of all the people was made. . . . Those who were the richest were (appointed) chiefs and governors. . . . Each family had its own saint, some San Sergio (Sv Srđ), some this saint, some that . . . And when men had come from Lower Vulasi (Wallachia), a division of the citizens was made, each class for itself. Many Wallachians were rich in possessions – gold, silver, cattle, and other things: among them were many *Chatunari*, each of whom considered himself a count, and had his own Naredbenizi (stewards). One was master of the horse, another looked after the cattle, another after the sheep and goats, another managed the household, another commanded the servants, but one chief was

above all the others, and called the Grand Chatunar.... These
Chatunari formed the *Sboro* (Council or Parliament), and for their
convenience divided the population into three parts: the first was
of gentlemen, the second of burghers, the third of serfs. Many
serfs had come from Wallachia with cattle, and it seemed to them
a mean thing to be called only shepherds. Some attended to the
house, some to the horses, some to the person of their master, but
the latter were few in number. The third part was of gentlemen;
for at the beginning there were many who had fled from Bosna and
Albania, and who were not men of low condition, but of much
account, having been captains or counts or Naredbenizi, and these
were of noble origin ... Those who were gentlemen were made
governors of the land or were given other offices, and they alone
entered the Sboro or General Council. The other part was of the
people, *populani*, or villeins. Although these villeins were of low
status, some were in the houses of gentlemen as guardians, and
therefore enjoyed benefits'.

This account is somewhat confused and difficult to understand. As
far as can be made out, the people were divided into three classes,
i.e., the nobles, who alone formed the Grand Council, and were either
the descendants of the original Latin refugees from Epidauros and
Salona, or those among the newcomers who were of noble birth; the
middle class, consisting of non-noble burghers, the stewards, and
chief retainers of the nobles, and the men of small property; the third
class was composed of serfs and of the poorest citizens. The General
Assembly was presided over by the Head of State, the Byzantine
Duke, Prior, or Praeses. After Dubrovnik had made submission to
Venice in 998 we find Venetian counts instead. During the intervals
when the city was independent, and no foreign rulers were appointed,
the head of the government was chosen by the Council, as it was in
later times, but even when sent from Venice or Constantinople he
does not seem to have exercised much direct influence on the internal
affairs of the republic.

   Besides the Count and the General Council, there was the Assembly
of the People, or *laudo populi*, to whom the decisions of the Council
in all the more important cases had to be submitted. Lampridius,
praeses of Dubrovnik in 1023, sanctioned a decree 'una cum omnibus
ejusdem civitatis nobilibus', 'temporibus Sanctorum Imperatorum
Basilii et Constantini'. Petrus Slabba, prior to 1044, issued another

decree, 'temporibus piissimi Augusti Constantini scilicet Mono-
macho . . . cum parited nobiles atque ignobles'.[39] Thus we have the
aristocratic principle represented by the Council of Nobles, and the
democratic principle by the Assembly of the People, who were
summoned 'cum sonitu campane'.

In the Italian city-republics, besides the Head of the State, the
Council of Nobles, and the Assembly of the People, there was also a
minor or privy council of special advisers. It is very probable that
there was something of the kind at Dubrovnik even at this time, as
there was later. As the constitution evolved, the *laudo populi* gradually dropped into disuse, and Dubrovnik finally developed into a
purely aristocratic community on Venetian lines. Next in authority
to the Head of the State was the Bishop, later the Archbishop, by
whom the acts of the government had to be countersigned. The question as to who should appoint this dignitary was frequently a subject
of dispute between the republic and the Venetians, on account of
his political influence.

Saracens and Pirates

After 806 AD when the coastal towns were subject to Byzantine
authority Dubrovnik gradually consolidated its position as a trading
town on the east Adriatic coast, but not without its difficulties. Dubrovnik's citizens provided for the defence of their city by surrounding
it with walls 'un muro di masiera e travi' (a wall of rubble and
beams)[40] and these fortifications stood them in good stead. Between
the middle of the seventh to the end of the ninth century there was
a great need for timber throughout the eastern Mediterranean for
shipbuilding, due to the incessant wars between the Califat and
Byzantine Empire. The shores of the east Adriatic had a plentiful
supply and this led to numerous Arabic Saracen expeditions to obtain
wood for the Muslim arsenals of Syria and Egypt.[41] Increasing
demand eventually led to Arabic raids into Byzantine territory (including Dubrovnik). The town's fortifications enabled the citizens to
hold out against the Saracens, who in 866–867 AD beseiged Dubrovnik for fifteen months. The citizens implored help from the Byzantine
Emperor Basil the Macedonian, who at once sent a fleet according
to Porphyrogenitus which relieved the beleaguered city from the
raiders.[42] Again there is confusion over the dates. According to tradition, Dubrovnik had been delivered from the Saracens in 783 AD by

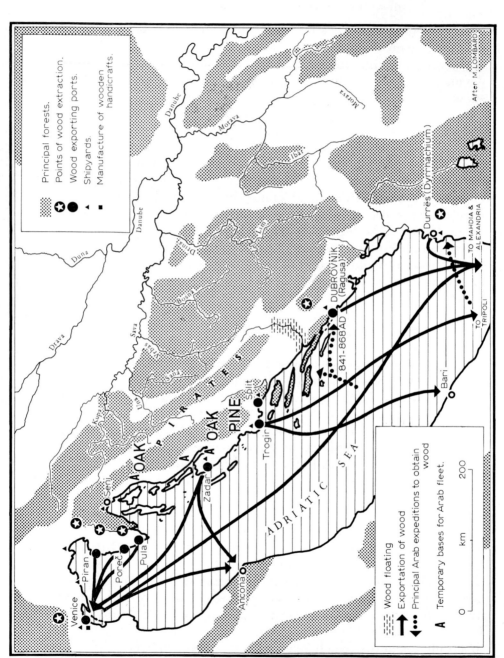

Fig. 13. Wood trade in the Adriatic, seventh to ninth centuries.

Legend (map):

Principal forests.
Points of wood extraction.
Wood exporting ports.
Shipyards.
Manufacture of wooden handicrafts.

Wood floating
Exportation of wood
Principal Arab expeditions to obtain wood
A   Temporary bases for Arab fleet.

km
0   200

After M. LOMBARD

Place names: Duna, Danube, Danube, Drava, Sava, Bosna, Vrbas, Una, Kupa, Sava, Drina, Morava, Ibar, Lim, Morava, ADRIATIC SEA, PIRATES, OAK, OAK, PINE, Venice, Piran, Poreč, Pula, Zadar, Seni, Trogir, Split, DUBROVNIK (Ragusa), 841-868 AD, Ancona, Bari, Durrës (Dyrrhachium), TO MAHDIA & ALEXANDRIA, TO TRIPOLI

Orlando, or Roland the Paladin. The legend probably has its origin in a confusion between Charlemagne's suzerainity over Dalmatia and the Saracen siege of Dubrovnik in 866. The Emperor wished to pursue the Saracens into Apulia, where they had established themselves, and the rendezvous for one part of the expedition was Dubrovnik. A large force of Serbs and Croatians in the pay of the Empire congregated there, and were transported to the Italian shore in Dubrovnik ships. The expedition was successful, Bari being recaptured, and the Saracen power in southern Italy broken.[43] This is the first time that Dubrovnik shipping is mentioned in documents, which was afterwards to play so large a part in the history of the Levant trade. The connection with the Islamic world, though greatly facilitated later by the extensive Dubrovnik trade connections, antedates the rise of the city to a position of first rate commercial importance. Particularly between 888 and the end of the tenth century there was an active traffic between Dalmatia and the Iberian peninsula, and Dubrovnik's ships and merchants were not wholly responsible for its development. During these years the Arabic Saracens were at peace with the Byzantine Empire. From Dalmatia to Spain it was a four weeks' trip in a fast sailing ship, and adventurous minded Slavs were attracted by the prospect of employment in the famous Slave Guard of the Moorish rulers of Córdoba. In the mid-tenth century the 'Slave' (Slav?) army of Omayad caliphs in Spain numbered 13,750 men, and the Venetians also used to send Slav war prisoners to the caliphs of Córdoba for service in the Slave Guard.[44] There were even Slav governors and administrators of large districts of Moorish Spain, on several occasions especially at Almería. Relations between the Adriatic Slavs and the Saracens in Andalusia endured for more than three centuries. The overthrow at the beginning of the eleventh century of the brilliant civilization of Moslem Spain was a part consequence of the hatred and rivalry that existed between the Slav and Berber elements in the armies of the caliphs. Many Slavs certainly had embraced Islam by this time. A very noted Moslem writer in the tenth century was Habib the Slave (Slav?), who wrote among other things a strong defence of the Slavs in the Moorish service. Evidently his treatise was designed to counter attack those being made upon them at this time. His work cited the literary and artistic accomplishments of the Slavs, among whom he included the Croats, in the Andalusian caliphate.[45] Córdoba's fall in 1013 to a new wave of Berbers from Africa led to the splitting up of the Moorish Empire in Spain into many small states, some of which had Croatian rulers. The Croats continued to be regarded as the elite troops of the Saracen army of Abd-ur Rahman III and other caliphs, their only rivals being the equally famous Moldavian guards. There were numerous links, too, between the Croats of the Adriatic shore and the Moslems settled around Lucera in southern Italy. In fact a Croatian bishop, Agustin Kožotić, came to convert this Moslem colony in the fourteenth century.

Of all the Slavonic tribes settled in Dalmatia, the most lawless and uncivilized were the Narentans, the Arentani of Porphyrogenitus (Cap. XXX). This hardy race of mariners occupied the land about the mouth of the Narenta (Neretva) and the coast, between that river and the Cetina together with the islands of Brač, Hvar, Korčula, Vis, Mljet and Lastovo. Connected by racial ties with the Serbs and the Croatians, they obeyed the laws of neither. The ancient Illyrians were famous for their piracy, which first called the attention of the Romans to the country, and the Narentans proved worthy successors. The coast with its numerous inlets, well-sheltered harbours, safe refuges and countless islands lends itself to this type of occupation. The Narentans ravaged the coastal towns of Dalmatia with their swift galleys, plundered peaceful merchantmen, and so harried Venetian trade that the republic was forced to pay them blackmail for a hundred and fifty years. On more than one occasion it sent its fleets to attempt their subjugation, at first with but little success. At the beginning of these wars Dubrovnik was a friendly harbour for the Venetian galleys, their most southern port of call in the Adriatic, where they could take on stores and their crews rest from the fatigues of the voyage.[46] Nevertheless, Dubrovnik very soon began to look askance at the Venetians as a possible danger to their own independence, and adopted the practice of secretly, or even openly, supporting the pirates against the Venetians. This naturally caused trouble later when the Venetians were strong enough to act energetically against the Narentans: it affords a curious insight into the policy of Dubrovnik, which, while anxious to preserve its own civilization and culture, was never averse to siding with barbarians, whether they were Narentans or Turks, against the Christian Powers, but especially against Venice.

As early as the reign of the Doge Giovanni Particiaco I (829–836) the pirates of the Narenta had begun to seize Venetian galleys, and his successor, Pietro Tradonico (836–864), sent two punitive expeditions against them without definite result. After the Venetian fleet had been defeated by the Saracens, the Dalmatian pirates were audacious enough to make a raid on the Lagoons. In 887 the Doge Pietro Candiano I sent a first unsuccessful expedition against them, and a few months later led a second himself. This too was defeated, and the Doge killed. Probably there was another in 948 under Pietro Candiano III, and this time operations were directed against Dubrovnik itself, the town being saved only through the special intercession of San Biagio (Sv. Vlah) who became the patron of Dubrovnik. The Venetian fleet designed to capture Dubrovnik by treachery, but the plot was revealed to a priest, who thus relates his vision:

> 'I was in the church of St. Stephen about midnight, at prayer, when methinks I saw the whole fane filled with armed men. And in the midst I saw an old man with a long white beard holding a staff in his hand. Having called me aside, he told me that he was San Biagio, and had been sent by Heaven to defend this city. He told me further that the Venetians had come up to the walls to scale them using the masts of their ships as ladders, but he, with a company of heavenly soldiers, had driven back the enemy; but he desired that in future the Ragusans should defend themselves, and never trust armed neighbours'.[47]

Ragnin dates the event 971.[48]

In the course of the tenth century Dubrovnik was again beseiged by barbarians – they were Bulgarians this time, under the Tsar Simeon who invaded the western provinces of the Eastern Empire. According to Cedren, his attack on Dubrovnik failed, whereas the Presbyter of Doclea writes that the town was burnt down.[49]

Territorial Growth

It was during this same century that Dubrovnik first began to acquire territorial possessions. The acount of the manner of these acquisitions is in part legendary; but, according to Gelcich, it has some substratum of fact. Pavlimir Belo or Belus, King of Rascia (synonymous for Serbia, and is derived from the River Raška), having been deposed and exiled, took refuge in Rome, and married a Roman lady. In 950 he returned to Illyria, and landed at Gruž, near Dubrovnik, with a large suite of Roman nobles, and is believed by some chroniclers, probably erroneously, to have founded the city. The Dubrovnik citizens received him with great honours, and he in return helped them to enlarge their city, and sent a number of his followers, including some Romans, to increase the population. After this he returned to Rascia and regained his throne. As Gelcich observes, Rome is evidently a mistake for Rama, a country which forms part of Herzegovina, and takes its name from a small river tributary of the Naretva. The territory of Dubrovnik had been hitherto confined to their rock; but in 1050 Stephen, King of Dalmatia and Ban of Bosnia, and his wife, Margaret, came to Dubrovnik in order to fulfil a vow which the former had made to St. Stephen when his wife was ill, that he would visit the saint's church in the city if she recovered. They were received with great honour and as a reward for the welcome accorded to him by the citizens he made a donation to them of 35 km of coast, including the fertile valleys of Breno and Rijeka Dubrovačka, together with Gruž, Zaton, and Brgat.

Venetians, Magyars, and Normans

From the beginning Dubrovnik was a rival of Venice. As early as 791 the Venetians attacked the city but suffered a defeat.

The Venetians, in 791, frequented the southern Adriatic sea for the purpose of rooting out pirates from the neighbouring Neretva who infested the Adriatic. Coveting the security and convenience of Dubrovnik's position the Venetians sought to subjugate it to their authority; but its strength being beyond their force, they attempted its possession by strategem. A fleet of galleys was seen from the towers of Dubrovnik coming from the north, the alarm passed from battlement to battlement, and the town was in a state of readiness: but while a part of the fleet anchored in Gruž, to the north of the island on which Dubrovnik was built, the other drew up under Lokrum Island to the south; and the Venetian commander, landing with his officers in a pacific manner, gave out that he was on a voyage to the Levant, and only wanted water and provisions. Suspicion was allayed, the Venetians went and came between the north gate leading to Gruž and the south gate opening on the small port; but a priest named Stoico, having by some means overheard, or got intelligence of, the Venetian plans to assault the town the following night, gave information to the government; and no sooner were the gates closed at sunset, than every citizen was at his post, waiting for the attack with breathless expectation. The first hour passed without alarm; but after midnight the warder on the tower above the Postijerna saw galleys from Lokrum getting under way, and suddenly bearing up to the southern port. Scarcely was the alarm passed, and preparation made to receive them when a large body of the men of the other fleet in Gruž suddenly landed, and silently ascended the steep hill to the north of Dubrovnik. They expected to scale the walls and enter the city; but to their surprise, on reaching the brow of the hill, they found themselves vigorously assaulted by a large body of citizens, and driven down the hill to the boats, suffering much slaughter. The diversion to the north having completely failed, the citizens re-entered the city, and found that the Venetians had been struck with a panic, and retired to their galleys on seeing all the southern wall armed with men, who poured a torrent of stones and heavy beams on the assailants. For some time after this event the attention of both of these maritime rivals was fully occupied by the necessity of dealing with the Moslem sea rovers.

Nearly fifty years had passed since the last Venetian expedition to Dalmatia in 948; but when the great Doge Pietro Orseolo came to the throne in 991, he was determined to put an end to the depredations of the Narentans once and for all. The annual tribute which the Venetians had been forced to pay to the freebooters only secured a very imperfect immunity, and the Adriatic trade was never really safe. Orseolo suspended the tribute, and immediately the Narentans recommenced their attacks so an expedition under Badoer was sent out which destroyed the town of Vis. The Venetian admiral took a great many prisoners, but failed to attack the pirates' chief strongholds at Lastovo and mouth of the River Neretva. They retaliated on the Latin towns of the coast, and the latter, unable to obtain help from their natural protector, the Greek Emperor, placed themselves under the suzerainty of the Venetians, whom they implored to intervene once more. The Croatians, to whom the towns in the northern and central parts of the country had paid tribute, now declared war on all who obeyed the Venetians, ravaged the territory of Zadar, and attacked the islands of the Kvarner. Dubrovnik was then a tributary to the Serbs, by whom they were surrounded, and fearing the Narentans, who were so close at hand, separated their cause from that of the rest of Latin Dalmatia, and maintained an ambiguous attitude.[50] The Croatians, not content with terrorizing the towns, sent ambassadors to Venice to demand the tribute; but the Doge replied: 'Non per quemlibet nutiorum tributum remittre curo; sed ad hanc persolvendam dationem venire ipso non denegabo'. He at once fitted out another expedition on a large scale, which set forth under his command on May 9, 1000. According to Johannes Diaconus, the expedition started in the seventh year of Orseolo's reign, which would be 998; but Monticolo, who edits that writer in his Cronache Antichissime (p. 156, note 1), observes that Diaconus says that he only heard the news of the victory when the Emperor Otho III came to Pavia in his third descent into Italy, i.e. July 1000. Nevertheless, it reached Cres on June 5, and the Doge claimed the homage of the Dalmatians as their protector; this was paid both by the Latins and by a number of Slavs. He then proceeded to Zadar, which recognized his authority, and the Bishops of Arbe and Veglia came to swear fealty to him, promising that his praises should be sung in the churches after those of the Emperor. Negotiations with the Narentans were now opened; the pirates agreed to forego all tributes, and swore no longer to infest the Adriatic; but the moment the Doge's back was turned they recommenced their depredations. Orseolo then sailed with the fleet for Biograd na More, the residence of the Croatian King. The terrified inhabitants paid him homage, and he prepared to strike a decisive blow at the Narentans. He sailed down the coast and received the submission of Trogir and Split, and on hearing that forty Narentan 'nobles' (pirate captains) were returning from Apulia, some of his galleys lay in wait for them, and captured them off the island of Sušac. The Narentans then sued for peace, which was granted them on a promise of future good behaviour, and all the prisoners were liberated save six, who were retained as hostages. The pirates on the islands of Korčula, Hvar and Lastovo still held out. The first two were easily captured, but the Lastovans hearing that the Doge meant to raze their stronghold to the ground, made a desperate resistance. The Venetians and their Dalmatian allies attacked the town, poured in through a breach in the walls, and put all the inhabitants to the sword. After the capture of this important fortress the power of the Narentans was broken, and the whole of Dalmatia lay at Orseolo's feet.

With regard to the subsequent proceedings and the dedition of Dubrovnik there is considerable divergence of opinion between Venetian and Dubrovnik writers. The latter wish to prove that their city remained independent, at all events until the beginning of the thirteenth century, whereas the Venetians affirm that in 998 (1000) Dubrovnik made full submission to Venice.

The first account of this dedition is that of Johannes Diaconus who writes:

'This (the capture of Hvar, Korčula and Lastovo) having been accomplished, the victorious prince went to the church of St. Maximus; there the Archbishop of Dubrovnik and his suite came and did great homage to the said prince, all partaking of the sacrement'.

Dandolo[51] uses almost identical language, and Sabellico adds that the Archbishop and the Dubrovnik envoys made formal submission to the Doge and the Venetians,[52] and that Counts were appointed to govern the Dalmatian towns, Ottone Orseolo being chosen for Dubrovnik. To this a Dubrovnik writer,[53] calling himself 'Albinus Esadastes de Vargas', replies that the church of St. Maximus must mean that of Maslina at Hvar, and that this island is so far away that the Dubrovnik envoys would hardly have come there to tender their submission. Jadesta, which is also alluded to, does not exist. The Dubrovnik citizens, who had resisted other attacks, both by the Venetians and the Saracens, so valiantly, would not have surrendered now without striking a blow; and, moreover, the Greek Emperors, Basil and Constantine, would not have authorized the submission. With regard to the first and third objections, it is most probable that when the fate of Lastovo had become known to Dubrovnik citizens, they would have gone to tender their submission to Orseolo wherever he happened to be. Jadesta is simply an old name for Lastovo. As for the Greek Emperors, they were far too much occupied in holding their own against the Bulgarians to be able to make any objections. The former attacks on Dubrovnik had all been on a small scale, whereas this expedition was a large and well-equipped force, against which it would have been madness for the tiny Dubrovnik to resist. Then 'Estadastes' shifts his ground, and asserts that the envoys went to the Doge merely to reclaim a ship captured by the Venetians. Also that they actually threatened reprisals on the part of the Emperors if satisfaction were refused, but it is most unlikely that for so trifling a cause the Archbishop and chief citizens would have been sent to the Doge. This version, however, is accepted by Mauro Orbini.[54] Ragnina does not even mention the expedition. Resti[55] says that Ottone Orseolo was sent to Dubrovnik merely to make a commercial treaty; but as Pisani observes, if the magistrates appointed to the other Dalmatian towns were sent to govern them, there is no reason to suppose that an exception was made for Dubrovnik. There is, on the whole, the strongest evidence that the city did actually submit to Venetian supremacy, together with the other coastal towns, in 1000,[56] and received a Venetian Governor. Local usages and laws, however, were respected, according to the Venetian practice of the time; nor was imperial authority wholly disregarded, and prayers for the Emperor continued to be sung in the churches of Dubrovnik. In 1001 a treaty of peace and friendship was made between Venice and Dubrovnik by which the Venetians were annually to give Dubrovnik fourteen yards of scarlet cloth, and an armed galley, in token of perpetual amity, and Dubrovnik to return the compliment with two white horses, three barrels of Ribola wine, and an armed galley.

Venetian rule was not of long duration. On the death of Pietro Orseolo in 1008, his son Ottone became Doge; and during this reign a strong opposition to the House of Orseolo was aroused, which ended with Ottone's expulsion in 1026. During the reign of his successor, Pietro Centranico, faction feuds broke out, greatly weakening the republic, and the Dalmatian towns revolted, as Venetian suzerainty was of use to them only so long as Venice was powerful. Some of them went over to Dobroslav, Prince of the Tribunian Serbs, and elsewhere Byzantine authority revived. Thus in 1036, instead of a Venetian Count at Zadar, it was Gregory, Jadertinus Prior, Pro-consul and Imperial Strategos for all Dalmatia.[57] But his authority was disputed by the Croatians, whose sovereign now proclaimed himself King of Dalmatia. Against this act the Venetians issued a protest, and the Doge Domenico Contarini (1043–1071) reasserted the authority of the republic.

In the year 1071 the Normans from Apulia made their first appearance in Dalmatia; they crossed the Adriatic, and threatened the Eastern Empire. The Emperor Alexius Connenus having implored the help of the Venetians, the Doge Selvo set sail for Dyrrhachium (Dürres) in command of a fleet. Alexius had also asked help from Dubrovnik, which was now practically independent; but they feared the Normans more, and in 1081 cast in their lot with them. The Græco-Venetian fleet encountered the Normans off Dyrrhachium; but in spite of the valour displayed by the allies they were defeated, and the town fell into the enemies' hands. It is said that the Dubrovnik contingent distinguished itself by hurling clouds of arrows, which wrought havoc among the Venetians.[58] As a reward they obtained important commercial privileges in southern Italy. In 1085 the

Venetians again attacked the Normans, and partially defeated them at Corfu, for which action Alexius granted the Doge Vitale Falier the Golden Bull, conferring upon him the title of Protosebastus, and created him Duke of Dalmatia and Croatia. Thus the Venetian Republic regained all its lost influence on the eastern shore of the Adriatic.

Yet another power now begins to interfere in the affairs of Dalmatia, a power which was to play a most important part in its subsequent history. In 1091 Ladislas, King of Hungary, was summoned by the Slavs of inland Croatia, who as usual called in foreign aid when quarrelling among themselves and willingly recognized him as their King. He did not wait to be asked a second time, but at once entered the province and appointed his nephew, Almus, Count of Cismontane Croatia. On his death in 1094 he was succeeded by another nephew, Koloman, who in the following year crossed the Velebit mountains and invaded maritime Croatia. He defeated and killed the Croatian King, Kresimir, at Petrovogora, became master of the littoral from Istria to the Neretva, and prepared to conquer the Serb states of Rascia and Tribunia. By marrying Busita, daughter of King Roger, he allied himself with the Normans, and enlisted their help for his schemes. At Biograd na More he crowned himself King of Dalmatia and Croatia. These conquests were not at all to the taste of Dubrovnik citizens who had every interest in the maintenance of a number of weak but independent Slavonic buffer states in their hinterland, whereas they dreaded the advance of a powerful military monarchy like Hungary. At first they tried to conciliate Koloman with gifts, but as this availed them little they applied to their old enemies, the Venetians; the latter made a treaty with the Hungarian King, by which the Latin municipalities of Dalmatia were recognized as outside the Hungarian sphere. It was not respected for long. The Emperor Alexius, annoyed with the Venetians for their action in the First Crusade and in the Levant generally, laid plans with Koloman, and induced him to violate his pledges. The Magyar King needed little pressure, as the conquest of the Dalmatian sea-board was one of his chief ambitions. When the Venetians sent their fleet to Palestine in 1105 he occupied Zadar, Trogir and Split and forced the citizens to swear fealty to him. Dubrovnik was not disturbed, but sent him another deputation. The Venetians, exhausted with their last efforts in the Holy Land, were unable to do anything for the moment.[59] In 1116 hostilities recommenced, and ended in 1118 with the defeat of the Venetians, who agreed to a five years' truce with Hungary. War broke out again in 1124, and lasted for several years, with varying success. Bela II who succeeded Koloman, crossed the Neretva and conquered the Serb principalities of Tribunia, Zachulmia and Rama, and, while the Venetians were occupied elsewhere, tried to induce the coastal towns to rebel against Venice. Dubrovnik once more applied for Venetian help, and even requested that Venetian Counts should be sent to govern them; both requests were granted.

Between 1124–1152 there is little to tell of Dubrovnik's history. 'Esadastes' mentions the names of four Venetians Counts – Marco Dandolo, Cristiano Pontestorto, Jacopo Doseduro or Dorsoduro, and Pietro Molina. Resti mentions a plague in 1145, which, he says, carried off three-quarters of the inhabitants, evidently an exaggeration. In 1148, according to the same writer, the Serbian Prince Dessa, ancestor of the Nemanjas, granted the island of Mljet to three Benedictine monks, with the provision that its civil government should be entrusted to Dubrovnik. This is the most distant possession in which the republic had, as yet, acquired importance.

In 1152 the series of Venetian Counts in Dubrovnik came to an end,[60] the last of them having apparently received notice to quit from the citizens themselves, who sent him home in one of their own galleys, with many gifts, as a reward, 'Esadastes' says ironically, for having ruled the city so well for thirty years; but he adds the following extract from an early chronicle:

> 'These counts had begun to tyrannise, and, moreover, whilst Dubrovnik was at war with the Bosnians, five hundred soldiers who had come from Venice to aid us outraged our women and committed countless robberies. To free the city from them the Council ordered them to be so placed in the van of the army that they should all be killed. This stratagem having succeeded, they sent the Venetian Rector back to Venice'.

Whether this story be true or not, it is characteristic both of the customs of the time and of the feelings with which Dubrovnik regarded the Venetians. For the latter and their government no native historian ever has a good word to say.

The reason why the Venetians submitted so tamely to being turned out of Dubrovnik lies in the general political situation of Dalmatia. In 1148 Venice had formed an alliance with the Emperor Manuel Comnenus against the Normans, whose incursions in the Adriatic constituted a menace for both powers; but Venetians and Greeks were on the worst of terms, and at the siege of Corfu the Emperor's name had been grossly insulted. Manuel vowed vengeance on his allies, and sent emissaries to stir up the Dalmatians against Venice. The latter was at war on the mainland with Hungary and in Syria, and therefore found it expedient to ignore the Dalmatian question for the time being. Venetian authority did not cease altogether, even at Dubrovnik, where Venetians continued to be appointed as arch-bishops. Thus in 1150 or 1151 the dignity was conferred on a certain Domenico of Venice, and in 1153 on another Venetian named Tri-buno; the latter in 1155 made formal submission to the Patriarch of Grado, with the consent of the clergy and people of Dubrovnik.[61] The town continued, in fact, to be regarded as one of those under Venetian protection, or, at least, as friendly to the republic of the lagoons.

In 1169 Manuel Comnenus was determined to conquer Dalmatia, and even Italy. He sent a squadron up the Adriatic to molest Vene-tian shipping, and encouraged pirates to do the same. The imperial fleet occupied the towns protected by Venice, treating them as con-quered territory. Dubrovnik too was occupied, and was doubtless not unwilling to get rid of all Venetian authority; the imperial stan-dard was raised on a tower expressly built for the purpose. On March 7, 1171, the Emperor had all the Venetians at Constantinople arrested and their property seized. Venice immediately declared war, and, in spite of the scarcity of men and money, a fleet of one hundred and twenty ships, with ten Dalmatian galleys added, was fitted out in a hundred days.[62] It set sail in September under the command of the Doge Vitale Michiel, and most of the Dalmatian towns willingly re-turned to Venetian suzerainty. Dubrovnik too surrendered, though not without resistance and the event is thus described in the *Cronaca Altinate*.[63]

'The Dubrovnik citizens, who, like the others (Dalmatians), were under oath of fealty to the lord Doge, would not go forth to do him homage, but they came out in arms as though to insult the host. Wherefore the Venetians, in high dudgeon, marched against them, and pursued them even to the gates of the city. The same day, at the ninth hour, they began the attack with so much vigour that many of the citizens were killed, and, having stormed the battlements, they captured some of the towers, on which they raised the ducal standards. The assault was kept up with great energy until evening. At dawn on the following morning, while men and machines were being prepared for the battle, Tribuno Michiel, the Archbishop of Dubrovnik, issued forth from the city with the clergy and the nobles bearing crosses, and they cast themselves at the feet of the Doge, imploring mercy for themselves and all the citizens, and declaring that they and their city made full submission. The Doge, calm and prudent, was moved by pity, and on the advice of his followers received them. And all the citizens sang the praises of the Doge, and those above twelve years of age swore the oath of fealty to him and his successors. In addition, they provided money and wine for each galley, and in obedience to the Doge's orders demolished part of their walls, that tower which had been expressly built for the Emperor. They consented that their archbishopric should be subject to the Patriarchate of Grado, provided that the Pope permitted it. (This stipulation appears in nearly all the subsequent treaties of dedition by which Dubrovnik surrendered to Venice. By this act the Dubrovnik Church came under the authority of a Venetian prelate.) When these things had been accomplished the Doge appointed the noble youth Raynerius Joannes (Renier Zane or Zen) as Viscount, and set sail with his fleet for Romania'.

(By 'Romania', mediaeval historians meant the Eastern Empire.)

Dandolo's account is almost identical, and so is that of Sabellico, save that the latter does not mention the actual storming of the town. He merely says that the citizens sued for peace through their archbishop, and that they themselves demolished the tower on which the imperial standard had been raised. Whichever version is accepted it is clear that Dubrovnik again made full submission to the ducal authority, and came once more under Venetian supremacy. We must not forget that Tribuno Michiel, the Archbishop, was a Venetian, and probably there was a Venetian, as well as a Byzantine party in the city. When it became evident that the Venetians were in earnest, the faction which favoured them at once prevailed. 'Esadastes', as usual, casts doubts on the whole story, because Dandolo and Sabellico do not agree as to the attack, but he does not even mention the account of the *Cronaca Altinate*. Resti denies the submission altogether. It should be remembered that whereas Dandolo and the author of the Altinate Chronicle wrote barely a century after the events related, the Dubrovnik historians flourished in the sixteenth, seventeenth, and eighteenth centuries, and wrote with the express purpose of combating all Venice's claims over the city. As before, the surrender did not greatly affect Dubrovnik's internal affairs, which continued to be managed by the citizens themselves. Nor did Venetian suzerainty last long. The campaign against the Eastern Empire ended most disastrously; the fleet was decimated by disease, and returned to Venice in 1172 a complete wreck. Venetian influence in Dalmatia was greatly reduced in consequence, while that of the Empire revived proportionately, and lasted until Manuel's death in 1180. Dubrovnik was still regarded as connected with Venice and in the treaty of peace, which the latter made with William of Sicily in 1175, he promised not to invade 'the lands which are under the rule of the Doge of Venice and of the Venetians'.[64] Dalmatia was included among them.

In 1186 the Normans made another raid into Dalmatia, and occupied Dubrovnik and several other coastal towns. Norman rule lasted until 1190, and does not seem to have left any traces beyond a few documents. The peace treaty dated September 27, 1186,[65] was drawn up

'at the court of the most glorious King William and of the Lord Archbishop of Tribunus, in the presence of Tasilgard, the Royal Chamberlain, of all the nobles, of Gervase the Count (of Dubrovnik), and of all the people'.

This shows that Dubrovnik was under a Norman Count. There is also a peace treaty between Dubrovnik and the Cazichi (another name for the Neretva pirates):

'And on the side of Dubrovnik, Gervase the Count swore to preserve this peace, without prejudice to his sovereign lord. . . . In the year of our Lord (1190), in the month of February, on the day of St. Blaize (the 3rd), the Assembly having been summoned by Gervase the Count to the sound of the bell, we decided . . .'[66]

Another treaty exists between this same Count from Dubrovnik and Miroslav, Prince of the Serbs, in which Gervase promises that the latter should receive hospitality in his city if he ever required it, *salvo sacramento domini nostri regi Tancredi.*[67]

The ocupation of Dubrovnik by the Normans is evidently an episode in the wars which they waged against the Eastern Empire, and the town was probably seized merely as a basis for further operations.

D

Gervase, who ruled the whole time, does not seem to have been an absolute despot, as the consent of the Assembly was required for all the acts of the government. Norman rule in Dalmatia did not survive the death of Tancred and the consequent collapse of the Sicilian kingdom in 1190. In documents of a date later than this, such as the treaty with Fano in 1199,[68] with Ancona[69] the same year, with Bari of 1201,[70] and with Termoli of 1203,[71] no mention either of Venetian or Norman counts is made, so that we may conclude that for the time being Dubrovnik enjoyed freedom from foreign rulers.

But Venice was preparing to re-occupy the whole of Dalmatia, and the Fourth Crusade of 1202 provided her with the desired opportunity. The Crusaders began their expedition to the Holy Land by storming and sacking Zadar where they wintered. In 1204 they captured Constantinople, subverted the Greek Empire, and set up the ephemeral Latin Empire of the East in its place, with Baldwin of Flanders as Emperor. The Doge of Venice, Enrico Dandolo, the prime mover and leader of the expedition, became 'Lord of a quarter and a half of Romania'. In 1205 the Venetians, at the height of their power, demanded the submission of Dubrovnik, which was at once tendered. Dandolo (the historian) thus describes this fourth surrender:

> 'Tommaso Morosini, who had been nominated Patriarch (of Constantinople) by Innocent III, returned to Venice, carrying the Pope's letter; he set sail with a fleet of four triremes and made war against the city of Dubrovnik, who, at the suggestion of the Greeks, had rebelled against Venice. The citizens, no longer trusting in the strength of the Greeks, surrendered their city to the Venetians'.

Two other chronicles[72] gave similar accounts of the event. The indefatigable 'Esadastes' of course tries to prove that Dubrovnik did not surrender, because the people who had held out so bravely and successfully against the Saracens 340 years previously would not have tamely submitted to a squadron of four ships commanded by a priest. The Dubrovnik apologist, however, forgets the enormous prestige acquired by the Venetians as a consequence of their exploits in subverting the Eastern Empire, after which event Dubrovnik could not hope to oppose the greatest power in the Adriatic with any chance of success. A further corroboration, if any were needed, of the surrender is found in the treaty of friendship between Stephen, Grand Župan, and Giovanni Dandolo, Count of Dubrovik.[73] No date is given, but it must be prior to 1222, as in that year Stephen received the title of King from Pope Honorius III, whence his designation of Prvoviencani, or First Crowned.

With this act of submission ends the first period of Dubrovnik history, during which the possession, or rather suzerainty over the city was a matter of dispute between the Venetians and the Greeks, with intervals of absolute independence, and four years of Norman rule. As Byzantine influence, not necessarily political, predominated even in Venice itself, it may be called the Byzantine period. For the next 150 years (1204–1358) save for one short interruption, Dubrovnik was under Venetian supremacy.

The Slavonic Hinterland

Meanwhile Dubrovnik was developing relations of a different character with the Slav principalities of the interior. During the earliest times Dubrovnik territory was limited to a small part of the actual city, and for a long time did not extend beyond the walls. Constantine Porphyrogenitus informs us that it bordered on the two states of Zachumlja and Tribunia (Travunia). The vineyards of Dubrovnik were on the territory of these tribes, and the citizens paid a yearly tribute of thirty-six numismata (gold pieces) to the Prince of Zachumlja, and as much to the Prince of Tribunia. As the population increased they gradually extended their cultivation to the whole of these districts. The Tribunian vineyards were in the Župa of Žrnovica; those of Zachulmja in the Župa of Rijeka as far as Zaton and in that of Poljico.[74] The tribute which Dubrovnik paid for this privilege was called 'margarisium' or 'magarisium',[75] its value varied considerably. In 1363 that due to the Zachumljans was of sixty ipperperi, paid by the owners of the vineyards in proportion to the extent of their holdings. The Zachumljans, on their side, sent a cow, called the 'vacca di margarisio', which was divided between the Count of Dubrovnik and some of the 'boni homines' (optimates) of the city. Besides the tribute, Dubrovnik paid a tithe in kind to the Slav princelings. From time to time they made special treaties with their neighbours, usually of a commercial character. By one of these, which Resti dates 831,[76] Svetimir, King of Bosnia, agreed to send fifty oxen, 500 sheep and goats, and 200 loads of oats to Dubrovnik and to treat their citizens in his territory as though they were his own subjects, while they were to send him fourteen braccia[77] of red cloth. This indicates the city's economic position, which enabled it to send manufactured articles from the West into the Balkan lands, while it bought from the latter the cattle and foodstuffs which its own limited territory could not provide. Even in later times most of the grain consumed by Dubrovnik was imported from abroad.

Dubrovnik's hinterland is the main massif of the Dinaric mountains, the central mountainous area of present-day Yugoslavia and this region is of special importance in the economic significance and role of Dubrovnik. In some areas, as for example the hinterland of Split, parallel mountain chains obstruct the journey inland; in others, as along the Bay of Kotor, the mountains reach the coast, but at Dubrovnik, they only rise gradually, so that this zone is relatively easy to cross right to the Morava valley, the main artery of southeast Europe. Livestock-breeding was developed over these plateaux at an early date, and became the basis of the region's economic importance, its social structure and political role. The Vlach shepherds had a long experience of animal husbandry and adapted their life accordingly.

With the different seasons the shepherds lived in the summer mountain pastures and wintered in the coastal zone or the basins of the hinterland.[78] In this undeveloped economy with its insecure mountainous conditions cattle were of great value, and referred to as 'wealth' (Blago) in the local language. Among the animals, sheep were called the 'mother of the poor' for they provided the necessary wool, fat and meat. The summer pastures were located in the limestone plateaux to the east and west of the River Drina. The mingling of the shepherds from the coastal and inland areas during the summer led to closer contact, and responsibility to undertake obligations which were to be of importance for Dubrovnik's commercial growth.

The nature of transhumance demanded mutual understanding and co-operation among those who practiced it; transhumance stimulated and maintained tribal organization. It also necessitated the regular acceptance of pasture rights and free movements of animals. In fact, transhumance, stockbreeding and the associated legal customs provided the economic and legal basis for the first independent Slav states. These developed first and lasted longest in the livestock breeding hinterland of Dubrovnik: Rascia (Raška), Tribunia (Travunia,) Zachumlja, medieval Serbia, Bosnia and Hercegovina. Unfortunately, relations with the Slavs were not always peaceful and Dubrovnik was often engaged in small wars with its turbulent neighbours. The gradual extension of Dubrovnik's vineyards was a frequent source of dispute (*lis de vineis*),[79] as the republic claimed and finally obtained the right to govern the territory in question. Another cause of dispute was the arrest and ill-treatment to which Dubrovnik merchants were often subjected when travelling in the interior. At other times Dubrovnik aroused anger in the neighbouring princes by giving shelter to their rebellious subjects. The story of Bodino, in spite of its legendary character, illustrates this very clearly. This Slav prince, having deposed his uncle, Radoslav,[80] and made himself King of Dalmatia and Croatia, conquered Bosnia and Serbia. He wished to get rid of Radoslav's sons, who still ruled over a small territory on the River Drina, and succeeded in this by treachery, but their children managed to escape to Dubrovnik and placed themselves under the protection of the republic. Bodino demanded that they should be returned to him, and on the refusal he beseiged the city for seven years. At the end of this time, finding that his efforts were useless, he put his cousins to death, and retired with the bulk of his army. In order to molest Dubrovnik further he built a castle at the head of the bridge connecting the town with the mainland, and left a small containing force behind. Dubrovnik cunningly obtained possession of this stronghold. After having bribed the commanders of the garrison by promising them land and honours in the city, they allowed a large consignment of wine to fall into enemy hands; while the latter were making merry on it, the burghers issued forth and put them all to the sword. The castle was destroyed, and the church of St. Nicholas (Sv. Nikola) in Prijeki was erected on its site. These events are recorded as having occurred some time during the eleventh or twelfth century, but the accounts are by writers who lived several hundred years later. Probably there were wars with the Slavs in which incidents of a similar character occurred, but the seven years' siege is pure fiction, and the name of Bodino is not found in any history of the Serbs or Croats.

Another Serbian war, on which we possess somewhat more reliable information is that which broke in 1184 between Dubrovnik and Stephen Nemanja, King of the Serbs. An army, commanded by the King himself attacked the city from the land side,[81] while a fleet under his brother, Miroslav, attacked it by sea. The citizens under Michele Bobali, completely defeated the Serbs who were ignorant of siege operations and quite unprovided with the necessary equipment. On the Feast of the Three Martyrs,[82] (September 27, 1186), peace was concluded.[83] Both sides agreed to forget past events and

Nemanja granted Dubrovnik permission to trade in all parts of his dominions, while his own subjects were to be protected in the city; but it was also stipulated that rebels should be prevented from using the city as a place for conspiracy against their sovereign. There was another stipulation, that should the King or his brother ever need a safe refuge, Dubrovnik should be open to them – a clause found in many subsequent treaties. It is interesting that Venice allowed Dubrovnik's citizens to do as they pleased in all that concerned her relations with the Slav states, even during the period when Venetian Counts presided over Dubrovnik's government. It was only in questions concerning maritime affairs that the Queen of the Adriatic asserted her authority over Dubrovnik from time to time.

Beginnings of Slavicization

The original significance of Dubrovnik's defensive position was lost in later years when the channel separating the Romanized population on the island from the Slavic settlement on the neighbouring shore, was filled in.[84] Fusion of the Roman and Slavic elements of the population ultimately occurred, but naturally cannot be precisely dated. Skok believes this fusion took place in the tenth century[85] coinciding with the victory of the Christians over the Pagan Slavs in Dalmatia. As Constantine Porphyrogenitus did not mention this fusion of settlements, it is safe to suppose that it was accomplished after 949 AD when his work appeared, and sometime before 1270 the year the first documents appear in the Dubrovnik Archives, because then the two settlements were synonymous. The question therefore arises when did the Slavs penetrate into Dubrovnik? The most probable answer is when the Roman population did not look upon the neighbouring Slavs as a source of danger. From the oldest documents Slavic names appear at the beginning of the eleventh century. Three documents act as proof; first is the charter for the foundation of Lokrum Monastery, dated during the reign of Basil II, the Byzantine Emperor, secondly the testament of Petrus Cerni of Split in the second half of the eleventh century, and thirdly a trade contract between Dubrovnik and Monopoli (southern Italy) at the beginning of the twelfth century. In each of these documents the Slavic and Roman names are mixed up together often with a Latin root and Slavic suffix, for example Lampridius becomes Lampre, Maurus appears as Mooreša, etc. Further evidence is dated from 1294 when the citizens of Dubrovnik rose against their Venetian rulers. When a Venetian administrator exiled a Dubrovnik nobleman it is said 'the crowd cried in a Slavic tongue "Podc z Bogom" ' (Leave with God's help).[86] This could indicate that during the last quarter of the thirteenth century the Dubrovnik laymen only knew the Slav language, whilst the noblemen were bilingual.

With the infilling of the small channel separating the Roman from the Slav population, there was an extension of the streets across the 'paludazzo' towards Mount Srđ. It is thought that the first Slavic inhabitants of Dubrovnik lived in the part known as Prijeko and around the area of the present day Minčeta Tower. Also tombs found here from this early period contained no Roman names e.g. Dabiživ and Matko Bogčinović, Radonja Vukotin, Brajko Mladijenović etc.[87] It is quite possible that the weakness of Byzantine rule in this area during the eleventh century allowed the slavicization process to proceed more rapidly. Further analysis has shown that between 1200 and 1300 of the 211 women's names cited in the city's acts, 129 of them were Slavic, whilst often names were bilingual e.g. Blanca and Biela.[88] Haumant has also suggested that most of the women spoke the Slav language and in that way it was gradually introduced into family life.

Early Trade Links

With the fusion of the two settlements and the ensuing peace Dubrovnik was able to continue the commercial functions of the old Epidauros, for according to Roglić 'everything indicates that this role was not developed on the inaccessible cliffs, where the refugees from Epidauros took refuge, but that it was inherited from the abandoned city'. In the organization of the new town a close contact was maintained between the backward shepherds of the hinterland and the richer town merchants and as Roglić states 'the selection of the site for the new community was not accidental; it was in harmony with earlier experiences', which 'explains the successful and rapid advancement of the new settlement on the defensible but otherwise valueless rocky island'. Roglić further maintains that 'the commercial orientation and close relationship with the hinterland explains the rapid coalescence of the refugee centre of Ragusium with the Slavic settlement'.[89]

Dubrovnik's land trade in the Balkan peninsula grew from its

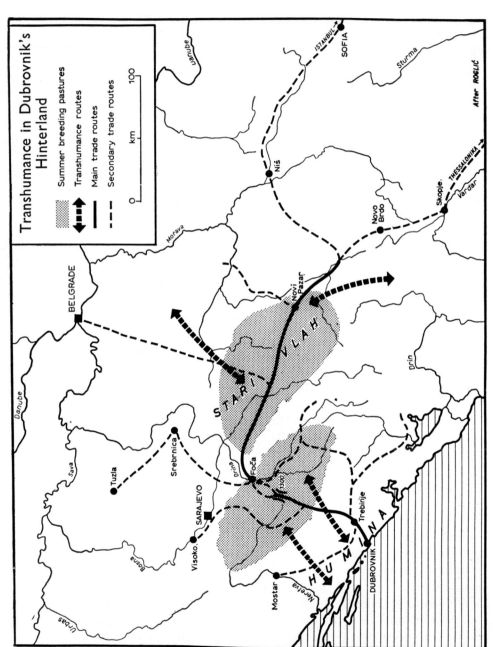

Transhumance in Dubrovnik's Hinterland

Summer breeding pastures
Transhumance routes
Main trade routes
Secondary trade routes

km 0 100

After ROGLIĆ

FIG. 14.

immediate hinterland to include much of Bosnia and Serbia, i.e. with the Slavonic principalities of the interior. Already in the tenth century trade was lively in the Balkan peninsula. Trade links between northern Europe and the Near East, came via the Danube to the Black Sea, on the well known Belgrade–Constantinople road. After the tenth century Dubrovnik and Salonika together with Belgrade and Constantinople were to be the four most important towns on the main trade routes of the Balkan peninsula. However it is not definitely known when Dubrovnik began to trade with the hinterland but it is thought to have been in the tenth century. These trade connections may quite probably have been earlier due to the impetus given by coastal trading experience and the fact that Dubrovnik had to extract from a wide hinterland the resources for its very existence, but documentary evidence is lacking to prove this point.

The main areas which entered into Dubrovnik's land trade during this early period of its history were Bosnia and Serbia. The Ban (kingdom) of Bosnia was a small state concentrated around the upper reaches of the Vrbas and Bosna Rivers. From time to time Dubrovnik made special treaties with its Bosnian neighbours, usually of a commercial character. Kulin (1180–1204), the first great figure in Bosnian history, allowed the trade of his country to be developed by merchants from Dubrovnik. In 1189 he concluded a trade treaty with Dubrovnik giving merchants from the town considerable privileges including free movement and trade throughout Bosnian territory without the need for customs duty. Much of this early trade consisted of exchanging Bosnian stock rearing products for salt and Italian manufactured goods.

More important for Dubrovnik, however, were trade connections with Serbia. This Slavic state had been created at the expense of the Byzantine Empire during the Middle Ages and bordered around Dubrovnik. Serbia remained an entirely inland state until the twelfth century, when it began to expand seawards both to the south along the Vardar valley and west along the Drin. This expansion brought the Serbian borders up to and around those of Dubrovnik. Stephan Nemanja, Župan of the Serbs, granted Dubrovnik merchants permission to trade in all parts of his dominions, while his own subjects were to be protected at Dubrovnik. This was a valuable commercial treaty for by the end of the twelfth century Serbian territories included northern Albania and Hercegovina reaching the coast between the Neretva River and Kotor; northwards their expansion was checked by the Ban of Bosnia.

By the twelfth century Dubrovnik's overseas trade must already have been important, for the Arab geographer Idrisi noted (in 1153) that 'Dubrovnik was a large maritime town whose population were hard-working craftsmen and possessed a large fleet which travelled to different parts'.[90] This statement is supported by twelfth and thirteenth century[91] trading treaties from the Dubrovnik Archives, which show that trade existed between Dubrovnik and the west Adriatic coast (Molfetta 1148, Termoli 1203, Ancona 1199, Venice 1232) together with Pisa 1169 and the region of Emilia 1235, but do not specify commodities transported. They indicate that by the thirteenth century Dubrovnik was an important trading town and according to Matković 'it is possible that, before there were written documents between these towns treaties by word of mouth existed between Dubrovnik, Sicily and the mid-Italian towns'.[92] Dubrovnik ships were too small and weak to make the long journeys to the Near East but a Dubrovnik merchant is recorded as making the voyage to Acre, via Constantinople and Cyprus, in 1143 on a Venetian boat.[93]

Thus Dubrovnik, blessed with a good natural position on the coast, and a safe haven of refuge, went through its embryonic stages of commercial development between the seventh and thirteenth centuries. It had satisfied the prerequisites for the emergence of such a city, namely 'a situation conducive to repeated contacts among peoples of divergent cultures',[94] which in turn permitted a constant accretion of social and technological skills in the area, and the emergence, through its merchant class, 'of a well-developed social organization, particularly in the political and economic spheres'.[95] Until the beginning of the thirteenth century Dubrovnik, like most of Dalmatia, was under the control of the Byzantine Empire. She found herself surrounded on all her land frontiers by powerful Slavonic states who at times were friendly; but envied her wealth and above all her splendid port; of this they tried on more than one occasion to gain possession. With the weakening of the Byzantine power and the creation of independent Slavic states in the interior, Dubrovnik accepted the protection, in 1205, of the then powerful Republic of Venice.

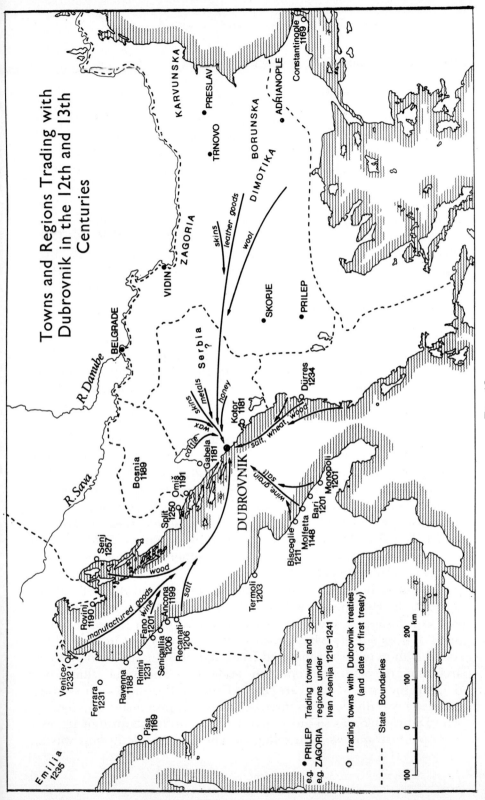

Towns and Regions Trading with Dubrovnik in the 12th and 13th Centuries

R.Danube

R.Sava

BELGRADE

Bosnia 1189

Serbia ?

Seni 1257

Split 1250

Omiš 1191

cattle

wax

skins

metals

honey

Gabela 1181

Kotor 1181

DUBROVNIK

wood

salt

wine grain

salt

salt, wheat, wool

Dürres 1234

VIDIN

ZAGORIA

KARVUNSKA

PRESLAV

TRNOVO

skins

leather goods

wool

DIMOTIKA

BORUNSKA

ADRIANOPLE

Constantingple 1169

SKOPJE

PRILEP

Venice 1232

Rovini 1190

manufactured goods

Fano wine 1201

Senigallia 1206

Ancona 1199

Recanati 1206

Ferrara 1231

Ravenna 1188

Rimini 1231

Pisa 1169

Emilia 1235

Termoli 1203

Bisceglie 1211

Molfetta 1148

Bari 1201

Monopoli 1201

salt

km

100   0   100   200

●PRILEP   Trading towns and
e.g. ZAGORIA   regions under
        Ivan Asenija 1218–1241

○   Trading towns with Dubrovnik treaties
        (and date of first treaty)

- - - -   State Boundaries

Fig. 15.

The Church

An important question in connection with the growth of Dubrovnik is its ecclesiastical history. Native historians have attempted to prove that the city was an archiepiscopal see from the earliest times, and that it succeeded to Salona, whence some of its first settlers had come, as the metropolis of all Dalmatia. This latter contention proving quite untenable (the Archbishop of Salona, together with the majority of the surviving inhabitants, took refuge at Split, which became an archiepiscopal see in consequence), they declare that the Dubrovnik archibshops had succeeded to those of Doclea. That city, they assert, had been destroyed by the Bulgarian Tsar Samuel, and its archbishop fled to Dubrovnik, which became *ipso facto* an archiepiscopal see. A more accurate account is that contained in the *Illyricum Sacrum*.[96] Doclea was destroyed, not by Samuel, who became Tsar of the Bulgarians in 976, but by Simeon. In fact Porphyrogenitus, who wrote in 949, mentions the event as having occurred during his own lifetime. According to the *Illyricum Sacrum* the exact date was 926. John (the Archbishop) actually did take refuge at Dubrovnik, where, on the death of the local bishop, he succeeded to the see, retaining his superior title by courtesy. His successors wished to continue in the dignity, and even began to assume metropolitan authority, refusing to obey the Archbishop of Split. The dispute lasted many years, and the bishops of the newly-created see of Antivari (Bar) claimed that they were the true successors to the archbishops of Doclea. Pope Gregory VII apparently refers to these contentions in his Epistle to Michael, Kings of the Slavs, dated 'Ides of January, Indict. I' (1078). The Roman Pontiff hereby summons 'Peter, Bishop of Antivari, the Bishop of Dubrovnik, and other suitable witnesses, by means of whom the contention between the Archbishop of Split and Dubrovnik may be judicially examined and canonically defined,' to repair to the Holy See. It will be noticed that Dubrovnik is alluded to first as a bishopric and then as an archbishopric in the same document. It does not say what Gregory's decision was, but in the end the see of Dubrovnik was separated from that of Split and made into an archbishopric with metropolitan authority. The same thing was done in the case of Antivari (Bar). Thus by the thirteenth century Dalmatia was divided into three ecclesiastical provinces. The reasons why Dubrovnik was so anxious to have an archbishopric of its own were political no less than religious. The Dubrovnik Bishop was an important personage in the constitution, and if he were to owe obedience to a prelate in a foreign and possibly hostile State, he might be induced to act in a manner prejudicial to the interests of the republic. The existence of a separate province also constituted a further assertion of Dubrovnik's independence.

The importance of the Dubrovnik Church was further enhanced by the conversion of the neighbouring Slavs, to whom Dubrovnik was the nearest religious centre. Dubrovnik missionaries went among them to preach the Gospel, and ecclesiastics from Constantinople made the city their headquarters and starting-point. The part which Dubrovnik played in these conversions explains the gifts which the Serbian princes and nobles made to its churches.[97] In later times religious controversies arose between the citizens and their neighbours, in consequence of the heretical and schismatic sects which were spreading throughout the Balkan lands. Dubrovnik was orthodox, and used all her influence to second the Papacy in trying to suppress these movements, which were often countenanced by the kings and princes of Serbia and Bosnia. Bernard, Archbishop of Dubrovnik at the end of the twelfth century, wished to bring the bishops of Bosnia under his authority, and the Ban Kulin, who at that time professed himself a Catholic, consented. But while Bernard was in Rome, Kulin abjured Catholicism for Bogomilism,[98] and set up Bogomil bishops in opposition to those consecrated by Bernard. Vulkan, Grand Župan of Zachhulmja, did likewise, and convoked a synod at Antivari (Bar).[99] In 1023 the Benedictine Order came to Dubrovnik from the Tremiti Islands under one Peter, and established itself on the island of Lokrum. Various Serb princes and Dubrovnik citizens made gifts of land to the monastery, the remains of which may still be seen today.

Cultural Development

Artistic and intellectual development was still in its infancy and of the few buildings of this period with any Byzantine architectural pretensions only the smallest traces remain. The town was built chiefly of wood, save for the walls and a couple of small churches. The oldest edeifice of which anything remains is the church of St. Stephan (Sv. Stjepan) mentioned by Constantine Porphyrogenitus as the most important in the town. Four ruined walls in a court near the old diocesan seminary are believed to have belonged to this very ancient building. The tradition is that it was erected by Stephen, Ban of Bosnia, or by his widow. Gelcich describes what the building must have been like:

'In the church of St. Stephen at Ragusa we must picture to ourselves not a work of art, but a chapel capable of containing few beyond the ministers at the altar; low-vaulted, decorated internally and perhaps externally, with frescoes; an apse just large enough for the altar, lit by such few rays of sunlight as could penetrate by an irregular number of holes piercing the stone slab which closed the single-arched window placed over the altar'.[100]

On the outside wall there is a fragment of bas-relief of two arches, each containing a cross on a design of foliage. Close by is the area of a larger church, also in ruins, of a later date, to which St. Stephen's later served as a sacristy.

Another church of the Byzantine period is that of St. Jacob (Sv. Jakov) in Peline (Serbo-Croat for 'wormwood') on the slopes of Mount Srd mentioned in thirteenth century documents (1225) as already very ancient. Seen from outside, there is nothing to tell one that it is a church at all, but internally it is in good repair. It is quite plain, and has round arches and vaultings. It consists of a nave, three bays, and an apse. The single window, which is a later addition, is to the left of the altar. A small fourteenth century painting is the main ornament. Two other churches – St. Nicholas (Sv. Nikola) in Prijeko, and St. Maria (Sv. Marija) near the Rector's Palace – although both of this epoch, were entirely rebuilt in the sixteenth and seventeenth centuries. The best piece of Byzantine scultpure in the town is a handsomely carved doorway in a chapel near the cathedral. The design, though simple, is elegant and graceful. On the island of Lokrum an inscription marks the burial-place of Vitalis, Archbishop of Dubrovnik from 1023 to 1047. This, then, is the sum of Byzantine remnants at Dubrovnik. The name of Mount Srd (Monte Sergio) is the only relic of the Oriental Church;[101] while the name of the west gate, Porte Pile, is possibly derived from the Greek πύηαι. Of literary production it is as yet too early to speak, for Dubrovnik literature only begins with the Renaissance.

2. Notes

1. G. Sjoberg, *The Preindustrial City Past and Present*, The Free Press, New York and London (1965).
2. E. A. Freeman, *Historical Essays*, Third Series, London (1881), pp. 22–23.
3. C. T. Smith, *An Historical Geography of Western Europe before 1800*, Longmans, London (1887), p. 2.
4. T. G. Jackson, *Dalmatia, the Quarnero, and Istria*, Vol. I, Oxford (1887), p. 2.
5. G. Novak, 'Problems and chronology of the finds in the Cave of Grabak', *Archaelogia Iugoslavica*, Vol. III, Belgrade (1959), pp. 11–39.
6. K. Jireček, 'Die Wlachen und Maurowlachen in der Denkmälern von Ragusa', *Sitzungsberichte der böhm. Gesellschaft der Wissenschaften*, Prague (1879), p. 120.
7. K. Jireček, *Handelsstrassen und Bergwerke von Serbien und Bosnien während des Mittelalters*, Prague (1879), pp. 22–25.
8. *Ibid.*, pp. 25–27.
9. *Ibid.*, pp. 27–35.
10. B. Gušić, 'Naše Primorje (Historijsko-geografska studija)', *Pomorski Zbornik*, Vol. I, Zagreb (1962), p. 19–60.
11. A. A. Vasiliev, *History of the Byzantine Empire*, Second Edition, Madison, University of Wisconsin (1952);
S. Painter, *A History of the Middle Ages 284–1500*, A. A. Knoff, New York 1956;
H. Mundy and P. Riesenberg, *The Medieval Town*, D. Van Nostrand, Princeton (1958).
12. I. Rubić, 'Zadar-Split-Dubrovnik', *Geografski Horizont*, God. VII, Broj. 1–2, Zagreb (1961), p. 25.
13. E. Falcon-Barker, *1,000 years under the Sea*, London (1960).
14. J. G. Wilkinson, *Dalmatia and Montenegro*, London (1848).
15. *Scriptores*, Vol. I, *Annales Ragusini Ananymi* 1883 states that Epidauros was destroyed by an earthquake, *circa* 365 AD after the death of Julius Apostata (363 AD); Idatius, a Portuguese bishop born 395 AD wrote two chronicles of his own time and mentions a terrible earthquake in 395 A.D. felt in Italy, Germany and Illyria, E. Falcon-Barker, *op. cit.* pp. 12–13.
16. P. J. Schafarik (Šafařik), *Slawische Altertümer*, Leipzig (1843–44), Vol. II, p. 238;
J. B. Bury, *History of the Later Roman Empire*, Vol. II, Book IV, Part II. Ch. IV.
17. Among writers accepting this version are:
J. Bradford, *Ancient Landscapes*, Ch. V., 'The changing face of Europe: classical and medieval town plans', pp. 273–274;
T. G. Jackson, *op. cit.* Ch. XIX;
P. Skok, 'L'Importance de Dubrovnik dans l'Histoire des Slaves', *Le Monde Slave*, Vol. VIII, (2), Paris (1931), pp. 161–171;
J. Roglić, 'The geographical setting of medieval Dubrovnik', *Geographical Essays on Eastern Europe*. (N. J. G. Pounds, ed.), Vol. 24, The Hague (1961), p. 141;
I. Sindik, 'O Naseljima, i Migracijama u Dubrovniku i Okolica', *Glasnik Geografskog Društva*, Vol. 9, Belgrade (123), pp. 35–56.

18. P. Skok, 'Les Origines de Raguse', (Etude de toponymie et de linguistique historiques) *Slavia Časopis pro Slovanskou Filologii*, Prague (1931), pp. 449–500.

19. Constantini Porpherogeniti, *De Administrand Imperio*, Bonn (1898), Ch. XXIX, p. 128.

20. A. J. Evans, 'Antiquarian researches in Illyricum', *Archaeologie*, Vol. 48, London (1885), p. 4, footnote.

21. Constantini Porphyrogeniti, *op. cit.* pp. 141, 151, 163.

22. K. Jireček, *op. cit.* p. 9, footnote.

23. *Enciklopedija Jugoslavije*, Vol. III, Zagreb (1958), p. 127.

24. Pauly-Wissowa, *Real-encyclopadie der class. Altertumswissenchaft*, Stuttgart (1901); it is assumed that the name is probably of Illyrian origin.

25. P. Skok, 'Les Origines . . .', *op. cit.* p. 477.

26. K. Jireček, *Handelsstrassen . . .*, *op. cit.* p. 10.

27. W. Tomashek, 'Zur Kunde der Haemus Halinsel', Ch. II, *in Trade Roads at the Time of the Arabian Idrisi*, p. 61, Sitzungberichte der phil. Hist. Classe der Kais Academie, Bd. 113, Vienna (1881).

28. B. Korkut, *Arapski dokumenti u Državnom Arhivu u Dubrovniku*, Sarajevo (Orientalni Institut) Posebna Izdanja III, (1969), uses the term 'Rakuza' (راكوزا).

29. W. B. Turrill, 'Plant life of the Balkan peninsula', Oxford (1929), Ch. 10, *in Influence of Man on Flora and Vegetation*, pp. 188–239.

30. Ž. Muljacić, 'O Imena grada Dubrovnika', *Zadarska Revija*, Vol. XI, No. 2, Zadar (1962), pp. 147–154.

31. P. Re'is, *Kitabi Bahriye*, (ed.), Istanbul (1935).

32. F. Babinger, *Ewliâ Tschelebi's Reisewege in Albanien*, Berlin (1930); also Evliya' Celebi wrote an analogy of Venedik (Venice) *circa* 1670.

33. B. Krekić, *Dubrovnik (Raguse) et le Levant au Moyen Age*, Paris–The Hague (1961).

34. G. Gelcich, *Dello Sviluppo Civile di Ragusa*, Dubrovnik (1884), p. 6.

35. W. G. East, *An Historical Geography of Europe*, 3rd Edition, London (1947), p. 59.

36. H. Schreiber, *Teuton and Slav*, London (1965), p. 38.

37. E. A. Freeman, *The Historical Geography of Europe*, 3rd Edition, London (1903), p. 115.

38. D. Waley, *The Italian City Republics*, McGraw-Hill Book Co., New York, (1969);
    Their mutual statutes present many analogies with those of Italy.

39. G. Gelcich, *op. cit.* p. 9.

40. N. Ragnina, *Annali di Ragusa*, South Slavonic Academy, Zagreb (1980), p. 30.

41. M. Lombard, 'Le Bois dans la Mediterranée Musulmane (VIIᵉ–XIᵉ siècles) Un problème cartographiqué', *Annales-Économies, Sociéties, Civilisations*, 14ᵉ Paris (1959), p. 238, 243.

42. Constantini Porpheregeniti, *op. cit.* cap. XXX.

43. Constantini Porpheregeniti, *op. cit.* cap. XXX;
    M. Mollat, C. Denoix, O de Prat, 'Le Navire et L'Economie Maritime du Moyen Age au XVIIIᵉ siècle'; 'Le port de Ragues et sa Flotte au XVIᵉ siècle', J. Tadić, p. 10, *Travaux du Second Colloque International d'Histoire Maritime*, Paris (1959).

44. F. Rački, *Documenta historiae Croatiae periodum antiquam illustratia*, Zagreb (1877), p. 420–423.
45. S. Guldescu, *History of Medieval Croatia*, Ch. XVII 'Ragusa and the Moslem Croats', The Hague (1964), pp. 297–305.
46. G. Gelcich, *op. cit.* p. 2.
47. S. Razzi, *Storia di Raugia*, Lucca (1588), Ch. 10.
48. N. Ragnina, *Annali di Ragusa*, Zagreb (1890).
49. Cedrenus, Vol. I, 1,019;
Presbyter Docleas, 'De Regno Dalmatiæ et Croatiæs', in G. Lucio, *Regnum Slavorum*, Rome (1666).
50. Abbe Paul Pisani, *Num Ragusini ab omni jure Veneto a saec. X usque ad saec. XIV immunes fuerunt*, Paris (1893), cap. II.
51. A. Dandalo, 'Chronicum Venetum', in G. Muratori, *Rer. Ital. Script.* Vol. XII, Rome (1890).
52. Sabellico, *Historia rerum Venetarum*, Dec. I, lib, IV, cap. 3, Rome (1880). (Seque suosque Orseolo Venetoque nomini dedunt.)
53. P. Pisani, *op. cit.*, thinks this to be Sebastiano Dolci (anagram for Sebastianus Slade de Ragusa), a Dubrovnik monk of the seventeenth century, in a work entitled *Libertas perpetua reip. Ragusine ab omni jure Venete reipub.*, in the Museo Correr in Venice, and copies in Zadar and Dubrovnik.
54. M. Orbini, *Regno degli Slavi*, Pesaro (1601).
55. G. Resti, *Chronica Ragusina*, South Slavonic Academy, Zagreb (1884), p. 272.
56. *Prospetto Cronologico della Dalmazia*, Zadar (1850), p. 112.
57. G. Gelcich, *op. cit.* p. 3.
58. J. C. von Engel, *Geschichte des Freistaates Ragusa*, Vienna (1807), § 6.
59. H. Brown, *Venice an Historical Sketch of the Republic*, London (1893), p. 87, states that between 1096 and 1105, Venice had put 300 ships on the sea.
60. S. Razzi, *op. cit.* p. 41.
61. G. Romanin, *Storia Documentata di Venezia*, Venice (1853), Vol. VIII, p. 455; D. Farlati and J. Coleti, *Illyricum Sacrum*, Venice (1751–1819), Vol. VI, pp. 60–80.
62. H. Brown, *op. cit.* p. 101.
63. *Archivo Storico Italiano*, Rome (1896), Vol. VIII, lib. V.
64. Venetian Archives, *Liber Pactorum*, Vol. II, p. 117 verso.
65. *Monumenta Spectantia Historiam Slavorum Meridioanalium*, South Slav. Academy, Zagreb (1879), Vol. I Document XVII.
66. *Ibid.*, Document XXII.
67. *Ibid.*, Document XXIII, dated June 13th 1190.
68. *Ibid.*, Document XXVI.
69. *Ibid.*, Document XXVII.
70. *Ibid.*, XXVIII.
71. *Ibid.*, XXIX.
72. G. Romanin, *op. cit.* Vol. VIII, p. 455.
73. *Monumenta Spectantia . . .*, *op. cit.* Vol. I. Document XXXIX.
74. K. Jireček, *Handelsstrassen*, *op. cit.* p. 12.
75. In Serbo-Croat 'mogoriš', which Miklosich (F. Miklosich, *Monumenta Serbica*, Vienna, 1858) believes to be of arabic origin (إيجار وَقَّة جَهْر rent, rented).
76. Probably this date is too early.

77. Braccio (Serbo-Croat 'lakat') a cloth measure 78 cm, an arm's length, in which there were 3–4 braccia to one English ell (or 2½–3 English yards). See F. Edler, *Glossary of Medieval Terms of Business* (Italian Series 1200–1600), Medieval Academy of America, Cambridge, Massachusetts (1934), pp. 52 and 59.

78. J. Roglić, 'Prilog poznavanju humljačkog stočarstva', *Geografski Glasnik*, Vol. 18, Zagreb (1956), pp. 1–12.

79. K. Jireček, *Handelsstrassen*, *op. cit.* p. 12.

80. The name is sometimes spelt Radosav.

81. J. C. von Engel, *op. cit.* § 19 gives the figures as 20,000 soldiers on horses and 30,000 on foot, but these are probably exaggerated.

82. The Three Martyrs of Kotor were saints murdered by heathens, or heretics.

83. *Monumenta Spectantia* . . ., *op. cit.* Vol. I, Document XVII.

84. P. Skok, 'Les Origines . . .', *op. cit.* p. 469;
    J. Engel and C. Stojanović, *Povijest Dubrovâcke republike*, Dubrovnik (1922), p. 10;
    B. Stulli, *Pregled državno-pravne historije dubrovačke*, Dubrovnik (1956), p. 2.

85. P. Skok, 'Les Origines . . .' *op. cit.* p. 474.

86. P. Skok, 'L'Importance . . .', *op. cit.* p. 165.

87. P. Skok, 'Les Origines . . .', *op. cit.* p. 480.

88. E. Haumant, 'La Slavisation de la Dalmatie', *Revue Historique*, Vol. CXXIV, Paris (1917), p. 292.

89. J. Roglić, *op. cit.* p. 150.

90. W. Tomashek, *op. cit.* p. 6.

91. Dubrovnik Archives:
    (i) 15/IX/1229. Safe conduct granted to Dubrovnik citizens trading in Fermo. *Facsimile II*, No. 53;
    (ii) 3/III/1231. Safe conduct to Dubrovnik merchants coming to Rimini. *Facsimile III*, No. 242;
    (iii) 26/III/1231. Safe conduct for all merchants from Dubrovnik coming to Senna (modern Senigallia) and district. *Facsimile II*, No. 55;
    (iv) 1/VIII/1235. Safe conduct to 'our chosen friends' of Ravenna to trade in Dubrovnik and district on the same footing as citizens of Dubrovnik. *Facsimile II*, No. 62;
    (v) 24/V/1249. Safe conduct for all merchants and merchandise of Dubrovnik trading in Fanum (modern Fano). Similar grants to be made by Dubrovnik within two months. *Facsimile II*, No. 140;
    (vi) 6/V/1429. Dubrovnik merchants can come to Firmum and Port of St. George with trade for five years, free of customs and exactions. *Facsimile III*, No. 167.

92. V. Foretić, 'Nekoliko pogleda na pomorsku trgovinu Dubrovnika u srednjem vijeku', *Dubrovačko Pomorstvo*, Dubrovnik (1952), p. 119.

93. R. Morozzo della Rocca and A. Lombardo (eds.) *Regesta Chartarium Italiae. Documenti del commercio veneziano nei secoli XI–XIII*, Vol. I, Rome (1940), pp. 85–86.

94. G. Sjoberg, *op. cit.* p. 27.

95. G. Sjoberg, *op. cit.* p. 31.

96. D. Farlati and J. Coleti, *op. cit.*

97. G. Gelcich, *op. cit.* p. 10.

98. A. Solovjev, 'Bogumulentum und Bogomilengräber in den Südslavischen Ländern', *Völkern und Kulturen Südosteuropas*, München (1958), pp. 173–199; M. Spinka, *A History of Christianity in the Balkans*, Chicago (1933).

99. J. C. von Engel, *op. cit.* § 20.

100. G. Gelcich, *op. cit.* pp. 13–14.

101. R. von Eitelberger von Edelberg, 'Kundstdenkmale Dalmatiens', Vol. IV of his *Gesammelte kunsthistorische Schriften*, Vienna (1884), p. 314.

3
Under Venetian Rule
1204–1358

For the past three centuries, the main interest of Dubrovnik as much of Dalmatia, had lain not in the dying shadow of Byzantine rule, but in the repeated attempts of the Slavic hinterland and Venice to intervene in an area, which by the nature of its coasts, favoured independence and piracy. In 1000 AD Peter Orseolo II, Doge of Venice, assumed the title of 'Duke of Dalmatia' after defeating the Croats and crushing the Slav pirates at the mouth of the Neretva River. Although two more centuries were to pass before Dalmatia, including Dubrovnik, became Venetian it was

> 'Nevertheless, of the highest importance; it raised the prestige of the Venetians, it opened to them a long line of factories down the Dalmatian coast, and it advanced their claim to free trade in the Adriatic'.[1]

Venice had a growing interest in the Levant trade and wished to control the sea-routes that led to her markets, but it was essential that the piracy, to which the Dalmatian coast was so well suited, should be kept down, and forests of the seaboard could be exploited to provide wood for the building of the Venetian galleys. After the fall of Norman power in southern Italy, the situation allowed Venice to take full control in the Adriatic for both Croatia and Hungary were too weak to benefit from the opportunity. Also, after the Fourth Crusade (1202–1204) Venetian interests in the eastern Mediterranean were greatly increased, and the need for controlling Dalmatia grew correspondingly greater. During 1204–1205 Venice began this task by systematically capturing towns along the coast from Trieste to Dubrovnik, all 'in the name of Christ'.

Venetian Domination

Having been mainly under Byzantine and for some time under Norman sovereignty, Dubrovnik became a Venetian dependency at the time of the Fourth Crusade (1204) and remained so for a period of over 150 years. This period was decisive for the direction Dubrovnik's commercial interests were to take. Her overseas trade, which had been developing for some time, was severely handicapped by the Venetian policy directed towards a monopolization of the Mediterranean area, particularly the Adriatic. The Adriatic stood in great contrast to other parts of the Mediterranean basin for its hinterland gave little opportunity for political interplay. It was the sea of a single power, as proved previously by the Romans. These waters, which deeply indented southern Europe, constituted the greatest single factor that conditioned Venetian history. The Dalmatian coast provided wood and the flat Italian coast prevented the rise of competitive cities, and so Venice strong in her own sea, was free to expand beyond. She received in her own phrase, 'a half and a quarter of the Roman Empire' in the Levant, in Asia Minor, and in the Black Sea. 'Never' it said, 'was there a state so completely dependent upon the sea'. Structurally it consisted of a series of strategic points, calling stations, merchant quarters in cities, small pieces of hinterland, and many islands – all strung along the greatest of medieval trade routes. Venetian activity led to an overall increase in the Levant trade, from which Dubrovnik was fortunately not altogether eliminated.[2] Nevertheless, because of the restrictive Venetian trade policy, Dubrovnik was forced to seek more lucrative markets elsewhere. These were found in the Balkan interior, and at the beginning of the thirteenth century were greatly expanded as a result of developments in the mining industries.[3]

Venetian domination in the Adriatic also leads into the legal aspects of such control and the theory of the *mare clausum*. This was an important concept in medieval maritime trade and therefore of consequence for Dubrovnik. Roman law had held the sea to be free and common to all, but in the Middle Ages many seas came to be recognized as private political domains, and their appropriation to be justified by legal principle. The sovereignty of the sea was that of a political sovereignty existing as a matter of right and implying a monopoly of authority and jurisdiction similar to that exercised on land. It usually meant too, an exclusive control over the sea as part of the territory of the realm, and in some cases made foreign trade dependent upon a permit or indeed, forbade such traffic entirely. This in substance was the doctrine of the *mare clausum*. An enclosed sea had the advantage of a geographical unit, allowing close grouping of its ports and constant interchange. The shores of the sea became economically linked by trade routes, and opposing shores sometimes had more affinities with each other than with their respective hinterlands. The enclosed sea thus emerges as a cultural and historical entity developing a unified civilization around its shore.[4]

Venetian application of this theory led to a continued struggle by all the Istrian and Dalmatian towns against the 'Queen of the Adriatic', in which Kopar, Pula and Zadar suffered the most, from repeated attacks and plunder. The first twenty years of Venetian rule in Dubrovnik have left few records. Between 1204 and 1222 only one Venetian count is mentioned – Giovanni Dandolo[5] – who may have ruled during the whole period. About this time there occurred a curious event in the history of the town. It is variously represented as having occurred about 1221–1223 or 1230–1232 but the earlier date appears more probable. Apparently for a few years previously Dubrovnik had been enjoying what was practically absolute freedom, as no Venetian count had been appointed. About 1221 a certain Damiano Guida or Juda was elected Count by popular assembly, but instead of resigning the dignity after six months, which had been the usual period during the intervals of independence, he continued in office illegally for two years. Giuda tyrannized the people, subjected his enemies to arbitrary arrest, exile, and confiscation, and kept a bodyguard of mercenaries. (Resti erroneously records the date as 1202.) The citizens became tired of this misgovernment so a conspiracy was set to bring about the tyrant's downfall, under the leadership of his own son-in-law, Pirro Benessa. Increased discontent in Dubrovnik was felt because Venice had ceased to protect the city against piracy, and their maritime trade had suffered in consequence. Giuda's arbitrary proceedings had also caused trouble with other Dalmation towns. A group of nobles met to discuss the matter, and although some, including Vito and Michele Bobali, opposed any suggestion that Venetian aid should be resorted to, their objections were overruled, and it was decided to send a deputation to Venice, headed by Pirro Benessa himself. On its arrival it was well received, and the government sent a squadron of six galleys down the Adriatic, ostensibly to escort the Patriarch of Constantinople. It weighed anchor at Dubrovnik, where Benessa landed and visited the tyrant, advising him to come and pay his respects to the Patriarch and the Venetian admiral. Not suspecting treachery Giuda agreed, and went on board the principal galley. He was instantly seized, locked in chains and the fleet sailed away. When he found himself thus out-witted he committed suicide in a fit of rage and despair by beating his head against the sides of the vessel. In exchange for this deliver-ance Dubrovnik agreed to readmit the Venetian counts.

How far this story is authentic is not known, but its main features are probably true. It may be that Damiano Giuda was a patriot. whose object was to consolidate Dubrovnik as a free city, indepen-dent of all Venetian tutelage, but felt that the community was still too weak to stand alone unless ruled by a strong personal govern-ment. He may have been, as most historians make him out, merely an ambitious citizen, like those who made themselves masters of the various Italian city-republics, but the important point is the subse-quent connection between Dubrovnik and Venice. There is a letter addressed to one Velcinno,[6] Podestà of Spalato, which alludes to 'Zellovellus ragusiensis comes', and to the story of Damiano Giuda. This Velcinno is probably the same as Buysinus, who was podestà[7] from 1221 to 1223 and would indicate that the episode was over not later than 1223, when Zellovellus came as Venetian Count. Damiano tyrannized Dubrovnik for two years, so he must have entered office as early as 1221 at least, but as he had been elected by the people and not appointed by the Doge, Dubrovnik must at that time have been semi-autonomous of Venice. In some documents dated 1224 and 1226 Dubrovnik is reprimanded for having failed to send hos-tages to Venice and otherwise fulfil its promises, but the final treaty of submission regulating Venetian suzerainty over Dubrovnik is dated 1232. Pisani concludes from this that the Zellovello letter is a forgery; that Dubrovnik shook off Venetian supremacy between 1224 and 1226, remained free and independent until 1230, when Giuda became tyrant; and that the submission of 1232 was the price which Dubrovnik paid for being freed from him.[8] Gelcich, however, holds to the authenticity of the Zellovello letter,[9] but does not allude to the documents of 1224 and 1226 regarding the hostages and the pro-hibition of Dubrovnik against trading with Alexandria. (Venice had received the same prohibition from the Pope.)

It is probable that these documents refer to a later rebellion against Venetian authority. Venice had helped Dubrovnik to shake off domestic tyranny, about 1223, exacting in exchange certain promises of allegiance and a number of hostages. These stipulations were not fulfilled; hence the protests referred to in the documents of 1224 and 1226 but Venice did not press her claims, and Dubrovnik remained more or less independent.[10] Finally, on finding that the city could not yet stand alone, or fearing that Venice was preparing to re-establish her authority by force of arms, the citizens made a voluntary submission in 1232. This view is corroborated by the fact that in the treaty of 1232 no mention is made either of Damiano Giuda or of Pirro Benessa, who headed the conspiracy against him and the deputation to Venice. The negotiations were carried on between the Venetian government and two Dubrovnik nobles, Binzola Bodazza. (Binzola Bodazza is always alluded to in this connection as one person, but in other documents, especially in the series *Reformationes* in Dubrovnik's archives the names Binzola and Bodazza are found as those of two separate noble families.)

In 1232 a treaty was signed between Dubrovnik and Venice which finally determined the relationship of the two, and fixed the terms of Dubrovnik's dependence. It begins,

'We, the envoys of Ragusa (Dubrovnik) seeing that it appears to us of great advantage that our country should be subject to Venetion domination, beg that you should grant us a Venetian Count according to our desires'.

Dubrovnik was always to have Venetian counts in future, who were to be chosen by the Doge with the majority of his councillors.

'The Count shall swear fealty to the Doge and to his successors, and thus will all future Counts to all future Doges for ever. Also all the men of the county (of Dubrovnik) above thirteen years of age shall swear fealty to the lord Doge and his successors, and they shall renew their oath every ten years. They shall also swear fealty to the Count and all his successors for ever, "salva fidelitate domini ducis ad honorem Venecie et salutem Ragusii"'.

Should the Doge ever visit Dubrovnik he was to be honourably lodged in the Archbishop's palace.

It was further agreed that Dubrovnik should always choose a Venetian for their Archbishop, namely, a man born at any place between Grado and Cavarzere, and that he should be subject to the authority of the Patriarch of Grado, if the Pope permitted it. (This stipulation is repeated in various subsequent documents, but it was not always observed.) He, too, had to swear allegiance to the Doge and his successors, whose praises the clergy had to solemnly sing in the cathedral at Christmas, at Easter and on the feast of San Biagio (Sv. Vlah).

The treaty specified the mutual obligations of the two cities in naval matters. When the Venetian fleet put to sea for war beyond Brindisi and Dürres, for every thirty Venetian galleys Dubrovnik had to provide one, and the ships from Dubrovnik were to remain in commission as long as those of Venice. Dubrovnik might levy the same tolls on all foreign ships as those levied at Venice, and the proceeds were to be divided in equal parts between the Count, the Archbishop, and the commune. The friends of the Venetians were to be the friends of Dubrovnik, and the enemies of the Venetians their enemies. They might not have any dealings with the Almissans (from Omiš), the Narentans, and other pirates, and Dubrovnik was to provide at least one good ship with fifty men. As regards tribute,

> 'the Ragusans must give 12 ipperperi to the Doge and 100 gold ipperperi of the right weight to the Venetian commonwealth on the feast of San Biagio (Sv. Vlah). At the same time the commune must give 400 ipperperi to the Count, as well as all the other usual revenues and honours, save the salt revenue. Dubrovnik must send twelve hostages, belonging to as many noble families, to Venice; of these, half are to be changed every six months'.

They were to pay 5% on all goods which they brought to Venice from the Eastern Empire, 20% on those from Egypt, Tunis, Barbary and 2½% on those from Sicily. Merchandise from the hinterland was free of duty. Dubrovnik could only send four ships of seventy miliari (sometimes written *miari*) to Venice each year on these terms; all further traffic was subject to higher duties; and they could not trade with foreigners in Venice, nor with countries where the Venetians could not trade.

The document ends with renewed oaths of allegiance to Venice on behalf of Dubrovnik.[11] 'Esadastes' admits that Dubrovnik really did submit to Venice in 1232, but declares this treaty to be a forgery. He bases his contention, first, on the fact that the provision as to the archbishops being Venetians was not always complied with. This, however, proves nothing, as there is no reason why Venice should not sometimes have allowed Dubrovnik to choose some foreigner if no suitable Venetian were forthcoming. He adds that Dubrovnik's envoys had no authority to surrender the city without consulting the Great Council, and as Damiano Giuda was then ruling, it could not be summoned. This is merely an ingenious quibble; for nine years had elapsed since the expulsion of the tyrant, and thus the argument has no value at all. Then he changes his line, and insists that Dubrovnik merely contracted a *foedus* or *fidelitas*, i.e. a treaty of friendship, with Venice, and not a *deditio* or true submission, and that in agreeing to have Venetian counts Dubrovnik did nothing more than what Florence and other Italian cities did when they chose foreigners for the position of *podestà*, without thereby prejudicing their liberty. It is easy to see that there is a considerable difference between the action of the Italian republics, who chose their rulers now from one town and now from another, and that of Dubrovnik, which was obliged to accept Venetian counts appointed by the Doge.

This chronicle of 'Esadastes', is quoted not because of the value of its arguments, but as characteristic of Dubrovnik's individuality, and of the way in which it made every effort to prove and to secure its own independence. Dubrovnik regarded itself not only as independent of Venice, but as distinct from the rest of Dalmatia. It was always afraid that the great Venetian Republic might one day claim its allegiance. Hence efforts to prove that this allegiance had never really existed, or at least that it had no practical effect.

Venetian rule was now stronger than it had been previously; the count made his influence felt for no important state business could be transacted without his authority, and Dubrovnik was obliged to pay a tribute both in money and ships to the *Dominante*. The ceremonial observed on the arrival of the new Count was very elaborate; described in detail in the statute-book of Marco Giustiniani (1272):

'We decide that the lord Count who will come to Ragusa for a period, shall swear in the public assembly summoned by the sound of the bell, to govern the city well, to maintain and guard its ancient constitutions and statutes, and to give judgment according to their provisions. After swearing this oath the standard of San Biagio (Sv. Vlah), Pontiff and Martyr, shall be delivered into the hand of the said lord Count by the Commune of Ragusa, and thus will he be invested in the piazza with the countship and governorship. Afterwards he will immediately repair with the standard to the principal church, where he will receive holy water, incense, and a Bible, on which he shall renew his oath, from the cathedral chapter. Then one of the canons preaches a sermon praising the Doge and the Count. The latter returns to the piazza with the standard, to receive the homage of the people, who, after the standard of St. Mark has been raised, swear to maintain the pact made with the Venetian Republic. One citizen shouts, another shouts, all shout together: "Long live our Lord N.N., the magnificent Doge of Venice!" and all and sundry in Ragusa and its territory vow to be loyal to the said Doge and the Commune of Venice for ever, gladly accepting the standard of the blessed St. Mark the Evangelist presented unto them by the lord Doge himself'.[12]

This account gives us a vivid picture of medieval municipal life with all its picturesque splendour and its characteristic admixture of religion and politics. The piazza of Dubrovnik, with what was then the castle, the imposing church, thick walls, and small wooden houses – for it was still mostly of timber – formed a suitable setting for the ceremony. The Count was assisted by two lieutenants or viscounts, usually, but not invariably, Venetians, each of whom received a salary of fifty Venetian pounds, paid by Dubrovnik, and two new suits of state robes every year. The Count remained in office on an average two years, and during his tenure was expected not to leave the city even for a single day. He could, however, obtain special permission from Venice to leave Dubrovnik for not more than eight days, but only on public business, such as arranging treaties with neighbouring princes.

Apparently there was another break in Venetian rule about 1235. In a treaty of that year with Koloman, Count of Almissa (Omiš).[13] (This Koloman was evidently the son of Andrew, King of Hungary, by whom he had been appointed Duke (or Count) of Croatia and Dalmatia (1226–1241),[14] and in another with Rimini,[15] mention is made of the Venetian Count. In January 1236 Dubrovnik envoys went to Venice to renew the treaty of 1232, but with modified conditions in favour of greater independence. The Signory, however, would not give way, and the treaty was reconfirmed in June on almost identical terms.[16] From this date Venetian over-lordship continued without interruption and without modification until 1358. Nevertheless, Dubrovnik continued to struggle against Venetian rule, as evidenced by documents from 1236, 1252 and 1265. In 1235 there was a temporary cessation in Venetian sovereignty as a result of Dubrovnik's demands for protection from Fridrika, Queen of Sicily, and the Statute of 1272 describes the long and bitter struggle of the city maintaining that Venice was the main stumbling block to Dubrovnik's legal and commercial development.[17] Furthermore, in 1236 the Venetian government forbad Dubrovnik boats entering harbours north of a line drawn from Ancona to Poreč, or from calling at ports where Venetian vessels were not allowed. Similarly with customs duty, for that paid by Venetian boats might not exceed the amount paid by Dubrovnik's merchants, which indirectly completely restricted competition from the latter.

Dubrovnik's relations with Venice in the second half of the thirteenth century were on the whole satisfactory. There were occasional complaints on the part of the Venetian government that Dubrovnik did not fulfil its treaty obligations and failed to send the promised galleys to take part in the expeditions against the Almissan pirates and other enemies.[18] On other occasions they were blamed for delaying goods (chiefly grain) which passed through the city on the way to Venice. However, when in 1296 Dubrovnik was almost entirely destroyed by fire, the Venetians showed generosity in providing money and building materials,[19] and the Count Marino Morosini (1296–1298) issued a decree for rebuilding the city on a more handsome scale.[20] During the Genoese War Dubrovnik lent four galleys to the Venetians, which took part in the battle of Korčula, and after that disastrous defeat the Dubrovnik ships lent aid to the scattered remnants of the Venetian fleet (1298).

Relations with Venice during the first half of the fourteenth century were more settled, mainly as both Dubrovnik and the 'Dominante' were continually having problems with the hinterland peoples. Domestic issues took second place and remained undisturbed save for one or two small disputes about certain 'Prava Statuta' which denied all value to the evidence of Venetian witnesses at Dubrovnik.[21] Also in 1307 a Venetian order stated that citizens from Dubrovnik and Zadar were not allowed to buy boats if they could not guarantee that they would handle Venetian business transactions. In these and many other ways Venice managed to obstruct Dubrovnik's development both internally and commercially, but in her relations with the Slavic hinterland, Venice allowed her to enjoy a considerable measure of self-management. By the middle of the fourteenth century the conditions of Venice were far from prosperous. The plague of 1348 had carried off three-fifths of the population, in spite of the most stringent precautions.[22] In 1350 the fratricidal war with Genoa was again renewed in consequence of disputes about the Black Sea trade. The battle of the Bosphorus (1353) was indecisive; in that of Cagliari the Venetians were successful, but dared not attack Genoa, because the city had placed itself under the protection of the Visconti. But in the same year they were totally defeated at Sapienza in the Greek Archipelago and their whole fleet captured. In 1354 the conspiracy of Marin Faliero broke out, and kept the whole state in a turmoil for many months, until the execution of the Doge and his accomplices.[23] His successor, Giovanni Gradenigo, made peace with Genoa, and the Venetians set to work to rebuild their fleet and restore their exhausted treasury by means of new commercial enterprises in the Levant. But their possession of Dalmatia and the land frontier north of Treviso were now threatened by Ludovik of Hungary. The latter allied himself with the Count of Gorizia and the Carraresi of Padua against Venice, and invaded the Trevisan march, defeating all the forces sent against him and capturing city after city. A five months' truce was concluded in 1356, but when it expired hostilities broke out once more, and the treasury was soon empty. Merchandise might arrive by sea, but with the mainland in the hands of the enemy there was no outlet for its distribution.[24] New taxes were raised, causing much discontent, and the Venetian Republic was at last forced to sue for peace. Ludovik made the cession of Dalmatia an express condition of his retirement from the Trevisan march. After much discussion and expostulation the Senate was forced to agree to these humiliating terms, and Dalmatia, which had been acquired and maintained at such great sacrifices, was now given up (February 1358).

The Slavic Hinterland

During the twelfth century the Slav lands were beginning to assume a semblance of order, and early in the thirteenth century, out of the chaos of barbarous and more or less independent tribes, four principal states had taken shape. They were Serbia or Raška, Bosnia, Hlum or Hum, and Doclea. The most important of these was Serbia, welded into a kingdom by the Nemanja dynasty, who had extended their frontiers southwards and eastwards at the expense of the Eastern Roman Empire. It included, besides modern Serbia, as far as the Rivers Ibar and Morava, a part of Bosnia to the east of the water-shed between the Rivers Bosna and Orina, the district of Novipazar and Old Serbia, and a part of Albania. It had no regular capital in the modern sense, but the kings resided usually at Prizren, at Skadar[25] or at Skopie (Uskub). It touched the sea-coast at the Bay of Kotor and in Albania; and the town of Kotor was sometimes under Serbian protection. The country's importance does not begin until the reign of Stephen Nemanja (1169). As Grand Župan he extended his territory to include Bosnia, and reduced all the semi-independent župans (feudal lords) to subjection. He was still under Byzantine suzerainty, but after the death of Manuel Comnenus in 1180 he refused to pay tribute to his successor, conquered Niš, and made Priština his capital. In 1185 he shook off all allegiance to the Greeks, and assumed the title of King of Serbia, but was not crowned. By 1186 he had united Zeta to Raška, and the cities of Skadar and Kotor, together with a stretch of the Adriatic coast, were now within his grasp. According to Temperley

> 'For the first time a real centre of unity and a real national ruler existed to educate, to govern, and to discipline the Serbians'.[26]

In 1196 he abdicated in favour of his son, Stephen Uroš, who was crowned by his younger brother, St. Sava, the first Archbishop of Serbia. Stephen Uroš's reign was peaceful, and Serbia flourished under him. His brother, Vukan, had inherited the Zeta and part of Hum from his father, but owed allegiance to Stephen Uroš. When the Latin Empire of Constantinople was established in 1205, Baldwin recognized him as independent King of Serbia, Bosnia and Dalmatia. Uroš died in 1224. His son, Stephen III, captured the town of Vidin from the Bulgarians, and the district of Syrmia between the Sava and the Danube. His brother, Ladislas, who succeeded him, abandoned Vidin on marrying the Bulgarian Tsar's daughter. A third brother, Stephen IV the Great, succeeded in 1237. With Stephen Uroš II Milutin (succeeded 1275) Serbia is almost at the height of her power. He conquered a large part of Macedonia, capturing the town of Serres, beseiged Thessalonika in 1285, and invaded Albania. He added Bosnia, which had been under Hungarian vassalage, once more to Serbia, by divorcing his first wife and marrying Elizabeth, the daughter of the King of Hungary, who gave him Bosnia as a dowry. His grandson, Stephen, who was called Dušan, succeeded in 1331, and extended his power over the greater part of the Balkan peninsula.[27] He conquered the rest of Macedonia and Albania, and reduced Bulgaria to a state of vassalage. In 1346 he had himself crowned 'Tsar of the Serbs and Greeks'.[28]

Bosnia, which corresponded to the modern region of that name, minus the eastern districts under Serbia and the north-west corner, was ruled by a Ban who owed allegiance to Hungary. The first Ban, whose name is recorded in authentic documents, is Borić, who reigned from 1154 to 1163. During the next twenty years the country was under Byzantine suzerainty, represented at times by Greek governors, at others by native princes with imperial diplomas. In 1180 the great Ban Kulin or Čulin came to the throne, shook off Byzantine authority and ruled the country wisely and well for twenty-four years. He cultivated friendly relations with his neighbours, including Dubrovnik. 'The days of Čulin' became proverbial in later and less happy times to indicate a golden age. After Čulin's death the country's prosperity declined, but revived to some extent under Matthew Ninoslav (1232–1250). After the death of his successor in 1254 Bosnia fell once more under Hungarian vassalage, and was divided into Bosnia proper (afterwards Bosnia-Mačva) under a native vassal Bani, and the district of Usora and Soli ruled by Hungarian magnates. After a short period under the Croatian House of Šubić the native prince, Stephen Kotromanić, became Ban under Hungarian suzerainty and reigned until 1353, when his nephew, Stephen Trvartko or Tvrtko,[29] succeeded him and crowned himself King.

The land of Hlum or Hum had in early times formed part of the kingdom of Doclea, and included, besides the modern Hercegovina, Tribunia (or Travunia), the Pelješac peninsula, a long stretch of Dalmatian coast, and part of Montenegro. In 1015 it was conquered by the Bulgarian Tsars, whose empire had spread to the Adriatic. The Greek Emperor, Basil II (Bulgaroktonos), reconquered it in 1019, and in 1050 the native prince Radoslav drove out the Greeks, and made himself ruler of the country. Among his successors was Bodin, who is said to have beseiged Dubrovnik.[30] During the twelfth century the Serbians attacked Doclea, and in 1143 King Radoslav II asked the Greek Emperor for help against them; but in 1150 Hum was conquered by Dessa (or Stephen Nemanja), brother of the King of Serbia, re-occupied by the Greeks a few years later, and in 1168 added once more to the kingdom of Serbia. From 1198 to the beginning of the thirteenth century it was connected with Croatia, after which it returned once more to the Serbians. The latter were extremely anxious to possess Hum, because it afforded them their best opening to the sea (to the north they were cut off by Bosnia and Croatia). In all probability it continued to form part of Serbia until added to the Bosnian Banate by Štephen Kotromanić in 1325.

Dubrovnik was, therefore, surrounded on all her land frontiers by powerful Slavonic states, who at times were friendly, but envied her wealth, and above all her splendid port; of this they tried on more than one occasion to gain possession. One such occasion occurred in 1276 when the King of Serbia, Stephen Uroš II Milutin (1275–1321) made another attempt to convert Dubrovnik into a Serbian seaport; he crossed the mountains with a large army and raided the territory of the republic. A Dubrovnik force sent against him was defeated, and its leader, Benedetto Gondola, captured and hanged. Elated by this success, the King marched forward and tried to capture Dubrovnik itself by a *coup de main*, but the citizens were prepared, and the city put in a state of defence. The massive walls and well-armed battlements baffled the Serbian King, and the Count Pietro Tiepolo, who had called in a Venetian contingent to stiffen the Dubrovnik levies, defeated the enemy. The Venetian government sent a deputation to the King threatening him with severe reprisals if he dared to attack the cities under Venetian protection, whereupon the Serbians retired and peace was made.[31] Ten years later the King of Serbia was again offended by the republic. He harried and plundered its merchants, raided Dubrovnik's territory, and tried to capture the city, but was again defeated.

Some of Dubrovnik's neighbours were not so aggressive, such as Ninoslav, Ban of Bosnia who expressed friendly relations towards the republic. In 1234 he had signed a treaty with Dubrovnik confirming the privileges granted by Kulin in 1189. On March 22, 1240, he paid a solemn visit to the city with a splendid retinue of nobles, and renewed the old treaties with the following proclamation:

'It was the will of our Lord Jesus Christ, and I, Matthew Ninoslav, the Grand Ban of Bosnia, had the good thought of coming to Ragusa to my old friends the nobles and commoners; I came with my magnates, and we found Niccolò Tonisto, the Count of Ragusa. I, with my magnates made oath to him of eternal peace and friendship'.

He adds:

'My subjects and my people and my officers shall love you, and with true faith protect you from the wicked.'

He granted them full commercial freedom throughout his Banate, and alludes to a dispute between Stephen Vladislav, King of Serbia, and promises not to abandon them should they actually have to make war. This treaty was renewed in 1249.[32]

The next few years were peaceful, save for a small religious dispute, and Dubrovnik continued to develop her resources quietly. The new Count Niccolò Tonisto, however, complained to the Pope that the Archbishop Arrengerius was a Roman and not a Venetian, and even accused him of heresy because he had consecrated a priest of Patarene tendencies as Bishop of Bosnia. Arrengerius was thereupon transferred elsewhere, and succeeded by a Venetian named John, to whom the diocese of Antivari (Bar) was assigned as well,[33] much to the gratification of Dubrovnik. The clergy and congregation of this second diocese, however, were not so pleased, and refused to recognize his authority. John's attempts to compel obedience only resulted in inducing Stephen Uroš, surnamed the Great, King of Serbia, to take up the quarrel of Antivari and make a raid on Dubrovnik's territory (1252). Uroš complained that Dubrovnik was strengthening its fortifications – a very natural precaution – and on this pretext attacked the city. The new Count Marsilio (or Marino) Giorgi was sent as Venetian ambassador to expostulate with him, but on reaching Dubrovnik he refused to proceed further, and two citizens were sent instead. (Dubrovnik writers frequently complain that the Venetians did not protect the city effectually against the Slavs, but it is difficult to see what they could have done against an almost inland state.) The latter proceeded to stir up and doubtless bribe Uroš's vassals, so that he thought it best for the present to renew their privileges but hostilities soon broke out again. Dubrovnik made an alliance with Michael, the Bulgarian Tsar, and with Radoslav, Count of Hum, against the Serbs which brought Uroš to reason, and in 1254 the differences were settled.

Radoslav had visited Dubrovnik in person that same year, and the treaty of friendship which was thus concluded is embodied in two documents. In the first Dubrovnik swore to the Župan Radoslav and his magnates that the city would be at peace with them according to

E

ancient custom, and that they should always have free access to its market.

'And all this we wish to do and maintain to you and your people, with prejudice to our oaths to the lord Doge and the commonwealth of Venice, and to the Lord Michael, Tsar of the Bulgarians'.

It is interesting that in the various histories of Serbia no mention is made of this coalition, and in fact the reign of Stephen Uroš is described as peaceful.[34] On the other hand, the treaty between Radoslav and Dubrovnik expressly mentions the alliance with Bulgaria against Serbia. Probably the Mongol invasion of 1255 induced him to make peace with his neighbours.

In the second document Radoslav promised to make war with all his strength against King Uroš and to defend Dubrovnik by sea and land; he also added that he would remain at peace with Michael for so long as the latter's treaty with Dubrovnik lasted.[35]

The Archbishop, who had been the original cause of all the trouble, had naturally become extremely unpopular, and when in his zeal for Venetian supremacy he proposed to carry out the provision of the treaty of 1232 by placing himself under the authority of the Patriarch of Grado, his position became untenable, and he was forced to abdicate (1257). Dubrovnik obtained from the Pope that his successor should not be a Venetian; another Venetian, however, was appointed in 1276.

In 1266 the quarrel with Serbia broke out afresh. The King was angry, because a number of his nobles quitted the country and settled in Dubrovnik. This statement, if true, is interesting, as it is the first immigration of Slavs on a large scale into the city after the early settlements between the seventh and the tenth centuries. Again the quarrel was settled and Dubrovnik agreed to pay Uroš a tribute of 2000 ipperperi in exchange for increased privileges and the confirmation of their rights over the disputed territories at Zaton, Brgat etc.

In 1301 there was another Serbian war, in which Venice and Dubrovnik co-operated, caused by a quarrel over Kotor. This town was now under Venetian protection, but continued to have illicit underhand connections with the Slavs. The Venetians protested, and Stephen Uroš, who called himself King of Serbia, Melinia, Albania, Chelmo, Doclea, and the maritime region,[36] made another raid on Dubrovnik territory, burning the houses, destroying the crops, and murdering many of the inhabitants and taking prisoners. The Venetians, however, came to the rescue, and ordered their 'Admiral of the Adriatic', to remain with the fleet at Dubrovnik as long as the city was in any danger. The Serbs were defeated on several occasions, and finally induced to listen to the remonstrances of the Venetian ambassadors.[37] In 1302 peace was made,[38] and as Dubrovnik had suffered greatly during the war, from devastating raids, and famine, they were allowed to retain the grain destined for Venice, and received loans and other favours. In 1316 another quarrel broke out with Uroš, who arrested and plundered a number of Dubrovnik traders. Venetian attempts at conciliation proved fruitless,[39] and in 1317 war broke out. The Count Paolo Morosini wrote that

> 'much serious damage has been done to the commune and people of Ragusa in their persons and property by Uroš and his people, who have again raided our territory'.

Among other damage, the Franciscan monastery outside the Pile Gate was burnt.[40] The Venetians sold arms to Dubrovnik and deferred claiming payment until the following year. These arms included 'many breast-plates, 100 cross-bows, 10,000 arrows, and 5,000 falsatores'.[41] The outcome of this war is unknown but apparently Dubrovnik was reconciled with Serbia in 1322, for in that year Stephen Uroš IV, (1321–1330) granted the city an accession of territory with the districts of Bosanka and Osojnik.[42]

About 1323, for some unrecorded reason, a quarrel broke out between Dubrovnik and the feudal family of Branivoj in Hum on April 8, 1325. The republic decreed warlike preparations against the Branivoj lord and his sons.

> 'qui fecerunt offensionis multas, depredationes, et rubarias contra comune et speciales personas civitatis Ragusii'.

A few months later Dubrovnik sent envoys to Venice to request the Doge's intervention on account of the King of Serbia's attitude, which appeared to be insincere.[43] Hostilities were commenced, and conferred with a barbarity unusual even for those times. The following year Braico, one of Branivoj's sons, was captured and condemned to be shut in a cage and starved to death. Some time afterwards his brother Grubaza (or Grubeza) was captured, and their mother, who had asked for Dubrovnik hospitality on her way to Bosnia, was detained as a hostage. The third brother, Branoe, was arrested by the

King of Serbia, who was now friendly towards Dubrovnik. The latter requested him to hand the prisoner over to the commune of Kotor where he would have less chance of escaping. Uroš agreed, but the republic was still unsatisfied, and private citizens offered rewards out of their own pockets for the heads of the surviving members of the Branivoj family. The Serbian King apparently had another slight disagreement with Dubrovnik about 1327, but when war broke out between him and and the Bulgarian Tsar Michael, he required their help to obtain Italian mercenaries,[44] and hostilities ceased.

Another dispute with the fickle Serbian King broke out in 1330, because Dubrovnik had given shelter to the widow of the Bulgarian Tsar, who had been forced to escape after the defeat and death of her husband by the Serbs at the battle of Velbužd. Stephen wished to secure the fugitive, and demanded her from the republic. The latter refused the demand, in spite of a promise of still further territories and privileges, and sent the Empress safely to Constantinople.

This story is somewhat confused. Dubrovnik writers declare that the princess in question was deposed, together with her son, by a rebellious noble, Alexander, who made himself Tsar and offered to place Bulgaria under Serbian suzerainty if Stephen secured the fugitives for him. After Velbužd, Michael's widow fled, his first wife, Anna, Milutin's daughter, was placed on the throne jointly with her son Šišman II by the victorious Serbs. Stephen Uroš died and his son Stephen Dušan, held Bulgaria as a vassal state. Then came the rebellion of Alexander, who forced Šišman and his mother to flee from Bulgaria and induced Dušan to marry his sister. Anna fled to Dubrovnik and perhaps this may be the princess to whom the local historians allude. On the other hand, it does not seem likely that Dušan would wish to capture her, his own kinswoman.[45] Stephen then raided Dubrovnik territory but had to retreat to defend his northern frontier against the Hungarians. Peace was made in 1335, and in 1336 a solemn Dubrovnik emissary was sent to honour him at Skadar.[46] In 1348 there was another disagreement with King Stephen for the Venetian government authorized Dubrovnik to purchase a further supply of arms;[47] in 1349 and 1350 Venetian emissaries were sent to Serbia to protest against raids on Dubrovnik territory, a Venetian galley was stationed in the habour for protection,[48] and two *mangani* or catapults were brought in for the citizens.[49] Some of the Venetian documents on the subject allude to Bosnian as well as Serbian raids; Klaić says that the Ban Stephen Kotromanić actually did make raids before 1345, but in that year made peace and never molested Dubrovnik again. His nephews, the Nikolić Counts of Hum and Popovo, had many quarrels with Dubrovnik and raided its territory, according to documentary evidence.[50] War now broke out between Serbia and Bosnia, because the Ban would not consent to his daughter's marriage with the King's son, Uroš. The King invaded Bosnia on two occasions with a large army, and beseiged the Ban in the royal castle of Bobovac, but could not capture him. These quarrels between Bosnia and Serbia, like those between Serbia and Bulgaria, were paving the way for the Turkish conquest and the obscure battles in the Bosna and Drina valleys formed the prelude to the fatal day at Kossovo and Ottoman conquest (1389). Ban Kotroman died in 1353, and was succeeded by his nephew, Stephen Tvrtko, who was the first King of Bosnia and friendly to Dubrovnik granting it important privileges.

Trade with the Hinterland

Despite periods of intermittent war Dubrovnik gradually developed closer trading relations with the Slavic hinterland. Admittedly she relied for safety on the various dissensions of the inland rulers and on Venetian protection, but in the meantime also made the most of her position by exploiting their territory for commercial purposes. After the beginning of the thirteenth century Dubrovnik was no longer content with the part it had formerly played in Balkan trade, which was hardly more than that of a transit port, but started to equip its own caravans. This grew into a thriving business, and Dubrovnik colonies were founded all over the peninsula, extending northeastwards to the River Sava and to Bulgaria. The merchants from Dubrovnik were quick to see that they had too many strong competitors in the Mediterranean and therefore turned to the extensive hinterland and exploited that, as Novak maintains

'Around the year 1200 the city began a systematic development of its trading politics, which was to remain for six centuries, until its fall'.[51]

It imported from the Balkans, cattle products (skins, wool etc.), furs, wax, honey, various forest products (charcoal, resin, staves, hoops for barrels, firewood, sumach), some rough woollen textiles, minerals (silver, lead, copper, iron), and slaves; and exported mainly manufactured goods such as textiles (drapery, silk and cotton) and arms besides wine, oil, spices, sweetmeats, gold and silver work, all kinds of metal goods and refined salt.

Throughout its early history Bosnia was an important stock raising area. The cattle herders practised transhumance, profiting from the short summers in the high limestone mountain pastures, and the warm, damp pasture of the coastal areas in the winter months. In a document of 1333 the Ban of Bosnia asked the Dubrovnik government for permission to bring his cattle to the coastal zone during the winter months as Dubrovnik citizens owned the grazing rights in this region.[52] The Vlah shepherds sold the surplus animals to Dubrovnik merchants who bought large quantities of wool, hides and cheese, and fat cattle for slaughter. In 1280 one Vlah shepherd paid a Dubrovnik furrier with a large quantity of cheese for some coats he had made him.[53]

In the second half of the thirteenth century Dubrovnik intensified its trade relations with Bosnia.[54] There appears to have been a considerable trade in slaves sent from Bosnia to Dubrovnik, where they were re-exported to western Europe.[55] The tragedy of the Bosnian slaves is seen from a letter of Prince Črnomir sent to Dubrovnik in 1253. He states

'You said previously that you would remain true and friendly with me and my people, but I, as ruler, really cannot believe this, or that you intend to keep your word. Your people come and catch my people from Luka and plunder them; I send you this message, return them to me, for you could give me no more pleasure, for already too many Luka people have been sold for slaves. Recently you have enslaved three men and one woman. Again, if that was not enough, you have sent some across the sea and others to wherever you could; after you caught one man, named Ruhota, you sold him, together with other men which the Dukljanin (people from the Kingdom of Duklja, in Dalmatia) already now hold. I would wish to say more to you, but words fail me'.[56]

Documents now begin to include other trade commodities. For example in 1296, one document refers to 350 lb of wax being sent from Vrhbosna (later Sarajevo) to Dubrovnik.[57] Another document dated 1296 refers to two loads of wax and a load of dried skins transported from Bosnia to Dubrovnik.[58] In return for these products, Dubrovnik imported and supplied the shepherds with salt. In 1215 salt was imported into Dubrovnik from Dürres in Albania and re-exported to Bosnia,[59] and several other documents refer to salt being sent from Dubrovnik to Bosnia at the beginning of the fourteenth century.[60] Salt was needed both for the people and their cattle since it was entirely lacking inland.

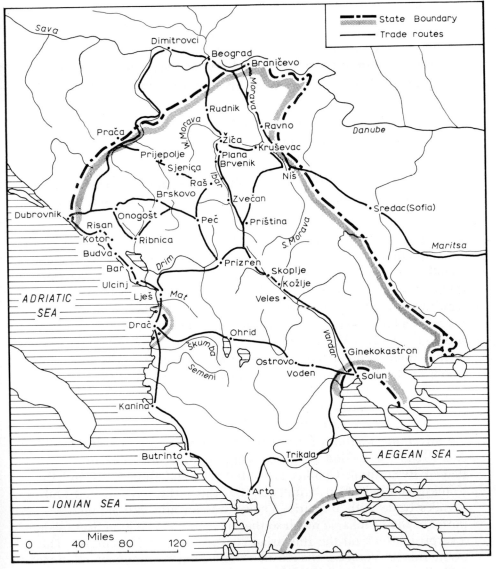

FIG. 16. Serbia during the reign of Stefan Dušan, 1331-1355

Stefan Dušan inherited the Serbian Crown in 1331 and was to give the Serb state its greatest extent and power. From its focal area about Skoplje, Dušan extended his power mainly southward to include more of northern Albania, Macedonia and northern Greece, but failed to capture the Aegean outlet of Salonika. Of Stefan Dušan, Temperley states that he made

'every effort to encourage commerce and stimulate industry by the importation of foreigners as well as by diplomacy and treaties. Saxons, Ragusans (from Dubrovnik), Venetians, Greeks, Albanians . . . peopled his cities, worked his mines or garrisoned his fortresses'.[61]

Good trade relations between Serbia and Dubrovnik continued throughout Dušan's reign until his death in 1355. In Article 118 of his Code, Stefan maintained that

'No man, noble or other, may molest merchants who travel about the Tsar's (his) dominions, nor rob them by force, nor scatter their merchandise, nor take their money by force'.

This clause was evidently inserted for the sake of ratification and promulgation from the text of the commercial treaties with Dubrovnik, the party most vitally interested in the trade of Dušan's dominions, as the security of their numerous agents, depots and caravans was of capital importance. Even at the very beginning of his reign, before he assumed the imperial title, Dušan issued a decree prohibiting anyone from hindering the men of Dubrovnik from dealing freely in meat and corn, 'under fear of the king's displeasure'.[62] Much of the trade was a direct exchange of raw materials, metals (especially lead and silver),[63] wax, wool, honey, hides and the products of domestic handicrafts, for manufactured Italian goods, mainly in the form of textiles and salt.[64]

Early trade relations existed between Dubrovnik and Bulgaria.[65] After 1186 the second Bulgarian Empire was formed from part of that of Byzantium. Conflict arose between the Bulgarians and the Franks, who held Constantinople, and this indirectly affected Dubrovnik's trade with Bulgaria. Venice was an ally and staunch supporter of the Franks, so much so that in 1256 the Venetian fleet made a surprise attack on the Bulgarian coastal town of Mesembria. This event ruined Venice's chance of establishing commercial relations with Bulgaria and even jeopardized the trading prospects of their fellow Italian merchants, the Genoese, who after this date rarely ventured into the Bosphorus, or Black Sea. Apparently Italian commerce neglected Bulgaria during the thirteenth century, thus creating less competition for Dubrovnik's traders. They had besides, the advantage of sharing a common Slavic origin which assured them a good reception. Tsar Ivan Asen II (1218–1241) called the traders from Dubrovnik 'his beloved and trusted guests' and gave them important trade privileges as is seen from the following document:

> 'The Emperor gives Dubrovnik citizens the authority to bring their goods to Vidin, Trnovo, and to Zagorija, or to Preslav, Karvunska, Borunska, Odrin (Adrianople), Dimotika, Skoplje or Prilep, Albania and Solun and there to buy and sell their goods. Signed – Asen Czar in Bulgaria and Greece 1230 AD'.[66]

In 1253 these privileges were renewed on the conclusion of a political alliance with Dubrovnik.[67] This was between the Bulgarian Tsar Michael II Asen, and Dubrovnik against the Serbian state as follows:

> 'as it was in the old treaty, from the River Neretva to the River Drin Dubrovnik shall have the monopoly in the salt trade'.

Unfortunately this monopoly was not realized because salt was sold in Kotor and Sv. Srđ on the Bojana River from which the Serbian government received half the profits. Dubrovnik had considerable intercourse with the neighbouring Dalmatian townships, especially with Kotor, which was one of the oldest city-republics on the coast. Nevertheless there were frequent quarrels between the two communities, partly through the intrigues of the Slavonic princes, and partly on account of commercial rivalries, both towns being competitors for the salt trade from the coast to the interior. Kotor had sometimes been under the protection of the Serbian kings, who used it as their seaport and sometimes under that of Venice. In 1257 a treaty was made by which Kotor promised in the event of a war between the Serbs and Dubrovnik to do their best to harass the former without openly espousing the latter's cause, and each republic was to try and promote arbitration if the other was at war. It is not known how this curious pact was carried out, but it was by no means an unusual arrangement among these semi-independent Dalmatian townships.

E*

Maritime Trade

Although the Venetian Republic suppressed much of Dubrovnik's commerce at sea, the small republic did manage to pursue some maritime activity, even though her vessels were small, and the sea-borne trade of a very limited character. Navigation was of three kinds, coastwise traffic, navigation 'intra Culfum', (within the Adriatic) and navigation 'extra Culfum'.[68] Coastwise traffic was comprised between the Molunat peninsula (north-west of Kotor Bay) and the Ston Kanal, (35 km north-west of Dubrovnik) a distance of about 70 kilometres in all, with ten harbours. Navigation 'intra Culfum', which extended from the vicinity of Split to Apulia and Dürres in Albania, was of considerable importance during the Byzantine epoch. Fine Milan cloths, skins, tar and canvas for sails were brought on Dubrovnik ships from the ports of the Marche and Apulia and forwarded to all parts of the Eastern Empire and the Slavonic lands.

Evidence of this commerce is seen from extant thirteenth century documents written in Latin now in the Dubrovnik Archives:

i) *1229, Saturday 15th.* Firmum (Fermo)
Lord Guido del Andriano grants safe conduct to Lord John, Count of Ragusa for his citizens till February 1st next. This was opposed by certain citizens in Firmum.[69]

ii) *1231, March 3rd.* Rimini
Solemn confirmation of safe conduct to Ragusans, if they observe statutes and regulations of the town.[70]

iii) *1231, Monday, March 26th* at Senna (mod. Senigallia)
Safe conduct granted by Lord Giovanni de Conziponzis to Lord Andrea de Balislava, Ambassador of Ragusa for all merchants from Ragusa coming to Senna and district.[71]

iv) *1235, August 1st.* Ragusa
Theodore Crosius and Peter Ballislav, Viscounts of Ragusa, grant safe conduct to 'our chosen friends' of Ravenna to trade in Ragusa and district on the same footing as citizens of Ragusa.[72]

v) *1249, May 24th* at Fanum (mod. Fano)
Safe conduct for all merchants and merchandise of Ragusa, trading in Fanum. Similar grants to be made by Ragusa within two months.[73]

vi) *1249, Sunday, May 6th* Firmum
Ragusans can come to Firmum and the Port of St. George for a
period of five years, free of customs and exactions. All penalties
granted to citizens of Firmum against Ragusans to be suspended
till then.[74]

Examination of a document embodying an agreement between
Ancona and Dubrovnik (April 4, 1292)[75] reveals details of some of the
goods transported. For instance

'the Ragusan can bring in freely from Slavonia (which the document defines as land between the Naretva and Drin-Bojana rivers)
leather goods, domestic and wild hides, wax and pelts (both wild
and domestic) and can sell them to the Anconans tax free'

and again

'grain can be imported into Ancona from Slavonia by Dubrovnik
boats',

whilst in the reverse direction

'if Anconans carry wine and salt to Ragusa (Dubrovnik) or its
district they may export it beyond Ragusa free of duty'.

Tax was placed on two commodities, silk and rope cordage which
Dubrovnik merchants imported from Ancona, but the reason for this
is not given. Moreover Dubrovnik traders

'who carry or cause to be carried goods into Ancona from Tuscany,
Lombardy and Romandiola (region of present-day Romagna) and
the whole seaboard of these places, by land or sea shall pay
Anconan taxes but as for merchandise from Apulia, let it continue
as before, as regards: wheat, grain, wine, salt and articles made of
wood, which they bring into Ancona'.

The full text of the treaty is as follows:

'*June 4th 1292.* This is the form of treaty contracted by Lord
Grubesia Radigne, ambassador and sindic of Ragusa, on the one
part, and the Lord Dominic Prandi, sindic of Ancona, and his
colleagues Lord Bonbaron Petri and Lambertinus Rustici on the
other part. They made the following agreements, to be ratified by
the Lord Andrea Dandolo, son of the once-famous Lord John
Dandolo, doge of Venice and Count of Ragusa, and the judges,
council and commune of Ragusa.

The former arrangements re taxes and immunities by treaty and custom have given rise to various obscurities (footnote : and much to the detriment of the community). Therefore Lord Grubesia de Radigne, citizen, sindic, and procurator of Andrea Dandolo and the (men of) Ragusa, agreed that a fully detailed treaty should be drawn up and written down by Aczonem, son of a certain Jacopo di Titullo, notary public for Dominicus Prandi, sindic of Ancona and procurator for the noble knight Lord Thomas de Henzola, ruler of Ancona, and by me, Karlectus, son of master Peter of Ragusa. 1. All men of Ragusa, safe or shipwrecked (which God avert), may come, drop anchor, remain in the port, city and district of Ancona freely and without hindrance, with all goods and merchandise which originates in Slavonia. They can sell it to Anconans, and buy from them, and can return home without paying any tax not legally due from them or from Anconans who buy from them; except in the case of silk, spun or not, and on rope/cordage. If the Ragusans import these they must pay customs duties, at the rate of 40 Anconan soldi per hundred pounds of denari (dinars).

Corn from Slavonia cannot be disembarked in Ancona without being declared to the customs or other officials of Ancona, who are deputed to inspect it and establish whether it comes from Slavonia or Romania. If the said grain is ascertained to be Slavonian, it is duty-free. If, however, it is found to be Roman, they must pay Anconan imposts like other foreigners, i.e. 40 Anconan soldi per hundred pounds denari. If the Ragusans do not produce the grain for examination as stated, they must pay on the Slavonian corn twice what they would pay on Roman corn, i.e. 4 Anconan pounds per hundred pounds of denari.

The Ragusans can bring in freely from Slavonia : leather goods, domestic and wild hides, wax and pelts, wild and domestic, and also dutiable goods. They can sell these to Anconans, and Anconans can buy them, tax free. If the Ragusans do not wish to sell, and wish to export them from Ancona by land or sea, they may do so if they pay the Anconan duties, i.e. 40 soldi per hundred pounds of denari of the value which they have exported.

Ragusans who come by sea into Ancona shall not be liable for duty if they discharge and then reload goods, but if they discharge and do not reload they shall pay harbour dues.

Ragusans who carry or cause to be carried goods into Ancona from Tuscany, Lombardy, Romandiola, and the whole seaboard of these places, by land or sea, shall pay Anconan taxes at 20 soldi per hundred pounds of denari. As for merchandise from Apulia, let it continue as before, conforming to the decrees of Ancona, as regards: wheat, grain, wine, salt, and wooden goods, which they bring into Ancona.

Ragusans who import goods from the Levant or Barbary coast intending to put in at Ragusa, should they put in and discharge at Ancona, and wish to sell the merchandise there, are liable for duty as follows: 40 soldi per hundred pounds denari. If, however, they do not wish to sell in Ancona, and wish to remove the goods from Ancona to Ragusa, they can do so duty-free, provided that they guarantee that they are taking the goods to Ragusa and nowhere else.

If the Ragusans shall take ships in any part of the whole seacoast of Slavonia, bound for the said seacoast or as far as Venice, or returning from Venice to Slavonia, and because of bad weather, high tides, or waterlogged ships, they put into Ancona, they can disembark and reload the said goods tax-free, provided they are carrying the goods on to that Slavonian coast or Venice. If, however, they carry them to *this coast, viz.* to Romandiola, March of Ancona, Reggio, or Apulia and district, they must pay duties at the rate of 40 soldi per hundred pounds of denari.

If at any time the Anconans generally prohibit any foreigner from selling merchandise from Ancona in the territories of Rome and the Levant and beyond the Gulf, or coming from those parts to Ancona, without certain punishment or surcharges, then Ragusans shall be treated in Ancona as foreigners of the better sort. This prohibition shall be notified at the time to Ragusa by the Anconans.

Conversely, the said Lord Grubesia agreed that Anconans should come and go freely to Ragusa with merchandise from anywhere, and buy and sell there tax-free. But if they wished to discharge and transport the merchandise beyond Ragusa by land, they must pay Ragusan taxes at the rate of 40 soldi per hundred pounds of denari. If they wished to convey it by sea, Anconans, like other foreigners, could do so tax-free unless they convey them into Slavonia, in which case they must pay tax at 40 soldi per hundred pounds of denari. By the said Slavonia is understood from the place which is called 'Orenta, to the estuary of 'Lessi. If Anconans buy merchandise in Slavonia, they must pay tax at 40 soldi per hundred pounds of denari if they convey it to Ragusa by land. But if Anconans put in to Ragusa on account of bad weather, high tides, because their ships are waterlogged, or through any other necessity, with goods and merchandise from overseas, they may discharge and reload and depart duty-free. If, however, the Anconans sell in Ragusa, they must pay one-fifth of the value of the said merchandise sold.

If Anconans put in to Ragusa for shelter they shall not be liable for any payment.

If Anconans carry or cause to be carried to Ragusa or its district wine or salt, they may export it beyond Ragusa tax free, provided that the said salt or wine is not discharged and sold or given away in Ragusa itself.

If at any time the Ragusans generally prohibit any foreigner from selling merchandise from Ragusa in the territories of Rome and the Levant and beyond the Gulf or coming from thence to Ragusa, then Anconans shall be treated in Ragusa as foreigners of the better sort. This prohibition shall be notified at the time to Ancona by the Ragusans.

Every single thing written down here is promised and guaranteed by the various rulers and officials individually.

Penalty for infringement 200 silver marks.

Signed: Karlectus, notary public, 1292, June 4th, at Ancona.'

This shows that by the thirteenth century Dubrovnik's citizens were transporting valuable and much needed goods, not only between the Balkan peninsula and Italy, but also between Italian markets themselves and her merchants were therefore important trading intermediaries.

All trade to places situated beyond the Adriatic Sea came under the heading of navigation 'extra Culfum' which began to grow to important proportions in the thirteenth century. The Levant trade became extremely active. From the commercial provisions contained in the various treaties between Dubrovnik and Venice[76] it can be seen that the former traded with all parts of the Eastern Empire, Syria, Tunis, Barbary, Italy, Sicily and Egypt. At Constantinople, the Latin Emperors, Baldwin I and Henry, granted Dubrovnik citizens the privilege of having a colony in the city. Her merchants traded especially with the Morea, in southern Greece, and the feudal duchy of Chiarenza or Clarence, in the Peloponnesus. From these places they brought silk to Ancona and other parts of Italy. At the same time they kept up their connection with the Greek princes who held sway over the fragments of the Greek Empire, namely the Emperors of Nicaea and Trebizond[77] and the Despots of Epirus, After the capture of Constantinople by the Latins, Epirus continued to hold out against their arms, and was ruled by the Despots Michael I (died 1214), Manuel (1214–1241) and Michael II (1241–1271), all of whom granted valuable privileges to merchants of Dubrovnik.[78] When the Greek Empire was re-established in 1261 all the exemptions and privileges were reconfirmed, first by Michael Palaeologus and later in 1322 by Andronicus II.[79]

With regard to Egypt and Syria little information exists before 1280, the time when documents were conscientiously preserved in Dubrovnik Archives. In 1224 Egypt was placed under interdict and the Venetians forbad Dubrovnik's citizens to trade 'in terra Alexandrie vel Egipti'.[80] Dubrovnik merchants before starting on a journey had to swear that they would not visit Egypt, but in all probability the prohibition was often disregarded.[81] Subsequent attempts to enforce the interdict were equally unsuccessful. The object of the prohibition was above all to prevent the Egyptian Sultans from obtaining timber and iron, which were rare in their own country, for military purposes. Traders were attracted by the enormous profits of the venture, for which they were willing to brave ecclesiastical displeasure. For example in 1304, three Dubrovnik merchants were captured whilst engaged in illicit traffic with Alexandria, finally being granted absolution by the Pope.[82]

Internal Organization

Commercial development could not have grown without some form of solid internal organization within the republic. Dubrovnik was an aristocratic republic in which the nobility were received and esteemed according to the value of their possessions.[83] The Prince (Knez) was carefully selected and held office for only a short period. He was expected to have an intimate knowledge of his city and republic, and to exploit its advantages to his full ability. The motto over the entrance to the Prince's palace is somewhat significant in this context – 'Privata obliti publica curate' (Forget yourself, look after the public). The site of the Prince's residence was also carefully chosen for from the garden terrace he had a clear view of the port,

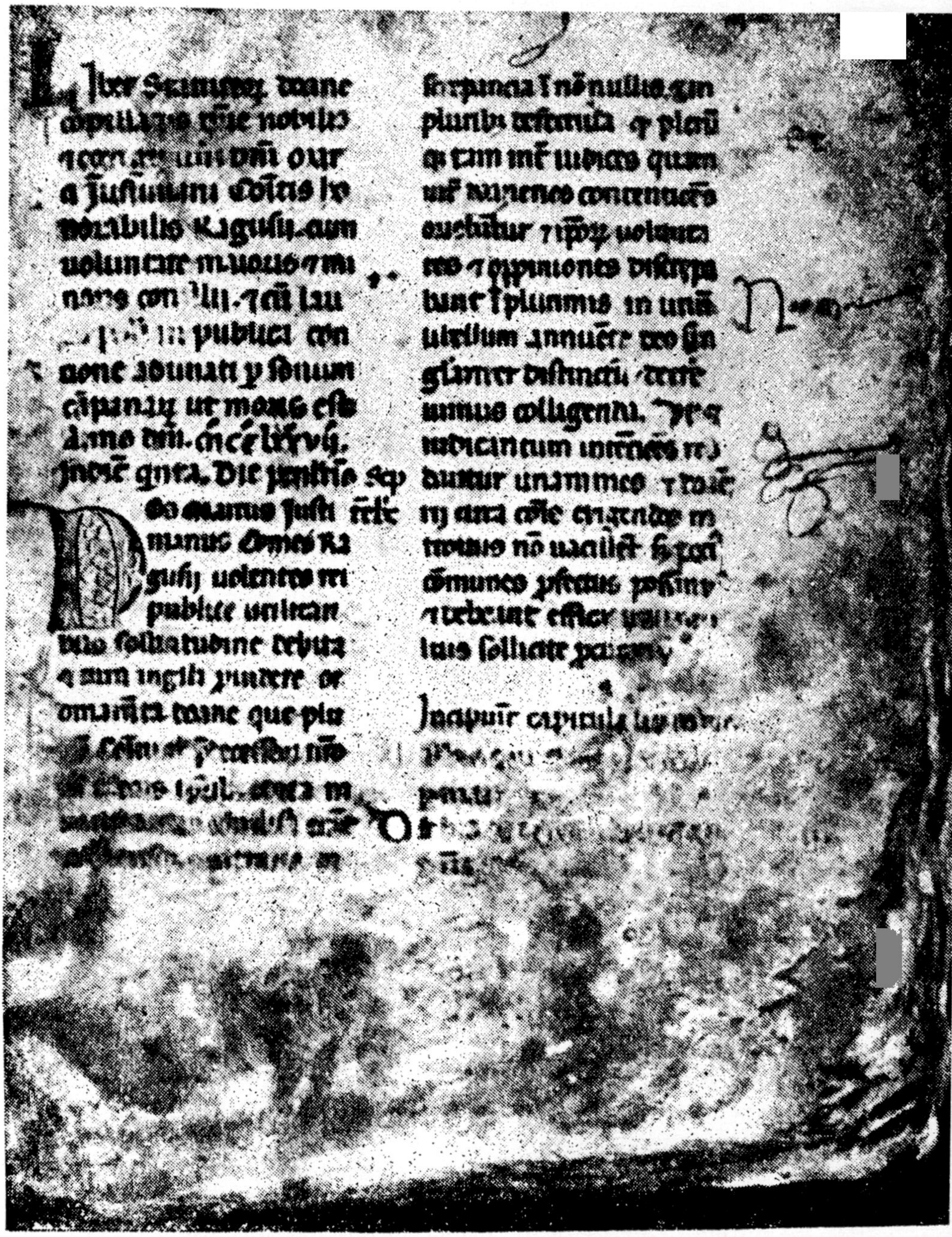

FIG. 17. First page of Liber Statutorum Doane – from the Dubrovnik Archives, dated 1277.

the caravan route out of the town, and the quarantine area, the three main foci of the business life of the small state.

The constitution of the republic was strictly aristocratic, with the population divided into three classes, the nobles, the commoners or 'cittadini' and the peasants. The latter had no voice in government and were not admissable for any office. A few offices were open to the commoners, but only such as had no political importance. The whole government was entrusted to the nobility, a close aristocracy which never permitted any admixture of plebian blood by inter-marriage with the inferior orders, and which was limited to certain families inscribed in the Dubrovnik 'Libro d'Oro' (Specchio di Maggior Consiglio). For the most part the nobles of Dubrovnik were merchants like those of Venice and there were only a few who lived purely from their rents, because the territory of the republic was small and for the most part sterile. There was therefore no oppor-tunity for the formation of a landed or feudal aristocracy but the increased wealth from commerce did mean that the gap between the nobles and commoners grew accordingly.

By the end of the thirteenth century the Dubrovnik constitution had assumed the form which, with certain alterations, it preserved until the downfall of the republic in the nineteenth century. Even the fact that in 1358 the Venetian Counts were superseded by native Rectors did not change the internal constitution of the state to any considerable extent. The constitution since the early days of the city's existence had undergone much the same transformation as that of Venice, and tended to become even more aristocratic. The *laudo populi* was still maintained, but it was resorted to less and less fre-quently as years went by, after having been an empty formality for some time. At the end of the period of Venetian suzerainty it had ceased to exist although theoretically laws were confirmed 'per populum Rhacusinum more solito congregatum', but by that time all power was invested in the aristocracy. Only nobles might aspire to any but the humblest offices of the state, and every noble had a voice at least in the Great Council. The nobles were, as a rule, the descend-ants of the original Latin colonists from Epidauros and Salona, or, in a few cases, of those early Slav refugees who were nobles in their own country. The names themselves have an Italian sound, although most of them are unlike any real Italian names. The commonest are : Bassegli, Bobali, Bodazza, Bona, Bonda, Bubagna, Caboga, Ghetaldi, Gondola, Gozze, Luccari, Raguina, Resti, Sarac, and Sorgo. Only a few, such as Zlatarich, are purely Slavonic.[84] There was a fairly large part of the population of Slavonic origin, but the official, and to a great extent the popular, language was Italian. The laws, deliberations and official documents are all either in Latin or Italian and the general character of the community was prevalently Italian, modified to some extent by Slavonic influences. The latter tended to increase especially after the end of Venetian suzerainty, and by the middle of the sixteenth century the bulk of the lower classes spoke the Slav language. The Head of State was the Count, who represented Venetian authority, summoned the councils, and signed all public acts. No act was valid without his approval, but, on the other hand, he could not make decrees without the assistance and consent of the councils. Of these there were three – namely, the Consilium Majus, the Consilium Minus and the Rogati or Pregati. The Great Council was the ultimate basis of the state, and was composed of all nobles above twenty years of age, (the age was afterwards lowered to eighteen years) including Minor Councillors, the Senators, and all the officials. Its numbers usually ranged from 200 to 300. It met in September, and the list of vacant offices was read out by the Count. The Secretary called up the Councillors one by one, drawing the numbers of all the seats from a bag. Each Councillor then drew a ball from an urn, which contained a number of gold balls equal to that of the offices to be filled; those who drew the gold balls took their seats beside the Count and Minor Council and ordered the Secretary to nominate three Councillors for each office. As each name was called out the Councillor in question and his nearest relatives left the hall and waited outside. Then all the remaining Councillors were given linen balls, which they were to drop into another urn divided into two sections, one for the ayes and one for the noes. If none of the three candidates received more than half the votes recorded, the election was repeated. No one might refuse the office thus conferred upon him, save a small number of persons who could obtain a dispensation by paying a small fine. (This account is based on that given in Luccari, save for such changes as occurred between the Venetian period and the late eighteenth century, when Luccari's book was published.)[85]

The Great Council ratified all the laws of the republic; it gave the final decision for peace or war, although the diplomatic function was reserved to the Senate; it could recall exiles, it received petitions, and it managed many of the daily affairs of the city. Sixty members (including the Count and the Minor Council) formed a quorum.

The Small Council, which had in all probability existed in a rudimentary form from the earliest times had now developed into an important body. It acted as the Count's privy council, it arranged all official ceremonies, and gave audience to foreign ambassadors and envoys to Dubrovnik. It also acted as a sort of Court of Chancery, protected widows and orphans from injury, and watched over the morals of the citizens. It examined the deliberations of the other bodies on taxes, dues, and the rents, income, and real property of the state. On simpler matters it gave decisions, and others it referred to the Senate. It was an intermediary between private individuals and the state, and heard all complaints against the magistrates and other officials. It consisted of the Count and eleven members, of whom five formed the *Corte Maggiore*, or High Court of Justice, for all important cases. (The number of members varied at different times.) The members were all men of mature age, and remained in office for a year only. Six made a quorum.

The Senate (Rogati) was the most influential of the three Councils, and transacted a great part of the business of the State. It imposed all taxes, tributes, and customs duties, decided how the money of the state should be spent or invested, and dealt with many other financial matters. It conducted the foreign affairs of the republic, and nominated ambassadors and consuls. It was the Supreme Court of Appeal for criminal cases, and after 1440 for civil cases as well. It appointed a number of state officials, such as the Provveditori of the Arsenal, the financial secretaries, and the functionaries who attended to the supply of provisions. The number of Senators varied considerably. In 1272 there were thirty-five members;[86] later the number rose to sixty-one. The body included the Count or Rector, the eleven Minor Councillors, various high functionaries, and a number of unofficial members. They met four times a week, and remained in office for a year, but might be re-elected,

'for the republic desires that her sons should exercise themselves in this kind of council, so that they may become Senators of judgment, and learn by long and continual experience the method and practice of governing excellently'.

By a decree of 1331 it was decided that thirty Senators made a quorum.[87]

Besides the three Councils, there were a number of special bodies appointed for different purposes. Thus there was the *Corte Maggiores* or *Major Curia*, whose sentences in civil matters were without appeal until 1440; the *Minor Curia* or Lower Court, with special advocates attached to each; the *Advocatores Comunis*, or Public Prosecutors, and many other functionaries. The three *Camarlenghi* kept the public accounts, and the *Doanerii* supervised the customs. The four Treasurers of Santa Maria had important fiscal duties in guarding the state treasury and paying out the public money according to the decrees of the Senate. They also had certain charitable duties, and spent the income of invested surpluses in providing poor girls with dowries, and later in ransoming Christian slaves from the Turks or the Barbary pirates. Private citizens, and even foreigners from Slav lands, often appointed them executors of their wills. Originally they had been the guardians of the relics and treasury of the cathedral, but as they gradually came to have so large a share of the financial business of the republic on their hands, in 1306 another board, called the *Procuratores Sanctae Mariae*, was instituted to manage the affairs of the Church, and act with powers of attorney for various religious confraternities. A similar body was formed when the church of St. Blaize (Sv. Vlah) was erected in 1349. The notary of the republic, who drafted all public acts, patents, diplomas, etc., was usually an expert Italian lawyer.

There were numbers of other officers for different departments of the administration and for purposes of defence, such as those *super sale, super blado comunis, super turribus,* and the *capitani di custodia,* who were elected every month, and the captains of the *sestieri* or six wards, into which Dubrovnik was divided. All the citizens in turn had to bear arms for the defence of the town, and certain nobles, who were changed very frequently, commanded the guard, and saw that the gates were securely fastened at night. The rest of the republic's territory was ruled by officers appointed by the Great Council, called counts, viscounts, or captains. They governed despotically, and no native of the territory had any voice in the administration. In many cases the government was very tyrannical and arbitrary. Dubrovnik's ideas of liberty were not only restricted to a limited class, but did not extend a yard beyond the walls. Only the island of Lastovo, purchased in 1216 from Stephen Uroš, King of Serbia, was permitted to retain its own customs and laws.

It will thus be seen that the Constitution was essentially copied from that of Venice, and was designed above all to make personal government impossible. None of the officials, save the Venetian Count, remained in office for more than a year, and the great majority of them could not be re-elected for two years afterwards. Everything was done to prevent individuals from acquiring undue influence, and to make the government as collective as possible. All business was executed by boards and committees, and hardly anything by single individuals. Every detail was carefully regulated, so as to leave no loophole for tampering with the institutions or suspending the continuity of the government. The result was from some points of view satisfactory. In the whole history of Dubrovnik only three or four revolutions are recorded – almost a unique distinction among the city-republics of Italy and other European lands, whose history is one long tale of civil wars and seditions. Venice alone enjoyed a similar though less complete immunity. On the other hand, it gave the executive very little power of acting energetically and pursuing a bold, broad-minded policy, and prevented Dubrovnik from expanding into a first-class maritime state, as it had more than one opportunity of doing. At the same time, had it become really powerful, and acquired a hegemony over a large part of the Adriatic littoral and of the Slavic hinterland, it would later have run greater risks of opposition from the Turks. Venice, who felt the need for a swift and silent executive, instituted the Council of Ten, to which the Dubrovnik constitution offers no parallel. The Dubrovnik Senate was too numerous a body to act in the same way, and in it those who hesitated and doubted usually carried the day.

The character of the Dubrovnik constitution is seen from the fact that so few individuals have left their mark on the town's history. There were various noble families whose names appear again and again in the public records, but hardly any single citizen emerges high above the others. The few names which are remembered are those of scholars, men of letters, or scientists. Even the ambassadors were alway sent in pairs, although in the Middle Ages this was not peculiar to Dubrovnik alone.

Another aspect was that the three Councils who had to transact all the weightiest matters of the republic were also overwhelmed with the petty details of municipal administration. This of course was difficult to avoid in the case of a small city-republic, but it constituted the radical feeling of that type of state, for its government was a parliament, a court of justice, and a town council all in one. The same body might be called upon to decide on an alliance with Hungary and on the seaworthiness of a ship in the same sitting.

In diplomatic affairs, however, Dubrovnik was a past-master. The republic was in constant danger from the powerful enemies which surrounded it on all sides. The Venetians, who claimed the monopoly of the Adriatic were ever anxious to increase their influence and to become absolute masters of the city, as they were of the other Dalmatian towns, and after their retirement from Dubrovnik in 1358 they made many attempts to reinstate their authority. On the mainland there was the King of Serbia, the Ban of Bosnia, the Lord of Hum, all watching for an opportunity to occupy Dubrovnik, whose splendid harbour they envied. But the city fathers, by a policy which was often tortuous and not always straight-forward, certainly achieved their object of preserving the republic's autonomy. Although Dubrovnik was never absolutely independent – for she either had a Venetian Count or paid a tribute to this or that power – she was always free from foreign control in her internal affairs, and to a great extent in her external relations. The government always knew when to give way and when to hold out; this feature became particularly conspicuous later in the republic's dealings with the Turks.

The continued existence of the small republic for so many centuries is the greatest tribute to the sagacity of its rulers. Its position according to Wilkinson

> 'exposed it to constant alarms, surrounded as it was by trouble-some neighbours, and subject alternately to the intrigues and ambitions of Venice, the unsettled and discordant projects of the Slavonian princes, the unstable friendship of the Hungarians, the selfish views of the Spaniards, and the capricious insolence of the Turks, to the ignomy of whose protection the hostility of Venice obliged it to submit; and the whole career of the Dubrovnik republic was a struggle for self-preservation, and the maintenance of its independence in the midst of constant danger'.[88]

The lives and influence of the non-noble citizens are less well known, save that they played no part in the government, and were ineligible for all but the very lowest offices. On the whole they seem to have accepted the oligarchial constitution, and apparently had little desire to take part in public affairs. The 'cittadini' did not form an individual group and were looked upon as the 'populus' as opposed to the 'nobilies'. Many were poor, employed in manual work, were artisans or provided various menial services. Already in 1272 statutes mention millers, butchers, seamen and fishermen. Water mills were found throughout Dubrovnik's territory especially in Župa Dubrovačke, Rijeka Dubrovačke and in Pile.[89] Venice exploited this situation and encouraged the division between the nobility and the people seeing it as a means of keeping the republic weak. The situation changed slightly in 1332 after the famous 'Closed' (Zatvaranje) Great Council. At this meeting the power of the Venetian Prince was greatly diminished and Dubrovnik's rulers were able to put forward proposals often against Venetian wishes. Also it inadvertently gave greater scope to the development of the town's traders and the varied handicraft guilds. The government gave merchants certain commercial concessions and the right to own land on newly acquired territory (e.g. Pelješac), but they were never given a chance to participate in the republic's rule. Guilds of various trades were formed, which had a beneficial effect for

> 'The guild sought order and proportion in the economic sphere, notably by serving as the master of the town's externalities. Only guildsmen could occupy shops; foreigners and others could only trade in the open town market. The history of medieval trade was an uninterrupted struggle between the chaos of free trading, which might destroy the traditional accommodation among economic interests, and the excess profit of the monopoly situation'.[90]

The third social group were the peasants. Between 1205 and 1358 Dubrovnik's territory was considerably increased, which led to a growth in the number of peasants under its control. It is interesting to note at this point the peasants' attitude and perception of the city. Stoianovich maintains that

> 'Balkan peasants of Slavic speech alluded to the village and peasant way of life as "črni svet" or "the dark world" . . . On the other hand the names of several Balkan towns specifically signified "white city". They were so designated less because their ramparts (or house walls) were occasionally white than because of their history as nuclei of protection and religious communion . . . Like peasants elsewhere, Balkan peasants succeeded in preserving a double or polar view of the city'.[91]

There were two types of peasants; those residing in the older territory of the republic, who were feudal serfs ('kmet') and found mainly on the church estates, and the free serfs who lived in the suburbs of the city and on the islands of Koločep, Lopud, and Šipan. It is difficult to understand why, but the peasants' situation did not fit the classic feudalistic situation. It may have been the result of a difference between Latin and Slav, or the critical need for food in the economic life of the commercial city. The main form of agricultural production allowed the peasant to till the land as he wished which was usually his own private possession. In turn he received money or part of the produce, but this system ensured that the city was not short of food. The free serf regime was first established on Lastovo sometime in the thirteenth century and also by 1340 there were specific relations set up on Mljet Island between the serfs and the Benedictine Abbey.

On the whole the 'cittadini' and peasants were ruled with wisdom and without oppression, free from faction fights, and many of the former had identical commercial interests with those of the aristocracy, for both classes derived their wealth from trade, whilst the latter in their role of food supplier were well cared for and protected by the government.

The Church

Increased trade with the hinterland gradually led to a growth in the influence of the Dubrovnik Church, especially by the Franciscans and Dominicans, the latter being very active in Serbia (Brskovo). The Church of Dubrovnik was also active in the important political questions surrounding the Bosnian Bogomils, but above all it helped commercial interests, particularly in the attitude towards Bosnia of the Roman court. The Dubrovnik Church had also been increasing in wealth and dignity at home with the growth of the republic, and a number of handsome ecclesiastical buildings were begun during the fourteenth century. In the eleventh, twelfth, and thirteenth centuries, the Slavonic princes gave the churches many valuable gifts of land, gold and silver ornaments, and relics, but during the thirteenth and fourteenth centuries Bosnia, Hum and Serbia were torn by religious wars owing to the spread of that strange heresy called Bogomilism. Of the origin of this heresy as of its tenets there is very little reliable evidence. In all probability it was an offshoot of Armenian Paulicianism, itself derived from the earlier Adoptionist creed.[92] Paulician colonies had been settled in Europe as early as the ninth century by the Emperor Constantine Copronymus, and the heresy spread to Bulgaria, Serbia, Bosnia and Macedonia. Jireček gives an account of the beliefs of the Bogomils based on research by various Slavonic scholars. They believed in the existence of two principles, equal in age and power, one good personified in God, and one evil personified in Satan. They recognized the New Testament, but not the Old; all matter and all the visible world were essentially evil; the body of Christ was only an apparent, not a real, body; the sacraments were corporeal, therefore evil. They had no hierarchy, but an executive consisting of a bishop and two grades of Apostles, and besides the ordinary Bogomils there was a special Order of the Perfect, who renounced all worldly possessions, marriage, meat, and lived like hermits. They had no churches or images but had a deathbed ceremony, without which one went to hell. They also did not believe in purgatory.[93] As Bury remarks, it is doubtful if this is a true presentation of the Bogomil creed. Hardly any of their books of ritual survive, and all the accounts of them which have been preserved are written by their prosecutors. It is more probable that they were a monotheistic sect, believing in one God only, and rejecting the Trinity. This view is supported by the fact that at the time of the Turkish conquest such numbers of Bogomils became Muhamedans. It was not merely that they went over to the conqueror's creed from motives of mere self-interest; there was really more similarity between that religion and Bogomilism than between the latter and either the Eastern or the Western Church. In the tenth century there was a bishopric of Bosnia, which until the eleventh century was in the ecclesiastical province of Split. In 1067 it was transferred to Antivari (Bar). Later in the same century it was added to the archbishopric of Dubrovnik, but the dioceses of Bar and Split continued to dispute Dubrovnik's supremacy and in the conflict of authorities Bogomilism found scope to increase its adherents. The Bosnians were mostly Roman Catholics, although there were Orthodox Christians among them. Ban Kulin was himself a Catholic, but when in 1189 the Pope, at the instigation of the King of Hungary, Bela III, transferred the Bosnian bishopric once more from the Dubrovnik province to that of Split, he went over to Bogomilism, so as not to be in any way under Hungarian authority. His conversion gave the heresy a fresh impetus, and it spread all over Bosnia, Slavonia, Dalmatia, and Croatia, even to the coastal towns. Pope Innocent III had to induce the King of Hungary to make a crusade against the Bogomils in Bosnia, but Kulin declared that they were good Catholics, induced the Archbishop of Dubrovnik to go to Rome with several of the heretics to be examined by the Pope, and asked for a Papal envoy to be sent to Bosnia to study the question. The Pope agreed, and sent his chaplain, Johannes de Casamaris, to Bosnia in 1203. The heads of the Bogomil community, who were also heads of monasteries, congregated at Bjelopolje on the River Bosna, and met the Ban Casamaris, and Marinus, the Archdeacon of Dubrovnik. They presented an address in which they affirmed their orthodoxy and their attachment to the Roman Church,[94] and declared themselves ready to obey the Pope in everything; Kulin himself abjured all heresy. They renewed these declarations before the King of Hungary and the Ban at Pest. The Papal legate was quite content, and advised the Pope to erect some new bishoprics in Bosnia.

In 1218 the heresy was again rampant, and Honorius III sent a legate to Hungary and Dalmatia to preach a crusade against the Bogomils, but no crusade was organized, and the legate went alone to Bosnia, where he died in 1222. The quarrels between the Pope and Hungary gave the Bogomils a respite, and they became even more numerous in consequence. In 1222 Andrew II, King of Hungary, placed Bosnia under the ecclesiastical jurisdiction of Ugolin, Bishop of Kalocsa, on condition that he stamped out the heresy and Pope Honorius confirmed the donation. Unfortunately the crusade never came off, and the Bogomils became so powerful that they deposed the Ban Stephen and succeeded in placing their co-religionary Matthew Ninoslav on the throne (1232). James, the Papal legate, went to Bosnia and found that the greater part of the inhabitants were tainted with the heresy, including the Catholic Bishop; the Archbishop of Dubrovnik knew of this and did not trouble about it, so that the legate reconfirmed the union of the bishopric to that of Kalocsa. He succeeded, however, in inducing Ninoslav to become a Catholic, and endow a new cathedral, which was to be in the hands of the Dominicans and many magnates followed his example. The Bogomils soon raised their heads once more, and the Ban was either unable or unwilling to extirpate them. A crusade was therefore proclaimed against them, which lasted from 1234 to 1239. Bosnia was ravaged with fire and sword, and finally conquered by the crusaders under Koloman, the King of Hungary's son. In 1238 the Dominican Ponsa was made Bishop of Bosnia, and by 1239 Bogomilism seemed to have been suppressed. The moment the crusaders retired the heretics who were supported by the nation, rose in arms once more and became independent of Hungary. In 1246 Innocent IV ordered a second crusade, but this time without success. After Ninoslav's death Bosnia again fell under Hungary, but no very severe measures were taken against the Bogomils. The Bogomil Church of Bosnia became an established institution, and the Catholic bishops themselves no longer resided in the country, but at Djakovar, in Slavonia, and various attempts to organize crusades against them failed. The Bani were afraid of persecuting them lest they should rise in arms and put themselves under the protection of the King of Serbia, who as a Greek Christian was also an enemy of the Catholics. Moreover, the missionary efforts of the Catholic Church were hindered by the quarrels between the Franciscans and Dominicans. Bogomilism spread to Croatia and Dalmatia, and found adherents even at Trogir and Split. Pope Benedict XII ordered the Croatian barons to make war on the heretics (1337), but they were too busy fighting among themselves to achieve much result. The Ban Stephen declared himself a good Catholic in 1340, and protected the Roman Church in Bosnia once more, agreeing to the establishment of two more bishoprics. Little more is heard of the heresy after this date until the crusade of 1360.[95]

The Dubrovnik Church suffered in consequence of the heterodoxy of so many of the Slav princes, and no longer received rich gifts from them. On the other hand, both an account of its convenient situation and because it was a stronghold of Catholicism, Dubrovnik became the centre of all this missionary activity. In 1225 the Dominican Order was established here, and occupied a small house attached to the church of St. Jacob in Peline. When the Order became more numerous it moved to the Ploča quarter, where a large new church was erected for it in 1306, and a monastery about 1345. The Franciscans first came to Dubrovnik in 1235, twenty-eight years after the foundation of the Order by St. Francis of Assisi, who is said to have visited the city himself on his return from the Holy Land, although there is no foundation for the legend. In 1250 a monastery was built for them outside the Pile Gate; it was destroyed by the Serbs during the raid of 1319.[96] A concession of land was granted to them within the walls in the Minčeta quarter, and by the middle of the fourteenth century they were established in the large, handsome monastery which still exists, built partly at government expense and partly by the munificence of private citizens, including the guild of Ghent merchants established there.[97] The two Orders gave battle to the heretics, and helped to organize crusades against them. They are amongst the most barbarous examples of religious persecution known. On the other hand, according to Dubrovnik legend, the Bogomils themselves persecuted the Catholics in the Kotor district, and the bodies of three martyrs who were murdered by them were brought to Dubrovnik where a church was built in their honour.[98] It is somewhat difficult to unravel the tangle of contradictory accounts on this subject, especially as Dubrovnik writers often confuse the Bogomils with the followers of the Oriental Church.

Territorial Growth

For an understanding of the characteristics and potentialities of Dubrovnik in this early period, a knowledge of its territorial development is essential. Until the second half of the thirteenth century, Dubrovnik was limited to the small coastal area of 'Astarea' (from *Astaria*, a medieval Latin word meaning a flat tract of sea-coast), at the foot of Mount Srđ The richest of the citizens in Dubrovnik gradually and cautiously extended their private holdings up to the territory of the Slavic princes in the hinterland (e.g. Žrnovnica). At the end of the thirteenth century Dubrovnik included the islands of Lastovo, Šipan, Koločep, Lopud and Daksa. During the fourteenth century up to the end of Venetian rule it added the Pelješac peninsula, Mljet Island and Kurilo inland. The territorial expansion of Dubrovnik was mainly attained by purchase and compromise, by benefiting from political competition and constantly avoiding wars.[99]

Perhaps the most important territorial acquisition obtained between 1205 and 1358 was the Pelješac peninsula, which converted Dubrovnik from a city-republic, with only a few kilometres of coastline beyond its walls, and some islands, into a fairly respectable territorial state. The Pelješac peninsula[100] is a long mountainous peninsula jutting out from the Dalmatian coast in a north-westerly direction, with a sort of spur or branch promontory stretching towards the south-east and forming a deep bay. It is 71·2 km long, varies in breadth from 3·1 km to 7·1 km and covers an area of 355 km. Parts of the peninsula are very fertile, especially for vineyards, and its population totalled 12,035 inhabitants in 1961 which in the Middle

FIG. 18. (facing page)   Territorial growth of the Dubrovnik Republic.

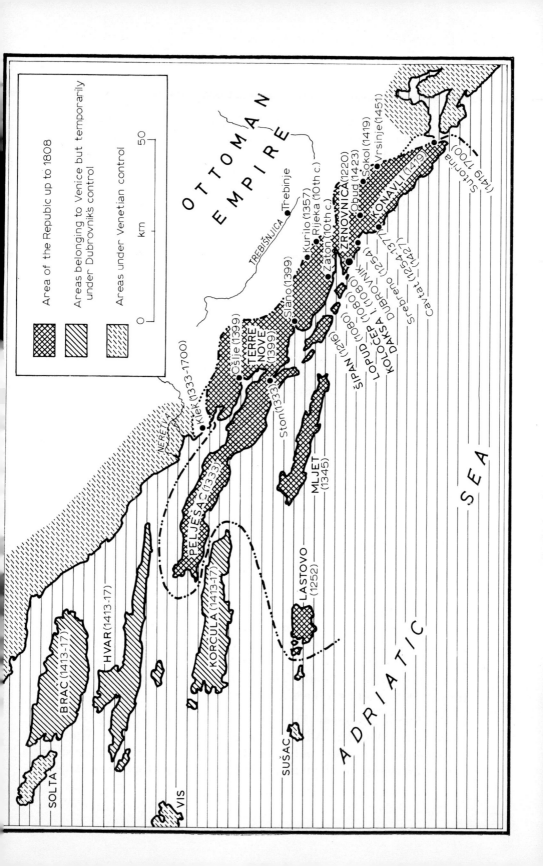

Area of the Republic up to 1808

Areas belonging to Venice but temporarily under Dubrovniks control

Areas under Venetian control

0   km   50

OTTOMAN EMPIRE

TREBIŠNJICA ●Trebinje

TREBIŠNJICA

Klek (1333–1700)

NERETVA

Ošlje (1399)

TERRE NOVE (1399)

Ston (1333)

Slano (1399)

Zaton (10th c.)

Rijeka (10th c.)

Kurilo (1357)

ZRNOVNICA (1220)

Obud (1423)

Sokol (1419)

KONAVLI (1419)

Vrsinje (1451)

Sutorina (1419 1700)

ŠIPAN (1216)

LOPUD (1080)

KOLOCEP (1080)

DAKSA

VINIK (1254)

DUBROVNIK

Srebreno (1254–1377)

Cavtat (1427)

PELJEŠAC (1333)

MLJET (1345)

KORCULA (1413–17)

HVAR (1413–17)

BRAC (1413–17)

SOLTA

VIS

SUŠAC

LASTOVO (1252)

ADRIATIC

SEA

Ages was probably even more. It is joined to the mainland by a
narrow isthmus 1½ km across, with two small towns Veliki Ston, looking towards Dubrovnik, and Mali Ston, on the north towards the
Neretvanski Kanal, each with a good port. On both shores of the
peninsula there are several small harbours. On the southern coast,
opposite the island of Korčula rises the imposing mass of Sv. Ilija
(961 m) with the town of Orebić at its foot. The importance of this
territory for Dubrovnik was partly strategic, as it formed a bulwark
against invaders from the north, whether by sea or by land, and partly
commercial, on account of the valuable salt-pans of Ston, which
afterwards formed one of the chief sources of revenue for the republic and are still in use today. This territory had formed part of the
principality of Hum which was originally joined to Doclea, and
recognized Serbian overlordship from about 1222 until in 1325 it
was added to the Ban of Bosnia under Hungarian suzerainty. Hum
was divided into a number of *župe*, like the other Serb lands, under
different feudal families. Ston and the Pelješac peninsula were ruled
by that of the Branivoj, with whom Dubrovnik had hitherto lived on
terms of friendship and commercial intercourse. The republic sent
them an annual gift of 100 ipperperi[101] which may, however, have
been blackmail to secure immunity from piracy, to which so many
of the Slav tribes were addicted. It is probable that Dubrovnik rulers
had had their eyes on this district for some time, and in 1320–21
they gladly obeyed the injunctions of the Venetian Senate to act
against the pirates of Ston and Kotor.[102]

Stephen Dušan (1330–1355) the Serbian King was well disposed
towards Dubrovnik and soon after inheriting his position went on a
state visit to Dubrovnik. The Serbian King was received by the
citizens with their usual magnificence (1332) and Niccolò Bucchia
(Nikola Buća), who finally induced the King formally to cede the
coveted territory to Dubrovnik, was presented with land and houses
on Pelješac and a house in Dubrovnik itself. He was afterwards
granted citizenship and a seat in the Great Council, and became the
founder of a famous family. The document ceding Ston in exchange
for a tribute read as follows:

'We, Stephen Nemanja Dušan, by the grace of God, King of Serbia,
Dalmatia, Dioclia, Albania, Zeta, Chelmo, and the Maritime
Region, ... concede and grant to the community of Ragusa by
hereditary right to them and to their successors the whole Pelješac

and coast of Stagno (Ston), beginning from Prevlaca (Prevlaka) to the confines of Ragusan territory, with all the towns and villages and houses therein contained, and also Posrednica (Osinj – a small island at the mouth of the Neretva River) . . . in exchange for which they must pay to us and to our successors annually on the day of the Resurrection of our Lord Jesus Christ 500 *soldi* in Venetian *grossi*, on pain of paying double in case of delay'.[103]

In addition he was to receive a sum down of 2,000 ipperperi, and Stephen Kotromanić, Ban of Bosnia, who had certain rights over the Pelješac, was to receive 600 ipperperi a year. According to Resti, it was necessary for the republic to bribe several of the King's nobles and councillors so that they should influence him in favour of the grant, and they influenced the Ban of Bosnia through his secretary, Domagna Bobali, who was a native of Dubrovnik. The contract was carried out save for the island of Posrednica, which Dubrovnik was not allowed to occupy until 1345. The fate of the Branivoj family, whether it was entirely wiped out or whether the surviving members were merely expelled, is unknown.

The republic at once set to work to partition the land in the new territory among its citizens. Three-quarters of it was granted to the nobles, and the rest to townspeople; the grantees were forbidden to sell any land to the Slavs. A colour of piety was lent to this conquest by the determination of Dubrovnik to stamp out Bogomilism, and schism from the peninsula. The caloyers (a name usually given to the Greek monks) and heretical priests were exiled, and their places occupied by Roman Catholics; at the end of the century the Franciscans were established as an additional bulwark of the Church. In order to protect Ston from more earthly dangers an elaborate system of fortifications was begun, which were to serve the republic in good stead on more than one occasion. Both Veliki and Mali Ston were surrounded with massive walls (linked in 1335 at a cost of 120,000 ducats), and a castle was built in each town. A third wall was erected at the top of the hill, between the two seas; a long wall with towers at intervals was carried right across the isthmus, and other walls from both towns to the castle on the hill. These defences may be seen to this day, and although in a woeful state of neglect and disrepair, still form a most conspicuous feature in the landscape.

The following year (1334) King Stephen rather repented his generosity, and demanded back the gift on the pretext that Dubrovnik was incapable of defending it securely. His envoys, who visited Ston, were convinced by the sight of the fortifications, and perhaps by that of Dubrovnik gold, that it was being rapidly made quite secure, and induced him to confirm the grant. This he did, and forbade his subjects to attempt to enter the ceded territory.

During the Venetian epoch the territory of the republic had expanded considerably, and when the last Count departed it consisted of the following districts: in the immediate neighbourhood of the city it possessed the valleys of Gionchetto (Šumet), Bergato (Brgat), and Ombla (Rijeka), with the Bay of Gruž and the Lapad peninsula, but the frontiers were very near, and on the crest of Mt. Srđ, immediately behind the city, watchmen were posted day and night. Part of this territory had been acquired in the earliest times, but small additions had been made at intervals. Beyond the Ombla the citizens owned the stretch of coast known as 'Starea' or 'Astarea'. Of the islands, they possessed in the thirteenth century Mercana (Mrkan) – a small rock opposite the promontory of Cavtat, with a monastery of St. Michael (mentioned in 1254) – and the islands of Lopud, Koločep and Daksa, the group known to the ancients as the 'Elaphites Insulæ' were added in 1080.[104] In 1252 the more distant island of Lastovo had been acquired, and at an early date that of Mljet had been granted by the Serbian King to the Benedictine monks, with the condition that the civil government should be entrusted to Dubrovnik, which finally took complete control in 1345. Stephen the First-Crowned gave them Šipan in 1216. Between 1220 and 1224 Stephen, Nemanja's son, granted the same monks a stretch of land around Žrnovica and Ombla (Rijeka Dubrovačka). As a consequence of Dubrovnik's alliance with Michael Asen, the Bulgarian Tsar, against Stephen Uroš I, King of Serbia, in 1254, the republic's southern frontiers were extended so as to include the vineyards of Breno (Srebreno) and the peninsula on which the ruins of Epidauros lie. Here a new town arose called Cavtat. In 1333–1334 Ston and the peninsula of Peljašac and the coast as far as the Neretva's mouth were acquired. In 1357 small additions were made around Srebreno and Šumet between the Ljuta River and the village of Kurilo (north of Rijeka). The districts of Carine and Drieno although on the Dubrovnik side of the mountain above Srebreno, remained beyond the frontier; eventually they became Turkish territory, and remained so until 1878.[105]

The End of Venetian Rule

For a century and a half, Dubrovnik attempted to establish more favourable relations with the envious and unscrupulous Venetian Republic, while at the same time making the most of her position by expanding her sea-borne trade, and by exploiting her Slavonic hinterland for commercial purposes. After the victory of King Ludovik of Hungary and Croatia over the Venetians in 1358, Dubrovnik passed under the protection of the Hungarian kings and entered into a new phase of her development. Even earlier the citizens of Dubrovnik were delighted at the successes of Ludovik; they had received him with great honour when he called at their city in 1349 on his return from the Neapolitan expedition.[106] From that moment they began to contemplate the possibility of placing themselves under his protection. They had been afraid of the Hungarians when they threatened to conquer Bosnia and Hum, but now there was little fear of that, and Hungary not being a great naval power, could not threaten their liberties by means of the fleet as Venice always did. In 1356 the Venetians sent commissioners to claim Dubrovnik's contingent for the war against Hungary. The Great Council made professions of friendship, and agreed to send it, but were at the same time negotiating with the Hungarian King for the surrender of their city to him. On July 7, 1357, Ludovik confirmed their possession of Ston, which, having formed part of Bosnia, was in a measure under his authority, and it is probable that a preliminary treaty of dedition was signed at the same time. When, by the peace of February 1358, Venice gave up the whole eastern shore of the Adriatic, from the Kvarner to Dürres, she attempted to retain her hold over Dubrovnik on account of that very claim to separation from the rest of Dalmatia which she had hitherto always combated. Blandishments were tried, and by a rescript of the Doge Giovanni Dolfin (January 2, 1358) Dubrovnik's citizens were granted Venetian citizenship and commercial equality with the Venetians.[107] Unfortunately Dubrovnik had no wish to retain even a vestige of Venetian authority, and a few weeks later Marco Soranzo, the last Venetian Count, left the city by order of the Doge. Dubrovnik treated him with courtesy and envinced no ill-feeling against him, whereas the Venetian officials in the other Dalmatian towns had departed amidst the jeers and curses of the inhabitants. A triumvirate of Dubrovnik nobles was elected by the

F

Great Council to carry on the government while arrangements with King Ludovik were being completed. By a curious irony they sent commissioners to Venice in March to order

'unum gonfalonem et aliquas banderias cum armis D.N.D. Regis Hungariæ pro galleis et lignis nostris',

and later

'unum gonfalonerium ad modum penoni de sindone torto cum arma (sic) Regis Hungariæ cum argento albo et cum argentum (sic) deauratum pro duc. auri xxx'.[108]

On June 27 the final treaty was signed by Ludovik of Hungary and Giovanni Saraca, Archbishop of Dubrovnik at Višegrad. Dubrovnik placed itself under Hungarian protection, but was allowed to retain its own internal liberties more fully than under Venice. The King's praises, instead of those of the Doge, were to be sung in the churches of Dubrovnik three times a year, the Hungarian standard was to be adopted as well as the banner of San Biagio (Sv. Vlah), and 500 ipperperi a year were to be paid to the King. Should Hungary be engaged in naval warfare Dubrovnik must provide one galley for every ten Hungarian galleys whenever the Dalmatian fleet put to sea; if the royal fleet alone were employed, Dubrovnik need only provide one for every thirty. The supreme government of the state was no longer to be vested in a foreign count, but in three Dubrovnik citizens (afterwards reduced to one) to be chosen by the Council. The only representative of the King was the captain of the Hungarian and Bosnian guard, but he too was really in the service of the republic and had no political authority. From this moment Dubrovnik may be considered an independent state, as Hungarian authority, save for the tribute, was little more than a formality.

3. Notes

1. H. F. Brown in *The Cambridge Medieval History*, Vol. IV, Cambridge (1923), p. 406.
2. B. Krekić, *Dubrovnik (Raguse) et le Levant au Moyen-Age*, Paris–The Hague (1961).

3. I. Božić, 'Ekonomski i društveni razvitak Dubrovnika u XVI i XVII veku', *Istoriski Glasnik*, Vol. I, Belgrade (1949), p. 22.
4. H. C. Darby, 'The mediaeval sea-state', *Scottish Geographical Magazine*, Vol. 16, Edinburgh (1932), p. 136.
5. He is mentioned in a treaty between Dubrovnik and Taddeo, Count of Montefeltro and Podestà of Ravenna and Cervia 1216–1238 (*Monumenta Spectantia Historiam Slavorum Meridionalium*, S. Slavonic Academy Zagreb, (1879), Vol. I, Document 49, pp. 35–36; also other documents in that collection between 1204 and 1226).
6. *Monumenta Spectantia . . . op. cit.* Vol. I, p. 40.
7. 'Podestà' – Magistrate in Italian municipalities, chief magistrate in medieval Italian towns.
8. P. Pisani, *Num Ragusini ab omni jure Veneto a saec. X usque ad saec XIV. immunes fuerunt*, Paris (1893), cap. vii.
9. G. Gelcich, *Dello Sviluppo Civile di Ragusa*, Dubrovnik (1884), p. 29.
10. Dubrovnik was not completely independent as seen from the 'Promissiom' of March 6th 1229, by Doge Jacopo Ziepolo which states 'And we are to receive the tributes of Cherso (Cres) and Ossero (Lošinj) as well as of the country of Arbe and Ragusa (Dubrovnik)' *Cod. Marc. DLI, class viii* quoted in G. Romanin *Storia Documentata di Venezia*, Venice (1853).
11. *Monumenta Spectantia . . . op. cit.* Vol. I, p. 75.
12. Dubrovnik Archives *Liber Reformationes*, Vol. II, p. 322; *Liber Statutorum*, Vol. I, p. 1–2; G. Gelgich, *op. cit.* pp. 30, 31.
13. *Monumenta Spectantia . . . op. cit.* Vol. I, p. 78.
14. V. Klaić, *Geschichte Bosniens*, Leipzig (1878), p. 92.
15. *Monumenta Spectantia . . . op. cit.* Vol. I, p. 79.
16. *Ibid.* p. 80.
17. *Enciklopedija Jugoslavije*, Vol. 3, Zagreb (1958), p. 134.
18. *Monumenta Spectantia . . . op. cit.* Vol. I, p. 204 (1293–1331) and p. 261 (1294).
19. *Ibid.*, p. 237.
20. Dubrovnik Archives, *Liber Reformationes*, p. 57.
21. *Monumenta Spectantia . . . op. cit.* Vol. I, p. 327.
22. H. Brown, *op. cit.* p. 196.
23. *Ibid.*, p. 198–205.
24. H. Brown, *op. cit.* p. 211.
25. William of Tyre speaks of the 'Rex Sclavorum' residing at Skadar when the Crusaders were in Dalmatia, and this was the Župan Vukan (1089–1105). See W. Miller *Essays on the Latin Orient*, Cambridge (1921), p. 446.
26. H. W. V. Temperley, *History of Serbia*, London (1919), p. 39–40.
27. F. W. Carter, 'An analysis of the medieval Serbian oecumene: a theoretical approach', *Geografiska Annaler*, Vol. 51, Ser. B., Stockholm (1969), No. 1, p. 39–56.
28. B. Kallay, *Geschichte der Serben*, Leipzig (1878); W. Miller, *The Balkan States*, London (1896).
29. V. Klaić, *op. cit.* p. 95.
30. D. J. Mandić, *Crvena Hrvatska*, Chicago (1957), p. 132; note 4, p. 138.
31. G. Lebret, *Staatsgeschichte der Republik Venedig*, Vol. I, Leipzig (1879), p. 598; J. C. von Engel, *op. cit.* attributes the attack to the Ban of Bosnia, but this is incorrect as he was on good terms with the republic at this time.

32. V. Klaić, *op. cit.* p. 101.
33. J. C. von Engel, *op. cit.* 25.
34. B. Kallay, *op. cit.* p. 51.
35. F. Miklosich, *Monumenta Serbica*, Vienna (1858), p. 60;
    V. Klaić, *op. cit.* p. 137–8.
36. Dubrovnik Archives. *Liber Pactorum*, 79.
37. *Monumenta Spectantia . . . op. cit.* Vol. I, p. 294–97.
38. Dubrovnik Archives, *Liber Reformationes* (May 1303), maintains that the Serbian war was still in progress, but was probably limited to sporadic raids and brigandage.
39. *Monumenta Spectantia . . . op. cit.* Vol. I, p. 254.
40. Dubrovnik Archives, *Liber Reformationes*, (1316).
41. *Monumenta Spectantia . . . op. cit.* Vol. I, p. 469.
42. G. Gelcich, *op. cit.* p. 34.
43. Dubrovnik Archives, *Consilium Rogatorum*, 40;
    G. Gelcich, *op. cit.* p. 34–35.
44. J. C. von Engel, *op. cit.* 28.
45. K. Jireček, *Geschichte der Bulgaren*, Prague (1876), p. 290–298.
46. Dubrovnik Archives, *Liber Reformationes* III, p. 365.
47. *Monumenta Spectantia . . . op. cit.* Vol. III, p. 16.
48. *Monumenta Spectantia . . . op. cit.* Vol. III, p. 182, 256, 272.
49. *Ibid.*, p. 274.
50. Dubrovnik Archives, *Liber Reformationes* I, p. 155–57; 162–3; 169; 248–9.
51. G. Novak, *Naše More*, Zagreb (1932), p. 147.
52. I. Sindik, 'Dubrovnik i okolica-naselja i porijeklo stanovništvo', *Srpski Etnografski Zbornik*, Belgrade (1926), Kniga 38.
53. F. Miklosić, *Monumenta Serbica Substantia Historium Serbiae, Bosniae Ragusii*, Vienna (1858), p. 102.
54. Dubrovnik Archives, Statute 1282, Book III, Article 52, *Liber statutorum civitatis Ragusii*.
55. Dubrovnik Archives, *Diversa Cancellariae* (1281–1301).
56. Enciklopedija Jugoslavije, *op. cit.* p. 133.
57. Dubrovnik Archives, *Diversa Cancellariae* (1296).
58. Dubrovnik Archives, *Diversa Cancellariae* (16–24/XII/1296).
59. F. Muller, *Acta et Diplomatica graeca medii aei*, Vol. III, Vienna (1880), p. 58.
60. Dubrovnik Archives:
    (i) (1319), salt sent from Dubrovnik to Foča in Bosnia, *Liber Reformationes* VI, folder 51′;
    (ii) (1329), salt sent from Dubrovnik to Drijeva in Bosnia. *Diversa Cancellariae* IX, folder 94;
    (iii) (7/V/1331), salt sent from Dubrovnik to Bosnia. *Liber Reformationes* X, folder 17.
61. H. W. V. Temperley, *History of Serbia*, London (1919), p. 65.
62. M. Burr, 'The Code of Stephen Dušan', *The Slavonic and East Europe Review*, Vol. XXVIII, No. 70 (1950), pp. 198 *et seq.*
63. Dubrovnik Archives:
    (i) (II/V/1333), 51 litres of silver sent from Novo Brdo to Venice via Dubrovnik. *Diversa Cancellariae* 10, folder 23.
    (ii) (21/I/1355), 14 litres of auriferous silver sent from Novo Brdo to Venice via Dubrovnik. *Diversa Cancellariae* 12, folder 30;

(iii) (20/XI/1336), silver worth 191½ perpera (64 ducats) was sent from Novo Brdo to Dubrovnik. *Debita Notariae* 2, folder 129'.

64. F. Miklosich. *Monumenta Serbica, op. cit.* p. 38;
 (i) (1253). Dubrovnik merchants sold salt to people from Raška (Central Serbia);
 (ii) Dubrovnik Archives: a, (18/VI/1318), salt sent from Dubrovnik to Serbia. *Liber Reformationes* 6, folder 5; b, (1319), salt sent from Dubrovnik to Serbia. *Liber Reformationes* 8, folder 7'.

65. Dr. I. Sakazov, 'Obšestveno i stopansko razvitie na Blgarija pri Asenevcit'. *Blgarija Istoričeska Biblioteka*, God. 3, Tome III, Sofia (1930), p. 114.

66. F. Miklosich, *Monumenta Serbica, op. cit.* p. 2.

67. *Ibid.*, p. 5.

68. G. Gelcich, *Delle Instituzioni Marittime e Secritarie delle Republica di Ragusa*. Trieste (1892) p. 3.

69. Dubrovnik Archives fasc. II n. 53.

70. Dubrovnik Archives fasc. III, n. 242.

71. Dubrovnik Archives, fasc. II, n. 55.

72. Dubrovnik Archives, fasc. II, n. 62.

73. Dubrovnik Archives, fasc. II, n. 140.

74. Dubrovnik Archives, fasc. III, n. 167.

75. Emperor's Archives, Vienna: document on skin.

76. T. Smičiklas, *Codex diplomaticus regni Croatiae, Dalmatiae et Slavoniae*, Jugoslavenske akademije znanosti i umjetnosti, Vol. III, Zagreb (1905), p. 354; Vol. IV, Zagreb (1906), pp. 8–11.

77. The documents on this subject are lost, but the privileges are frequently mentioned by later writers.

78. R. Tafel and G. Thomas, 'Griechische Urkunden' in the *Sigzungsberichte der Kaiserlichen Wiener Akademie der Wissenschaften, philosophisch-historischer Classe*, Vol. VI, Vienna (1851), pp. 508–529.

79. W. Heyd, *Histoire du Commerce du Levant au Moyen Age*, Vol. I, Leipzig (1923), p. 475.

80. S. Ljubić, *Historija o odnošajih između Južnoga Slavenstva i Mletačke Republike*, Vol. I, pp. 33–4.

81. V. Makušev, *Monumenta historica Slavorium Meridionalium*, Vol. I, Warsaw (1874), p. 40;
 W. Heyd, *op. cit.*, Vol. I, p. 308.

82. A. Theinen, *Vetera Monumenta Slavorum Meridionalium historiam illustrantia*, Vol. I, Zagreb (1875), p. 121;
 M. Λ. Andreeva, 'Torgorij dogvor Vizantii i Dubrovnika i istorija ego podgotorki' *Byzantinoslavica*, Vol. VI, Prague (1935–1936), p. 139.

83. B. Bogošic, *Le Statut de Raguse Codification inédite du XIII siecle*, Paris (1894); K. Vojnović, 'O Državnom ustrojstvu Republike dubrovačke', *Rad. J.A.*, Zagreb (1891);
 K. Jireček, 'Die mittelalterliche Kanzlei der Ragusaner', *Archiv für slavische Philologie*, Vienna (1904);
 W. Anderssen, 'Verfassungsgeschichte von Raguse', *Zeitschrift für Vergleichende Rechtswissenschaft*, Bd. 50, Stuttgart (1936).

84. I. Manken, *Dubrovački Patricijat u XIV Veku*, Srpska Akademija Nauka i Umetnosti. Posebna Izdanja Kniga CCCXL. Odeljenje Društvenih Nauka. Kniga 36. Belgrade (1960).

85. G. Luccari, *Copioso Ristretto degli Annali di Ragusa*, Dubrovnik (1790).
86. G. Gelcich, *op. cit.* p. 32.
87. Dubrovnik Archives, *Liber Reformationum* V. (1331), p. 307.
88. J. G. Wilkinson, *Dalmatia and Montenegro*, London (1848), Vol. I, p. 351.
89. K. Vojnović, 'Sudbeno ustrojstvo republ. Dubrovačke', *Rad. J.A.*, Vol. 108, p. 121–122;
    ibid., Vol. 114, p. 181;
    Dubrovnik Archives, *Croceus Ordo pro molendinis ad Pillas supro civitatem*, Vol. 52;
    K. Jireček, *Važnost Dubrovnika trgovačkoj Povijest srednjega vjeku*, Dubrovnik (1915), p. 68.
90. J. E. Vance, 'Land assignment in the precapitalist, capitalist, and post-capitalist city, *Economic Geography*, Vol. 47, No. 2, Worcester Mass. (April 1971), p. 105.
91. T. Stoianovich, 'Model and Mirror of the Premodern Balkan City', *Studia Balcanica*, Vol. 3, Sofia (1970), p. 109.
92. E. Gibbon, *History of the Decline and Fall of the Roman Empire*, (J. B. Bury ed.), London (1901), Vol. VI, Appendix 6, p. 540;
    D. Obolensky, *The Bogomils: A Study in Balkan Neo-Manichaeism*, Cambridge University Press (1948).
93. K. Jireček, *Geschichte der Bulgaren*, Prague (1876), pp. 176 sqq.
94. A. Theiner, *Vetera Monumenta Slavorum Meridionalium Historiam spectantia*, Rome (1863), Vol. I, p. 20.
95. V. Klaić, *Geschichte Bosniens*, Liepzig, 1885, pp. 3–8.
96. Dubrovnik Archives, *Liber Reformationum* V (14/IV/1319), p. 139.
97. G. Gelcich, *op. cit.* p. 21.
98. *Ibid.*, pp. 17–18, 23, 25.
99. J. C. von Engel and T. Stojanović, *Povijest Dubrovačke republike*, Dubrovnik (1922);
    B. Stulli, *Pregled državno-pravne historije dubrovačke*, Dubrovnik (1956);
    B. Cvjetković, *Dubrovačka diplomacija*, Dubrovnik (1923);
    B. Krizman, *O Dubrovačkoj diplomaciji*, Zagreb (1951).
100. B. Milojević, 'Stonski Rat', *Hrvatski Geografski Glasnik* Broj. 1–4 (1929–30), pp. 266–68;
    N. Z. Bjelovučić, 'Poluostrvo Rat (Pelješac)', *Srpski Etnografski Zbornik* Srpska Kraljevska Akademija, Knijiga XXIII, Belgrade (1922), pp. 175–248;
    V. Taljeran, 'Zrnca za Povijest Stona', *Prigodom 600 godišnjice pripojenja Stonskog Rata Dubrovačkoj Republici* 1333–1933, Dubrovnik (1935), pp. 45–52, 80–90.
101. G. Gelcich, *op. cit.* p. 34.
102. A. Theiner, *op. cit.* Vol. I, p. 204.
103. *Monumenta Spectantia* . . ., *op. cit.* Vol. I, p. 589.
104. G. Gelcich, *I Conti di Truhelj*, Dubrovnik (1889), p. 22.
105. K. Jireček, *Die Handelsstrassen* . . . *op. cit.* p. 13–14.
106. G. Gelcich, *Dello Sviluppo* . . . *op. cit.* p. 44.
107. J. C. von Engel, *op. cit.* Appendix VIII.
108. Dubrovnik Archives, *Liber Reformationes* (1358);
    G. Gelcich, *op. cit.* p. 44.

4
The Trading Organization of the Dubrovnik Republic

The whole basis of Dubrovnik's prosperity was trade. The republic's territory was too small, and in part too barren, to provide sufficient foodstuffs for the population, and consequently it was upon trade and industry that the citizens had to depend for their means of livelihood. C. T. Smith has recently claimed that the growth of Dubrovnik depended essentially on its position between Christian and Moslem Europe, and on the failure of Venice to exploit a potentially similar intermediary role in the Adriatic.[1] Apart from shipbuilding, manufacturers never assumed great importance at Dubrovnik, and it was not until the fourteenth century that any other industries were established (see Ch. 7). Trade on the other hand, both sea-borne and overland, received a great additional impetus from the extension of Venetian traffic and from the increasing civilization of the Slav states. At Dubrovnik, as at Venice, Florence, Sienna and elsewhere in Italy, the aristocracy as well as the middle classes were all interested in trade and its organization.

One of the main problems in Dubrovnik's trading organization was the opening and maintenance of trade routes both on land and at sea. Her maritime trade routes were dependent on efficient shipping. From the earliest days of the republic shipbuilding was an important industry. The timber was obtained from the forests of Mount Srđ, now alas disappeared, and from those of Lastovo and Mljet Islands, of which traces still remain, as well as from Bosnia. The iron came from the interior and was manufactured at Venice or locally, the canvas from Ancona and the Marche, pitch from Dalmatia and cordage from Dubrovnik itself.

The dangers of navigation, even in the Adriatic were by no means trifling. The storms of that narrow sea, the sudden gusts of 'Bora' or

'Sirocco' which sweep down among the countless islands, channels, and promontories of the east coast with terrific violence, often meant that the light sailingcraft of the Middle Ages ran great risks. But, piracy was the chief source of anxiety. Almissa (present-day Omiš), between Split and the Neretva River, was the chief centre, whose inhabitants were almost exclusively engaged in piracy. The Dubrovnik statutes contain numerous provisions forbidding all intercourse with them.[2] The Almissans were finally subdued by the Venetians in 1444. Other piratical communities were found in northern Dalmatia and Croatia – the district formerly known as the Kraina[3] – and from the ports of Apulia,[4] Sicily and even from Kotor, pirate vessels often issued forth to ravage the Dalmatian coast or prey upon Adriatic trade. Another risk which Dubrovnik's traders ran was that their ships and goods might be seized and confiscated in foreign ports by local authorities. Bar, Ulcinj, Dürres and Trani in Italy were the worst offenders in this respect, but even at Venice and Alexandria the citizens of Dubrovnik were not always safe.

Land Trade Routes

The overland trade of the Balkans developed remarkably in the thirteenth and fourteenth centuries, and regular trade routes were established from the Adriatic coast through the interior to Constantinople and the Black Sea. There were several of these routes which, together with that from Hungary, formed the connecting link between western and eastern Europe. One was from Split, one from the Neretva mouth, one from Dubrovnik, one from Kotor and one from the mouth of the Bojana. They all joined the Belgrade-Constantinople route at different points, and all had branch routes to the various mining and commercial centres of Serbia, Bosnia, Albania

FIG. 19. (facing page)   Land routes connecting Dubrovnik with the Balkan peninsula.

■ Leskovac   Dubrovnik trading posts (Colonies) before Turkish conquest.

▲ Prokuplje   Dubrovnik trading posts (Colonies) established after Turkish conquest. Circa 1450.

● Kumanovo   Places mentioned in Dubrovnik documents.

———————   Main Caravan routes.

----------   Secondary Caravan routes.

    Mining areas.

    Salt pans.

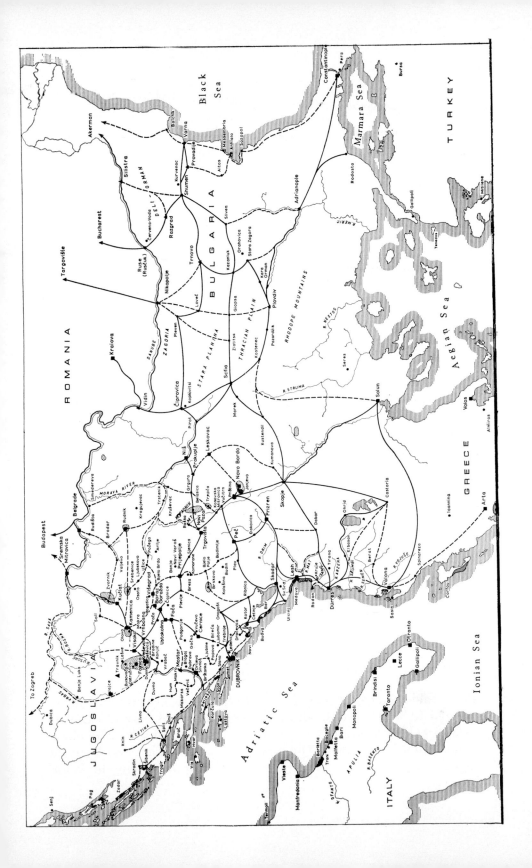

and Bulgaria. Dubrovnik, owing to her geographical position, was always the chief market in the Adriatic for the Balkan hinterland, and Dubrovnik's caravans were constantly travelling along the various routes.

The land trade was carried on entirely by means of caravans. There is no direct confirmation as to when Dubrovnik's caravan trade began, but it appears to have been well-developed by the time the first documentary evidence was recorded in the last quarter of the twelfth century. There were no carriage roads since the decay of those built by the Romans, and all goods were transported by pack-animals, chiefly horses, reared in the mountain pastures by the Vlachs. The name for this method of transportation was originally 'turma', from the Latin but later the Persian word 'caravannus' was adopted (or Arabic 'caravanana' or 'garauanus'). Each caravan was under the charge of Vlach drovers who were nearly all shepherds or horse and cattle drovers and had markedly nomadic habits. Many of the caravans which left Dubrovnik for the Balkan interior, appear from archival material to have been small in size. Most of the goods carried were small, textiles, salted fish, saltpetre etc. which were rarely carried in large quantities. The following table gives some indication of their size.[5]

Table II

Number of Horses/Caravan	Number of Caravans
1—10	71
11—20	67
21—30	36
31—40	27
41—50	10
51—60	9
61—70	4
71—80	6
81—90	1
91—100	2

From Table II it can be seen that 94% of the caravans that left Dubrovnik had 50 horses or less, whilst there are only two cases of caravans using 100 horses and they were for the transport of salt.[6] The oldest known information about Dubrovnik's caravan trade dates from the first decade of the fourteenth century,[7] but according to Rubić

Fig. 20. A typical Balkan caravanserai – Hanul Lui Manuç (Bucaresti).

caravans are first referred to in Dubrovnik archives in 1359.[8] Most of the traders were from Dubrovnik, or natives of the other coastal towns but Slavonic merchants also took part in this trade, especially those who had settled at Dubrovnik. Some of them even became naturalized so as to enjoy the same exemptions and privileges as the Dubrovnik citizens. The journey was by slow stages, as the paths were steep and rocky and many precautions were necessary but the importance of this traffic was very considerable as it was then the chief link between the West and the Slavonic lands; Dubrovnik merchants in fact probably did more to civilize the latter than was attempted by the Greeks, with whom the Slavs were always in eternal conflict.

Four principal communication lines radiated from Dubrovnik, two by land across the Balkan peninsula and two by sea. The principal land route from the coast was that from Dubrovnik to Niš in Serbia, where it joined the great road from Hungary to Constantinople via Belgrade. The caravan left Dubrovnik following the road to the east which gradually ascended the slopes of Mount Srđ to Brgat on the Republic's frontier. Here a low col, Brgat Pass (251 km), cuts through the coastal range of the Dinaric mountains into Popovo Polje, providing one of the easiest access points to the interior along the whole Dalmation coast. From Brgat the path descends into the broad fertile valley of Popovo to the town of Trebinje,[9] (five or six hours by caravan from Dubrovnik). From Trebinje the march was resumed up the course of the Trebišnjica River past Ljubomir to Bileća; then along what is now the Montenegrin frontier through dense forests to Cernice,[10] where in 1380 a Dubrovnik colony was established; thence into the basin of Gačko[11] close to the watershed between the Adriatic and the Black Sea. The country here was fertile and offered good pasturage. The Sutijeska gorge was entered next, where during the fifteenth century an important customs station stood which levied a toll on all caravans. On emerging from the gorge the banks of the Drina were reached on which there were several trading stations the most important being Chotca (Foča). Another station was at Ustokelina, where a Dubrovnik colony was established in 1399.[12] A day's march further on was the town of Goražde after which the main route proceeded in a south-easterly direction to Plevlja. From Plevlja the route continued to Prijepolje on the Lim River, a favourite halting place for Dubrovnik merchants in the fourteenth century on account of its nodal position. Here the route from Dubrovnik joined the one from northern and eastern Bosnia,[13] continuing eastward through Sjenica[14] to Novi Pazar. Near here lay Trgovište,[15] often mentioned between 1345 and 1459, as the site of a Dubrovnik colony. From here the route bifurcated one branch going southwards to Solun, and the other eastwards, across the Ibar valley, through the mining district of the Kopaonik Mountains to Grgura, Prokuplje and Niš. The whole journey from Dubrovnik to Niš took fifteen days in favourable weather. From Niš onwards the Dubrovnik caravans followed the great road to Constantinople (total 30 days from Dubrovnik), or branched off to various parts of Bulgaria, where they had considerable trade and an important colony at Vidin as a result of the privileges obtained from the Bulgarian Tsars.[16]

Another much frequented route was that which started at the mouth of the Neretva and passed through Bosnia and Serbia. Goods from Dubrovnik were transported either wholly by sea round the Pelješac peninsula or via Ston to Drijeva in the Neretva delta. Drijeva possessed a large customs station, salt stores and a Dubrovnik colony. The caravans travelled from the mouth of the Neretva following the course of the river to Blagaj, then on past Konjić, over the Iron Pass to Visoko the centre and capital of Bosnia.[17] Between 1348 and 1430 this was also the commercial capital of the country and the seat of important trading communities. From Visoko the route proceeded to Vrhbosna (later Sarajevo) where it bifurcated, one branch going to Borać and the other to Olovo. At Olovo the route branched off into three. One led eastward to Srebrenica, the centre of the silver-mining district (Srebro meaning 'silver') and Rudnik; another went northwards to Soli; the main route went to Kučlat, well known as a trading colony in the fourteenth century with a large Dubrovnik colony, to Zvornik, and across the Drina River to Sremska Mitrovica and Belgrade. At Sremska Mitrovica, Dubrovnik merchants had a flourishing settlement protected by the Kings of Hungary, until the town was burnt by the Turks in 1396. Its importance was due to its position as a starting point for Dubrovnik traders going to all parts of Hungary.[18]

These various routes were called collectively the 'Via de Bossina' in the Dubrovnik documents and formed the first of the major lines of communication. The routes which started from the coast at points south of Dubrovnik were denominated the 'Via de Zenta',[19] which was the second important communication link by land. Vessels sailed southwards along the coast from Dubrovnik, and either discharged their goods at the ports of Bar or Ulcinj, or sailed for some distance up the various rivers – the Bojana, the Drin, the Mat, the Ishm, the Shkumbi, the Seman and the Vojuše. This river trade was described in documents as 'ultra marinis partibus', whilst this stretch of coast was under Serbian rule from 1180 to 1440.

'In Serbian times,' writes Jireček, 'this region now so desolate, was in the most flourishing condition, and had a large population and numerous beautifully situated towns . . .' 'the ports plied a busy trade for from hence goods were transported to the Byzantine districts of Macedonia and Thrace and as far as Bulgaria and the Black Sea'.[20] From the ports of Bar and Ulcinj the caravan route went past Skadar along the Drin River to be joined by the route from Lesh and thence proceeded to Prizren which was reached in thirty-three hours by a road reputed to be one of the most difficult in the Albanian mountains.[21] At Prizren, Dubrovnik merchants had their chief commercial factory for Albania and from here the route crossed into the fertile and well populated plain of Kossovo. At Janjevo it crossed the route from Bosnia to Solun, reached Novo Brdo and finally went via Niš to Sofia. The first mention of a Dubrovnik trader in Sofia was in 1376; the Dubrovnik colony became very important at the end of the fourteenth century in Turkish times, when Sofia was the residence of the Beglerbeg of Rumelia.[22]

Another branch of the Via de Zenta' ran from Bar along the coast to Budva and then inland to Cetinje via Kotor. The route proceeded over well-wooded mountains, now bare and desolate, to Ribnica (a day and a half's march from Kotor); here the route bifurcated one branch going northward to Brskovo, the chief commercial centre of Serbia, and the other eastward via Plava Lake, both joining again at Peč. Peč like Brskovo enjoyed considerable traffic and had a Dubrovnik colony in the fourteenth century.

Sea Routes

Of the two principal sea routes, one was found 'intra Culfum' and the other 'extra Culfum'. The former ran northward from Dubrovnik through the channel between Korčula Island and the Pelješac peninsula on to the vicinity of Hvar Island, and still using the safe passage of the Dalmation Islands went northwards past Zadar to Lošinj. At this point it crossed the Adriatic Sea to Venice. The other sea route went southwards along the Albanian coast near to the island of Corfu and the Gulf of Corinth. It then rounded the Peloponnesus to Crete

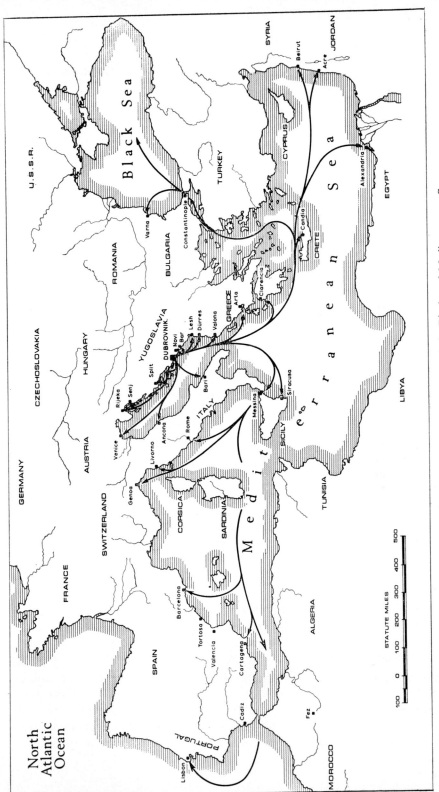

Fig. 21. Sea routes connecting Dubrovnik with the Adriatic, Black and Mediterranean Seas.

and Rhodes and there bifurcated, one arc turning northwards into the Aegean, and the other southwards towards the Levant and Alexandria.

Colonies in the Balkans

Closely connected with the opening and maintenance of trade routes was the establishment and support of Dubrovnik colonies. Although they were found throughout Dubrovnik's trading area they were most numerous in Bosnia and Serbia particularly in the fourteenth and fifteenth centuries. As a rule mining was the chief industry and it was in the mining districts that the commercial settlements were to be found. Each mining centre usually consisted of a castle on a hill, wherein dwelt the feudal lord (the Vojvod), and a town below with a market, where the miners and merchants dwelt. (This division is reflected in the prefixes Gornji and Donji – upper and lower – which are frequently found attached to the names of Bosnian and Serbian towns.)

During the fourteenth and fifteenth centuries Bosnia was undoubtedly the most important trading region for Dubrovnik due to its wealth in natural resources and its comparative nearness in terms of distance. Therefore Dubrovnik colonies were established and developed in Bosnia as early as 1382.[23] This development can be traced in greater detail from archival evidence between the years 1400–1465, the period of most intensive trading activity by Dubrovnik merchants in Bosnia. This information gives the number of Dubrovnik merchants recorded[24] as having either visited the colony for a short time, or having permanently stayed in the town. From a closer analysis certain noticeable factors emerge. Firstly, colonies were usually situated either at an important communication centre, or in a mining town. Secondly, two colonies appear more important than the others – Visoko and Fojnica, Visoko was, until the Turkish conquest in the second half of the fifteenth century, the principal commercial centre within the Bosnian core area of the Sarajevo basin. It was a significant exchange mart for Dubrovnik merchants who brought Italian cloth here, trading it for wool, grain and silver from the local mines. Fojnica was basically a mining colony, developing after 1430 as a result of the discovery of silver there. Also being centrally placed within the mining area, the town acted as a mineral collecting centre. Thirdly, the distribution of colonies show a concentration in central

and eastern Bosnia. This may be accounted for not only by the
natural wealth of this part of Bosnia, but also because the shortest
caravan routes from Dubrovnik to Serbia passed through this region.
Dubrovnik merchants were also found in north-west Bosnia with a

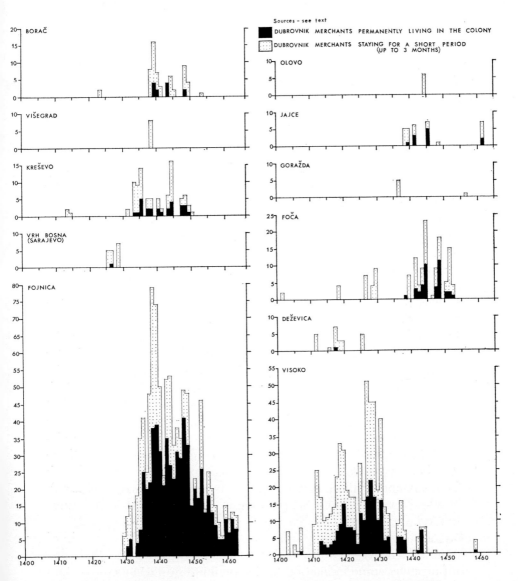

FIG. 22.   The development of Dubrovnik colonies in Bosnia between 1400–1465.

colony at Jajce, but here traders from the north Dalmatian towns especially Split, provided stronger trading competition.

Some Dubrovnik colonies existed in Serbia during the fourteenth and fifteenth centuries, but fewer than in Bosnia. The reasons for this appear to be a greater distance from Dubrovnik, the constant threats of Turkish danger, the disorganized political life of the Serbian state, and that many of the commodities the Serbians had for sale could be bought much nearer in Bosnia. Dubrovnik colonies did exist in the mining towns of Novo Brdo, Trepča, Rudnik and Janjevo (given in order of mining importance for Dubrovnik) and the market towns of Priština and Trgovište. Novo Brdo was the most important Serbian mining town in these two centuries, especially for silver and gold. Dubrovnik had a colony there from 1387[25] until 1455 and it was to be their largest 'settlement' in Serbia. Constant raids by the Turks in the early part of the fifteenth century tended to diminish the significance of the town for Dubrovnik, Turkish soldiers finally occupying Novo Brdo in 1455.[26] Rudnik was an important silver mining centre, but during the early fifteenth century it lost much of its attraction for Dubrovnik traders, as they were able to get enough silver from the Bosnian mines. Priština was the commercial centre for the rich agricultural area of Kosovo, but after the Turkish victory there in 1389 its importance declined for Dubrovnik citizens. Trgovište was the main market centre for the whole agricultural region of the Ibar basin.

After the conquest of the Slav states by the Turks during the second half of the fifteenth century some of Dubrovnik's old colonies in Bosnia and Serbia were destroyed (Visoko, Srebrenica, Novo Brdo, Rudnik) but others arose in their place. Of the older towns only Belgrade maintained its former importance under the new rulers. But now Vrhbosna (Sarajevo) arose,[27] and instead of Novo Brdo there was Novi Pazar, Prokuplje, Skoplje, Travnik and Mostar also being elevated into commercial and administrative importance. In all these towns there were wealthy Dubrovnik colonies, each with its church and consul, and of these new colonies Sarajevo (formerly Vrhbosna), Belgrade, Novi Pazar and Skoplje, were of the greatest importance, commercially.

Bulgaria figures quite prominently in Dubrovnik's network of colonies. There were twelve such colonies in Bulgaria and their distribution gives some indication to the regional importance of certain parts at this time. Firstly, seven of the colonies were located in the rich cattle-breeding area of north-east Bulgaria emphasizing the significance of skins and wool in Bulgaria's exports to Dubrovnik. Secondly, four of the colonies were sited on the Danube, acting as communication centres between one of the major European river routeways and roads leading to further markets in Wallachia.[28] From Bucharest and Trgovište routes led to the markets of central Europe and Poland. Thirdly only two colonies lay south of the Stara Planina mountains. These were both sited on the main Belgrade–Constantinople trade route – Sofia and Plovdiv. The high Rhodope mountains to the south proved an effective barrier to trade exploitation and the many small villages of the Thracian Plain tended to patronize either Sofia, or Plovdiv, as a market centre.

The gradual growth of Dubrovnik's trading organization and influence in Bulgaria[29] can be seen from the dates when different colonies were established in the country. Four different periods emerge – the early colonies *circa* 1500 (Sofia 1470, Plovdiv 1502), colonies founded during the mid-sixteenth century (Varna 1536, Vidin 1541, Provadija 1541, Nikopolje 1556, Trnovo 1562), those established late in the century (Ruse 1581, Silistra 1581, Razgrad 1581, Shumen 1581) and finally those of seventeenth century origin (Čiprovica 1676).[30] Theoretically Vidin[31] had the oldest Dubrovnik colony in Bulgaria (established 1365), but as this was destroyed in the Turkish advance on the Balkans and had to be re-established much later, Sofia,[32] in fact, claims this title. The earliest mention of a Dubrovnik colony in Sofia was 1470 and by 1559 her merchants owned twenty-one houses in the town.[33] The Turks established a large army garrison here, whilst the town itself was also a considerable market for local and distant commerce, having trading connections with the Carpathians, White, Black and Adriatic Seas. Plovdiv was the other early Dubrovnik colony in Bulgaria.[34] Situated on the Marica River, it was, like Sofia, on the main trade route from Belgrade to Constantinople. Dubrovnik traders sold quantities of English and Dutch textiles in the town often in exchange for the agricultural products gathered there from the rich Thracian Plain, of which Plovdiv was the commercial centre.[35]

Five colonies were established between 1536 and 1562. One of these was Varna, the only port on the Black Sea coast of Bulgaria to possess a Dubrovnik colony. It enjoyed an international trade prior to the Turkish invasion but when the Turks made the Black Sea a 'mare clausum' for all but Dubrovnik shipping it left Varna dependant only on localized trade. Dubrovnik merchants were to re-vitalize the harbour by sending a large variety of commodities produced in Dobrudja – wheat, wood, fat, buffalo and ox skins etc. – through the port for the Adriatic and Mediterranean markets, and importing textiles especially from Ancona, for the hinterland of Varna. Of the remaining colonies from this period (Nikopolje, Trnovo, Provadija, Vidin), Provadija had the greatest significance, for just as Varna was the seaward outlet for Dobrudja, this town was the inland gateway to this rich agricultural region.

Dubrovnik consolidated its interests in Dobrudja and north-east Bulgaria by founding four new colonies towards the end of the sixteenth century. All these colonies were outlets for Dobrudjan products especially skins and wool. Silistra and Ruse on the Danube were collecting centres for goods to be transported up river via Nikopolje, Vidin and through Serbia to Dubrovnik, whilst Razgrad and Shumen were important exporting centres for raw skins sent via Trnovo and Sofia to Dubrovnik. Only one colony was established in the seventeenth century, at Čiprovica 1676. This had been an important silver and copper mining town, which the Turks carefully guarded against outside exploitation. Not until this late date were Dubrovnik merchants allowed to found a colony there, probably when its mining role had become only negligible. It was prominent as a caravan station and skin collecting centre en route from Vidin to Sofia and a good market for foreign textiles.

Colonies Overseas

All the colonies so far mentioned were primarily concerned with land trade, but Dubrovnik established some colonies in the more important ports of the Levant, Italy and western Mediterranean. In the Levant, Constantinople, Solun, Alexandria and Candia had prominent Dubrovnik colonies. In 1169 Dubrovnik merchants were allowed to establish a colony in Constantinople, and about the same time obtained the right of citizenship, granted to them by Manuel, and confirmed by his son Alexius II.[36] These privileges were renewed by the Latin Emperors Baldwin I and Henry, and even in the fifteenth century Runciman on describing Constantinople states

'The Venetians had a prosperous quarter down by the harbour; and the streets allotted to other Western traders, the Anconitans and the Florentines, the *Ragusans* and the Catalans, and to the Jews were close by'.[37]

Solun was also a city of great prosperity and one of the chief ports for the Balkan peninsula. A document dated March 1234 records how the Despot of Solun gave Dubrovnik merchants the freedom of trade and the right to found a colony in the city.[38] Its annual fair was the meeting-place of merchants of all nations, and, in particular, the town was a source of cereals for Dubrovnik traders. Her merchants were still living in the colony towards the end of the fifteenth century.[39]

Commercial intercourse between Egypt and Christian Europe was at first interrupted owing to the hostility which reigned over the Mediterranean Sea; in the twelfth century, despite Papal prohibitions on the export of arms and iron, trade relations were established between the Italian cities, Dubrovnik, and the ports of the Nile Delta.[40] Any strong development of a Dubrovnik colony in Alexandria was looked upon unfavourably by other Christian European powers yet even as late as 1561 Lane quotes

'The Venetians had two such 'fondachi' (house) at Alexandria, the other 'nations', the Genoese, *Ragusans* and French, who were less numerous having one (2/V/1561)'.[41]

'Candia, on the island of Crete had a Dubrovnik colony as early as 1271'.[42]

Its strategic position on the shipping routes of the Levant and rich source of cereals, made it a valuable centre for Dubrovnik's commerce. Unfortunately for Dubrovnik's merchants it remained a Venetian possession from 1204 until 1669, so that a strong colony was never allowed to develop, but even so it was an important market for Dubrovnik's traders.

Dubrovnik merchants also established colonies in Italy and the western Mediterranean. Italy's west Adriatic coast had old established colonies which were founded on the strength of early contacts and trade treaties with the ports of Apulia, of Venice and of Ancona. Not only did Dubrovnik benefit from their relatively close proximity (given favourable south-east winds a sailing ship could cross the Adriatic Sea in twenty-four hours) but also the more advanced stage of their economic development. The central position which Sicily occupied in the Mediterranean gave it both commercial and strategic importance for Dubrovnik, which reached a climax during the reigns of Alfonso I (1416–1458) and his son Ferdinand (1458–1494). During their reigns friendly relations between Sicily and Dubrovnik were at their greatest and most of the colonies on the island date from this period. Of much later significance were the colonies of Livorna (Leghorn) on the west coast of Italy, and those of the Iberian peninsula. During the seventeenth century Livorna became the funnel through which the Turkey trade of the British, French and Dutch all ran. Use was made of Dubrovnik shipping and a colony existed in the town to organize it.[43] Despite early contacts with the Iberian peninsula little evidence exists to prove the establishment of colonies there before the sixteenth century. In this century many Spanish ports, like Valencia, Tortosa, Cadiz and Barcelona[44] hired Dubrovnik boats to carry goods between the Iberian peninsula and other parts of the Mediterranean. Dubrovnik colonies in these towns provided Spanish and other merchants with a valuable service.[45] There was even a Dubrovnik colony at Fez in Morocco.[46]

Transport Costs

Given the distribution of Dubrovnik's colonies and the pattern of her trade routes it is now possible, however tentatively, to examine transport costs. Several reservations should be borne in mind. Firstly, transport costs were never automatically recorded with each consignment in documents, so that a full transport cost network cannot be given. For most areas the period of Dubrovnik's greatest commercial activity has been taken, e.g. Bosnia 1350–1450, Levant 1350–1500 etc. so that with the larger number of documents there was a greater chance of transport information. Secondly, due to the lack of published work on transport costs, especially in the Balkan peninsula, there are few means of comparing results. Thirdly, data on transport costs are found in various forms, different currencies, time of year, inclusive/exclusive of tolls or customs duties, etc. so that costs have been averaged from minimum and maximum prices charged, taking into account the possibilities of inflation or deflation. Therefore conclusions drawn from this information can only be of the most general nature.

Inland transportation for Dubrovnik's trading empire had many problems. The shortcomings of the roads were in part counterbalanced by the widespread use of rivers, although most streams had some natural defect; too rough and fast, spring floods, rapids, etc. Safety was more important than speed and the human enemies might be worse than the physical. Dubrovnik's caravan traders' greatest fear was the Turks. Until the Dubrovnik government made official agreements on their behalf during the first half of the fifteenth century, they were constantly terrorized by small bands of marauding Turks, especially in those territories as yet unoccupied by the Turks. To the physical dangers of travel were added the financial burdens. The Romans had collected tolls from travellers and traders but had spent at least part of the revenue on the roads. Medieval kings, bishops and lords continued to make the levy but spent little of it on roads, bridges or river improvement. Rivers were heavily dotted with new toll collecting stations (in gorges and mountain passes) often appearing in places not previously utilized for this purpose. From the beginning of the fifteenth century all forms of tolls and custom duties were applied over a wider area.

All these facts had some bearing on overland transport costs. With reference to the caravan trade between Dubrovnik and certain places in Bosnia and parts of western Serbia, information was taken from the series *Diversa Cancellariae* for the years 1350–1450, because this yielded the most consistent amount on such costs. All prices charged for carrying a load from a certain place to Dubrovnik were noted. Loads varied in size from one of lead (97 kg) to one of wax (149 kg), with several weights in between. An 'average load' of 126 kg was taken for a matter of convenience.[47] The prices charged for transporting the merchandise were then scaled for each place, ranging from maximum to minimum price, with some slight alterations for inflation. Then an average transport cost was found for each settlement, which had enough statistical information, and plotted.

From this certain basic conclusions may be drawn. Firstly, transport costs from certain market towns on, or near, the Drina River (Višegrad, Goražde, Borač) were higher due to the importance of these places as market centres for Dubrovnik merchants. Secondly, the mining towns of Olovo and Kamenica have transport costs nearly as high as the main trading centres in central Bosnia, like Visoko and Prača. Thirdly many of the places on major caravan routes had higher transport costs than places situated on secondary routes. This was probably due to a larger number of toll stations on the straighter, safer major routes increasing the price, together with the higher transport costs charged by Vlach drovers for the more popular runs.

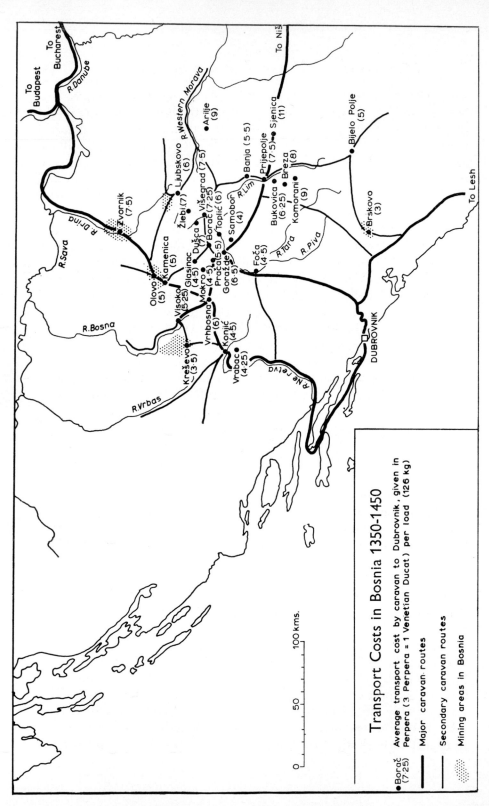

FIG. 23. Source: Dubrovnik Archives (1350–1450) *Diversa Cancellariae* Nos. 14–60.

Transport Costs in Bosnia 1350–1450

• Borač   Average transport cost by caravan to Dubrovnik, given in
  (7·25)   Perpera (3 Perpera = 1 Venetian Ducat) per load (126 kg)

━━━ Major caravan routes

───── Secondary caravan routes

⠿ Mining areas in Bosnia

To Budapest
To Bucharest
R. Danube
R. Western Morava
To Niš
Arilje (9)
Bijelo Polje (5)
Sienica (11)
Prijepolje (7·5)
Ljubskovo (6)
Banja (5·5)
Breza (8)
Žlebi (7)
Višegrad (7·5)
Zvornik (7·5)
R. Drina
R. Sava
Dušca (7)
Borač (7·25)
Toplić (6)
R. Lim
Bukovica (6·25)
Komorani (9)
Brskovo (3)
To Lesh
Kamenica (5)
Samobor (4)
Olovo (5)
Glasinac (4·5)
Pračat (5·5)
Goražde (6·5)
Foča (4·5)
R. Tara
R. Piva
Mokro (4·5)
Visoko (5·25)
Vrhbosna (6)
R. Bosna
Konjić (4·5)
DUBROVNIK
Kreševo (3·5)
Vrabac (4·25)
R. Neretva
R. Vrbas

100 kms.
50
0

Likewise places not even on a secondary route like Komorani, (9 perpera), Breza (8), Arilje (9), Žlebi (7), had higher prices, but this was probably related to more difficult access and greater risks from bandits so that the Vlachs charged more for their services. It is interesting to note at this point that it was not the Vlach drovers and small dealers who profited from this trade but the landed gentry. This is seen from the following example. One group of Vlachs under Vojvod Radoslav Pavlović must pay him 100 ducats if they held a trading contract for transporting goods to Dubrovnik.[48] Therefore many of the contracts between the Vlach drovers and Dubrovnik merchants were by word of mouth, in order to avoid paying such feudal dues, unfortunately leaving less documentary evidence for analysis. Fourthly, distance did not affect transport costs as much as may have been expected. It cost only the same price to send a load to Prijepolje, Višegrad or Zvornik, (7½ perpera), yet the time needed to reach these places was 4, 5 and 8 days respectively. Conversely mining areas do seem to have higher transport costs with greater distance from Dubrovnik although only ½ perpera difference between Brskovo (3) and Kreševo (3½), seems a little difficult to understand.

Finally two facts should be remembered when considering these results. In the first place in order to simplify the data all loads irrespective of contents are the same, but it is possible that the Vlachs had different transport rates for each commodity, e.g. lead, wax, textiles, etc. just as Dubrovnik's merchants stipulated what goods could and could not be mixed together in one caravan.[49] In the second place a seasonal variation appeared in the use of caravan routes, probably giving seasonal changes in transport costs, but sufficient information is lacking to prove this point. According to archival material the routes were most used in autumn – September, October and November; December to February were the worst months when many of the higher passes were blocked by snow, whilst April was a sowing month and July–August harvest time, both periods of the year when labour was most needed on the land.

The second reliable source on inland transportation costs comes from the account books of *Benedict Resti* under the series *Privata*. Resti was a Jewish merchant from Dubrovnik who lived in Sofia from 1590 until 1605 and who kept fairly extensive trade books, which fortunately have been preserved in Dubrovnik's archives. His trade connections covered much of Bulgaria at a time when the Dubrovnik Republic was enjoying its greatest period of commercial prosperity in that country. Resti's information on transport costs is not large and is often mentioned incidentally but as he dealt almost exclusively with land transport, and his statistics give costs for separate commodities, the evidence should be cited here.

One document dated 1594 relates to the amount paid a carrier for transporting ox and cow skins from Silistra overland to Dubrovnik.[50] On the first stage of the journey from Silistra to Nikopolje the carrier charged 2·6 aspri each (120 aspri=1 venetian ducat). From Nikopolje to Užice in Serbia, the skins cost 7·0 aspri each and from Užice to Dubrovnik 10·7 aspri. The total journey cost 20·3 aspri per skin. The average cost of cow and ox skins at this time (1594) in Silistra was 60·0 aspri per skin, so that when the pelts reached Dubrovnik the merchant had incurred an expenditure of 80·3 aspri each, twenty-five per cent being spent on transport costs, assuming that no other costs were involved, which the document fails to relate.

Another document dated 1598 gives information on the transport of wool. In this year Resti bought 105 sacks of wool (9,030 kg) in Sofia for 79,998 aspri (667 ducats). For transporting this wool from Sofia to Dubrovnik by the main trade route via Niš, Grgura, and Novi Pazar, he paid the carrier 26,559 aspri (222 ducats). Total expenditure on the wool equalled 104,557 aspri (889 ducats) on reaching Dubrovnik, of which, as with skins twenty-five per cent had been spent on transport costs (assuming no other expenses incurred). Resti received 3% commission for the transaction.[51]

A transaction, recorded by Resti at the beginning of the seventeenth century, gives valuable information on Bulgarian wax. During 1600, Resti together with some other traders, bought a large quantity of wax, 16 kantars (896 kg) for 40,808 aspri (340 ducats).[52] A carrier in 1601 was paid 21,350 aspri (178 ducats) to transport this load to Dubrovnik, on the main route through Serbia and Bosnia. Transport costs therefore totalled 34% of the expenditure on the wax when it arrived in Dubrovnik.

Two documents refer to textile imports. The first one dated 1601 refers to Resti buying 74 packets of Flanders 'Kersey' cloth in Venice for 107,942 aspri (900 ducats). (A type of heavy woollen cloth, woven like serge and rough on both sides, used for making clothes and for bed covers. The best kersey was made in France, Holland and England). He paid a further 18,907 aspri (158 ducats) to cover insurance, customs duty and transport costs from Venice to Sofia via Dubrovnik and equal to 18% of the total expenditure on the cloth when it arrived in Sofia.[53]

The second document, dated 1602, mentions 12 bales of kersey cloth (one bale of cloth was equal to 2–3 topa; a 'topa' averaged 56 lakats – 1 lakat = 2 feet) being sent from Ostende to Venice for 23,873 aspri (199 ducats). In Venice, Resti (or his agent) bought five of these bales for 18,750 aspri (158 ducats). He then paid 4,950 aspri (41 ducats) for customs duty, transport costs and insurance for this cloth to send it from Venice via Dubrovnik to Sofia, in other words about 21% of the total expenditure.[54] Unfortunately these two documents do not differentiate transport costs from other commitments like customs duty and insurance and it is also impossible to tell the individual transport route by land from Dubrovnik to Sofia.

Finally, a Dubrovnik document written in 1602 shows the seasonal price variation for transporting goods from Dubrovnik to Sofia. In this particular agreement, relating to the previous year, caravans were expected to arrive in Skoplje a month after leaving Dubrovnik and in Sofia ten days later. During the winter, transport costs from Dubrovnik to Sofia were fixed at 10 ducats for each caravan consignment, whilst in summer the rate was one ducat less.[55]

Throughout the Middle Ages and later, sea transportation was cheaper and safer than movement overland, but this also had its perils, some of them natural, some contrived by men. Thus the danger of shipwreck to which the small craft of the time were frequently exposed, was aggravated by the survival of the right of wreck ('jus naufragii'), by which lords and communes were permitted to seize all goods thrown up on the shores of their territory. But the greatest menace to merchant shipping was piracy which some maritime communities made their principal occupation. Even when the use of the compass facilitated long-distance navigation in the open sea, the lack of security, especially in foreign waters maintained the habit of travelling in convoy. In spite of such dangers, sea communication was still the most preferred method of travel even for journeys that could be made by land, because it offered the means of transporting heavy, bulky and inexpensive goods. Although merchant ships were of small tonnage,[56] after the thirteenth century they tended to increase in size especially those destined for the distant Black Sea.[57]

Information in Dubrovnik documents tells little of the cost of sea transport. Work has been done on this problem for Italian shipping

notably by Sapori,[58] Luzzato[59] and Sombart.[60] Of particular interest
is an analysis of eight documents by Fanfani[61] of merchant ships
travelling between Italy and Sicily at the end of the fourteenth
century. These vessels were performing similar operations to those
of Dubrovnik at this time and therefore his results prove of interest.
His main conclusion was that despite the slowness and risks taken by
sea transport its costs were much lower than by land. In fact, transport
costs, customs duty, insurance and other incidental expenses only
represented a fraction of a commodity's selling price (usually about
1/20). Luzzato also states that transport costs by sea were 'avea
sempre un costo infinitamente pui basso del transporto terrestre'.[62]

Despite Dubrovnik's lack of evidence on maritime transport rates
the town's documents give information on freight costs. Freight costs
are frequently referred to in documents and Krekić[63] has calculated
them for the Levant from 1358 until 1450. From the 111 trade contracts, he found that nearly 50 were based on weight. Another 40
cases showed that a lump sum was agreed upon by merchants, whilst
lengths of voyage and number of crew were less frequent methods.
Even so in some cases length of voyage and distance did have a
bearing on the freight costs as seen for example with wheat in the
following table:

Table III

Average Freight Costs/Cubic Metre for Wheat in the 15thC

Place	Average Return Voyage Dubrovnik	Ducats
Corfu	25 days	·12
Santa Maura	1 month	·14
Zante	1 month	·155
Arta	1½ months	·165
Patras	3½ months	·20
Clarencia	3½ months	·23
Livadia	3½ months	·25
Volos	4 months	1·00
Rhodes	4 months	1·00
Chios	4 months	1·00
Constantinople and Pera	4½ months	1·33
Famagousta	7 months	1·50

Table III shows that the more time needed to complete a voyage, and therefore the greater distance involved, so the increase in average freight cost per cubic metre of wheat. This ties in with Fanfani's findings, whereby the greater the distance, and therefore longer duration of capital investment in a voyage, the higher the transport costs.[64]

Marine Insurance

Distance was also an important criterion for Dubrovnik's marine insurance.[65] Dubrovnik documents are particularly rich in information on marine insurance which began in the town during the second half of the fourteenth century. Its organization was not properly completed until the sixteenth century when each owner of a boat or cargo had to insure it for the length of a journey (i.e. distance) and against such risks as piracy, shipwreck, fire and other mishaps. All such evidence was recorded in *Diversa Cancellariae, Diversa Notaria* and a special book for this purpose *Securtà e nolegiamenti di notaria*. The contracts were registered almost always by the same men who were engaged in the insurance business. The insurance policy was made either for a single voyage or for a period of 6 to 12 months.

The premiums had to be paid immediately and they differed according to the length of voyage. Figure 24 shows this distribution. The smallest rates were paid from Dubrovnik to the Adriatic ports i.e. 'intra Culfum',[66] these show distances fetching a 2–3% premium. The Ionian Sea, Sicily and the west coast of Italy cost 3–5%,[67] whilst the Aegean, Marmora and Black Sea ranged from 5–9%.[68] The Near East, Egypt and Spain had rates between 6–8–10%[69] with England and Constantinople 12–15%.[70] These were the average insurance costs assessed by special committees appointed by the Dubrovnik government. They acted as naval courts of justice. The highest premium paid was 15% of which there are three examples, one for a voyage from Dubrovnik to Alexandria[71] (reason not given) and twice in 1543 for fine textiles travelling from London to Dubrovnik.[72] Marine insurance also increased during war-time.[73]

If these marine insurance rates of the sixteenth century are compared with the freight costs for wheat in the fifteenth century (Table III) the same overall picture emerges, with distance/length of voyage the main criterion applied. Only the high marine insurance rate of

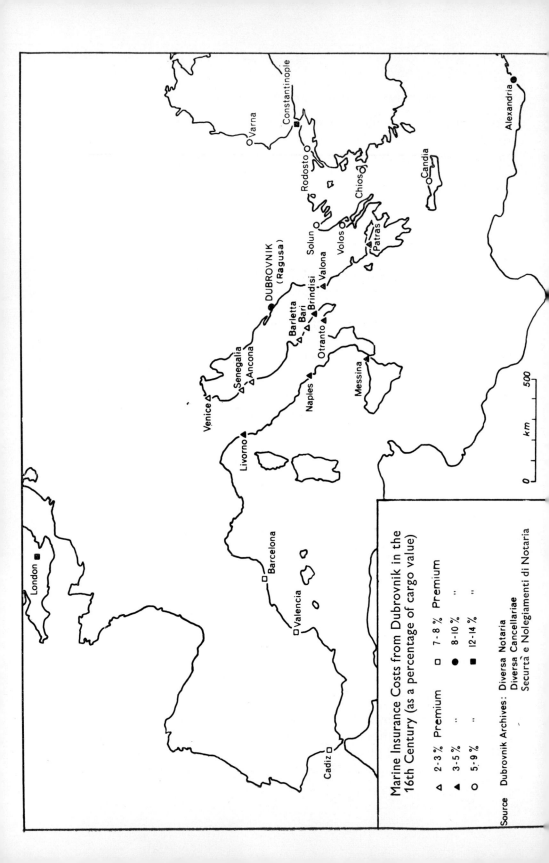

Marine Insurance Costs from Dubrovnik in the
16th Century (as a percentage of cargo value)

△ 2-3 % Premium   □ 7-8 % Premium
▲ 3-5 %   "   ● 8-10 %   "
○ 5-9 %   "   ■ 12-14 %   "

Source   Dubrovnik Archives: Diversa Notaria
                              Diversa Cancellariae
                              Securtà e Nolegiamenti di Notaria

Constantinople is the exception to this rule and that is probably on account of its significance and popularity as a market centre.

The Time Factor

Between the collapse of the Roman Empire and the eighteenth century good road making was almost a lost art. In general a road was a strip of land on which people had the right to travel, rather than an improved surface. Over the moors, through the passes and forests, or across the swamps it might be a little more than a path. In easier country it was often wide enough for a horseman to ride quickly, while cattle could wander along but wheeled vehicles found the going hard in wet weather. On such roads the normal speed was the walking pace of man or animal; 32 km was a good day's journey and some daily stages were shorter. When news and mail had to be carried quickly, couriers might cover 64–80 km in a day, and some cities or large business firms ran regular fast services. A journey of 1600 km from Calais to Rome took a relay of express riders twenty-seven days to complete in 1200. By the early fifteenth century a regular mail service carried letters from Bruges to Venice in about twenty-five days, but the Romans were able to do the journey in about the same time a thousand years before. In the carriage of goods the packhorse or the two wheeled wagon, moving at the easy pace of a horse or oxen, set the speed and the day's journey. A drover who steered a small herd of cattle and a large flock of sheep along 208 km of fairly level English road in thirteen days probably made good time.[74]

From an analysis of Dubrovnik documents it is possible to get some idea of the time factor in the Balkan peninsula. Most contracts were done by merchants keeping their word, or by paying messengers 'kuriri', couriers (Latin 'cursares', Ital. 'curieri' Slav. 'knjižnici, listonoše, knjigonoše') a system adopted at the beginning of the fourteenth century which continued until the fall of the republic in 1808. The Dubrovnik government would receive a letter from a respective colony, or consul, which worked through the same lawyer in Dubrovnik. Private letters were allowed only for sending an answer which usually went by caravan and was very slow. Large numbers of trade agreements were carried out by word of mouth. In winter messages took twice as long as in summer. Goods naturally travelled much slower than letters. In the fourteenth century a messenger took on average 15 days to get from Dubrovnik to Constantinople.[75]

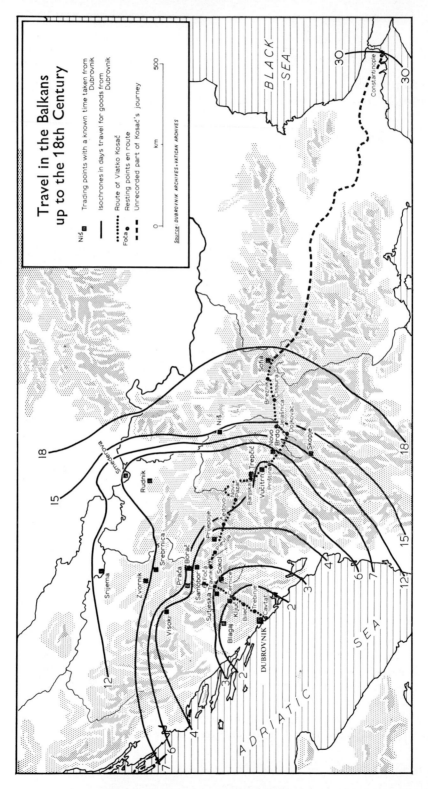

Travel in the Balkans up to the 18th Century

Niš ■   Trading points with a known time taken from Dubrovnik

——   Isochrones in days travel for goods from Dubrovnik

········   Route of Vlatko Kosač

Foča ●   Resting points en route

‒ ‒ ‒   Unrecorded part of Kosač's journey

SOURCE: DUBROVNIK ARCHIVES · VATICAN ARCHIVES

FIG. 25.

Probably one of the best sources of information on this problem was a letter discovered in 1935 which told of two travellers who went from Constantinople to Dubrovnik in the sixteenth century.[76] Unfortunately the first few pages are missing but it tells of the latter half of the voyage from Sofia to Dubrovnik.[77] After one day in Sofia they went through Bazar Bristina (Breznik) to the west of Sofia, and their itinerary afterwards was as follows:

(i) 31st July arrived Clissura, on the present-day Bulgarian/ Yugoslav border.

(ii) 1st August arrived Gelassinizza (or Jelašnica) village, north-east of Vranje.

(iii) 2nd August arrived Dojkovica village, north of the confluence of the Decivojka and Kriva Rivers tributaries of the South Morava.

(iv) 3rd August passed near Novo Brdo and at noon arrived in Priština.

(v) 4th August passed through Vučitrn (Bazar Buciterna) where 'there is a large polje (Kossovo Polje) and arrived in Mitrovica where there is a fortress, and then arrived at Banjska where there are two hot springs'.

(vi) 5th August at noon arrived in Novi Pazar and stayed here resting all next day.

(vii) 7th August arrived in Čedovo village (today 2 km north of Sjenica).

(viii) 8th August passed Mileševo monastery and arrived in Prijepolje.

(ix) 9th August spent night in Plevlja.

(x) 10th August spent night at caravan centre (?).

(xi) 11th August they were in Foča, rested two hours, then crossed River Čehotina, slept in a village (?) from where they crossed a river on a ferry called Brod on River Drina south-west of Foča.

(xii) 12th August arrived Ternovaluch (which could be a mistake for Travnik) in the Foča district near the confluence of the River Sutjeska with River Drina.

(xiii) 13th August in Cernica (now a village in the south-western part of Gačko (Gatačko) Polje.

(xiv) 14th August slept in a small house which was *en route* somewhere near Bileč.

G

(xv) 15th August slept in Trebinje.

(xvi) arrived in Cavtat (Ragusavecchia).

(xvii) 17th August arrived Dubrovnik.

They had followed the old route from Constantinople to Dubrovnik, and the section from Metrovica (in Kossovo Polje) was known as the 'Dubrovnik Way'; they rested one day in Sofia and one in Novi Pazar and the whole journey from Constantinople had taken 33 days.

Within the Balkan hinterland Dubrovnik maintained taverns, warehouses and consulates in certain key centres. The most important of these were at Belgrade, Borač, Foča, Fojnica, Kosovska Mitrovica, Mostar, Niš, Novo Brdo, Prijepolje, Prokuplje, Sarajevo, Sjenica, Skoplje, Smedereva, Sofia, Temišvar, Vidin and Visoko.[78] It must be remembered that in the economic life of these centres merchants from Dubrovnik played an important role. Besides their own special quarters in the cities they also built beautiful monuments, such as the 'Kursumli' tavern in Skopje, and underlines the importance of and big investment in these commercial connections.

The time factor in maritime commerce seems less complicated. From maritime insurance costs, previously quoted, it appears that the average travelling time in the Adriatic was about ten days, and rarely more than fifteen days. The travelling time of voyages to Albania, western Greece, southern Italy and Sicily was between ten to twenty days, whilst journeys to eastern Greece, the Black Sea, Syria, Alexandria or Spain was usually about a month in duration. Journeys further afield for example to England could take up to a year to complete the round trip.[79]

Conclusion

Such was the organization behind Dubrovnik's trading empire. The need for a good network of trade routes was vital if the city's commercial prosperity was to be maintained. Dubrovnik's fortunate position gave her easy access to the main commercial links of the Balkan peninsula whilst from her port, connections could be made with the Levant and Italy without much difficulty. Dubrovnik lay, according to the classic work by Demolins,[80] between 'La route des Ports maritimes – Le type Vénetien' and 'La route des Plateaux – Les types Albanais et Hellène'. It was located near the southern end of the main longitudinal sailing route through the Adriatic Sea between the

Dalmatian islands, but at the same time it lay on the open sea. It did not need to come into conflict with the Venetian galleys which in full sight of Dubrovnik, sailed the high seas from the Korčulan gate, where the island route began. The main advantage of the position on the sea was that it was on an open coast and a short distance away from the great sailing route. Even so, Roglić states that

> 'obviously the city's prosperity was not derived from the seacoast, nor did it come from the sea. For an appreciation of the import- ance of Dubrovnik and of its development, its position and con- nection with the hinterland are of major significance'.[81]

In some areas, as in the hinterland of Split, for example, parallel mountain chains obstruct the journey inland; in others as along the Bay of Kotor, the mountains themselves come to the coast, but at Dubrovnik they gradually rise, so that this zone is relatively easily crossed all the way to the Morava valley, the main commercial artery of south-east Europe.

The strong, cheap and well-organized caravan transport facilitated the shipment of valuable goods from the hinterland, especially ores of silver, lead, copper and gold, as well as other products, while in the return direction came valuable and expensive products of the Italian handicraft industries. The caravans were the bridge across the Dinaric mountains, and the trade routes were important in ex- tending the cultural and political influences of Dubrovnik. Her system of colonies ensured the smooth working of her commercial empire, where merchants could rest and organize their wares. Although most heavily concentrated in the Balkans, Dubrovnik's colonies were found throughout the Mediterranean giving the city's merchants command over a large trading area. Thus again quoting Smith

> 'Trade was not only with the Adriatic ports of Italy but also to a wider sphere beyond. Dubrovnik's ships took wine, spices and raisins to London in return for cloth and metal goods, and sailed regularly to eastern Spain and the Levant. The overland route from Dubrovnik to Constantinople was also of importance since it by- passed the dangerous waters of the Aegean, and Bosnian gold and wool as well as timber came by it from the hinterland'.[82]

Therefore by the end of the fifteenth century, thanks to an effective and efficient trading organization, the small republic could boast of the largest fleet in the Adriatic and merchants who had contacts in all the important towns of the Mediterranean.

4. Notes

1. C. T. Smith, *An Historical Geography of Western Europe before 1800*, Longmans, Green and Co. London (1967), p. 420.

2. Dubrovnik Archives, *Liber Statutorum VI* (1301), folders 21–22.

3. Dubrovnik Archives, *Liber Reformationes* I (18/VII/1325), folder 176.

4. Dubrovnik Archives, *Liber Reformationes* I (17/X/1325), folder 184. A complaint was made by Dubrovnik town to King Robert of Naples because of the acts of piracy committed by the people of Manfredonia.

5. M. J. Dinić, 'Dubrovačka Srednjevekovna Karavanske Trgovina', *Jugoslovenski Istoriski Časopis* God. III, Belgrade (1937), Sveska 1–4, p. 140.

6. Three of the largest loads of salt which left Dubrovnik were:
   (i) Dubrovnik Archives, *Diversa Cancellaria*, 41, (22/III/1418), folder 246, 337 loads to Konjica;
   (ii) *ibid.* (6/VI/1443), 57, folder 261', 442 loads to Goražde;
   (iii) *ibid.* (9/VIII/1428), 44, folder 31', 600 loads to Podvisoko.

7. V. Ćorović, 'Sr. najnoviju raspravu o Brskovu', *Glasnik Geografskog Društva*, Vol. XX, Belgrade (1934), p. 40.

8. I. Rubić, 'Utjecaj pomorskih i kopenih faktora na razvoj grada Dubrovnika', *Dubrovačko Pomorstvo* Dubrovnik (1952), p. 314.

9. Dubrovnik Archives, *Diversa Cancellaria* 2 (1285).

10. Dubrovnik Archives, *Liber Reformationes* 24 (18/XII/1378), folder 252; *ibid.* (10/XII/1381).

11. Dubrovnik Archives, *Diversa Cancellaria* 2 (1285) referred to as Gescecha or Gececha and mentioned as early as 1275.

12. Dubrovnik Archives, *Consilium Minoris* (23/VI/1399); *Liber Reformationes* 31 (1397–99), folder 199.

13. Dubrovnik Archives, *Liber Reformationes* 7 (1322), folder 16, 'Litterae praeceptorie et citatorie, et de praeconcicationibus'; *Diversa Cancellaria* 14 (7/VII/1343), folder 28 – the first time that Prijepolje is mentioned in Dubrovnik documents.

14. Dubrovnik Archives, *Lettere e Commisioni* (*Lettere di Levante*) 20 (1526–31), folder 274.

15. Dubrovnik Archives, *Consilium Minoris* (4/VII/1412); *Liber Reformationes* 34 (1412–1414), folder 318.

16. Benedetto Ramberti, *Libri Tre delle cosi dei Tarchi* Book I, Dubrovnik (1539) – gives further details on this route.

17. Dubrovnik Archives, *Diversa Cancellaria* 25 (16/VI/1382); *Lettere e Commisioni* (*Lettere di Levante*) 11 (1430–35), folder 282.

18. K. Jireček, *Die Handelsstrassen und Bergwerke von Serbien und Bosnien wahrend des Mittelalters*, Prague (1879), pp. 75–82.

19. Zenta or Zedda was the name of a district comprising Montenegro and that

part of Albania between Lake Skadar and the Adriatic coast as far as Dürres. See Dr. G. A. Škrivanić, *Imenik Geografskih Naziva Srednjovekovne Zete,* Istoriski Institut, N. R. Crne Gore. Titograd (1959).

20. K. Jireček, *Die Handelsstrassen* . . . *op. cit.* p. 63.
21. *Ibid.,* pp. 66–67.
22. K. Jireček, *Die Handelsstrassen* . . . *op. cit.* p. 68. The Beglerbeg of Rumelia was the commander-in-chief of the Turkish armies in Europe.
23. Dubrovnik Archives, *Liber Reformationes* 2 (2/X/1382), folder 8. Dubrovnik merchant bought a slave from Visoko colony.
24. *Liber Reformationes,* 32 (20/IV/1400), folder 35;
    Diversa Cancellaria, 35 (1405), folder 160;
    Testamenta Notaria, 9 (1406), folder 101;
    Liber Reformationes (1407), folders 14, 36;
    ibid., 34 (1412–1414), folders 11, 23, 29, 50, 52, 69, 89, 122, 123;
    Diversa Cancellaria, 39 (1412), folder 142;
    ibid., 45 (1428), folder 31;
    Lamenta de Foris, 2 (1413), folder 9;
    ibid., 8 (1429), folder 189;
    Diversa Notaria, 12 (1418), folder 234;
    ibid., 16 (1429–1430), folders 151, 238;
    in the book *Consilium Minus,* 1 (1415–1418);
    ibid., 2 (1418–1422);
    ibid., 3 (1422–1426);
    ibid., 4 (1426–1439);
    ibid., 5 (1430).
25. Dubrovnik Archives, *Liber Reformationes* 27 (23/IX/1387), folder 23. Dubrovnik citizens given right by Serbian ruler to found a colony at Novo Brdo.
26. Dubrovnik Archives, *Consilium Rogatorum,* 14, folder 240. Letter dated 19/XII/1455 states Novo Brdo taken by the Turks.
27. Previously only mentioned once in a treaty. Dubrovnik Archives, *Diversa Cancellaria* 34 (29/IX/1409), folder 159.
28. N. Iorga, *Geschichte des rumänischen Volkes,* Vol. II, Gotha (1905), p. 258; W. Heyd, *Histoire du commerce du Levant au Moyen-Age,* Vol. I, Leipzig (1885), p. 258, and Vol. II, Leipzig (1886), p. 347.
29. Dubrovnik Archives, *Liber Reformationes,* 10 (1332), folder 293;
    ibid., 12 (1343), folder 341, 345;
    ibid., 18 (1362), folder 157, 158. 'Item in eodem consilio captum fuit, quod Petrucius de Barleto factor domini imperatoit Bulgariae, possit extrahere de Ragusio illas mercationes, qua investivit de furmento suo, sine aliqua doana solvenda amore dicti domini imperatoris'.
30. I. Sakazov, *Stopanskite Vrzki Mezdu Dubrovnik i Blgarskite Zemi Prez 16 i 17 Stolitija,* Sofia (1930), Chapter II. 'Organization of Dubrovnik colonies in the Bulgarian lands'.
31. Dubrovnik Archives, *Diversa Cancellaria,* 27 (15/X/1387), folder 45, mentions caravan from Vidin carrying skins 'per viam Pristine et in Prepaglie et de Anagast versus Ragusium'.
32. Dubrovnik Archives, *Lettere e Commisioni* (*Lettere di Levante*), 2, folder 105, first mention of a Dubrovnik trader in Sofia (1376).
33. Dubrovnik Archives, *Diversa Notaria* 117 (29/I/1559), folder 108'.

34. Dubrovnik Archives, *Diversa Notaria* 81 (18/I/1502), folder 45.
35. I. Sakazov, 'Dubrovnik i Blgarija v Minaloto', *Blgarska Istoričeska Biblioteka* God. V (1932–33), Vol. 1, p. 87–109, Vol. II, p. 56–76;
ibid., 'Stopanskite Vrzki na Blgarija s Čuzbina prez XIV veku', *Godišnike na Sofiaskija Universitet Uridiceski Fakultet*, Vol. XXX, No. 7, Sofia (1934–1935), pp. 4–100.
36. V. Makušev, *Monumenta historica Slavorium Meridionalium*, Vol. I, Warsaw (1874), document XIV.
37. S. Runciman, *The Fall of Constantinople 1453*, Cambridge (1965), p. 11.
38. G. Ostrogorsky, *Histoire de l'Etat byzantium*, Paris (1956), pp. 459–460; Dubrovnik Archives, *Diversa Cancellaria* 80 (23/VII/1483), folder 21.
39. *Regesta chartarum Italiae. Documenti del commercio veneziano nei secoli XI–XIII* (R. Morozzo della Roca – A. Lombardo, eds.) Vol. I, Rome (1940), pp. 85–86.
40. F. C. Lane, 'The Mediterranean spice trade', *American Historical Review*, Vol. XLV, No. 3 (April 1940), p. 582;
B. Korkut, *Arapski Dokumenti u Državnom Arhivu u Dubrovniku*, Knijiga I, Sveska 3, Sarajevo (1969), 60 pp.
41. B. Krekić, 'O Nekim Našim Ljudima na kritu u srednjem veku', *Godišnjak Filozofskog Fakulteta*, Kniga V, Novi Sad (1960), pp. 1–10.
42. *Documenti della colonia veneziana di Creta I*, Imbreviature de Petro Scardon (1271) (A. Lombardo, ed.) Torino (1942). Nos. 86, 195, 196, 451.
43. M. Popović-Radenković, 'Dubrovački Konzulat u Alexandriju od Šešdesetih do Osamdezetih Godina XVIII Veka', *Istoriski Glasnik* Kniga 4, Belgrade (1954), p. 41.
44. Dr. I. Rubić, *op. cit.*, p. 319.
45. J. Tadić, 'Le Port de Raguse et sa Flotte au XVIe Siècle', *Travaux du Second Colloque International d'Histoire Maritime*, Paris (1959), p. 20.
46. S. Guldescu, *History of Medieval Croatia*, The Hague (1964), p. 301.
47. Dubrovnik Archives, *Diversa Cancellaria*, 29, (21/V/1390), folder 98. This document records '100 salmas salis de tribus modiis pro singula salma' – 'One hundred loads (of merchandise) with three "modia" (42 kg) for each load. 126 kg'. Most of the 'loads' mentioned in the documents were between 120–140 kg.
48. Dubrovnik Archives, *Diversa Notaria*, 20 (12/VI/1435), folder 23.
49. Dubrovnik Archives, *Diversa Cancellariae*, 48 (9/II/1434), folder 57. Merchants forbad the Vlachs to carry *salted fish* and *textiles* in the same caravan.
50. Dubrovnik Archives, *Resti*, (1594), folder 64. 'Cori bovini e vachini del anno passato deve dare addi ultimo Genero aspri 7920 sono per pezze 132 di cori . . . addi detto aspri 4683 sono per pezze 58 . . . auti da Dimitrie Georgie di Cora Harmanluck . . . aspri 719 per vittura di cori pezze 273 da Silistra a Nicopoli . . . aspri 2849 sono per vittura di pezze 407 da Nicopoli fino Ušiz ad aspri 7 . . . 4375 sono per vittura di pezze 407 da Ušiz a Ragusa'.
51. Dubrovnik Archives, *Resti*, (1598), folder 155. 'Lana tosata fina di qui deve dare addi 27 di Maggio aspri 79,998 sono per costo e spase . . . in sacca 105 . . . addi 26 Luglio aspri 26,559 sono per vittura e spese a fachino . . . 7 Luglio aspri 3,197 sono per mia provigione di lor compra a 3 per cento.'
52. Dubrovnik Archives, *Resti*, (1600), folder 157.
53. Dubrovnik Archives, *Resti*, folder 178.

54. Dubrovnik Archives, *Resti*, folder 178.
55. Dubrovnik Archives, *Diversa Notariae*, 130 (3/VII/1602), folder 182.
56. J. Tadić, 'O pomorstvu Dubrovnika u XVI i XVII veku', *Dubrovačko Pomorstvo*, Dubrovnik (1952), pp. 165–189.
57. The first mention of Dubrovnik boats in the Black Sea was in 1270: Š. Ljubić, *Histoire . . . op. cit.* Vol. I, pp. 113–114.
58. A. Sapori, *Una compagnia di Calimala ai primi del Trecento*, Firenze (1932), pp. 64–99.
59. G. Luzzato, *Storia economica, L'età moderna*, Padora (1934).
60. M. Sombart, *Der modern Kapitalismus*, Leipzig (1916).
61. A. Fanfani, 'Costi e profitti d'un mercante del Trecento', *Saggi di Storica Economica Italiana*, Milan (1936), pp. 3–15.
62. G. Luzzato, *op. cit.* p. 48.
63. B. Krekić, *Dubrovnik (Raguse) et le Levant au Moyen Age*, Paris – The Hague (1961), p. 81.
64. A. Fanfani, *op. cit.* Transport costs from Constantinople to Trapani in Sicily = 3.1% of total expenditure on the voyage (18/XI/1391 – 20/XI/1392) whilst from Genoa to Pisa = 0.5% (28/I–28/III/1392).
65. J. Tadić, 'Pomorsko Osiguranje u Dubrovniku XVI Stoljeća', *Rešetarov Zbornik iz Dubrovačke Prošlosti*, Dubrovnik (1931), p. 109–112;
    A. Marinović, 'Stari dubrovački zakon o pomorskom osiguranju', *Osiguranje i privreda*. Vol. 9, No. 6, Zagreb (1968), p. 21–28.
66. Dubrovnik Archives, *Diversa Notaria*, 106, (1539–42), folder 5′, 77′, 78′, 117, 173;
    ibid., 106 (1542–44), folder 16′, 18′, 109, 143′, 182′;
    Diversa Cancellaria, 132 (1546–1548), folder 8′;
    Securtà e Nolegiamenti, Notaria (1566–67), folder 1, 7;
    ibid. (1587–88), folder 1, 32, 36, 125′, 215′, 264′;
    ibid. (1588), folder 32′, 211′;
    ibid. (1588–89), folder 71′;
    ibid. (1598), folders 31, 37, 44, 57′, 223′;
    ibid. (1604–1605), folder 4′.
67. Dubrovnik Archives, *Diversa Notaria*, 98 (13/I/1519), folder 6;
    Securtà e Nolegiamenti Notaria (1570–71), folders 106, 123;
    ibid. (1539–42), folders 98′, 155′, 178′, 190, 193′;
    Diversa Cancellaria, 132 (1546–48), folder 9;
    Securtà e Nolegiamenti Notaria (1566–67), folders 40, 43;
    ibid. (1587–88), folder 267;
    ibid. (1598), folder 1.
68. Dubrovnik Archives, *Diversa Notaria*, 106 (1539–42), folder 194, 196′;
    ibid., 107 (1542–46), folder 110;
    Securtà e Nolegiamenti Notaria (1587–88), folders 37′, 144′;
    ibid. (1588), folders 117, 142′;
    ibid. (1598), folder 134′.
69. Dubrovnik Archives, *Diversa Notaria*, 106 (1539–42), folders 73′, 82, 149′, 170, 176′, 180;
    ibid., 110 (1549–50), folder 57′;
    Securtà e Nolegiamenti Notaria (1588), folder 254;
    Diversa Notaria, 107 (1546), folder 87;

Securtà e Nolegiamenti Notaria (1566–67), folder 62'.

70. Dubrovnik Archives, *Diversa Notaria*, 107 (1542–46), folders 139', 154', 155', 156', 162', 172', 175';
Diversa Cancellaria, 136 (1549–50), folder 245;
Securtà e Nolegiamenti Notaria (1587–88), folder 176';
ibid. (1588–89), folder 63.

71. Dubrovnik Archives, *Diversa Notaria*, 95 (8/II/1520), folder 42.

72. Dubrovnik Archives, *Diversa Notaria*, 107 (1543), folders 172', 175'.

73. Dubrovnik Archives, *Securtà e Nolegiamenti Notaria* (8/VII/1571), folder 80.

74. H. Heaton, *Economic History of Europe*, New York (1948), p. 158.

75. Dubrovnik Archives, *Consilium Minoris* (25/II/1397) in *Liber Reformationes* 30 (1395–97), folder 145;
B. Krekić, 'Kurirski Saobraćaj Dubrovnika sa Carigradom i Solunom u prvoj polovina XIV veka', *Zbornik Radova* SAN, knj. XXI Biz. Inst. kng I, Belgrade (1952), p. 118;
Z. Šundrica, 'P'tepis na Dubrovnińkite Pratenici s haradža ot 1673 g.', *Izvestija na B'lgarskototo Istoričesko Družestvo*, Vol. 25, Sofia (1967), pp. 250–260.
P. Petrov, 'Dubrovnińki P'tepis prez B'lgarskite Zemi ot 1792 g', *op. cit.* Vol. 26, Sofia (1968), pp. 267–274.

76. A. Urošević, 'Putovanje Vlatka Kosać iz Carigrad u Dubrovnik u 16 veku' *Glasnik Geografskog Društva*, Vol. XXII, Belgrade (1936), pp. 86–89.

77. Vatican Archives, *Code A.A.Arm.I–XVIII* (6511), folder 12[re-vo].

78. I. Rubić, *op. cit.* p. 316.

79. J. Tadić, *Pomorska Osiguranje . . . op. cit.* p. 112;
A. Tenenti, *Naufrages, Corsaires et Assurances maritimes à Venise 1592–1609* (S.E.V.P.E.N.) Paris (1959), pp. 59–65.

80. E. Demolins, *Comment la route crée le type social* (*Les Routes de l'Antiquité*), Paris (1901), pp. 347–412.

81. J. Roglić, 'The geographical setting of medieval Dubrovnik', *Geographical Essays on Eastern Europe* (N. J. G. Pounds, ed.), Vol. 24, The Hague (1961), p. 147.

82. C. T. Smith, *op. cit.* p. 420.

5
Political Relations of
the Dubrovnik Republic
1358–1500

The year 1358 was an important landmark in the political life of
Dubrovnik. The victory of King Ludovik of Hungary and Croatia
over the Venetians in 1358 marked the end of one of the more
significant struggles between the two powers and greatly affected
the future of Dubrovnik. By the treaty of Zadar the whole eastern
shore of the Adriatic as far as Dürres was ceded to Hungary, but as
a matter of fact, that power only extended its occupation as far as
Dubrovnik. Not having a strong fleet, King Ludovik feared that the
more southern cities would be difficult to hold and he therefore never
exercised his treaty rights over them. Venice, having lost, with Dalmatia, her chief naval base of Dubrovnik, turned her attention towards Albania and the adjoining Slavic countries. She had at one
time occupied Dürres (1205–1208) and through her colonies in Dalmatia had come into contact with the Albanians. Now that her influence in the former country was destroyed, and that she had lost
a large part of her mainland possessions, the population devoted
itself to 'the bee-like task of accumulating wealth and extending its
commerce'.[1] Relations were once more established with Albania, and
trade with the country was encouraged.[2]

The exchange of Hungarian supremacy for that of Venice brought
about less change in the internal situation of Dubrovnik than might
have been expected, but the dignity of the republic was enhanced
by the further extension of its autonomy, for it became to all intents
and purposes an independent state. When the last Venetian Count
departed a commission of three Rectors, elected by the citizens, was
appointed to carry on the affairs of the government, and they were

G*

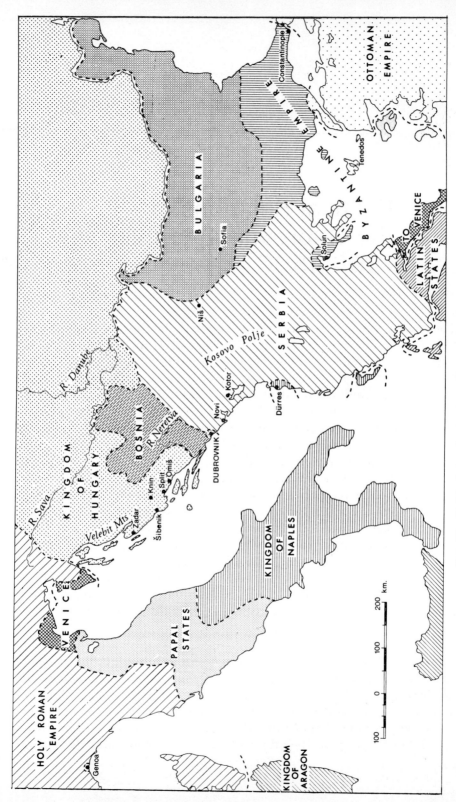

Fig. 26. Political situation in the Balkans and Italy, *circa* 1358.

changed every two months; but a few months later the number was reduced to one and his tenure of office limited to one month. (After 1358 the series *Liber Reformationes* alludes to the 'Rector' and no longer to the 'Rectores'.) No other important changes were made in the constitution from this date until the fall of the republic in 1808.

Dubrovnik's international position, however, was now considerably altered. The King of Hungary allowed the citizens the most absolute liberty to manage their own affairs, and not only had he no Hungarian representative in the city, but he did not even attempt to interfere indirectly with the government. Dubrovnik was merely bound to pay him a tribute and to provide a naval contingent in time of war on the terms set forth in the treaty of Višegrad.[3] She always remained the faithful friend and ally of Hungary, and was quite content to render this not very onerous allegiance; in her relations with Hungary there was no trace of the constant recriminations and bickering that there were with Venice.

The reason for this difference of feeling towards the two powers lies in the character of Venetian as compared with Hungarian policy. Venice was ever extending her influence down the Adriatic coast, consolidating her dominion and destroying local autonomies. Above all, Venice was a great maritime power and could swoop down on Dubrovnik or any other Adriatic town with her swift galleys at any moment; commercial rivalry, too, had its effect, for Venice aspired to the monopoly of the same trades as those in which Dubrovnik dealt, for example salt. Hungary, on the other hand, was purely a military state. Its aims were internal consolidation and the security of its own immediate frontiers. It did not aspire to distant dominions, as it had no powerful navy, and it merely desired to possess Dalmatia so as to secure a wider outlet to the sea than the Croatian coast; and it had no seaborne trade to interfere with that of Dubrovnik. On the land side it wished to secure the allegiance of the Bosnian Bans, but there was little danger of its establishing an absolute sway over the Slav lands immediately behind Dubrovnik.

Dubrovnik citizens now set to work to consolidate their independence and develop their trade for they realized that small states

'obviously cannot use their size or depth as an aid in defence. Surrounded by neighbours many times larger they have to rely on other forceful means to preserve and protect themselves'.[4]

It is at this point one realizes the importance of Dubrovnik's nobility in the commerce of the town. The noble families were as a rule the descendants of the original Latin colonists from Epidaurum and Salona, or, in a few cases, of those early Slav refugees who were nobles in their own country.

Relations with the Slavonic Rulers

The conditions of the Slavonic states behind Dalmatia were at this time extremely disturbed. During the brilliant reign of Stephen Dušan, the Serbian people were at the height of their greatness and power. Macedonia, Albania and other parts of the Greek Empire, and a part of Bosnia, as well as Serbia proper, acknowledged the rule of the Serbian Tsar, and even Bulgaria paid him tribute. The great position of Serbia under this ruler is now generally appreciated by historians of the Eastern Empire; Dušan, was not only a great warrior, but a great legislator, and drew up the *Zakonik* or code of laws,[5] comparable with that of Jaroslav for Russia. Had he lived a few years longer, and been able to crush the turbulence of his feudal vassals and consolidate his possessions, the battle of Kossovo might never have taken place, and the Balkans never have been subjected to the horrors of the Turkish conquest. On his death in 1355 the whole fabric of his Empire split up into a number of separate principalities. He was succeeded by his son, Uroš IV (1355–1367), who was not strong enough to carry on his father's work, and the Magnates and governors soon began to show signs of insubordination. Not only had he to deal with internal discontent, but he was also attacked by foreign neighbours. In 1358 Ludovik of Hungary made war upon him with such success that he conquered the erstwhile Hungarian district of Mačva, (the 'Machova' of Dubrovnik documents) south of Sava River, and placed Nicholas of Gara to rule over it.[6]

The most powerful Serbian Magnates were the brothers Vukašin and Ulješa Mrnjavčić, Prince Lazar Grebljanović, who was afterwards to achieve immortal fame on the field of Kossovo, Vuk Branković, the brothers Balša, and Knez Vojislav Vojinović. The latter and the Balšas obtained their independence during the lifetime of Uroš. In 1367 the last of the Nemanjas died; Vukašin himself, who had been greatly favoured by Dušan and appointed, by the terms of the Tsar's will, chief State Councillor to Uroš, succeeded to the throne. Unfortunately this only hastened the disruption of the Empire, for Prince Lazar, Vuk Branković, and Nicholas Altomanović (the Governor of the Danubian provinces) rose against him, and not only proclaimed their own independence, but occupied part of his immediate possessions.

(The decline of Serbia can be traced in the titles of its rulers. Uroš IV was the last Tsar, Vukašin was only King, and his son was Marko Kraljević, 'the King's son').

Of the various states into which the Serbian Empire split up the first to be formed was the Zedda (Zeta or Zenta) ruled by the Balša family. A Balša had served in Dušan's armies, and was afterwards made Governor of the Zedda. In a privilege of 1360, in which Stephen Uroš IV grants trading rights in his states to Dubrovnik, the 'Zedda of Balša' is mentioned, showing that the province was still under Serbian suzerainty. It consisted of the region round Lake Skadar and is another name for the ancient Doclea. It was always regarded with especial affection by the Nemanjas as their original home, and in 1195 they made it into a Grand County. The first Balša died in 1361, leaving three sons, Stračimir, George, and Balša II, and a daughter. The sons reigned jointly, the eldest being merely 'Primus inter pares'. (This form of succession was a very usual one in the Serb lands.) They at once began to aspire to become independent of Serbian authority and to expand their own territories. Their first move was an alliance with Dubrovnik, who made them honorary citizens of the republic. Between 1362 and 1370 they conquered Skadar and threw off all allegiance to Dušan's successor. South of the Zedda lies Albania proper. Formerly a province of the Eastern Empire, it had first been conquered by Charles of Anjou (1266), then by Stephen Uroš II, Milutin, and then again by Philip of Taranto for the Angevins. Finally, after many vicissitudes, it came under the rule of the native prince Charles Topia, who, after he had captured Dürres from the Neapolitans in 1364, made himself master of the whole of middle Albania and independent of Serbia. In southern Albania and Macedonia other vassal nobles, such as the Gropa of Ochrid, Radoslav Hlapa in the Verria district, and Alexander at Valona, rose to power.

In the immediate hinterland of Dubrovnik was the land of Hum (Humina), ruled by Prince Vojislav Vojinović, who owed allegiance both to the Serbian Tsar and to the Ban of Bosnia. He too after Dušan's death made himself independent of his successor, and with Hungarian help also of the Ban. His territory extended from the River Morava via Sjenice and Gačko to Kotor and Dubrovnik, and included the coast between those two towns. He was the bitterest enemy of

Dubrovnik and never ceased from molesting them. He is described in their chronicles and documents as a 'homo perfidus', who 'tamquam infidelis male servat fidem'.[7] On his death in 1363 he was succeeded by his nephew Nicholas Altomanović, who fixed his headquarters at the important commercial town of Rudnik.

Whereas Serbia had reached the peak of its power before 1358 and was now in decline, Bosnia reached the summit of its medieval power under the leadership of Stefan Tvrtko 1353–1391. He took advantage of the now disorganized Serbian state and obtained large tracts of Serbian land in return for help against the Turks. Apparently some of his magnates were inclined to rebellion and encouraged in their disloyalty by the Tsar Dušan, who thus hoped to annex the whole Banate; in this Dušan might have succeeded had he not been cut off by death while on the march to Constantinople (December 20, 1355). But as soon as the power of Serbia was broken, Ludovik of Hungary changed his policy towards Bosnia, and obliged Tvrtko to agree to very onerous conditions. His possession of the Banate was recognized, but he had to give up his rights over Hum to Elizabeth, Ludovik's wife. (These were allowed to lapse in favour of Vojslav Voinović.) At the same time he was reduced to the position of a vassal of Hungary, and various feudal lords on the frontier were encouraged to shake off their allegiance to him. A general rising of the Bosnian barons ensued, and the sect of the Bogomils, taking advantage of this state of anarchy, became so influential that Pope Innocent VI proclaimed a crusade against them early in 1360. This was more than Ludovik had bargained for, and he sent an army into Bosnia (June 1360) which put down the revolt and restored Tvrtko's authority.

Another rebellion broke out in 1365, and Tvrtko was driven from the country and forced to apply once more for Hungarian help; a small contingent was granted to him, and after severe fighting he managed to regain the throne in 1366; his brother Vuk, a Bogomil, who had been among the rebels, fled to Dubrovnik. Shortly after Tvrtko visited that city in full state, accompanied by a train of nobles, confirmed all the privileges granted to it by his uncle Stephen, and contracted a treaty of perpetual alliance with the republic, 'save for what shall do injury to the honour of the King of Hungary'.[8] Unfortunately he failed to achieve the main object of his visit, the surrender of Vuk. Dubrovnik refused to release him and on becoming a Catholic he enlisted the sympathy of the Pope (Urban V) for his claims to the Bosnian throne. But Ludovik of Hungary would not support him, having turned his attention to Poland, where he hoped to become King. Tvrtko was thus able to enjoy a period of peace, and to consolidate his somewhat disturbed Banate. Dubrovnik set to work to consolidate its independence and develop trade, but it was not destined to enjoy a long period of absolute peace. The first quarrel was with Vojislav Vojinović, Count of Hum ('Comes Chelmi Magnus Procer Imperatoris Sclavoniae').[9] Early in 1359 the republic sent an envoy to him, offering to pay a sum of 4,000 perpera as tribute due to the Emperor of Slavonia; but shortly after he raided the Dubrovnik districts of Astarea and Šumet, burned the houses and churches, cut down the vineyards, took a number of prisoners, and arrested Dubrovnik traders in his territories. Vojislav was known to be thinking of an expedition against Ston and even Dubrovnik city, so that defensive measures were taken. All the city gates except two were walled up, a special guard of night watchmen was formed, troops and sailors levied throughout the republic's dominions, and a band of mercenaries was raised at Korčula with the permission of the Venetian Count for the defence of Ston. A master-mechanic was sent for from Messina to superintend the war engines, and a master-crossbowman from Italy. In the meantime the Senate sent envoys to the King of Hungary and to his lieutenant the Ban of Croatia and Dalmatia, complaining of Vojislav's conduct, and asking for assistance against him.[10] He was described as being 'like a wolf who wishes to devour us lambs',[11] and a price of 10,000 perpera was put on his head the following year.[12] Dubrovnik also tried to resort to another measure against Vojislav. The latter's territory reached as far as the neighbourhood of Kotor, which served him as a port; Dubrovnik now proposed an alliance with Kotor and suggested that they should break off all relations with the Lord of Hum and cease to provide him with provisions and salt. Kotor was unable to accede to this plan from fear of Vojislav's power. Dubrovnik was then determined to punish that town, and made an alliance to this end with the Balšas, Lords of Zedda. Negotiations were opened with the Serbian Tsar Uroš and his most powerful vassals, and envoys were sent to the Ban of Bosnia to arrange a plan of campaign against Hum. Operations began by sea, and on July 6, 1361, Dubrovnik itself appears to have been attacked by Vojislav's ships.[13] The republic confiscated the money which that prince had deposited in the town (the Slavs used Dubrovnik as their banking centre) and a naval expedition was fitted out to operate against Kotor. Raids were also made into Vojislav's territories on the landward side. The quarrel with Kotor and Vojislav lasted nearly two years, and only ended through Venetian and Serbian mediation.

Another war took place in 1363–64 between Hum and Dubrovnik. During this war the Balšas, in order to consolidate their power, began to make political and commercial alliances with their neighbours. For this purpose they applied to Dubrovnik requesting the honour of its citizenship for themselves. The Senate was well pleased to accede to this desire, as the republic was feeling by no means safe from Vojislav, and Hungarian help was delayed in coming. A treaty of offensive and defensive alliance was concluded, by which it was agreed that the Balšas should attack Kotor, Vojislav's ally, by land and Dubrovnik by sea. The Dubrovnik envoy, Clemente Dersa, informed the Balšas that Vojislav was meditating a *coup de main* on Budva, and that this would be a serious menace to their territory. (Budva is a small town on the Adriatic, just south of the entrance to the Bay of Kotor.) It was under the direct protection of the Serbian Tsars and independent of the vassal feudatories. Dubrovnik had quarrelled with the town in 1359 owing to the alleged acts of piracy committed by its inhabitants, but afterwards peace was made when Budva became subject to the Balšas and helped them in their revolt against Serbia. During the hostilities Kotor citizens beseiged Budva and nearly captured it taking several prisoners until finally a Dubrovnik flotilla came to the rescue and drove them back.[14] In April 1362 Dubrovnik ships blockaded Kotor by sea, while the Balšas attacked it by land.[15] (During these hostilities Dubrovnik captured the property of some Venetian merchants as contraband of war, and this caused some unpleasantness with Venice.) Kotor then requested Venetian mediation, and in January 1362 Paolo Quirini and a Hungarian representative were sent to Dalmatia to arbitrate, but without success. At last, in August, the Serbian Tsar intervened and on August 22 peace was signed at Onogošt (Nikšić).[16] All parties regained their former privileges, prisoners were liberated, and compensation paid for injuries. The chief result for Dubrovnik was the introduction of the plague from the interior.[17] The Balšas, however, were able to extend their territory along the coast as far as Ulcinj and in 1367 the dignity of warden of Budva passed to George Balša, and he and his brothers thenceforward styled themselves 'magnificent barons of Maritime Slavonia'. They were now able to negotiate with Venice, and became an important power in the Adriatic. This ultimately proved advantageous for Dubrovnik, to whom they granted many privileges and opened the trade routes up the rivers of northern Albania. They also obtained for the republic from the Serbian Tsar the full possession of the island of Mljet.[18]

Peace failed to prevent the lawless Count of Hum, Nicholas Altomanović, cousin of Vojislav Vojinović.[19] In April 1371 Dubrovnik wrote to the King of Hungary complaining of his raids,[20] and describing him as 'the worst of all the Slavic barons, although they are all false and infamous'. Not content with the gifts they had made to him, he had demanded the tribute due to the Serbian Tsar, and on refusal he invaded Dubrovnik's territory and tortured its prisoners. Dubrovnik added that the Ban of Mačva, who was the King of Hungary's vassal, had done nothing to restrain Altomanović, but was secretly his friend. The whole of the interior being in a state of anarchy, inland trade was almost at a standstill, and the Dubrovnik Republic requested the Hungarian King to intercede with the Pope to allow two ships every year to be sent to the lands of the Infidel.

Dubrovnik's forces did manage on several occasions to defeat Altomanović's raids and later in 1371 the republic joined the alliance of Prince Lazar and Tvrtko, Ban of Bosnia, against Altomanović. The latter now had the Balšas on his side but the coalition succeeded in conquering a large part of Altomanović's possessions. Prince Lazar occupied Rudnik, and Tvrtko the upper valley of the Drina, and drove George Balša from Trebinje. The Ban of Bosnia's possessions were thus extended by 1376 over the greater part of the Serbian lands as far as Trebinje, Kotor and Nikšić in the south, to Sjenice in the east, and included the important monastery of Mileševo. He was now the most powerful ruler in this part of the Balkans, and had himself crowned at Mileševo with two crowns, styling himself 'Stephen Tvrtko in the name of Our Lord Christ King of Serbia and Bosnia and the Primorije (coast land)'.[21] Dubrovnik was the first state to recognize him, and proved quite willing to pay the 2,000 perpera a year due to him as Lord of Serbia.

Unfortunately, now that the Bosnian King had humbled his neighbours and become the most powerful sovereign of the Southern Slavs he began to assume an unfriendly attitude towards Dubrovnik. His kingdom possessed a stretch of coast from the Bay of Kotor to the mouth of the River Cetina, but the two best ports of that region – Dubrovnik and Kotor – were independent republics owing allegiance to the King of Hungary, who was by no means likely to be always friendly to a powerful and independent Bosnia. If Tvrtko wished to establish a really strong Serbian state he would have to occupy those cities. While still Ban he had granted the freedom of his territories to Dubrovnik in a charter dated at Bobovac, February 5, 1375.[22] On April 10, 1379, he came to Žrnovica, very near Dubrovnik, accompanied by his magnates. The republic sent out a commission of nobles to greet him, and a new and advantageous commercial treaty was concluded, Dubrovnik agreeing to pay Tvrtko and his successors 500 perpera a year for freedom to trade in Bosnia, and 2,000 a year as lord of the Serbian lands.[23]

This friendship did not last long, for on July 26, 1379, we find the republic complaining to Ludovik of Hungary that the people of Kotor having offered their city to the King of Bosnia, the latter refused to allow foodstuffs to be imported into Dubrovnik. Ludovik defended his faithful vassals, and Tvrtko was forced to desist from his annoyances. When, in 1382, Ludovik died, he left a widow, Elizabeth, who was Tvrtko's cousin, and two daughters, Mary and Hedwig. He had declared Mary his successor, and betrothed her to Prince Sigismund, son of the Emperor Charles IV, King of Bohemia; but on his death the Poles, who were united to the Hungarians under the same dynasty, refused to be ruled by Mary, and elected her younger sister Hedwig as their Queen instead, and even in Hungary and Croatia a considerable party was opposed to Elizabeth and Mary. Civil war broke out and devastated Hungary, Croatia, Dalmatia, and Slavonia for the next twenty-five years. Tvrtko was determined to take advantage of these disturbances now favouring Elizabeth and Mary, now Charles of Dürres (who as an Angevin also claimed the throne of Hungary) and his son Ladislas, always with an eye to his own profit.[24] Tvrtko's thought was to capture Dubrovnik. He knew that he could not capture the town without a large fleet, for Dubrovnik shipping had revived since 1358, and was now very formidable; he also knew that its inhabitants lived entirely by trade, and was determined to injure them by establishing a rival trading centre at the entrance of the Bay of Kotor, making it the chief port and the commercial capital of Bosnia. He called it Sveti Stjepan (San Stefano), but the name was soon changed to Novi, and then to Erzegnovi (Herceg Novi). In violation of his treaties with Dubrovnik he opened salt-pans at Herceg Novi which soon became an important trading station not only for the neighbourhood but for the whole of Dalmatia and Croatia. Dubrovnik complained bitterly, and as they obtained Hungarian support, Tvrtko deemed it prudent to give way for the moment, and he promised to close the salt market.[25] Again in 1383 he re-opened Herceg Novi and the republic sent Pietro Gondola and Stefano Luccari to Budapest to complain of this breach of the treaty to Queen Mary. The latter at once issued a decree forbidding the inhabitants of Dalmatia and Croatia to trade at Herceg Novi.[26]

Tvrtko, not feeling strong enough yet to attack Dubrovnik openly, allied himself with the Venetians. The latter sold him a large galley fully armed and equipped, and allowed him to have two others built in Venice, sent Niccolò Baseio to him as admiral, and made Tvrtko honorary citizen of the Venetian Republic.[27] These movements disturbed not only Dubrovnik, but also the two Hungarian Queens, who feared that Tvrtko might avail himself of the discontent in Croatia and Dalmatia to raise further trouble. They therefore sent Nicholas of Gara to his court at Sutijeska to try to come to some arrangement. Finally Tvrtko was induced to agree not to disturb Dubrovnik nor the Hungarian dominions, for which promise he was rewarded with the town of Kotor[28] (July 20, 1385). This occupation brought him into conflict with the Balšas of Zedda, but after some fighting peace was restored through Venetian mediation. On April 9, 1387, Tvrtko concluded a treaty with Dubrovnik in which he promised to protect the city from all enemies, and its citizens granted him the right of asylum should he ever be in need of it. It was added that if he should come to the town for any reason, and Queen Mary, who was then a prisoner in the hands of the rebels, should escape, he should be warned in good time and allowed to leave.

By the following year the King of Bosnia's power in Croatia and Dalmatia had greatly increased, and he came into possession of such important castles as Klis, Vrana, Ostrović, and probably Knin, the key to Croatia.[29] He now tried to get hold of the Dalmatian coastal towns, as the whole country was in the turmoil of war and revolution, Dubrovnik alone remaining quiet and loyal to Queen Mary and her husband Sigismund. Various Dalmatian towns promised to pay allegiance to Tvrtko, including Split which raised the Bosnian Standard on June 15, 1389. But on that very date the death-knell of the Southern Slavs sounded on the fatal 'Field of Crows' (Kossovo Polje).

While Tvrtko was thus consolidating his kingdom at the expense of his neighbours, while Hungary was a prey to civil war, while the princelings of Serbia were eternally fighting among themselves, the Turks were ever marching onward. The native princes continued to fight among themselves regardless of their impending doom, and Tvrtko, who was the most powerful of them, thought more of occupying Dalmatia and Croatia than of strengthening his southern frontier. His enterprises were fairly prosperous; he succeeded in conquering the whole country from the Velebit mountains to Kotor and Zadar, with Dubrovnik alone remaining true to Sigismund, while the three islands of Brač, Korčula and Hvar recognized the suzerainty of the Bosnian King (1390). He died in 1391, leaving Bosnia in such a position as she had never enjoyed before, but her power was not based on a solid foundation, and therefore short-lived. His brother, Stephen Dabiša, who succeeded him, soon lost the greater part of Dalmatia and Croatia.

George II Stračimirov Balša, who now styled himself 'absolute Lord of all the Zedda and of the coast', and had established a court at Skadar,[30] was equally unconscious of the danger, and thought only of capturing Kotor. He began by occupying the Krivošije mountains behind Kotor and blocked all the roads leading into the town. Dubrovnik at the request of Kotor acted as mediator, and peace was made, probably on an understanding on the part of Kotor's citizens that they would pay a tribute to George.[31] Dubrovnik was beginning to be really alarmed at the progress of the Turks in Albania, and saw the necessity of allying herself with the other Dalmatian townships, 'propter oppressionem Turcorum'. In 1390 the Senate had tried in vain to mediate between the Kings of Bosnia and Hungary, so as to end the war which was desolating the country,[32] and now it made a proposal of this kind to Hungary and Venice. At the same time it granted a subsidy of arms and ammunition to George Balša. But mutual jealousies prevented the idea from being realized,[33] and in 1392 George himself was a pioneer in the hands of the Turks.[34] He was soon ransomed, but he lost Skadar, and his power was seriously shaken.

The year 1395 proved an unfortunate one for Dubrovnik. In the first place, one Constantine Balša, a relative of George II, who had obtained a trade monopoly in the Zedda and inland as far as Prizren and Novo Brdo, laid heavy impositions on Dubrovnik trade so as to exclude it from the country.[35] At the same time heavy rains flooded the city and its immediate neighbourhood, destroying all the crops, and on May 19 a severe earthquake – the first great shock felt in Dalmatia for many centuries – wrought great havoc.[36] Also during this period the Adriatic was infested with the pirate ships of Gabriele da Parma. There was another quarrel with George Balša on account of a certain monk named Marino of Ulcinj, who intrigued with the Slavs near Dubrovnik. However, this was soon settled to the satisfaction of all parties, the Albanian markets were re-opened, Constantine Balša recovered Skadar from the Turks for his kinsman, and declared himself Despot of the town. In 1395 George visited Dubrovnik where he was splendidly received as Prince of Albania.

Although Dubrovnik was usually on bad terms with its immediate neighbours it had been for some time good friends with the Bosnian magnate Vlatko Vuković. On his death in 1392 his estates descended to his nephew Sandalj Hranić, to whom Dubrovnik sent an embassy of homage in 1395. He was a true type of South Slavonic lord of that time. His one object was to consolidate and enlarge his territories, so as to carve out a principality for himself and be independent of the King of Bosnia or the Despot of Serbia. Like all his colleagues, he completely failed to appreciate the terrible significance of the Turkish danger, and while he began by

> 'proclaiming his misfortunes from the mountain tops, he ended by descending into the plain to declare himself the vassal of the powerful invader'.[37]

He was certainly less cruel than most of his neighbours, and, unlike them, was guilty of no particularly heinous murders. The result of his ambitious schemes was the formation of a duchy, afterwards called St. Sava or Herzegovina. In 1396 he contemplated an attack on Kotor in order to round off his dominions. This town was also coveted by Radić Črnoević, Lord of Montenegro. Radić got into trouble with Balša, who defeated and killed him while Sandalj, although he could not take Kotor took Budva, probably at the secret instigation of Venice. For his services Sandalj was granted the honorary citizenship of Venice.

The kingdom of Bosnia was subject to constant incursions on the part of the Turks, whom it was incapable of resisting, for under the reign of King Dabiša and Queen Helena Gruba the Vojvods had risen to power once more, and had become almost independent. Of these the most important were Sandalj Hranić, Lord of Hum; Hrovje, Duke of Split and Paul Radinović. Sandalj ruled over a great part of Hum as far as the River Drina. Hrvoje ruled over middle Dalmatia, a large part of Bosnia, including the town of Jajce, and some districts in Hum, including Livo. Paul Radinović was Lord of Trebinje, part of Konavle and other lands as far as Prača. His sons, Peter and Radosav, took the name of Paulović. Queen Helena lost her throne owing to a rebellion in 1398/1399, and was succeeded by Stephen Ostoja, probably a son of Stephen Tvrtko.[38] Ostoja had to depend for his authority on the goodwill of his magnates, but his reign was at first successful. He defeated Sigismund of Hungary, who tried to enforce his claims on Bosnia, and had invaded it at two points. Also on the Turkish frontier things were more peaceful for Bayazet had to hurry off to Asia to defend his Empire against Timur.

For a few years after his accession Ostoja had been friendly to Dubrovnik and in 1399 he granted them a further stretch of coast from Ston to Klek, near the mouth of the River Neretva. For this the citizens had given him a palace in the city and made him an honorary citizen; they granted the same favours to Hrvoje for his intercession. (A few years before, in 1391, they had received part of Konavle, with Dolnja Gora and Soko, from Paulović, so that now the territory of the republic extended from the Neretva to the Bay of Kotor.)

Ostoja, finding himself with no coast-line save the bit between the Rivers Cetina and the Neretva, repented his generosity, and tried to induce Dubrovnik to recognize Bosnian supremacy. When in 1400 the envoys brought him the tribute he suggested that the city should throw off the Hungarian yoke and come under his protection. But the republic would not hear of the proposal, preferring to obey the distant and complaisant King of Hungary rather than the near and untrustworthy King of Bosnia. The latter did not yet feel strong enough to attack the city openly with any chance of success where Tvrtko had failed, so he resorted to intrigue and secretly fomented a conspiracy of ambitious nobles. A conspiracy took place within the city during the early part of 1400 the offenders being finally beheaded. Nevertheless this was one of the few instances of internal revolution in an otherwise law-abiding city. It may also have been an early

symptom of the disagreements between the Latin and Slavonic
elements of Dubrovnik's population, but Ostoja's actual complicity
in the plot is unknown.

Ostoja, after having received the homage of Šibenik and Trogir
renewed his request that Dubrovnik should recognize his supremacy;
but again the citizens refused, and renewed their oath of fealty to
Sigismund, merely promising to take no part in the hostilities
between Bosnia and Hungary, and to refuse to admit Bosnian rebels
into the city. The following year a number of Sigismund's opponents
in Hungary, Croatia, and Dalmatia collected at Zadar, and Ladislas
crossed over from Italy and was crowned by the Hungarian Primate
King of Hungary, Croatia, and Dalmatia. Ostoja himself, however,
was not altogether satisfied, for although he had favoured Ladislas's
cause as long as the pretender was in Italy, the moment he landed
in Dalmatia, the Bosnian King felt that his own interests along the
seaboard were menaced. Hrvoje, Duke of Split, maintained an ambiguous attitude, and Ostoja was determined to make use of this
confusion to declare war on Dubrovnik. He found a pretext in the
fact that two Bosnian rebels had been given hospitality in the town;
he began by demanding back the Primorije which he himself had
ceded, as well as other territory given by his predecessors, and he also
insisted that Dubrovnik should recognize his full suzerainty. His demands being rejected he sent a force of 8,000 men under the Vojvods
(Dukes) Radić Sanković, Sandalj Hranić, and Paul Radinović into
Dubrovnik's territory. Hostilities lasted from August 1403 to the
spring of 1404.[39] Encounters took place at Brgat and Šumet in which
4,000 well-armed Dubrovnik citizens commanded by Giacomo Gondola tried to induce the enemy to give battle, but without success, as
the latter retired to Trebinje. Fortunately for Dubrovnik, Ostoja was
deposed. Stephen Tvrtko II, son of Stephen Tvrtko I, was elected
King and Ostoja retired to Bobovac, now occupied by a Hungarian
garrison. The new King owed his position to Hrvoje and Sandalj, who
were the real masters of the country, and Dubrovnik applied to them
to obtain a lasting peace with Bosnia. The Rector wrote to Sandalj,

'For what you desire, that also the lord King Tvrtko and the Duke
(Hrvoje) and all Bosnia desire too, for God has granted you the
favour that this should be so'.[40]

Eventually Tvrtko gave them back all the territory that had been
theirs and some more lands besides. The republic made him and his

brothers, as well as Sandalj, citizens of Dubrovnik, and gave them palaces in the town.

This friendship with Bosnia and loyalty to Hungary greatly tested Dubrovnik's diplomatic skill in 1405. Sigismund, King of Hungary, prepared to make war on Tvrtko as a usurper and reinstate Ostoja as the rightful King. Dubrovnik would not side openly with Tvrtko against this suzerain, but it did not wish to lose the valuable and freshly won favours of Bosnia; Dubrovnik therefore placed its arsenals at the disposal of Tvrtko's agents, who bought large supplies of arms for the war.[41] Sigismund sent three armies into Bosnia but after a few ephemeral successes the Hungarians were defeated at all points, and Tvrtko's position was thereby considerably strengthened. Ostoja fearing for his life, asked for a safe conduct to Dubrovnik in April 1407, and the Senate, much to his surprise, granted it, forgiving him all his former hostility,

'for any man who from Bosnia or from the land of any other lord takes refuge in our city, according to the law, may enter freely and live here undisturbed'.

Even so he did not avail himself of the permit, either because he mistrusted Dubrovnik or because he still hoped to regain his throne. While Tvrtko was trying to win Kotor and Budva from the Balšas, Sigismund was preparing his revenge, and in 1408 invaded Bosnia with a large army, defeated the usurper and captured him, together with a large number of magnates, of whom 126 were beheaded at Dobor. Ostoja was replaced on the throne, and Sigismund retired to Budva with Tvrtko.

Also of interest is Dubrovnik's relations with the Balšas. When George II died in 1403 he was succeeded by his son, who styled himself Balša III. The Zedda was now surrounded by jealous rivals; the Turks claimed tribute, Venice wished to establish posts in the country against them, and various native princelings aspired to enlarge their estates. Dubrovnik being at war with Bosnia, allied herself with the lords of Njegoš (near present day Nikšić) and with Kotor, and tried to conciliate Venice. Balša was determined to oust the Venetians from Albania and invited the Turks to help him to capture Drivast (Drishti) and Skadar. Thus Dubrovnik and he were in opposite camps. Drivast fell, and so did the town of Skadar, but the castle held out (1404). With the help of Sandalj Hranić and the Albanian magnates Venice soon recovered all that she had lost, and by June 1407, Balša and his ambitious mother Helena had to sue for peace and give way on all points. Ambitiously, in 1410, Balša again raided the Venetian possessions and attacked Skadar with a large force. Benedetto Contarini defended the town with great skill, and received much assistance from a Dubrovnik flotilla operating on the lake.[42] Balša also threatened Kotor so that town offered itself to the Venetians, who were ready to occupy it; but now Sandalj came forward with his claims on it, which caused further complications. Dubrovnik although allied to Venice, tried to better her relations with Balša on account of her Albanian trade, but this ambiguous attitude was not quite successful, and Dubrovnik's merchants ended by suffering molestations both from the Venetians and from Balša's subjects. In 1412 peace was concluded, and Balša restored everything.

There was now fresh disturbances in Bosnia, and Trvtko, who had been deposed in favour of Ostoja, was causing trouble. He raised a band of rebels, with which he defeated his adversaries, and obliged some of them to take refuge in Dubrovnik's territory. Tvrtko, as an old friend of the republic, complained of this hospitality but the citizens replied that it was better for malcontents to fly to Dubrovnik, where they usually ended by making peace with their King, than to other lands. For a few months Tvrtko was quite powerful, but soon after he was again defeated. Hrvoje, who had been deprived of his duchy, now called in the Turks to aid him against Hungary and Bosnia, and the Sultan Mohammed I thereupon sent a force into the latter country, which defeated the Hungarians near Usora, and obtained much booty. As soon as the Turks retired civil strife broke out again, a consequence of the murder by Ostoja of Paul Radinović, a powerful Bosnian noble. Hrvoje died in March 1416 and in October a Dubrovnik despatch declared that 'the whole of Bosnia is laid waste, and the barons are preparing to exterminate each other'. The rebel magnates met in a diet, and forced Ostoja to fly to Hum, where he succeeded in establishing a precarious rule, but after the year 1418 nothing more is heard of him. The magnates elected his son, Stephen Ostojić, as King, and Dubrovnik at once sent an embassy to try to obtain from him the rest of Konavle, of which a part had been given by Sandalj and a part by Paul Paulović. This request Ostojić granted, and in exchange for a yearly tribute of 500 perpera promised to protect the city. Sandalj and Paulović still retained a part of that territory, but on Paulović's death in 1419 Sandalj sold all his remaining share to Dubrovnik for 18,000 ducats, and included that of

Paulović. The latter's son, Radosav, protested, asked for Turkish help and continued to disturb Dubrovnik for years to come.

Meanwhile between 1417 and 1421 Balša had been at war with most of his neighbours, including Venice and Dubrovnik but in 1421 his stormy life came to an end, and with him the house of Balša died out, for he left no sons. Stephen, the Despot of Serbia, Sandalj Hranić, and a native prince named Stephen Maramonte, laid claim to his estates, but Venice obtained the main share, as Drivast, Ulcinj and Bar surrendered spontaneously to the Venetian Republic and thus the Zedda principality disappeared. Around 1420 Bosnia was fairly quiet; the Turks had been driven out of the country, and their leader, Isak Beg, defeated in a raid into Hungary, so that King Tvrtko was able to reoccupy Vrhbosna (later Sarajero) and Sandalj Hranić recognized his supremacy for the time being. The long civil war in Croatia and Dalmatia between the partisans of Sigismund and those of Ladislas had resulted in the acquisition of the littoral by Venice, and the only prince who remained independent of the republic was Ivan Nelipić, Count of Cetin, Klis and Rama. His estates comprised western Bosnia and some districts of Hum and Dalmatia. All through the summer of 1426 there were 4,000 Ottomans in Bosnia and they seized a number of towns and raided Croatia, Usora, and Srebrnica, while King Tvrtko did not dare to do anything against them.[43] The Dubrovnik colonies in Novo Brdo and Prizren were beseiged by the Turks and in great danger; the routes through Albania, Bosnia and Slavonia were interrupted,[44] and the inland trade at a stand-still.

Sandalj Hranić for a moment seemed to appreciate the danger, and after a visit to Dubrovnik in 1424, made peace with Radosav Paulović, who now seemed ready to sell his share of Konavle to Dubrovnik for 13,000 ducats down payment and 600 a year. The republic created him and his son Dubrovnik nobles, and gave them a palace in the city.[45] He soon repented his generous bargain, and demanded back the territory, with the excuse that Dubrovnik was fortifying it contrary to the treaty. Dubrovnik refused to evacuate it, and Radosav collected a large force to make war on them. The republic raised local levies and mercenaries in Italy, Albania, the Neretva Valley, the Krajina and Hum. More troops were levied in Dubrovnik and 2,000 more mercenaries obtained from Albania and Italy, while envoys were sent at the same time to the Hungarian court to protest against Radosav's conduct and to request that troops should be sent against him from the town of Usora. Finally, Sigismund did intervene directly, and formed an alliance with Bosnia, Dubrovnik and Sandalj against Radosav, and an agreement[46] was concluded by which the republic retained the territory it had purchased, and was to keep the interest of the money invested by Radosav at Dubrovnik for twelve years as compensation; prisoners were to be released on both sides without ransom; certain special enemies of the republic were to be exiled from Radosav's court, and all damage done to Dubrovnik's territory in future by his vojvods (dukes) was to be paid for by him (1432).

In 1431 the Council of Basle had met, and one of its most active members was Johannes Stoicus of Dubrovnik who made every effort to promote the union of the Eastern and the Western Churches, and end the religious strife in the Balkans with a view to common action against the Turks. He requested the Dubrovnik Senate to try to induce the chief princes of Serbia and Bosnia, whether schismatics or Bogomils, to send envoys to Basle. The attempt was actually made, but the whole country was in such a state of anarchy and rebellion that none of them were able to pay any attention to the matter.[47]

A war had broken out between the King of Bosnia and Stephen Lazarević, Despot of Serbia, which was destined to last for thirty years. All the Slav princes were fighting amongst themselves, and Dubrovnik had another opportunity of extending her dominions far into the interior had she been so minded. It appears the main reason why she abstained was that she realized that the Turks had earmarked all that country, and that for her to occupy it would be to court annihilation. The town of Trebinje, which was now offered to her, was refused. It seemed more prudent to content herself with a small compact territory and with acting the part of intermediary between East and West, civilization and barbarism, Christianity and Islam, than to aspire to dangerous conquests. In 1443 Stephen Turtko died and was succeeded by Stephen Thomas who in September 1444 held a diet of magnates at Kreševo, where Dubrovnik envoys came to greet him on his accession. He confirmed the republic's possession of the Primorije and of Konavle, for which he was to receive the Serbian tribute of 2,000 perpera and the Bosnian tribute of 500. This shows that Bosnia was once more the chief South-Slavonic state and had annexed all the western part of the former dominions of the Serbian Tsars. Serbia itself was little more than a vassal state of the Turks. Even so Stephen Kosača, Duke of St. Sava had important relations with Dubrovnik. Like so many other Serbian princes he was a Bogomil by religion, and when Stephen Thomas, King of Bosnia, abjured that heresy and became a Catholic, many of his Bogomil subjects fled into the Duchy to escape persecution, and others into Turkish territory, while his Orthodox subjects took refuge in Serbia. This caused further discords between Bosnia and Serbia. Like his predecessor Sandalj Hranić, Kosača was one of the fated rulers of the Balkans; his attitude contributed to the Turkish conquest of the South Slavonic lands although he tried to resist them later. His aim was simply to consolidate and extend his own dominions at the expense of his neighbours, and he availed himself for this purpose of the assistance which the Turks were always only too ready to give. He also proved Dubrovnik's most inveterate enemy. In July 1450 he was still on good terms with the republic,[48] but in 1451 a minor dispute arose, and Kosača, out of revenge, raised customs duties on Dubrovnik trade, opened salt-markets in the Naretva, reoccupied part of Konavle, and laid waste the republic's territory. A more likely reason is probably to be found in Kosača's over-mastering ambition. Fortunately for Dubrovnik the King of Bosnia was hostile to Kosača on account of certain indignities suffered by the latter. For the same reason his son Vladislav left Dubrovnik and raised a rebellion against his father, allying himself with the republic, to whom he promised to give back Konavle as soon as he was master of the Duchy. In December 1451 Dubrovnik contracted an alliance with Stephen Thomas, who undertook

> 'to declare war without delay and carry it on without interruption against the Duke Stephen Vukčić (Kosača), his government, his cities, and his servants, with all the glorious strength of Our kingdom, with Our servants, and Our friends in open warfare, as is suitable to Our lordship and Our kingdom, provided that no obstacle impede us and no Turkish army attack us'.[49]

The Despot of Serbia and other minor potentates joined the league against 'this perfidious heretic and Patarene'.[50] Hostilities commenced in 1452, and at first Kosača was unlucky, for a number of his barons rose against him and joined Dubrovnik, and the commander of the league's forces was his own son. Soon after a civil war broke out in Bosnia, while Kosača was devastating Dubrovnik's territory. In July 1453 Vladislav expressed a wish to make peace with his father, and the Duke, thus strengthened, again invaded Konavle, took Cavtat and captured a Dubrovnik contingent under Marino Cerva near Brgat. Peace was at last made through the intervention of the Papal legate and a Turkish Vizir, and signed at Novi, April 10, 1454, confirming the *status quo*. Kosača promised Dubrovnik that he would never attack them again 'save by order of the Grand Signior, the Sultan of Turkey, Mehmet Beg' (Mohammed II).[51] It is thus clear that already the Sultan's influence in this part of the world was predominant.

The Balkans were indeed in a most terrible condition at this time – the Turks threatened it from the south, the Ban of Croatia from the west, and internally the Bogomils were in open revolt and protected by the Duke of St. Sava. The Papal legate managed, however, to bring about a reconciliation between the latter and Stephen Tomašević (son of King Stephen Thomas), who now retired to Jajce. There he collected his magnates around him, and was solemnly crowned, being the first and last Bosnian king who was crowned with the favour of the Catholic Church.[52] He granted many privileges to Dubrovnik, confirmed the republic in possession of all its territories, and promised to pay his father's debts.[53] By the end of 1461 he managed to make peace with the Ban of Croatia and his own rebels and obtained help against the Turks from Venice, Dubrovnik and elsewhere. Kosača himself was in danger from the Turks, who only supported him as long as he was of any use to them; he too applied to Dubrovnik for money and ammunition. Nevertheless the Bosnian King's Catholicism had alienated his Bogomil subjects, many of whom had taken refuge among the Turks, while several of the magnates were holding treasonable intercourse with the enemy. When the time came the Turks were in no doubt as to what to do with Stephen Tomašević. The Queen-mother, Catherine, was forced to escape by way of Ston to Dubrovnik, like many of the countless fugitives from Bosnia who now fled to the Dalmatian cities, especially the ever-hospitable Dubrovnik.

Hercegovina was still ruled by Kosača, but Turkish raids from southern Bosnia were frequent, and it was important to keep the enemy from the Neretva's mouth. The town of Počitelj, came to be the centre of a series of operations against the Turks which lasted until 1470. In 1466 Dubrovnik gave '4 schopetos parvos, 4 tarassios de minoribus', 200 lb of powder, 1,000 beams, and 1,000 'clavos' for the defence of Počitelj, and two carpenters, two *marangoni*, (shipbuilders) and some boats. Three bombards, building materials, ropes, bullets, provisions and more firelocks and boats were added later, together with a staff of boat-builders and engineers.[54]

In 1466 Kosača died, having deposited his will at Dubrovnik. By its terms his estates were divided between his three sons, Stephen, Vladislav, and Vlatko, but their possessions were constantly menaced by the Turks, and the youngest brother became a renegade and took the name of Achmed Beg. The other two soon quarrelled among themselves, and each asked for Turkish assistance. In 1469 Hamsa Beg raided Dubrovnik's territory, and an attack on the city was momentarily expected. A second raid was made in 1470, and Postranja and Konavle were laid waste, the castle of Soko alone holding out; Dubrovnik merchants in Trebinje were also plundered. As Hamsa refused to hear reason, the garrison was increased, the galleys armed, and the moat before the Porta Pile dug.[55] Also at this time Počitelj was being beseiged. In fact this was not the last time.

Relations with Venice

The Dubrovnik Republic was not only in constant danger from the powerful landward enemies which surrounded it on all sides, but also from the sea. The Venetians, who were always trying to claim the monopoly of the Adriatic, were ever anxious to increase their influence and to become absolute masters of Dubrovnik, as they were of the other Dalmatian towns, and after their retirement from Dubrovnik in 1358 they made many attempts to reinstate their authority. Venice, having lost Dalmatia with Dubrovnik her chief naval base, turned her attention towards Albania and the adjoining Slavonic countries. Trade was encouraged, and the foundations were laid for the revival of Venetian influence in the Adriatic.[56]

In 1378, in consequence of the intrigues of Venice and Genoa to obtain a predominant position at Constantinople, war broke out between the two republics – the famous Chioggia War – in which Dubrovnik too was involved. The Genoese induced Francesco Carrara, Lord of Padua, who had been humbled but not subdued by Venice to join them, and further help was obtained from Ludovik of Hungary. Dubrovnik, as vassal of that potentate, joined the coalition, but Venice, undismayed, made all preparations for war, and invested Vettor Pisani with the supreme command at sea. A Venetian victory off Cape Antium (Anzio) was won on May 30, and Pisani took Šibenik and Kotor by storm; these and other towns on the Adriatic coast

which his garrisons occupied were harried and blockaded by Dubrovnik vessels, who also seized this opportunity to destroy the salt-
pans of Kotor thus ridding Dubrovnik of a dangerous competitor.[57]
The republic was in great fear of an attack by the Venetian fleet and
made desperate efforts to strengthen the defences of the city and at
Ston. The government also asked for assistance from Tvrtko, King of
Bosnia, who offered them a contingent; but on hearing that he was
bargaining with the Venetians, possibly with a view to a move
against Dubrovnik, it was refused. On October 14, 1378, the Genoese
fleet under Fieschi put in at Dubrovnik,[58] where a local galley joined
it, and the admiral received two bombards and a present of money
from the republic. Armed barques issued forth from the city to
scour the Adriatic and obtain news of the movements of the Venetian fleet, which were at once transmitted to the Ban of Dalmatia
and Croatia at Zadar, while privateers cruised about to plunder the
enemy's merchantmen. Dubrovnik's ships were, in fact, the eyes of
the allied fleet.

The Senate sent a squadron out under the Stefano Sorgo to capture
all Venetian or Kotorian ships found in south Dalmatian waters,[59]
while envoys went to Kotor to stir up the people to rebel against
Venice and return to Hungarian allegiance. At first Kotor refused
still fearing the Venetians, but then a joint Genoese-Dubrovnik fleet
made a demonstration against the town, and the authorities promised
to raise the Hungarian standard on a certain date. They failed to do
so, and intrigued instead with the King of Bosnia against Dubrovnik
plundered its grain ships, and captured the sentinels guarding the
approaches to the city on Mt. Srđ. After the total defeat of the
Venetian fleet off Pula in May Dubrovnik pursued its operations
against Kotor by land and sea with renewed vigour, and on June 26[60]
the town once more returned to Hungarian allegiance.[61]

Meanwhile the Genoese had carried the war almost to the very
gates of Venice, and were besieging Chioggia. A Dubrovnik contingent under Matteo Giorgi was of great assistance to them in the
siege, owing to Giorgi's knowledge of the use of artillery,[62] and would
have prevented the blockade of the Genoese fleet, by closing the
harbour with sunken boats, if only his advice had been followed.[63]
On the defeat of the Genoese the Dubrovnik galleys managed to
escape, and saved a number of the fugitives whose vessels had been
sunk (June 24, 1380). Desultory fighting continued for a few months
longer, in which Dubrovnik's galleys took part, and in 1381 peace

was signed at Turin. Although in the end the Genoese had been defeated, Venice was by no means victorious, and had to confirm her renunciation of Dalmatia, much to the satisfaction of Dubrovnik.

Two aspects of this war directly affected Dubrovnik. Firstly the out-come of the struggle for Tenedos island in the Levant, and secondly the action taken against Venetian re-occupation of Dalmatia particularly Kotor. The possession of Turkish held Tenedos Island was the 'raison d'etre' of this war.[64] Its strategic position at the entrance to the Dardanelles was important for both Venetian and Genoan policy. In the three-cornered fight the Turks held the island, whilst Venice and Genoa continued their own struggle in the Adriatic. With the problem of Tenedos Island resolved Dubrovnik continued and extended her trading influence in Asia Minor where much needed corn supplies could be bought from the Turks. Secondly the Republic of Kotor continued to remain in a state of semi-independence. It was usually on good terms with Venice, and the town contained a flourishing commercial colony of Venetians. Ensconced in the deep and well-sheltered inlet known as the Bay of Kotor its trade was active and its mercantile fleet large. Its relations with Dubrovnik were characterized by mutual jealousy, owing partly to commercial rivalry (especially on account of the disputed salt monopoly), and partly to the intrigues of Venice, who wished to prevent all possible coalitions of the Dalmatian townships against her own supremacy,[65] but now Venetian influence in the port declined.

Nevertheless, amidst all the confusion in the Balkans, and the internal complications of the Hungarian kingdom during the first decade of the fifteenth century, Venice was able to obtain virtual control of almost the whole of the Dalmatian coastline. In 1409 the Venetians began to re-establish their rule over Dalmatia. In that year Ladislas of Naples, who claimed the throne of Hungary sold his potential rights to Venice for 100,000 ducats[66] together with the port of Zadar. This caused an outbreak of hostilities between the Venetians and Sigismund, who regarded Dalmatia as an integral part of his dominions. While the two powers were fighting the common enemy was advancing, and in 1411 a Dubrovnik despatch announced that the Turks had taken and burnt Srebrnica. In 1413 negotiations were opened between Hungary and Venice, in which Dubrovnik took part, and while Sigismund agreed to give up the greater part of Dalmatia, Dubrovnik asked for and obtained the lease of the three coveted islands of Hvar, Korčula and Brač. Dubrovnik had hoped to obtain full ownership, but even the lease was a great point gained, and the republic thought that it would eventually become vested into absolute possession. The islanders, however, were not well disposed towards their new masters, and were only forced into submission by a naval demonstration. A Count was appointed for each island, to remain in office for six months, with a salary in which Dubrovnik was to pay one-third and the islanders the remainder.[67] This acquisition might have been the beginning of great things for the republic had its policy been a little less narrowly provincial and nervous. Its territory was now fairly large, its commerce and finances flourishing, and with its intimate connection with the dying kingdom of Bosnia it might have extended its influence far into the hinterland, establishing a strong Latin-Slavonic state as a bulwark against the advancing Turks. At this time, however, Dubrovnik's hostility against Venice revived and the Senate wrote to protest against Venetian depredations in Albanian and Sicilian waters. Dubrovnik still desired the supremacy of Hungary in the Adriatic, and although that cause was lost, it tried to bolster it up by inducing Kotor to return to Hungarian allegiance. The maze of intrigue and counter-intrigue between Venice, Hungary, Dubrovnik, Bosnia and the various Slav and Albanian princes now became hopelessly involved, and no one trusted each other. Dubrovnik's policy is well explained in a despatch,[68] in which it is stated that the republic

'had to be on good terms with these lords of Slavonia, for every day our merchants and our goods pass through their hands and their territory, and we fear lest they (the merchants) should suffer injury'.

When Balša demanded a number of Dubrovnik shipbuilders to repair his vessels for operations against Venice the Senate refused, fearing to incur the latter's displeasure.

The protection and promotion of trade was the key-note of Dubrovnik's policy, and everything was done with that end in view. In the meantime the Dubrovnik Senate acquired much knowledge concerning the affairs of Italy and of the East from Dubrovnik traders, and communicated the information to Sigismund. Thus the latter learned about the advance of the Turks in Bosnia at the instigation of Vuk, the son of Prince Lazar, who wished to get possession of his brother's principality. Ladislas continued to send piratical fleets to

H

Dalmatia, which did much damage to Dubrovnik's commerce, but its citizens revenged themselves by relieving Korčula, which was attacked by the Apulian fleet.

'With the favour of St. Blaize (Sv. Vlah) we shot so many arrows and javelins against the enemy, and did their ships so much damage with our bombards, that many of their men were killed or wounded. They abandoned much property and arms, and not only desisted from the siege, but abandoned these parts altogether'.[69]

The year 1420 opens a new epoch in the history of Dalmatia, for it marks the final reconquest of the country by Venice and the withdrawal of Hungary from the Adriatic. In 1409 the great republic reoccupied Zadar, and in 1412 Šibenik. She seized the opportunity of Sigismund's engagement in the Hussite war in 1420 to seize Hvar, Brač, Korčula and Omiš. Trogir defended by a strong Hungarian garrison, held out for a little while, but ended by surrendering too. Split fell next, and Kotor after having for some time owed allegiance to Sandalj Hranić, now spontaneously surrendered to the Venetians, who took possession on March 8. Thus they regained the whole of Dalmatia, including the Croatian towns of Novigrad, Nin and Vrana. Dubrovnik alone remained outside their sphere and it is likely that Venice may have thought of uniting her Dalmatian possessions by re-occupying Dubrovnik.

A disadvantage of this situation is that a single state sometimes attempts to dominate and monopolize the whole basin. This is what had happened in the Adriatic for by the close of the thirteenth century Venice had assumed sovereign jurisdiction over the whole sea, but during the fourteenth century this position had gradually been broken. After 1420 Venice was again able to assert the idea of 'mare clausum' on the Adriatic, with the Dalmatian coast supplying the republic with raw materials and providing markets, while the smooth Italian coastline, offered few sites suitable for the rise of rival ports, and prevented the establishment of competing cities. This situation affected Dubrovnik in the years after 1420 for her fleets fought a number of battles up to 1444 when Venice joined Aragon, the Papacy, and the Holy Roman Emperor in recognizing Dubrovnik's neutrality.[70] Even so, the old jealousy of Venice was by no means dead, and Dubrovnik was suspicious of her every movement, fearing that by a *coup de main* she might capture the city, and thus unite her Dalmatian possessions with Kotor and gain an unbroken line of posts all down the Adriatic. Dubrovnik's fears of Venetian hostility were justified in the following year. Venice was then at war with Alfonso of Ferrara; the causes of that war offer a curious parallel with those of Venetian hostility towards Dubrovnik. Like Dubrovnik, Ferrara was an independent state placed between the main Venetian possessions and an outpost – in this case Ravenna. In addition there

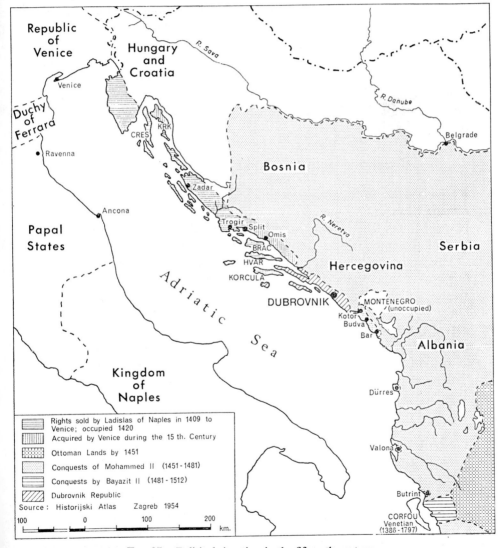

FIG. 27. Political situation in the fifteenth century.

were disagreements on account of the salt monopoly and the navigation dues, as in the case of Dubrovnik. A Venetian flotilla was block-
ading the entrance to the Po and besieging the city. Some Dubrovnik
galleys happened to be on the River Po, and were detained by Ippolito
d'Este, who utilized them and their crews for the defence. When the
Venetian fleet under Angelo Trevisan attempted to sail up river it
was repulsed by shore batteries, helped by Dubrovnik gunners. The
Venetian government out of revenge issued a decree which greatly
hampered Dubrovnik's trade with Venice and her possessions (September 21, 1484). Dubrovnik residents and merchants were expelled
from Venice, and all her ships forced to pay 100 ducats as anchorage
dues, while some of them were seized as compensation for the
damage suffered at Ferrara.[71] Other impositions were also levied,
and although the dispute was settled soon after, mutual distrust
continued as before.

Relations with the Turks

A new power now made its appearance as a factor in the history
of Europe, the Ottoman Turks, who were destined in the space of
two centuries to conquer the whole of the Balkan peninsula, a large
part of Dalmatia, and nearly the whole of Hungary.

The Dubrovnik Senate had the foresight to understand the growing importance of the Ottoman Turks, and obtained from Urban V
an exemption to trade with the Infidel. It was formerly thought that
Dubrovnik contracted commercial agreements with the Sultans of
Egypt, Syria, and Konia in 1359, and in 1365 obtained from the
Sultan Murād a firman granting the citizens of Dubrovnik freedom
to trade in all parts of the Ottoman dominions and protection for
their commercial factories, in exchange for a yearly tribute of 500
ducats. However it has more recently been proved that the charter
which Dubrovnik was supposed to have obtained from Sultan Murād
I (1359–89), or even from Sultan Orhan (1326–59) does not exist.[72]
Nevertheless it still appears that Dubrovnik was probably one of the
first Christian states to make a treaty with the Ottoman Turks, and
its citizens were enabled to penetrate into the remotest parts of the
Turkish Empire and form permanent settlements there at a time
when other Christians were either excluded altogether or limited to
a few coastal towns. The tributes the city paid for these advantages
proved a most profitable investment, although its amount was re-

peatedly increased with the passage of time. The first Turkish invasion of Europe occurred in 1341, when Osman I (1288–1326) crossed the Bosporos to intervene in the civil wars of the Eastern Empire. Several minor raids followed, while Orhan, who may be regarded as the founder of the Ottoman power, established his capital at Brusa. In 1358 his son Suleiman again invaded Europe, and Thrace was soon filled with Turkish colonies. In 1359 Gallipoli, 'the key of Europe', was occupied and rebuilt as a Turkish town. In 1360 both Orhan and his son Suleiman died, and his second son Murād succeeded to the throne. The latter in the following year captured Adrianople, which henceforward was to be the seat of the Turkish government, and the headquarters for the attacks on the Greek Empire, the Serbs, and the Bulgarians. In 1370 a Turkish army of 70,000 men under Murād spread into Macedonia, but was driven back by the Serbs under King Vukašin and his brother Ulješa. Feudal disunity characterized the latter days of the Second Bulgarian Empire, so that when during the fourteenth century, the rising tide of Turkish expansion reached their very doorsteps, these feudal lords failed to take energetic action against the common foe. At first the Turks were content to obtain control through alliances, and where force had to be used, to restore the defeated local rulers as their vassals. After the fall of Niš in 1375, and of Sofia in 1382, almost all southern Bulgaria was in Turkish hands and only northern Bulgaria retained nominal independence as a vassal state. In 1392, all Bulgaria passed under the Turkish yoke and was to remain so until the nineteenth century. Meanwhile Sultan Murād I prepared a further expedition against the Slavs. The Serbian-Bosnian army, under the leadership of Prince Lazar, with Marko Kraljević as chief lieutenant, had its headquarters at Priština, in the Kossovo plain – a long plateau surrounded by mountains extending from Verisović to Mitrovica. The Turkish army was commanded by the Sultan Murād in person; the right wing was led by his son Bayazet, and the left by his son Yakub. The fight began early on Wednesday, June 15, 1389, and raged all day. For a long time the fortunes of the battle seemed doubtful, and both sides fought with heroic courage. At last Bayazet succeeded by a sudden attack in throwing the Serbian left wing into confusion. Then Vlatko Hranić and the Bosnian contingent began to give way, and the main body of the Serbs was driven slowly back. At first it was thought the Slavs had won and the Dubrovnik Republic congratulated the Bosnian King on his victory. Even when the true

result was known no one realized at the time what a crushing blow
had fallen on the Slavonic peoples of the Balkans. Even so the Turks
did not follow up their victory. Unfortunately the Serbs and other
South Slavonic peoples, by their civil wars and mutual jealousies,
prepared the way for their greatest enemy and that of all Christendom. In these events the part played by Dubrovnik was a curious
one. At one moment the republic actually tried to arbitrate in the
quarrels of the Serbian princes and to induce them to unite against
the invader. From the point of view of general European history
Dubrovnik's chief interest lies in the action of its government in
obtaining information as to the movements of the Turkish armies.

Dubrovnik citizens were subsequently on good terms with the
Turks and permitted to visit all parts of the Empire, even when other
Europeans were excluded. (Dubrovnik merchants and agents sent
home despatches which are preserved in the city records, giving each
stage of the Turkish conquest.) As in the 1350's so again in the 1390's
did the citizens of Dubrovnik realize the impending danger of the
Turks in Europe. During the last decade of the fourteenth century
the Turks occupied Macedonia, and pressed into southern Serbia.
According to Dubrovnik documents relations were renewed with the
Turks in 1392 when one Teodor Gisli travelled from Novo Brdo to
see the 'Imperator Turchus' on behalf of Dubrovnik traders who were
being arrested by Turkish soldiers.[73] The results of this venture are
unknown but four years later a letter of safe conduct (litera
securitatis) is mentioned as coming from the Turks; in the same letter
Dubrovnik traders were given permission to trade in Serbia.[74] In
1397 a treaty was drawn up between the Republic of Dubrovnik and
the Turkish Sultan, allowing Dubrovnik's citizens the freedom to
trade in any part of his empire.[75] At the same time the Dubrovnik
government had friendly relations with the Pasha of Skoplje with
whom there is a noticeable amount of correspondence.[76] In 1399 the
first Turkish ambassador arrived at Dubrovnik with a letter of safe
conduct from Sultan Bayezit I.[77] So great was the skill of Dubrovnik
diplomacy that such events were allowed to take place without
offending the Hungarian throne, the citizens of Dubrovnik realizing
that they had to live by trade irrespective of who were the political
rulers of a country.

During the first half of the fifteenth century Dubrovnik came more
and more into the Turkish sphere of influence, although continuing
to recognize Hungarian sovereignty until the battle of Mohács in

1526. Gradually all Dubrovnik's neighbouring territories were directly incorporated into the Ottoman Empire, yet from the beginning the city was determined to maintain good relations with the new rulers of its markets. Even so many Dubrovnik citizens were convinced right up to the middle of the fifteenth century, that the Turks would soon be expelled from the Balkans. Meanwhile the Turkish war machine pressed relentlessly forward. The enemy's headquarters were at Üsküb (Skopje) where many raids into Bosnia and Albania were made. In 1415 the Turks invaded Bosnia for the third time, and raiding parties came as far as Šibenik and Omiš, so that the Dubrovnik Senate ordered its islanders to arm light galleys to co-operate with those of Dubrovnik and Ston. The ridges dividing the hinterland from the sea were anxiously watched, for fear of Turkish attack. In 1416 Sigismund announced to Dubrovnik his intention of making war on a grand scale against the Turks, and declared that the property of all those who helped the enemy would be confiscated. In the same letter he declared that the three islands of Hvar, Brač and Korčula were withdrawn from Dubrovnik's suzerainty (September 21–23, 1416). No reason was given for the withdrawal of the concession, but it was probably due to the somewhat high-handed manner with which the republic had governed its new possessions. Curiously enough, the Senate did not seem very unwilling to lose them. Until 1430 direct contact by Dubrovnik officials with the Sultan was avoided, as it was feared that such relations would ultimately lead to his demanding a tribute. Nevertheless Dubrovnik did maintain friendly relations with local Turkish officials such as the Sandjakbeg of Skopje, who in turn provided Dubrovnik merchants with letters of introduction to certain Albanian towns (Kruja, Valona) after the Turks had captured them from Venice. Also various local rulers in Bosnia requested Turkish intervention in settling local disputes, and similarly Dubrovnik did not hesitate to call for Turkish mediation when a war broke out over Konavle with a neighbour who had already submitted to Turkish vassaldom.[78] Meanwhile the Slavonic princes were averse to settling their differences, and continued to war among themselves, while Turkish inroads were made through the weak defensive wall that Bosnia still provided. By 1430 all southern Bosnia was a Turkish dependency and in 1436 the Sultan Murād II (1421–51) again invaded Bosnia, and captured Vrhbosna (Sarajevo), which henceforth became the Turkish headquarters in the country.[79]

King Tvrtko now returned with Hungarian help, but he found his whole kingdom devastated, Usora, Srebrnica, and Zvornik held by the Despot of Serbia, and the rest by the Turks, or by vojvods who were Turkish vassals. He was therefore forced to agree to pay the Sultan a yearly tribute of 25,000 ducats. The real ruler of Bosnia was now Murād, who in 1439 annexed the territory of Serbia, and invited Dubrovnik to send envoys with a tribute. The envoy was duly dispatched, but without the requested tribute. Thereupon, the Sultan had all Dubrovnik merchants in his dominions thrown into gaol, and refused to release them until the republic gave way. After lengthy negotiations the republic's government conceded and agreed to pay an annual tribute of 1,000 ducats. In exchange Dubrovnik received the treaty ('Ahd-name') of 1442, which was to be the basis of all future relations between Turkey and Dubrovnik. In this privilege the Sultan alludes to Bosnia as part of his own dominions, and allows Dubrovnik merchants to trade 'in Romania, Bulgaria, Wallachia, Serbia, Albania, Bosnia, and all other lands, places and cities under my rule'.[80] Nevertheless Dubrovnik continued to play a double-edged game. By 1440, Murād had conquered the whole of Serbia with the exception of Belgrade which was gallantly defended by the Hungarian garrison commanded by Giovanni Luccari from Dubrovnik. The Sultan retired baffled, but the Serbian Despot, George Branković was forced to escape and took refuge with his treasure at Dubrovnik. The following year the Sultan, Isak Beg, and the Pasha of Romania sent to demand the surrender of the Despot, offering the republic his treasure and an increase of territory between Kotor and the River Drina as a bribe. The citizens refused to violate the laws of hospitality, maintaining that

> 'We should rather give up our city, our wives, and our children than George or his family, for we have nothing but our good faith; and we should do the same with you if you came here under our safe-conduct'.

Even so it was hinted to George that he had better leave the city. He agreed, and went to Hungary instead on a Dubrovnik galley. Murād was determined to punish the republic for this refusal, and arrested all the Dubrovnik citizens in his dominions, the ambassadors escaping with difficulty to Constantinople. He then prepared to attack the city by land and sea, and the citizens strengthened their defences, increased their military forces, enlisted foreign merccnaries, and secured the services of an Italian engineer. The Turkish menace was notified to the Pope and to the King of Bosnia, while at the same time the Senate tried to bribe the Sultan by offering to raise the tribute to 1,400 ducats. Murād finally respected the laws of hospitality; but the real reason is probably to be found in his alarm at the attitude of Hungary, and in the fact that the city's defences promised a long and difficult siege. In any case Murād was pacified, and in 1443 Ali Beg arrived at Dubrovnik, and a treaty of peace was signed which returned to the *status quo*.[81]

The easy Turkish conquests in the Balkans could have been the direct result of religious strife between the Bogomil and Catholic Croats. It was the view of the former that, if they had to choose between Catholicism and Islam, the latter was the lesser of the two evils. As for the more or less religiously indifferent nobles they accepted Islam in order to conserve their estates and their privileges.[82] The perennial threat of Turkish conquest did not put an end to the nobles' anarchical feuds. They called in the Turks to judge these disputes and, when necessary, they purchased Ottoman good-will by paying annual tributes. Their whole mentalities and energies revolved around the winning of bits of land from one another. They do not seem to even have thought of combining to present a common front against the Ottomans. Nor did the Church of Rome do anything to heal this feudal anarchy with all its fateful consequences for the Christian world. On the contrary the Papacy stimulated the disorder through its continued persecution of the Bogomils. Until the very end Rome put the duty of fighting the Bosnian heresy ahead of the necessity of opposing the Turks. Hence the triumphal march of the latter could not long be stayed.[83] More foresighted was Pope Eugene IV (1431–1447) who prepared an international crusade against the Turks, and also sent a brief to Dubrovnik. In it he requested that a contingent of two galleys should be provided by the republic, as well as the loan of three more, to be paid for by himself, to escort his legate, the Bishop of Corona, which request was granted.[84] Shortly afterwards the Senate informed the King of Hungary that nineteen galleys had touched at Dubrovnik and that they were now anchored at Corfu, while some more Burgundian vessels, and seven from Aragon, were expected at Modon. The land war in the Balkans began badly for the Christians. On November 11 the Hungarians were utterly routed at Varna, in Bulgaria, and King Ladislas was killed. The young Ladislas Posthumus was then elected

H*

King of Hungary. One of the Sultan's first acts after this fight was to raise the Dubrovnik tribute as a punishment for sending galleys to join the Christian fleet.[85] George, Despot of Serbia, with characteristic treachery, had arrested and imprisoned the famous leader John Hunyadi after the Hungarian defeat. The Dubrovnik envoy, Damiano Giorgi, who had come to Belgrade to return the Despot's treasure, made every effort to obtain Hunyadi's release, but as George would not hear reason, he induced the Serbs to liberate him without the Despot's consent. Giorgi and his family were afterwards taken into the Hungarian service by the new King, Matthew Corvinus, as a reward, and given high emoluments. It is interesting that former citizens never ceased to work in the interests of their native city by means of their influence at Court. The efforts of Dubrovnik's citizens in foreign countries were among the chief causes by which the republic attained and maintained its international position. Also it should be noted that during the war Dubrovnik had made gifts and paid tribute to the Sultan to secure immunity for the Dubrovnik merchants in Turkish territory and obtained the renewal of the privileges; the King of Hungary does not seem to have taken much exception to this.[86]

In 1447 war between Hungary and the Turks broke out anew, and Hunyadi led an expedition across the Danube, but the following year he was defeated on the ill-omened field of Kossovo. On this, as on other occasions, Dubrovnik sent a number of boats to Albania to pick up the fugitives who had escaped across country from the fury of the invaders, and sent them back to Hungary or gave them asylum in the city. Peace was concluded, but fighting continued in Albania, and we now find the name Skanderberg, the great Albanian hero, mentioned for the first time in Dubrovnik's annals. The Senate informed the Hungarian King that the Turks were besieging Kruja, Skanderberg's stronghold. Dubrovnik had furnished him both with money and provisions, and he frequently came to the city to refit his fleet. He was now successful, raised the siege of Kruja, and expelled the Turks from a large part of his country.

In 1453 the whole of Europe was shaken to its foundations with the capture of Constantinople by the Turks.[87] This event, however, did not have much direct effect on the Balkans, particularly Bosnia, as the Turkish conquest there had already begun. Every month some fresh raid was made, dealing death and destruction, and yet everywhere the invaders found Slavonic princes ready to help them against others who still held out.[88] The first consequence which the fall of Constantinople had on Dubrovnik was the raising of her tribute to the Sultan to 5,000 ducats,[89] and the second, her city became a haven of refuge for fugitives from the territories invaded by the Turks. Many were of distinguished families, who when given food and shelter were then sent to Ancona free of charge.[90] This again shows Dubrovnik's diplomacy, for the Senate feared that as many of them were such distinguished people (many were Greeks from Constantinople) the Sultan might use this as a pretext for aggression.

After the capture of Constantinople it was hoped that Mohammed II (1451–81) would content himself with being overlord of the remaining Balkan lands not under his direct sway; but he soon evinced more dangerous intentions, and proceeded to establish his complete ascendancy, destroying all the independent or semi-independent states. Of these the first to be attacked was Serbia. Mohammed's object was to prepare for the struggle with Hungary, the only power which he seriously feared, for Genoa was now weak, and Venice's first thought was

'not to recover the bulwark of Christendom from the hands of the Muslim, but to preserve her own commercial privileges under the Infidel ruler'.[91]

In 1454 the Turks invaded Serbia captured Ostravica and Smederevo, and in the following year captured Novo Brdo with its valuable mines.[92] The republic suffered ill-effects from this capture because the Dubrovnik merchants who had a flourishing trade there were driven out. There was little they could do and by 1459 the whole of Serbia including Belgrade was under Turkish rule.

In this same year, 1459, the final conquest of Bosnia was begun, the Sultan finally completing the campaign in 1463. Dubrovnik's main concern during this period was to try and induce the Sultan to reduce their tribute, stating that the constant troubles in Slavonia and Serbia had made them very poor, but this request was refused.[93] Negotiations were then conducted with the Beglerbeg of Rumelia, and in 1458 a new agreement was finally drawn up stipulating that the annual tribute must now be 1,500 ducats.[94] There was nothing for it but to pay as the Turkish block-houses were only a few kilometres from Dubrovnik's gates, and an attack was feared at any moment. The tribute was not paid without reward, for the citizens of Dubrovnik obtained many new privileges in trade; moreover the increase was in part due to the fact that the Turks were the successors to various native princes whom they dispossessed,[95] and to whom the republic had formerly paid tribute. The one danger was that the Turks should suddenly desire to capture the city, as on more than one occasion they had been at the point of doing. It required all the skilful diplomacy of the Senate to avoid this contingency.

This fear of Turkish attack led to the strengthening of the fortifications on the churches outside the city; houses in the suburbs of Pile and Ploče were pulled down, wells at Rijeka, Dubrovačka, Gruž and the neighbourhood poisoned, and the government was authorized to destroy the aqueduct if necessary. The fortifications at Ston were improved, and a local count entrusted with the defence of the frontier. All Dubrovnik galleys in Dalmatia and elsewhere were recalled to defend the home waters, crossbowmen and rowers were levied in all the islands, a corps of infantry and lances raised in Apulia and a Herzegovinian contingent under Ivaniš Vlatković was formed; also a loan of 15,000 ducats was raised to provide for war expenses.[96] During his raid through the Duchy, the Sultan came very near to Dubrovnik, which he was determined to attack and occupy in person, as it would be a most useful port on the Adriatic and a basis for operations against Venice and Italy. While processions and prayers of intercession were being held in the city a messenger arrived from the Beglerbeg of Rumelia ordering the republic to pay homage to Mohammed. This was done; but the Sultan demanded that the citizens should give up all their territory to him, and that the ambassadors should follow him to Thrace as hostages. The Senate was filled with consternation, as the surrender of the territory would be only a preliminary to the capture of the city itself. One of the Senators, Serafino Bona, proposed that a reply should be drafted to the effect that while the republic was ready to give up its territory to the Turks, it would place the city itself under the direct protection of Hungary and admit a Hungarian garrison. This diplomatic answer saved the situation, for the Sultan, who had heard of the great preparations which were being made in Hungary, had no mind to be attacked by the enemy from the south-west as well as from the north.

In 1474 the Turks renewed their incursions into Albania. Turkish influence was being felt in Albania as early as 1417, (the local tribesmen sold the port of Valona to Venice in 1417; the Turks attacked and took the town in the same year) and by 1479 they had the whole country under their control, leaving the Venetians with little influence in that area. Venice now held only Dürres, Bar, Valona and Butrint, all the rest of Albania being occupied by the enemy. As some citizens from Dubrovnik had taken part in the defence of Albania, the Sultan again raised the republic's tribute this time to 10,000 ducats.[97] (Growing Turkish influence on Dubrovnik's border had resulted in a series of such increases in the annual tribute until by 1481 it had risen to 12,500 ducats.) During these operations Dubrovnik was more than once in serious danger, and Pope Sixtus V (1471–1484) granted full indulgence to all those who contributed to the defence of the city whether natives or foreigners.

'In oculis Turchorum quasi propugnaculum sita existit, maribus satis munita, florenti populo decorata ac armis et aliis intrumentis bellicis abundans, et hominum suorum virilitate parata adversus prædictorum incursus semper existit'.

He believed the Sultan was planning to attack Dubrovnik with an immense army, and it could not hold out unless other Christians came to its assistance.[98] The city, however, was saved once more by the crushing defeat of the Turkish army by the Hungarians in Transylvania.

In 1481 Mohammed II died, and on the succession of his son Bayazit II, many of the pashas used this as an excuse to make fresh conquests, stating that on the death of the Sultan all the treaties made by him were invalid unless renewed by his successor. Venice found that the negotiations proved difficult, and lasted over a year. Dubrovnik was more fortunate; all her privileges were confirmed and the tribute, which had been 15,000 ducats for the year 1480, was reduced to 12,500 ducats,[99] and 500 to his Ministers as a bribe, while it agreed to pay an additional 100 a year to Aliza, the newly-appointed Sandjakberg of Hercegovina. It is said that Aliza had already come to an understanding with the commander of the Hungarian guard in Dubrovnik to enter the town, but the Senate discovered the plot in time.[100]

In 1482, Bayazit successfully conquered the whole of Hercegovina, and Dubrovnik's contact with the Turks became even closer. Therefore by 1500 the whole of Bosnia,[101] Hercegovina, all Albania, excepting a few Venetian towns, parts of Croatia, Slavonia and Hungary were in Turkish hands. Dalmatia as far as the mouth of the Neretva River was still Venetian, and so was Kotor, although the Turks held a strip of the coast around the bay. Dubrovnik's land frontier was thus encompassed on all sides by the Infidel save on the north, where the marshy delta of the Neretva divided it from Venetian territory.

Relations with Southern Italy

During the second half of the fifteenth century difficult conditions prevailed in the hinterland, which subsequently caused a decline in trade for Dubrovnik. Coupled with this was the need for a constant watch to be kept on Venetian activities in the Adriatic. Dubrovnik found it therefore a refreshing change to possess a stable political relationship with southern Italy. There had always been friendly relations between Dubrovnik and southern Italy, but these reached a climax during the reigns of Alfonso I (1416–1458) and his son Ferdinand I (1458–1494), in the Aragonese kingdom of Naples, and, like Dubrovnik, adversaries of Venice.

Alfonso realized that southern Italy would stagnate without its trade and maritime relations[102] and saw Dubrovnik as a useful commercial partner. In 1442 he united Aragon and Sicily which inadvertantly increased Dubrovnik's trading area at the expense of Venice. This came at a most appropriate time, for Dubrovnik during the mid-fifteenth century was going through a difficult period with the Turkish conquest of Bosnia and Serbia disrupting commerce in her hinterland. Further, southern Italy's richness in wool and corn together with its relative proximity proved strong reasons for cementing Dubrovnik's political relations with this part of Italy. Dubrovnik also had connections through Skanderbeg the Albanian hero. He passed through Dubrovnik on his way to Apulia to obtain help from Alfonso V, King of Naples, and having received promises of a contingent of Neapolitan troops, he returned in disguise to Dubrovnik, when he was given a ship to go to Rodon in Albania. Albania was then placed under Neapolitan protection; 1,000 men and 18 guns were sent from Naples to Skanderbeg. In 1458 Alfonso died, and his son Ferdinand found his succession disputed by John of Anjou, who had the support of most of the barons. He then appealed to Skanderbeg for help, and the chivalrous Albanian, who was not forgetful of past services, being at the time undisturbed by the Turks, crossed over to Apulia in 1459, defeated Ferdinand's enemies, established the King securely on the throne, and returned to Albania the following year. Unfortunately the final succession of the Spaniards, Ferdinand and

Isabella to the kingdom of Naples in 1490 caused a deterioration in the relations between Dubrovnik and the Aragonese kingdom probably due to the Spaniards resentment of Dubrovnik's close ties with the Turks.

Relations with Hungary

Finally, some evaluation should be made of Hungarian rule in Dubrovnik during the later Middle Ages. Generally speaking, Croatian historians, publicists and politicians have given their old Magyar associates little credit for the centuries of union between the two peoples. Yet in many respects this union was as much to the advantage of the Croatians as to that of the Magyars, particularly in the case of Dubrovnik.[103]

Certainly throughout the period of Hungarian control over Dubrovnik the Magyar kings did not behave tyrannically towards their subjects. Indeed throughout Hungarian rule few occasions provided for constitutional quibbling. Dubrovnik's citizens made their own laws, in their own Senate under their own ruler, and promulgated laws without the King's sanction. As a general rule the Hungarian kings and their councillors respected the laws of Dubrovnik and their political, economic, religious and social as well as cultural attitudes. Indeed the Magyar rulers had too many other interests, in Italy, in the Empire, in the Balkans, in the Czech, Austrian, Russian and Polish lands, and overseas, for them to take effective action over the affairs of a distant Croatian city.

The relationship of Dubrovnik towards Hungary was also considerably altered after 1420 as the Magyars were no longer on Dubrovnik's borders. Henceforth Dubrovnik was even more independent, but from the despatches to the King of Hungary apparently still recognized his suzerainty. Dubrovnik citizens maintained that 'We are the subjects of the Crown of Hungary, and whoever is actually King of Hungary is our suzerain'. A symbol of Hungarian suzerainty, is the so-called statue of Orlando. In many mediæval towns a pillar was erected in the chief square, from the summit of which the public crier proclaimed the enactments of the government; the pillar also served as a support for the city standard. It was usually adorned with a statue of a warrior, hence it was called in German towns the *Rolandssäule* or *Rolandsbild*, Roland being the symbol of imperial authority. Such a monument did not exist at

Dubrovnik until the fifteenth century when Sigismund, King of Hungary, the city's protector, was elected Emperor of Germany.

Hungary was, however, no longer able to afford Dubrovnik valid protection, for she was weak on her southern border, and much occupied with the German wars in the north; but although Dubrovnik could hope for little help in that quarter, she kept on good terms with the King, and continued to furnish him with information as to the movements of the enemy, and to pay him the tribute of 500 ducats at irregular intervals. This she did partly for commercial reasons, the Hungarian trade being still important, and partly because she hoped that the cause of Christendom in the western Balkans might yet triumph under Hungarian auspices. Furthermore, Dubrovnik did not trust the Venetians; this explains its subsequent attitude towards the Turks, whom it was now obliged to conciliate, lest it should suffer the fate that was soon to befall its neighbours. Even so dependence on the Sultan amounted to little more than the payment of a tribute.

For the next hundred years Dubrovnik remained under Hungarian protection (until 1526), but bound by ties so vague that for all practical purposes she may be regarded as an independent state. In spite of the ever-present Turkish danger Dubrovnik continued to grow in wealth, splendour and importance. She flourished as a centre of learning and the arts no less than as an emporium of trade, and all this took place while she remained singularly free from internal troubles and constitutional changes. She pursued the even tenor of her way undisturbed, conservative, aristocratic, narrow-minded, but on the whole successful and prosperous, and her population contented.

Perhaps the best testimony to the maintenance of Dubrovnik's individuality *vis-a-vis* Hungary, and to the general toleration on the part of the Magyars of this individuality, is the surprising lack of material reminders of Hungarian rule in Dubrovnik itself. This absence of material remains of the Hungarian dominion becomes significant when it is compared with the relics of Venetian domination in Dalmatia, where the Lion of St. Mark, carved in stone, together with public monuments, distinctive architecture and innumerable forts are found at every turn. Also in Dubrovnik's folk-lore there are few traces of enmity, whilst on the other hand it overflows with indications of grievances against Venice. The conclusion is inevitable, that the Dubrovnik-Hungarian union during the Middle Ages was a harmonious one as far as the bulk of the peoples of both nations were concerned. In the light of subsequent developments it is only regretted that this union did not find a lasting political expression.

Conclusion

In studying Dubrovnik's political relations during the later Middle Ages, three characteristics emerge – in order of importance – firstly, the growth of Turkish power in Europe, secondly, the Venetian reoccupation of Dalmatia, and thirdly the essentially loose relationship that prevailed between Dubrovnik and Hungary. These three factors must be thoroughly understood before an appreciation of the city's commercial relations can be attempted. The link between politics and commerce was strong. The quest for profits dominated the minds of Dubrovnik citizens. Their achievements of commercial prosperity depended, however, very largely on the vagaries of political events. The foresight of Dubrovnik's government in seeing the rise of Turkish power is to be commended, together with the skilful diplomacy used in her contacts with the Infidel. The fear of Venetian hegemony in the Adriatic is understandable seeing that the Lion of St. Mark had similar commercial interests to her own. The easy rule of the Magyar kings is to be applauded for they allowed Dubrovnik to develop her commerce during a period of intense unrest and mistrust amongst the powers of the eastern Mediterranean and south-east Europe.

5. Notes

1. H. Brown, *Venice*, London (1893), p. 212.
2. G. Gelcich, *La Zedda e la Dinastia dei Balšidi*, Split (1899), Preface.
3. Dubrovnik Archives, *Liber Reformationes II* (27/VI/1358). An annual tribute of 500 gold ducats to be paid together with one galley for every 10 Hungarian galleys whenever the Dalmatian fleet put to sea.
4. V. K. Shaudys 'The external aspects of the political geography of 5 diminutive European States', *Journal of Geography*, Vol. LXI, Chicago (1962), p. 29.
5. M. Burr, 'The code of Stephan Dušan', *The Slavonic and East European Review*, Vol. XXVIII, No. 7 (1950), pp. 198 *et seq.*;
F. W. Carter, 'An analysis of the medieval Serbian oecumene: a theoretical approach'. *Geografiska Annaler*, Vol. 51, Ser. B, No. 1, Stockholm (1969), pp. 39–56.

6. V. Klaić, *Geschichte Bosniens* (Von ültesten Zeiten bis zum Verfulle des Königreichs), Leipzig (1885), p. 197.

7. G. Gelcich, *La Zedda e la Dinastia dei Balšidi*, Split (1899), p. 13;
K. Jireček, *Die Handelsstrasen und Bergwerke von Serbien und Bosnien wahrend des Mittelalters*, Prague (1879), p. 36 sqq.

8. F. Miklosich, *Monumenta Serbica*, Vienna (1858), p. 176.

9. Dubrovnik Archives, *Liber Reformationes* II (January 1359);
M. Zečević, *Rašobanje Vojislava Vojinovića sa Dubrovnikom*, Belgrade (1908);
I. Manken, *Dubrovački Patricijat u XIV veku*, S.A.N., Belgrade (1960), pp. 194, 298, 327, 388.

10. *Diplomatarium relationum Reipublicæ Ragusinæ cum Regno Hungariæ*, (G. Gelcich and V. Thalloczy, eds.) Magyar Tudomanyos Akademia, Budapest (1887), (1359) 4, 5, 8; (1360) 12; (1361) 20.

11. Dubrovnik Archives, *Liber Reformationes* II (February 1360).

12. Dubrovnik Archives, *Consilium Maius* (1/VII/1361).

13. Dubrovnik Archives, *Liber Reformationes* II (July 1361).

14. *Monumenta Ragusina* (G. Gelcich and F. Rački, eds.), Zagreb (1879), p. 3.

15. Dubrovnik Archives, *Liber Reformationes* II, Vol. 8, pp. 276–280;
Lettere e Commissioni di Levante, Vol. II (1350–80) – August 31st 1359;
Liber Reformationes, Vol. III, pp. 91, 98, 99;
ibid., Vol. IV, pp. 24, 117, 133–34, 139, 140.

16. F. Miklosich, *op. cit.* p. 169.

17. G. Gelcich, *La Zedda . . ., op. cit.* p. 38.

18. G. Gelcich, *La Zedda . . ., op. cit.* p. 53.

19. M. Dinić, *O Nikoli Altmanoviću*, Knjiga 90, Belgrade (1932), S.A.N. 46 pp.

20. *Diplomatarium . . ., op. cit.* p. 42.

21. V. Klaić, *op. cit.* p. 200.

22. F. Miklosich, *op. cit.* pp. 184–5;
Lj. Stojanović, *Stare srpske povelje i pisma*, Vol. I/1, Belgrade (1929), No. 81 (5/II/1375).

23. *Ibid.*, p. 188;
Lj. Stojanović, *op. cit.* No. 83 (10/IV/1379).

24. V. Klaić, *op. cit.* p. 206.

25. F. Miklosich, *op. cit.* pp. 201–202.

26. I. Kukuljević-Sakčinski, *Iura regni Croatiae, Dalmatiae et Slavoniae*, Vol. 1, Zagreb (1861), pp. 150–151.

27. A. Theiner, *Vetere Monumenta Slavorum Meridionalium Historiam spectantia*, Vol. IV, Rome (1863), pp. 187–8, 194–5, 200–203.

28. V. Klaić, *op. cit.* p. 211.

29. V. Klaić, *op. cit.* p. 226.

30. G. Gelcich, *La Zedda . . ., op. cit.* p. 140.

31. Dubrovnik Archives, *Lettere de Commisioni di Levante*, Vol. IV, folder 78.

32. Dubrovnik Archives, *Liber Reformationes* II, Vol. 29 (17/IX/1390 and 26/I/1391).

33. G. Gelcich, *op. cit.* pp. 161–163.

34. A. Theiner, *op. cit.* Vol. IV (7/X/1392), p. 295.

35. Dubrovnik Archives, *Liber Reformationes* II, Vol. 30 (1395–97), folders 75, 78.

36. G. Gelcich, *La Zedda . . ., op. cit.* p. 175.

37. G. Gelcich, *La Zedda . . ., op. cit.* p. 183.

38. V. Klaić, *op. cit.* p. 274.
39. *Diplomatarium* . . ., *op. cit.* pp. 91–102.
40. O. Medo-Pučić, *Spomenici Srpski*, Vol. I, Belgrade (1858), pp. 56, 61.
41. F. Rački 'Pokret na slavenskom jugu koncem XIV i početkom XV vieka', *Rad. J.A.*, Vol. IV (1868), p. 85;
    V. Klaić, *op. cit.* p. 297.
42. G. Gelcich, *La Zedda* . . ., *op. cit.* p. 271.
43. *Diplomatarium* . . ., *op. cit.* p. 202 (8/VI/1426).
44. *Ibid.* (31/VII/1427), p. 206.
45. F. Miklosich, *op. cit.* (31/XII/1427), pp. 336–350.
46. G. Resti, *Chronica Ragusina*, Book X.
47. V. Klaić, *op. cit.* pp. 351–52.
48. F. Miklosich, *op. cit.* p. 441.
49. V. Klaić, *op. cit.* p. 386.
50. *Diplomatarium* . . ., *op. cit.* p. 274.
51. F. Miklosich, *op. cit.* pp. 457–60;
    V. Klaić, *op. cit.* p. 386.
52. V. Klaić, *op. cit.* p. 419;
    M. Dinić, 'Zemlje hercega Svetoga Save', *Glas S.A.N.*, Vol. 182, Belgrade (1940), pp. 151–257.
53. F. Miklosich, *op. cit.* pp. 485–91.
54. Diplomatarium . . ., *op. cit.* (5/II/1466–16/IX/1470).
55. G. Resti, *op. cit.* (1470–1471).
56. G. Gelcich, *La Zedda* . . ., *op. cit.* (preface);
    J. Tadić, 'Venecija i Dalmacija u Srednjem Veku', *Jugoslovenski Istoriski Časopis*, Vols. 3–4, Belgrade (1968), pp. 5–17.
57. G. Gelcich, *Delle Sviluppo Civile di Ragusa*, Dubrovnik (1884), p. 44.
58. Dubrovnik Archives, *Liber Reformationes II*, Vol. 24 (14/X/1378).
59. Diplomatarium . . ., *op. cit.* No. 62 (13/III/1379).
60. Dubrovnik Archives, *Liber Reformationes II*, Vol. 24 (20–26/VI/1379).
61. D. Gruber, 'Borba Ludovika I s Mlečanima za Dalmacija, *Rad. J.A.*, No. CLII, Zagreb (1903), pp. 32–161;
    D. Gruber, 'Dalmacija za Ludovika' I (1358–1382);
    ibid., No. CLXVI (1906), pp. 164–215;
    No. CLXVII (1907), pp. 163–240;
    No. CLXX (1907), pp. 1–75.
62. J. C. von Engel, *Geschichte des Freystaates Ragusa*, Vienna (1807), §32.
63. S. Razzi, *La Storia di Raugia*, Lucca (1588), Book 1, Ch. XXI.
64. F. Thiriet, 'Venise et l'occupation de Tenedos au XIVᵉ siecle', *Melanges d'archeologique et d'histoire*, Tome LXV, Paris (1953), p. 219;
    B. Krekić, 'Dubrovnik i rat oko Tenedosa (1378–1380)', *Zbornik radova Vizantaloškog Instituta Srpske akademije nauke i umetnosti*, Vol. V, Belgrade (1958), pp. 21–46.
65. G. Gelcich, *Memorie storiche sulle Bocche di Cattaro*, Dubrovnik (1879);
    La Zedda . . ., *op. cit.* p. 14.
66. *Enciclopedia Italiana*, Vol. XII, Milan (1931), p. 252.
67. G. Resti, *op. cit.* (1413).
68. G. Gelcich, *La Zedda* . . ., *op. cit.* p. 294.
69. '*Diplomatarium* . . .', *op. cit.* (21/VII/1409).

70. S. Ljubić, 'O odnošajih medju Dubrovčani i Mletčani za ugar.-hrv. vladanja u Dubrovniku (1348–1526)', *Rad. J.A.*, XVII (1871), 1–69 give later Dubrovnik-Venetian relations.

71. J. C. von Engel, *op. cit.* §40.

72. I. Božić, *Dubrovnik i Turska u XIV i XV veku*, S.A.N., Belgrade (1952), pp. 6–7;

L. Vojnović, *Dubrovnik i Osmansko carstvo. Prva knija. od prvoga ugovora s Portom do usvojenja Hercegovine* (1365–1482), S.K.A., Beograd (1898), p. 23; K. Jireček, 'Novakovic, Serben und Türken im XIV–XV Jahr'. *Archiv für slav Phil.*, Vol. XVII, Vienna (1895), p. 260 states, 'In dem Rathsprotokollen von Ragusa, die in diesen Jahren bis 1368 erhalten sind, ist nicht dergleichen zu lesen; die esrten Beziehungen mit den Türken beginnen urkundlich erst seit 1396'.

73. Dubrovnik Archives, *Consilium Minus* (12/V/1392).

74. M. Pučić, *Spomenici Srpski*, Vol. I, Belgrade (1858), pp. 7–8.

75. *Ibid.*, p. 9.

76. *Ibid.*, pp. 14–15, 19.

77. *Ibid.*, p. 25.

78. N. H. Biegman, *The Turco-Ragusan Relationship*, Mouton and Co., The Hague – Paris (1967), p. 49; I. Božić, *op. cit.* pp. 55–56.

79. K. Jireček, *Handelstrassen . . .*, *op. cit.* p. 85.

80. I. Božić, *op. cit.* pp. 92–96; F. Miklosich, *Monumenta Serbica . . .*, *op. cit.* pp. 409–11; V. Klaić, *op. cit.* pp. 335–336. The annual tribute was fixed at 1,000 ducats on 7/II/1442.

81. G. Resti, *Chronica . . .*, *op. cit.* (1441–1443); I. Božić, *op. cit.* p. 98–107.

82. Z. Jakić, *Povijest Hrvatskoga naroda*, Zagreb (1941), p. 9.

83. S. Guldescu, *History of Medieval Croatia*, Mouton and Co., The Hague (1964). pp. 258–259.

84. *Diplomatorium . . .*, *op. cit.* pp. 268, 270.

85. J. Hammer-Purgstall, *Histoire de l'Empire Ottoman*, Vol. I, Paris (1835–42), p. 453.

86. *Diplomatarium . . .*, *op. cit.* 266.

87. S. Runciman, *The Fall of Constantinople 1453*, Cambridge (1965), pp. 133–144,

88. F. Miklosich, *op. cit.* pp. 465–469.

89. Dubrovnik Archives, *Traduzioni di Capitulazioni et de Firmani* (7/III/1459). The annual tribute was now 1,500 ducats.

90. F. M. Appendini, *Notizie Istorico – Critiche de Ragusei*, Vol. I, Dubrovnik (1803), p. 204.

91. J. B. Bury, *Cambridge Modern History*, Vol. I, Cambridge (1923), p. 68.

92. Dubrovnik Archives, *Lettre di Levante*, 16 (4/VI/1455), folder 201. ('Totam religionem Christianam libidinoso ambiciosoque animo dicioni suæ ascripsit, flagratque cupidine mundi', as the Dubrovnik reports informed the Hungarian King.)

93. J. C. von Engel, *op. cit.* §40.

94. I. Božić, *op. cit.* pp. 153–154.

95. Istanbul Archives, *Basbakanlik Arşivi, Tapu defter*, No. 16, folder 56, pp. 265–279.
96. *Diplomatorium* . . ., *op. cit.* (30/IV/1463);
    Č. Truhelka, 'Tursko-slovjenski spomenici dubrovačke arhive', *Glasnik Zemaljskog Muzeja Bosne i Hercegovine*, Vol. XXIII, No. 47, Sarajevo (1911), (30/XII/1475) signed in Constantinople.
97. J. Hammer-Purgstall, *op. cit.* Vol. III, p. 191.
98. J. Hammer-Purgstall, *op. cit.* Vol. IV, p. 4.
99. G. Elezović, *Turski spomenici*, Vol. II, Belgrade (1952), pp. 3, 4, 37, 44, 48, 51, 57, 58 (from 1,500 ducats in 1458 it rose to 5,000 in 1468, 10,000 in 1472 and 12,500 in 1478. In 1480 this amount was increased to 15,000, but Bayazet II brought it down to 12,500 the following year);
    Ć. Truhelka, *op. cit.* No. 71 (1482), p. 63.
100. J. C. von Engel, *op. cit.* §40.
101. H. Šabanović, 'Turski dokumenti u Bosni iz druge polovine XV vijeka', *Istorijsko-Pravni Zbornik*, No. 2, Sarajevo (1949), pp. 184–92.
102. A. Beccadelli, Fr. Carucciolo, C. Porzio, *Alfonso I und Ferrante I von Neopel*, Jena (1912), pp. 34–35;
    B. Krekić, 'Trois fragments concernant les relations entre Dubrovnik/Raguse et Italie au XIVe siecle', *Godišnjak Filosofskog Fakulteta u Novom Sadu*, Vol. 9 (1966), pp. 19–37.
103. B. Nedeljković, 'Položaj Dubrovnik prema Ugarskoj 1358–1460', *Godišnjak Pravnog Fakultet u Sarajevu*, Vol. XV, Sarajevo (1967), pp. 448–64.

6
Balkan Trade through Dubrovnik 1358–1500

After the declaration of independence from Venetian rule in 1358 and in spite of Ottoman raids and political intrigue, the Republic of Dubrovnik prospered. The city was the starting point for journeys into Turkey, and the ambassadors of foreign powers passed through the city on their way to Constantinople. Its traders were to be found in every part of the Mediterranean. The permission granted by the Popes to trade with the Infidel contributed enormously to this situation. In 1433 the Synod of Basle confirmed the Papal decision of 1341 by giving Dubrovnik permission to trade freely with infidels and schismatics. In 1433 the Bull 'Coena Domini' granted by Pope Eugene IV and based on the decrees of the Council of Basle was issued as follows:

> 'To the city of Ragusa, situated on a hard rock, on the coast of the sea and therefore exposed to its ire and in a most sterile land, wholly devoted to the Church of Rome and ever obedient to Her, constantly faithful to the King of Hungary . . . is granted permission to navigate with its ships even unto the Holy Land and to the ports of the Infidel for the purpose of conveying pilgrims thither, and of trading; to maintain consuls, erect churches and establish cemeteries in these countries'.[1]

The increase in Dubrovnik's trade continued throughout the first half of the fifteenth century but, owing to the Turkish invasion of and the constant wars in the Slav lands it tended more and more towards the sea. Italy, the Greek Empire, Asia Minor and Egypt were the chief markets for Dubrovnik merchants, and such special exemptions as the Bull of 1375 were granted to them to trade with the Infidel,[2] although they were forbidden to sell timber, corn and arms

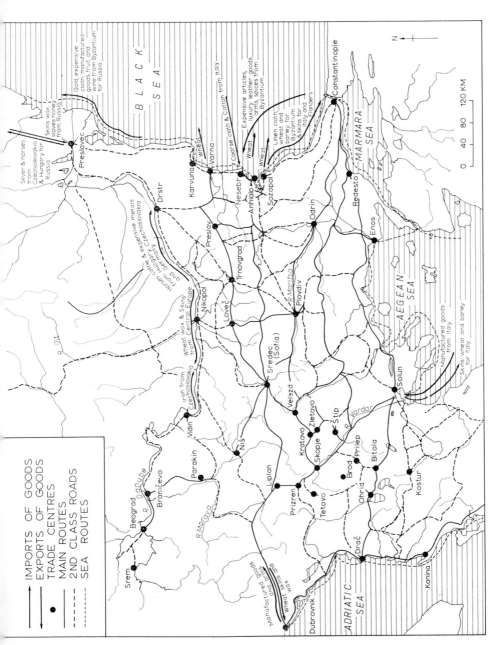

FIG. 28. Main features of east Balkan trade in the later Middle Ages.

Traduzione della Capitulazione di sultan Mehmed 2º dell'anno 1459, stata concessa in tempo delli ssigri ambasciatori ser Palladino Marino de Gondola e ser Palladino Luccari tradotta dal greco l'anno 1730, e trascritta in questo libro l'anno 1758.

Io grande Imperatore, e Gran Prencipe Mehmed Begh figlio del Gran Imperatore e Gran Prencipe Sultan Murat Begh giuro per il sigr. Iddio del Cielo, e della Terra, e per il Grande Mio Profeta Mahomete, e per i sette Capitoli dell'alcorano che abbiamo, e confessiamo Noi Muslimani, e per li cento centiquatro migliaia di Profeti di Dio, e per l'anima del Mio Avo, e del Mio Padre, e per la vita mia, e dei miei figlioli, e per la spada, che cingo, che dal giorno d'oggi, che corre, io amo l'onorato Rettore di Ragusa, con i suoi Consiglieri, l'interessi loro, i mercanti loro, et universalmente tutti i sudditi loro, et avendo mandato li ssigri ambri con la ricognizione verso la Porta del mio Imperio il Sigr Palladino Gondola e il sigr Palladino Lucari, affinche intraprende, e conservi il puro amore verso di loro, e verso tutti quelli, che si dicono Ragusei, ovunque siano sempre, e per tutto il tempo e che nessuno faccia guerra ne io, ne li miei Vesiri, ne gli Subasci miei, ne gli altri miei officiali, ne contro loro, ne contro il Popolo loro, ne contro il Paese loro, e che alcuno Esatore Tributario dell'Imperio mio non tratenga, ne noccia loro, e che siano le Citta loro, et il Paese loro, et i lor Sudditi imuni dalle contribuzioni di questi, e siano imuni da tutte le cose di qualunque genere, e che possano andare nelle citta loro, e nel distretto loro, e per mare, e per terra senza paura, e senza impedimento, e che per cio non habbiano alcuna molestia ne dall'Imperio Mio, ne da quelli, che danno il Harac al mio Imperio: Ordina la Maestà mia, che li Mercanti loro, et i loro Vomini con il loro essere, e con i loro negozij caminino liberamente, e senza paura, e senza impedimento alcuno il Paese mio dell'Occidente, e dell'Oriente per mare, e per terra, per Bulgaria, per Valachia, Servia, Albania, Bossnia, e per tutte le citta e luoghi del Mio Imperio: che nessuno prenda dazio delle merci di transporto in fuori di quello, che è imposto, cio e quando rendono aspre cento aspre due, secondo la tassa d'Adrianopoli, Fillipopoli e Cratoa, ma se non avranno venduto le mercanzie loro, che le prendano, e transportino senza impedimento dove vogliono. Di piu commando, che, se sara loro preso dazio, che non dovarano pagare, giurino due, o tre Ragusei d'esserli stato preso do dazio, vengano al giudicato Mussulmano, presentandosi al Cadi, qual determini, giusta il giudizio di Dio, che sia fatto, e non contrasti uno contro l'altro ma quel che deve sodisfi. Se qualche d'uno avendo preso alcuna cosa d'un altro sara andato à Ragusa, che se li faccia giostizia secondo che la fanno à loro stessi, e nessuno audisca d'aprir la bocca contro il giudicato. Se qualche d'uno dei Ragusei morira nello stato mio, che nessuno prenda il suo essere ne io, ne alcuno del mio Imperio, ma venga il suo Congionto, o Parente per prenderlo. E se i nemici miei mi farano guerra o all'Imperio mio d'Occidente, o dell' Oriente o per mare, o per terra il Rettore, Consiglieri, et il Popolo di Ragusa stiano zenza paura, senza molestia per riguardo dell'Oltraggiatori, e li mercanti loro caminino il paese mio senza paura. Ordina ancora la Maesta mia, che nessuno li faccia oltragio, o danno nelli Paesi loro, o ai loro mercanti, o alli loro Omini, o alli negozij loro, e chiunque sara che paghi il danno à loro. Il Rettore, e Consiglieri di Ragusa, che mandino ogni anno, cio e a capo del anno del mese di Genaro i loro Nobili al mio Imperio flori, ossiano Ongari annui mille cinque cento.

Scritto li 7 del Mese di Marzo dell'indizione 6967, quali corrispondono all'anno 1459.

FIG. 29. Transcript of original Turkish document into Italian whereby a new Turkish Sultan (Mehmed II), and friend of Dubrovnik, gave his merchants all rights to travel in both eastern and western parts of his Empire (Bulgaria, Wallachia, Serbia, Albania, Bosnia etc.). In return, Dubrovnik had to pay 1,500 ducats in gold annually. Also Dubrovnik traders had only to pay taxes once a year direct to Constantinople, and therefore no need to pay local taxes. Dated 7/III/1459 No. 6967. Dubrovnik Archives, *Traduzioni di Capitulazioni et de Firmani.*

in those countries. The relations with the Turks were satisfactory, and they often sent envoys to the Emirs and Sultans.[3] At the same time, this did not interfere with their good understanding with the Christian powers, and they did much business with Constantinople and the rest of the Greek Empire, both by sea and by land. The trade with the Slavonic hinterland, although subject to frequent interruptions, was still active, with new and flourishing commercial colonies being established in Bosnia, Serbia, Bulgaria and Albania. Active trade continued also with Hungary, both by way of Bosnia, Serbia and the Danube, and by sea via Croatia. Trade with Italy continued to develop and expand, and late in the fourteenth century direct intercourse with Florence was established.[4] In 1406 the Florentine government declared that the merchants of Dubrovnik had brought so much silver to Florence, from the Balkan mines, 'that we have almost purchased Pisa with it.'[5] In 1429 a five years' treaty between the two republics was concluded, the citizens of Dubrovnik agreeing to bring gold, silver, skins, wax and other Balkan produce to Florence in exchange for Italian wares.[6] Close relations were maintained through frequent visits of the Florentine ambassadors on the way to Constantinople,[7] and many Florentine merchants resided in the city. Various other Christian powers made use of Dubrovnik for their relations with the Turks, and even Francis I of France is said to have had recourse to a member of a Dubrovnik nobility in his negotiations with the Sultan.[8]

Gelcich quotes the opinions of a number of foreign writers on Dubrovnik's trade in the fifteenth century[9] which provide further insight into the commercial activities of the city. The Abate Denina wrote :

'The Ragusans were ever a nation of merchants and traffickers, and are well satisfied to do what the Neopolitans have failed to do, monopolizing the export trade of the Kingdom (of Naples), and visiting with their ships all parts of the Mediterranean'.

Amalthaeus in a letter to a friend advises him to settle at Dubrovnik, as there were in that city many opportunities of becoming rich by trade, for there was much active traffic with the West, and the most industrious nations of Europe, such as the French, the Spaniards, the English, the Flemings, and even the Germans had established colonies there.

If Dubrovnik was as important commercially as all this evidence suggests, upon what regions and commodities was the commercial pre-eminence of Dubrovnik based? There was an important commerce in raw materials, which can be subdivided into precious commodities – various metals, slaves, spices and salt, and into cheaper goods such as skins, wax, wool, wheat, flax and other victuals; and also into manufactured goods concerned mainly with the importation of textiles from western Europe for the Balkan and Levantine markets. The primary products came to Dubrovnik principally from east-central Bosnia and western Serbia, the 'oecumene' in the later Middle Ages of the Bosnian and Serbian states. The connection between the export of these commodities to Dubrovnik and their origin in these areas becomes clearer when one realizes the function of the oecumene.

The Concept of the Oecumene and Core Area

Most European states have grown by a process of accretion from germinal areas, which have come to be called after Derwent Whittlesey 'oecumene'. He states

'The oecumene is the portion of the state that supports the densest and most extended population and has the closest mesh of transportation lines'.[10]

This should not be confused with the narrower concept of a 'core-area', which Whittlesey defines as 'the area in which or about which a state originates'.[11] Other definitions of an oecumene have been put forward, as for example by Jefferson, who maintains that

'the oecumene is the utilized land of a country, the part from which the people draw life',[12]

and Trewartha –

'Distribution of people in its broadest aspect, involves dividing the land portions of the earth into permanently inhabited as compared with uninhabited or temporarily inhabited, parts'.

The terms oecumene and non-oecumene have been employed to represent these two major subdivisions.[13] In fact a suitable definition of an oecumene would be a community, or district, which may be considered as an entity, to some extent self-sufficing and not primarily dependent on other regions for its population or supplies.

This definition would fit Karl Deutsch's idea that such an area must have considerable advantages in order to permit it to perform within itself against enroachment and conquest from neighbouring areas and it must have been capable at an early date of generating a surplus income above the subsistence level, necessary to equip armies and to play the role in contemporary power politics that territorial expansion necessarily predicates.[14] In terms of the medieval period, this meant a fertile soil, well cultivated within the limits of contemporary technology, a population dense enough to derive maximum advantage from local resources and generally a long distance commerce to enable it to obtain materials not locally available. Both Bosnia-Hercegovina and Serbia had these necessary qualifications and were by 1358 both consolidated medieval states.[15] For Dubrovnik citizens the main incentive was the purchasing of these precious raw materials in the Balkan peninsula and selling them at a profit to the wealthier areas of western Europe and the Levant. During the period 1358-1500 this entrepreneural activity was characterized by intensive trading in the western half of the Balkans, buying Bosnian and Serbian commodities and selling there 'materials not locally available'.[16] Deutsch further distinguishes between population density and a network of communication as determinants of oecumene growth:

'It should be noted that the density that makes an oecumene is one of traffic and communication rather than mere numbers of passive villagers densely settled on the soil'.[17]

This ties in with Whittlesey's idea of a close mesh of transportation lines.[18]

During the thirteenth and fourteenth centuries the economic awakening that was abroad over the whole of Europe began to be felt in the Balkan lands. Agriculture was developed, cattle and pigs were important, and there were plenty of cereals – hemp, flax, wine and oil; Serbian flour became famous. Amid the highlands of Raška, the fertile basins (or polja) of Kossovo along the upper Ibar, of Metohija along the upper Drin, of Tetovo along the upper Vardar and of Skoplje-Kumanova in the region of the Vardar-Morava watershed, were all floored with rich soil, the relic of former lakes. Indeed, it seems likely that the population of some of these basins was greater in the fourteenth century than it is today.[19] It is not surprising therefore that the capital of the growing Serbian state should have been

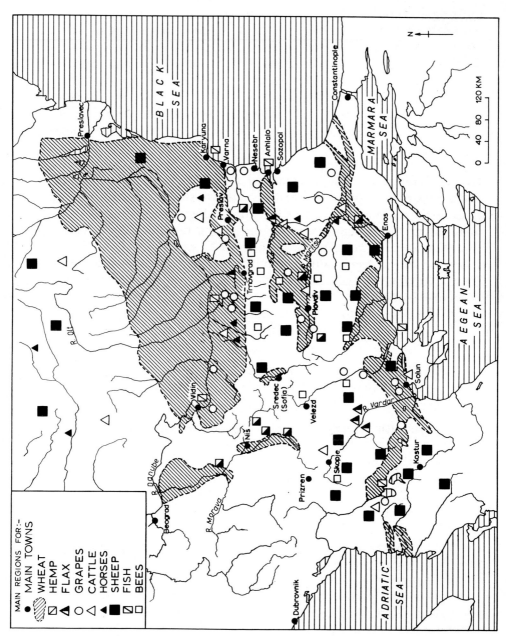

Fig. 30.   Agricultural distribution in the east Balkans during the later Middle Ages.

moved from the older centre of Raš to Skoplje in a region at once more fertile and more in touch with the vital south-eastern frontier. The new religious capital, too, was at Peč in the Metohija region. Here, then around the headwaters of the Ibar, the Vardar, the Drim and the Morava, was the oecumene of medieval Serbia. Gordon East[20] has stated that

'Medieval Serbia, affords an interesting study of what may be called the "oecumene" of a state. In sharp contrast with medieval France, it had its political centres and its base in a region not of confluents, but of river sources. The physical geography of the western half of the Balkan peninsula offered many difficulties and few aids to state building. . . . In one respect, however, the physique of the land afforded possibilities in an area of relatively level country where communication was not difficult, where pasture was available and productive cultivation was possible'.

It was from within this area that Stefan Dušan was able to build the great medieval Empire of Serbia. He made a striking impression on his contemporaries both by his ability and by his commanding presence, and his reign has always been regarded by later Serbians as the most glorious epoch in their history. The work of earlier Serbian rulers was now to be carried forward to its logical conclusion, for Dušan brought genius both to the development of the internal resources of the Serbian lands and the execution of a daring foreign policy.

Serbia of course remained fundamentally an agricultural state, but every effort was made to encourage industry and commerce. An important economic development was that of mining. Copper, tin, silver and gold, well known in Roman times, began to be mined again with the help of German colonists from Hungary (known as Saxons), and of immigrants from Dubrovnik and Italy. Temperley states[21] of Stefan Dušan that

'he made every effort to encourage commerce and industry by the importation of foreigners as well as by diplomacy and treaties: Saxons, Ragusans, Venetians, Greeks, Albanians ... peopled his cities, worked his mines, or garrisoned his fortresses'.

The Kopaonik mountains, each of the upper Ibar, were particularly important for their mining centres. Gold, silver and copper coins began to be minted by the Serbian rulers,[22] and they provided an

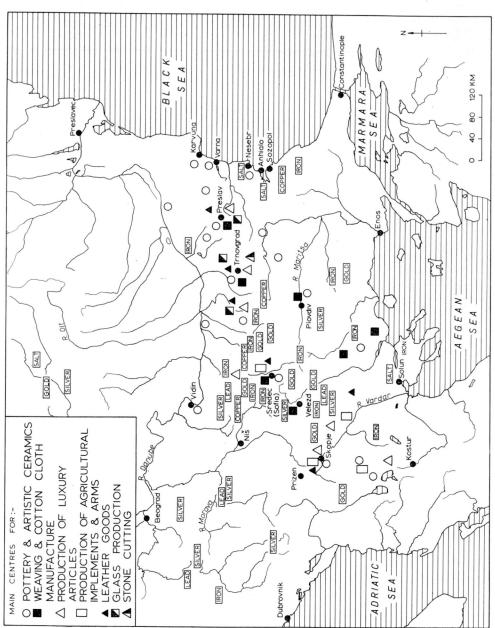

MAIN CENTRES FOR:-

○ POTTERY & ARTISTIC CERAMICS
■ WEAVING & COTTON CLOTH
  MANUFACTURE
△ PRODUCTION OF LUXURY
  ARTICLES
□ PRODUCTION OF AGRICULTURAL
  IMPLEMENTS & ARMS
◢ LEATHER GOODS
◪ GLASS PRODUCTION
▲ STONE CUTTING

Fig. 31.   Industrial distribution in the east Balkans during the later Middle Ages.

index of the economic advance of the state. It was this wealth that enabled the Serbian kings to hire mercenaries to fight against the armies of Bulgaria and the Byzantine Empire. In commerce, Dubrovnik merchants, in particular, received trading privileges throughout the entire realm. The east-west Roman roads from the Adriatic into the interior carried an exchange of commodities, which was to some extent stimulated by the contrasted character of the different geographical regions; from the coast oil, wine, manufactured and oriental goods; from the highlands, timber – for ships and wine casks – cattle, gold and silver, honey, wool, skins and leather. The industries of the coastal towns were based on the raw materials derived from the mountainous hinterland; thus for example Kotor worked gold and silver, tanned leather, prepared wax, made shoes and armour and built ships.

Expensive Raw Materials

Metals

Minerals seemed to have the greatest significance for Dubrovnik's entrepreneurs in Bosnia-Hercegovina and Serbia. Geologically the mineral deposits in both Bosnia and Serbia were associated with the igneous intrusions in the ancient resistant rock against which the Alpine Dinaric mountains were folded. In Bosnia two main mineral basins were found, a larger one lying to the west and east of Visoko, and a smaller basin containing Srebrenica and Zvornik. Serbia had two major mining areas, in the north around Rudnik and Rudišta, and in the south the Kopaonik and Novo Brdo (New Mountains) of the Ibar-Kossovo mineral basin.

In medieval industry mining showed a great diversity of organization. Where minerals were found near the surface, or in outcrops, little capital was needed and the mining unit was small. German farmers called 'Sasi' or 'Teutonics' from Saxony, migrated to the western Balkans,[23] and in their spare time dug out the minerals and smelted them with charcoal. Deeper deposits required larger outlays for the mine and for the smelting and refining equipment. In many cases Dubrovnik merchants either provided the capital or bought a lease on the right of the mine,[24] granted as a concession in return for

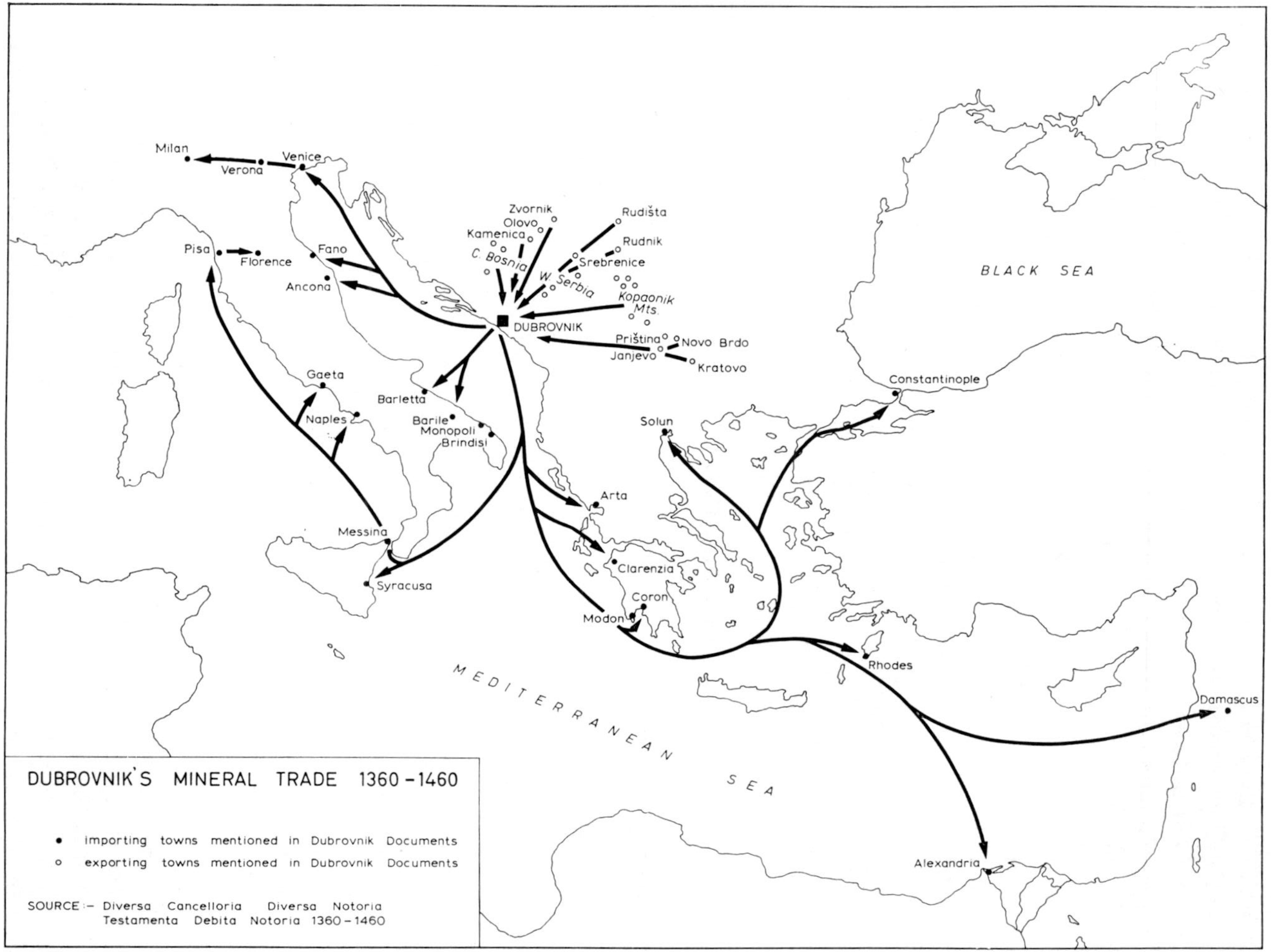

DUBROVNIK'S MINERAL TRADE 1360–1460

• importing towns mentioned in Dubrovnik Documents

○ exporting towns mentioned in Dubrovnik Documents

SOURCE – Diversa Cancellaria   Diversa Notaria
Testamenta   Debita Notoria 1360–1460

FIG. 32

Labels on map:

BLACK SEA
MEDITERRANEAN SEA

Damascus
Alexandria
Constantinople
Rhodes
Solun
Arta
Clarenzia
Coron
Modon

Rudišta
Rudnik
Srebrenice
Zvornik
Olovo
Kamenica
W. Serbia
C. Bosnia
Kopaonik Mts
Priština
Novo Brdo
Janjevo
Kratovo
DUBROVNIK

Brindisi
Monopoli
Barile
Barletta
Syracusa
Messina
Naples
Gaeta
Ancona
Fano
Florence
Pisa
Venice
Verona
Milan

some loan, or handed over as collateral security. Mining therefore became a field for investment, by Dubrovnik merchants bringing their capital to the mountains and backwoods of the western Balkans.

ΜΛСΤΝЮ БЖΝѠМ Η ПОѠЕΛ(Е)ΝΝΙЄΜ ГΔΝΑ ΜΗ ΑΜΗР СꙊΛΤΑΠ Ц(Α)РᲐ
ΜЕХΜЕΤБЕГΑ ΜΗ ѠЕѠѠΔΑ ЕСБЕГЬ ΔΑѠΑΜ ΝᲐ ЗΝΑΝЬЕ СѠЕΜ Η СОΛΚꙊΜꙊ, ΚꙊΜꙊ
СЕ ΠΟΔΟБΑ ΠΟΚᲐЗΑΤЬ СЫ ΝΑШЬ ѠЕРѠОΔΑΝΝ ΛΝСΤЬ, ΚᲐΚО ꙊЧΝΝΗХ Μ(Н)Λ(О)СΤЬ
Η СΛОБОΔꙊ ΤРЬГОѠ ЦЕΜ ΔꙊБРОѠЬЧЬΚΙЕΜ ΠОѠЕΛЕΝΝΕΜ Г(О)СПОΔΑРΑ ГОΛЕΜОГΑ, ΔΑ
ΗΜЬ ЈЕ ѠЕРΑ Η СΛОБОΔΑ, ΔΑ ГРЕΔꙊ СѠОЕΜ ΤРЬГОΜЬ Ꙋ ЦΑРЕОꙊ ЗЕΜΛЮ, ΔΑ ΗΜЬ
ΝЕ БꙊΔЕ ѠБꙊРΗѠᲐΝΝΙΑ, ΝΝ ΝΑ ΠꙊΤꙊ ЗΑΠΠΗРᲐΝЬΙΑ, ΝΗ ЕΔΝΕ ХꙊΔОБЕ, ΝΗ ЕΔΝΗ
ЧΛ(О)Ѡ(Е)ΚЬ ΔΑ ΗΜЬ ΝЕ ѠОΛЬΝ ꙊЧΝΝΗΤ, ΝΝ ΜꙊСРОΜΑΝΝΗ ΝΗ ХРΝСΤЬΙΑΝΗΝ:
ΠО ЦΑРЕѠЕ ЗΑΠОѠЕСΤΗ ΔΑ ΝХЬ ΝΜΑΜО СЬБΛЮСΤЬ, ΝΗХ Η ΝΝΗХ БΛ(Α)Гѡ. Η ΚΤО
БΗ ΝΝΗХ ΤОѠΑРЕ ΠОСΝΛᲐ, ΛΝΗ БꙊΔꙊ ΛЮΔΙЕ ХЕРЬЦЕГОѠΗ, ΛΝΗ БꙊΔꙊ ΛЮΔΙЕ ѠЕѠѠΔЕ
ѠΛᲐΔΗСᲐѠΑ, ΔΑ ΗΜЬ Е ѠЕРΑ ЦΑРЕѠΑ Η ΜОΙΑ, ѠОЈЕѠОΔЕ ЕСБЕГΑ, СΛОБОΔΝО ΔΑ
ΛОГЮ Ꙋ ЦΑРЕОꙊ ЗЕΜΛЮ Η ΤОѠΑРЕ ΔΑ ΔОΝЕСꙊ Η ѠΠЕΤ ЗΔРΑѠО Η ѠЕС(Е)ΛО ΔΑ
СΗ ΠОГЮ СѠОЕΜΗ ΚОΝΜΗ Ꙋ СѠОЮ ЗЕΜΛЮ: ΔΑ СЕ ΝЕ БОЕ ΝΗ ΠОРОБΛΕΝЬΙΑ, ΝΗ
ѠБꙊЗЕΤΙΑ, ΝΝΗ ЕΔΝЕ ЗΛЕ ΜЕΙЬΚРΝЕ: ΔΑ ΗΜЬ ΝЕ ѠОΛЬΝΗ ΝΗΚΤОР ꙊЧΝΝΗΤ ΝΗ
СꙊБΑШΑ ΝΗ ΝΝΗ ΤꙊРЧΝΝЬ ΝΗ ΜΑРΤОΛОЗΝΗ, ΔΑ ΗΜЬ ΝΗΚЬΤОР ЖΑѠ ΝЕ ꙊЧΝΝΗ.
ΚΤО ΛΗ СЕ ЗΑ ΝΗХ ЗΑΔЕΝЕ, ЩО Е ѠРЕΔΝО ЕΔЬΝО ѠΛᲐΚΝО ΔΑ ΗΜЬ ꙊЗЬΜЕ, Ꙋ
ΝЕѠЕРꙊ Η РΑСЫΠ СѠОѠΜ ГΛΑѠОΜ ΔΑ ΠΛΑΤΗ, Α ΗΝЕΜ ΝΗЧΗΜ ΔΑ СЕ ΝЕ ѠΔΚꙊΠΗ.
ΠΝСΑ ΝОЕΜѠРΝΙΑ ᲐΙ ΔΝЬ.

FIG. 33. Transcript of document giving Dubrovnik merchants trading rights in Herce-govina, and stating that punishment would be served on any Turks who killed Dubrovnik traders. Dated 14/XI/1454 at Poslija. (Original in Dubrovnik Archives on paper 26 cm × 13 cm.)

The three most important minerals, according to Dubrovnik documents, were silver, lead and copper in that order together with less significant ones like iron, mercury, lapis lazuli and antimony. The years 1360 to 1460 appear to have been the period of Dubrovnik's greatest interest in Balkan mining. A generalized picture of mineral trade movements can be constructed but this does not give complete accuracy since documentary sources fail to record all the transactions which took place. Such references as occur are often accidental, occurring in wills, lawsuits, or accidents, rather than as the result of systematic recording of merchants' agreements. Many transactions, particularly concerning precious metals like gold and silver, were never committed to paper. Sometimes Dubrovnik documents mention the actual mine where a mineral was bought, but in other cases reference is only made to the market town in which it was purchased.

Silver had an international market in the Middle Ages and at the beginning of the modern era, for credit was then little developed and supplies of silver played a greater part in determining the wealth and political power of sovereign states. Stefan Dušan in the first half of the fourteenth century developed and exploited the Serbian mines in order to finance his wars of expansion leaving Saxon miners and Dubrovnik traders and financiers in control of the mines. In this way Dubrovnik achieved the monopoly in silver based on privileges granted to its traders, by the Serbian and later Bosnian rulers.

The most famous mine in Serbia, and indeed in the whole of the Balkan peninsula was at Novo Brdo (New Mountain) which was first mentioned in Dubrovnik documents in 1326[25] and continued to have connections with Dubrovnik until the Turkish occupation of the mine in 1455. Here, as in the Kopaonik mountains, auriferous silver was contained in the serpentine rocks of the area, and was referred to in documents as 'argento de Glama', 'argento indorato' and 'argento di oro'. Auriferous silver was exported from Serbia only via Dubrovnik to Italy and contained according to a document of 1436, one sixth gold.[26] The price and amount of gold is rarely mentioned.

Srebrenica (silver town) was, after Novo Brdo, the most important mining centre for Dubrovnik, and a source of constant quarrels between the Bosnian and Serbian rulers. The quality of silver from this town was of much higher value than from the rest of Bosnia. The ordinary Bosnian silver had several impurities and was called 'pliko' (a piece) – 'argento plicho de Bosne'.[27] Srebrenica silver was much purer, 'argento fino', not being found in the other Bosnian silver mines at Kreševo, Fojnica, Dusina, Deževica and Ostružnica. Fine silver is mentioned in many documents,[28] and was sometimes the centre of court cases.[29] Dubrovnik had the lease on the Srebrenica mine and received the following yearly incomes from it:

1389 –   3,400 ducats
1417 – 24,800 ducats
1458 – 30,000 ducats[30]

showing clearly the expansion of this mine.

After Novo Brdo and Srebrenica, Rudnik (the mine) in northern Serbia appears to have been the next in importance to Dubrovnik despite the distance involved. With silver, distance did not appear to matter for the profit margin must have been so great. As transport costs in the Middle Ages were paid according to the size and not the value of the load, and due to the poor road conditions, the lesser valued minerals like lead and iron were bought by Dubrovnik traders much nearer home in Bosnia. In the case of silver the nearer mines at Fojnica, Kreševo, Ostružnica and Leževice appear from documentary evidence to be of secondary importance.

Lead, like silver had an international market despite the problem of weight in transportation. This metal was used either in the pure form for domestic utensils, church ornaments and church roofing, or mixed with other metals to make armour, trapping for horses, chains for livestock and prisoners, candlesticks, arms, etc. and, like silver, it was exported in large quantities by Dubrovnik merchants to Italy and the Levant. In contrast to the search for silver, Dubrovnik's citizens rarely went outside Bosnia to obtain lead, firstly because transport costs could have seriously affected the profit margin and secondly, because there appeared to be enough lead mined in Bosnia to satisfy Dubrovnik's needs.

The most important lead mine in Bosnia was at Olovo ('Lead town'). Two reasons made this place known to merchants, firstly because of the large reserves of lead found in the Lower Trias beds there, and secondly because of the high quality of the ore which contained few impurities. Merchants distinguished between Olovo lead 'plumbum dulce' or 'plumbum subtile', in comparison with lead from the igneous rocks at Srebrenica, Krupanj, and Deževica calling this 'plumbum durum'.[31] The 'hard' lead from Srebrenica was combined with antimony and silver, which technologically at this time was difficult to separate. Therefore Olovo lead had a higher price and was in greater demand in foreign markets than lead from the other Bosnian mines. Olovo was first mentioned in conjunction with Kamenica; in April 1377 merchants from Dubrovnik went to Kamenica and bought 90,000 lb of lead.[32]

Copper was apparently of less importance than either silver or lead especially in the second half of the fourteenth century, and there is a surprisingly small amount of information on it in Dubrovnik's archives.[33] The reasons for this are obscure. Possibly it was more difficult to extract and smelt than other minerals, or that many of the

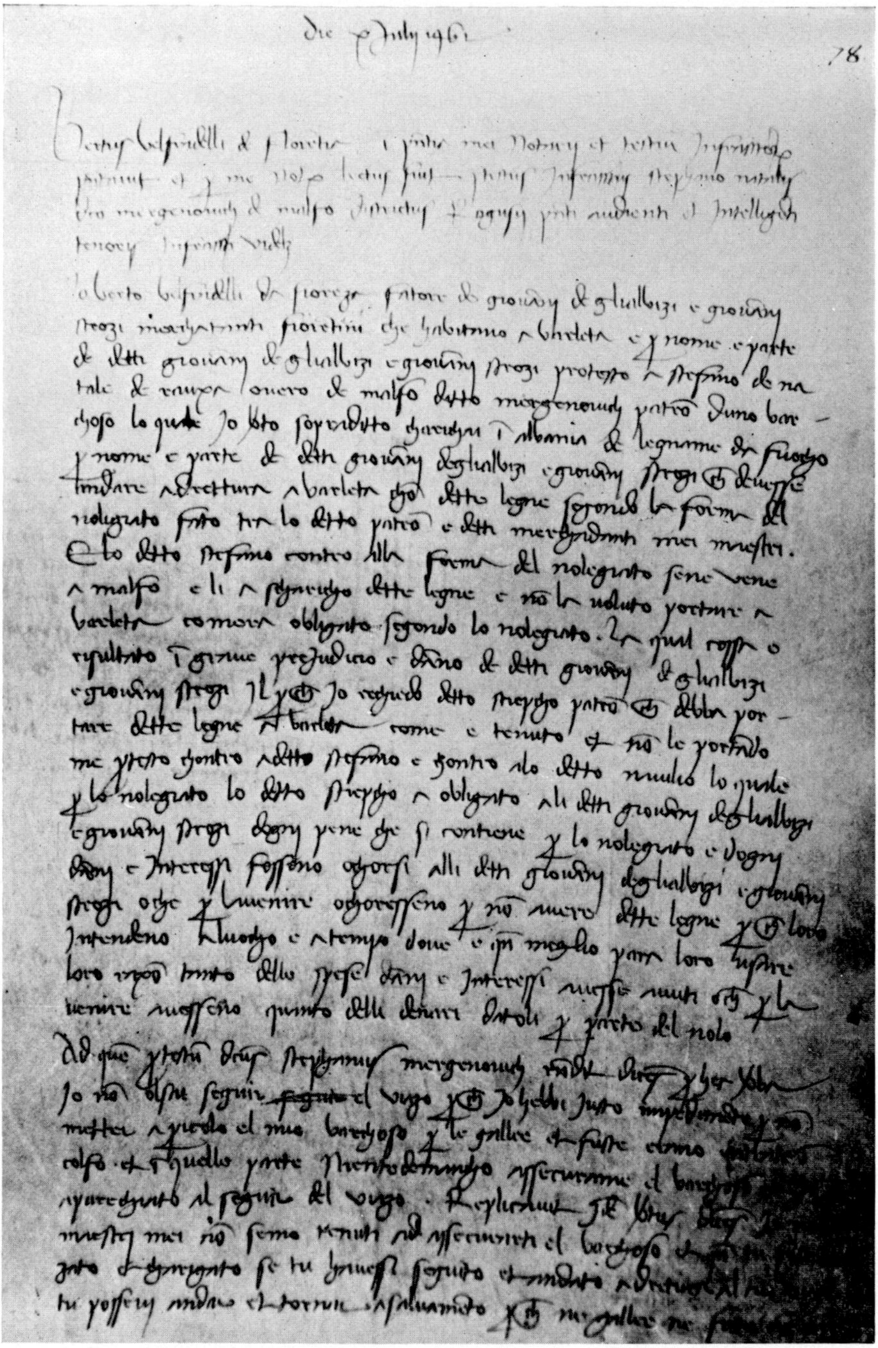

Fig. 34. Dubrovnik Archives. 10/VII/1462. Document recording the dispatch of lead from Olovo and kermes from Trgovište to Dubrovnik. *Diversa Notaria* 46 fol. 78′.

uses for copper could be substituted by lead. Lead plaques were extremely fashionable in medieval Italy. However copper was used for armaments especially in the production of cannons, and for currency.

Rudnik appears to have been one of the few Serbian mines producing copper for Dubrovnik, this mine having a higher production of copper than most of the other mines in the Balkan peninsula.[34] Dubrovnik merchants bought copper in Rudnik as early as 1321, and copper is mentioned on several occasions in the fifteenth century.[35]

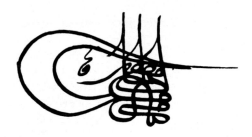

мⷨлостїю божїю мн ѡⷷл(н)кь гⷭпⷪдарⷶ н ѡⷷл(н)кь амнн҃ре сѵⷶлⷮⷶн мⷹхамеⷣ
по свⷷⷯ зⷷмлаⷯ гⷭпⷪстⷪа м(н), по роⷨ(л)нⷷ, по анатолⷷ, по ѡлашⷠⷩ
зⷷмⷧн, по срⷠннⷯ, по арⷠанⷶнⷶсⷩⷯ, по боⷭннⷯ сⷪⷷⷨ санчⷶⷨꙛ н кⷶднⷷⷨ,
сⷠⷩшⷨⷶⷨ н тⷩмⷶⷢⷪннкоⷨ, царⷷннкоⷨ н сⷪⷶкⷪн ѡрⷠстⷷⷨ лⷹдⷷⷨ, кто ѥ подⷠ
гⷪⷭпⷪстⷪⷪⷨ-ⷮ алⷩ кто мн харⷶчⷩ лⷶⷣⷶ, зⷶпоⷪⷶⷣ мн, да тⷢⷪ нⷷⷢⷷ нⷶ сⷷ
прⷩмнⷮ гⷪⷷ н роⷠⷩстⷪⷪ о гⷪⷭпⷪстⷪⷶ мн, нⷷ зⷶⷣⷷнн сⷷ нⷷⷢⷩⷨ злⷪⷨ н нⷷпрⷶⷣⷪⷨ
алⷩ коноⷨ нзⷶдⷪрⷠⷮннⷪⷨ зⷶ ѡлⷶстⷷⷧⷷ лⷪⷠроⷪⷶчⷩⷨⷷⷨ н ннⷯ грⷶⷢⷩⷯⷷⷨ
н трⷠⷢⷪⷪ цⷷⷨ, (к)он кⷷ холнⷮ н трⷠⷢ роⷪⷶтн ꙋ зⷷмлⷷⷯ н гⷪⷭпⷪстⷪⷶ м(н) нⷷⷢⷪ
ⷮ оⷠзⷶⷣⷩⷨ сⷯрⷶннⷮ н снⷠⷶꙋⷣⷩⷮ н прⷩⷶтⷷⷧⷪⷶтⷩ кⷶк сⷪⷷ моⷷ ѡⷶⷢⷩⷷ. н лⷶ
нⷨ сⷷ нⷷ ꙋчннⷩ нⷷⷪⷩⷪⷩннⷶ нⷩ ꙋ ѥдⷩоⷨ мⷷⷭто, нн да плⷶтⷷ пꙋⷮнⷷ
цⷶрⷩнⷷ, нⷷⷢⷪ глⷷ продⷶлꙋ лⷶ плⷶтⷹ ⷪ аспрⷮ ѡⷣⷠ р̅ аспрⷮ а ѿшто¹) нⷷ
продⷶлꙋ лⷶ понⷷⷭ кꙋⷣⷷ мꙋ ѥ драго. а ко л̅ бн сⷷ зⷶⷣⷷноⷭ²) зⷶ нⷷ
кⷮⷪⷢⷪⷣⷷ нⷷпрⷶⷣⷪⷨ коноⷨ, да сⷷ пⷷⷣⷷнⷭⷷ ˙н прⷩⷨн гⷪⷷ н роⷠⷭтⷪⷪ пⷶⷣ
сⷪⷠⷪⷨ.

пнса на снннцаⷯ мⷭца юлⷩ з̅ лⷶнⷠ н почⷷⷧⷠ сⷪⷶⷮⷶ з̅ сⷠⷠ н а сⷶⷮн
н ѿⷶ лⷠⷮⷍ.

Fig. 35.   Transcript of document instructing Turkish officials to collect only 2% customs duty on goods carried by Dubrovnik merchants in Rumania, Anatolia, Wallachia, Serbia, Albania and Bosnia. Dated 7/VII/1463 No. 6971 at Sjenica. (It is 33 cm × 13 cm and on the back is written 'Chomandamento in schiauo per li merchadanti aduse ser Illia de Bona e ser Nicola de Palmota, 21/VII/1463'.)

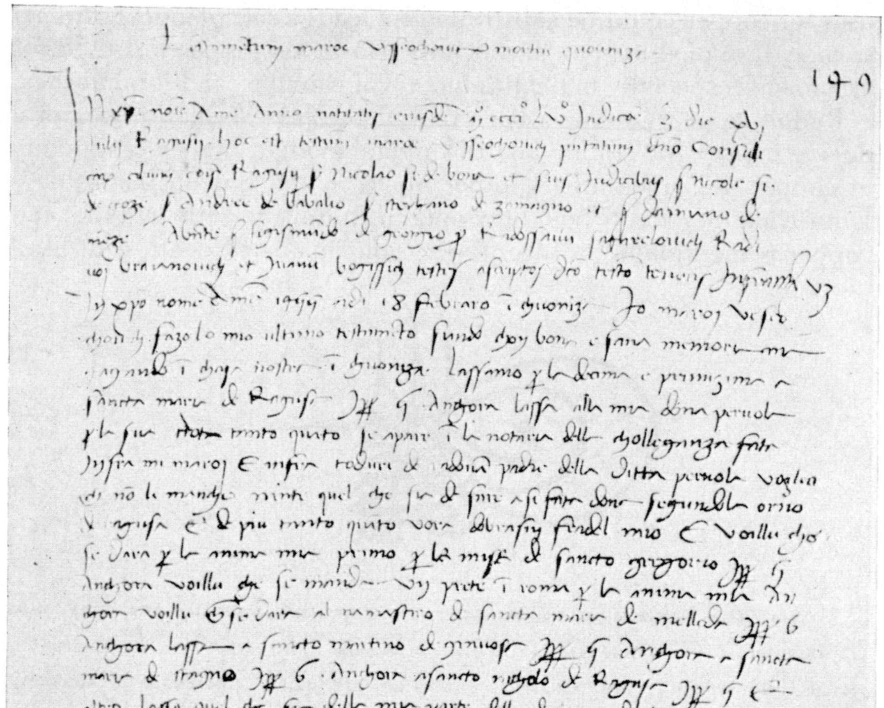

Fig. 36. Dubrovnik Archives. 16/VII/1455 Part of a document recording the dispatch of wheat from Fojnica and Kreševo, cheese and 280 litres of copper from Fojnica, together with skins, honey and wax from other parts of Bosnia to Dubrovnik. *Testamenta Notaria* 15, fol. 149–150′.

Evidence of Bosnian copper being sent to Dubrovnik is seen in the will of a Dubrovnik trader who died at Fojnica, and mentions sending 280 litres of copper to Dubrovnik,[36] and again in 1411, five litres of copper were conveyed to Dubrovnik from the market town of Foča,[37] but much of the remaining information on copper is unreliable.

Of the other minerals exported to Dubrovnik, mention should be made of lapis lazuli. From this stone the most expensive blue dye was obtained, but it was not exported in large quantities as it was a rare mineral.[38] Kermes (a natural occurring amorphous trisulphide compound of antimony, of brilliant red), also used for dyeing, was sent to Dubrovnik in large quantities, especially between 1440–1460, coinciding with the period of increased textile production in Italy.[39] Antimony and mercury were also exported from Bosnia for medicinal purposes, the latter as an important antidote for venereal disease. Iron, due to its weight and high transport costs, was less important in the mineral export trade for Dubrovnik merchants usually obtained their supplies by sea. Rarely in the Dubrovnik Archives is iron mentioned as being sent from Bosnia via Dubrovnik to Venice.[40]

Two questions remain regarding Dubrovnik's mineral exploitation of Bosnia-Hercegovina and Serbia, firstly at what period(s) was the mineral production most intensive, and secondly, what were the causes for the decline of mineral exploitation. According to Nef

'The production of silver in Bohemia, Saxony and most of the mountainous districts peopled by the Germans, Slavs and Magyars probably reached a low point during the Hussite Wars of the 1420s and 1430s'.[41]

This fact is not borne out by documentary evidence from Dubrovnik's archives referring not only to silver but to all mineral production from Bosnia and Serbia between 1400 and 1450.[42] Maximum production was achieved in or near 1430 at most of the important mines. The explanation appears to be firstly that this was the period of maximum effort by the Bosnian and Serbian rulers finally to repulse the Turks from the western Balkans, therefore needing silver to purchase materials and lead and copper to produce arms, and secondly with a decline in silver production in central Europe, Serbia and Bosnia were seen as an alternative source of supply, in which Dubrovnik acted as entrepreneur for western Europe, especially Italy.

After 1460 there was a distinct decline in mineral exploitation throughout Bosnia and Serbia, and Dubrovnik entered upon one of the most difficult periods of her trading history. This period coincided with the final conquest of medieval Bosnia (1463) and Serbia (1459) by the Turks, and all the causes of decline in mineral production stem from this fact.

One of the basic factors which influenced the mining industry in the fifteenth century was warfare, which the rulers of Bosnia and Serbia continually waged against either the Hungarians or the Turks, gradually sapping the whole economy of its strength. Secondly, during the Turkish occupation the mines were often the scene of armed struggle. The Turks tried to induce the miners to increase output, often with the threat of death or enslavement elsewhere, for failure to co-operate. This led to struggles and open resentment on the part of the miners, especially those working in the silver mines, for the Turks were always demanding more of this metal to finance wars of further conquest. Thirdly, when the Turks occupied the region they completely upset the trading life of these mining towns. Much of the mining organization was in the hands of foreigners, Saxons, Venetians and merchants from Dubrovnik, who, due to repeated attacks on the mines (Novo Brdo was attacked in 1413, 1427, 1439 and 1455) felt insecure and gradually left. In 1466 the Saxon settlers at Novo Brdo left *en masse*[43] probably leaving other mining areas as well. This meant that metal craftsmen, financiers, miners etc. who left the area could not easily be replaced for neither the

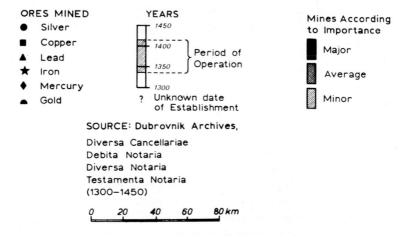

FIG. 37. (facing page)   Mining in Bosnia and Serbia, 1300–1450.

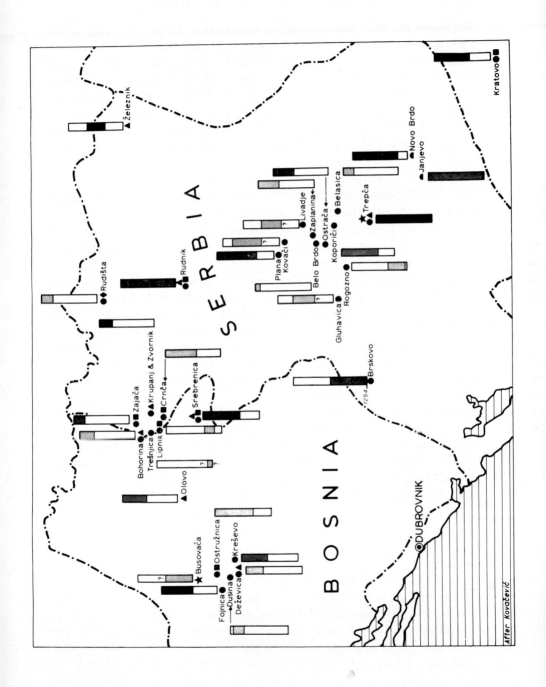

After Kovačević

Turks nor Serbs had much mining experience. Fourthly, many mines were situated in difficult terrain, mountain areas often well above sea level (Novo Brdo and many mines in the Kopaonik mountains were over 3,000 feet) which together with poor roads made exploitation an arduous task even in peace time and impossible in war time. Fifthly, many traders, especially from Dubrovnik, were attacked and robbed by Turkish soldiers whilst transporting minerals along the caravan routes. Many mines were also sacked by the Turkish army. Sixthly, the Turks transported *en masse* many people from Bosnia and Serbia to Turkey, to work as slaves. In 1467 a large number of the 40,000 population of Novo Brdo were resettled in Constantinople.[44] Finally, the Turks, on occupation forbad the exporting of all minerals from newly gained Turkish territory. This decree was later rescinded but even then the export of minerals was discouraged by means of a high tariff.

The destination of minerals exported from Dubrovnik must next be considered. The pattern can be effectively divided into two – exports to western Europe, particularly Italy, and exports to the Levant. Western Europe was slow to discard the economic customs of the Middle Ages but progress began in Italy during the twelfth century gathering momentum in the following two centuries and became evident in Europe in many spheres of economic life. Changes occurred in the trend and distribution of population. Larger territorial units were formed, which extended the range of local and foreign trade. In north and central Europe new peoples were brought within the orbit of commercial life, which for much of the Middle Ages had been almost closed to them. The domain of money economy was widened, spreading to countries which had previously occupied only a secondary place in the economic life of western Europe. The consequent rise in demand for precious metals eventually outstripped production, and for a period of several decades, beginning in the thirteenth century, there were general complaints of a serious lack of silver.

Minerals proved to be one of Dubrovnik's major exports to north and mid-Italy, up to the time of the Turkish Conquest. Given that there was important industrial growth in north and mid-Italy in the thirteenth and fourteenth centuries, nourished by markets created from increasing population and urbanization, what part did Dubrovnik's mineral exports play in this development? Unfortunately for Italy, industrial growth was hampered by notoriously poor mineral resources. Efforts were made at exploiting more unrewarding resources within the country, for example, the sands of certain Alpine streams were washed for gold, and silver was dug from small mines in Trentino and Cadore, Tuscany and Sardinia,[45] but supply could not satisfy demand. Consequently minerals had to be imported from central and eastern Europe, so that Dubrovnik, with a virtual monopoly in the rich Bosnian and Serbian mines, became an important supplier of Italian needs. The main market for Dubrovnik's lead exports was Venice, and from there it was distributed to the industrial centres of northern Italy. Lead was used in many ways including for roofing, drainage and other building purposes. The earliest firearms appeared in the West during the first half of the fourteenth century,[46] and according to Luzzato[47] the arms industry reached the peak of perfection and production in fourteenth century Milan. The industry was greatly stimulated by the rapid increase in demand for weapons which accompanied the replacement of urban militias by mercenary troops after the middle of the thirteenth century. Here again lead was an indispensable mineral, being used for a variety of purposes including the manufacture of cannon-balls,[48] body armour etc. The popularity of pewter cutlery also stimulated demand for lead besides its uses as a base for paints and dyes.[49] The trade in lead probably increased considerably after the first difficult decade of non-Venetian rule in Dubrovnik, and Table IV shows the incidence of lead exports from Dubrovnik to Venice.[50]

Two points should be noted from this table. Firstly the comparative insignificance in volume of medieval trade if one compares it with the volume of present-day commerce. But it must be remembered that the demand for foreign wares was very small in volume, because the population was much less dense than now and the lower orders of society, often on a subsistence level of economy, both in the country and to a greater extent in the town, had no share in foreign trade whatever. Secondly, the gap in trade between 1377 and 1382 coincided with one of the numerous wars between Venice and Genoa which raged both in the Adriatic and Levant during the fourteenth century. Dubrovnik as an ally of Genoa reduced her trade with Venice for the war period and only one document mentions the export of lead to Venice during this time and then only together with other goods.[51]

There seems little documentary evidence to support the view that Venetian merchants travelled to the Balkan interior to buy lead during the period preceding the Turkish occupation. It appears that the inland rulers worked together with Dubrovnik merchants, like the noted Zore Bokšić,[52] usually sending their lead and other goods to Dubrovnik or her warehouse at the mouth of the Neretva. Therefore the Venetian interest only lay on the door-step of the Balkans, her merchants restricting themselves to the financial and maritime share of the business.

Table IV

Year	Sent by	Original quantity	Present-day quantity	Sent from
1372	Venetian merchant	170 Venetian milijari	81,090 kg	Neretva
1372	Venetian merchant	80 Venetian milijari	38,160 kg	Neretva
1372	Venetian merchant	30 Dubr. milijari	10,743 kg	Dubrovnik
1372	Dubrovnik merchant	120 Dubr. milijari	42,972 kg	Neretva
1375	Dubrovnik merchant	100 Dubr. milijari	35,810 kg	Dubrovnik
1375	Dubrovnik merchant	10 Dubr. milijari 14 libri Dubr.	3,586 kg.	Dubrovnik
1377	Dubrovnik merchant	20 Venetian milijari	9,540 kg	Dubrovnik
1382	Dubrovnik merchant	150 peccias	6,124 kg	Dubrovnik
1386	Dubrovnik merchant	30 Dubr. milijari	10,743 kg	Dubrovnik
1387	Dubrovnik merchant	4 Dubr. milijari	1,432 kg	Dubrovnik
1387	Dubrovnik merchant	9 Dubr. milijari	3,223 kg	Dubrovnik
1387	Dubrovnik merchant	120·5 Dubr. milijari	43,152 kg	Dubrovnik
1387	Dubrovnik merchant	37·5 Dubr. milijari	13,429 kg	Dubrovnik
1391	Dubrovnik merchant	27·5 Dubr. milijari	9,848 kg	Dubrovnik

TOTAL   309,852 kg (305 tons)

One 'peccia' of lead equalled about 41 kilogrammes.
A Venetian milijari weighed 477 kilogrammes.

Bosnian and Serbian lead was sent to other towns in north and mid-Italy. Ancona[53] was a receiving port for Dubrovnik's lead exports, but despite much friendlier relations and a shorter distance it never seemed to possess the attraction which the Venetian market had for this commodity. Part of the answer to this enigma may have lain in the availability of transport and communications. The enormous expansion in the range of Italian commerce was not matched by any comparable improvement in the means of transport and communications. River navigation had considerable importance in the Po valley especially between Piacenza and the coast[54] and even towns which did not lie along it, in particular Milan,[55] Bergamo and Bologna, were all connected with it by rivers or canals and all maintained their tiny ports. Therefore to transport a heavy commodity like lead inland from Venice proved no great obstacle. Conversely Ancona, despite a good road to Florence, was backed by the Apennine mountains, and consequently conditions of travel were far worse, for there was little investment in road building. The hinterland of Ancona bristled with difficulties and dangers, and it is therefore not surprising that Dubrovnik's merchants commonly preferred to go by sea the extra distance to Venice.

Examples of lead being sent to Florence from Dubrovnik do exist,[56] but it appeared more common to ship the lead by sea to Pisa,[57] and was probably then transported up the Arno to Florence. Milan as an important metallurgical and armament manufacturing centre[58] was sometimes mentioned directly as receiving Dubrovnik's lead exports,[59] but one suspects that many of the transhipments for Venice eventually found their way to the Milan workshops.

Silver also found its place in Dubrovnik's mineral exports to Italy. The small silver resources, which Italy possessed, were never able to satisfy demand, especially for coinage production. The only money generally coined in Italian mints down to the fourteenth century was the silver penny (dinaro) which varied in alloy and weight from one mint to another and from one period to another with a constant and uniform tendency to debasement. The rapid growth of Italian trade in the Mediterranean and western Europe had revealed the inadequacy of silver currency of any kind as a means of exchange. Although this shortage was partially offset by the introduction of gold coins (e.g. Florentine 'florini', Genoese 'genoino' and the Venetian 'ducato') silver coins in the form of the 'grosso' and the piccolo [27 piccolo to 1 grosso (containing 96·5% silver in total weight= 2·18 grammes)] still persisted. The former was destined to serve the needs of large scale commerce and credit, whilst the latter was used in local trade of town and countryside and in payment of wages.

Unfortunately there is not a lot of information on silver exports in Dubrovnik's archives. Silver, as a precious metal was always treated with great care by Dubrovnik's merchants, who often accompanied loads in transit, and rarely made official statements on its movement. What information exists, hints at its possible importance in trade. Often large quantities were sent to Venice by individual merchants,[60] and while the town was probably Dubrovnik's main silver market,[61] it is recorded as having been sent to Tuscany (Florence[62] and Prato[63]) and the Papal States (Ancona[64] and Pesaro[65]). As with lead, silver was also sent to north Italian towns on an exchange basis for textiles.[66] But despite all this information the quantity of silver transported to Italy from the Balkans could not have been so great in the first half of the fifteenth century, for it was only after 1450 that the search for new supplies began to yield measurable results notably in Saxony and the Tyrol.

Other Balkan metals found their way through Dubrovnik to north and mid-Italy. Copper was used (with tin) for making bronze, and with tin and calamine (hydrous zinc silicate) for making brass for bells, cannons and other monumental and ornamental 'dinanderie'.[67] Consequently shipments of Bosnian and Serbian copper ores were sent during the fourteenth century through Dubrovnik to be refined in Venice,[68] but in the following century the ores were refined in Dubrovnik before being sent to the Venetian market.[69]

In Italy iron smelting was especially well developed in the valleys behind Bergamo and Brescia.[70] The Milanese arms industry acquired an international reputation by manufacturing corselets of the finest steel mail,[71] always in demand during this period of frequent wars. Dubrovnik satisfied some of the demand for iron ore by exporting Bosnian supplies,[72] although much less frequently than lead, silver or copper.

In contrast to western Europe the Levant was far less frequently mentioned, as a market for Balkan minerals, in Dubrovnik's documents. Firstly, the Levant was an underdeveloped region, with little or no industrial development unlike northern Italy, so the demand for minerals was much less. Secondly, part of the Levant belonged to the Infidel and it was forbidden by the Pope to carry to these lands minerals which could be utilized for the manufacture of arms. This does not imply that the boycott was successful, but it certainly discouraged what could have been a much larger export commodity from Dubrovnik.

Lead from the Bosnian mines was being exported to Alexandria by the middle of the fourteenth century. In 1359 just after Dubrovnik's break with Venice, a Venetian commander of a boat sailing for Alexandria refused to take lead on board at Dubrovnik.[73] Venetian competition, although strong in some commodities was not able to compete with Dubrovnik in the lead trade, because Dubrovnik had the advantage of proximity to raw materials. Lead was also exported to Syria[74] in the fourteenth century and information from the fifteenth shows a continuance of this trade to the Near East. Despite the Dubrovnik government's forbiddance of iron exports to the Levant, doubtless some reached their ports through contraband. Iron, like copper and lead was in popular demand for the manufacture of arms, particularly in Greece;[75] but due to weight and poor financial return (compared to lead) iron was usually in small quantities. It is possible that the manufactured arms in Greece were then sold illegally to the infidels at a substantial profit.

Slaves

Another precious commodity exported from the Balkans through Dubrovnik, besides minerals, was slaves. Even in Roman times slaves had been exported from the Balkans to Italy,[76] and by the thirteenth century, Dubrovnik had an organized trade in this commodity. A large number of slaves were female as seen from the documents, where the name and often age were included in the details. Most of these females were young girls, sold in Dubrovnik as concubines to traders from western Europe. The other slaves were used in domestic service, or employed in agriculture. In Dubrovnik itself the male slaves were also used in shipbuilding and the maritime service. The slave trade continued in the fourteenth century with Dubrovnik merchants transporting slaves, mainly from Bosnia, to the west, especially Italy, but slaves were also bought by Dubrovnik's citizens in the Levant.

A larger number of slaves came from Bosnia than from Serbia. The reason Bosnia figured largely in Dubrovnik's slave trade was due to the number of Bogomil schismatics living there at this time. These people proved an easy prey to merchants, because it was not generally looked upon as a sin to put these disbelievers into slavery. Many of the slaves came from the easily accessible areas of Bosnia, like Popovo Polje, the Sarajevo basin, and several river valleys like the Urbas, Usore and Neretva. Slaves were recorded as coming from Serbia, for example Skoplje was a noted slavery centre for Dubrovnik, but unlike Bosnia, Serbia did not have so many Bogomil heretics so one finds many Serbian slaves having come originally from Russia, Hungary and Roumania. Apparently, two major routeways were used, the one through eastern Bosnia collecting the majority of

Serbian slaves, whilst the Neretva valley was used in transporting slaves from central and north-west Bosnia.

Although Bosnia was the main source of slaves for Dubrovnik's merchants some were imported from the Levant, but as in Serbia, these slaves were of diverse origins. The majority of slaves bought in Greece or Turkey were usually from Russia or Tartary whilst those from Egypt[77] were Arabs or negroes,[78] all fetching varying prices according to skin colour, age (most of the slaves were aged between ten and thirty years old), sex and beauty.

The slave trade was no doubt a profitable business in which Dubrovnik's participation centred on transporting Balkan and Levantine slaves to the Venetian and other north Italian markets. Again, like minerals, demand outstripped supply as Luzzato maintains,[79]

'The insufficiency of slave labour (in Italy) may seem hard to reconcile with the unambiguous evidence of slave trading in this (tenth century) and later centuries. But the fact is that the international slave trade was now no longer supported by massive wars of conquest, but only the petty raids and forays of the Balkan and other tribes of eastern Europe; and so the slave market could only furnish labour enough for domestic service and specialized crafts'.

By the end of the thirteenth century documents gave precise information on their traffic to the west. According to documentary evidence the main buyers were from Florence, Ancona and Venice. Whether the slaves went to these towns is not always known for often these Italian buyers were acting as intermediaries for other western towns. Slaves were specifically mentioned in the Dubrovnik–Ancona Treaty of 1372,[80] whilst Venetian merchants had continuously visited the Dubrovnik market throughout the fourteenth century.[81] Slaves were also sent to Milan,[82] probably to be used for labour in the industries of that town. In southern Italy the main slave importers were the towns along the Apulian coast – Trani, Bari and Brindisi. Slaves must have been a profitable commodity for Dubrovnik's merchants. In the fifteenth century Genoese merchants found that

'Though both the Turks and Christians continued to capture and purchase white slaves in the Balkans and Asia Minor and to offer them at high prices in the markets, the supply could not meet demand. Merchants of Genoa trebled the prices of such white slaves as could be found and tried to fall back on Negro slaves'.[83]

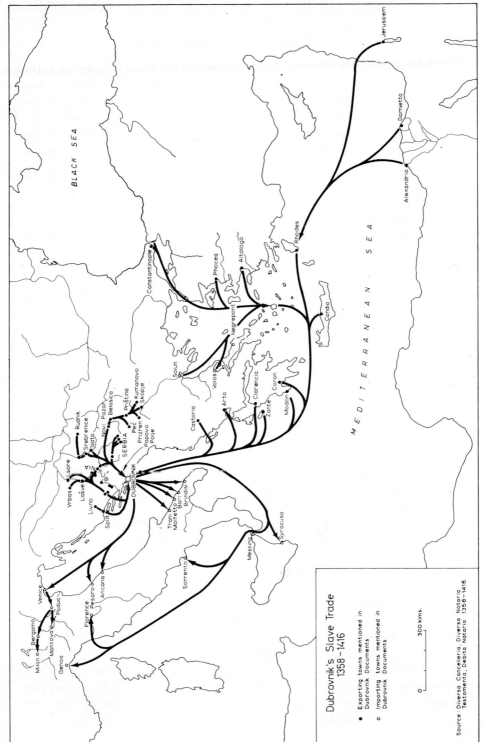

BLACK SEA

MEDITERRANEAN SEA

Jerusalem
Damietta
Alexandria
Rhodes
Candia
Altologo
Phocea
Negrepont
Constantinople
Soun
Volos
Arta
Castoria
Clarencia
Zonte
Coron
Modon
Messina
Syracusa
Sorrento
Ancona
Pesaro
Florence
Padua
Venice
Mantova
Bergamo
Milan
Genoa
Brindisi
Molfetta
Trani
Bari
DUBROVNIK
Split
Livno
Lašve
Vrbas
Isore
BOSNIA
SERBIA
Rudnik
Srebrenice
Osata
Peć
Prizren
Popovo
Polje
Novi Pazar
Belasica
Priština
Kumanovo
Skopje

Dubrovnik's Slave Trade
1358–1416

• Exporting towns mentioned in
   Dubrovnik Documents

○ Importing towns mentioned in
   Dubrovnik Documents

0   300 kms.

Source: Diversa Cancelleria, Diversa Notaria
        Testamenta, Debita Notaria 1358–1416

Fig. 38.

Unfortunately for Dubrovnik's citizens, the slave trade like the mineral exports suffered a decline in the mid-fifteenth century, but this was due more to an awakening of western consciences and the ensuing opposition to slavery, rather than from prohibitive measures by the Turkish authorities. There were two reasons for the marked change in Dubrovnik's slave trade. First, at the beginning of the fifteenth century the Bosnian government protested against the collection and selling of its people. This protest terminated in the Dubrovnik government law of 1416 forbidding the use of slaves in the town, but not forbidding their transit through the port,[84] so that Dubrovnik merchants still continued their trade even if on reduced terms. The second and more important factor was the general disappearance of slaves in western Europe during the fifteenth century. For example, the Venetian government in 1446 forbad its citizens selling slaves from Dubrovnik, if they had come from the Turkish (i.e. Bosnian and Serbian) hinterland.[85] Thus it appears as much an economic as moral factor which caused a decline in Dubrovnik's slave trade.

Spices

Increased trade by Dubrovnik's merchants with the Near East in the twelfth and thirteenth centuries saw a growth in spice exports to the town. Salzman[86] states

> 'Medieval men had neither a delicate palate nor the means of gratifying it with choice meats; their meat was coarse and they liked it highly flavoured'.

Consequently the spice trade grew in importance throughout medieval times, but it was a trade which had many intermediate stages and innumerable middlemen; Dubrovnik's merchants were amongst those who took on this role.

By 1358 spices were by no means a new commercial venture for Dubrovnik but in the second half of the fourteenth and in the fifteenth centuries, they were her major import from those parts of the Levant known as 'Ash Sham' (Syria, Lebanon and Israel) and Egypt. They were often cited in documents as either 'spices' or 'aromata', but sometimes the actual variety is mentioned. Of these varieties pepper seems to have attracted the most attention, coming chiefly through Alexandria. The Arabs knew that pepper grew on the Malabar coast,

and they bought it at Serif in Aden, from there it passed through
Egypt in the usual manner and the Venetians monopolized the
greater part of the trade in western Europe. The Sultans of Egypt
realizing the importance of this commodity made it their own
personal monopoly. The Venetians complained about extortionate
prices and in 1438 their merchants were shocked that 'pepper could
be had cheaper at Constantinople, Bursa and Trebizond than Alexandria'.[87] No documents indicate the profit Dubrovnik merchants
made on pepper but they did re-export it to Venice[88] whence in turn
it was distributed to other parts of Europe.

Other spices referred to in Dubrovnik documents as coming from
Egypt and Ash Sham included cloves, which were used extensively
in medicines, as well as in cooking and aromatic drinks;[89] capers used
for pickling purposes, and the herb saffron, a popular ingredient in
many medieval sauce recipes. Saffron was the most costly of all herbs,
coming from the saffron crocus; only the stigmas of the flowers were
used and it took about 75,000 flowers to make one pound of saffron.[90]
Consequently Dubrovnik's merchants only bought small quantities.[91]

Salt

In the geological composition of the Balkan peninsula there was a
noticeable lack of salt-bearing rocks. The deposits that existed were
small or remained undiscovered until after the Turkish occupation, so
that the demand for salt from external sources, was high. As the
Bosnian and Serbian economy was largely dependent on livestock
for its existence, there was a dual demand for salt, for the people
themselves, and for their cattle. Salt panned from the sea (called in
documents 'sal de marina'), therefore assumed great importance
commercially and Dubrovnik's merchants exploited this situation
from early times; salt could have been the earliest stimulus to trade
between Dubrovnik and the hinterland. Unfortunately many documents referring to the salt trade have been lost but those that survive
show that it was an important branch of Dubrovnik's commerce.

During the last decade of the fourteenth century there was a
marked increase in salt imports by Dubrovnik from western Greece.
Much of this salt during the fourteenth century had come from Corfu,
where in the south-west part of the island pans were located for
trapping sea water during the winter months. In 1386 Venice
occupied Corfu, an occupation lasting until 1797. Venice was

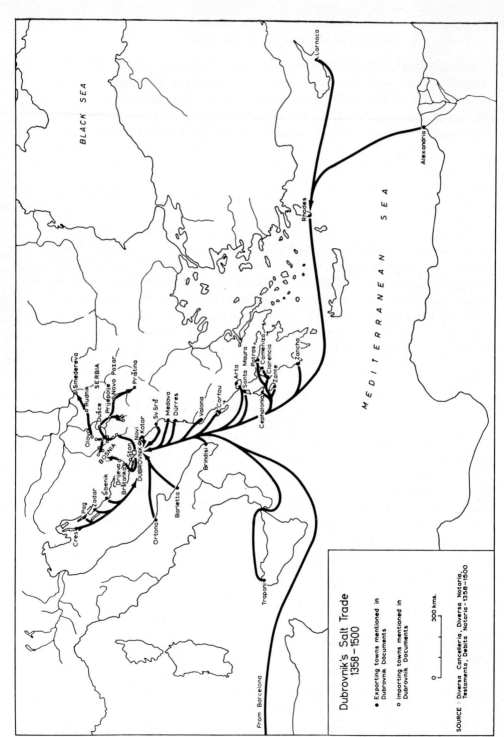

Dubrovnik's Salt Trade
1358–1500

• Exporting towns mentioned in
  Dubrovnik Documents

○ Importing towns mentioned in
  Dubrovnik Documents

0 ————— 300 kms.

SOURCE : Diversa Cancelleria, Diversa Notaria,
          Testamenta, Debita Notaria – 1358–1500

BLACK SEA

MEDITERRANEAN SEA

Larnaca

Alexandria

Rhodes

Smederevo
Rudnik
SERBIA
Novo Pazar
Dušče
Prijepolje
Priština
Olovo
BOSNIA
Sv Srđ
Medova
Durrës
Novi
Ston
Kotor
DUBROVNIK
Drijeva
Brštanok
Šibenik
Zadar
Pag
Cres
Ortona
Barletta
Brindisi
Volona
Corfou
Arta
Santa Maura
Patras
Cephalonia
Camenitza
Clarencia
Zante
Zoncha

From Barcelona

Trapani

FIG. 39.

naturally resentful of Dubrovnik's merchants utilizing the island's resources particularly to feed the Balkan markets, for the Venetians themselves were intent at this time on capturing them. Consequently Santa Maura (present day Levkas), which did not become Venetian till 1684, took Corfu's position as Dubrovnik's chief supplier in the fifteenth century.

Other centres in western Greece used by Dubrovnik merchants for buying salt included the islands of Cephalonia and Zante, together with the coastal towns of Arta, Patras, Clarencia and Zancha. Unfortunately Dubrovnik's trade was continually harassed by Venetian intervention. In 1417 for example, the Venetians protested to the Dukes of Arta and Cephalonia for favouring traders from Dubrovnik when selling salt.[92] Much of this rivalry only ended on Venetian occupation of these centres. Despite competition from the other salt pans trading with Dubrovnik, western Greece, and particularly the Ionian Islands, managed to produce enough salt, and at the right price, to attract merchants from the city. Also much of this salt was not for Dubrovnik itself but for the inland Balkans, importing via the Neretva valley. Albania also provided a partial answer to the shortage of salt experienced by Dubrovnik's merchants during the latter part of the fourteenth century.

Salt was imported to Dubrovnik from three main places. First, from the main market centre of Sveti Svd, a settlement on the left bank of the Bojana River centred around a Benedictine monastery,[93] where Dubrovnik merchants bought their salt supplies.[94] They are also mentioned as buying it at Medova, the outport of Lesh.[95] The second salt market was at Dürres.[96] This town was the main port for mid-Albania possessing a good harbour at the northern end of Drim Bay, and within close proximity to salt workings along the marshy coast. Finally salt was purchased by Dubrovnik from Valona.[97] This was the main market centre of southern Albania and noted for its ability to accommodate large boats. It is noticeable that Dubrovnik's imports of Dalmatian salt are smaller than would be expected considering the nearness of the Dalmatian salt pans and the hinterland markets. The reasons were twofold, for Dubrovnik-Dalmatian trade relations between 1358 and 1500 experienced two main pressures. The first of these, in a wider context, was the rivalry between Venice and Dalmatia as a whole, the second, on a smaller scale, competition between Dubrovnik and other Dalmatian towns. Competition was largely confined to the southern part of Dalmatia, towns along the southern coast had the same hinterland as Dubrovnik and were all about the same distance from the Italian coast. Dubrovnik's competitors included from north to south, Drijeva in the lower Neretva valley, Novi, Risan and Kotor in the Bay of Kotor, and Budva and Bar on the coast to the south. All these places possessed, or were near salt-pans and the capturing of Balkan markets for this commodity provided the main bone of contention between Dubrovnik and her neighbours. Southern Italy was also a source of salt supplies particularly during the reigns of Alfonso I and Ferdinand. The shore between Barletta[98] and Manfredoni provided ideal sites for salt-panning. Similarly the coast near Trapani[99] in Sicily is low and faced by extensive areas of shallow water where even today salt pans line much of the shore.

Dubrovnik therefore imported salt mainly from western Greece, Albania, Dalmatia and southern Italy, and by efficient organization and monopolistic treaties[100] was able to exclude other coastal towns, like Kotor and Dürres, from the market. The main market for Dubrovnik's salt exports was Bosnia. The reason for this could have been due to Bosnia's closer proximity, but there may also have been another reason. In eastern and central Serbia, Dubrovnik's merchants were faced with competition from Hungarian traders[101] who had controlling interests in the rock salt deposits of Hungary and Roumania. In southern Serbia and Macedonia, Greek merchants using salt supplies from the Aegean Sea reduced the market potential for traders from Dubrovnik. This forced the city's merchants to concentrate on the Bosnian salt market with a resulting growth in its exports there in the late fourteenth and early fifteenth centuries.[102] Two major routeways, the Neretva valley and the mountain route to the Drim valley, were used with a third route by sea to the port of Novi. The latter was probably discouraged amongst the city's traders for fear of attaching too much importance to the harbour for political reasons. Most of the importing places mentioned in Dubrovnik's documents were market centres. This was particularly so in central and eastern Bosnia where towns like Borač, Goražda, Prača and Visoko were distribution centres for all sorts of goods coming not only from the coast but other parts of the Balkan hinterland. In comparison places like Drijeva and Brštanka at the mouth of the Neretva were mainly storage centres where Dubrovnik's merchants had warehouses, despatching the salt up the valley to the markets of inland Bosnia. Also market centres like Borač, Goražda and Foča were all on the main trade routes to western Serbia and although Dubrovnik documents only register them as going to these towns the salt supplies may have travelled further eastward.[103] Finally, the Lim valley was important as a routeway for supplying Prijepolje and further south, Plevlje and Brežnica. From these towns salt supplies may have been forwarded to the agricultural areas of Kossovo polje .

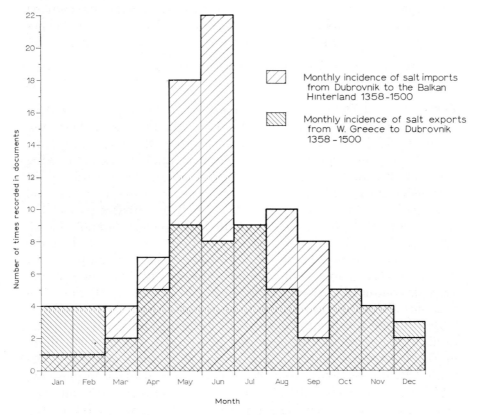

Monthly incidence of salt imports from Dubrovnik to the Balkan Hinterland 1358 -1500

Monthly incidence of salt exports from W. Greece to Dubrovnik 1358 -1500

Fig. 40. Source: Dubrovnik Archives; *Diversa Cancellaria*; *Diversa Notaria*; *Testementa*; *Debita Notaria*, 1358–1500.

This situation persisted, even after the Turkish occupation, only changing with the capture of Hercegovina by the Turks in 1483. Rock salt deposits in Hercegovina were found and exploited by the Turks so that one cannot say, as Kostić maintains, that 'the *exclusive* selling of salt to the Bosnians by Dubrovnik merchants existed during the time of Turkish rule'.[104] A further setback for Dubrovnik happened in 1484 when the Turks re-opened the port of Novi in the Bay of Kotor. All salt imports now had to go through Novi, as did the four main export products at this time lead, silver, kermes, and wax.[105] This meant the Turks could easily collect the heavy customs duties placed on those commodities either going to, or coming from Dubrovnik, naturally cutting down the profit margin for Dubrovnik's merchants. The city continued to export salt to Bosnia-Hercegovina and Serbia but with her monopoly broken it failed to hold its former position in Dubrovnik's trade structure.

Cheaper Raw Materials

Fortunately for Dubrovnik her economy was not solely dependent on trade in precious raw materials. Otherwise the decline of these products would have had a disastrous effect on the city's economy, through reasons quite beyond her control. Luckily the flourishing state of Italian towns, which were amongst Dubrovnik's best customers during this period, was not built exclusively on trade in high quality merchandise; in practice much the greater part of the goods which Italians imported from the Balkans consisted not of lead, silver or slaves, but of skins, wool, wax and timber[106] – in fact the cheaper commodities. These were produced in the Balkan peninsula and what is more important were not subject to prohibition after the Turkish conquest. Consequently Dubrovnik's trade with the West was not affected so disastrously as was at first feared.

Prior to the fourteenth century the Bosnians and Serbs had practised little agriculture but possessed many cattle; later, particularly in the fourteenth century, agriculture made some advance. The central basins, or poljes, were floored with a rich black humus soil, which was both well watered and sheltered, and cereals, hemp, flax and beans were all cultivated there. In the Sarajevo basin, the Metohija basin between Peč and Prizren, and the basin of Kossovo, nucleated villages were very numerous and population was abundant – greater in the fourteenth century than it is today.[107] Cultivation was in some measure increased by deforestation, but in the late fourteenth century it was in some cases forbidden 'to plough up the pastures of the mountain'. Cattle, pigs, and horses were the chief source of wealth; transhumance was practised, cattle were led up from the winter pastures of the Mediterranean coastlands to the summer pastures of the interior mountains.[108] Other features of this

ѡдь херьцегове земле санжакбегу и новскому кадиѣ.

када вамь ован моа книга доге, такон да знате: прѣге овоган ѡд велике ми порьте заповѣдь послахь, ѡд новске скале амалдари, тко ю по еннебегу, сь дубровачьком г(ос)п(о)домь парбу су имали, сви на юдно мѣсто да догють и тефьтишь учините и да видите, ако ми иманю нѣка щета некѣ бити, на нихь уговорь амальдарь ако пристанеть, такон да учините. ако ли путем друзѣмь щета буде, ѡд щете путь, ѡд циа ю, лѣпо исьписавше да ми на порту пошлете и путь ѡд моѣга имана, ѡд кога се гѫде векина види, тѣмь путем да учините. и по овѣзѣхь рѣчехь ако с(е) щета не види, како они веле, ако би такон било, да буде и у дубровник свила, олово, восакь и црваиь: ове четири ствари да не идуть, друге трговине да идуть: такон самь бию заповидию.

а сада за друге трговине задѣваю се. що ѣ прѣ речено инако да не буде и сада да не учините. ако ли за тон узиманѣ у амалдара моа кома книга будеть, у писмю да ми кажете. такон самь бии заповидию. по ѡвонзи монои заповѣднои книзи сви на юдно мѣстѡ да се скупите и дубровачке поклисаре туи доведите, тефьтишь учините. речени дубровачки поклисари ѡдговорь такон дадоше: ѡд новьске сланице сѡ када се продаа, ми нашу сѡ ѡд друзѣхь, како они узимаю, такон и ѡд нас да узимаю, са амальдаромь сѡ дѣлеки на половину, да учинимо. ѡд оне .д. ствари ину трговину ако наши люде доносе и ѡдносе, за царину да не имаю рѣчь. на ови уговаи стауши за нѣколико дана дубровачка сѡ дошадьчи ‚в‚в аспри продано ю соли, такон ми сте уписали.

да и сада, када ви ован книга догѣ, требуѣ, прѣге овоган кон ю уговаи бию да и сада на том стану.

инако да нѣсте учинили. али такон требе да ми иманю не буде нѣка щета. ако ли ѡд вась знамь, да не будете за велику срамоту врѣдии. такон да знате, тако ви мои лѣпи нишаи да вѣруѣте.

писань мсца шабана лѣта мехемета ѡѕ.

FIG. 41. Transcript of document issued by Sultan Bajazid II in which he states that salt from Dubrovnik can be sold in the port of Novi, but silk, lead, wax and kermes cannot be sent through Dubrovnik. Dated August/September 1485, Dubrovnik Archives, *Liber Privilegiorum* Vol. I, p. 118b.

inland Balkan economy were trapping, hunting and fishing in lake and river, timber felling in the high lands for ships and wine casks, whilst apiculture for honey, wax and mead was deliberately extended.

Skins

In the second half of the fourteenth century skins were already a noteworthy export article from the western Balkans and this continued during the fifteenth century. Skins were one of the main by-products from the stock-raising activities of these inland peoples being used in innumerable ways—for shoes, coats, carpets, saddles, leather bags etc. There appeared to be two types of skins – the ordinary hides from cattle, goats, sheep and buffalo, and the rarer skins from wolf, marten, fox, lynx and other wild animals living in the forest areas. These rarer skins were greatly treasured in Italy as linings for coats, shoes and hats, being made up by Dubrovnik furriers and then exported to Italy at a high price. Unlike Serbia, the skins of wild animals were rarely mentioned in documents from Bosnia, and this may be explained by the much greater importance that Bosnian merchants attached to skins from domestic livestock.

Skin exports from the Balkan hinterland have an interesting distribution pattern. Central and eastern Bosnia figured largely in the skin trade for the main exporting places, like Goražde, Prača, Borač and Foča, were all collecting centres and market towns for their respective districts where skins were probably bartered or sold; also settlements in the poljes behind Dubrovnik – Gačko, Vučevo, Cernice and Vrm – provided a substantial number of skins for Dubrovnik's traders. The proximity of these poljes naturally attracted the city's merchants whereas Serbia appears less important. This may be due to lack of documentary evidence, but it is equally possible that when Dubrovnik's merchants could get supplies in the near vicinity of the city, there was no need to travel into Serbia except for skins of the rarer wild animals. Most of the expensive raw materials had followed the safer river valleys of the Ibar and Lim. Skins, which had much less intrinsic value, could be transported along the shorter but more dangerous routes through the north Albanian mountains to the ports of southern Dalmatia which tended to specialize in the transporting of cheaper commodities. Also Dubrovnik merchants would never have risked sending precious products through Ulcinj for this

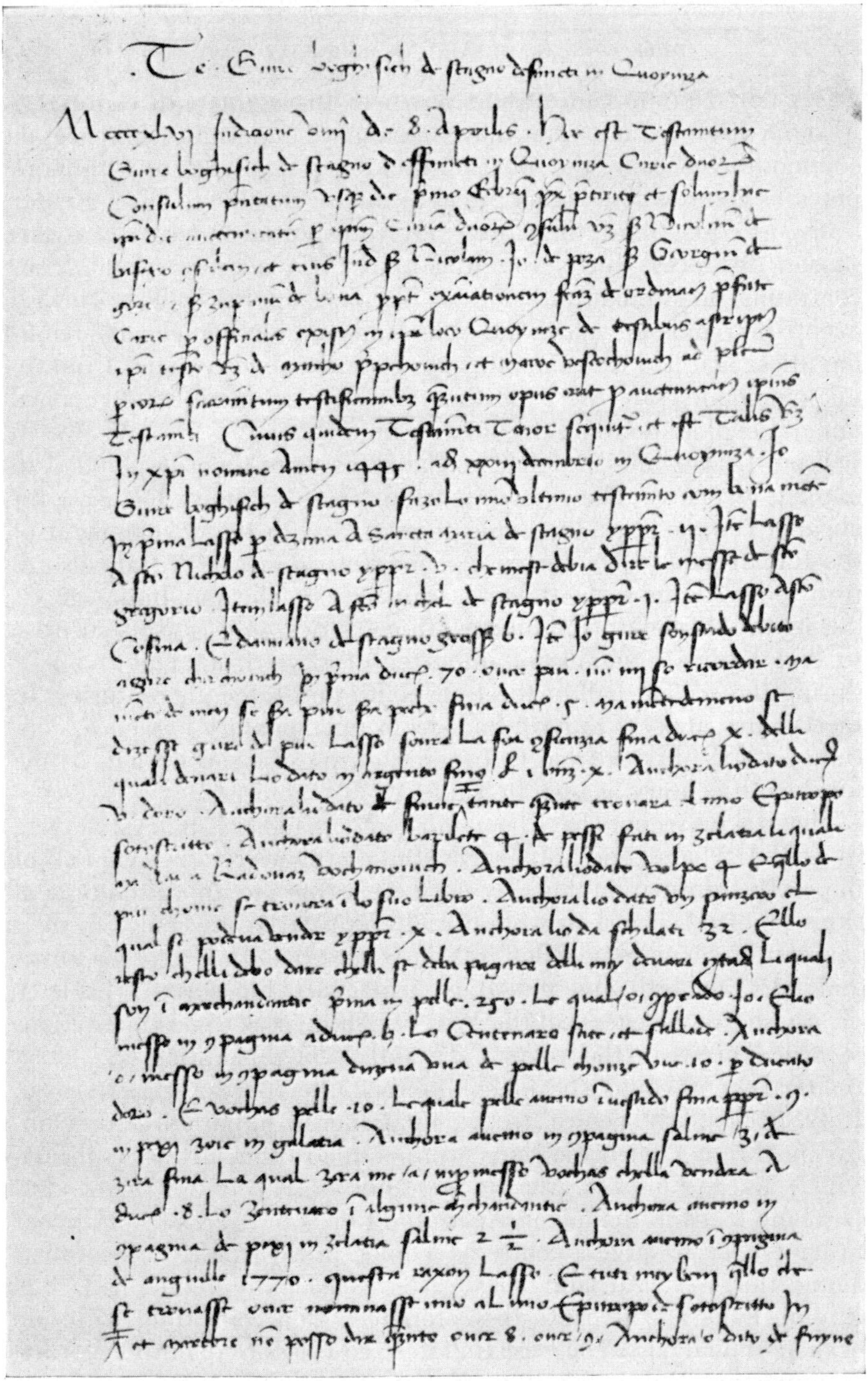

FIG. 42.   Dubrovnik Archives 8/IV/1446 Document recording the dispatch of tanned skins from Bosnia to Dubrovnik. *Testamenta Notaria* 14, fol. 31.

was a noted pirate centre right down to the eighteenth century.[109] Also the distance factor must have been more important with cheaper commodities because the profit on them was smaller than with more precious goods whose higher prices abroad were able to offset greater transport costs. Skins, therefore, were transported in larger caravans shorter distances, thus accounting for Dubrovnik's merchants concentrating on Bosnian rather than Serbian supplies.[110] The Turkish occupation did not affect the skin trade and other cheaper commodities, as it had the mineral exports. Consequently many Dubrovnik merchants saw the exporting of skins as an alternative once mineral exploitation had declined in importance.

From Dubrovnik's warehouses the skins were then despatched to markets overseas. The most important were in Italy. Demand for cheaper commodities, like skins, increased with the development of the Italian fairs.[111] The increase of markets in medieval Italy also in turn led to large-scale Italian commerce in cheaper bulky goods during the thirteenth and fourteenth centuries, so it is of no surprise to find Venice a significant importer of skins from Dubrovnik,[112] during the second half of the fourteenth and fifteenth centuries. In fact Venice appears to have had, from documentary evidence, continued trade in skins from Dubrovnik during the second half of the fourteenth century as seen in Table V.

Sheep skins seem to have been most in demand (237 bales) followed by lamb (12 bales) and lastly cattle, but owing to the large amount of imprecise information this may not give a true picture of the type of skins exported. The skins were usually transported to Venice in their raw state[113] being remodelled in Venice and then sent to other towns and fairs in north and mid-Italy, especially Florence.[114] Table V clearly shows the effects of the War of Chioggia with no transactions recorded between the years 1377 and 1382 illustrating the effect political events could have on commercial intercourse. Skin exports to Italy, particularly Venice, were of paramount importance for Dubrovnik. From Venice the skins were sent to other towns in the Po Valley and to Florence. Ancona was another distribution centre despatching loads to the inland Apennine towns but it does not appear to have been so large a centre as Venice in this trade. Other towns along the west Adriatic coast are occasionally mentioned, e.g. Rimini, Fano and Recanti, the reference often coinciding with one of their annual fairs. The west Italian coast is less frequently recorded as importing Dubrovnik skins but it is probable that some loads

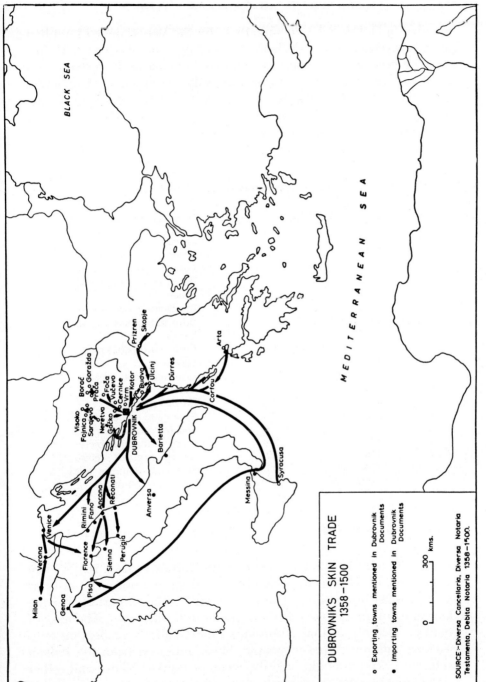

DUBROVNIK'S SKIN TRADE
1358–1500

○ Exporting towns mentioned in Dubrovnik Documents

● Importing towns mentioned in Dubrovnik Documents

300   kms.
0

SOURCE:–Diversa Cancellaria, Diversa Notaria Testamenta, Debita Notaria 1358–1500.

FIG. 43.

recorded in Dubrovnik's documents as for the Venetian or Florentian markets, eventually found their way to towns on this coast. Unlike the more precious commodities, skins could be carried overland with less risk of loss, so the sea route around Italy was much less frequently used. The two-way traffic in skins from Sicily is not so surprising, because due to their demand merchants would take them as return cargo always knowing they were a saleable commodity. As with Bosnia and Serbia, one suspects that the times Greece and Albania

Table V

Year	Quantity in Bales*	Type of Skins
1358	3	Lamb
1358	2	Sheep
1359	2	Lamb
1366	192	Information not precise
1367	15	Sheep
1370	26	Information not precise
1372	160	Information not precise
1372	7	Lamb
1376	37	Information not precise
1377	73	Sheep
1377	250	Information not precise
1382	25	Buffalo
1382	32	Cattle (cow oxen)
1382	8	Sheep and goats
1382	18	Sheep
1387	10	Information not precise
1389	700	Information not precise
1390	129	Sheep (at 13 ducats/bale)
1390	13	Information not precise

TOTAL 1,702 (170,200 skins)

*1 bale = 100 skins. (Information given only where correct quantities are known.)

are mentioned in documents is not representative of their importance for Dubrovnik. This is supported by the larger amount of times skins are mentioned as exported from Dubrovnik, than imported. Yet the skins must originally have been imported into the town. The answer could lie in the fact that Dubrovnik's merchants were dealing with two very different types of people. Skins imported from the Balkan hinterland were bought mainly from peasants – Vlahs and other inland stockbreeders who rarely demanded any written confirmation of a transaction. Also skins were not of great value so there were less court cases, disputes, etc. in which they were recorded. Conversely skins exported from Dubrovnik were sent to Italian merchants trained in the art of recording commercial transactions.

'The magnitude and modernity, so to speak, of large-scale Italian commerce during the thirteenth and still more the fourteenth and fifteenth centuries was clearly displayed in the complex and systematic organization of business houses'[115]

and further

'no great merchant at that time could neglect opportunities in small trade. Without the addition of substantial cargoes of cheap bulky goods (like skins), it would have been impossible to maintain the convoys of Venetian, Florentian and Genoese galleys, which carried luxury goods on longer voyages'.[116]

Wax

Wax was another cheap Balkan commodity which Dubrovnik merchants found worth exploiting. Bee-keeping was a significant feature of Slavonic settlements throughout the Balkans during the Middle Ages. Domestically, apiculture was a source of honey and mead, which took the place of sugar in the diet, for sugar was difficult to obtain, having to be imported from the Levant. Commercially, wax was produced and sold in large quantities to churches and monasteries, not only in the Balkan peninsula but in western Europe. Beeswax together with tallow fat were the basic ingredients for producing candles – the main form of artificial light in medieval times. Besides its obvious use for candles in both home and church it became of special use in business life. With the increased organization associated with western European business life there arose the need for more documentation. Consequently quantities of wax were required for the sealing of letters and legal documents, since without a proper seal the authenticity of any medieval communication was suspect.

Bosnia-Hercegovina and Serbia possessed rich forests and luxuriant vegetation, which were extremely important for bee-keeping. The wax was taken to the local market centres like Foča, Goražda and Borač by the peasants, for sale, just as they did with skins, and there Dubrovnik's merchants bought large quantities for export. For transportation purposes wax had an added advantage. It was easy to mould to the most convenient shape for carriage compared with a load of the more unwieldy lead.[117] Dubrovnik purchased more wax than was needed to satisfy her own needs and had the distinction like lead and silver of being mentioned separately in documents, as compared with other goods which on many occasions were just referred to as 'alias mercancias'.[118] This special treatment must have been due to its large market in western Europe.

In the first half of the fifteenth century there appears to have been a great growth in wax exports to Italy,[119] coinciding with the economic expansion in Italy at this time. Prior to the Turkish conquest wax from the Balkans and Levant (Arta and its hinterland were noted for wax) was transported freely by Dubrovnik's boats to the coastal towns of north and mid-Italy – Pesaro in particular, which specialized in the wax trade.[120] In March 1484 the Turkish Sultan decreed that a heavy tax must be placed on the export of wax (together with lead, kermes and silver), from Bosnia-Hercegovina and Serbia to Dubrovnik.[121] The profit margin on wax could not have been so great for the dues and tariffs imposed by the Turkish Sultan had the effect of temporarily stopping the wax trade with Italy at the end of the fifteenth century but it was renewed and extended in the following century.

Livestock Products

Other livestock products were sent to Dubrovnik for sale, but these came mainly from Bosnia-Hercegovina, little mention being made in Dubrovnik documents relating to Serbia. Cattle and sheep were often brought live to Dubrovnik slaughter houses, to help supply the large town population with meat, or to be exported to Italy, especially Apulia.[122] Hercegovina seems to have figured prominently in this trade with live cattle and especially sheep. This phenomenon is probably accounted for by weight loss in cattle if walked over large distances, so that Dubrovnik's traders bought livestock within close proximity to the town. Horses,[123] as the main form of transport in southern Europe at this time, and as a source of meat, were always in demand in Dubrovnik, either for export to Italy, or for local use, whilst pigs, besides providing meat, were a source of skins for the Dubrovnik leather workers. Trade in live cattle was probably much greater than is suggested by documentary evidence, because livestock was brought to Dubrovnik from the hinterland often without any formal transaction being signed.

Cereals

Lack of arable land within the Republic of Dubrovnik meant that their cereal crop scarcely sufficed for more than four months of the year, there was thus a constant need to procure grain for the remaining eight months. More documentation exists on cereal imports than many other commodities traded by Dubrovnik's merchants, probably because of its constant concern by the republic and the close watch kept on its reserves. Four main areas emerge in Dubrovnik's cereal imports – the western coast of Asia Minor, the Black Sea, Greece, and southern Italy. The western coast of Asia Minor has increasing references to grain exports during the last two decades of the fourteenth century, particularly the coastal settlements of Phocea, Smyrna, Altologo (Ephesus) and Palatia.[124] This coincided with the expulsion of the Venetians and Genoese from Tenados island during the War of Chioggia (1382). The islands of Mitilene (Lesbos), Chios, and Rhodes[125] also exported cereals to Dubrovnik. Constantinople with its adjoining suburb of Pera was also a cereal mart for Dubrovnik during this period. Cereals, especially wheat, barley and millet were imported from Bulgaria and Wallachia through the Black Sea ports of Varna, Mesembria and Moncastro (Akkerman) into Constantinople and from here Dubrovnik's merchants took the grain by sea to their own and other granaries in the Adriatic. The disadvantage of distance (60 days voyage from Dubrovnik) was partially offset by the favourable trade concessions the city had in the Byzantine capital. Dubrovnik merchants had a customs duty of only 2% of the value of goods imported or exported from the town, whilst most foreign traders paid 5%.

Greece is first mentioned as a grain exporter to Dubrovnik in 1294, Arta, the Peloponnesus, Volos and Solun being the main suppliers.[126] Arta, according to documentary evidence, became increasingly important in the fifteenth century[127] having as its great advantage, nearness to Dubrovnik. The question of proximity to Dubrovnik was a noticeable factor. Western Greece is mentioned more frequently than eastern Greece as a source of cereals, with Corfu[128] the major grain exporter to Dubrovnik. One notable grain market of the fourteenth and fifteenth centuries which was rarely mentioned in Dub-

K

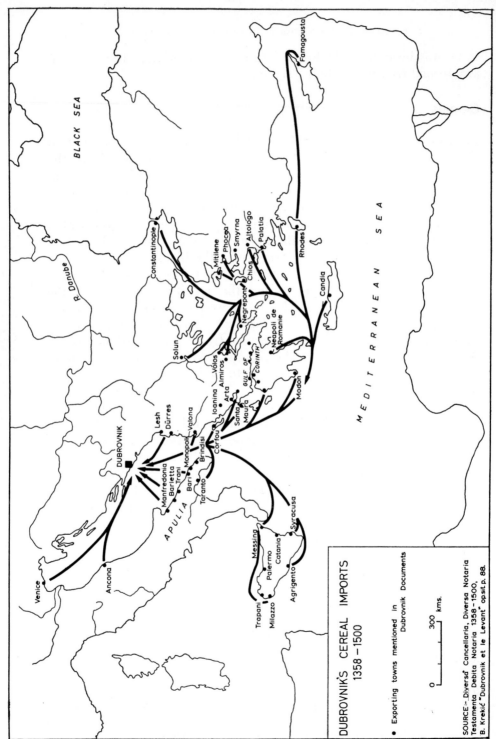

DUBROVNIK'S CEREAL IMPORTS
1358 – 1500

• Exporting towns mentioned in
  Dubrovnik Documents

0   300 kms.

SOURCE:- Diversa Cancellaria, Diversa Notaria
Testamenta Debita Notaria 1358-1500,
B. Krekić "Dubrovnik et le Levant" opsit.p. 88.

BLACK SEA

MEDITERRANEAN SEA

R. Danube

Famagousta

Constantinople

Mitilene
Phocea
Smyrna
Chios
Altologo
Palatia
Rhodes
Candia

Negrepont
Neapoli de
Romanie
Solun
Volos
Almiros
GULF OF
CORINTH
Modon

Ioanina
Arta
Santa
Maura
Corfou

Lesh
Dürres
Valona
DUBROVNIK
Manfredonia
Barletta
Trani
Bari
Monopoli
Brindisi
Taranto

APULIA

Venice

Ancona

Syracusa

Messina
Palermo
Catania
Agrigento
Trapani
Milazzo

FIG. 44.

rovnik's documents is Crete. This Venetian-held island provided its rulers with a large part of their corn supplies from the Levant[129] and so became a carefully guarded monopoly against outside intrusion. Southern Italy was the fourth largest area exporting to Dubrovnik. The ports of Apulia and Sicily were most frequently mentioned as exporting cereals to the city.[130] It is interesting that as a result of close proximity, lower transport costs and an advantageous political situation, *vis-a-vis* southern Italy, there were no famines recorded in Dubrovnik during the whole of the fifteenth century. It may be significant that with the succession of the Spaniards, Ferdinand and Isabella to the kingdom of Naples in 1490, commercial relations deteriorated and famines are recorded in Dubrovnik in 1502 and 1503 – the first for two hundred years.[131]

Flax

One commodity which probably enjoyed a greater share in Dubrovnik's trade than documentary evidence suggests was flax. Flax figured prominently in Levantian exports to Dubrovnik, particularly from the region of western Greece. This supply was not to satisfy the demand of Dubrovnik's own textile factories, as they were not developed until the fifteenth century, but to be re-exported from Dubrovnik to the manufacturing centres of Italy, mainly through the port of Ancona. Flax was first recorded in Dubrovnik's documents[132] in 1278 and was frequently noted in the next two centuries. Clarencia was the principal exporting harbour,[133] some of the flax undoubtedly coming from the plains of north and north-west Peloponnesus,[134] but it is probable also that the port was a collecting point for other areas, for it was known to have been an important crop in Negrepont.[135] Again from documentary evidence Corfu seems to have been the origin for much of Dubrovnik's flax imports, but the island was probably only an intermediary stage in its transportation.[136] Most probably it was originally bought in the Peloponnesus, or Arta and then shipped via Corfu to Dubrovnik.

Manufactured Goods

Textiles

One of the main branches of trade during this period dealt with the import and export of cloth. Dubrovnik was a station on the most important axis of Florentine trade whose key points were Florence itself, Ancona, Dubrovnik and Constantinople; to the west the route extended in two main directions: to the wool ports of eastern Spain and to the Florentine-dominated emporium of Lyons; to the east the route split at both Dubrovnik and Constantinople into many parts leading to all the great cities of the Ottoman Empire. It was to the East that nearly all Florentine cloth not sold in Italy was consigned[137] and with the abandonment of the Florentine galley system,[138] cloths to the East were being directed more and more along the overland routes across the Balkans.

Textile imports from north and mid-Italy were of two types – foreign cloth of north European origin and home produced stuff. The foreign cloth came mainly through Venice and Ancona from northern Europe. The English textile industry had a wide reputation specializing in both high grade and cheap woollens for home and foreign markets. Dubrovnik's merchants even visited England and are first recorded as sailing to 'Inghilterra' to buy woollen cloth in 1443, returning by the land route via Lyons and Milan.[139] Unfortunately, a voyage like this took over a year to complete and the dangers involved often made insurance costs total 15 per cent of the outlay on a voyage.[140] English textiles were occasionally mentioned in the second half of the fifteenth century but it was in the following century that a considerable growth in their imports took place. Although less frequently recorded than that from England, Flemish cloth nevertheless had some attraction in the markets of south-east Europe. Cloth from 'Ypre' (Ypres – centre of the linen industry) was mentioned as early as 1272,[141] and during the reorganization of Dubrovnik's own textile industry, Flemish textiles (frixoni, cariseae blanchetae) were allowed into the port, but had to be sold on a small scale,[142] to avoid too much competition.

Italian home produced cloth was frequently mentioned in Dubrovnik's documents sometimes giving the town of origin; Florence appeared quite often as a source of textiles. In the course of the Middle Ages the merchant families of Florence succeeded in making their city the leading commercial and financial centre of Europe, whilst the wool trade was at its zenith there in the fourteenth century. English wool, and dyes from the East, together with the secrets of the Florentine 'arta di Lana' (Wool Guild) produced the heavy red cloth which was marketed throughout the civilized world.[143] But the

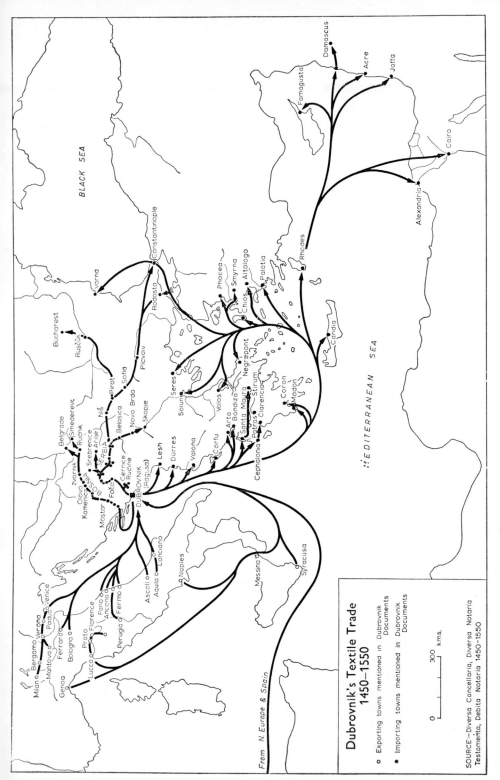

Dubrovnik's Textile Trade
1450–1550

o Exporting towns mentioned in Dubrovnik
   Documents

• Importing towns mentioned in Dubrovnik
   Documents

SOURCE:—Diversa Cancellaria, Diversa Notaria
Testamenta, Debita Notaria 1450–1550

FIG. 45.

BLACK SEA

MEDITERRANEAN SEA

From N. Europe & Spain

0   300   kms.

Damascus
Acre
Jaffa
Famagusta
Cairo
Alexandria
Rhodes
Constantinople
Varna
Rodosto
Bucharest
Ruscuk
Picvaiv
Sofia
Pirot
Niš
Belasica
Novo Brdo
Skopje
Phocea
Smyrna
Chios
Aitologo
Palatia
Candia
Seres
Solun
Volos
Negrepont
Stirum
Arta
Bondiza
Santa Maura
Patras
Clarencia
Cephalonia
Coron
Modon
Corfu
Valona
Durres
Lesh
Cernice
Rudine
(Fagusa)
DUBROVNIK
Mostar
Kamenica
Olovo
Zvornik
Srebrenice
Arilje
Rudnik
Smederevc
Belgrade
SERBIA
Foĉ
BOSNIA
Naples
Ascoli
Aquila
Lanciano
Fano
Ancona
Fermo
Perugia
Prato
Florence
Lucca
Bologna
Ferrara
Genoa
Mantova
Po
Padu
Venice
Verona
Bergamo
Milan
Messina
Syracusa

drab single coloured cloth usually went to the commoners in south-east Europe – the landed gentry and inland rulers demanding more variegated and shiny material. Farther down the Arno valley was situated the town of Lucca, the first place in northern Italy to engage in silk manufacture. For more than a century the Lucchese silk industry maintained an unchallenged supremacy, the town later becoming responsible for the growth of similar industries in Florence, Bologna, Venice and Genoa. The textile industry flourished in the larger communes of northern Italy, particularly Verona and Padua, and the main export commodity was woollen cloth, sometimes referred to specifically in Dubrovnik's documents.[144] Dubrovnik's export markets were those of the south-east European and Near East regions, where textiles from western Europe had a great attraction, both for their superior quality and different styles. The regions of western Greece, Anatolia and the Near East provided substantial markets for Dubrovnik's cloth exports, but documentary evidence does not support Roller's viewpoint[145] that western Greece exported its own high quality textiles, although poor grade wool and linen cloth were occasionally recorded as having come from this area. Heyd's view[146] that a two-way traffic in textiles did exist in the Levant is borne out by archival material, but this was an exchange of good quality wool and linen cloth from the West going to the Levant with silk and cotton textiles, mainly from Syria and Egypt, being exported in the reverse direction; both Greece and Anatolia remained pre-dominantly consuming centres for textiles. In Greece the west coast had the largest importing centres, but this in itself is misleading, for many of these towns like Arta, Corfu, Clarencia and Cephalonia, were only transit harbours similar to Dubrovnik so that many of the textiles were re-exported from these places to the eastern parts of Greece and Asia Minor. The fourteenth century only furnishes a small amount of information on textile exports to Greece, but several government decisions show that the trade existed.[147] The fifteenth century, par-ticularly between 1425–1450 gives a clearer picture. Venice in her bid for commercial hegemony, was jealous of Dubrovnik's Levantian textiles markets and she exerted pressures on other Italian towns to discontinue the supply of material. Therefore Dubrovnik had to develop her own textile production in order to reinforce the general economic life of the town. Already, by 1430, Dubrovnik cloth 'panni Ragusii' was often mentioned as exported to the Levant,[148] but never in the quantities that it was sent to the Balkan interior.

Although the inland peoples of the western Balkans produced their own type of textile, a rough linen known as 'rasa', it did not satisfy the demand of the whole home market. Textiles therefore had to be imported from abroad. Two types of textiles were imported – firstly 'drappi panni fostagni' which included varied high quality cloths made from wool, linen, cotton or silk and sold mainly to the feudal lords[149] and landed gentry, and secondly cheaper, drabber cloths for

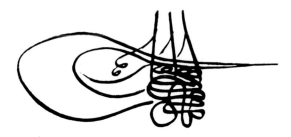

ѠД ѲЄЛИКОГА ГСПДАРА И СЇЛЬНОГА Ц(А)РА И ѲЄЛИКАГѠ АМИРА СꙊЛЬТАН МꙊХАММЄТЬ КНЄЗꙊ И ѠЛАСТЄЛѠМЬ ДꙊБРѠѲАЧЇЄМ МНОГО ЗДРАѲЇЄ И ѲЄСЄЛЬЄ ДА ИМАТЄ.

ПОТОЛЄ ТАКО ѲИ ДАѠ̈АМЬ ѲЄДЄТИ, КАКО Є ѲИЛА ЗАПОѲЄСТЬ Ц(А)Р(С)ТОА МИ ЗА ТАИ ГЮМРꙊКЬ, ДА ПЛАКЬ̈Ю ѠАШИ ЛꙊДИ ѠД СТО ПО Є̈ А ПАШИ ЛꙊДИ ѠД СТО ПО Д̈ ДА ПЛАКЬ̈Ю. А ДАѠ̈АЛИ СꙊ АМАЛДАРИ ЗА Г̈ ГОДИНЄ Ї ТИСꙊК ДꙊКАТ ЗЛАТЄХ̈ Ц(А)Р(С)ТОꙊ МИ. ТАКОИ СЄ СТЄ МОТНО ПОТꙊЖИЛЄ Ц(А)Р(С)ТОꙊ МИ, КАКО ДА СЄ ТАИ Ц(А)РИНА ѠД ѠАС ѠДИНМИ. А ТОГАИ РАДИ ꙊЧИНИХ̈ ОИ МИЛОСТЬ ЦРЬСТОА МИ ТЄРЬ СЄ С ѠАШИМИ ПОКЛИСАРМИ ТАКОИ ЛОГОѲОРИСМѠ И ꙊТАКМИСМО, КАКО ТАИ ЦАРИНА ѠД ѠАС ДА СЄ ѠДИНМИ, А ДО САДА СТЄ ПЛАКЬ̈АЛИ Ц(А)РСТОꙊ МИ ХАРАЧ Ї ТИСꙊКЬ ДꙊКАТ ЗЛАТЄХ̈ НА ѠСАКꙊ ГОДИНИꙊ, А ѠД СЬДА ДА ПЛАКЬ̈ТЄ НА ѠСАКꙊ ГОДИНꙊ ЗА ХАРАЧ И ЗА ГЮМРꙊКЬ ПО Ї̈В ТИСꙊК И ПО ПЄТСАТЬ ДꙊКАТЬ ЗЛАТЄХ̈ ТЄРЄ М̈ЦА НОЄМБРИА, КАКО ТО СТЄ И ѠД ПРЄГЄ Ꙋ ТОИ ѠРЄМЄ ДОНОСИЛЄ, А ѲЄКЄ ТОГАИ ГЮМРꙊКА ДА ГА НЄ ИДЄ. НАПРЄДА ИЄКА ДОСАДА ѠАМЬ НЄЧИМЬ ДА НЄ БꙊДЄ.

ПС М̈ЦА МАРТА Ѿ̈ ДНЬ ѠЬ ЛЄТО Ӓ И ЧЄТИРИСТА Ѿ̈ Ӥ ѠД РОЖЬДЬСТОА ХРИСТОѠА.

FIG. 46. Transcript of document in which Sultan Mehmed II states that he wishes to place a 5% customs duty on goods carried by Dubrovnik merchants, and that the annual tribute must be increased from 10,000 ducats to 12,500 ducats. Dated 2/III/1478, the original paper in Dubrovnik Archives measuring 40 cm × 15,5 cm and on the envelope is written 'Comandamento del imperator sultan Mechmet 1478 per achonto de charaz de ducati 2,500 ultra li 10,000 et questo per giumruch'.

the general market. Markets reveal a concentration in east and central Bosnia, with a wider dispersal in west and central Serbia. The proximity of Bosnia could partially explain this pattern, but other factors have to be taken into account. In 1382 the Dubrovnik government allowed the Bosnian King to buy textiles from the town,[150] creating a trade link which was to grow in the ensuing years. Less contact was made in north and west Bosnia for there were fewer markets there and in these areas Dubrovnik's traders faced stiffer competition from local Dalmatian merchants, who came from ports along the coast. Similarly the Serbian market was not so secure as that of Bosnia, because Dubrovnik's merchants had to compete with cloth imports from Cologne, Czechoslovakia, Braşov and Wallachia,[151] which came to Serbia by overland routes. This did not mean Dubrovnik's citizens were not important in the Serbian textile market, for there are many examples of them bringing cloth to Prijepolje, Novo Brdo,[152] Smedereva and Trgovište.

Documentary sources show there was a large increase in textile exports to Bosnia-Hercegovina and Serbia during the fifteenth century, for in the preceding century they were rarely mentioned. This could of course be due to a lack of extant documents, but more probably it was related to a steady growth of population inland and increased demand. In 1420 the Dubrovnik government arranged for a colony of traders from the Italian textile town of Prato to live in the city specially to concentrate on the Bosnian trade.[153] This move could have been a direct consequence of Venetian attempts to forestall supplies of textiles from other Italian towns reaching Dubrovnik but far more important was the general economic decline of the Dubrovnik Republic during the decade 1460–1470 resulting from the Turkish advance into the Balkans. Consequently increased cloth exports to Greece was seen by Dubrovnik as another, if not alternative, market for western material, but it was not a completely successful venture. Inevitable conflict with Venice, in the race for markets grew, and the Venetian occupation of Corfu (1482) at the entrance to western Greece weakened Dubrovnik's position. Venetian control of many west Grecian textile workshops in the second half of the fifteenth century, reduced Dubrovnik's trade in the area, but fortunately by 1500 conditions in the Balkan interior were again more settled for the textile trade, for unlike some commodities, e.g. silver and lead, where the decline was permanent, textiles experienced some resurgence. The reason was apparently the Turkish demand

милостю божм ӣ велики гсподрь и силни царь ꙗ велики амирь сꙋлтан
мꙋхаметь давамь [ведети и] ꙋзнати вьсакомꙋ чл҃вкꙋ, како ꙋчини м(и)л(о)сть
цр҃ство ми кнезꙋ и властелом дꙋбровачцѣм, моемь вѣрнѣм и правѣм
слꙋгамь, за землю и за държавꙋ свою и за нихь бащинꙋ, за малѣхь и за
велицѣхь, колико имають ꙋ свою рꙋкꙋ и ꙋ свою заповѣсть и кою сꙋ
ѿ прво држали како свою истинꙋ и правꙋ бащинꙋ и за све люди, кое
имають по сꙋхꙋ и по морꙋ и на отоцѣхь и за град, и кащеле, коѣ
имають ꙋ свою рꙋкꙋ и за тои ми сꙋ до сада плакꙗли ꙇ҃ дꙋката златѣхь
харача а за гюмрꙋкь две тисꙋкѣ и петь сать дꙋката златѣхь. а пакь
сада заповѣда цр҃ство ми, да ми даю савише тогаи две тисꙋкѣ и петь
сать дꙋкать златѣхь, како за све за тои да се плакꙗ цр҃ствꙋ ми ꙇ҃е дꙋката
златѣхь харача на годинꙋ. нꙋ такои се заповѣда, како ови харачь да
се донесеть по прꙋем харачꙋ, кои се кѣ платити ꙇ҃в҃ꙇ дꙋката златѣхь;
по темь на годинꙋ да се почметь плакꙗти ован реченни харачь ѿ
ꙇ҃е дꙋката златѣхь.

нꙋ такои заповѣда цр҃ство ми, како векѣ ѿ нихь да не ище ничюрь
ни за ютнꙋ сатварь или работꙋ, ни санжакбегь, ни сꙋбаша, ни кадиа,
ни харачникь, ни травникь, ни емин, ни канфьсоржиа, ни ини цклавь
цр҃ства ми ами, кои доходи на мою послꙋ а на тѣхь странахь, кои
ꙋсьхокѣ, да не ꙋпадьнеть ꙋ гневь цр҃ства ми; и ако с ꙗвить или сьтворить
ѿ моихь люди нѣкоѣ зло или напасти више реченѣмь дꙋбровчаномь
или нихь земли или владанье, да га цр҃ство ми педепьсать, како ѥ
подобнꙋ.

и нихь трьговци да ходеть са нихь трьг и са нихь иманье и да
трьжѣть землю цр҃ства ми безь никꙑедне забаве, нꙋ да плакꙗють царине
и бродꙋꙗкꙑомꙋ по земли цр҃ства ми, кꙋде ходе и и[проходе] како сꙋ
и ѿ прво до сада плакꙗли а да не имають ни ѿ ꙑеднога чл҃вка [некою
злобꙋ] или некою завртицꙋ.

и даде се сѣ писанѣ и заповѣсти цр҃ства ми више реченимь дꙋбровчаномь, како да имь бꙋде ꙋтрьгꙑенꙑе и непотвореиѣ.

такои да се зна, инꙗко да не бꙋде.

вь лѣтѡ ѕ҃.ц҃.п҃.и҃. мсца маꙗ дань ꙁ҃ ꙋ цариградꙋ.

м(и)л(о)стю божмь ꙑа велики гсподрь и сильни цр҃ь и велики амирь
сꙋлтаи баꙗзить хаи, синь присвѣтлꙑга и веле ꙋзьможнога поконнога
сꙋлтан мехемеда.

понеже честити и почтени кнезь и властеле дꙋбровачки ꙑесꙋть до
сада право и вѣрьнꙋ и сь вьсемь чистѣм и целемь срцемь слꙋжили
привꙑсокꙋмꙋ и веле ꙋзьможномꙋ поконномꙋ сꙋлтань мꙋхамедꙋ родителю
цр҃ства ми, кꙑга да б(ог)ь помене, и сада паки више речени кнезь и
властеле ꙑесꙋ послали вь своꙑехь вѣрьни и почтени властеле, кнеза инꙑкꙑшꙋ
палмꙋтикꙗ и кнеза влахꙋшꙗ кабꙋжикꙗ ꙋ поклисарьствꙋ на портꙋ моꙑеи
вꙑсоти, опеть поновити мирь и приꙗꙁань ꙋтьрдити и ꙋ слꙋжбꙋ припо-
вѣдати и казати моꙑемꙋ величаствꙋ, кою сꙋ до сеть[1]) имали ѿ прꙋехь
врѣмень.

тои видѣвь мою вꙑсота и ꙋчиних имь масть и ладох имь сеи
барать[2]) и клетовꙑиꙋ книгꙋ цр҃ства ми, како ѿ донешнꙗгꙑи дна напреда

Fig. 47   See p. 267 for legend

да бꙋдеть мегю нами миръ и приꙗзнь и лꙋбовъ непотворена с ними и
са нихьни град и са нихъ землю и люди и съ нихъ трговци и съ всѣмь
нихъ владаꙑемь, що ѣ нимь пот рꙋкꙋ и ꙋ запоѡѣсти до мала и до
многа, или ю по морꙋ или на сꙋхꙋ и да имъ не ꙋчиним размирые ни
нио нѣкое зло, ни мало ни великω, ни нихъ градꙋ, ни нихъ земли, ни
нихъ владаꙑю ꙗ нихь людемь ни нихъ отоцемь ни нихъ имаꙑꙋ ни
ꙗ ни мои везꙑри ни мои санжаци ни мои вон(во)д(е) ни мои сꙋбаши ни
кадие ни мои склави ни нии мои члвкъ, кон сꙋть подрꙋчни царствꙋ
ми, ни малъ ни великъ, него да ѣ нихъ градⸯ и землꙗ и нихъ люди
ꙋ нихъ законꙋ слободⸯω. и люди всакога езика по морꙋ и по сꙋхꙋ да
могꙋ кь ними приходити и ꙋ владаꙑю нихъ како ꙋ всако слободно
мѣсто и ꙋ слободии град и за тон да не имають забавꙋ ниѣднꙋ ни
ѡд цр̇ства ми ни ѡд иного чл̇ка.

и вꙑше тога имъ ꙋчинихъ м(и)л(о)сть кнезꙋ и властелом дꙋбро-
вачкем, како харач и гюмрꙋкъ, що сꙋ давали ꙋ врѣме присвѣтлога и
вели ꙋзможнога покоинога родителꙗ цр̇ства ми мꙋхамеда, по петьнаде-
сете тисꙋки дꙋката златѣхъ бнетачцѣхъ на годинꙋ, тон имъ ꙋчинихъ
м(и)л(о)сть и оставихъ имь две тисꙋкѣ и петьсат дꙋкат златѣхъ бнетачцѣхъ, како ѡд данашнагон дна напрѣда да давають пω дванадесете
тисꙋки и по петьсат дꙋкать златѣхъ бнетачцѣхъ харача на годинꙋ а
две тисꙋкѣ и петь стотинь дꙋкать златѣхъ да имъ сꙋ прости, а осташни
дванадесете тисꙋкъ и петь стотинь дꙋката златѣхъ да ихъ посилаю на та
гꙋдинꙋ съ своѣхъ вѣрни поклисари на порьтꙋ царства ми по ѡбичаю,
како сꙋ и доселе посилали.

и още имъ ꙋчинихъ м(и)л(о)сть, да могꙋть нихъ трговци и нихъ
трговци и нихъ люди съ иманьемь и са нихъ трговⸯ ходити слободⸯнω
безъ нѣдне забаве по всꙋ землꙋ и владаꙑе царства ми по романию и
по анатолию, по морꙋ и по сꙋхꙋ и по бꙋгарскои земли и по срⸯбскꙋ и
по босанскꙋ и по арбанасѣхъ и по херьцеговине, по всѣхъ градове и
земле царства ми и да имь се не ꙋзима попꙋтна царина ѡд нихъ
трⸯгове, него да плакꙑю ꙋ мѣсто, где трⸯгъ продаю, законꙋ царинꙋ
ѡд сто аспри две аспре, како тон ю законь ꙋ дренополе и ꙋ пловдинь
и ꙋ кратовꙋ. и ако си трⸯгове не продадꙋ, да си га ѡднесꙋть, гдѣ ним
бꙋдеть драгω.

и още имъ ꙋчинихъ м(и)л(о)сть, да си ꙋзимають дꙋгове своѣ, где
имають. ако ли тко ꙋдари ꙋ бахъ, да се заклинають по законꙋ два или
тре дꙋбровчани, да имъ плакꙑю дльжници. ако ли бꙋдꙋ имали кон гдѣ
сꙋть съ тꙋрькⸯе, да погꙋть прѣдъ кадию, како е волꙗ и повеление божие,
такон да бꙋде.

и да не бꙋде принꙋзма ꙗедному за дрꙋгога, него тко бꙋде дꙋжанъ,
он да плакꙑ.

ако ли би тко ꙋзель тꙋгѣ иманье тере би пошелъ ꙋ дꙋбровникъ,
да мꙋ се сꙋть по законꙋ ꙋчинить, да не изгꙋби чл̇вкъ иманѣ.

и още имъ ꙋчинихъ м(и)л(о)сть: ако би кон дꙋбровчании ꙋмрео ꙋ
земли царства ми, да мꙋ се не ꙋзметь иманⸯе, негω да се предасть ꙋ
дꙋбровчанѣхъ рꙋкꙋ до мало и до многω.

for western-style material[154] in exchange for their own oriental types of silk cloth, brocaded woollen goods and ribbons.[155] Dubrovnik again therefore became a trading mediator between the Balkans and the West.

Wine and Oil

Besides wheat, the other two stalwarts of the Mediterranean economy were wine and oil.[156] In normal years Dubrovnik produced enough of both wine and oil for herself and for export, but if it happened to be a bad year then Apulian and Sicilian produce was bought.[157] Venetian restrictions after 1420 forbad any of the Dalmatian towns under her control to send either wine or oil to Dubrovnik in a general attempt to boycott all goods going to the city.[158] Dubrovnik also imported 'special' wines like that from Zante in western Greece – the noted 'malvoisie' type which always attracted the western European markets.

Miscellaneous Goods

Besides textiles, wine and oil, the only other products worthy of mention were the various manufactured articles from Italy. These included paper, silver-ware, ornamental belts, needles, glass and medicines, usually being shipped from the ports of Venice and Ancona to Dubrovnik,[159] where they were re-exported to the villages and towns of the inland Balkans or Levant.

Commodity Prices

In the thirteenth and fourteenth centuries money began to play a greater part in economic life in the Balkans. Nevertheless it is not so easy to find out what the prices really were in the past, or once discovered to interpret the information correctly. There are many difficulties to overcome including changes in the intrinsic value of coins, regional differences in weights and measures, and fluctuations according to the season of the year. Therefore information gleaned from

FIG. 47. Transcript of document in which it states that all Dubrovnik merchants must now pay 15,000 ducats annually for the trade rights they possess. Dated 7/V/1480 No. 6988 and signed in Constantinople. Copied from *Liber Privilegiorum* page 116 in Dubrovnik Archives. Original firman in the Emperor's Archives in Vienna.

И ако би цр҃ство ми имало размирїе с нѣкемь г(о)сп(ода)ромь или
источникѣмь или западнѣмь али коѣ ине земле по морȣ и по сȣхȣ, дȣбровачки люди тргофци да стоють и тргȣють по ниҳь земьлȣ слободно и
доброволнѡ.

И още имь ȣчинихь милость виш(е) реченомȣ кнезȣ и властеломь
дȣбровачскѣмь, ако би се тко нашао да имь коѣ годе зло ȣчинить,
нимь или ниҳь земли или ниҳь людемь или ниҳь тръговцемь или ниҳь
иманю, мало или много, кон годерь бȣде чл҃вкь ѿ земле цр҃ства ми,
маль или великь, да имь се иманїе и землы врати а цр҃ство ми оноган
чл҃вка по достояню да педепшеть.

А више речени честитни кнезь и властеле дȣбровачки да посилають
више речени ҳарачь дванадесете тисȣкы и петь сать дȣката златѣхь
бнетачкеҳь сь свои вѣрни поклисари по прьвемь законȣ и по обичаю на
портȣ моѣ пресвѣтлости ката гднȣ прьви дань месеца новембриа.

И више овоган нашега писаны се заклина цр҃ство ми: тако ми ѿчине
и дѣдине дȣше и тако ми животь лѣтцаҳь моиҳь и тако ми пȣть, що
пȣтȣю и саблю, кономь се опасȣю, и тако ми ҏ.к҃.д҃ пророкь божниҳь
и великога пророка нашега мȣхамеда и тако ми .з. мȣсафь, што верȣемо
и посведȣѣмо ми и почитамо ми мȣсломани и тако ми вѣрȣ, кою вѣ-
рȣемо, и тако ми гспда, кон ѥ сьтворнѡ нибѡ и з:млȣ, како, докле
кѣт кнезь и ѻластеле дȣбровачки право и вѣрнѡ слȣжити присвѣтломȣ
прѣстолю моѣга величаства, коѣга да богь ȣмножи за многа лѣта, ован
савнше писана и ѡбетованы цр҃ства ми да имь бȣде кнезȣ и властеломь
дȣбровачицѣмь вь ȣторгѣнѣ а ва непотвореиѣ до вѣка.

Такон да с(е) зна.

Вь лѣтѡ ҂s.ч҃.s. мѣца новембра к҃в дань ȣ дренополȣ а рожаства
ҳристова ҂а.ȣ.п.а.

FIG. 48. Transcript of document issued by one of the most powerful Turkish Sultans
(Bajazid II) in which he lowered the annual tribute paid by Dubrovnik from 15,000 ducats
to 12,500 ducats. Dated 22/XI/1481 and signed in Adrianople, Dubrovnik Archives,
Liber Privilegiorum p. 116–117, (Original Turkish manuscript in the Emperor's Archives,
Vienna.)

documentary evidence should be regarded as mainly for the record
rather than possible interpretations for a wider sphere.

Information for metals is mainly on lead. For example, in 1410 a
Dubrovnik merchant bought 1,230 pieces of lead from Bosnia weigh-

ing 143,465 lb. This cost him 932 ducats (approx. 6½ ducats/1,000 lb). He then hired a boat in Dubrovnik to transport the lead to Alexandria, sharing equally with the boat owner whatever profit was made on the voyage.[160] Information on the price Venetians paid for lead is rare. One document[161] dated 1482 mentions a Venetian merchant paying 228 ducats for 20 milijari (9,540 kg) of lead (i.e. about 42 kg/ducat) sent him from Dubrovnik. On another occasion[162] a Venetian in 1488 bought 10,000 lb of lead (3,586 kg) for 70 ducats (i.e. about 51 kg/ducat). Another piece of information[163] dated 1479 states that 144 milijari (51,552 kg) and 833 litres[164] (9,412 kg) of lead were bought by a Venetian for 1,833 ducats (i.e. 33 kg/ducat). Two other examples of 26 kg/ducat[165] and 33 kg/ducat[166] show quite a variety of prices for lead going to Venice, but it was often quite common to send it on an exchange basis for textiles.[167]

Continued demand pushed up the average price of slaves in Bosnia from 1–2 ducats each around 1350, to 35–40 ducats by the end of the century.[168] According to Božić[169] there was a great variance in prices at the turn of the century, a Bosnian slave fetching anything between 20 and 150 ducats in the Dubrovnik market. Prices paid by north Italian merchants, from places like Bergamo, Mantova and Padua, for Dubrovnik's slaves varied between 100 and 1,600 ducats.[170] Similarly, Dubrovnik slaves, which in the fourteenth century had fetched on average 200–300 lira (50–75 ducats) each in Genoa were fetching 800 lira (200 ducats) the following century.[171] Information on spices is seen in a Dubrovnik document dated 1442. In this year Nicholas Martinić bought 30 'sportas' of pepper in Alexandria for 1,800 ducats[172] (i.e. about 4p per pound).[173] Mahuan[174] in 1409 noted that pepper was sold in Cochin at 5 taels the Poho, which would work out at less than ½p a pound on the Malabor Coast.[175] This meant the Sultans sold pepper at nine times the price it had originally been bought for in India. In England at this time pepper fetched about 10p a pound.[176]

It is interesting to compare the buying and selling prices of salt paid by Dubrovnik's merchants, which are particularly revealing for the second half of the fourteenth century. Within the Dubrovnik Republic salt was bought in Ston at an average price of 2 ducats per 100 modia. It then had to be transported 50 kilometres down the coast by boat to Dubrovnik city where it was sold on average for 6 ducats/each modia – a threefold increase in price, from which had to be deducted freight costs, insurance etc. Prices paid by Dubrov-

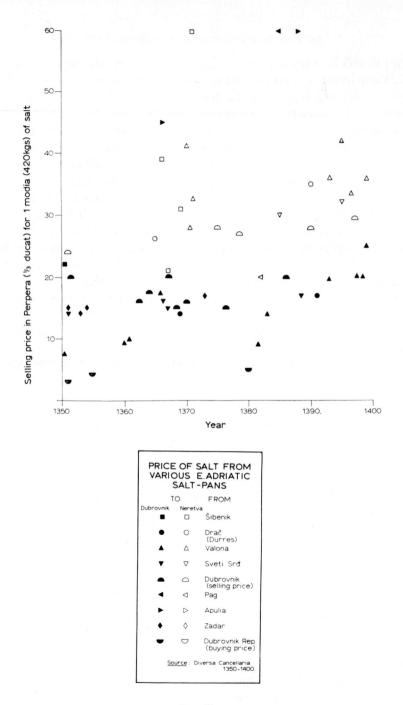

FIG. 49.

nik merchants buying salt outside the republic, averaged between 3–8 ducats/each modia, whilst selling prices averaged between 8–13 ducats/each modia, which gave them a possible twofold increase on their buying prices. Thus profits made from salt, as with other commodities, show how commercial cities in the Middle Ages were able to exist and thrive, often as in the case of Dubrovnik, in a very difficult geographical environment. Salt selling was also a seasonal affair reaching peak output during the months of May, June and July, coinciding with the period of greatest evaporation of the trapped seawater in the pans (Fig. 40).

The proximity of Albania's salt-pans had quite a bearing on the price of salt for Dubrovnik's merchants in the second half of the fourteenth century. Salt from Albania cost much less than that which had been bought in western Greece. The most noticeable features

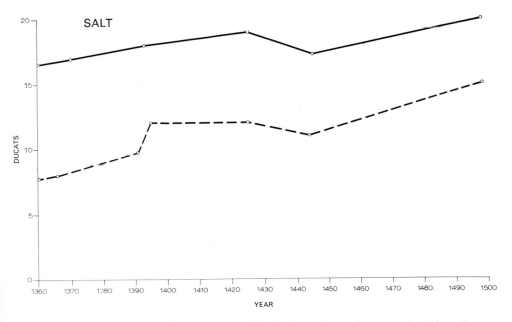

FIG. 50. ——— Average freight cost, paid by Dubrovnik merchants, per boat for salt, from western Greece to Nerevta; – – – – purchasing price, paid by Dubrovnik merchants, in western Greece for one Modia of salt (420 kg).

are the Albanian prices varying between 3 and 7 ducats for each modia of salt compared with 7 to 12 ducats for western Greece. More long term features are seen in the freight costs and purchasing price of salt from western Greece (1360–1500) which remained fairly constant throughout the period, with a slight rise in price during the last half of the fifteenth century. This was in keeping with the general trend for costs and prices throughout Europe at this time,[177] the slight rise in prices after 1450 resulting from the increase in the quantity of money connected with renewed silver mining in central Europe and the influx of American silver. Previous to 1450 salt from western Greece seemed stable at about 10 ducats each modia, 100 modia are equal to 4,200 kilogrammes (about 4·2 tons), despite temporary fluctuations. The profit gained on salt from western Greece is difficult to ascertain. Only one reliable document shows the profit made though unrepresentative is of interest. In 1425 a Dubrovnik merchant bought salt for an unspecified price at Santa Maura.[178] If he sold the salt in Dubrovnik he would receive 5·75 ducats/each modia, but if he took it as far as the Neretva (a further sea journey of 144 km) he could sell it for 17·5 ducats/each modia – a gross profit of over 200% (cf. with Dubrovnik's selling price) from which extra freight costs, customs duties, insurance etc. had to be deducted but even then the pure profit must have been considerable.

Comparative prices of wheat in Dubrovnik and western Greece are of interest. Information on prices is more forthcoming here than for other areas but whether it is representative of other wheat exporting regions is impossible to say. Gross profit on each cubic metre of wheat gave a 30–50% profit margin, but from this was deducted freight costs, insurance etc. Therefore a fair average estimation of 30% pure profit for a merchant can be assumed. To some extent this reflects the general pattern of cereal prices throughout Europe at this time. The rise was common in Europe after 1450 coinciding with the steady growth of population, slight agricultural recovery and increase in the quantity of money following increased silver production.

The small number of extant documents on flax in Dubrovnik's archives does not allow a greater understanding in this trade, but from the information available, flax like salt seems to have enjoyed stable prices for much of this period. The sudden rise in flax prices around 1377 could be attributed to the Chioggian War, whilst the fall in both salt and flax prices around 1447 may have resulted from disruptions brought about in trade by the Turkish conquest. The rise in prices after 1450 is noticeably in keeping with the general trend throughout Europe. The higher price of flax for a similar weight of

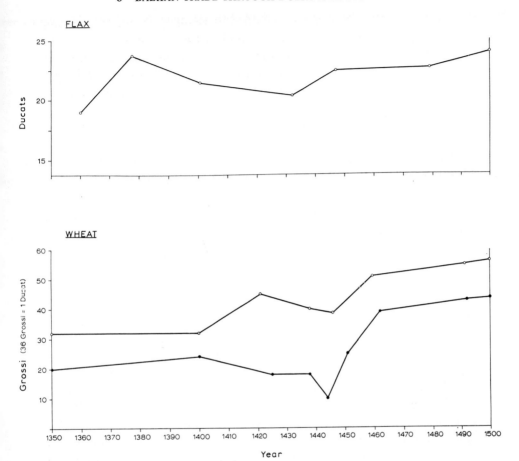

FIG. 51. Upper: ○——○ price of flax in Dubrovnik (from western Greece) per milijari (358 kg); lower: ○——○ price of wheat per cubic metre in Dubrovnik; ●——● price of wheat per cubic metre in western Greece.

salt (358 kg as against 420 kg) is explained by the fact that one was the price paid in Dubrovnik (flax) while the other was paid in western Greece (salt).

Trade Treaties with Ancona

Trade with Italy continued to develop in the fourteenth and fifteenth centuries on the same lines as it had previously. One of the oldest trading partners was Ancona which first signed a treaty with Dubrovnik in 1199. During the eleventh and twelfth centuries, Ancona played a part in the commercial revival in the Mediterranean, associated with the Crusades and like Dubrovnik became a centre of opposition to Venetian power in the Adriatic. Unfortunately for Ancona growing Venetian strength resulted in a humiliating commercial treaty of 1264 which checked further development.[179] Ancona achieved its greatest commercial importance during the first half of the sixteenth century, but it is of interest here to record trade treaties between Dubrovnik and Ancona (one also with Fermo) dating from a period between these peaks of commercial significance.

1372, 27th November[180]

Copy of the declarations and payments and exemptions of Ragusan customs compiled from Anconans.

Anconans shall be treated in Ragusa (Dubrovnik) and district as full citizens of Ragusa for tax purposes.

All merchandise imported into Ragusa by Anconans or others conveying Anconans from any part of the world within or beyond the Gulf, is to be tax-free except that on every half-thousand vessels of wine import duty of 8 Ragusan grossi is due, just as Ragusans themselves pay. If this merchandise is exported from Ragusa by Anconans or Ragusans who have bought it, to any place not mentioned below, no handling charge is to be made. The exceptions are all the kingdom of Rascia, the part of the kingdom of Hungary called Sremia, the Banat of Bosnia, the cities from Ragusa eastwards along the coast of Slavonia to Dyrrachium (Dürres), and the islands of Melita (Mljet), Curzula (Korčula), Farra (Hvar), and Braza (Brač). On such exports they must pay two and three-quarters per centum. If the goods are exported to Dyrrachium (Dürres) itself, or the whole coast from Dyrrachium to Avlona (Valona) then the duty is two per centum. If fustian is exported to the above places, the duty is one Ragusan grosso per piece.

If the said merchandise is sold in Ragusa to Slavs or men of the aforesaid places, except Dyrrachium and Avlona, Anconans and Ragusans alike must pay three and one-third per centum.

If such goods are sold to men of Dyrrachium or Avlona, or any other foreigners not mentioned, then these foreigners should pay duty at the rate Ragusans pay in their cities. Anconans are not liable for duty if they sell to such foreigners in Ragusa.

If Anconans buy in Ragusa from a Ragusan, Slav, or man of the aforesaid places, except Dyrrachium and Avlona, and export the goods to Ancona or any place not mentioned, they owe no tax. If they convey the merchandise to the places mentioned, they should pay as stated above. Ragusans, Slavs or men of the places mentioned except Dyrrachium and Avlona, may buy from Anconans tax free.

If Anconans buy in Ragusa from men of Dyrrachium, Avlona, or any other foreigners not mentioned, they can export the goods to Ancona or places not mentioned, tax free. If they export them to the places mentioned above, they are liable to tax. Men of Dyrrachium etc. who sell to the Anconans should pay as much handling charge as the Ragusans pay in their cities. Men of Dyrrachium etc. buying from Anconans in Ragusa, pay nothing.

For every transaction taking place in Ragusa involving Anconans in any merchandise of the value of 20 soldi of grossi upwards, buying or selling, brokerage is due to the commune of Ragusa at the rate of 3 Ragusan grossi for each 100 soldi of grossi, of which half should be paid by the seller, and half by the buyer. No brokerage charge is levied for gold or silver. As for grain of any kind, or pulses, imported and unloaded by Anconans in Ragusa, they shall be treated exactly like citizens of Ragusa – no duty payable. As for wine, they are on the same footing as Ragusans, i.e. no foreign wine may be imported into Ragusa under any circumstances. As for salt, tallow, olive oil, cheese, salt, flesh, cattle of any kind, linen cloths, long cloaks (from Slavonia), cloth called 'rassa', falcons and other animals, slaves and maidservants, Anconans shall be treated like Ragusans.

For every 1,000 lb of merchandise sold by the pound, they must pay 25 parvuli per pound for selling. The buyer pays nothing. If he wishes to have the goods weighed without concluding a sale, he must pay half of the said 25 parvuli.

If any Anconan shall carry or send goods to the places mentioned above where tax is payable, he should pay over and above what is stated 1 Ragusan grosso for each pack horse load. For iron or wool so carried he must pay three Ragusan grossi per 1,000 lb extra.

Vessels who put into harbour are not liable for dues. Any Anconan vessel running for shelter because of bad weather, high tides, or damage to the ship, can unload and reload duty-free. If they sell any of their goods, however, or convey them to the aforesaid places where tax is due, they must pay as stated.

Questi sono li ordeni, como debiano esser tratadi Ragusini in Ancona in fato de doane per patti fati.

1. (CXC). Per tute e zascaune mercadantie entra le quale se intenda eziamdio le sclavine, che sera condute per Ragusini o per altri a lor nome ala zitade o distreto de Ancona, le qual fosse condute da Ragusa, overo dentro del colfo per tera, e serano cargate in qualunqua parte del Saxeno in qua, e da cavo de Otranto[1] in qua, se debia pagare per conduta de quele mercadantie. Ma se le dite mercadantie se trazera dela zitade de Ancona per Ragusini o per Anconitani, ali quali le dite mercadantie fosse vendute, pagi colui, chi tra pizoli tre per libra del valore de quelle, zoe uno e quarto per C⁰ de quele mercadantie, che se trara. Ma se le dite mercadantie se vendera a forestieri, e queli forestieri trazesse quele, pagi quel forestier, che tra pizoli VI per libra de pizoli del valor de quele mercadantie, zoe doy e mezo per cadauno centenaro de quele mercadantie, sicome pagano li forestieri comprando dali Anconitani. Salvo e reservado, che in le dite mercadantie non se intenda le spezie: zucaro, coton, ne seda de Chiarenza, ne de Tartaria, over dele contrade de Chiarenza, ne de Gazaria, ne drapi de seda, over d oro dele dite parte o contrade, per le qual se di pagar come per mercadantia del Levante, zoe VI per C⁰ de quele come de soto se contien.

2. (CXCI). Per oro, argento, moneda, perle, piere preziose, che se condura in Ancona per Ragusini o altri per loro, se s vendera over non se vendera, per conduta over trata de quele niente se pagi.

3. (CXCII). Per mercadantie de merzaria e draparia, che se condura per Ragusini o altri per loro ad Ancona, per mare over per tera, per portar over condure quele a Ragusa o ad altre parte de Sclavonia, se tale mercadantie non se vendera in Ancona, debia se pagare uno e quarto per cadauno centenaro de quele. Et se li trazera de Ancona niente altro se pagi. Et ad Ancona se vendera, pagare debia come zitadini de Ancona, zoe quatro per cadauno centenaro de draparia, e cinque per cadauno centenaro de merzaria, che se vendesse. Et per tute altre mercadantie quale se sia, exceto merzaria e draparia, che se contien in lo presente capitolo. Et excepto mercadantie e cosse in li capitoli de sopra e de soto contegnude, da esser condute per Ragusei, over altri per loro ala zitade de Ancona per mare o per tera, per portare o condure quele ala zitade de Ragusa, o ad altre parte de Sclavonia, o per condure in Ancona, sia tratadi li Ragusini over altri per so nome condugando, sicome zitadini de Ancona.

4. (CXCIII) Ancora de tute mercadantie de Puglia e de Sizilia, siano tratati li Ragusini in Ancona e in lo distreto come zitadini de Ancona.

5. (CXCIV). Ancora per tute mercadantie da esser comprade per Ragusini dali Anconitani, tali Anconitani venditori ali diti Ragusini sian tenuti a pagar per meter in Ancona le dite mercadantie uno e quarto per cadauno centenaro de quele. Ma se li forestieri vendesseno a Ragusini, tali forestieri vendendo pagi do e mezo per cento de quele mercadantie, per mettere quele in Ancona. Salvo che per draparia o merzaria, se quele li zitadini o forestieri de Ancona vendera a Ragusini, non pagi queli zitadini o forestieri per mettere tal mercadantie in Ancona; salvo uno e quarto per cento de quele mercadantie; e li Ragusini trazando quele de Ancona sia tenuti pagare uno e quarto per cento de quele.

6. (CXCV). Ancora de tute mercadantie de fuora del colfo, li Ragusini siano tratadi in Ancona com zitadini de Ancona, zoe che per mercadantie, che seran trate de Ancona per li Ragusini per portare ale parte de Levante fuora del colfo, pagi li diti Ragusini per trata tre per cento de quele. Et per le mercadantie de fuora del colfo, de esser condute per li Ragusini da qualunqua luogo ala zitade de Ancona, pagi li Ragusini condutori VI per cento de quele mercadantie, le qual se condura de fuora del colfo per li diti Ragusini o per altri o per loro de qualunqua luogo,

Fig. 52, See p. 278 for legend

possa li diti Ragusini vendere sei a zitadini del Ancona come a forestieri. Et etiamdio tanto li deli Ragusini quanto li compradori prediti possa quele mercadantie trare libere e franche senza pagare alguna doana ; salvo che eli siano tenuti pagare pizoli XII de Ancona per la boleta, per la trata de quele per cascauna fiada, che se trara le dite mercadantie dela zitade de Ancona ; salvo e excepto che per cenerazo de sapone pagi li diti Ragusei per trata soldi XX per cadauno migliaro, e per trata de sapone do e mezo per centenaro, e soldi XXX de anconitani pizoli per cadauno migliario de quelo, e pizoli cinque per cascaduno pesso del dito sapone.

7. (CXCVI). De vino, sale, olio, biave de cadauna generazione, semenze de lino, fige, noxe e pomi, de le qual se paga la regalia ala camera dela ecclesia de Roma, da esser condutti ad Ancona over al so destreto, over de la trati per alguno de Ragusa, sia tratadi li Ragusini conducando o trazando come zitadini de Ancona.

8. (CXCVII). Ancora che grano e biave, che se condura ala zitade de Ancona o al so destreto per Ragusci, e descargara in Ancona per vender, se possa vender li diti Ragusei, o per altro modo alienar solamente ali zitadini de Ancona e non ad altri, e niente per questo siano tenuti a pagare, salvo quanto pagano li zitadini de Ancona, zoe a queli, che tien le mesure de la biava, per le mesure pizoli oto dela moneta de Ancona ; e li comperadori de quele pizoli XVI per salma cadauna dela dita biava.

9. (CXCVIII). Se alguni navilii de Ragusini o mercadantie de queli arivasse, o se conducesse ala zitade de Ancona o al so destreto, per fortuna del mare o per paura de corsari over de altra gente, o per algun defeto del navilio, possano li diti Ragusini le soe mercadantie predite descargare in Ancona, e quele cargare e portar liberamente et expeditamente senza pagare alguno dazio, doana, o altro pagamento; salvo che le dite mercadantie in tutto o in parte se vendesse in Ancona, che solamente per quele, che se vendera, sei per la conduta, come per la trata se debia pagare secondo se contiene in li capitoli e pati presenti.

10. (CXCIX). Ancora che nisuno navilio de Ragusini in Ancona ne in lo so destreto debia pagare arborazo.

11. (CC) Per le mercadantie, che se condura ala zitade de Ancona, o al so destreto per li Ragusini, o per altri per loro, queli che chondura abia termene a pagare in Ancona la doana uno ano, dal di dela conduta proximo che vignera. Ma se infra l ano tal mercadantie se vendesse o translatase, over se trazesse de Ancona, in tal caxo, zoe quando se vendesse o translatasse, se debia pagare per conduta. E se le trazesse, alora e anche per la trata sia tenuto a pagare al tempo, che se trara secondo la forma deli presenti capitoli. Ma se infra quel ano le dite mercadantie non se spazasse o non se tracesse, in tal casso le dite mercadantie siano extimate ; e secondo la extima, che se fara, debia se pagare solamente per la conduta dele dite mercadantie. E quando se trazera debiasse pagare per la trata de quele.

12. (CCI) Ancora che li diti Ragusei possano liberamente tute le mercadantie, che per loro o per altri per loro se condura de qualunque luogo ala zitade de Ancona vendere, ali zitadini de Ancona come a forestieri, e quele trahere pagando come in li diti capitoli e declarato; salvo, che grano e qualunqua biava se condura per li Ragusini, o per altri a so nome, ala zitade de Ancona per vendere, a nesuno la possano vender ne alinear, salvo ali zitadini de Ancona come de sopra se contiene.

13. (CCII) A levare ogni dubio el qual potesse nascere per alguno modo, dove in li presenti capitoli se fa menzione de merzaria, declaremo che merzaria se intenda ogni generazione de arme, item ogni lavoriro de corame conzo; item ogni lavoriro de fero, de stagno e de rame, e generalmente tutte le cose, che se contien expressamente in lo statuto del commune de Ancona, che parla de merzaria in lo volune deli statuti dela doana.

14. (CCIII) A presso oltra quelo, che e de sopra declarato per tutte le mercadantie, che se vendera per li diti Ragusei facandosse el mercado per sensali, se die pagare uno pizolo dela moneta de Ancona per ogni libra de prexio dele dite mercanzie, zoe la mitade per li venditori el altra mitade per li comperadori, in quanto tal mercanzie non se trazesse dela citade de Ancona. Ma sel esse trazera per mare o per terra, pagasse do pizoli dela deta moneda per libra del prexio de quelle, che se trazera: la mitade per li venditori e la mitade per li compradori. Ma se l mercado dele dite mercadantie se fesse senza messeta, alora li venditori e li comperadori non sono tenuti a pagar ne uno ne do pizoli prediti.

15. (CCIV) Anco a de tutte mercadantie de Ragusini, che se die pessare per li officiai del commune de Ancona, se di pagare per lo comperadore V pizoli de Ancona per cadauno pesso de quelle.

16. (CCV) Ancora che ultra le cosse predite in li diti capitoli expresse e declarate nessune altre execeione se debia fare dali diti Ragusei, over da altri per so nome per le dite soe mercadantie in la zitade, contado, distreto de Ancona per alguna rasone e ocaxone.

17. (CCVI) Tutte mercanzie e cosse de Ragusei in ogni navilii e barche, fosse che navegasse a qualunqua parte del mondo, passando per le aque de Ancona possano intrare liberamente senza alguno dazio over gabella in li porti de Ancona, e de li levar se a suo piaxer senza pagare alguna gabella over dacio si veramente non descargandola. E se voluntariamente li alguna parte over cosse fosse scargate, quella cossa, la qual li se scargasse, si aserva ali ordeni dele mercadantie, zoe mercanzie, le qual se meteno in Ancona per li Ragusei. E le altre che non se descargasse, siano libere e franche come e deto. E se in Ancona over in alguna altra parte intra quello tempo, che la nave ove barcha fosse in lo porto de Ancona per portezare se fosse venditta de alguna cossa, che fosse in la naue predita, simelmente per la dita cossa dela qual se fesse vendita se debia pagare gabella, come se in Ancona fosse scargatta. E le altre cosse dele qual non fosse fata vendeta, vadi libere e franche da cadauna gabella.

18. (CCVII) Ancora che cadauno Raguseo, che vora, possa navegare con mercanzie e cosse con le nave de Anconitani, e che mercanzie e cadaune cosse de Ragusei, le qual se portasse de le parte de Levante, o dele parte fora del Colfo, in nave de Anconitani, e descargasse dentro del colfo a questa riva de Albania e de Sclavonia, comenzando dal Saxeno (Sasino) fina a Sebenico e per tutti li scoli de Sebenico, se possa descarigare libere e franche senza pagare alguna gabella o dacio del (!) commune de Ancona, de la qual eeiamdio gabella sian sibere le nave e li patroni de quelle.

19. (CCVIII) De sale e altre victuarie, che se conducesse per Ragusei in navilii de Ancona, sia sotoposti ali ordeni del commun de Ancona.

20. (CCIX) Per panni, e fostagni e altre cosse de lana o de lino, le qual li Ragusini conducesse o trazesse de Ancona, sia tratadi come forestieri in fato de doane secondo li ordeni de Ancona, si veramente che li panni e fostagni e altre cosse de lana e del lino, di Ragusini per portizare in lo porto de Ancona sian libere da ogni gabelle, come altre merzancie e cosse de Ragusei, come de sopra se contien in le dite condicioni, e conte se contiene.

I sopradetti patti firmati in MCCCLXXXXVII, indcione V, a di VI mazo, deno durare anni XXVIIII proximi che seguira. Deo laus et gloria in secula seculorum. Amen.

FIG. 52. Transcript of the trade agreement between Dubrovnik and Ancona dated 6/III/1397. (Dubrovnik Archives *Capitulare della Dogana grande* No. 321 written on skin.)

1372, 19th December[181]
Ancona authorizes Jacopo Pauli to ratify the existing treaties with Ragusa for the next five years.

(circa 1373)[182]
Pope Gregory IX writing from Avignon, March 30th to Ragusa.

His Vicar General, Cardinal Peter, has authorized towns in the Papal States to renew old treaties for five years. This letter solemnly ratifies the treaty between Ancona and Ragusa.

1379, 6th March[183]
Customs Regulations for Ragusa and District to Last for Twenty-Nine Years.

  (i) Anconans who sail with Ragusan fleets within or without the Gulf unload duty-free except for cargoes of salt and other victuals which shall be liable to tax in Ragusa.

  (ii) Anconans trading by sea in woollen cloth and fustian shall pay the same duty as other foreigners less 1 per centum.

  (iii) Woollens, fustian, and other goods of wool and linen from Ancona can be carried into Ragusa tax free like other Anconan goods contained in the above list.

Regulations for Ragusans trading in Ancona, as Agreed.

  (i) For every kind of merchandise including Slavonic imported by Ragusans into Ancona by sea or land, loaded up in any district from Sasino (island near Valona) on the one side to Otranto on the other, duty is payable. If it is sold by Anconans or Ragusans in Ancona, they must pay 3 piccoli per pound of value, i.e. one and one-quarter per centum of the goods. If the merchandise is sold by a foreigner, he must pay 6 piccoli, or two and one-half per centum.

    This merchandise does not include spices, sugar, cotton, silk from Chiarenza (Clarenza) or Tartary or the country districts round Chiarenza or Gazaria, nor cloths of silk or gold from the said areas, which pay duty like goods from the Levant, i.e. 6 per centum as below.

  (ii) Ragusans are not liable for duty on gold, silver, coinage, pearls and precious stones imported into Ancona, whether to be sold or not, for import or handling.

  (iii) As regards mercer's or draper's wares brought in by Ragusans or their agents to Ancona, by sea or land, to be carried or conveyed to Ragusa or other parts of Slavonia, if they are not sold in Ancona they pay one and one-quarter per centum only. If they are sold they must pay 4 per centum for cloth and 5 per centum for mercer's wares, like Anconans. For all other merchandise not specified above or below, Ragusans are on a par with Anconans.

(iv) For merchandise from Apulia and Sicily, Ragusans are on a par with Anconans.

(v) Anconans selling to Ragusans pay the customs one and one-quarter per centum. Foreigners similarly selling pay two and one-half per centum, except that for draper's and mercer's wares, Anconans and foreigners alike pay 1¼ per centum. Ragusans trading in Ancona pay 1¼ per centum.

(vi) Ragusans are on an equal footing with Anconans as regards merchandise from beyond the Gulf to the Levant and Ancona, i.e. merchandise dealt with in Ancona to be carried beyond the Gulf to the Levant pays 3 per centum, merchandise brought from beyond the Gulf to Ancona pays 6 per centum, on sales to Anconans or foreigners. Purchasers to pay 12 piccoli of Ancona per transaction. Except that for trading in alkali, Ragusans must pay 20 soldi per 1,000, and for soap 2½ per centum and 30 soldi per 1,000, and 5 piccoli per measure of soap.

(vii) Ragusans are on a par with Anconans as regards wine, salt, olive oil, grain of any kind, flax seed, figs, walnuts, apples, and everything that pays a levy to the Papal treasury.

(viii) Wheat and other grain imported by Ragusans can be sold or disposed of to Anconans only, not to foreigners. The usual duties apply, i.e. 8 piccoli per measure of corn. The buyer pays 16 piccoli per salma (i.e. 1,000 lb).

(ix) Ragusan ships may shelter from weather, pirates, etc. tax-free. If they sell any goods, tax is payable.

(x) No duty is payable for mooring (short term period).

(xi) Ragusans can have one year from the date of import to pay import duties. If they sell or otherwise dispose of their goods, they must pay the sales tax at the time. Goods remaining unsold after a year shall be valued and pay import duties at valuation price. When they are disposed of, sales tax is due.

(xii) Ragusans can sell any goods to Anconans or foreigners in Ancona according to the terms of the treaty, except grain which must only be sold to Anconans.

(xiii) To remove any possible doubt, mercer's wares includes all types of armour, manufactured leather goods, and goods made of iron, copper and tin, and everything included in the excise regulations of Ancona under 'Mercer's Wares'.

(xiv) If the business is conducted through a broker, duty must be paid in addition at the rate of 1 piccoli per pound of the price, if it is not sold in the city of Ancona, 2 piccoli if it is; half to be paid by the purchaser, half by the vendor. This duty does not apply if no broker is employed.

(xv) If Ragusan merchandise is weighed by Anconan officials, the purchaser must pay 5 piccoli per weighing.

(xvi) No other duties are to be levied on Ragusans except as specified here.

(xvii) Any goods may be brought in duty-free provided they are not unloaded. If the cargo is discharged it becomes subject to Anconan regulations. If sold while the ship is in harbour tax must be paid on the part sold.

(xviii) Ragusans can transport their goods in Anconan ships. Merchandise from the Levant and beyond the Gulf discharged on this side of the Gulf from Sasino to Sebenico (Šibenik) is not liable to Anconan taxes, neither is the ship or shipowner.

(xix) Salt and other victuals conveyed for Ragusans in Anconan ships are subject to Anconan regulations.

(xx) Ragusans trading in cloth, fustians, and other types of wool and linen in Ancona shall be on a par with other foreigners for tax purposes. If the cloth etc. is merely brought into harbour it is tax-free as above.

1426, 16th March. Ragusa[184]
Letter to ambassador from Ragusa to Ancona.

The treaty of friendship from time immemorial is due for renewal on April 8th. Renew on the same terms if possible.

The Anconans may object that they have lost money because Ragusan merchants do not come to Ancona as they used to. Reply that that is true enough, but merchants always go where the money is, and we cannot force them to go to Ancona. You still have the whole seaboard of Slavonia from the Cuman Gulf to Cattaro (Kotor) with ports to put into. We are interested in preserving friendship, not making profits.

It was twenty-nine years ago that an Anconan ship came with a cargo of wax and other goods from the Levant which should have been charged more than 400 ducats at our customs. Out of the kindness of our hearts we remitted those duties.

Again, only last year one of your ships came to the harbour of Malonto and was attacked, robbed and burnt by the inhabitants. The shipowners complained to us, and although we did not own Malonto at the time, we put our citizens to considerable trouble and expense to make good the damage done.

We are always doing our best for your benefit and honour. How about a little consideration from you?

1426, 4th June. Ragusa to Ancona[185]
So you say the treaty is to your disadvantage and you do not want to renew it. We have had this treaty for over seventy years, and when it was renewed thirty years ago there were no complaints about disadvantages. You complain that our ships shelter in your harbour and then trade elsewhere. We've had hundreds of your ships doing the same and we aren't fussing. You're reasonable people, so are we. Why not make some new agreements for twenty years, or even ten? There is no point in quarrelling, let us discuss the matter sensibly.

1426, 18th June. Ragusa to Fermo[186]
Message for the chancellor, Baptista de Fermo to take to Lord Lodovico di Megliorati, ruler of Fermo.

Your Magnificence promised full safe conduct for Ragusan merchants in all places under your jurisdiction provided they paid their customs dues. This has lapsed last year and this year and it would be to your advantage to renew it. If you don't want to renew it in full, can we have the same concessions that merchants from Pesaro and Fano get? If we get our safe conduct, we will treat your citizens here just as ours are treated there.

1440, 13th June[187]
Paul son of Honfrid de Polidorus, Nicolas son of Leonard de Bonarellis, Kyriac son of Lippo Pizecollis, Paglaresius son of Simoli de Pisanellis, and Antonio son of Bertucci de Amandulanis (in the absence of Stefano son of Thomas de Fatatis) on behalf of Ancona are to consolidate the treaties with Ragusa.

These treaties were drawn up on December 24th, 1372 by Astorelli, son of Nino de Tudento, notary public and treasurer of Ancona, with additions and amendments dated May 7, 1397, by Silvester de Collestade.

The agreements were discussed with Signor Marino, son of Michael de Restis, sindic of Ragusa, and his notary and chancellor, Egidio de Jugo of Cremona, on April 20th, and ratified by the commune of Ancona on May 14th.

The following additional clauses were agreed.

On all Ragusan merchandise coming from or bought within the Gulf, from Sasino to Otranto inwards, except gold, silver, precious stones and pearls, which is imported into Ancona (i.e. between St. Clement and St. Colphus) harbour dues must be paid: 1 gold ducat and ⅜ ducats per 100 ducats estimated value.

If Ragusan ships run for shelter into Ancona for any reason, they can discharge and reload without paying anything more than the aforesaid harbour dues of 1⅜ ducats. If the cargo is discharged in any other circumstances, or if any part of it is sold, duty shall be paid as provided for in the agreements. If there are any causes for disagreement or dispute or restrictive practices, let them be at an end from now on. Ragusans and their people shall be on an equal footing with Anconans in Ancona, and vice versa.

Any Ragusan avoiding or defrauding the customs of Ancona shall pay a summary fine of 25 ducats per 100 of value of the fraudulent goods only, and vice versa.

This treaty is to be observed for twenty years. Infringements are punishable by a fine of 1,000 ducats plus customs expenses. The treaty to continue nevertheless with the strength of oak. Signed: Barnabas de Vitalis, notary-chancellor of Ancona.

Conclusion

All this evidence – the different commodities, the various markets and regions of importance, show how Dubrovnik came to have a prominent position in the commerce of the later Middle Ages. Dubrovnik proves in fact Gras' point that

'the real interest of the medieval town seems to have been the development of purely local trade and the most profitable part of distant or international commerce'.[188]

The city was a link in the chain for transporting the products of underdeveloped regions, like the Balkans, to the more developed areas of the west and the Levant. However evidence suggests, in the case of Dubrovnik, that Gras was not correct when he assumed

'there was no effective large-scale organization of the commerce of a wide compact area or hinterland'.

The repeated recurrence of central and east Bosnia and western Serbia in the trade patterns of the city tend to suggest that Dubrovnik's citizens did have an effective large-scale organization for hinterland commerce. Without it they would not have been able to participate in 'the most profitable part of distant or international commerce', but in fact Dubrovnik 'managed to develop and prosper as a trading city during the later Middle Ages'.[189]

7. Notes

1. Dubrovnik Archives, (22/XII/1433). *Acta Sanctae Mariae Maioris*, facs. XV century; *Diversa Notaria*, 18, folders 215–217.
2. Dubrovnik Archives, (24/III/1373). *Acta Sanctae Mariae Maioris* XIV century. Bull issued by Pope Gregory XI.
3. Ć. Truhelka, *Tursko-Slovenski Spomenici*, Sarajevo (1911), p. 77, No. 88 (April/May 1485).
4. V. Foretić, 'Nekoliko pogleda na pomorska trgovinu Dubrovniku u srednjem vijeku', *Dubrovačko Pomorstvo*, Dubrovnik (1952), p. 138.
5. V. Makušev, *Monumenta historica Slavorium Meridionalium*, Warsaw (1874), p. 345.
6. V. Makušev, *op. cit.*, p. 440.
7. G. Muller, *Documenti sale Relazioni delle Citta Toscane coll'Oriente*, Tuscany (1881), p. 227.
8. I. von Düringsfeld, *Aus Dalmatien*, Vienna (1883), p. 25.
9. G. Gelcich, *Dello Sviluppo Civile di Ragusa*, Dubrovnik (1884), p. 70.
10. D. Whittlesey, *The Earth and the State*, 2nd Edt. New York (1944), p. 2.
11. D. Whittlesey, *op. cit.*, p. 597.
12. M. Jefferson, 'The problem of the Ecumene', *Geografiska Annaler*, Vol. 16 (1934), p. 146.
13. G. T. Trewartha, 'A case for population geography', *Annals of the Association of American Geographers*, Vol. 43 (1953), p. 92.
14. Karl W. Deutsch, 'The growth of nations: some recurrent patterns of political and social integration', *World Politics*, Vol. 5 (1952–53), pp. 168–95.
15. N. J. G. Pounds and S. S. Ball, 'Core-areas and the development of the European states system', *Annals of the Association of American Geographers*, Vol. 54 No. 1 (March 1964), p. 37.

16. K. W. Deutsch, *op. cit.*, p. 170.
17. K. W. Deutsch, *op. cit.*, p. 174.
18. D. Whittlesey, *op. cit.*, p. 2.
19. J. C. Russell, 'Late Medieval Balkan and Asia Minor population', *Journal of Economic and Social History of the Orient*, Vol. III (1960), pp. 265–274.
20. W. G. East, *An Historical Geography of Europe*, Methuen, London (1956), p. 179.
21. H. W. V. Temperley, *History of Serbia*, London (1919), p. 65.
22. D. M. Metcalf, *Coinage in the Balkans 820–1355*, Institute of Balkan Studies No. 80 Thessaloniki (1965), Ch. XII, pp. 253–258.
23. Dubrovnik Archives (1370–1373), *Lamenta de Foris* 'Si aliquid vis a me, eamus coram curia communis Ragusii uel ad racionem curie de Bossina uel ad furiam Teutonicorum.'
24. C. Mijatović, 'Studije za Istoriju Srpske Trgovine XIII-og i XIV-og Veka' *Glasnik Srpskog Učenog Društva Knj. XXXIII*, Belgrade (1872), pp. 191–230; p. 226 – 'Dubrovnik merchant (Đurda Branković) in 1400 took under lease, gold and silver mines at Janjevo, Kratovo, and Novo Brdo for 200,000 ducats/year.'
25. T. Smičiklas, *Codex diplomaticus regni Croatiae, Dalmatiae et Slavoniae*, J. A. Z. U. Vol. IX, Zagreb (1918), p. 278.
26. K. Jireček, *Istorija Srba*, Belgrade (1952), p. 175.
27. Dubrovnik Archives, *Caboga*, folders 3, 5, 6, 7, 8, etc. 'pliko' silver is mentioned many times.
28. Dubrovnik Archives, (8/IV/1446). *Testamenta Notariae*, 14, folder 31. Dubrovnik trader received 'in argento fino' from Srebrenica; (21/VIII/1451). *Consilium Rogatorum*, 12, folder 125. In a treaty between the Bosnian King and Dubrovnik it mentions 'argenti fini' from Srebrenica.
29. Dubrovnik Archives, (13/IX/1446). *Diversa Notariae*, 30, folder 106. A court case arose over the ownership of 61b of silver from Srebrenica 'd'argento fino'.
30. V. Makušev, *op. cit.*, Volume II (1904), p. 204.
31. V. Simić, *Istoriski razvoj našeg rudarstva*, Belgrade (1951), pp. 36, 145.
32. K. Jireček, *Die Handelsstrassen und Bergwerke von Serbien und Bosnien während des Mittelalters*, Prague (1879), p. 50.
33. Dubrovnik Archives, (15/11/1376). *Diversa Cancellariae*, 24, folder 111.
34. M. Dinić, *Za istoriju rudarstva sredjevekovnoj Srbiji i Bosni*, Part II, (Belgrade) 1962, p. 10.
35. Dubrovnik Archives, (4/VI/1321). *Diversa Cancellariae*, 6, folder 101. 3,000 litres of copper sent from Rudnik to Dubrovnik.
36. Dubrovnik Archives, (16/VII/1455). *Testamenta Notariae*, 15, folders 149–150.
37. Dubrovnik Archives, (12/IX/1411). *Lamenta de Foris*, 2, folder 89.
38. B. Hrabak, *Dubrovački ili bosanski azur*, Belgrade (1923), pp. 33–41.
39. Dubrovnik Archives, (14/VII/1441). *Debita Notaria*, 20, folder 185; (10/VII/1462). *Diversa Notaria*, 46, folder 781; (10/I/1449); C. M. Cipolla, 'The trends in Italian economic history in the later Middle Ages,' *Economic History Review* 2nd series II (1949–1950) p. 183.
40. Dubrovnik Archives, (16/VIII/1387). *Diversa Cancellariae*, 28, folder 54'.
41. John U. Nef, 'Silver production in central Europe 1450–1618', *Journal of Political Economy*, Vol. XLIX, no. 4, (August 1941), p. 575.

42. D. Kovačević, 'Dans la Serbie et la Bosnie medievales: Les Minies d'or et d'argent', *Annales, economies, societies, civilisations*, Vol. II (March–April 1960), p. 248–258;
ibid., *Trgovina u srednjovekovnoj Bosni*, Sarajevo (1961), pp. 135–146;
A. Handžić, 'Zvornik u drugoj polovini XV i u XVI Vijeku', *Godišnjak Društva Istoričara Bosne i Hercegovine*, Godine XVIII, Sarajevo (1970), pp. 141–196;
D. Kovačević, 'Le Rôle de l'industrie minière dans le développment des centres économiques en Serbie et en Bosnie, pendant la première moitié du XVe siècle,' *Studia Balcanica*, Vol. III, Sofia (1970), pp. 133–138.

43. V. Simić, *op. cit.*, p. 52.

44. M. Dinić, *op. cit.*, p. 85.

45. R. S. Lopez, 'Contributo alla storia delle miniere argentifere della Sardezna', *Studio economico-guiridici della R. Universitat di Cagliari*, Cagliari (1936).

46. A. C. Crombie, *Augustine to Galileo: The History of Science A.D. 400–1650*, London (1952) p. 191.

47. G. Luzzato, *An Economic History of Italy*, London (1961) p. 107.

48. A. C. Crombie, *op. cit.*, p. 193. Lead shot was used from the fourteenth century with smaller guns.

49. A. C. Crombie, *op. cit.*, p. 196.

50. Dubrovnik Archives, (1372–1391). *Diversa Cancellaria*, Vols. 23–29.

51. Dubrovnik Archives, (10/IX/1377). *Debita Notaria*, 8, fold 82′: 250 bales of skins, and 20 milijari of lead sent from Dubrovnik to Venice.

52. D. Kovačević, 'Zore Bokšić, Dubrovački Trgovac i Protovestijar bosanskih kraljeva', *Godišnjak Drustva Istoričara Bosnia i Hercegovina* Godina XIII Sarajevo (1962) pp. 289–310.

53. Dubrovnik Archives, (1377). *Diversa Notaria*, 9, folder 179. 20 milijari 'plumbi de Bossina' and 10 female slaves sent from Dubrovnik to Ancona.

54. A. Solmi 'Le Diete imperiati di Roncaglia e la navigazione del Po presso Piacenza', *Bollettimo della soc. di storia patria per le prov. parmenisi*, Piacenza (1910).

55. G. Biscoro, 'Gli antichi navigli milanesi', *Archivio storico lombardo*, Milan (1908).

56. Dubrovnik Archives, (1375). *Diversa Cancellaria*, 24, folder 34. 40 milijari (14,344 kg) of lead sent from Dubrovnik to Florence.

57. Dubrovnik Archives, (1393). *Diversa Cancellaria*, 30, folder 58';
31, folder 173–74; 177′–179.

58. A. Schulte, *Geschichte des mittelalterlichen Handels u Verkehes zwischen Westdeutschland u Italien*, Leipzig (1900).

59. Dubrovnik Archives, (3/VI/1489). *Consilium Rogatorum*, 26, folder 39.

60. Venetian State Archives, (2/VIII/1409). *Senato Misti*, 48, folder 95. 'Cum pridie fuerit captum in isto consilio et mandatum galeis nostris culphy quoddeberent ire Ragusium et levare argentum illus quod ibi erat conducendumVenetias'.

61. Dubrovnik Archives, (27/VII/1388). *Diversa Cancellariae*, 27, folder 141'.
6 litres of silver sent from Novo Brdo to Venice via Dubrovnik.

62, 63. Dubrovnik Archives, (1419). *Diversa Notaria*, 12, folders 207′, 242, 242′, 248, 248′, 252′, 254.

64. Dubrovnik Archives, (15/V/1380). *Consilium Rogatorum*, 21, folder 6;
(21/VII/1380). *op. cit.*, 20, folder 181;
(10/VIII/1381). *op. cit.*, 20, folder 243.

65. Dubrovnik Archives, (1420). *Diversa Notaria*, 13, folders 33, 34′, 132′, 176′, 214′, 221.
66. Dubrovnik Archives, (1480). *Diversa Notaria*, 77, folder 155. Silver sent from Srebrenica to Verona in exchange for Italian linen.
67. A. C. Crombie, *Augustine to Galileo: The History of Science A.D. 400–1650*, London (1952), p. 190.
68. Dubrovnik Archives, (8/II/1371). *Diversa Cancellaria*, 23, folder 3′. Zore Bokšič sent copper worth 360 ducats to Venice;
    (1376) *Diversa Cancellariae*, 24, folder 144′. 12 milijari of copper 'ad pondus ragusium' (totalling 4,296 kg) sent to Venice.
69. K. Jireček, *Die Bedeutung von Ragusa in der Handelsgeschichte Mittelatters*, Almanach Kaiserlichen. Akademie der Wissenschaften. Vienna (1904), p. 90.
70. C. Baudi de Vesme, *Dell' industria delle miniere nel territorio di Villa di Chiesa*, Turin (1870).
71. A. Schulte, *op. cit.*, p. 4.
72. Dubrovnik Archives, (16/VIII/1371). *Diversa Cancellariae*, 23, folder 54′. 30 Milijari of iron 'ad pondus venetum' (14,310 kg) bought in Bussovac (Brsovac) was sent to Milan via Venice at a price of 20,½ ducats/milijari (i.e. 23,25 kg/ducat.)
73. Dubrovnik Archives, (30/VIII/1359). *Lettere di Levante*, II, folder 10′.
74. Dubrovnik Archives, (29/XI/1377). *Debita Notariae*, 8, folder 107′.
75. Dubrovnik Archives, (12/II/1435). *Diversa Cancellariae*, 48, folder 323. Dubrovnik merchant took 29 ducats worth of iron to Greece for sale.
76. G. Novak, 'Pogled na prilike radnih slojeva u rimskoj provincije Dalmaciji', *Istoriski Zbornik*, Broj. 1–4, Godina I, Zagreb (1948) pp. 129–153.
77. B. Krekić, *Dubrovnik (Ragusa) et le Levant au Moyen Age*, Paris (1961), p. 135; V. Vinaver, 'Črno Roblje u Dubrovniku' (1400–1600)', *Istoriski Časopis*, Vol. 5, Zagreb (1954–1955), pp. 437–442.
78. Dubrovnik Archives, (4/V/1399). *Diversa Cancellariae*, 33, folder 142. Dubrovnik merchant bought a negro slave from Damietta (Dumyat, Egypt) later selling him to a Venetian merchant;
    (28/III/1454). *Diversa Notaria*, 34, folder 30. Two negro slaves were bought in Syracuse and Alexandria, sent to Dubrovnik, being then shipped on further to Florence and Valencia.
79. G. Luzzato, *An Economic History of Italy*, London (1961), p. 62.
80. Dubrovnik Archives, (27/XI/1372. *Lettere e Commissioni di Levant*, Vol. II (1359–1380).
81. V. Vinaver, 'Trgovina Bosanskim Robljemi tokom XIV veka Dubrovniku', *Annali Istoriskog Instituta u Dubrovniku*, Dubrovnik (1953), p. 136.
82. Dubrovnik Archives, (1375). *Venditae Cancellariae*, 2, folder 44′. Two sisters from Bosnia were sold as slaves in Dubrovnik and sent to Milan via Venice.
83. R. S. Lopez, 'Market expansion: The case of Genoa', *Journal of Economic History* Volume XXIV, (December 1964), No. 4 pp. 458–459.
84. V. Vinaver, *op. cit.*, p. 127.
85. M. Ivanović, 'Prilozima za istoriju Carina u srednjevokovnim srpskim državama', *Spomenik Srpski Akademija Nauka*, Kniga 97, Belgrade (1952), p. 22.
86. L. F. Salzman, *English Trade in the Middle Ages*, Oxford (1931), p. 420.
87. Venetian State Archives, (1438), *Senato Misti*, 59, folders 144–151, 172.

88. S. Ljubić, *Listine o odnošajih izmedju južnoga Slavenstva i mletačke republice*, Vol. I Zagreb (1868), p. 289.

89. Dubrovnik Archives, (13/I/1452). *Diversa Cancellariae*, 63, folder 70. Merchant in Alexandria bought 285½ lb of cloves and 2,552 lb of pepper.

90. Margaret W. Laborge 'The Spice Account', *History Today* Vol. XV No. 1, (January 1965), p. 34.

91. Dubrovnik Archives, (15/VI/1373). *Lemanta de Foris*, I, folders 118–118'. A merchant bought 50 lb of pepper but only 14 lb of saffron from Alexandria.

92. N. Jorga, *Notes et extraites pour servir a l'histoire des croissades au XVe siècle* Vol. I, Paris (1899), p. 266.

93. Dr. G. A. Škrivanić, *Imenik Geografskih Naziva srednjovekovne Zete*, Istoriski Institut N.R. Crne Gore. Titograd (1959), p. 97.

94. Dubrovnik Archives, (1366). *Diversa Cancellaria*, 18, folders 98';
(1367). *op. cit.*, 21, folder 83';
(1368). *op. cit.*, 21, folder 114.

95. Dubrovnik Archives, (22/V/1393). *Diversa Cancellaria*, 30, folder 28, 'Medua portus fluminus de Lesso'.

96. Dubrovnik Archives, (13/IV/1368). *Diversa Cancellaria*, 21, folders 182–1, 360 modia of salt, (57,120 kg) taken from Dürres to Dubrovnik.

97. Dubrovnik Archives, (25/VI/1417). *Diversa Notoria*, 12, folder 177';
(January 1419). *op. cit.*, 12, folder 252;
(1420). *op. cit.*, 12, folders 139', 288';
op. cit., 13, folder 119.

98. Dubrovnik Archives, (1385). *Reformationes*, 26, folder 71'. Salt sent from Barletta to Dubrovnik;
Dubrovnik Archives (22/XI/1380) *Consilium Minus*, 9, folder 18. 998 sacks of salt sent from Brindisi to Dubrovnik.

99. Dubrovnik Archives, (November 1392). *Diversa Cancellaria*, 30, folders 138–139, 154.

100. *Monumenta Slavorium . . . op. cit.*, Vol. II, p. 184 – mentions treaty dated 19/V/1357 in which the Bosnian king Stefan Tvrtko I gave Dubrovnik merchants the monopoly of supplying salt to his kingdom.

101. Dubrovnik Archives, (7/V/1414). *Lamenta de Foris 1412–1414* – with reference to customs duty on salt 'sal de marina sol (uit) unciam unam argenti pro salma uel unum iperpirum, sal de Ungaria sol decem'; Dubrovnik merchant testified 'si aliquis emebasal pro argento, soluebat pro qualibet libra argenti grossos octo'.

102. M. Gečić, 'Dubrovačka Trgovina solju u XIV veku' *Zbornik Filosofskog Fakulteta*, Kniga III Belgrade (1955), pp. 94–153.

103. J. Tadić, 'Privreda Dubrovnika i srpske zemlje u prvoj polovini XV veka', *Zbornik Filosofskog Fakulteta* Kniga X, Broj. 1 Belgrade (1968). pp. 519–539.

104. K. Kostić, *Trgovinski centru i drumovi po srpskoj zemlji u srednjem i novom veku*, Belgrade (1899) p. 95.

105. Dubrovnik Archives, (August/September 1485, šaban 980). *Liber Privilegiorum* Vol. I, p. 118 b;
Ć. Truhelka, *op. cit.*, p. 103 Doc. 116, (August 1491) (7 ševala 896), concerned with tax from salt trade.

106. G. Luzzato, *op. cit.*, p. 114.

107. K. Jireček, *La Civilisation Serbe au Moyen Age*, Belgrade (1920), p. 48.

108. J. Roglić, 'Prilog poznavanju humljačkog stočarstva', *Geografski Glasnik.* Zagreb (1956), No. 18, p. 3.

109. V. Vinaver, 'Pomorstvo Ulcinja u XVIII veku', *Istoriski Zapisi*, Vol. 20 (1), Zagreb (1963), pp. 51–69.

110. Dubrovnik Archives, (8/XI/1434). *Diversa Cancellariae*, 48, folder 263 (when 30 horses carried skins from Borač via the Neretva valley to Dubrovnik.)

111. Reference is frequently made to fairs even in the sixteenth century – for example, Dubrovnik Archives, (January 1523). *Consilium Rogatorum*, 37, folder 16, – goods taken to the fair at Recanati.

112. Dubrovnik Archives, (1363). *Testamenta Notaria*, 5, folders 303′ – 304′. Several hundred skins were in the shop of a Dubrovnik merchant which he had received from Prizren. The bill for them was noted as being paid in Venice.

113. D. Roller, *Dubrovački zanati u XV i XVI stoljeću*, Zagreb (1951), p. 144; I. Božić, 'Ekonomski i drustvenu razvitak Dubrovnika u XIV i XV stolječu', *Istoriski Glasnik*, I, Belgrade (1949), pp. 31–32.

114. Dubrovnik Archives, (1383). *Diversa Cancellariae*, 25, folder 32′; (1390). *Testamenta Notaria*, 7, folders 248–250′.

115. A. Sapori, *La crisi delle compagnie mercantile dei Bardi e dei Peruzzi*, Florence (1926).

116. G. Lopez, *op. cit.*, p. 456.

117. Dubrovnik Archives, (19/VI/1449). *Testamenta Notaria*, 14, folder 123′. Five loads of wax weighing 2,223 litres arrived in Dubrovnik from Bosnia. (i.e. 148 kg per load), compared with a load of the more unwieldy lead which averaged only 97 kg, (12/IX/1411). *Lamenta de Foris*, 2, folder 89.

118. Dubrovnik Archives, (11/V/1436). *Diversa Notaria*, 20, folder 234′. Three traders from Goražda sent 'ceram uel alias mercantias' to Dubrovnik.

119. Dubrovnik Archives, (10/V/1403). *Diversa Cancellaria*, 34, folder 218′. Bosnian wax sent from Dubrovnik to Ancona; (18/V/1445). *Testamenta Notaria*, 13, folders 219′–220. Bosnian wax sent from Dubrovnik to Pesaro in Italy.

120. Dubrovnik Archives, (1481). *Diversa Cancellaria*, 79, folders 185, 186; (1486). *Diversa Notaria*, 65, folder 62′.

121. Dubrovnik Archives, (March 1484). *Liber Privilegorium*, p. 118.b.

122. Dubrovnik Archives, (6/I/1399). *Diversa Cancellaria*, 32, folder 214. Merchant from Trano bought cattle in Dubrovnik from Bosnian trader (Foča).

123. Dubrovnik Archives, (8/XI/1393). *Diversa Cancellaria*, 30, folder 77′. Bosnian merchants who sold horses in Dubrovnik came from Foča and Goražda; (1395). *op. cit.*, 32, folder 214; (6/II/1456) *Diversa Notaria* 40, folder 135.

124. Dubrovnik Archives, (11/IX/1383). *Diversa Cancellaria*, XXV, folder 245′; (19/VI/1385). *Reformationes*, XXVI, folder 34′; (24/II/1393). *Diversa Cancellaria*, XXX, folders 20–20′; (1/II/1414). *Diversa Notaria*, XII, folders 12–12′.

125. Dubrovnik Archives, (9/X/1407). *Diversa Cancellaria*, 36, folder 233′. Two grain merchants from Rhodes visited Dubrovnik with cereals.

126. T. Smičiklas, *Codex Diplomaticus Regni Croatie, Dalmatiae et Slavoniae* J.A.Z.U. Vol. VII (Zagreb 1903–1934), p. 175: boat from Dubrovnik was attacked in Dalmatia which had come from Romania (Greece) carrying silk, wax, corn, and other goods.

127. Dubrovnik Archives, (28/II/1406). *Diversa Cancellaria*, XXXVI, folder 25′; (21/VII/1418). *Diversa Cancellaria*, XLI, folder 270; (22/VI/1423). *Consilium Minoris*, II, folder 75; (23/I/1435). *Consilium Minoris*, VI, folder 209.

128. F. Thiriet, *La Romanie Vénetienne au moyen age*, (*Le Dévelopment et l'exploitation du domaine coloniale vénetian*), (XII–XV Siècle) Paris (1959) p. 306.

129. Dubrovnik Archives, (7/II/1438). *Consilium Minoris*, VII, folder 198′; (16/I/1442). *Consilium Minoris*, IX, folder 56′.

130. Dubrovnik Archives, (18/VI/1380). *Consilium Rogatorum*, 24; (November 1457), *Lettere e Commissioni di Levante*, XIV, folder 179–180′.

131. D. Dinić-Knežević, 'Trgovina žitom u Dubrovniku u XIV veku', *Godišnjak Filosofskog Fakulteta u Novom Sadu*, Vol. 10, (1967), pp. 79–131.

132. S. Ljubić, *Listine . . . op. cit.*, Vol. I pp. 113–114 – a boat from Greece carrying flax to Dubrovnik was attacked by pirates.

133. Dubrovnik Archives, (1369). *Diversa Cancellariae*, 22, folder 24: 'linum album, longum' is recorded as having come from 'Puntam Chiarentie'.

134. W. Heyd, *Histoire du commerce du Levant au Moyen-Age*, Vol. II, Leipzig (1886), p. 282 – footnote 1 includes flax as one of the products grown in the Peloponnesus at this time.

135. F. Balducci – Pegolotti, *La practica della mercatora*, (A. Evans, ed.) Cambridge, Massachusetts (1936), p. 118.

136. Dubrovnik Archives, (23/II/1370). *Diversa Cancellaria*, 22, folder 104; (18/IX/1428), *Diversa Cancellaria*, 45, folder 88.

137. E. Alberi, *Relazioni Venete* 2nd series Vol. I 'Relazione di Firenze del clarissimo Marco Foscari, 1527', Florence (1839), p. 28.

138. M. E. Mallett, *The Florentine Galleys in the Fifteenth Century*, Oxford (1967), pp. 145–152.

139. Dubrovnik Archives, (18/IX/1443). *Lamentationes de Foris*, 19, folder 40.

140. Dubrovnik Archives, (1532–1546). *Diversa Notaria*, 107, folders 139′, 154′, 156′, 162′, 172′.

141. Dubrovnik Archives, (1272). *Liber statutorum civitatis Ragusii Compositus anno 1272*.

142. Dubrovnik Archives, (14/III/1483). *Liber Croceus*, 82.

143. Dubrovnik Archives, (10/VI/1476). *Consilium Rogatorum*, 23, folder 223; (24/XII/1477). *Diversa Cancellaria*, 79, folder 186; (1483). *Consilium Rogatorum*, 24, folder 53: Textiles sent to Serbia from Florence via Dubrovnik.

144. Dubrovnik Archives, (1482). *Consilium Rogatorum*, 22, folder 299′. Large quantity of textiles sent from Verona to Dubrovnik.

145. D. Roller, *Dubrovački zanati u XVi XVI stoljeća*, Zagreb (1951) pp. 22–23: His conclusions do not appear to be based on documentary evidence.

146. W. Heyd, *op. cit.*, Vol. II, p. 693.

147. Dubrovnik Archives, (1380). *Dogana*, III, folders 37′, 42, 46′, 47; (1381). *op. cit.*, folders 79, 79′, 95, 99, 128′, 136′. These documents include declarations by merchants in Dubrovnik for paying customs duty on cloth they had sent to Greece.

148. Dubrovnik Archives, (2/V/1430). *Diversa Cancellaria*, XLVI, folder 178.

149. Dubrovnik Archives, (11/XI/1402). *Diversa Cancellaria*, 34, folder 170. A Dubrovnik merchant sent to the Bosnian court 'benetini de Florencia' and linen from Como.

150. M. Dinić, *Odluke Veća Dubrovačke Republike*, Kniga I S.A.N. Belgrade (1951), p. 250.

151. K. Jireček, *Važnost Dubrovnika op. cit.*, p. 51.

152. Dubrovnik Archives, (November 1462). *Consilium Rogatorum*, 17, folder 146. Wax and silver were sent to Dubrovnik from Novo Brdo in exchange for textiles. There are several examples of silver being exchanged for textiles.

153. M. Popović, 'La penetrazione dei mercanti Pratesi a Dubrovnik (Ragusa) nella prima méta del XV secolo', *Archivio storico italiano* Anno CXVII, Venice (1959) pp. 508, 517, 518.

154. Dubrovnik Archives, (1492). *Diversa Notaria*, 71, folder 164'. Textiles from Naples, Perpignon and London were sent via Dubrovnik to Serbia.

155. Dubrovnik Archives, (27/V/1490). *Diversa Notaria*, 70, folder 218. Woollen cloth sent from Constantinople overland to Dubrovnik in several large quantities.

156. J. Luetić, 'Agrarno-proizvodni odnosi u okolici Dubrovnika od polovine XIV stoleća', *Zgodovinski Časopis*, Vol. 22 No. 1–2, (1968), pp. 61–96;
D. Dinić- Knežović, 'Trgovina vinom u Dubrovniku u XIV vijeku', *Godišnjak Filiosofskog Fakulteta u Novom Sadu*, Vol. 9, (1966), pp. 39–85;
Ibid., 'Prilog proučavanju mjera za vino u Dubrovniku XIV vijeku', *Historijski Zbornik*, Vol. 19–20, Zagreb (1966–67), pp. 419–427.

157. Dubrovnik Archives, (2/VI/1381). *Consilium Maius*, 51, folder 6;
(30/XII/1390). *Diversa Notaria*, folders 140–141;
(November 1457). *Lettere di Levante*, 14, folder 179–180'.

158. Zadar Archives, (23/X/1425). *Ducali e Terminazioni*, Listine IX, p. 7.

159. Dubrovnik Archives, (1381). *Consilium Rogatorum*, 24;
(1447). *Lamenta de Foris*, 21, folder 297;
(1449). *ibid.*, 22, folder 46;
(23/XI/1472). *Diversa Notaria*, 56, folder 152'.

160. Dubrovnik Archives, (25/VI/1410). *Diversa Cancellariae*, 38, folder 136'.

161. Dubrovnik Archives, (1482). *Diversa Cancellariae*, 81, folder 101'.

162. Dubrovnik Archives, (1488). *Debita Notaria*, 52, folder 100.

163. Dubrovnik Archives, (1479). *Diversa Notaria*, 63, folder 107.

164. Calculated on the assumption that the density of lead is 11,3 grammes.

165. Dubrovnik Archives, (1473). *Diversa Notaria*, 58, folder 99.

166. Dubrovnik Archives, (1473). *Diversa Notaria*, 58, folder 130.

167. Dubrovnik Archives, (1477). *Diversa Notaria*, 66, folder 78' – 531 ducats and 11 pieces of Verona cloth sent from Venice in payment for lead.

168. V. Vinaver, 'Trgovina Bosanskim Robljemi . . .' *op. cit.*, p. 142.

169. I. Božić, *Dubrovnik. i Turska u XIV i XV veku*, Srpski Akademija Nauka Posebna Izdanja CC Istoriski Institut Kniga 3. Belgrade (1952), p. 328.

170. I. Božić, *op. cit.*, p. 331.

171. V. Vinaver, *op. cit.*, p. 142.

172. Dubrovnik Archives, (12/IX/1442). *Diversa Notaria*, 26, folders 96'–97.

173. A 'Sporta' in Alexandria weighed 700 lb (see F. Edler *Glossary of Medieval Terms of Business*, Italian Series 1200–1600. London (1934), p. 277). If 30 sportas cost 1,800 ducats then 1 ducat bought 121 lb, 1 ducat = 45p gold, therefore one pound cost about 4p.

174. G. Phillips, 'Mahuan's account of Cochin, Calicut and Aden', *Journal of the Royal Asiatic Society*, London (1896), pp. 341–351.

175. The Poho is taken here to represent 534 lb and the tael at 33p. (see F. Edler *op. cit.*, p. 344). Pepper was apparently sold at Cochin at £1.66p for 534 lb or less than ½p a pound.

176. H. T. Turner, *Manners and Household Expenses of the Thirteenth and Four-teenth Centuries*, Roxburghe Club London (1841).

177. B. H. Slicher Van Bath *The Agrarian History of Western Europe A.D. 500–1850*, London (1963), Part III, p. 98.

178. Dubrovnik Archives, (18/IV/1425). *Diversa Cancellaria*, 43, folder 122'.

179. G. Luzzatto, 'I più antichi trattati tra venezia e le città Marchigiane' *Nuovo Archivio Veneto*, Venice (1906), pp. 5–42, 65–70.

180. Dubrovnik Archives, (1359–1380). *Lettere e Commissioni di Levante*, Vol. a, (in Latin).

181. Dubrovnik Archives, *Fasc. I*, n.50, (in Latin).

182. Dubrovnik Archives, *Fasc. I*, n.21, (in Latin).

183. Dubrovnik Archives, *Capitulare della Dogana grande* No. 321, (in Italian).

184. Dubrovnik Archives, (1423–27), *Lettere e Commissioni di Levante* Vol. a, (in Italian).

185. Dubrovnik Archives, (1423–27), *Lettere e Commissioni di Levante* Vol. a, (in Latin).

186. Dubrovnik Archives, *ibid.*, (in Italian).

187. Vienna State Archives, *Ancona* 163/5, (in Latin).

188. N. S. B. Gras, 'The economic activity of towns', Ch. 3, p. 461 in *The Legacy of the Middle Ages*, (C. G. Crump and E. F. Jacob, eds.), Oxford, (1926).

189. N. S. B. Gras, *ibid.*

7
Domestic Production in the Dubrovnik Republic

In a recent publication Thrupp has stated that

'Industrially, the function of medieval towns was to foster and
satisfy demand for things of better quality than village work could
supply. In the Mediterranean world there had been no break in
reliance on the market for this purpose, and current re-examination of the background of urban industrial revival in north-eastern
France and Flanders is discovering more and more scraps of
evidence pointing to some degree of continuity in urban production for sale and export throughout the early medieval centuries.
Wherever merchants wintered there were craftsmen. In Kiev and
Novgorod and other Russian trading towns they were making
copper icons and crosses for domestic export at least as early as
the tenth century. By the eleventh century Cologne and London
had a high reputation for fine goldsmiths' work, and Liege and
Milan for arms. By the twelfth century, demand for town-made
goods was clearly rising, and continued to rise more or less steadily
for nearly two hundred years. The largest bulk sales at fairs were
of cloth. Any stuff that was warm, and more regular in weave or
more smoothly finished than country cloth could find a market'.[1]

The whole basis of Dubrovnik's prosperity was trade. The republic's
territory was too small, and in part too arid, to provide sufficient
foodstuffs for the population, and threequarters of the grain which
was consumed annually had to be imported from abroad. Consequently it was upon trade and industry that the citizens had to
depend for their means of livelihood. Manufactures, except for shipbuilding, never assumed great importance at Dubrovnik, and it was
not until the fourteenth century that any industries were established

at all. Nevertheless, mercantile development naturally led to the formation of numerous guilds, or confraternities. Like many institutions they were based on Venetian models, and were really the beginnings of the modern mutual aid societies on a religious framework. Among the earliest of these were that of the joiners, founded in 1266, and that of the goldsmiths established in 1306. During the Venetian period they were under strict government supervision, but after 1358 they were invested with political privileges and exemptions.[2] Domestic production, although always subsidiary to other branches of commerce, did exist in Dubrovnik, and probably the most interesting is the rise and fall of the woollen cloth industry.

The Woollen Industry

Prior to 1450 the woollen industry in Dubrovnik was poorly developed. According to Novak[3] the woollen industry was established in Dubrovnik about 1380. The Dubrovnik merchants believed that the most profit could be made from cloth if they manufactured their own material in the town and its immediate vicinity, providing that standards did not fall behind the rest of western Europe. It was on this basis that Dubrovnik's woollen workshops were established, most of them privately owned but well supported by the town authorities, who passed suitable laws to protect and encourage the growth in the industry. The first real documentary evidence comes from January 30, 1416 when a law was passed establishing the posts of 'officials in charge of woollen handicrafts' whose main purpose was to obtain 'better profits from this handicraft and its adminstration'.[4] The new industry flourished possessing many modern buildings and concentrating on the production of unusual cloth widths, for which there was always a ready sale. Already by 1430, 'panni Ragusii' was mentioned as being exported to the Levant[5] but never in the quantities that it was dispatched to the Balkan interior, and Dalmatian towns then under Venetian rule.

The government of the Dubrovnik Republic took great interest in the woollen industry. The government agreed in 1440 that there should be no customs duty on imported wool for the next three years, in order to encourage increased production,[6] and satisfy above all domestic consumption. Further, a high duty of one ducat for imported drapery and half a grossi for exported raw wool placed on the statute books to help protect the industry from outside competition. According to the notes of one contemporary,[7] the woollen industry in the 1440's had an annual production of 4,000 'peča' annually.[8]

The problem of foreign competition was always uppermost in Dubrovnik minds. Venice, in her bid for commercial hegemony in the Adriatic and beyond, was jealous of Dubrovnik's Levantine cloth markets, and gradually exerted pressures on other Italian towns to discontinue supplying Dubrovnik with material. Therefore Dubrovnik had to develop her own textile industry, particularly for wool, to reinforce the general economic life of the town. Even this caused some friction outside the republic because the people of Kotor in 1446 wrote to Venice complaining about the large amount of cloth being sold by Dubrovnik merchants that had been produced in their own workshops, and as a result was 'stirring up trouble in Zeta, Bosnia and Sklavonija'.[9] Venetian competition in the Balkan interior was weak at this time, and there were even attempts to establish the industry by some inland rulers. For example a short lived attempt was made by Duke Stipan Vukčić (generally known as Stephen Kosača or Cosaze),[10] who tried to establish woollen production in Hercegovina, but failed probably due to the poor quality of local wools.

Each year the Great Council (Veliki Vijece) appointed three officials (Časnika, officiales artislanae, or commissioned officer) whose main duty was to watch the progress of the industry and report it to the Great Council.[11] Their major tasks were to assess which laws would prevent or discourage production, which workshops needed more equipment and what was required for helping in the dyeing of wool. On their recommendations the government then passed the necessary laws or orders.[12] At first the dyeshops were both state and privately owned; later the officials found it necessary to close the private ones, forcing each entrepreneur to take his wool to the state establishment for dyeing. In the laws of May 21, 1445 and January 15, 1454[13] the government passed legislation concerning the relations between the dye-houses and wool-workers. These laid down how the garments had to satisfy home demand in which customs duty of one ducat per peča of drapery was placed on imported goods and half a grossi per libre placed on the export of wool.

The growing importance of the woollen industry is reflected by the increasing number of laws passed by the Dubrovnik government during the second half of the fifteenth and first half of the sixteenth centuries. There appears to have been three basic reasons for this legislation. First, that the woollen industry was considered to be financially important enough both for private individuals and as a source of income to the state. Secondly, that there were signs of possible decline within the industry, and thirdly that the government realized the need to support it if the industry was to be a success. The first[14] of these many laws was passed on February 22, 1461 which ordered the construction of new dye works, for the wool industry. Similar laws on November 30, 1461 and August 19, 1463 issued leases for the opening of textile workshops up to a value of 6,000 ducats,[15] whilst yet another[16] of April 1464 established a new headquarters for the industry (Camera dell 'arte della lana') and would employ people to scrutinize production looking for bad workmanship and faulty material. This was important if the small republic was to maintain its position in competition with its great rival, Venice. Such competition caused added friction which came to a head in the Venetian Senate on September 28, 1462, when it was noted that competition was fiercest in the woollen industry. Further it was remarked that

'competition from Dubrovnik's merchants and drapery would destroy our own woollen industry for their products now extend into the Venetian seas, where we have jurisdiction, make laws and carry out orders in places and lands which do not belong to Dubrovnik'.

As a result of this meeting they proclaimed that in future Dubrovnik's transit ships on entering Venetian harbours, or harbours under their jurisdiction, must pay one tenth the value of cloth transported, and that even before leaving Dubrovnik these ships must have written permission to call at Venetian-held Kotor and pay 10% duty, under threat, on arrival, of losing all drapery carried. Also from now on, none of the Venetian towns, or dependencies, would be allowed to buy or sell Dubrovnik's cloth, or cloth from Novi, and places inside 'Our Gulf' (Adriatic Sea), under threat of paying a 500 ducat fine and having all material confiscated, which Dubrovnik merchants have either bought or sold against Venetian orders. This order applied to all towns in Dalmatia and Albania under Venetian rule, i.e. Zadar, Šibenik, Trogir, Split Cres-Orsov, Rab, Pag, Nin, Brač, Hvar, Korčula, Kotor, Skadar, Lješ, Ulcinj, Drač, Bar, Budva and Corfu.[17]

Coupled with this misfortune, Dubrovnik's merchants were also affected by the general economic decline in the Balkan peninsula, during the decade 1460–1470, as a result of the Turkish conquest, so that the trade in textiles fell off rapidly. Towards the end of the next

decade there was a growth in demand, for the Turks, once consolidated in the Balkans, provided a market for western cloth in
exchange for their own oriental styles of material. This is borne out
by the sitting of Dubrovnik's Great Council of May 25, 1478, when it
decided to increase import and export duty to 1% on all foreign cloth
from western Europe and on all sales to the Balkan peninsula, whilst
no Dubrovnik cloth was to be exported anywhere free of customs
duty.[18] This illustrated how the Dubrovnik government could obtain
increased revenue from the new demand, whilst at the same time
protecting her own industry. Nevertheless this was a time when
Dubrovnik had fears about the collapse of her woollen industry, for it
was now over 100 years old, with poor production facilities and in
need of reorganization if it was to meet the challenge of increased
output. The government officials realized the importance of this
industry for the livelihood of the town and remembered how prosperous it had been earlier in the century. Similarly the citizens of
Dubrovnik saw how much this would affect their economic life as the
woollen industry was a very important branch of the town's business.

The outcome of this discontent is seen from a meeting of the Great
Council of February 12, 1481, when it decided it must help woollen
manufacture in the town and ordered a complete overhaul of the
industry.[19] The ensuing enquiry recommended a need for new weaving sheds, places for dyeing, and more weavers, especially for finishing
the material, marking the owner's name and quantity of cloth. Protection was also suggested for the domestic industry so that Dubrovnik
cloth would be more saleable within Dubrovnik and her territories;
this meant that now foreign cloth, which had been bought for 20
grossi a lakat[20] must not be sold for less in Dubrovnik, under threat
that it would be regarded as smuggling and liable to punishment. The
law of 1481, therefore, not only tried to help the home industry but
limit imports of foreign cloth by raising their prices. People convicted
of wool smuggling were to be fined, one third of the fine going to the
informant, one third to the government, and one third to the official
in charge of documenting the evidence. Also all workshops which
had previously purchased foreign cloth for less than 20 grossi a lakat
had to go to the customs office and have it registered, before it could
be sold again. The law took immediate effect for after three days of
its passing not one workshop in Dubrovnik sold cloth which had not
been registered. Those merchants who had sold Dubrovnik cloth for
less than 20 grossi per lakat were not given official clearance until

L*

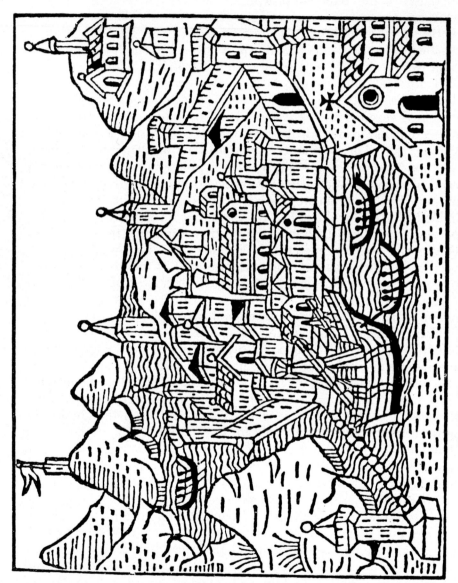

Fig. 53.   Woodcut of Dubrovnik in 1481 (8·2 cm × 6·4 cm).

they had sold it all. The law therefore controlled the selling prices of Dubrovnik cloth and forced great price reductions on domestic wool manufacture. This is further illustrated by the drastic price reductions ordered by the government for the selling of Dubrovnik cloth: a price scale was made based on the quality of wool of peča length. A peča of cloth valued at 50 ducats had to be sold for 10 ducats, 60 ducat quality for 12 ducats and 70 ducat standard for 15 ducats, in other words an 80% drop in price. Merchants who tried to deceive the law, or who stole cloth on a small scale were fined 50 perpera, and forbidden from ever selling cloth in Dubrovnik again. However, the law was not entirely one of suppression. A system of rewards was introduced whereby if a merchant sold a peča length of Dubrovnik cloth for less than 30 ducats, then the workshop where it was manufactured received one ducat bonus in return; further those workshops importing better quality foreign wool, i.e. fine French, Mantua and Verona wools, were freed of all customs duty by the Great Council.[21] All wool of 70 ducat per peča quality, or less, for weaving had first to be brought to the 'Komora vunenog obrta' (chamber of woollen handicrafts) for examination and classification and thereafter its quality could not be changed, or mixed with inferior wools. Strict measures indeed, but devised to deliberately keep up the standard of Dubrovnik woollen manufacture. Nevertheless, only two years after this law, there was further discussion in the Great Council regarding the buying and selling of imported foreign cloth.[22] The town officials now deemed it possible to allow Flemish textiles (frixoni, cariseae, and blanchetae) into Dubrovnik's port, providing they were only bought there on a small-scale. This does reflect, however, the increased growth and newfound strength of Dubrovnik's woollen industry which is confirmed by a Florentine merchant Pietro del Bantella who wrote in 1490 that

'in Dubrovnik the art of woollen cloth manufacture forms a small part of the gross earnings of the merchants, and sustains woollen cloth merchants and poor families'.[23]

Even so right at the end of the century a law was passed to ensure that severe punitive restrictions would be placed on anyone in the republic who tried to evade any of the new regulations.[24]

Changes can be seen in the textile trade of Dubrovnik after 1500. The first change concerned the purchase of raw wool. During the later Middle Ages, Dubrovnik had intensive trade connections with

Fig. 54. Dubrovnik between 1481–1485. Detail from statue of St. Blaise (Sv. Vlah) measuring 14·4 cm × 13·6 cm. *Key:*

1. The Minčeta Tower
2. Franciscan monastery and garden
3. Monastery of St. Thomas
4. Monastery of St. Claire
5. Onofrio's fountain
6. Monastery of St. Mary
7. Church of St. Peter
8. Orlando's column
9. Dubrovnik's flag (Sv. Vlah)

10. Church of St. Blaise (Sv. Vlah)
11. Stolna church
12. Church of St. Jacob in Pelina
13. Bell Tower
14. Prince's Court
15. Harbour
16. Church of St. Dominic
17. Chain across the harbour
18. St. Ivan's Tower

Bosnia-Hercegovina where raw wool was of particularly low quality.[25] Dubrovnik's merchants were formerly unable to compete successfully in the Italian textile centres, but now demand was so great that it made this commerce profitable. Also Dubrovnik's citizens were now having more extensive trade connections with Serbia and Bulgaria – the better raw wool producing areas of the Balkan peninsula. The second change was the undermining of the previous Italian domination in the Balkan and eastern Mediterranean textile trade by the rise of local merchants and shipping; Dubrovnik traders now found increasing markets for their own domestic woollen products. The third change was the decline of the Florentine textile industry which reflected the disruption in manufacture that followed the political and economic struggles of the late 1520's in that part of Italy combined with increasing competition from the sale of English and Flemish cloth brought overland.[26] Siena had now replaced Florence as the most important Italian source, but Dubrovnik's government realized the potential of the skilled Florentine wool workers and invited some of them to live in Dubrovnik and advise in the development of their own woollen industry.

In the context of these changes it is proposed to examine the reactions of the Dubrovnik authorities, through their different laws, on controlling the woollen industry and obtaining revenue from some of its trade. For example, in 1504 all duties on woollen cloth were lowered to encourage increased production.[27] Yet despite the legal stipulations for the woollen trade laid down in the laws of the previous century, Dubrovnik merchants continued to evade some of the rules. According to Dubrovnik law all its citizens were subject to its statutes wherever they might be, whether in their own or foreign vessels. Apparently there had been illegal transporting of woollen textiles from towns within and outside the Adriatic Sea by Dubrovnik merchants, who were not paying their government's customs duty. Consequently the Great Council on May 9, 1508 issued a decree in which they specifically referred to Dubrovnik traders carrying woollen goods from the western coast of the Adriatic, Sicily or places outside the Adriatic; if their merchants unloaded cloth in Alexandria, or Syria they were liable to pay the Dubrovnik customs duty of 2%; if the cloth was discharged in Anatolia, on Skyros Island (Cyclades), at Constantinople, Adrianople, or other Turkish ports, they must pay 5% customs duty to Dubrovnik. The value of the cloth was assessed according to the price it would have fetched in Dubrovnik. These merchants, who sold cloth they had either bought in western Europe or the Levant, must have been private traders under oath to the Dubrovnik customs officials, to tell them what goods they carried, what prices they paid etc. Violation of this decree was punished by a fine equal to double the original price paid for the material.[28] The purpose of this law was first, that the Dubrovnik government did not wish to create unnecessary competition for its own woollen industry, and secondly to differentiate, by less customs duty, for goods which could only be transported by sea, i.e. to Alexandria and Syria, rather than those products which could be delivered totally, or in part by the use of Dubrovnik's extensive land routes. A law passed in the same year did encourage the importation of certain quality wools by allowing them into Dubrovnik free of any tariffs, if they came from Solun (Thessaloniki), Plovdiv or Neapolitan Apulia, but it was forbidden to import similar wools from other places outside the republic.[29] Similarly, official rewards were given to those merchants who imported French and Spanish wools and for workshops producing cloth from these high quality raw materials.[30] Five years later another decree allotted prices for various cleaned wools and an order was made stating that workers were to be paid on a Saturday to Saturday basis in either money or woollen garments of their choice.[31]

Fifty years after the important law reform for woollen manufacture was passed in 1481, the industry again seemed to be in a critical position. In 1530 the Great Council admitted that the woollen industry

'was one of the most important industries in our town, providing a substantial part of its income, but which for some time now has been declining'.

A result of this situation was a meeting held between the officials of the woollen industry, and the cloth traders, to try and find out reasons for the decline. The basic proposal put forward after this meeting was that the Great Council should pass legislation for improving the woollen industry and this was accepted.[32] Whereas the law of 1481 was designed to nurture the Dubrovnik domestic woollen industry and limit the import of foreign cloth, this new legislation of 1530 was aimed at improving the quantity and quality of Dubrovnik's cloth. First, incentives were given to cloth manufactures to buy good quality raw wool; for every 'milijarij' (a milijarij weighed about 35 kilogrammes) of French wool bought, the manufacturer received a four ducat subsidy from the government; if it was Spanish wool the state gave him a two ducat subsidy per milijarij if it was washed and one ducat for unwashed material to be received on importation. This proved that there was now a free import of foreign wool, the Great

Council abolishing customs duty on all raw wool imports for the next five years, which arrived in the Dubrovnik port and were sold.

These incentives were also coupled with some restrictions. No-one was allowed to store raw wool without the express permission of the 'Veliki Umoljenih' (Great Council of Requests), nor to sell wool to the weaving workshops without governmental permission. Further, there was now to be strict supervision over the quality of woven wool. All cloth called 'sopramani' (superfine)[33] must be of good manufacture and finished in 'the Florentine manner'.[34] Thus the cloth had to have a number and the sign 'Garbo'[35] signifying its origin from pure wool imported from western Europe. A peča length of superfine woollen cloth had to have a woven weight of 87 libre,[36] which after dyeing must be at least 77 libre. Each piece of superfine cloth had to be 4·25 lakats long (i.e. 331·50 cm) together with a substantial margin for the official government stamp issued by the 'Komora' (Chamber of Commerce). Besides all this the 1530 law laid down the number of threads in the cloth's width and the quality of its selvage. Further the dyers were not allowed to dye the cloth just red and then supplement it with verzino,[37] or oricello (orchil),[38] nor to give short measure with these dyes when colouring cloth from Spanish and French wools. All these rules illustrate to what length the town officials went in trying to raise the standard of manufacture and bring their products up to the level of some of the better cloths from western Europe. Another section of the law enumerated the responsibilities of the 'officiales artislanac', whom the Great Council ordered to take care of all who worked in the wool trade and see that they were strong and healthy people. Even so there appears to have been some attempt to partly suppress the brotherhood of the woollen industry.[39] The 'Gastald' (members) of the brotherhood were not allowed to call a meeting of the 'Kapitul' (kaptol – collegiate body) without the consent of the government officials, and when given permission at least one woollen goods merchant had to be present.

As a result of this legislation the government was now able to carry out complete control of all cloth manufacture, through its own appointed officials. Each Sunday they visited the homes of woollen workers, and searched their dwellings with the help of assistants, to see if they were abiding by the government's regulations for the industry. In addition each month all the people who had been outside Dubrovnik were searched, for no matter how they tried to conceal cloth it was usually found. The Great Council ordered severe punishment for offenders who bought, or stole, wool. Merchants committing this offence were fined 500 ducats and expelled from the Ragusan Republic. Further Dubrovnik merchants were forbidden to sell, mortgage, or give away as presents, any piece of cloth that had been woven from Spanish, or any other fine quality wool. Wool pilfering was subject to heavy punishment. The raw wool either arrived as imported fleeces from farther afield, or sheared in Dubrovnik from sheep bought in the nearby Bosnian hinterland, but in both cases pilfering wool, by cutting bits here and there, was strictly punished. After the wool had been washed, sheared and dyed[40] by state workers it was stored for a period of time. All this had to be reported and registered in the 'Nova Komora' (New Chamber of Commerce) where the cloth received a number, its quality recorded, the time taken in its preparation and any obvious deficiencies. These deficiencies were then notified to shops and purchasers.

Fierce punitive regulations were enforced by the government for theft, for wool thieving was certainly prevalent. Usually wool was stolen to make white and coloured 'capo'[41] cloth. In 1530 the Great Council forbad the manufacture of such capo goods from the rougher wools, or wool left over after carding. A person who stole wool, sold stolen wool, or manufactured capo goods from fine quality wools, was subject to a scale of punishment according to the weight of wool stolen. If this weighed less than five libre, the offender only paid its value to the local official on encounter; should its weight exceed five libre and not more than ten libre, the guilty person was bound up to a post with a rope five times for disgrace, marked on the face in three places and exiled from Dubrovnik and its territories; from 10 to 15 libre of stolen wool led to the cutting off of the right hand, whilst more than 15 libre meant the person was hung 'until dead'.

Such were the extremes in Dubrovnik's woollen industry. Wariness, supervision and court rulings were prominent in all questions concerned with the industry and the three officials (officiales artislanae) were chosen to serve a calendar period of one year and a day. Each official was rewarded with a salary of 25 perpera annually, plus one third of the money received from all sentences passed, and one third of all confiscated goods. Officials chosen for this length of time, became *ipso iure* members of the Great Council, having the same responsibilities and privileges as criminal lawyers and consulates. Their period of service began in January and ended in December; during this time they could be chosen as Chancellor (Rector) of the small republic. Besides their role as criminal lawyers, the officials sat in judgement over civil matters, as well as having special judicial sittings for making new laws and trying particular cases pertaining to the woollen industry.

It is not known to what extent all these measures and elaborate procedure influenced the growth of the industry in Dubrovnik, but the expected prosperity in woollen manufacture never came. While 1530 was a year of crisis for the industry, the following year, 1531, saw Dubrovnik textile imports reach a peak when 31,407 pieces of cloth arrived in the port.[42] Unfortunately the largest part, 26,404 pieces, consisted of cloth whose origin is not specified, but the remainder of the majority came from west European workshops, showing the possible effect of the 1530 law allowing the free import of foreign wool and less protection for the home industry. It also appears that there was little connection between prosperity in the transit trade and growth of Dubrovnik's domestic industry. Much of the transit textile trade was in the hands of Jewish merchants[43] who had connections in many Italian and Balkan towns, but had little interest in the development of the republic's own small woollen manufacture.

Nineteen years after the law of 1530, there was repeated discussion in the Great Council on how it must help the woollen industry. It noted

'see how the woollen industry of our town is so weak; if it is not restored and helped with all the necessary resources there are fears of its decline'.

The town 'Providura'[44] was instructed to examine all earlier measures of support for the industry and recommended the need for more workshops and a serious attempt to be made in the production of coloured cloth. If the cloth colour was poor then all work expended on the material was of no avail. The 'Providura' suggested to the Great Council that it chose the best conditions and facilities for dyeing each piece of cloth, and that the minimum requirements should include the use of verzino, oricello and robbia[45] dyes; further some investigation should be made into how the other dye chemicals were produced, what were the best colours to mix, if the dyes faded after a certain time, and the reasons for failure to produce even colours, for they realized that when a cloth's colour faded then the price for it fell.

The Providura saw the dyeing process as the key to the future developments. It proposed to the Great Council that the Dubrovnik Republic should invite a dye works in Florence to send specialists to the city to teach local craftsmen the art of dyeing. The Dubrovnik state would give 500 ducats as a security for the safety of these Florentine dyers which would last over a period of six years. The Providura also laid down an order specifying how Dubrovnik's merchants should pay for the dyeing of cloth in red, green and other colours, and for the cloth woven from French and Spanish wools. Prices varied between three and twelve ducats for a peča length. As an incentive the Providura recommended that any person who would be responsible for the weaving of a 100 pečas annually, could borrow 2,500 ducats over five years at a reasonable premium. Those who accepted this loan had to begin production within six months, but failure to reach the 100 peča norm, meant a four ducat fine for each peča length below this target. Rules also existed concerning cloth quality. Cloth woven from Spanish wool which had 80 pegs[46] was equal in quality to 'settantini' (70) pegs woven in Venice; each peča of this quality cloth would count as two pečas of the soprameni (superfine) material. The Providura also suggested that any Dubrovnik merchants wanting cloth woven in the settantini Venetian style should be given preference in manufacture.

Other regulations existed regarding the use of various wool types. Selvaged cloth of 70 or 80 peg quality was not allowed to be woven from purely home-made, or Alexandrian wools, if those from Spain, Thessaloniki, or Apulia, were available. All wools were strictly categorized. A further regulation concerned agreements between producer and merchant. For example, if a merchant wanted cloth of 80 peg quality for the domestic market, and was prepared to provide French wool sent from England for its manufacture, the producer could obtain a loan of 500 ducats, from the state, to be repaid over a period of five years. Even so, every manufacturer who agreed to weave cloth from this wool must sell it to the merchant at a minimum price of four ducats per peča length, and guarantee to produce 30 pečas of this material annually. Should the producer fail to manufacture this amount he was liable to a fine of ten ducats per peča short of the agreed minimum. The Providura clearly stated

'If, by the Grace of God, our production from French wool is successful, and is equal in quality to French and Venetian cloth, then we shall forbid the selling, even on a small scale, of foreign cloth, and any one who does so, will be punished for smuggling'.

Besides the provision of new buildings, increased production of coloured cloth, price control and government loans, other ways were devised to bolster up Dubrovnik's woollen industry. New import regulations were suggested by the Providura to encourage the buying of superior foreign raw wool. Previously only French and Spanish wool had been encouraged for cloth manufacture in the town, but now the Providura advised the free import of raw wool from Thessaloniki, Apulia and other parts of the Levant. Nevertheless, restrictions still existed regarding the storing of these wools, for none of them were to be stored in warehouses, or workshops, which held wool from France or Spain. Further, it advised that a system of rewards should be set up for those merchants who bought wool from three specific places, Taro,[47] Arcadia and Passatuta in the Levant, which had a quality similar to that used to manufacture the 'sopramani' cloth in Florence. Similarly, all kinds of wool arriving in Dubrovnik not of pure quality, would be allowed in free of customs duty, a reversal of policy formerly operating in the port. Woven cloth from high quality wool must be produced from satisfactory material so that when completed each peča of sopramani material must weigh at least 80 libre. Finally, wool officials in the 'Nova Komora' were instructed to examine each peča of cloth, making sure that it came up to specifications and had no tears in the material. All those recommendations were accepted by the Dubrovnik Great Council on March 27, 1549.[48] In future the judicial administration of the wool industry was in the hands of the 'officiales artislannae', but the responsibility for continued progress in woollen manufacture was now with the town's Providura, who were ordered to meet every Sunday in the New Chamber of Commerce (Nova Komora) and discuss matters of urgency.

The success achieved in transit trade seems to have had little effect on the prosperity of domestic industries, as witnessed by the problems incurred in the development of Dubrovnik's woollen industry. Throughout the period 1450–1550 government legislation on cloth manufacture was continually trying to bolster up production and encourage new lines of growth, putting great strain on Dubrovnik officials in charge of the industry. The earlier attempts placed a customs duty on foreign cloth, deliberate legislation for dissuading

Dubrovnik merchants from selling foreign cloth even on a small-scale, and devising incentives for those same traders to sell home-made cloth in the Dubrovnik Republic and abroad. Even so much of their efforts failed to gain the required result. This was followed by alternative legislation for freeing the custom duty on foreign wools, and later giving rewards to those manufacturers who used such wools in the production of domestic cloth. Further, the Dubrovnik government decided to take direct control over all cloth weaving in the town in an attempt to introduce higher standards and better quality. It was found that greater attention should be paid to the dyeing of material so help was enlisted from a Florentine dyeworks, whilst other foreign specialists (weavers, dyers, tailors etc.) chiefly from Italy, but also from Germany and France, were encouraged to come and live in the town.[49] Also the government guaranteed financial support for the construction of a central workshop, together with protection for those manufacturers who would weave cloth from French and Spanish wools, in the hope that future production of material would be in the same class as those of Florence and Venice. Competition in the woollen trade was being felt with increasing effect during the sixteenth century, not least from north and mid-Dalmatian towns under Venetian rule. Dubrovnik's government on reading this situation began to invest in alternative domestic industries such as gold and silver working which by the second half of the sixteenth century had more importance for Dubrovnik's export trade.

The Shipbuilding Industry

Shipbuilding formed an important industrial branch of the Dubrovnik Republic from its earliest days. The timber was obtained originally from the forests of Mount Srđ, the islands of Lastovo and Mljet, as well as from Bosnia. The iron came from the Balkan interior, and was manufactured at Venice or locally, the canvas came from Ancona and Apulia, pitch from Dalmatia, and cordage from Dubrovnik itself. The republic was very jealous of its shipbuilding industry and would not allow its native builders ('calafato' or 'marangone') to work in the services of any foreigners, including their fellow Slavic neighbours. This rule was later wavered, the exception being made in favour of the Turks. The harbour at Dubrovnik was always busy in the middle ages with the arrival and departure of ships, whilst the workers in the arsenal were always employed in the building or repairing of all kinds of craft. Other shipping yards existed on Lopud Island, at Šipanska Luka, on Šipan Island, and later at Ston, Slano and Cavtat. Dubrovnik's vessels were famed throughout Dalmatia and the republic was frequently requested to lend some to this or that Slavic potentate, to the Hungarians and sometimes even the Venetians themselves.[50]

Dubrovnik received an early impetus in this trade. As a small Byzantine town, Dubrovnik had participated in many of the struggles waged by the Empire, and had contributed both warships and sailors to its fleet, so that by the end of the eleventh century Dubrovnik already had a strong mercantile marine, which was used for trading purposes within the Adriatic and later further afield. The great filip to the industry came in 1358 when Dubrovnik, together with the whole of Dalmatia came under Hungarian rule. Venice on retreating from this area, also withdrew all her shipping. The Dubrovnik Republic was left with hardly any vessels, and therefore began to intensively develop her own shipbuilding industry. New shipyards were established together with three arsenals, two in the City Harbour and one at Mali Ston in which galleons and other types of warships were anchored.[51] Although the first shipyards were situated in the small city harbour, and along some of the beaches in the district it soon became evident that a larger place was needed. Much of the boatbuilding had been done in the northern part of the city harbour (Stari Porat) probably according to Tadić[52] in the place below the Revelin fortress which today serves as a quay for small craft. The growth of trade with the Turkish hinterland meant that there was a need for boats larger than 100 kola (carro).[53] Work was begun on a new shipyard at Gruž (at a place called Kantafig) at the end of 1525 and completed the following June.[54] The new harbour was already employing nearly seventy boatbuilders by 1530 which later in the sixteenth century rose to over 100 during the periods of intensive production.[55] The actual building of larger boats took between eight and nine months, whilst those over 100 kola took two to three years, several after 1540 reaching over 200 kola in size. All the employees in the shipyards were from within the republic's territory, although on occasions famous shipbuilders from the nearby island of Korčula were engaged. Average pay for a shipbuilder at the beginning of the sixteenth century was 3,5 ducats for 30 working days. The skill of Dubrovnik's shipbuilders became well known as evidenced by two contemporary Italian naval authors, who ranked them on a par with

FIG. 55.   Carved relief of a Dubrovnik carrack (from the sixteenth century) on the Resti family house, Dubrovnik.

the craftsmen of Portugal and England.[56] Their vessels were no doubt of quality for many had a life span of over thirty years.

The types of vessels produced within the Dubrovnik Republic are also of interest. The most common was the carrack a large sailing vessel which was built between the fourteenth and seventeenth centuries. They were the largest type of cargo merchant ships built at that time, being also made outside the Adriatic in other Mediterranean and western European shipyards. A larger version of these ships was called a carrackoon. These ships voyaged to England with wine, dried grapes and other southern products, and were given the name of 'argosy' by the English merchants.[57] The other type of sailing vessel widely produced and used by the republic was the galleon, particularly in the sixteenth and seventeenth centuries. Galleons were ships with three masts, and sometimes four, and possessing two or three decks. On the forepart of the vessel there was an elevated superstructure, while aft there was an elevated poop. The figurehead was placed below the bowsprit. Dubrovnik's galleons usually carried three masts, each containing one top and one bowsprit; a sail (civadera) was set below each bowsprit and the foremast held two crosssails, the same as the main mast, while the smaller mast at the stern held a Latin sail.

The materials for shipbuilding were mainly imported. The timber came from the mouth of the River Bojana and the district along the River Drim in Albania, some from Senj in the north-east Adriatic and finally from Monte Gargano in Italy. For example, at the end of the sixteenth century Dubrovnik imported a lot of wood from Albania.[58] This was used not only for shipbuilding but also for making barrels, houses, etc. Good quality timber often cost more than four ducats a metre, but this varied according to width and length of beam. Sometimes completed boats were also imported from Albania and resold to owners in western Europe.[59] The rigging was manufactured in Dubrovnik or imported from Italy. Those ships built in Dubrovnik were usually preceded by two legal contracts: the shipowners made the first among themselves and the second one was between themselves and the shipbuilder. Owing to the great value of the ships and the great risks involved, they were usually owned by several individuals, and the value was divided into twenty-four parts, the so-called 'carats'. Although the dimensions of the vessel were usually stipulated in the contract with the shipbuilder, the actual ship's tonnage could not be calculated in advance. In the fifteenth and early decades of the sixteenth century the value of ships does not appear to have greatly altered, the cost of one kola (carro) being between 8–10 ducats. At the end of the sixteenth and in the seventeenth centuries, increasing inflation meant that prices rose to 28–30 ducats per kola.[60]

The activity of the shipbuilding industry is reflected in the tonnage of the Dubrovnik merchant navy. In 1530 the republic owned about 180 ships with a total loading capacity of up to 21,000 kola;

by 1585 there were still about the same number of ships but their collective weight was now about 38,000 kola, which somewhat diminished towards the end of the century to 25,000 kola. The value of the Dubrovnik merchant navy also increased from 200,000 ducats to 675,000 ducats, but in the seventeenth century this was only 225,000 ducats. It is interesting at this point to compare the English and Dubrovnik merchant fleets at that time. As Davis points out,

'In 1560 England ranked low among the maritime states; her merchant fleet was by European standards an insignificant one. It stood far behind that of the Dutch ... behind Venice or even *Ragusa* and Genoa'.[61]

By 1582 English merchant shipping totalled 76,000 tons, whilst that of Dubrovnik was about 40,000 tons.

The seventeenth century was a period of decline for Dubrovnik's merchant navy. This was due to the contemporary situation in the Mediterranean and general decline of commerce. Also the hostile attitude of Venice towards the republic hindered the development of Dubrovnik's fleet. Nevertheless shipbuilding revived during the middle of the eighteenth century and increased in importance particularly in the last decade. Many boatbuilders were employed from the nearby island of Korčula and shipbuilding again became one of the main industrial branches of the city.[62] Several types of vessel were manufactured including the 'polacre' (31–98 kola loading capacity), the 'nava' (66–148 kola), the 'pinq' (22–66 kola) and the 'tartan' (27–58 kola) but all much smaller than had been made in previous centuries. Some idea of the importance of maritime activity in the republic during the second half of the eighteenth century can be seen from the following figures. There were over 2,000 seamen sailing on Dubrovnik's ships outside the Adriatic, which is a high proportion when compared with the total population of the time estimated at 25,000. Over 380 shipowners should then be added to that figure. This does not include fishermen, coral and sponge-divers, shipbuilders, boatsmen, and dockworkers who together illustrate the dependence of the Dubrovnik Republic on shipping and the maritime trade. By 1805 the merchant navy totalled at least 278 various types of vessels sailing outside the Adriatic, which between them had a total loading capacity of 24,000 kola,[63] many of which had been built by local craftsmen. The Napoleonic Wars and the French occupation of Dubrovnik in 1806–08 ruined much of the republic's maritime life, and ended its importance as a naval power.

The Jewellery Industry

One noticeable factor between the years 1000 and 1500 A.D. was the growth in town-building in all parts of Europe. The larger towns were nodal points of a commercial network, which in south-east Europe stretched out to mix with Islamic trade. Members of the various moneyed groups in these towns were drawn together, competing socially and in ways of adornment. This led to a demand for skilled craftsmen, capable of producing objects of artistic beauty to satisfy the needs of the more privileged classes. From the main street or business centre there extended other commercial streets, in which there was usually a different craft or group of crafts, and the space allocated to them varied in accordance with their position in the city's heirarchy of values. This feature was apparent in Dubrovnik, where wealthy merchants dealt in precious stones, bright jewels, expensive articles of gold and silver, fine porcelain and other similar goods.[64]

Goldsmiths were already evident in the city in the thirteenth century, and by 1306 had their own guild. The import of gold and silver deposits from the hinterland is recorded in Dubrovnik as early as 1253,[65] and appears to have been part of a general trend in Europe for

'By the twelfth century there was active prospecting, resulting in a series of gold rushes to new discoveries of silver, copper, iron, tin, lead, and gold that went on through the thirteenth century'.

According to Sindik, by the fourteenth century Dubrovnik was divided into six administrative districts, but besides these, documents refer to the 'Get' (Ghetto). In fact Dubrovnik had two ghettos, one 'a porta Pusterlae versus S. Mariae' and the other 'prope ecclesiam S. Nicolai versus mare',[66] which could be earlier than the fourteenth century for Heer maintains that

'The twelfth century saw the beginnings of the Ghetto system and the isolation of Jews from their environment. Jews ceased to live in the Christian sectors of towns and settled in a specifically Jewish quarter . . .'[67]

Even today one of the streets of Stradun (Placa) is called Židovska Ulice (Jewish Street), which was in the heart of the goldsmiths' quarters, and lists preserved in Dubrovnik Archives give the names of the city's goldsmiths, several having Jewish names (e.g. Jakob Rućemanović, Radoslav Miošić). Two of the lists give the names of ninety-one goldsmiths in Dubrovnik between 1417 and 1471, forty-seven of them resident between 1417 and 1445, and forty-four between 1445 and 1471.

As in the cloth industry the government took an active part in the control of the goldsmiths' work. A law was passed in 1459 which forbad goldsmiths from finishing their work in private houses, or anywhere within the community except in the 'in ruga aurificum' (literally 'golden crease') or goldsmiths' district,[68] thus presumably allowing the government to keep a tighter control on production. Much of their work consisted of filigree making and in 1466 the Great Council issued a decree in the form of assistance to the goldsmiths so that they would not fall behind the standards set by the filigree industry of Venice.[69]

Individual documents also refer to specific cases concerning jewels. Some of the foreign merchants who had come to live in Dubrovnik, used jewels bought in the city as a form of security against default. One document dated January 28, 1457 mentions that a certain Florentine merchant, Nicolaus de Bono was indebted to a Dubrovnik jeweller, Jacob di Mozis, for the sum of 3,187 and 225 ducats on account of jewellery bought to the value of 30,000 ducats.[70] Also that the same J. de Mozis, a member of the 'Jacob and Peter de Pazis Society of Florence', had as a security, different jewels belonging to one Rombout de Wachter, a Bruges salesman, to the value of 7,080 ducats. Another documents dated March 28, 1463, states that the magistrate of Dubrovnik records that Eli Lampriz from Zadar declares that he has as a security, several jewels of R. de Wachter from Bruges, and that both parties had not notified this agreement with the authorities.[71] Besides their importance as a form of security, jewels were also worn by the women of noble families in Dubrovnik whilst it was a common habit for ordinary citizens' wives to wear gold ear-rings with silver wire attachments, denoting marital status. These were not the normal type of ear-ring for the pierced ear, but had silver clasps which were attached to a veil, and known locally as 'klizak' or 'riguletum' in Latin.[72] Also gold rings were worn, usually only by women, in the city and often of considerable value.[73] Simi-

larly the jeweller's craft was expressed in many of the church adornments throughout the city. (See Ch. 11.)

Salt Production

The salt trade formed one of the republic's chief sources of income,
as the interior, although rich in other minerals, was absolutely wanting in this necessary commodity. Salt pans were established at four
points along the south-east Adriatic coast – the mouth of the Neretva
River, Dubrovnik, Kotor Bay and Sv. Srđ on the River Bojana. Dubrovnik by means of old treaties with the Slavic hinterland, had almost
acquired a monopoly of the commerce in salt, and it was often able
to punish the depredations to which its territory was subjected by
cutting off the supply. The question of salt monopoly involved Dubrovnik in a war with Duke Stipan Vukčić (who also tried to ruin the
city's cloth trade) between 1451 and 1454, for he tried to break Dubrovnik's hold on the salt trade in Hercegovina, previously given it by

Fig. 56.   Salt pans at Ston, from the air.

King Tvrtko. The outcome of this was a final return to *status quo ante* in 1454. Similarly it was a constant bone of contention between Dubrovnik and Venice, the latter by various means of subterfuge constantly tried to erode Dubrovnik's position in this commodity. The largest salt-pans were in the neighbourhood of Dubrovnik itself, but after 1333 they were removed to Ston. The Neretva salt-pans were monopolized by Dubrovnik, who established a custom station at the river's mouth, and those of the Bojana, although outside its territory, were also in its hands; Dubrovnik's only other rival was Kotor, whence the innumerable quarrels with that city.

In medieval Europe salt was mined in a few central inland regions but for the most part was extracted from seawater by solar evaporation or by slow boiling with peat fuel. The evaporation pans, leased to part-time peasant salters who did the upkeep work, represented little or no investment on the part of the landlord. In the Dubrovnik Republic all the salt was produced from pans; prior to 1333 most of the salt came from the coast near Gruž, the island of Šipan and at Zaton, many of the employees in the fourteenth century having come here originally from Pag Island in the northern Adriatic and from Drač (Dürres) in Albania. Also documents between the thirteenth and fifteenth century mention salt workings on Mljet Island near the Benedictine monastery, where even today there is a small place called 'Soline' (from 'solana' the salt-pan). The addition of the Pelješac peninsula to the republic in 1333 saw the foundation of the present town of Ston on the site of the former Roman 'Turris Stagni', but prior to this date the republic had rented the pans there on five and ten year leases. In 1351 the pans were leased by the republic to three men (Junijo Kalić, Klimo Držič, and Junijo Kašić) for 1,060 perpera annually. They paid this sum in two parts (on March 1st and September 29th) and in return had the free use of all equipment needed for salt extraction together with a house each. All this had to be given up when the lease expired, but if it was terminated before the five years were complete they owed the republic nothing.[74] It appears that at the beginning of the sixteenth century the salt-pans at Ston had been in decline for many years, and were unfit for production due to negligence on the part of the local officials. The government, therefore, ordered that it would pay 7 perpera for every 1,000 stara [one Dubrovnik 'star' equalled about 100 litres (1 hl)] of salt produced to the four officials in charge.[75] After eleven years this agreement was cancelled, the officials now being given 2 grossi and

2 piccoli per star of salt produced.[76] This must have had some effect because a receipt showing income from Ston for the year 1575 revealed that the republic's revenue from Ston for meat, fish, wine, etc., totalled 1,830 ducats compared with that for salt of 15,900 ducats (i.e. 11%: 89%),[77] The Dubrovnik government was also active in protecting home production. It forbad Dubrovnik merchants from bringing salt purchased from Split in the north, or Dürres in the south for sale in the city.[78]

Miscellaneous Urban Industries

There existed in Dubrovnik many types of medieval handicrafts, often small and highly specialized. The most popular guilds were in carpentry, wall-building, furriers, blacksmiths, goldworkers, shoemakers, tailors and shipbuilders as well as the textile workers. According to Tadić there were eighteen handicraft workers' guilds (esnafa) in the city during the first half of the sixteenth century which included about two-thirds of Dubrovnik's active population.[79] One may imagine that in Dubrovnik as in other places,

'An inventory of fixed industrial capital inside the towns in this period would probably show the most valuable to have been the furnaces and moulds of bell-founders and other metal workers, bakehouse ovens and brewers' malting kilns and vats rating next in order of their size. Other equipment consisted of looms, storage bins, and the movable paraphernalia of heating, soaking and cleaning processes. Standing in the cramped workshops and cluttered yards attached to the living quarters, these bits of capital were for the most part the property of individual masters, or partners. Along with hand tools they were assembled by careful strategies of family saving and investment and with the help of loans from merchants'.[80]

Various industries were found in the city. During the second half of the fifteenth century the government established a soap factory, giving the monopoly to two brothers who were to use inferior materials. This idea failed miserably so a new government order stipulated that only suitable material should be used,[81] but there seems to have been a poor response on behalf of the local population to this private enterprise and at the beginning of the sixteenth century the republic built its own soap works.[82] Dubrovnik also had its own shoe factories which were located in one part of the city (između Crevljava). This was part of a brotherhood of shoemakers, who forbad any master shoemaker from buying skins from anywhere other than through their guild. Again the government stepped in and maintained that any shoemaker could buy up to twelve skins from whoever he wished and need not be a member of their guild.[83] The city had its own printing works, publishing books in both Greek and Latin,[84] and a glass factory at Pila which was established in 1422.[85] There were also factories producing arms for the city's arsenal, numerous scissor works located at Gruž, on the islands of Lopud and Šipan, at Slano and Ston, and in the first half of the eighteenth century a hat factory was founded in Pila.[86] Other factories, outside the city were engaged in brick and tile manufacture as in Župa Dubrovačke at Crijepi (present-day Kupari) which dates back to medieval times.[87]

Miscellaneous Rural Industries

Some historians have described any ancient or medieval city where the majority of the working population lived by industries with more than a local market, as examples of industrialization,[88] but seen in the perspective of the late twentieth century, successful industrialization is the attainment of self-sustaining economic growth. This means regular increases in output per head, and the produce of the land is included in the measure of total output. The rural industries within the Dubrovnik Republic were therefore significant in the overall economic life of the state. One of the most important was stock-breeding.[89] This consisted mainly of goats and sheep, for beef cattle were few in number; also the villages at higher altitudes tended to specialize in stock-rearing for milk, wool and cheese, whilst the lower villages were engaged in a greater variety of occupations. Many of the higher villages in the republic sent their stock to the inland areas of Hercegovina to the summer pastures, usually between Vidov-day (15th July) and Mihalj-day (29th September), where they were allowed to graze their flocks in exchange for payment in cheese and other dairy products.[90] A reciprocal arrangement was also made so that during hard winters oxen from Hercegovina were brought down to the lower villages and islands (Lopud and Šipan) of the Dubrovnik Republic, an agreement that was already common practice in the fourteenth century. Much of this transhumance work was done by

Vlach shepherds who lived in the surroundings of Dubrovnik, but may also have included some gypsies, who were first mentioned in Dubrovnik in 1423.[91] Pigs were reared in all the villages and suburbs of Dubrovnik, but usually only to satisfy home demand.

The lower villages tended to specialize in more sedentary forms of agriculture.[92] Wine production had an old tradition of government protection and control. For example, wine produced in 'Astarea' (between Zaton and Osojnik) was strictly regulated and people living there were not allowed to import wine or vines from any other territory.[93] Similarly, one family was not allowed to have more than three 'solad' (5,037 m²) of vineyards, which was checked by government officials every two years. The reason for this tight government control was to keep a strict proportion between the vineyards and area of ploughed land, much of which was given over to cereal production, which was constantly in short supply.[94] Furthermore, the government inflicted punishment on people who worked the vineyards carelessly (up to 15 days in prison), for many owners spent considerable money on the digging and maintenance of their vineyards.[95] The home market was also carefully protected, for Dubrovnik people were forbidden to purchase and import foreign wines from Split, but Dubrovnik's wine was allowed to be sold in the Neretva valley.[96] Other commodities were also protected, particularly the meat supply. No one was allowed to export beef, or any livestock under the threat of a twenty-five perpera fine and two months in prison. Only Dubrovnik's princes and members of the Small Council were allowed to export certain commodities, and then only during times of emergency.[97] There were also strict rules for olive oil production. In 1434 a building containing four warehouses for oil was constructed near the church of Sv. Nikola, but was only for the use of foreigners. This meant it was easier for them to sell their oil, and for which the government received a rent of thirty grossi per month for each warehouse. Under the same law home produced oil was not to be sent anywhere but to the state cellar.

A large part of the Dubrovnik Republic remained very rural, much as it is today.

'Up to a population size of about 1,500, or perhaps twice that size in Mediterranean areas, towns were still very rural. Successful craftsmen and traders still cultivated gardens or vineyards, the less successful merging into the peasantry; yards were noisy with pigs and geese and the streets at sundown filled with cattle strolling home from the fields'.[98]

One phenomenon typical in Europe was the late medieval development of a drift of industry from the towns to the countryside on account of lower costs, but this does not appear to have taken place in the republic. This was probably due to the government's strict control of all industrial undertakings, and the shortage of land for agricultural production.

Domestic production in the Dubrovnik Republic did not appear to reflect the success achieved in transit trade, as witnessed by the problems incurred in the development of the woollen cloth industry. Government legislation continually tried to bolster up production in several industrial branches, as well as protect the growth of domestic industries. Dubrovnik was also vulnerable to external influences. Factors that had enabled the port and its industries to expand during the late medieval period, also left the city in a precarious position. There was no particularly strong reason why commerce based on such distant centres as London, Antwerp, Constantinople and Florence should continue to pass through Dubrovnik. The use of alternative ports by foreign merchants in the seventeenth and eighteenth centuries in turn effected domestic industries, which likewise went into a period of decline. Nevertheless Dubrovnik had the comfort of knowing that she was not alone in this situation for it was felt by many other places in the Mediterranean basin, all of whom had seen more prosperous times.

7. Notes

1. S. Thrupp, 'Medieval industry 1000–1500', *The Fontana Economic History of Europe Series*, Vol. 1, Section 6, London (1971), p. 24.
2. G. Gelcich, *Dello Sviluppo Civile di Ragusa*, Dubrovnik (1884), p. 32.
3. G. Novak, 'Vunena Industrja u Dubrovniku do sredne XVI stoljeća', *Rešetarov Zbornik iz Dubrovačke Prôslosti*, Dubrovnik (1931), pp. 99–109.
4. Dubrovnik Archives, *Liber Viridis*, caput 152, 'Quod ut ars lanae melius et salubrius atque utilius conservetur et guberetur per manus oficialium Communis'.
5. Dubrovnik Archives, (2/V/1430). *Diversa Cancellariae*, 46, folder 178. Two pieces of 'panni Ragusi' – one blue and the other red, valued at 37 ducats were sent to Greece.

6. K. Vojnović, 'Sudbeno Ustrojstvo Republike Dubrovačke', *Rad. J. A.* Knjige CVIII, CXIV, Zagreb (1892, 1893), pp. 121–131.
7. Filipa de Diversis de Quartigianis, *Situs aedificiorum, politae et laudabilium consuetudinum inclytae civitatis Ragusii* (edt. Brunelli) Zadar (1882), (original manuscript in Dominican Library in Dubrovnik).
8. 'Peča' a piece of woollen cloth of regulation length between 42 and 49 lakats (3,276 – 3,822 cm).
9. *Enciklopedija Jugoslavije*, Vol. 3, Zagreb (1958), p. 139.
10. 'Omnes de progenie ipsius domini Sandali appellata Cosaze', *Glasnik Matice Dalmatinske*, Vol. XIII, Zadar (1902), p. 159.
11. Dubrovnik Archives, (1452). *Liber Viridis*, caput 426.
12. Dubrovnik Archives, (1434). *Liber Viridis*, caput 283, 284; *ibid.*, (1455). caput 485.
13. Dubrovnik Archives, (1445), *ibid.*, caput 239; (1454) caput 493.
14. Dubrovnik Archives, *Liber Croceus*, caput 10.
15. Dubrovnik Archives, *Liber Croceus*, caput 20.
16. Dubrovnik Archives, *ibid.*, caput 21.
17. S. Ljubić, *Listine o odnošajih izmedju južnoga slavenstva i mletačke republike*, Vol. X, Izdanje Jugoslovenskih akademije, Zagreb (1891), pp. 226–227.
18. Dubrovnik Archives, (1478). *Liber Croceus*, 79.
19. Dubrovnik Archives, *Ordo captus pro Arte Lanae in 1481. Die 12 Februarij Captus per Cansiliarios 160, Contra 19* (with 160 members voting for and 19 against the new wool law).
20. 'Lakat' a cloth measure = 78 cm an arm's length, a yard (about 2/3 of an English yard), but it varied from place to place. In Dubrovnik and elsewhere the Lakat was frequently used for cloth sold by the cut. See F. Edler, *Glossary of Medieval Terms of Business* (*Italian Series 1200–1600*), Medieval Academy of America, Cambridge, Massachusetts (1934), p. 52, ('Braccio' in Italian), further information in Horace Doursther, *Dictionnaire des poids et mésures*, which has recently been reprinted from the Brussels 1840 edition.
21. Dubrovnik Archives, (12/II/1482). *Liber Croceus*, caput 79.
22. Dubrovnik Archives, (14/III/1483), *Liber Croceus*, caput 82.
23. G. Luccari, *Copioso Ristretto degli Annali di Ragus*, Venice (1605).
24. Dubrovnik Archives, (15/II/1499). *Liber Croceus*, caput 117.
25. I. Božić, *Dubrovnik i Turska u XVI i XV veku*, S.A.N. Posebna Izdanja Kniga CC. Istorijski Institut Kniga 3, Belgrade (1952) pp. 303–304.
26. P. Earle, 'The commercial development of Ancona 1479–1551; *Economic History Review*, Vol. XXII No. 1, April (1969), p. 37.
27. Dubrovnik Archives, (29/V/1504). *Liber Croceus*, caput 126.
28. Dubrovnik Archives, (9/VI/1508), *Liber Croceus*, caput 135.
29. Dubrovnik Archives, (18/II/1508). *ibid.*, caput 135.
30. Dubrovnik Archives, (6/III/1510). *Liber Croceus*, caput 141.
31. Dubrovnik Archives. (16/V/1515). *ibid.*, caput 145.
32. Dubrovnik Archives, (11/I/1530). *Ordine dell' arte della lana 1530 a di 11 Genero a Carte 197* (with 133 members voting for and 30 against the new wool law).
33. See F. Edler, *op. cit.*, pp. 393–394 and p. 422.
34. A. Doren, *Studien aus der Florentiner Wirtschaftsgeschichte* (2 vols). Stuttgart (1901–1908);

M

G. Bonolis, 'Sull'industria della lana in Firenze' *Archivio storico italiano*, Series V, Vol. XXXII (1903), pp. 379–417; F. Edler, *op. cit.*, Appendices VI–IX, pp. 409–426.

35. C. Du F. Du Cange, *Glossarium Mediae et Infimae Latinitatis*, (L. Favre, ed.). 10 vols, Niort (1883–1887), section 'Lana'; R. Davidsohn, 'Garbowölle und Garbotuche' *Historische Vierteljährschrift*, N.F. Vol. II (1904) pp. 385–90.

36. Pound, which varied from place to place, in Italy and other countries. Most cities had two pound weights, a light and a heavy one. Florence had only one; so did Dubrovnik weighing 1,49 kilogrammes. See F. Edler, *op. cit.*, p. 158; *Mercatura* Medieval Academy of America, Cambridge, Massachusetts (1936), p. 142.

37. Brazil wood peelings, the valuable red core of the Brazil-wood, with the white outer layers removed, used for dyeing purposes. See A. Evans, *F. R. Pegolotti . . . op. cit.*, pp. 422 and 433.

38. Red or violet dye from lichen. See F. Edler, *op. cit.*, pp. 123, 208.

39. See R. de Roover's article in Volume I of *Studi in Onore di Amintore Fanfani:* 'La doctrine scolastique en matiere de monopole et son application a la politique economique des communes italiennes', Milan (1962).

40. A description of the steps in the manufacture of woollen cloth in medieval Italy, with which Dubrovnik production had close affinities, is found in F. Edler, *op. cit.*, pp. 324–329.

41. Or 'chapo' meaning article, item (of commodities). See F. Edler, *op. cit.*, pp. 62 and 394.

42. Dubrovnik Archives, *Registro de 'debitori per titolo di guimbrucho del' anno 1531–1534*.

43. J. Tadić, *Jevreji u Dubrovniku do polovine XVII stoljeća*, Sarajevo (1937), p. 136.

44. Chamber of Provisions (Italian 'Provveditore' contractor, purveyor).

45. Madder, herbaceous climbing plant with yellowish flowers used as a dye.

46. Part of unit, (Italian 'Paiuola'), usually of forty warp threads, arranged upon a peg of the warp-frame. Each frame had 50 to 110 pegs, and a corresponding number of warp threads, varying according to breadth and quality of the cloth. See F. Edler, *op. cit.*, p. 201 and p. 420.

47. In books of sailing directions (portolans) with descriptions of ports, this place is referred to as Taro, Tar and Lotal, now Cape Dolgaya, on the Sea of Azov.

48. Dubrovnik Archives, (27/III/1549). *Liber Croceus*, 217.

49. *Enciklopedija Jugoslavije*, *op. cit.*, 139.

50. Dubrovnik built boats for Venice *circa* 1650. A. Vučetić, *Dubrovnik za kandijskog Rata*, (Velikoga Državnoga Gimnazija) Vol. II, Dubrovnik (1895), p. 12.

51. J. Lučić, 'Prilog brodogradniji u Dubrovniku u drugoj polovini XV stoleća', *Historijski Zbornik*, (1951), broj. 1–4, p. 134; L. Beretić, 'Dubrovački arsenali', *Mornarički Glasnik*, Split (1956), broj. 5, pp. 577–586.

52. J. Tadić, 'Organizacija dubrovačkog pomorstva u XVI i XVII veku', *Istoriski Časopis* Vol. I, No. 1–2, S.A.N. Belgrade (1948), p. 3.

53. Old measure for the capacity of boats used throughout the Mediterranean, but varying in size. In Dubrovnik a kola weighed a little less than 2,000 dm 3. See I. Sišević, 'Računanje obujma broda u Dubrovniku, XVI veku', *Anali Historijskog instituta J.A.Z.U. u Dubrovniku*, Dubrovnik (1952), p. 166.

54. V. Ivančević, 'Brodogradilište Krile u Gružu', *Naše More*, Split (1955), p. 22.
55. J. Tadić, 'O Pomorstovo Dubrovnika u XVI i XVII veku', *Dubrovačko Pomorstvo*, Dubrovnik (1952), p. 178.
56. B. Crescentio, *Nautica Mediterranea*, Rome (1607), pp. 4–5;
    P. Pantera, *L'Armata Mavale*, Rome (1614), pp. 40–41.
57. There are many theories on the origin of this English word [*Oxford Dictionary*, 1959: *argosy* (hist. poet) Large merchant-vessel esp. of Ragusa & Venice; (poet) ship, venture (earlier reagusye, prob.f.It. Ragusea (nave), Ragusan (vessel)]; One theory is that the name comes from the Greek mythological name 'argo' i.e. from the ship used by the Argonauts taking the golden rune to the Black Sea. Another theory is that the term was derived from the Roman name given to the city of Dubrovnik. In the sixteenth century the English name for Dubrovnik was Aragouse, Arragouse, Aragosa (derived from Ragusa) *Encyclopedia Britannica* 'Argosy', American Edition published 1944;
    M. Bošnjak, 'Dubrovačko Pomorstvo u Literaturi', *Dubrovačko Pomorstvo*, Dubrovnik (1952), pp. 451, 457.
58. Dubrovnik Archives, *Diversa Cancellaria*, 177, folder 9, 62. August 1588, 60 beams of wood from Albania brought to Mljet island;
    Diversa Notaria, 125, folder 30. November 1589, 20 beams of wood from R. Bojana brought to Dubrovnik.
59. Dubrovnik Archives, (1590). *Diversa Cancellaria*, 180, folder 98'. Boat from Perast brought to Dubrovnik (600 kola) to be sent to Spain by a benevolent Pula merchant. Made from 1,300 beams and worth 3,900 ducats. Some confusion arose which ended in a law suit.
60. J. Luetić, 'Povijest Pomorstva Dubrovačke Republike', *Pomorski Zbornik*, Vol. II, Zagreb (1962), pp. 1699–1720.
61. R. Davis, *The Rise of the English Shipping Industry in the Seventeenth and Eighteenth Centuries*, Macmillan, London (1962), p. 2.
62. V. Ivančević, 'O brodogradnji u Dubrovniku potkraj Republike', *Anali Historijskog Instituta J.A.Z.U. u Dubrovniku*, Vol. III, Dubrovnik (1954), pp. 559–579.
63. Dubrovnik Archives, *Arboraggi* 56 – 3/16, folder 62–80.
64. T. Stoianovich, 'Model and mirror of the premodern Balkan city', *Studia Balcanica*, Vol. 3, Sofia (1970), p. 92.
65. D. Roller, *Agrarno-Proizvodni Odnosi na Području Dubrovačke Republike od XIII do XV stoljeća*, Grada za Gospodarsku Povijest Hrvatske, Zagreb (1955), p. 5;
    C. Fisković, *Dubrovački zlatari od XIII do XVII stoljeća*, Starohrvatska Prosvjeta, Vol. 3, Zagreb (1949), p. 1.
66. I. Sindik, 'Dubrovnik i okolica', *Etnografski Zbornik Srpska Kral. Akademije*, Vol. XXXVIII Belgrade (1926), p. 194.
67. F. Heer, *The Medieval World*, The New American Library, New York (1962), p. 310.
68. Dubrovnik Archives, *Liber Viridis*, caput 491.
69. Dubrovnik Archives, (27/X/1466). *Liber Croceus*, caput 27.
70. Dubrovnik Archives, *Diversa Notaria*, 41, folders 97'–99.
71. Dubrovnik Archives, *Diversa Cancellaria*, 71, folder 21'.
72. Filip de Diversis de Quartigianis, *op. cit.*, 'clizak, sue riguletum'.
73. V. Vukasović, 'Imena i preimena zlatara u Dubrovniku XV veku', *Zbornik iz dubrovačke prošlosti Milanu Rešetaru o 70-oj godišnjici života*, Dubrovnik (1931), p. 67.

324 DUBROVNIK (RAGUSA) A CLASSIC CITY-STATE

74. V. Taljeran, 'Zrnca za Povijest Stona', *Prigodom 600 Godišnjice Pripojenja Stonskog Rata Dubrovačkoj Republici 1333–1933, Dubrovnik* (1935), pp. 89–90.
75. Dubrovnik Archives, (13/XI/1504). *Liber Croceus*, caput 129, 'per ogni miaro di mogi grossi che usciranno dalle slanice de Stagno'.
76. Dubrovnik Archives, (5/XI/1515). *Ibid.*
77. V. Taljeran, *op. cit.*, p. 90.
78. Dubrovnik Archives, (18/XII/1464). *Liber Croceus*, caput 21.
79. J. Tadić, 'O društvenog strukturi Dalmacije i Dubrovnika u vreme Renesanse', *Zgodovinski Časopis Kosov Zbornik Leto 1952–1953*', No. VI–VII, Ljubljana (1953), pp. 552–565.
80. S. Thrupp, *op. cit.*, pp. 27–28;
    D. Roller, 'Dubrovački zanati u XV i XVI stoljeću', *Grada za gospodarsku povijest Hrvatske*, knj. 2, Zagreb (1951).
81. Dubrovnik Archives, (9/VII/1495). *Liber Croceus*, caput 66, 'Ordo sapone forensis';
    ibid., caput 94 and 108.
82. Dubrovnik Archives, (14/VII/1516). *Liber Croceus*, caput 187, 'Ordo saponarii Communis ad Pillas';
    Consilium Rogatorum 1670–71, (10/VI/1671).
83. Dubrovnik Archives, (14/XII/1492). *Liber Croceus*, caput 101.
84. M. Medini, *Provijest Hrvatske Kniževnost i Dalmaciji i Dubrovniku*, Zagreb (1902), pp. 65–66.
85. K. Jireček, *Važnost Dubrovniku Trgovačkoj Povijest Srednijega Vijeka*, Dubrovnik (1915), p. 87.
86. M. Rešetar, *Dubrovačka numizmatika*, Vol. I, Sremska Karlovac (1924).
87. K. Vojnović, 'Carinarski sustav republike dubrovačke', *Rad J.A.*, Vol. 129, Belgrade (1896), p. 154.
88. S. Thrupp, *op. cit.*, p. 7.
89. D. Roller, Agrarno-Proizvodni . . .' *op. cit.*, pp. 249–259.
90. J. C. Engel and B. Stojanović, *Povijest Dubrovačke republike*, Dubrovnik (1922), pp. 309–310.
91. K. Jireček, *Istorija Srba*, (trans. J. Radonić) Vol. IV, Belgrade (1952), p. 200.
92. Filipa de Diversis de Quartigianis, *op. cit.*, p. 34, refers to importance of vegetables grown by peasants in Župa for the Dubrovnik market 'sed olera, ut caules, blites, lactucae, radichium, raphani, radices, faerriculi, frondes, floresque, seu semina anetum, rosae, violae, lika et caetera talia, similiter, ceresa, amarena et ejusmodi fructus in fasciculis feruntur, vendun turque a rusticis'.
93. Dubrovnik Archives, (15/XII/1524). *Liber Croceus*, caput 184.
94. Dubrovnik Archives, (20/VI/1477). *ibid.*, caput 59;
    (26/XI/1487). caput 89;
    (22/X/1490). caput 89;
    (28/XI/1524). caput 178.
95. Dubrovnik Archives, (25/III/1465). *ibid.*, caput 22. 'Considerando che la maggior della spesa nostra va in lavoranti nostri delle vigne nostre, et veduto la grande malicia et pigricia delli lavoranti nostri li qusli lavorano le terre e vigne nostre'.
96. Dubrovnik Archives, (18/XII/1464). *ibid.*, caput 21.
97. Dubrovnik Archives, (17/XII/1471). *ibid.*, caput 80.
98. S. Thrupp, *op. cit.*, p. 20.

8
Political Relations of the Dubrovnik Republic 1500–1700

The last years of the fifteenth century and the first of the sixteenth were to prove a turning point in the life of Dubrovnik. During the sixteenth and seventeenth centuries the political, commercial and cultural relations of Europe became, for the first time in history, world-wide in extent. The early modern period was to see not only a new sea route with the East brought into use, thanks to the discoveries of the Portuguese navigators, but further the discoveries of Columbus and the Cabots opened up parts of the American continent to European colonization, exploitation and trade. In the Middle Ages European commerce developed new regions of activity in the North and Baltic Seas which were bound up by land and sea routes with the centres of Mediterranean culture. In that age the flourishing cities of Venice, Alexandria, Constantinople, Bruges and Lübeck, like Dubrovnik occupied sites which were stategically placed in relation to the contemporary routes of trade, whilst Egypt held pre-eminence as the best transit region for the Far Eastern trade.

Changes in Western Europe

The discovery both of the new ocean route to the East and of the American continent and West Indian islands effected a reorientation in European commerce. In 1487 Bartholomew Dias accidentally rounded the Cape of Good Hope and reached Mossel Bay on the Indian Ocean. Thus the way lay open to the trade of India, dazzling in its variety; but a decade passed before Vasco da Gama made his epochal voyage ending at the great spice port of Calicut in the early summer of 1498, and furthered the desire of the Portuguese to control the profitable trade in spices. Prior to 1500 this trade was almost exclusively in the hands of the Arab traders who transported the spices in dhows to the ports of the Red Sea and Persian Gulf; thence they were carried overland to the Mediterranean where the Venetians, and to a lesser extent Dubrovnik's merchants, took charge and sold them for large profits to an eager Europe. In the first decade of the sixteenth century the Portuguese not only established control of Socotra and Ormuz Islands the two main extremities of the Arab trade routes, captured Goa[1] and the Moluccas, but also entered the Chinese port of Canton, thus initiating the lucrative trade with China. Columbus' voyage in 1492, under the auspices of Ferdinand and Isabella of Spain, to the New World was a major event in world history. After many difficulties, he sighted Watling Island in the Bahamas later reaching northern Cuba which he firmly believed to be the mainland of Asia. Before Columbus made his last voyage in 1502 others were already continuing the work of exploration, which was to prove the basis for colonization and trade.

These two events changed the geographical values of European lands. The Baltic and the Mediterranean lost their former centrality and supremacy in European trade. In the new oceanic world those states which had more westerly situations, with sea-boards fronting the Atlantic and the North Sea enjoyed geographical advantages in relation to the sea routes to the Indies and the Americas.

It was a fortunate circumstance for at least some of these states that the new opportunities came at a time of political consolidation; certainly in Spain, Portugal and England the growth of royal power and national unity favoured economic advance. The Mediterranean and Baltic seas although they lost their importance, nevertheless continued to play an active part in European commerce. The former still distributed its own local products within and outside its shores, whilst the latter continued to supply western Europe with essential raw materials like timber. At the same time Egypt, and Alexandria in particular, declined in population and wealth, since not only were they outflanked by the new sea route to the east, but also subjected to this misfortune of Turkish rule. Moreover, Venice ceased to rule in European commerce. In 1503 Lisbon received its first big cargo of eastern spices by way of the Cape, and Venice began to lose its entrepôt trade in these lucrative commodities. Similarly what affected Venice was also felt by Dubrovnik for although they were competitors these external events were experienced by them both. In addition, the supply of accessible timber suitable for shipbuilding grew scarce – a scarcity which the whole Mediterranean region seems to have suffered in the course of the sixteenth century.[2] Thus although Venice long remained a vigorous maritime power and in fact built larger ships in the sixteenth century than in her more flourishing days, she restricted her activities to the Mediterranean thus intensifying her competition with Dubrovnik.

Events in South-Eastern Europe

These events basically affected the political life of western Europe, but Dubrovnik also had to take account of events in south-eastern Europe situated as she was on the borders between East and West. Dubrovnik was especially affected by Turkish influence, owing to her semi-independent position and her close intercourse with her power- ful neighbour. Turkish policy was always founded more on ex- pediency than on far-sighted diplomacy whilst Turkish aggression was usually a response to external pressure or foreign alliances. Thus prolonged war was often astonishingly indecisive. Four themes governed Turkish policy : first the hostility of the Persians; secondly the alliance with France; thirdly trade and war with Venice; and finally the opposition to the Hapsburgs in eastern Europe and the Mediterranean. These themes were often closely interrelated and in their turn were of relevance to Dubrovnik. So 'the sacrilegious union of the Lily and the Crescent'[3] confronted a Hapsburg who found willing helpers in the senators of the Venetian Republic and the Shütes of Persia.

The Persians were Shütes (a sect of Islam separated from their opponents by a bitter controversy concerned with the succession to the early Caliphate); the Turks were Sunnis which made the struggle even more bitter.

During the sixteenth century Persia had undergone a renaissance in power and culture under Shah Ismail and his successor Abbas the Great (c. 1557–1628). The declining hold of religious sanctions was thus confirmed by the strange spectacle of the Sunnite Turk relying on French Catholic help against the Catholic Hapsburg Emperor in the unusual company of the Shüte Shah of Persia.

The French alliance with Turkey arose out of expediency but long remained one of the constant factors in the complex story of south-

eastern Europe. The French King Francis I found the Ottoman
Sultan a reliable substitute who could be depended on to harass the
Hapsburg army in Hungary and the Hapsburg fleet in the Mediter-
ranean. Help from France in 1534–35 led to a treaty full of substantial
privileges for France being signed in 1536. Part of this treaty meant
the French were empowered to buy and sell throughout the Turkish
Empire on the same terms as the natives—an ominous sign for
Dubrovnik's future.

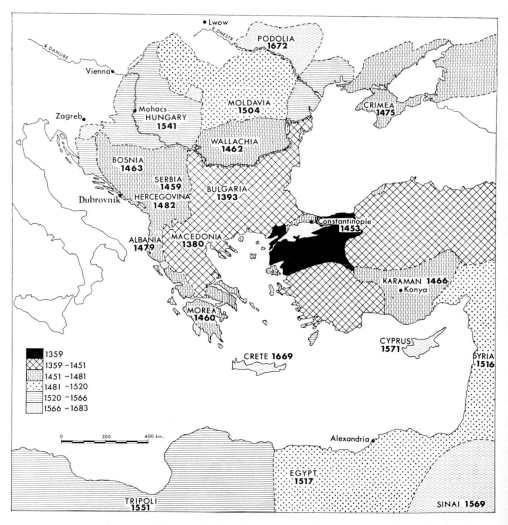

FIG. 57. The Turkish expansion into Europe, Asia Minor, and Africa, 1358–1683.

The opening of the western seaboard had already reduced the economic and political significance of Venice but the republic still ruled over a considerable territory, including the mainland along the Dalmatian coast and a number of islands in the Adriatic and Aegean seas. The Turkish armies made repeated onslaughts on Venetian territory while pirates pillaged the city's galleys; but Venetian policy was never consistent. War between the two powers was by no means continuous nor were the Venetians willing to sacrifice their valuable trade to support a crusade. Although Venice was still strong enough to hold the Turk in check, it could do little by itself to defeat him. This may help to explain the close connection which existed between the Venetian and Hapsburg policy. The hostility of the Hapsburgs to the aggresive moves of the anti-Christian Turk was indeed far more natural than Hapsburg-Valois rivalry.

The period opened with unusual peace in south-eastern Europe, The mild and studious son of the conqueror of Constantinople, Sultan Bayezid II (1498–1512) was too involved in struggles with the rising Persian state and the Mameluks of Egypt to pay much attention to events in the West, like his successor Selīm I (1512–1520). Suleiman the Magnificent (1520–1566) realized that the two chinks in Turkish armour were the fortress-city of Belgrade and the heavily fortified island of Rhodes, both important trading centres for Dubrovnik's merchants; the first endangered the security of his northern frontiers and the second threatened the communications between Cairo and Constantinople. Szabacs and Belgrade fell in 1521, thus opening the rich Hungarian plains to his invading armies. A year later Rhodes fell to Suleiman after a siege lasting four months – now 'the passages to Hungary, Sicily and Italy be open to him'.[4]

The year 1526 was a momentous one for Christendom. The Turkish Wars with Hungary had been going on intermittently for many years, now one side gaining the advantage now the other, but no decisive operations had taken place recently. In 1526 Suleiman again invaded Hungary, and in the great battle of Mohács the Hungarians were totally defeated and 20,000 soldiers including their King were killed.

Dubrovnik's dependence on Hungary now ceased. In 1527 Ferdinand of Austria, who succeeded to what remained of the Hungarian kingdom wrote to the Dubrovnik state, requesting them to remain faithful to him as overlord of Hungary, as they had been to his predecessors. At the time no attention was paid to this demand and the

M*

republic remained more or less under Turkish protection until its fall.[5] It obtained from the Turks all the commercial privileges granted by the King of Hungary, and its trade in the Ottoman Empire flourished under the Crescent as well as under the Cross.

Dubrovnik and the European Wars

The first years after the cessation of the Hungarian protectorate were again disturbed by a quarrel with the Venetians. Some of the grain ships bringing foodstuffs to Dubrovnik were captured by Venetian cruisers in the Adriatic, as the government of the great republic accused its small but enterprising rival of playing a double game. Dubrovnik's citizens wishing to retaliate started tampering with Venetian dispatches, one letter containing the announcement of an alliance against the Sultan was forwarded to the French ambassador at Constantinople. The Venetians threatened vengeance and her ships continued to harry the Dubrovnik coast for some time inflicting much damage.[6] This same year (1538) Pope Paul III, as head of the Christian League issued a decree against the Turks. It was probably inspired by the Venetians, and hostile to Dubrovnik, forbidding all Christians to sell arms, gunpowder, cables, ship-timber, iron, etc. to the Ottoman Empire. The Pope also ordered the republic to sever all allegiance to the Sultan, cease to pay him tributes and to immediately join the League against the Infidel, contributing five galleys and 10,000 ducats to the common war-chest. The citizens were filled with consternation at these peremptory commands, but by clever diplomacy the small republic proved equal to the emergency. Dubrovnik, situated between the Turks and the sea, she maintained, would be the first to fall victim to the wrath of the Infidel if she joined the League. Owing, moreover, to the small extent of her territory, she was dependent for three-quarters of the year on foreign grain; this came mostly from the Turkish provinces and she could not, therefore, exist without commercial intercourse with her neighbours. The only result of Dubrovnik's joining the alliance would be the destruction of the city with all her precious sacred relics falling into the hands of the Infidel without any advantage accruing to Christendom. The astute diplomats hinted that the Venetians were merely urging the Pope to take measures against Dubrovnik out of jealousy. These arguments had the desired effect, the Pope relenting towards the republic and exempting it from joining the League. There is no doubt that Dubrovnik's position was always a very risky one and it required all her diplomatic tact to save it from ruin. Although they were on good terms with the Sultan, danger from the turbulent Pashas and Sandjakbegs of Bosnia and Hercegovina had to be apprehended. Many of these men were the descendants of the lawless native princelings who had gone over to Islam and still maintained their old ambition to win their way to the seaboard. The whole of Dalmatia was now threatened, and by 1537 only the most important parts of Dalmatia, the Venetian coastal towns and the Dubrovnik Republic, remained under a Christian Government.

In 1538 the allied fleet under a Venetian commander sailed southwards along the east Adriatic coast encountering the Turks off the Gulf of Arta; the engagement proved indecisive so the Venetians then proposed to attack Novi much nearer to the Dubrovnik Republic. In fact it had been suggested that Dubrovnik itself should be attacked instead, as she had shown herself friendly to the enemy. But the Venetian commander refused to make war on a Christian city so Dubrovnik was once more spared. In the ensuing battle for Novi, the neutrality of Dubrovnik was respected and her territory remained intact, Novi finally staying in Turkish hands at the end of hostilities in 1540.

Dubrovnik's trade was now in a somewhat depressed condition owing to these various disturbances. Seven out of thirteen of Dubrovnik's ships in the service of Spain had been lost in an expedition to Algiers,[7] whilst pirates had wrought much havoc among her ships elsewhere. While the Emperor Ferdinand was invading the Hungarian provinces occupied by the Turks, the Dubrovnik colonies there suffered considerably; and the land trade was disturbed by the depredations of the Sandjakbeg of Hercegovina. In 1544 bankruptcies at Dubrovnik amounted to 80,000 ducats,[8] but by 1545 peace was concluded between the Sultan and the Christian powers. The Sultan issued severe injunctions to the Algerian pirates not to molest ships flying the Dubrovnik flag. In the somewhat quieter period which followed there was a partial revival of the city's trade, which now extended to America by means of the favour of Spain.

In 1566 Suleiman the Magnificent died, and his successor, Selim at once began to cast covetous eyes on Cyprus. War between the Turks and the Christian powers was again imminent, and Dubrovnik began to fear that she might get into difficulties with either of the belligerents. A Turkish army invaded Cyprus in 1570 quickly capturing the fortified cities of Nicosia and Famagusta. Meanwhile the fear of Turkish aggression had at last brought the Mediterranean powers together in some sort of unity, with the result that a Holy League was formed between Spain, Venice and other Italian states under the lead of Pope Pius V. In 1566 Dubrovnik's government applied to the Grand Duke of Tuscany, with whom it was then on excellent terms,[9] (Lorenzo Miniati was then Tuscan Consul at Dubrovnik, and was entrusted with the duty of informing his government of all the rumours he heard regarding the movement of the Turks) and he recommended the town to the King of Spain on the plea that if their trade failed so would the greater part of their income cease, and they would be unable to pay the tribute to the Sultan. The latter would seize on this as a pretext for occupying the town to the great detriment of Christendom.[10] The plea was successful, and moreover, the same year Pius V renewed the exemption to trade with the Infidel, because the city 'in fancis infidelium et loco admodum periculoso sita est'. Dubrovnik now acted once more as intermediary between Christian and Turk in her role as a neutral state.

Yet Venetian jealousy was ever present in the life of Dubrovnik. In a despatch to the Senate dated April 1, 1570 the Dubrovnik ambassador in Rome wrote as follows:

'This war gives food for reflection to the thoughtful, especially with regard to the State of Dubrovnik, considering the capital malignity of the Venetians against us ... The Emperor (Charles V) had expressly recommended the said republic to Venice and enjoined them to protect and guard it in the same manner as the cities of his own kingdom of Naples'.

On April 8th he added

'The Emperor's ambassador in Rome has been informed from Venice that the Senate has determined to place a garrison in Dubrovnik so that the Turks may not occupy the city; and if the Republic refuses to admit it, they have decided to seize it by force, which means that they wish to capture the town with the excuse of preventing the Turks from doing so'.[11]

The Spanish and Imperial ambassadors took the side of Dubrovnik's citizens and the Pope also favoured them. Venice believed 'that the only way of saving Dubrovnik from all danger on the part of the

Turks is to occupy the town herself'. In the face of these threats Dubrovnik diplomats obtained a treaty giving her the joint protection of Christendom, a clause being inserted to the effect that

'no acts of hostility are to be committed against Dubrovnik and its territory, the Pope for weighty reasons having so decreed'.

Thus by her successful diplomacy Dubrovnik was under the aegis of seven different Powers – Spain, the Papacy, the Empire of Naples, Venice, Hungary, the Turks and the Barbary Deys – whence the republic earned the sobriquet of 'Le Sette Bandiere' (the Seven Standards); and although subsequently they often were in difficulties with some of their protectors, they could always play one off against the other. This was the secret of Dubrovnik's long-continued independence.

One of the decisive events in the war between Turkey and the Holy League was the battle of Lepanto in which the Turkish fleet was completely defeated.[12] Lepanto was the true signpost to the decline of Turkish power – even though the road was to be long. It doomed Turkish maritime supremacy in the Mediterranean, and heralded a general slow decay with its feeble Sultans and prevailing inefficiency during the first half of the seventeenth century. Also incidentally the results of Lepanto meant the Turks were now more dependent on Dubrovnik's shipping for maritime trade. In 1573, a general peace was concluded, much to the disgust of the Venetians who saw that in spite of the victory over the Turks it was not properly followed up, and the enemy was allowed to recuperate. Dubrovnik, however, was delighted, for the peace removed the dangers from both quarters. Unfortunately even this period of calm was destined to be short-lived, for there now began a series of calamities for Dubrovnik which culminated in the great earthquake of 1667.

A new disturbance emerged with the Uskoks,[13] a group of Christian pirates. Originally these men were refugees from the lands occupied by the Turks and many had settled in Dubrovnik and other Dalmatian towns. Wherever the Uskoks resided they revenged themselves on the usurpers by raiding their territory, plundering their caravans and keeping up a constant guerilla warfare on the frontiers. The Austrian Emperor Ferdinand gave them refuge at Senj in the Kvarner, a town protected on the land side by impassable mountains and forests. From Senj they continued their raids into Turkish territory and also began operations by sea. They were always a trouble to

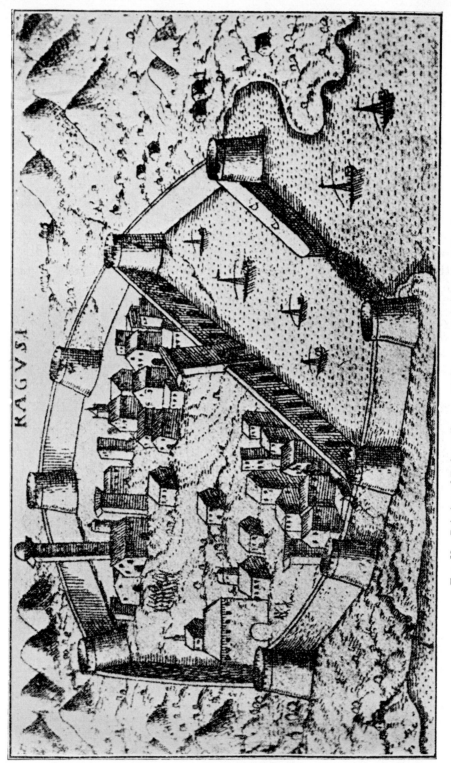

Fig. 58. Painting of Dubrovnik *circa* 1580, on wood (16·5 cm × 9·5 cm).

the citizens of Dubrovnik, because they captured their galleys, and also by attacking the Turks involved the Dubrovnik Republic in difficulties with the Porte. The latter accused Dubrovnik of protecting these freebooters mainly because they were Christians. In 1577 numbers of them were still living in the Dalmatian mountains and made raids as far as Trebinje, while others from Senj harried Turkish merchantmen. The Uskoks professed to regard Dubrovnik's citizens as vassals of the Sultan and plundered her ships and territory.[14] Peace was restored through the mediation of Austria, but the Turks persisted in regarding Dubrovnik's citizens as the pirates' accomplices and again the Sandjakbeg of Hercegovina threatened to lay waste Dubrovnik's territory. On the landward side the republic was vulnerable, while on the sea her shipping had suffered heavily from piratical attacks. The incident ended in the Dubrovnik government bribing the enemy into a more reasonable attitude.

In 1617–18 Dubrovnik was involved in further trouble through the Uskoks. In 1617 a treaty was signed between Venice, Austria and Spain, in which they agreed to force the Uskoks into the Croatian interior. A Venetian squadron sailed down the Adriatic, with the pretext of capturing the Uskok galleys but used the opportunity to blockade Dubrovnik itself. Spain on hearing of this incident sent a squadron up the Adriatic with the object of attacking Venice but the plot was discovered and the fleet failed in its main objective, but succeeded in forcing the Venetians to withdraw from the area. This, however, caused the Turks to accuse Dubrovnik's government of having allied themselves with Spain to the deriment of the Ottoman Empire. Again delicate diplomacy averted a catastrophe but Venice nursed a resentment against Dubrovnik for having been on good terms with Spain at the time of the blockade, and indulged in a 'policy of pin-pricks' towards the small republic. The latter also suffered annoyances from the Pashas of Bosnia, who were always imposing extortionate duties on Dubrovnik's goods and arresting her merchants as they passed through the country. These turbulent viceroys had to be pacified with presents and heavy bribes.

During the quieter period after 1631, Dubrovnik turned its attention once more to the development of commerce, but discovered that conditions had entirely changed from what they were a hundred, or even fifty, years previously. The whole of the Atlantic and East Indian trade was divided up between the English and the Dutch. Also much of the Mediterranean trade that was not in their hands,

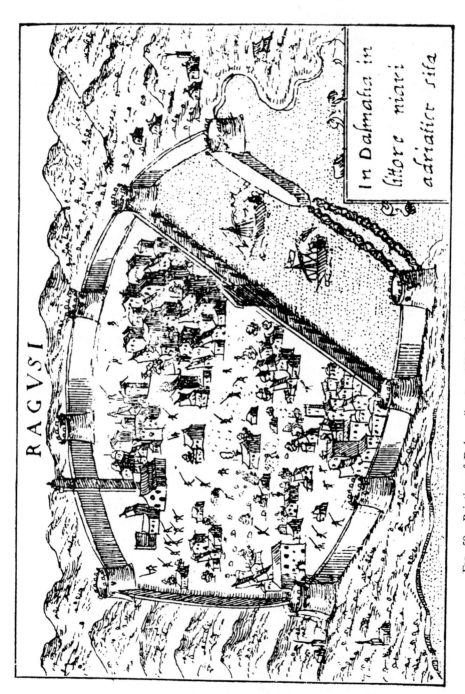

RAGVSI

In Dalmatia in
litore mari
adriatici sita

Fig. 59. Painting of Dubrovnik *circa* 1590, (probably based on painting in Fig. 58 with more detail).

FIG. 60. Painting of Dubrovnik, dated 1638, by M. Merian (1593–1650). The painting measures 33·3 cm × 11·5 cm. (Note the Turkish minaret.)

was in those of the Venetians. Dubrovnik's merchant navy had been for the most part lost in the service of Spain or captured by pirates, and its shipping was therefore reduced to little more than a few coasting vessels, and the republic's only source was now the land trade with Bosnia and Hercegovina. But that too was less brisk than it used to be, as the general trade of the Balkans was tending more and more to follow the Budapest, Belgrade and Sofia highway to Constantinople instead of the Adriatic routes. Decadence was setting in throughout Dalmatia, and the halcyon days of the Dubrovnik Republic had passed away. The Italian trade now consisted of little more than the transport of grain necessary for the feeding of its inhabitants and the Italian colony in Dubrovnik was very small.

When in 1645 the war of Candia broke out between the Venetians and the Turks, Dubrovnik feared that she too would be involved in the conflict,[15] and appealed to the Pope for protection. In 1645 a strong expeditionary fleet was sent from Turkey to capture the richest Venetian possession in the east Mediterranean – the island of Candia (Crete). Venetian efforts managed to repulse the Turks from Candian waters by 1647, but the struggle was then continued on the Turkish mainland. The conflict dragged on for the next twenty-two years, with much of the fighting centred on the Turkish/Venetian border in Dalmatia. Dubrovnik's appeal to the Pope succeeded in the town maintaining a neutral attitude without being molested, the Sultan's plan for concentrating his troops at Dubrovnik for an invasion of Dalmatia having been luckily abandoned. Neutral Dubrovnik, therefore, became the main port for oriental and occidental trade in the Balkans. The war ended in September 1669 with Venice evacuating the island of Candia. For Venice, the war had been 'a bottomless pit into which she poured men, money and supplies endlessly and without effect'.[16] For Turkey it meant success and a renewal of the aggressive policy against western Christendom which had been adopted by earlier Sultans, and for Dubrovnik a period of intense trading prosperity in which she acted as entrepreneur between the two enemies.

In retrospect, the early modern period had so far been one of mixed fortunes for Dubrovnik. The political scene had given Dubrovnik years of intense trading coinciding with her wartime stands of neutrality but this had been interspersed with economic depressions and fierce rivalry which tended to diminish her former role of trade mediator between the Orient and Occident. This was further

FIG. 61. From an oil painting of Dubrovnik painted sometime prior (1658?) to the earthquake of 1667. This is in the Franciscan monastery, Dubrovnik. (Venetian school, 170 cm × 11·5 cm).

Fig. 62.

emphasized by a dramatic event, for on April 6, 1667 an earthquake, followed by fire swept through the city killing an estimated 5,000 people and destroyed much of the town. Very slowly Dubrovnik rose from the ruins and the work of rebuilding began. Help came to the

FIG. 63.   View of Dubrovnik, 1678, by V. Coronelli (in '*Mari, Golfi, Isole, Spiagge, Porti, Città, Fortezze ed altri luoghi dell' Istria, Quarner, Dalmazia . . . 1678*,' Archives of Split Museum).

stricken city from all parts of Christendom and one of the first buildings to be repaired was the Customs House, the chief source of the republic's revenues. Unfortunately it was now a very different Dubrovnik to that which existed before the earthquake.[17] The merchant navy, save for a few coasting vessels, had now disappeared, and with it the sea-borne trade, while the land trade was also reduced.

FIG. 62.   Map dated 1664 by F. N. Sanson (1600-1667) showing the boundaries of the Dubrovnic Republic, Venetian Dalmatia and the Ottoman Empire.

FIG. 64. Map of the Dubrovnik Republic in V. Coronelli's atlas, Venice 1678.

The next major political event to affect Dubrovnik was the Austro-Turkish War 1683 to 1699. In 1683 the Turks attacked Vienna. Their repulsion revealed that Ottoman supremacy in the Balkan lands had passed its zenith and was a prelude to further disasters for the Turks. In March 1684 a new Holy League was formed between the Emperor Leopold I of Austria, the King of Poland, the Pope, and the Venetians, in which Dubrovnik was forced to join. Danger from such a proceeding was now less great, for the Turkish power was broken. As the Austrians had reconquered a large part of Hungary, Dubrovnik was considered to be under the protection of the Emperor as ruler of that country, and in August 1684 a treaty to that effect was signed in Vienna. The treaty declared that this protection was merely a renewal of the old Hungarian protectorate over Dubrovnik. The Emperor promised to protect and defend Dubrovnik, to confirm all the privileges and commercial immunities which the Kings of Hungary, his predecessors, had granted her, in exchange for which she was to pay him a sum of 5,000 ducats per annum. This payment, however, was only to be made if and when the Austrian armies conquered Hercegovina. The Empire was successful in the war, and the Turks were steadily driven back out of Hungary, where they now only held a few isolated posts.

Venice too displayed an energy and achieved a success remarkable for a decaying state. She conquered the greater part of the Morea in southern Greece, captured Athens and a number of islands, occupied Novi and the whole of the Bay of Kotor, as well as several positions in Hercegovina; Vlachs in the Venetian service made raids into Turkish territory, Venetian privateers threatened to destroy what remained of Dubrovnik's sea-borne trade, while the closing of the land routes practically stopped all commercial intercourse with Turkey. Dubrovnik's citizens applied now to their new protector the Emperor of Austria, who persuaded the Venetians to refrain from molesting the small republic.

The Austrian army failed to conquer Hercegovina, so Dubrovnik never paid its tribute to the Emperor. As soon as there was a prospect of peace on lines contemplating the maintenance of a *status quo* regarding the hinterland, Dubrovnik hastened to come to an agreement with the Porte, sending tribute arrears from 1684. After some years of fighting the Sultan was induced to sue for peace, due to the Tsar Peter's capture of Azov, the Austrian victory of Zenta and Venetian successes in the Adriatic. In the treaty of Karlovitz (southern

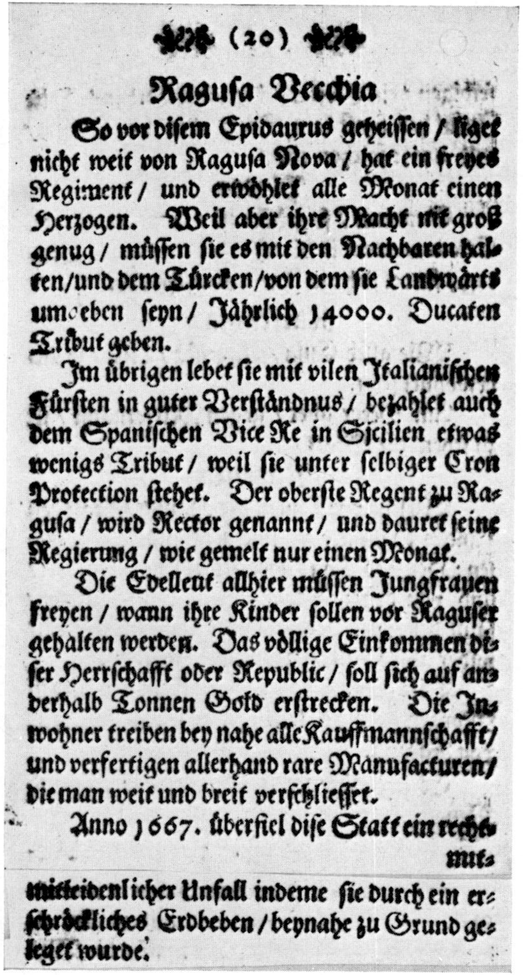

(20)

Ragusa Vecchia

So vor disem Epidaurus geheissen / liget nicht weit von Ragusa Nova / hat ein freyes Regiment / und erwöhlet alle Monat einen Herzogen. Weil aber ihre Macht nit groß genug / müssen sie es mit den Nachbaren halten / und dem Türcken / von dem sie Landwärts umgeben seyn / Jährlich 14000. Ducaten Tribut geben.

Im übrigen lebet sie mit vilen Italianischen Fürsten in guter Verständnus / bezahlet auch dem Spanischen Vice Re in Sicilien etwas wenigs Tribut / weil sie unter selbiger Cron Protection stehet. Der oberste Regent zu Ragusa / wird Rector genannt / und dauret seine Regierung / wie gemelt nur einen Monat.

Die Edelleut allhier müssen Jungfrauen freyen / wann ihre Kinder sollen vor Raguser gehalten werden. Das völlige Einkommen diser Herrschafft oder Republic / soll sich auf anderhalb Tonnen Gold erstrecken. Die Inwohner treiben bey nahe alle Kauffmannschafft / und verfertigen allerhand rare Manufacturen / die man weit und breit verschliesset.

Anno 1667. überfiel dise Statt ein recht-mit-

mitleidenlicher Unfall indeme sie durch ein erschröcklichés Erdbeben / beynahe zu Grund geleget wurde.

RAGUSA VECCHIA

Previously it was called Epidaurus and it lies not far from Ragusa Nova and has a free Regiment, every month a Duke is elected. Because however their strength is not large enough they have to live in harmony with their neighbours and the Turks, by whom they are surrounded and have to pay them 14,000 ducats annually.

Apart from that they live in peace with the Italian princes and also pay the Spanish Viceroy in Sicily a sum of money, as they live under their protection. The highest Regent in Ragusa is called Rector, his reign only lasts one month.

The nobility here have to marry titled girls (virgins) if their children are to become Ragusan citizens. The whole revenue of the republic is supposed to be one and a half tons of gold. The inhabitants are nearly all merchants and manufacture many rare objects, which are sold everywhere.

In the year 1667 this town was struck by a terrible disaster and was practically completely destroyed by an earthquake.

FIG. 65. From *Viridarius Adriaticus* (anon. author), Augsberg (1687), pp. 20–21.

Hungary) 1699 the Porte ceded to the Emperor all Hungary (save the Banat of Temesvar), Transylvania, Slavonia and Croatia as far as the Una River; Poland obtained Podolia, the Ukraine and Kameniek; Venice received the Morea, some islands and several fortresses in Dalmatia. From Dubrovnik's point of view, an important article referred to two strips of Turkish territory which should divide the

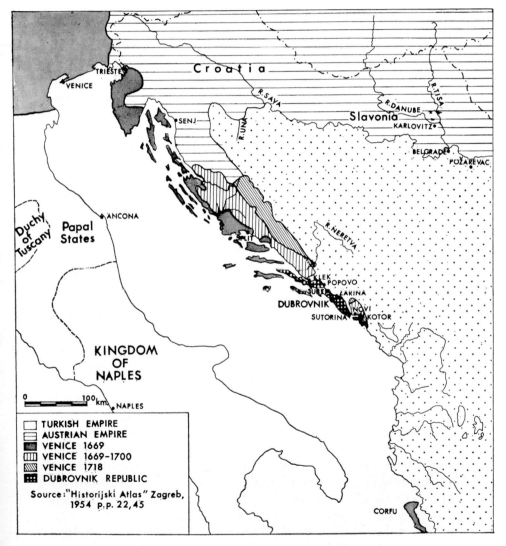

FIG. 66. Political situation *circa* 1700.

republic from Venetian territory, *viz.* the enclaves of Klek, near the mouth of the Neretva and Sutorina in the Bay of Kotor.[18] Dubrovnik thus became tributary to the Porte once more and deliberately preferred to be surrounded by Turkish territory rather than that of Venice.[19] This in turn was to bring about a partial revival of the republic's land trade.

Conclusion

Political events in the early modern period provided Dubrovnik with new problems for her commerce. The discovery of sea routes to Asia and America by the Spanish and Portuguese, diverted the old trade routes from the Mediterranean Sea. The wars in Europe, although sometimes placing Dubrovnik on the edge of extinction, were averted by her government's shrewd diplomacy, the ensuing policy of neutrality being turned to commercial advantage. Turkish foreign policy caused disturbances not only in the Balkans but in western Europe, Dubrovnik often finding herself walking on a political tightrope as a result of sudden incursions. Nevertheless, although Dubrovnik's situation did not allow her rulers to pursue a policy of real neutrality between Turkey and the Christian powers, their business-like minds were of a very neutral disposition.

Fundamentally, this disposition was a reflection of the two worlds in which Dubrovnik's citizens lived. As Slavs they were ethnically similar to the local rulers of the Ottoman hinterland, but their cultural tradition was predominantly Mediterranean, or more specifically, Italian. This may be the reason why the loyalty of several of its citizens lay individually with the Christian powers rather than with the Turks, but it was an attitude that was carefully supressed in all dealings with the Ottoman Empire. The practical attitude of Dubrovnik's government in respect to world affairs, often meant that the small republic was in a precarious position in the Empire, particularly at times of crisis. On many occasions its reputation could easily have been ruined by foreign representatives as well as by the Turkish officials, who maintained that Dubrovnik was following an anti-Turkish foreign policy. Therefore the diplomatic skill of Dubrovnik's political envoys played an important part in upholding her privileges and preserving the republic's autonomous position.

Finally it should be stressed that the political relationship between Turkey and Dubrovnik was one of mutual advantage. Dubrovnik's autonomy had hardly any disadvantages for the Turkish Sultan. The small republic presented no danger to the Ottoman Empire from a military point of view and it was unlikely to allow itself to be used as a base for an invasion of Turkey. Also the city was a useful point of contact for the Turks with the Mediterranean world particularly during wartime, and also a good source of strategic information. Similarly, Dubrovnik's importance as a commercial centre was based on a large measure of freedom and ensured the Turks of a regular annual tribute. This may have been reduced if the republic was annexed to the Empire proper, for it would inevitably have declined into the position of one out of many rather unimportant Turkish harbours in the Adriatic coast. On the other hand, the lasting fear of Venetian control kept Dubrovnik tied to the Ottoman Empire of its own accord, and allowed the republic a much freer hand in exploiting its commercial advantages.

8. Notes

1. S. Guldescu, *History of Medieval Croatia*, The Hague (1964), pp. 302–303. Guldescu maintains that
   ' . . . a few decades after this discovery there certainly were Dubrovnik's citizens at Goa. Their influence is apparent in the founding and decoration of the church in Goa of St. Blasius, the patron saint of Dubrovnik. Some Croatian academicians believe that Dubrovnik's merchants reached Goa long before the Portuguese did. When Vasco Da Gama and Albuquerque brought the power of Portugal to the Malabar coast they found the present day Portuguese holdings of Goa and Diu fortified and garrisoned by Europeans. These last were mostly Greeks and Slavs, but certainly there were Dalmatian and Dubrovnik Croats among them. Dubrovnik's influence can be detected in their fortifications as well as in the great trade emporiums that the Portuguese found existing. Indeed there are remarkable similarities between the general city plans of Dubrovnik and Diu and in the governmental spirit that prevailed in both localities.'
2. F. C. Lane, 'Venetian shipping during the commercial revolution', *American Historical Review*, Volume XXXVIII No. 2 (1933).
3. V. H. H. Green, *Renaissance and Reformation*, London (1954), p. 381; W. L. Wright, *Ottoman Statecraft*, Princeton University Press, Princeton N.J. (1935), pp. 21–28.
4. R. B. Merriman, *Suleiman the Magnificent*, London (1944), p. 33.
5. G. Gelcich, L. Thalloczy, *Diplomatorium . . . op. cit.*, p. 441.
6. S. Razzi, *op. cit.*, p. 42; J. C. von Engel, *op. cit.*, p. 91.

7. J. C. von Engel, *op. cit.*, p. 45.
8. S. Razzi, *op. cit.*, Vol. II, p. 17.
9. V. Makušev, *op. cit.*, p. 495.
10. V. Makušev, *op. cit.*, p. 501.
11. L. Villari, *op. cit.*, pp. 286, 287.
12. F. Braudel, *La Mediterranée et la Monde Mediterranean a l'Epoque de Phillip II*, Paris (1944), pp. 923–942.
13. M. Minuci, *Historia degli Uscochi, co i progressi di quella gente sino all' Anno MDCII*, Venice (1602);
    J. Tadić, 'Pogibije uskočkog vodje Djura Daničića', *Novosti*, Zagreb (1931), pp. 4–10.
14. Dubrovnik Archives (12/V/1584), *Lettere di Levante*;
    ibid., (17/V/1586).
15. A. Vučetić, 'Dubrovnik za Kandijskog Rata (Iz dopisovanja republike sa Mihom Sorgom-Bobaliem)' *Program C. K. Velikoga Državnoga Gimnazija u Dubrovniki za Skolsku Godinu 1894–1895*, Dubrovnik (1895), 84 pp.
16. *The New Cambridge Modern History*, Volume V, Cambridge (1961), p. 462.
17. R. Samardžić, *Borba Dubrovnika za Opstanak posle velikok zemljotresa 1667 G. (Archivska Grada 1667–1670)*. Belgrade S.A.N. (1960), 654 pp.;
    L. Vojnović, 'Louis XIV et Raguse (1667–1680), *Revue Historique diplomatique*, Vol. XXI Paris (1907), pp. 57–95.
18. Article IX and XI of the Turco-Venetian Treaty;
    see R. Knolles, *Turkish History 1604–86*, 2 vols, London (1687), and the continuation in Sir P. Rycant, *History of the Turks 1679–99*, London (1700).
19. T. G. Jackson, *op. cit.*, Vol. I, p. 163.

9
The Commerce of
the Dubrovnik Republic
1500–1700

The period between the consolidation of the Turkish Empire in the Balkan peninsula, *circa* 1500, and the renewal of Dubrovnik as a Hungarian protectorate at the end of the seventeenth century had special repercussions on the commerce of the republic. In spite of violent fluctuations or interruptions in trade, economic prosperity grew until about 1550, when economic advance in Europe was sharply checked by religious wars, the decline in mid-European mining, the extension of Turkish conquests in the Balkans and Hungary, and widespread royal defaults on debts. The rest of the century was disturbed and depressed in many respects but by 1600, when the clouds lifted, the shape of things to come was fairly clear. The New World had revealed some of its treasures; Spain and Portugal had become important because of the overseas empires they had staked out, but were not equipped for active participation in European trade; the Italian cities were well located for trade through the Mediterranean but not for ocean traffic; Holland, England and France were well placed for combining European commerce with that of the New World, and the Dutch were already started on the road to becoming the world's leading carrier and middleman.

Trade Decline in Expensive Raw Materials

Spices

It is now proposed to examine how Dubrovnik fitted in to this new European economic pattern and what changes she had to make in order to survive commercially. One of the most important products to decline were spices, but this was no over-night phenomenon. Mirković[1] states

'The economic history of the sixteenth and seventeenth centuries needs a number of fundamental revisions. There are too many assumptions which could not stand a thorough and conscientious re-examination of contemporary source materials. Most of these are connected with the question of the place of the Mediterranean world in the commercial revolution. It is true that during the sixteenth century the centres of world trade have shifted towards the Atlantic. On the other hand that process has not been by any means "clean" and exclusive. Some sections of the Mediterranean world have maintained their positions throughout the sixteenth century'.

He further maintains that

'One of the most interesting places in the history of the commercial revolution still asking for more classification is the Portuguese trade with the East Indies during the sixteenth century. The question is still open: was there a real Portuguese monopoly in the East Indian spice trade following the discoveries and conquests of 1498–1502, and what happened to the trade that was carried through the old trade routes of the Levant?[2]

In support of the thesis by Mirković[3] and Lane[4] following the pioneer work done by Lybyer[5] it may be possible to give some supplementary materials concerning Dubrovnik's Levant trade in spices, which might broaden the argument. Before this is done it is worth pausing to consider the relationship between the conquests of Selīm I and the immensely significant shift that was now occurring in East-West trade routes. For centuries spices and other commodities that Asia supplied to Europe had been funnelled mostly through the Mameluke ports of Syria and Egypt where they were purchased by Venetians and other middlemen (e.g. from Dubrovnik) for resale throughout western Europe. Suddenly the flourishing Mameluke Empire was struck by the direct sea access to India and to the coveted spice islands of the East Indies. Lengthy as the voyage was on the all-water route around the Cape of Good Hope, it still was infinitely

FIG. 67. (facing page)   Part of a letter from the Mameluke's Governor in Alexandria to the Rector of Dubrovnik, dated 25/VI/1510, in which Dubrovnik traders were allowed to reside permanently in the port of Alexandria.

بسم الله الرحمن الرحيم

الشافي أنعم وأفضل

خلّد الله تعالى ملكه

هذه المكاتبة من مولانا المؤلف المشرّف

الكريم العالي المولوي الأميري الكبيري العمدي

الذخري العالي الفاضلي المجاهدي المرابطي السيدي المالكي

المرابطي المسيفي خلّد الله تعالى في عين السادة للأمراء

معزّ بني الأولاد الديار المصرية ومملكة الأمراء الأيوب

الشريفة معزّ للإسكندرية والدور لمحمد الدين نوال نصارى غلاً

منارة ضماعي عزّه واقتدارة إلى الكفر والموقر

المنتظم الأسد للسلاسل للدرع غانم نحن لمّة محمل طائفة

لأد لفرسان بين تكون للنصارى ملك الهم اللتي نحن

هال الغفرة الحبسور والعصابة الصليبية دوك

للأردخون والهمة للقائده للسنبه التفرّط عين

وللسمف في ملكة ادام لله للعجنبة لأمّ مسرد صدّة

اليه دربقائب نورا الكفر لمرود دعلينا لثابه

مابو للوارد بركب الردّوزه لمواهل الى لكفر من يجو ازجوابا

يعني ما اشاره بالكفر ومن ورود المراسيم

على استمر نو لمن جاء نجار الركوز وكل من سرد بهمن لنحن

واختار المعدله لمرتب عليهم بلمر حصل لكفر وكلا لهل

ملكنا لواسطة تقد فرح به سرود والرى انثار الثابه

بحمده من لم يكون ايمانا الكعبه لعليهم على ثقية سر بنا

more economical than the old course through the Mameluke ports in the eastern Mediterranean. The latter route involved several loadings and unloadings to traverse the land barrier separating Alexandria from the Red Sea, and the Syrian ports from the Persian Gulf. Also there were customs duties to be paid at several points along the route as well as Bedouin marauders who had to be placated by money, or wares, or both. This combination of high transportation costs, customs dues and outright extortions raised the price of spices in Alexandria, and on top of this there still remained the west European merchants to levy their far from modest charges before the goods finally reached the consumer in France, England or Germany. It is not surprising then to find

> 'that in the four years 1502–1505, the Venetians were able to obtain an average of only 1,000,000 English pounds (avoir du pois) of spices a year at Alexandria, whereas in the last years of the fifteenth century they had averaged 3,500 pounds. Conversely Portuguese imports rose from 224,000 pounds in 1501 to a average of 2,300,000 pounds in the four years 1503–1506'.[6]

The Turks are frequently held responsible for this shift in the trade routes. According to this theory Selīm conquered Syria and Egypt and then proceeded to interfere with the flow of spices through those countries to such an extent that western Europe suffered a serious shortage. Hence the efforts of the Portuguese captains to find a direct route to the Far East, culminating in da Gama's successful voyage around the Cape of Good Hope. This reasoning appears incorrect because, da Gama reached Calicut in 1498; Selīm over-ran Syria and Egypt eighteen years later in 1516–1517. Not only did the Turks have nothing to do with the appearance of the Portuguese in the Indian Ocean, on the contrary, they made every effort to drive the Portuguese out in order to revive the prosperity of their newly won Syrian and Egyptian possessions.

The Lybyer-Lane-Mirković argument, suggests that the trade of Dubrovnik and Venice was not halted at the Levantine ports of Alexandria, Tripolis [in Syria (Tarabulus Ash-Sham) as distinguished from Tripolis in Lybia (Tarabulus al-Gharb)] and Beirut, but was carried by the merchants of these republics as far as Goa and possibly even Malacca and Batavia, thus penetrating the commercial empire of the Portuguese in India at a period when Portugal is supposed to have had a 'monopoly' of the spice trade. Mirković proves the existence of a Dubrovnik colony at Goa and subsequent trading activities of the town's merchants are discussed.[7]

In order to broaden the argument it is necessary to prove that Dubrovnik did import spices from the Levantine countries of Egypt and Syria during the sixteenth century. The failure of the Turks to counteract Portuguese expansion had far-reaching repercussions for the entire Near East. It marked the beginning of the end of Levantine predominance in world commerce, but the old routes did not disappear overnight. After the first shock of the Portuguese intrusion a gradual recovery occurred. There even were years when the volume of trade through Levantine ports surpassed that which rounded the Cape. The survival of the old channels is surprising in view of the natural advantages of the all-water route. The explanation seems to have been the excessively high rates set by the Portuguese and the corruption of Portuguese officials, who were willing for a consideration to permit cargoes to enter the Red Sea and the Persian Gulf.[8] It was not until some time in the seventeenth century, after the penetration of the more efficient Dutchmen into the Near East, that the balance swung decisively in favour of the Cape route. Consequently both Venice and Dubrovnik were active in the spice trade in the sixteenth century. Only two years after the Turkish conquest of Egypt, a document records spices being imported into Dubrovnik from Alexandria (1519).[9] In fact, between 1530–1540 Dubrovnik had a virtual monopoly in that trade. According to Lane

'Some of the German merchants had begun to do business through Dubrovnik, for the Venetian-Turkish War of 1537–1540 had enabled Dubrovnik's citizens to take a larger part in Levantine trade. At Venice, Germans were prevented from buying directly in the east. By trading through Dubrovnik they could send their own agents to the Levant'[10]

thus illustrating the benefits of Dubrovnik's political neutrality.

As the sixteenth century continued the spice trade if anything grew. Again quoting Lane

'the importation of spices from Alexandria to Europe about 1560 was as large or larger than it had been in the late fifteenth century. Evidently the consumption of spices or at least pepper increased greatly in Europe during the sixteenth century. Shipment from Alexandria went principally to Dubrovnik, Messina and Venice.

o

From these three harbours spices were sent to all Italy and Germany'.[11]

Moreover

'the Venetians had two fondachi (trading houses) at Alexandria, the other "nations", the Genoese, Ragusans (Dubrovnik) and French who were less numerous each having one'.[12]

About 1570 Dubrovnik's interest in the East Indian spice trade began to decline. This does not imply that her merchants entirely withdrew from the Levant[13] and India. Old commercial connections were kept up until the republic's disastrous earthquake of 1667. But the main fleets of Dubrovnik beginning in 1580, were transferred to the Atlantic and the West Indies. The main reasons for the Dubrovnik withdrawal from the Orient were the revival of Venetian trade in that region, and the political line up of Dubrovnik with Spain. Dubrovnik's ships were employed by Spain in defending her empire from the attacks of the English, Dutch and French.

Salt

Sea salt was another product to suffer decline for Dubrovnik after 1500, but again this was not an immediate process. Salt continued to be in demand from the hinterland peoples throughout the sixteenth and seventeenth centuries. Dubrovnik's merchants sought supplies for the hinterland market as far afield as Spain, North Africa, Sicily and Greece.[14] Each year three to six boats transported up to 4,000 tons of sea salt from these distant pans to the warehouses of Dubrovnik, Slano and Gabela in the Lower Neretva valley.[15] How much of this went inland is not known but a document dated 1577 mentioning these warehouses states that 'one third to a half the salt inside them was for Bosnia, Hercegovina and Serbia.'[16] Bosnia's salt supply[17] was mostly in the hands of Venice and Dubrovnik, apart from the Turkish production on the coast at Hercegnovi and in the interior at Tuzla. Dubrovnik merchants were the principal suppliers at Gabela and southwards. The trade was a state monopoly, both for the suppliers and the supplied. The Turks only allowed foreigners to sell salt at certain ports and kept a strict control over its importation. Dubrovnik worked through its official salt salesman, who was paid a certain percentage of the business completed or was on a fixed salary. The

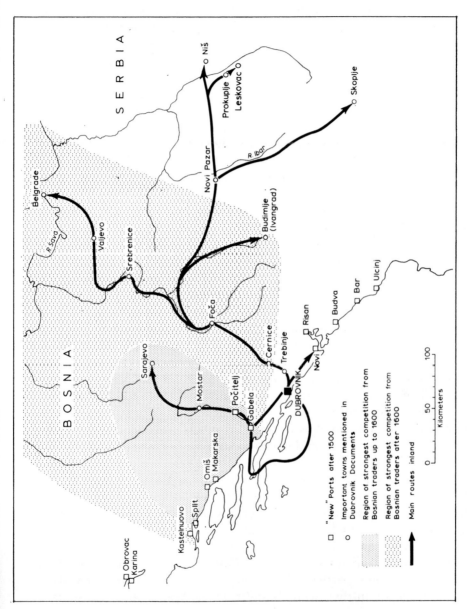

FIG. 68. Growth of Dubrovnik's competitors, 1500–1700. Source: Dubrovnik Archives, *Diversa Cancellariae; Diversa Notaria; Diversa di Foris; Debita Notaria 1500–1700.*

price was fixed by the Turkish authorities, as with grain, and every port had its own tariff. The sale of salt to the Turkish hinterland was carried out mainly at Gabela (formerly called Drijeva at the mouth of the River Neretva), Dubrovnik (Ploče), and Hercegnovi. Smaller quantities were sold in Slano and Risan, and after 1528 in Ston on the Pelješac peninsula.

The main markets for Dubrovnik's salt between 1500 and 1700 were in Bosnia, Hercegovina and Serbia. Prior to 1500 Bosnia had greater importance as a market for salt, than Serbia, but between 1500 and 1700 this situation seems to have been reversed. The main reason was the appearance after 1500 of the so called 'home' traders. These people were Bosnian merchants who wished to exclude Dubrovnik's middlemen, and trade directly with markets in western Europe and the Levant. Before the Turkish occupation, Dubrovnik had arranged with the Bosnian feudal lords that home traders who possessed such ideas were gaoled. Once the Turks had consolidated their power in Bosnia, many of these merchants, especially from Olovo and Goražda, were freed by the Pashas and Sandjakbegs of Bosnia-Hercegovina who saw these traders as a possible means of winning their way to the Adriatic seaboard and a lever against Dubrovnik's grip on hinterland commerce. Coupled with this growth of Bosnian home traders was the development of the 'new' ports. *New* for these harbours had existed prior to the Turkish occupation but had never managed to develop due to Dubrovnik's monopoly on trade. The Turks rejuvenated them or allowed them to be developed by Venice, for during peacetime Turks and Christians through familiarity became less hostile and did much business together. Also Turkey needed revenue and goods to support her war campaigns and as trade mediator, Dubrovnik found that alone she could no longer fill this role. Of particular importance were the new harbours of Gabela and Počitelj in the Lower Neretva valley. Dubrovnik's salt monopoly at the mouth of the Neretva River was seen by Venice[18] as another obstacle to her aspirations of complete hegemony in the Adriatic whilst Dubrovnik wished to maintain her coastal warehouses to facilitate inland trade.[19] Salt, for Dubrovnik, was one of her best sources of income particularly during the Candian War (1645–1669) when large quantities were bought from Apulia and transported inland.[20]

The eastward gravitation of Dubrovnik's merchants into Serbia between 1500 and 1700 was a direct result of intensified competition in Bosnia-Hercegovina from home traders. Curiously, Serbia did not possess home traders in anything like the quantity of Bosnia, perhaps due to their greater distance from the Adriatic, and less contact with Venetian and other foreign traders. Hungarian traders, who were previously strong competitors for Dubrovnik's merchants, were now discouraged by the Turks due to the Magyar-Ottoman conflicts of the sixteenth and seventeenth centuries. Dubrovnik's increased trade in Serbia saw a concentration of salt imports in the major Turkish administrative centres of Belgrade,[21] Novi Pazar, Niš, Skoplje and Budimlje, which were developed not only as administrative but also commercial centres by the Turkish authorities. This is also seen in Bosnia with Sarajevo and Mostar, both towns being developed under the Turkish occupation.

Two routeways, the Neretva valley, and the mountain route to the Drin valley, were major communication links with the hinterland together with the river valleys of the Lim and the Ibar in Serbia. The poljes within Dubrovnik's immediate hinterland were also significant consuming centres for salt; this appears particularly so in the case of Trebinje, which even after 1600 did not come directly under the influence of Bosnian home traders but remained entirely within Dubrovnik's trading sphere due to its proximity to the city.

Minerals

Not only spices and salt lost their meaning in Dubrovnik's commerce but also slaves and minerals. The slave trade[22] had already declined by 1500, but minerals were still entering the town's commerce in the first two decades of the sixteenth century. Their future, for Dubrovnik, depended unfortunately on the consent of the Turkish authorities, who realized the value of these minerals both for armament manufacture and the minting of coinage. Central-east Bosnia and western Serbia were the major mineral producing areas in the Turkish Empire, silver, lead and copper being needed in increasing quantities both to finance and supply the Ottoman war machine. Turkey, therefore, became reluctant to export minerals, particularly lead, to Dubrovnik knowing that a large part of them would be re-exported to Venice – Turkey's main adversary in western Europe. A document dated 1523, between Dubrovnik's government and the Turkish Sultan, Suleiman, stated that the export of lead (and other unspecified products used for war purposes) to Dubrovnik was strictly forbidden.[23] A second document dated 1538, and coinciding with one of the Turkish-Venetian wars, refers to an attempt by a Dubrovnik merchant to export lead from Bosnia; not only was the lead confiscated but the merchant was subjected to a heavy fine.[24]

The decrease in importance of spices, salt, slaves and minerals in Dubrovnik's trade structure meant that she had to find alternative commodities to trade in, but this in itself provided problems. Her merchants had acquired specialist knowledge in these products during the fourteenth and fifteenth centuries and built up connections with foreign traders willing to buy these goods. With the arrival of the Turks this balance was upset. Several old mining and commercial centres like Fojnica,[25] Kreševo, Visoko and Prača fell into complete decadence, whilst those that still remained active like Srebrenica, Olovo and Sarajevo either fell under the influence of the Bosnian home traders, or their products became subject to new Ottoman laws forbidding export. Similarly, the rise of the new ports, supported by Turkish encouragement, meant Dubrovnik now had to face increased competition in areas which she had previously held monopolistic control.

Trade in Cheaper Raw Materials

The result of all these changes was to cause a reorientation of Dubrovnik's trade. This change meant a decline in the *intensive* exploitation of Bosnia and Hercegovina, which had been so strong in the fourteenth and fifteenth centuries, and an attempt to create more *extensive* trading connections in other parts of the Balkan peninsula. The tranformation was already discernible by 1530, and only during wartime between the Turks and Venetians, was Dubrovnik again able to monopolize the markets of the Bosnia-Hercegovina region. Wartime meant the closure of all the new ports along the Turkish-Venetian border, neutral Dubrovnik being the only outlet for trade between the Balkan peninsula and western Europe. The new policy of more extensive trade connections for Dubrovnik was also helped for other reasons. The Turks, as a people, despised trade in commerce. Their society had no middle class and their nobility seemed little interested in the art of trading. Therefore it was left to foreign merchants to take over this role. This is probably why Dubrovnik was able, as early as the fourteenth century, to obtain trade concessions with the Turkish Empire. Furthermore, the Turks on conquest of Bulgaria (1393) and Serbia (1459) expelled all foreign merchants from these countries, with the exception of those from Dubrovnik, closed the Bosphorus and turned the Black Sea into a *mare clausum*. The reason that all other foreign merchants were expelled except those from Dubrovnik, was that the majority were from either Venice or Genoa. To quote Lybyer

'It is true with them (the Turks) commerce was secondary and conquest stood first. But they wished to encourage trade for the sake of revenue. They fought with Genoa and Venice, not because these were trading powers but because they owned lands, cities and exceptional rights within the area of Turkish political influence. With Florence, Ancona and other commercial cities (i.e. Dubrovnik) which had no lands in the Levant and strove for none relations were uniformly good'.[26]

This was equally true in Serbia and Bulgaria for merchants from Dubrovnik did not issue a threat to Turkish political expansion and yet with the advantages of closer proximity and old trade connections in the eastern Balkans they could develop monopolistic control of commerce in the face of competition from Anconian and Florentian merchants and also the Bosnian home traders who lacked contacts in this area. Therefore it can be said that

'the Turks were not active agents in deliberately obstructing trade routes. They did not by their notorious indifference and conservatism greatly if at all increase the difficulties of commercial traffic'.[27]

Yet despite these ideal conditions for Dubrovnik's citizens there was little intensive interest in the eastern Balkans until after 1500. Admittedly, Dubrovnik's privileged position in Bulgaria after 1393 had led to a growth in the number of her merchants in the towns of Sofia, Plovdiv, Provadija, Trnovo, Nikopolje and Silistra, but the preoccupation with her Bosnian, Hercegovinian and west Serbian markets in the later Middle Ages had led to limited commercial contact. After 1500 this pattern changed with much greater emphasis on trade in Serbia and Bulgaria. Furthermore, with the decline of the more expensive raw materials in Dubrovnik's commerce there was a greater emphasis placed on the cheaper raw materials – skins, wax and wool,[28] all of which were produced in large quantities throughout the Balkan peninsula.

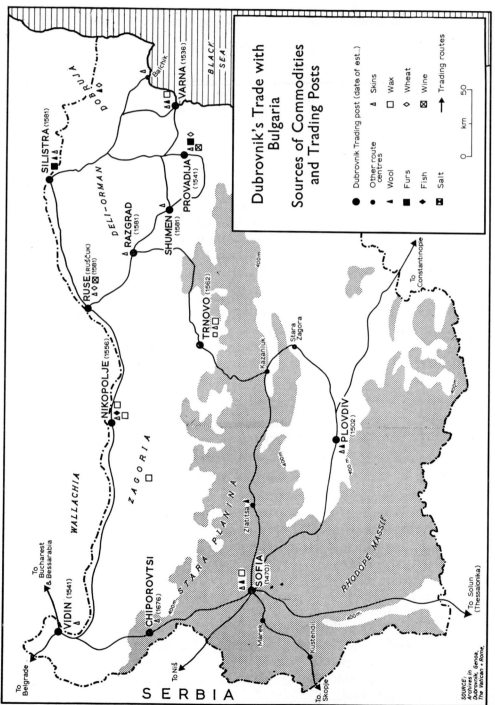

FIG. 69.

Skins

The period 1500 to 1700 coincided with the town's most active participation in the skin trade. Dubrovnik imported most of her skins overland, from collecting points along the Danube, Sofia and towns in central Serbia. Whereas Serbia had wool as its main exporting article, Bulgaria tended to place greater emphasis on different types of skins, obtained from nearly every region of the country. Both domestic and wild animal skins were exported, domestic skins usually coming from buffalo, oxen, cow, lamb and sheep. The raw skins were sent to towns like Plovdiv, Sofia, Silistra and Rusčuk where they were tanned and stored for transport. Together with tanning, other allied trades such as saddlery, fur dressing and slipper-making were developed. One particular branch of interest for Dubrovnik's merchants was the cavalry capes lined with rabbit skin – 'spalle di cavalli' highly prized in the Italian market. Many Bulgarian tanners and furriers developed their own style of skin called 'bulgaro',[29] and the export of astrakhan was one of their specialities. Cordovan (i.e. goat and sheep hides used for clothing, saddlery, etc.) was also a popular export, and Rambert, a French traveller, in 1534 recorded that in Bulgaria many towns had cordovan workshops.[30]

In Serbia the main buying centres for Dubrovnik's traders were Belgrade, Prokuplje and Novi Pazar. Large numbers of skins were brought to Belgrade from northern Spain and Hungary and transported by caravan to Dubrovnik. Her monopoly of this trade in Belgrade was shortlived, for by 1600 Dubrovnik documents complain of Bosnian home traders in Belgrade, together with those of Smederevo, Valjevo, Budimlje (present-day Ivangrad) Osijek and Sombor.[31] Skins from Prokuplje were sent via Novi Pazar to Dubrovnik, the most frequent mention given to cattle and buffalo skins,[32] which came from large herds kept in the damp pastures of the Leskovac basin. Novi Pazar, on the main caravan route from Bulgaria to Dubrovnik was an important skin centre, collecting skins not only from its local district but from other marketing centres. Hercegovina was still a reliable source of many livestock products particularly skins from Trebinje, Cernice, Onogošt and other small centres in the poljes near to Dubrovnik.

Skins also arrived in Dubrovnik by sea, particularly from Bulgaria's Black Sea ports. Varna was the exporting harbour of skins collected by Dubrovnik's merchants in Provadija, Silistra, the region of Dob-

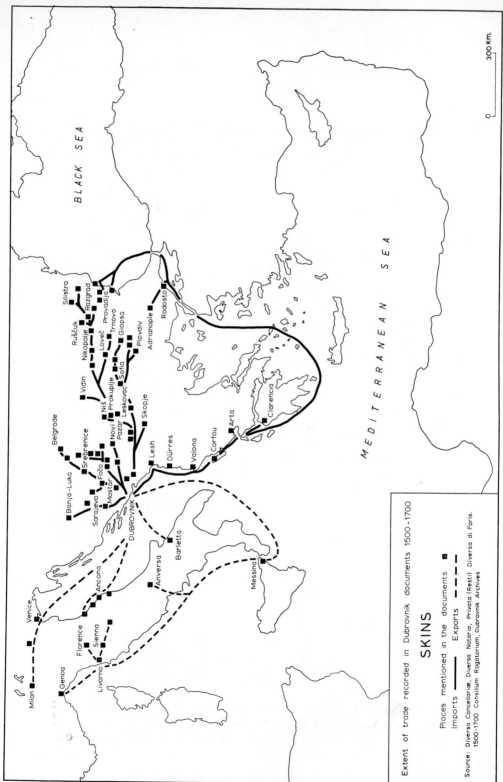

Extent of trade recorded in Dubrovnik documents 1500-1700

SKINS

Places mentioned in the documents ■

Imports ▬▬▬▬ Exports ▬ ▬ ▬ ▬

Source: Diversa Cancellariæ, Diversa Notaria, Privata (Resti) Diversa di Foris.
1500-1700 Consilium Rogatorium, Dubrovnik Archives

FIG. 70.

ruja and other inland markets of eastern Bulgaria. Varna had previously been important for Venetian and Genoese traders but when
the Black Sea became a *mare clausum* to all but Dubrovnik's shipping, the citizens of Dubrovnik took over their role. Rodosto on the
Marmara Sea coast was used by Dubrovnik's traders as a warehouse
and exporting centre for skins collected from the Thracian Plain.
Rodosto provided Dubrovnik's merchants with an alternative port
to Constantinople, because in the Ottoman capital there was a greater
threat of competition from Greek and Armenian traders, who may
have tried to break Dubrovnik's position in the skin trade, together
with the higher marine assurance costs incurred on voyages to the
Porte. Skins brought to Rodosto from the Thracian Plain by Dubrovnik's traders were dried and loaded on boats for the Dubrovnik
and Italian markets. In 1591 the Venetian ambassador in Constantinople (during a comparatively friendly period in Turkish-Venetian
relations) wrote that Rodosto was

'a great maritime town, port and warehouse where Dubrovnik
traders in wool, skins and wax have companies involved in this
trade'.[33]

Further purchases of skins were made from various ports along the
western Greek coast and Albania, but these appear from documentary evidence to be small compared with the inland markets of the
eastern Balkans.

Three towns, Ancona, Venice and Genoa stand out as Dubrovnik's
main customers for skins. Once the skins had arrived in Dubrovnik
from the Balkan hinterland, the shortest sea route to a large Italian
market was to Ancona.[34] Dubrovnik, therefore, became the main
warehouse for skins to Italy, for from Ancona routes led to Rome,
Florence and Lombardy. As early as 1578 one of the trading houses
in Sofia specialized in buying skins solely for the Anconian market.[35]
In 1592 Ancona received a further fillip. Previously Venice had been
Dubrovnik's main skin market, particularly during the sixteenth century, when wars with Turkey made neutral Dubrovnik the main exporting town for the Balkan peninsula. The opening of Split ferry, in
1590, during a period of comparative peace, greatly reduced Dubrovnik's significance as a source of Balkan skins for Venice, so her merchants concentrated on the other great importing centre of Ancona.
Although in partial decline since the loss of its full autonomy, Ancona
was still the only Italian port on the Adriatic seaboard completely

مو

ماهو المسطّر فيه ، مقرّر عـندي و انا الفـقـير احمد بن ولى بـقضاء

نوه ءئى عنهما

هيچ كس نديدم كه كمتر ازبنده ست

الفقير احمد بن ولى

٠٠٠راكى موجب رضاى خداست

سبب تحرير كتاب و موجب تسطير خطاب بودركه

حالیا بوسنه بكار بكیسى اولان حسن پاشا یدره الله تعالى فى الدّارین مایشا ، حضرتلرینك مهر شریفلریله مختوم و دفتردارى اولان محمد چلبى افندینك امضاسیله ممضى زعیم سلیان بیك یدندن بو فقیره خطاب ایدر مكتوب شریفلرى وارد اولوب ، مضمون منیفنده مندرج اولان اقدم یكرمى یوك مقدارى اقچه ایله دیار فرنكستانه تجارت ایدن خواجه حسین نام كمسنه فوت اولوب یتش اسكرلات چوقهسى و ایكى دنك قوماشى و ایكى نفرعبد مملوكى ، سائر نقود و اسبابى دوبرونیك كنزى و بیكلارى معرفتیله دفتر و محفوظ اولدوغى استماع اولندوغنه بنا ، بو خصوص ایچون افتخار الاماجد و الاعیان سربوایان زعیم سلیان زید مجده ارسال اولنوب و بو خصوص ایچون سیزه تذكره تحریر و ترقیم اولنوب دوبرونیك كنزى و بیكلارى نه داخى گوندر یلمشدر و صول بولدقده لازم و مهم اولان بودركه بوخصوصه اوكات و جمله مقیّد اولوب هرنه و جمله اقتضا ایدر ایسه حالیا دوبرونیك ناظرى اولان فخر الاقران چاوش صالح زید مجده و امینى اولان زعیم احمد چلبى معرفت و رضاله یله متوفاء مزبور تجارك بالجمله اسباب و اقچه سى هرنه بولنور ایسه نقیر قطمیر قلیل كثیر دفتر و ارسال و ایصالى بابنده دقت تام و اهتمام مالا كلام ایدمسز بونك خصوصار فرك طائفه سنك الارینده اولان عهدنامه ء سلطانیه اوكات وجمله مشروح و مؤكد بیوریلمشدر اولیه كه اهال ٠اولنه دیو مسطور و مقید بولنغین امتثالا بالمكتوب العالى قلعه دوبرونیك وارلوب مزبور زعیم سلیان بیك و ناظر صالح چاوش و زعیم احمد چلبى امین نام كمسنهلر ایله دوبرونیك كنزى و ولاستلارى قبلریندن وكیل و ادمیلرى اولان اندریه راستیك و مارتولیچه دیراغویك نام ، لاستلار ایله دوبرونیك كرك خانه ، نه واریلو ، نه خواجه حسین نام مرحومك مخلفاتى طالب اولندقده یاشل التش چیله چوقهسى یكرمى یكرمى التى دنك كه الى ایكى پاستاو اولور و لاجوردى التش چیله چوقهسى اون التى بچق دنك كه اوتوز اوچ پاستاو اولور و كوكونى التش چیله چوقهسى درت دنك كه سكز پاستاو اولور و قرمزى التش چیله چوقهسى اوچ دنك كه التى پاستاو اولور و مور التش چیله چوقهسى درت بچق دنك كه طقوز پاستاو اولور و سیاه یتش چیله چوقهسى بش دنك كه اون پاستاو اولوركه جملا التش طقوز دنك كه یوز اوتوز سكز پاستاو اولور و بر صندوق ایچینده قوماشى كه خربى قرمزى كمخا الى ایكى ذراع و خربى قرمزى اطلاس اللى بر ذراع دفعاخربى قرمزى كمخا الى سكز ذراع دفعا خربى قرمزى كمخا اللى ذراع دفعا خربى قرمزى كمخا یوز ایكى ذراع خربى ، مور اطلاس اللى بر ذراع دفعا خربى قرمزى كمخا اون بش ذراع دفعا خربى قرمزى كمخا اوتوز ذراع دفعا خربى ، مور كمخا سنجقاق قدرى خربى ، مور خاره التش ایكى ذراع دفعا خربى لاجوردى خاره اللى یدى دراع دفعا خربى ، آل خاره التش ذراع دفعا خربى قرمزى خاره اللى سكز ذراع دفعا خربى ارغوانى خاره التش بر ذراع دفعا خربى ارغوانى خار اللى التى ذراع دفعا خربى مور خاره اللى یدى

FIG. 71. Part of a transliterated document dated 25/V/–3/VI/1591 relating to commodities from Bosnia to Dubrovnik including various types of Balkan cloth in return for damask and satin (472 lakats) on which Dubrovnik customs duty had been paid. Zadar Archives, Document without code number, *Carte turche*, Book VI.

free of Venetian control. Indeed, during the sixteenth century, when the Ottoman fleet made conditions unsafe for maritime trade in the Aegean, Ancona acquired a certain importance as a port of embarkation for all those merchants travelling east, who preferred to go no further by sea than Split or Dubrovnik and then proceed by land to Solun, Constantinople and the Black Sea ports. Also the sixteenth and seventeenth centuries found Ancona better situated, than previously, with regard to inland communications which meant goods could go through the port more quickly.[36] With the intense competition that developed in the skin trade towards the end of the seventeenth century, Dubrovnik's monopolistic position in the Anconian skin market was broken. Skins were sent from Constantinople, Smirna and Solun not only by Dubrovnik's citizens, but also Anconians, Venetians and Jews. After 1690 there is little confirmed information about Bulgarian skins going to Ancona and Dubrovnik's merchants are rarely mentioned as buying them from the eastern Balkans after 1700.

After Ancona, Venice was the main overseas market for Balkan skins going through Dubrovnik. Venetian Jews, living in Dubrovnik, had their connections both in Venice and the major skin centres of the Balkans, like Sofia. They were extremely active during the Cyprus War of 1570–1573 and in the first two decades of the seventeenth century, but during the second half of this same century Venice began to encourage her own merchants to go and buy skins in Bulgaria shipping them through Constantinople, Rodosto and Varna direct to Venice.[37] The other important market was Genoa. Unfortunately many of the skins destined for Genoa,[38] were only recorded in Dubrovnik documents as having been sent to Ancona, so that the real importance of Genoa in Dubrovnik's skin trade cannot be estimated. After 1666 Genoese traders were again found in Asia Minor, but before this date any Serbian or Bulgarian skins which Genoa purchased must have come through a third party, and Dubrovnik's merchants must surely have been involved.

Wax

Dubrovnik's trade in wax had a very similar distribution pattern to that of skins. This is not surprising for most of the skin trading centres also dealt in wax. Again the greater dependence on eastern Balkan sources compared with the later Middle Ages, is noticeable,

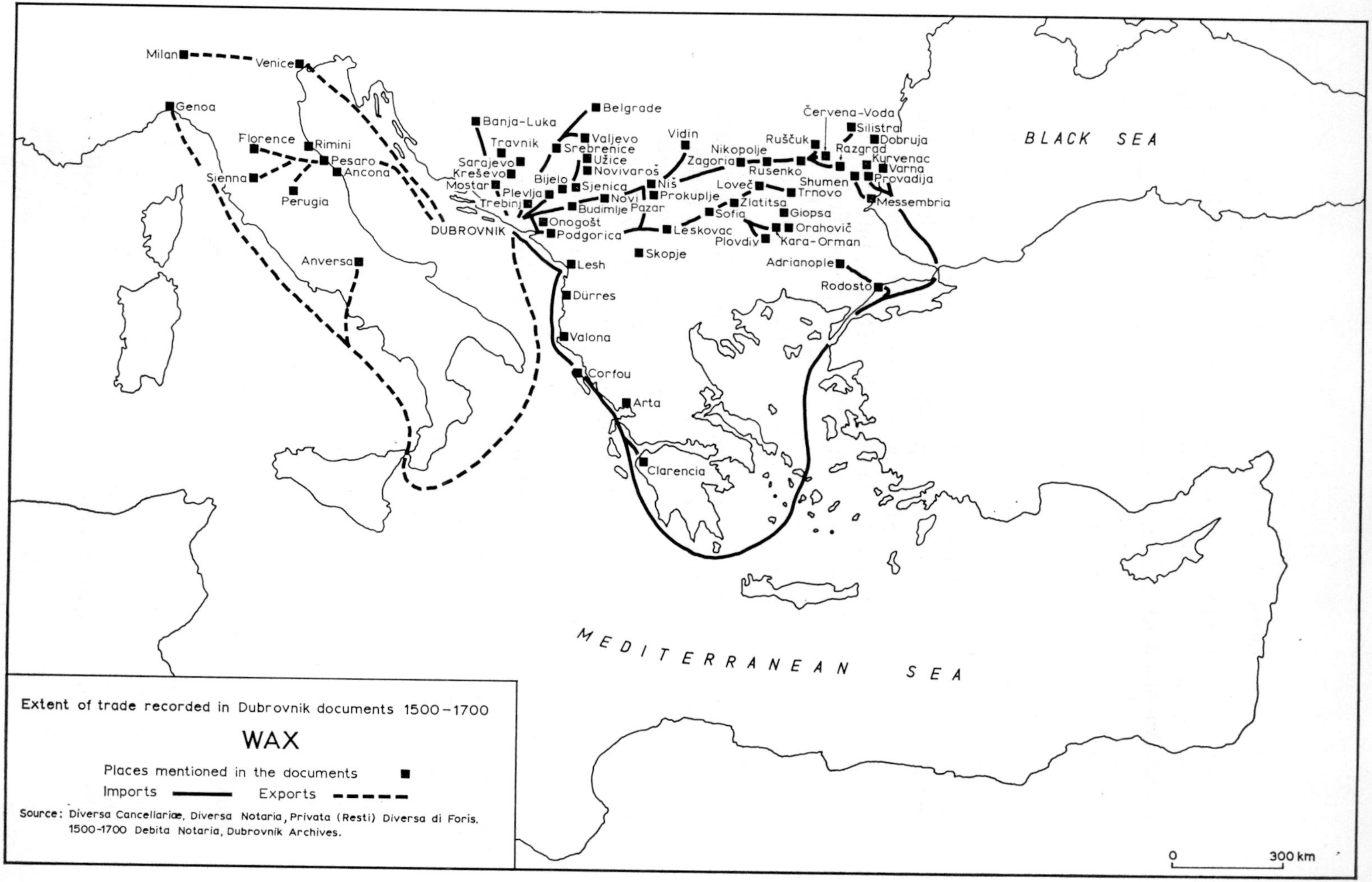

Extent of trade recorded in Dubrovnik documents 1500–1700

WAX

Places mentioned in the documents ■

Imports —— Exports ┄┄┄

Source: Diversa Cancellariae, Diversa Notaria, Privata (Resti) Diversa di Foris. 1500–1700 Debita Notaria, Dubrovnik Archives.

FIG. 72.

BLACK SEA

MEDITERRANEAN SEA

300 km

Červena-Voda · Silistra · Dobruja · Razgrad · Kurvenac · Varna · Provadija · Messembria · Ruščuk · Shumen · Rusenko · Trnovo · Zagoria · Loveč · Orahovič · Giopsa · Nikopolje · Zlatitsa · Kara-Orman · Vidin · Niš · Prokuplje · Sofia · Plovdiv · Adrianople · Rodosto · Belgrade · Valjevo · Srebrenice · Užice · Novivaros · Leškovac · Skopje · Banja-Luka · Sjenica · Bijelo · Budimlje Pazar · Travnik · Plevlja · Onogošt · Podgorica · Lesh · Arta · Clarencia · Sarajevo · Kreševo · Mostar · Trebin · DUBROVNIK · Durres · Valona · Cortou

Milan · Venice · Florence · Rimini · Pesaro · Ancona · Perugia · Anversa · Sienna · Genoa

merce profitable. Wool, therefore, became an alternative commodity for trade, after the decline in mineral and slave exports, to Italy and the west. Also Dubrovnik's citizens were now having more extensive trade connections with Serbia and Bulgaria – the better wool producing areas of the Balkan peninsula.

After skins, wool was the most important export from Bulgaria to Dubrovnik. The earliest information regarding wool exports dates from 1550, when a Dubrovnik merchant exported 230,000 ducats worth of Bulgarian wool, skins and cordovan from Constantinople to Venice.[43] Italian textile manufacturers used a large amount of Bulgarian wool in their products, so the Dubrovnik government realizing the profitable nature of this trade, managed to get a monopolistic position on wool collection throughout Bulgaria. This is borne out by documentary evidence. Two documents dated 1619 mention Dubrovnik's sole right to export wool from Sofia,[44] the main wool centre in Bulgaria. The Turkish authorities gave Dubrovnik's government this right because they knew her traders had good connections in the secure markets of Ancona and Venice.[45] Wool was the most important commodity exported from Serbia to Dubrovnik between 1500 and 1700. Most of it came from the region of Southern Moravlje which covered the area between Niš and Novi Pazar in the north and Kosovska Mitrovica and Leskovac in the south. Before 1500 it was a region of comparatively little value to Dubrovnik for it had no lead or silver mines, then the main part of Dubrovnik's export trade. With the change in Dubrovnik's trade structure, after 1500, and the new emphasis on livestock products, especially wool, this region came into prominence. The faulted basins, which have been developed on the crystalline rocks, contain fertile Tertiary soils, and the South Morava River, with its tributaries, has dissected the area into a subdued relief of wide valleys and long flattened crests. This provided an area well suited for livestock production.

Prokuplje[46] was the main wool collecting centre for Dubrovnik's merchants after the last decade of the sixteenth century, reaching its greatest importance during the middle of the seventeenth century (1620–1667). Of particular interest are the trade accounts of the Mili brothers,[47] who controlled the whole of Dubrovnik's wool exports to Italy from Prokuplje. The Mili accounts enable the area which Prokuplje served as a woollen trading centre to be discerned, revealing that besides the larger towns like, Leskovac, Niš and Trepča, supplies were also collected from many small villages within the southern Moravlje region.

The seasonal nature of the wool trade (March-August) is again seen from the Mili brothers' accounts,[48] for during the periods of intensive trading, it was obligatory to record all wool deliveries to Dubrovnik. The major source of income, for the remainder of the year, came from trade in other livestock products.[49]

Besides southern Moravlje, the region of Kossovo-Metohija was a source of wool for Dubrovnik's citizens. Prior to the Turkish invasion, Kossovo-Metohija was part of the Serbian core-area[50] and an important mining region. With the decline in minerals after the Turkish conquest, Dubrovnik's merchants, gradually deserted the region, and towards the end of the sixteenth century, the changed emphasis in Dubrovnik's trading structure caused them to return. The greater dependence on livestock products, particularly wool, caused Dubrovnik traders to make a re-assessment of the commercial potentialities of this region. The flat plain of Kossovo and the low, hilly region of Metohija, provided excellent grazing for cattle and sheep. Wool proved to have the greatest export value reaching, as in southern Moravlje, maximum production between the years 1620 and 1667. This period coincided with the decline of Bulgarian wool exports to Dubrovnik, and the increased demand by the Italian markets during the Candian War (1645-69). Vinaver has estimated[51] that Kossovo-Metohija provided seventy per cent of Dubrovnik's total wool exports, but as the region is not well documented this is difficult to verify. Despite the poorer quality of wool from Bosnia and Hercegovina, the demand was large enough to absorb or mix it with better quality wools. Wool imports from there mainly occurred during wartime when Bosnian traders had to bring their wool to Dubrovnik for sale due to the closure of the new harbours like Split. During peacetime wool from Sarajevo, Banja-Luka, Travnik and Mostar would have gone through Split harbour direct to Venice. Wool was also imported into Dubrovnik by sea. Bulgarian supplies came mainly from Varna and Rodosto, whilst the Albanian ports served Dubrovnik's merchants with a valuable source of wool mainly from the inland towns of Tirana, Elbasan and Berat; southern Italy also sent wool to Dubrovnik, particularly through the ports of Barletta, Molfetta, Bari and Brindisi.

Wool from Dubrovnik began to be exported in large quantities at the beginning of the sixteenth century, mainly to the markets of north and mid-Italy. The two main markets were Venice and Ancona. Venetian textile factories used large amounts of Balkan wool, especially from Bulgaria, for this seemed particularly suited to the manufacture of Venetian cloth.[52] After Venice, Ancona proved a sure market, valued as much by the Turks, as by Dubrovnik's citizens, for they saw both Venice and Ancona as secure markets for their raw materials and as a source of currency to buy western goods.

Grain

Lack of arable land within the Republic of Dubrovnik meant that their wheat crop scarcely sufficed for more than four months of the year, and there was thus a constant need to procure enough grain for the remaining eight months. More documentation exists on cereal imports than many other commodities traded by Dubrovnik's merchants, probably because of its constant concern and the close watch kept on its reserves.[53] Three main areas emerge in Dubrovnik's cereal imports. Firstly, the Aegean particularly the coastal settlements of Phocea, Smyrna, Altologo (Ephesus) and Palatia. These towns were ports for the agricultural produce of the Gediz and Menderes river valleys, where cereals grew well and Dubrovnik merchants frequently visited the granaries there for supplies. The islands of Mitilene (Lesbos), Chios and Rhodes, as well as Constantinople with its adjoining suburb of Pera were also cereal marts for Dubrovnik. The second area was the Balkan interior. After the Turkish conquest of the Balkans, no other nation except Dubrovnik was allowed to buy grain, but even then only for its own use. Due to the chronic shortage of grain since the mid-sixteenth century[54] one of the most difficult problems of the Ottoman government was supplying this item to both the army and the big cities. Dubrovnik managed to get a certain amount of grain from the Empire almost every year, being generally bought from the Sultan's own estates, but in cases of insufficient quantities, permission was given to buy elsewhere. By preference, the Dubrovnik merchants bought their wheat in the region of Volos or, when available, from the Gulf of Patras. Valona in Albania, ranked third in popularity, supplying mainly millet.[55] Southern Italy was the third large area exporting to Dubrovnik with the ports of Apulia and Sicily being most frequently mentioned as exporting cereals to the town.

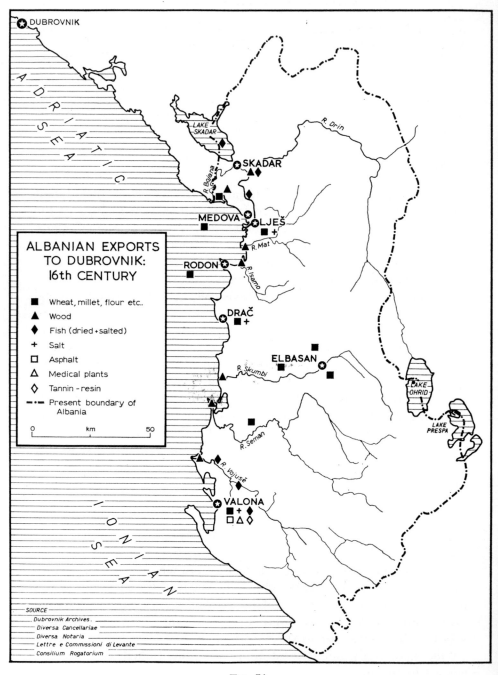

FIG. 74.

Trade in Manufactured Goods

Textiles

An equally significant branch of Dubrovnik's commerce was in secondary products, particularly textiles. West European textiles were the commodity most sought after in the Balkan markets and between 1500 and 1550 Dubrovnik had little competition in this field. Textile imports reached a peak around 1531 when 31,407 pieces of cloth were imported into Dubrovnik.[56] Unfortunately the largest part, 26,404 pieces, consisted of cloth whose origin is not specified, but of the remainder the majority came from west European factories. It has, indeed, been suggested that the industrial quadrilateral bounded by Genoa, Milan, Venice and Florence constituted a region of advanced industry in the late medieval world, but in the sixteenth century this industrial quadrilateral was beginning to take second place to the new industrial centres of north-western Europe. This is borne out by the Dubrovnik import list of 1531, with cloth also coming from Carcassone, Perpignon and London. At this time English cloth exports were increasing and invading the Mediterraean markets, for the fine, light cloths were eminently suitable to warmer climates. That Dubrovnik's trade extended[57] as far as England is further proved by the letter of Barbarigo, the Venetian ambassador to the Porte, who in 1513 passed through the city on his way to Constantinople;[58] and again in 1526 Pope Clement VII addressed a brief to the Chancellor and Councillors of the Duchy of Brittany, who had seized a Dubrovnik ship coming from England.[59]

If 1531 was the peak year for textile imports the following year saw a substantial drop, with only 15,000 pieces recorded as entering the port, 12,670 of which were 'kersey' cloth of unspecified origin. This decline continued until it was partly checked by the short war between Venice and Turkey from 1537 to 1540. Much of the textile trade was in the hands of Jewish merchants and this war saw an increase in their numbers living in Dubrovnik.[60] These traders had connections in many Italian and Balkan towns, and as Dubrovnik remained neutral during this, and the Cyprus War of 1570–1573, they channelled their trade through its port. With the conclusion of the Cyprus War and the restoration of peace throughout the Mediterranean, Dubrovnik's textile imports fell in face of competition from

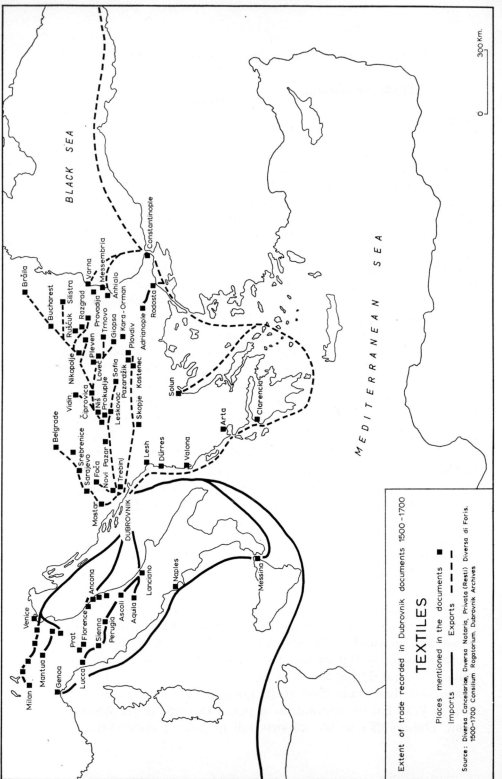

BLACK SEA

MEDITERRANEAN SEA

Brăila
Bucharest
Silistra
Razgrad
Ruščuk
Varna
Messembria
Provadija
Anhialo
Pleven
Trnovo
Giopsa
Kara-Orman
Lovec
Plovdiv
Vidin
Nikopolje
Sofia
Adrianople
Rodosto
Čiprovica
Niš
Pazardžik
Constantinople
Belgrade
Prokuplje
Leskovac
Skopje
Kostenec
Srebrenice
Novi Pazar
Solun
Sarajevo
Foča
Trebinj
Arta
Mostar
Lesh
Clarencia
Dürres
Valona
DUBROVNIK

Venice
Ancona
Lanciano
Naples
Mantua
Prat
Florence
Ascoli
Aquila
Milan
Lucca
Sienna
Perugia
Genoa
Messina

TEXTILES

Extent of trade recorded in Dubrovnik documents 1500-1700

Places mentioned in the documents ■
Imports ——— Exports - - - - -

Source: Diversa Cancellariae, Diversa Notaria, Privata (Resti) Diversa di Foris. 1500-1700 Consilium Rogatorium. Dubrovnik Archives

Fig. 75.

300 Km.

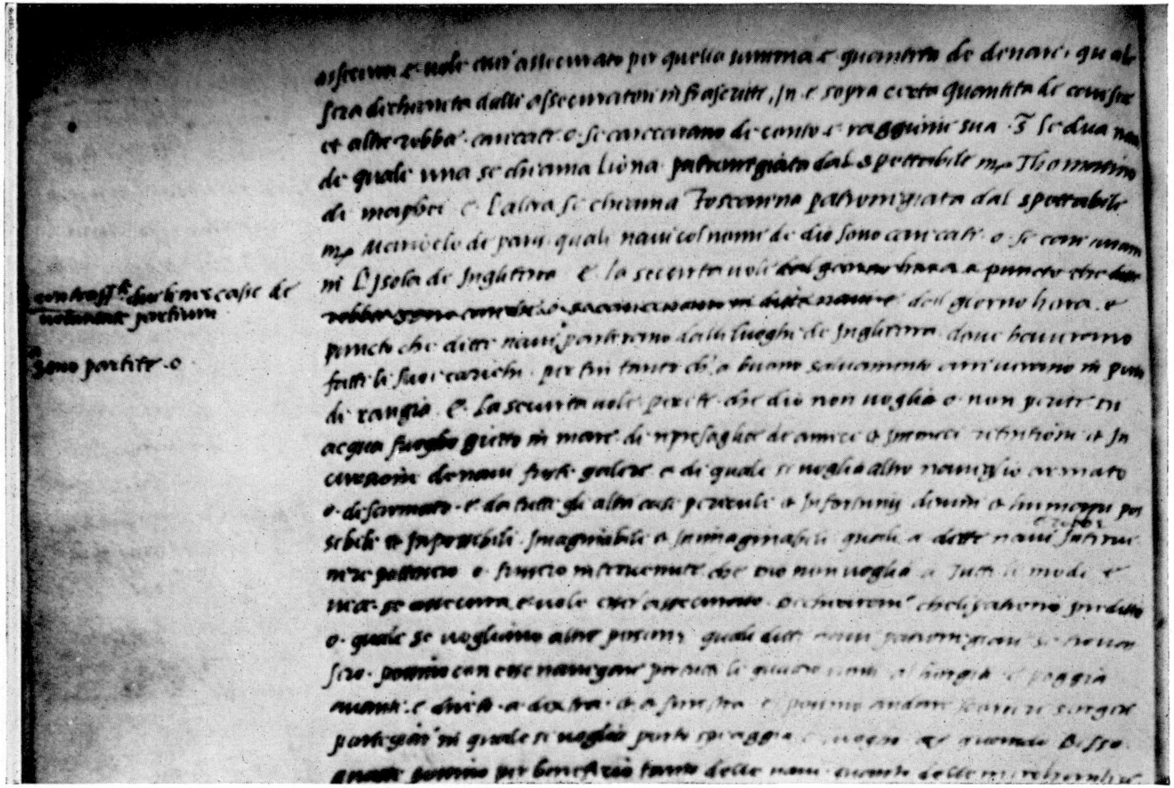

FIG. 76a. Legend on p. 376

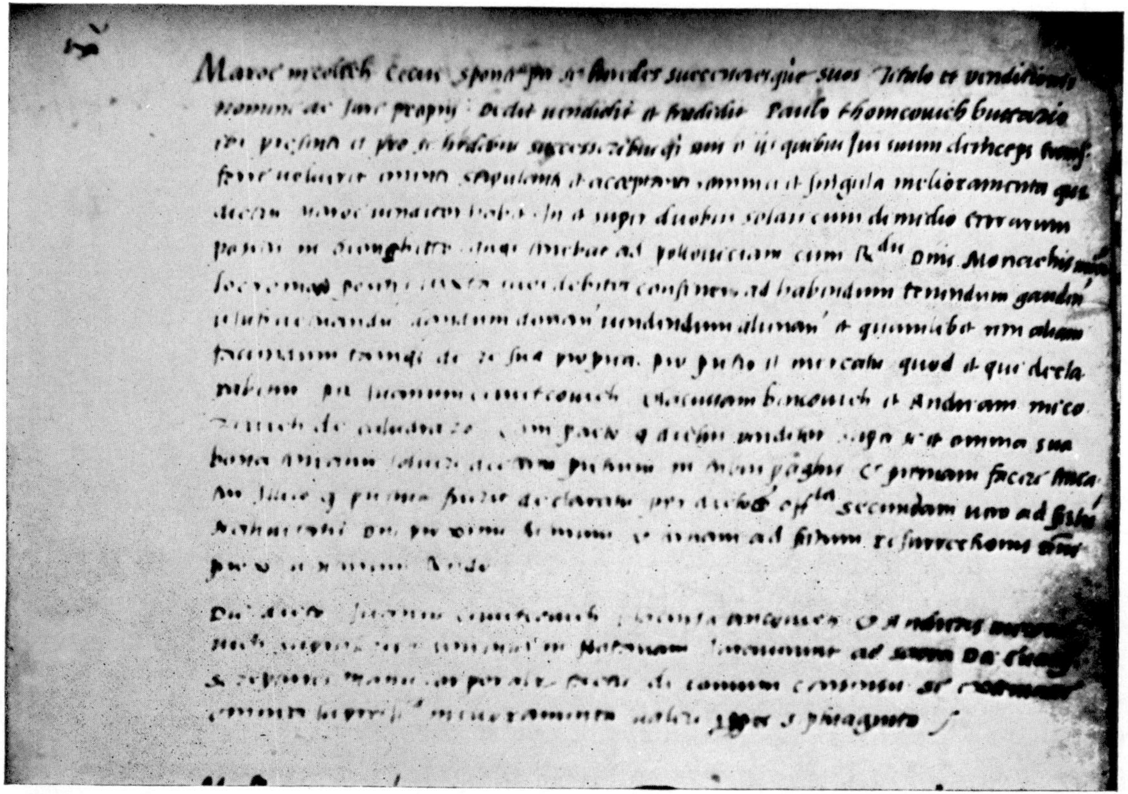

Fig. 76b. Parts of a document recording the purchase of fine textiles from London being imported into Dubrovnik. Dubrovnik Archives. (7/VII/1543). *Diversa Notaria*, 107, folders 172, 175.

the 'new' Dalmation harbours, although many Jewish traders remained in the town. Unfortunately they were not alone in Dalmatia, for an anonymous author at the time wrote

'Once the massacre was over the Turks spent much money, and thus after Novi (one of the new harbours) had been captured, plundered, and 4,000 Christians murdered, it became a source of great wealth. That is the reason why so many Jews from Spain settled on the Turkish shores of the Adriatic, especially at Novi'.[61]

Peacetime, in the second half of the sixteenth century was an extremely difficult period for Dubrovnik, particularly for textiles. During the first half of the sixteenth century, manufactured goods from western Europe, especially textiles, could always find a market in the Levant if not in the Balkans. The penetration of the new great powers, the English, Dutch and French, themselves important textile producers, after 1550 made competition for the Levantine

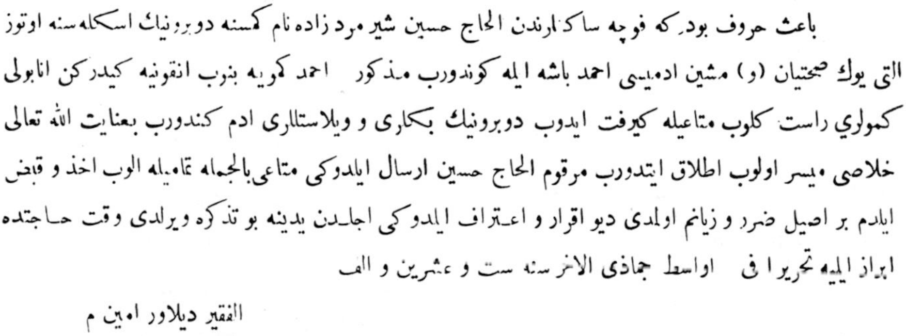

باعث حروف بودر که فوبه ساکارندن الحاج حسین شیر مرد زاده نام کمسنه دوبرونیك اسکله سنه اوتوز
التی یوك صحتیان (و) مشین ادمیسی احمد باشه اله کوندورب مذکور   احمد کوریه بنرب انقونیه کیدرکن انابولی
کمولری راست کلوب متاعیله کیوفت ایدوب دوبرونیك بکاری و ویلاستلاری ادم کندورب بعنایت الله تعالی
خلاصی ،میسر اولوب اطلاق ایتدورب مرقوم الحاج حسین ارسال ایلدوکی متاعی بالجمله تقامیله الوب اخذ و قبض
ایلدم بر اصیل ضرر و زیانم اولدی دیو اقرار و اعتراف ایلدوکی اجلدن یدینه بو تذکره ویرلدی وقت حاجتده
ابراز الیه تحریرا فی   اواسط جمادی الاخر سنه ست و عشرین و الف

الفقیر دیلاور امین م

FIG. 77.   Seven hundred loads of wax, 3,000 bales of ox skins, and 6,000 loads of wool sent from Bosnia via Dubrovnik to Ancona. Dragomanski Archive, Zadar (July 1647), Document (without a number), Book VI (Turkey).

market much keener. Dubrovnik and Venice were thus compelled to withdraw from the Mediterranean trade, and concentrate on the Balkan markets. This led to great rivalry, which was intensified when Venetian merchants began operating through Split's harbour in 1590, coming to a head in 1621 when the Venetian Senate forbad the export of goods by Dubrovnik merchants from Venice to Dubrovnik,[62] and so compelled the use of Split for goods bound for the Turkish lands.

This Venetian action affected Dubrovnik in two ways. Firstly, since the Venetian market had been the main source of western tex-

محمد بن ابراهيم خان مظفر دائما

اقضى قضاة المسلمين اولى ولاة الموحدين معدن الفضل و اليقين وارث علوم الانبياء (و) المرسلين حجّة
الحق على الخلاق اجمعين المختص بزيد عناية الملك المعين مولانا سراى قاضيسى زيدت فضائله و قدوة ارباب الاقبال
عمدة اصحاب الاجلال جامع وجوه الاموال عامل الخزاين بزيد عناية الملك البارى بوسنه
خزينه‌سى دفتردارى   دام علاوه توقيع رفيع همايون واصل اوليجق معاوم اولا كه و نديك بايلوسى اولان ·

قدوة امراء الملة المسيحيه   در سعادته عرضحال ايدوب اسپلت اسكله‌سنه كلان تجار قديمدن اوله
كلدوكى اوزره حين صلحده بوسنه خزينه‌سى دفتردارى طرفندن امين كلوپ اوتوردقده طرفندن تجارك كمرگى نه
مرتبه الندوغنى بوسنه خزينه سنده اولان دفتر خانه‌دن صورت دفتر اخراج اولنوب موجبنجه لازم كلان كمرگى بو
انه دكين   ويره كلمشكن حالیا امين اولنلر اول دفتر صورتنه مخالف ايپك يوكندن بيك بشيوز اتجه النوركن
اون التى ريال طلب ايدوب و ديبا يوكندن التمش غروش النوركن سكسان غروش ايله بر ربع طاب ايدرلر و
قاطيفه يوكندن اللى غروش النوركن يتش غروش طاب ايدرلر و قماش يوكندن اون دورت غروش النوركن يكرمى
غروش طلب ايدرلر و سايه چوقه يوكندن طقوز غروش النوركن اون اوچ غروش بر ربع طلب ايدرلر و اسكرلت
چوقه يوكندن بش غروش النوركن يدى بچق غروش طلب ايدرلر و بوندن ماعدا كمرك ايچون زياده غروش الميوب
يالدز التونى طلب ايروب تجاره زياده تعجيز و رنجيده ايدكندن اسكله اشلميوب ميريه و تجاره غدر ايدرلر ديو
بار روب صورت دفتر و عهدنامه؛ همايون موجبنجه عمل اولنوب خلاف قانون و دفتر زياده طلبيله رنجيده و رميد
ايتدرله‌لمك بابنده امر شريفم رجا ايلدوكى اجلدن خزينه؛ عامره‌مده محفوظ اولان باش محاسبه دفترلرينه نظر
اولندقده بوندن اقدم و نديك ايله اولان جنك و جدال دوستانه‌مه مبدل اولوب صلح و صلاح اولغله اردوى
همايونغنده و نديك جمهورينك المجيدى عرضحال صونوب اسپلت اسكله‌سى اجیاوب تجار طايفه‌سى كمركلرين قانون
قديم اوزره ادا ايلدكدن صكره خلاف شرع شريف و عهدنامه؛ همايون قديدينه مغاير اخزدن مداخله اولنامق
ايچون امر شريف رجا اتمكين جنكدن مقدم امين اولنلر زه محلده اوتوره كلمش ايسه يه اول محلده اوتوررۇوپ
كلان تجارك رسم كمركلرين قانون قديم اوزره ادا ايلدكدن صكره خلاف شرع شريف و مغاير عهدنامه؛ همايون
تجار طايفه سنه دخل و رنجيده اولنميه ديو سكسان تاريخنده امر شريف ويرلدوكى عرض اولندقده امدى عهدنامه؛
همايون موجبنجه و قانون اوزره عمل اولنمق فرمانم اولمشدر حكم شريفمله واردقده بو بابده صادر
اولان امرم اوزره عمل ايدوب دخى اسكله؛ مزبورهيه متاع كتورن تجار طايفه‌سى كتوردكارى متاعارينك ميريه
عايد اولان رسم كمركلرين عهدنامه؛ همايون و قانون قديم اوزره و دفتر موجبنجه ادا ايلدكدن صكره من بعد

FIG. 78. Brocade, silk, and Venetian (Scarlatini) cloth sent from Venice via Dubrovnik
to Bosnia. Dragomanski Archive, Zadar (2/III/1679), Document (without a number),
folder Cx.

tiles for Dubrovnik's traders, they now had to look elsewhere for sources of supply. Florence was the first alternative, but Florentian textiles were more expensive than those from Venice, and when these were not available Dubrovnik had to import cloth from London and Ancona.[63] This Venetian act gave opportunities for smuggling cloth from Venice to Dubrovnik, but even then prices were higher than before. Secondly, Turkish traders, especially those from Bosnia found sources other than Dubrovnik for buying Venetian goods, particularly the cheaper cloth, thereby making competition in the Balkan peninsula even sharper and contentious. The Venetian Senate also advised many of their Jewish citizens to leave Dubrovnik and for political and economic reasons many did leave the town between 1620 and 1630.[64] After 1630 Dubrovnik entered a period of decline and stagnation.[65] With the advent of the Candian War, Venice had to completely reverse her previous policy of attempting to isolate Dubrovnik and now channelled her goods, as did other west European ports, through the town. Textiles provided the bulk of the imports again attracting Jewish traders, especially from Venice to Dubrovnik.

The general pattern of places importing textiles from Dubrovnik shows Balkan sales were extended to include the whole of Bulgaria, whilst in the Levant only western Greece seems to have provided markets. In the Balkans, competition from the Bosnian home traders, resulted in Dubrovnik's merchants extending their cloth sales into Bulgaria. This proved a wise move for textiles were in great demand not only in the wealthier towns, but also in the villages. Much of the cloth came from Italy, especially Venice, Ancona and Florence, but material from Dubrovnik's own factories is rarely mentioned in documents. Her own textile industry appeared to have had a limited production, the town preferring to develop as a trading rather than industrial centre. Kersey cloth was most popular throughout Bulgaria, being first mentioned in Dubrovnik documents[66] as going there in 1547. Previous to this date the Venetians and Genoese had controlled the trade in this cloth, importing it into Bulgaria via Constantinople and Solun. After these merchants were expelled from these ports by the Turks, Dubrovnik's citizens took over their former role.

One of the main reasons for the success of this cloth was the direct dealing by Dubrovnik merchants with the Bulgarian peasants. Most of the villages were settled by Bulgarians, (compared with the towns which were largely inhabited by Turks, Jews, etc.) and cheap, rough, simple kersey cloth was within their means. Consequently when Dubrovnik merchants bought supplies of skins, wax and wool from the villages they often paid for them in kersey cloth on a barter basis. Kersey cloth also had large markets in the main towns. Resti imported large quantities of kersey cloth from Dubrovnik, sending supplies to all the principal markets like Plovdiv, Silistra[67] and Provadija. He also sent stuff on to Wallachia, (to such towns as Bucharest,[68] and Brăila), Constantinople and Rodosto. Besides kersey cloth, Dubrovnik's merchants imported other more expensive textiles into Bulgaria. These included Venetian and Anconian cloth, Florentian damask, and English stuff.[69] The most expensive cloths were silk and velvet, fetching between 300 and 350 ducats per topa (37 metres) and having very restricted markets due to their high prices. These cloths are only mentioned as being sold in the main administrative towns, like Sofia[70] and the Sultan's court in Constantinople.

Textiles were also exported to Persia for limited periods during the sixteenth century, for hostility to the Persians had formed one of the main themes of Turkish foreign policy. After the death of Selīm I in 1520, his successor Suleiman the Magnificent was too preoccupied with wars on the Danube and at Rhodes to worry about the Persians so there followed a period of appeasement and peace. Merchants immediately profited from this situation for in 1522 the first Persian traders appeared in Dubrovnik.[71] Prior to this date Selīm had forbidden Persians to brings goods across his lands.[72]

After this freedom two distinct trading periods were established between Dubrovnik and Persia according to documentary evidence. The first period lasted from 1522 to 1544. Up to 1535 commerce had remained uninterrupted but with the wars of expansion eastwards by Suleiman, trade with Persia was somewhat reduced because her merchants could not get through to Dubrovnik. After 1544,[73] Persians are not mentioned as visiting Dubrovnik until 1571, the beginning of the second trading era. This coincided with the town's neutrality during the Cyprus War when much of the Mediterranean trade was channelled through its port. Trade continued with Persia until the last decade of the sixteenth century[74] mainly by sea, for the Turks, wishing to monopolize their own land routes forbad Persian traders from crossing the Balkan peninsula.[75]

Much of the commerce with Persia was concerned with textiles. This was a two-way traffic for the Persians bought silks and camelots to sell in Dubrovnik in order to buy western textiles.[76] Other imports included carpets from Baghdad,[77] linen and cotton.[78] In the reverse direction Persian merchants returned from Dubrovnik with Italian textiles[79] and English kersey cloth,[80] whilst Dubrovnik's traders also visited Persia with cloths[81] but less frequently than their Persian counterparts visited the small republic.[82] In the Levant, competition from the English, French[83] and Dutch proved too much for Dubrovnik's traders, who now concentrated on the west Greek and Albanian markets, but here again they faced stiff competition. Venetian, Greek and Jewish traders, began sending their cloth direct from Italy, cutting out Dubrovnik's middleman role, so that towards the end of the sixteenth century it became a rare occasion for a Dubrovnik citizen to send a large shipload of textiles to Albania. Nevertheless, on occasions Albanian traders brought their goods (e.g. grain, wood and asphalt) to Dubrovnik and were repaid with textiles.[84]

Other Manufactured Goods

Other secondary products took a much smaller part in Dubrovnik's commerce. Ornaments and expensive luxury articles are occasionally mentioned, most of the ornaments coming from Venice and other Italian towns. Church adornments were sometimes noted as being transported to the Balkans, including silver crosses, cups, chalices, candlesticks,[85] gold and silver plates, iconstands and incense burners. Other expensive luxuries included precious stones,[86] pearls, rings, belts and decorated headscarves, but all of minor importance.

Commodity Prices

Price movements in the sixteenth and seventeenth centuries were influenced as in all centuries by many factors. In the first place, there were short-run oscillations, caused by plenty or famine, by news of the outbreak of, or end of, a war,[87] rumours and speculations. Secondly they were caused by alterations in the precious metal content or the official value of coins, whilst thirdly there was a long upward movement caused by the influx of treasure. As stated previously information gleaned from documentary evidence in Dubrovnik's archives should be regarded as mainly for the record rather than possible interpretations for a wider sphere.

The prices of skins in the Balkans cannot be calculated precisely

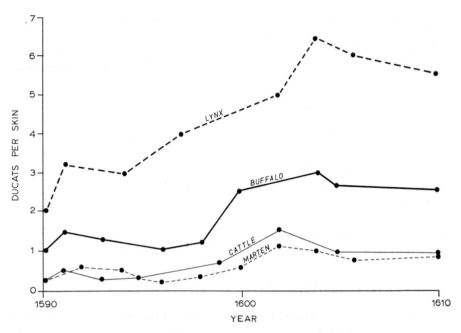

FIG. 79.   Skin prices paid by B. Resti in Sofia, 1590–1610. Source: Dubrovnik Archives, *Privata* (Resti) 1590–1605; *Diversa Cancellariae* 1605–1610.

for the whole period 1500–1700, but the preservation of Resti's trade books show price changes of skins, in Sofia, at the turn of the six-teenth century, and certain features can be noted. First, this period was one of inflationary tendencies, prices of all goods, not only skins, being closely linked with the fall in value of Turkish money at this time. This is particularly noticeable between 1602 and 1604 yet this was a peaceful period in Balkan history. Inflation had affected Italy as early as 1552–1560 when prices rose at an average of 5·2% per annum,[88] but it probably took longer to reach the more remote parts of Europe like Bulgaria. Second, buffalo skins usually fetched a higher price than cattle skins, probably due to their larger size and greater durability. Third, there was a large difference in the prices of wild animal skins from the rare and expensive lynx to the cheaper pelts of the marten. The profit gained by Dubrovnik mer-chants from the skin trade is difficult to assess due to lack of informa-tion, but one document dated 1596 does gives some indication into the sort of profit which was expected. In that year a relation of Benedikt Resti bought 1,200 ox and cow skins in Rodosto for 104,139

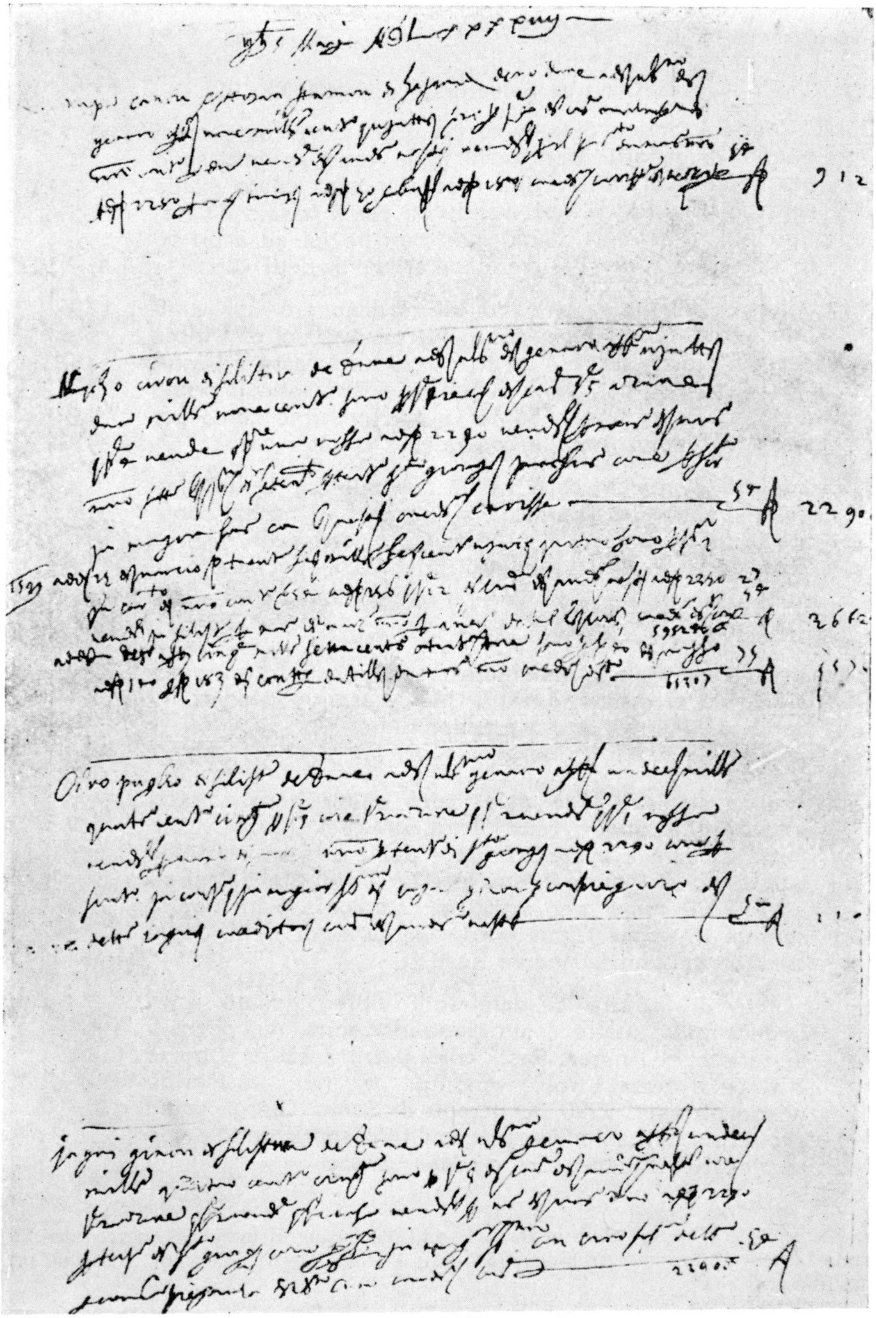

FIG. 80a. Legend on p. 384

Iesus Christus Salvator. Maria MDLXXXIIIJ —

Gusso Canov e Stojan Stamov di Hasgrad deve dare addi
ultimo di genaro aspri nove milla cento e vjntti sono
per pezze 4 di carisee dua rosa di nostro conto e dua
verde di Andrea di Resti vendutoli per il pasato da Marino nostro ad aspri 2250 per cori bovini ad aspri 50
e buffali ad aspri 180 creditor carisse di detti cori   54 as.   9120

Nicho Cirov di Silistria de dare addi ultimo di genaro aspri vintti
dua milla nove cento sono per pezze dieci di carisee
pezze 5 azure e pezze 4 verde e pezze una rossa ad aspri
2290 vendutoli per mano di Marino nostro sotto il primo
di setenbre per tempo Santo Giorgi prossimo come per
scrito in magior somma con questo creditor carisse   54 as. 22900

1595 addi 15 di marcio aspri trenta sei milla sei cento vjnti
quatro sono per pezze 1 in carnato di nostro conto
bracia 54 ad aspri 156 e pezze 12 di carise di Andrea
Resti ad aspri 2350 vendutoli in Silistra per mano di 27
Marino nostro per aver da lui li cori creditor detti carisse 54 as. 36624
                                                    ‾‾‾‾‾‾‾
                                                      59524

Addi detto aspri cinque milla sette cento otanta tre sono per
bracia 40 di rasso ad aspri 140 e aspri 183 di conto
datilli da Marino nostro creditor detto
                                         ‾‾‾‾‾‾   75 as.   5783
                                          65307

Ciro Pugliov di Silistria de dare addi ultimo genaro aspri
undeci milla quatro cento cinquanta per pezze 5 coie
pezze 2 azure e pezze 2 verde e pezze 1 rossa vendutoli
per mano di Marino nostro per tempo di Sto Giorgi ad
aspri 2290 come per scrito in conpagnia e in magior
somma di Jagni Ginov e con piegaria di detti Jagni
creditor carisse di Andrea Resti   54 as. 11450

Jagni Ginov di Silistria de dare addi ultimo genaro aspri
undeci milla quatro cento cinquanta sono per pezze 5
di carisse di Andrea Resti coie pezze 2 azure e pezze
2 verde e pezza 1 rossa vendutoli per, mano di Marino
nostro ad aspri 2290 per tempo di Santo Giorgi come
per scritto in magior somma con Ciro sopra detto e con
la piegaria di detto Ciro creditor carisse   54 as. 11450
                                         ‾‾‾‾‾‾
                                          22900

Fig. 80b.   Sale of kersey cloth in Bulgaria, and the buying of buffalo skins, recorded by
Andrea Resti. Dubrovnik Archives, (1594–95). *Privata* (Resti), folder 61. (Original (a)
and transcript (b).)

aspri (868 ducats). The skins had previously arrived from Provadija. These skins were then shipped via Dubrovnik to Ancona and sold for 149,820 aspri (1,248½ ducats). Therefore there was a difference of 380½ ducats between the buying price in Rodosto and selling price in Ancona, equalling 30% profit. But this was not pure profit. Compulsory insurance (ranging between 5%–9% of the cargoes' value from Rodosto to Dubrovnik and 2%–3% from Dubrovnik to Ancona) together with transport costs (2% of the cargoes' value) could have reduced the merchants pure profit to about 20% on the whole transaction.[89]

Wool prices in Sofia reached a peak in 1602 of 4·7 ducats per sack, a price not to be reached again until during the Candian War. Venetian textile factories used large amounts of Balkan wool, especially from Bulgaria, for this seemed particularly suited to the manufacture of Venetian cloth, and it may not be insignificant that the annual output of cloth in Venice soared from a paltry 2,000 pieces in the second decade of the sixteenth century to a peak of 28,729 pieces in 1602.[90] According to Resti's accounts, Venetian cloth fetched the highest price in 1601, of 140 ducats per topa. Political events also had an influence on the price of wool. The Candian War saw a doubling of wool prices, which reached a maximum in the 1660's. The end of the Candian War and the cessation of hostilities between Venice and Turkey saw a fall in wool prices only to rise again with the outbreak of the Austro–Turkish War of 1683–1699. Vinaver has made some analysis of wool prices in Serbia and Bulgaria for the second half of the seventeenth century.[91] He notes that about 1660 there was a distinct fall in wool prices in Italy due to a slump in the Italian economy, and its effect was felt in Balkan selling prices. In 1651 a kantar (56 kg) of fine wool in Sofia cost 5,5 talirs.[92] Table VI gives the average of a vreča (86 kg) of wool in Serbia and Bulgaria between 1656 and 1674, which reaches a peak in the early 1660's.

Table VI

Year	Price/Vreča	Year	Price/Vreča
1656	11,5 talirs	1663	12,5 talirs
1659	12,5 talirs	1664	11,0 talirs
1660	12,0–12,5 talirs	1667	11,0 talirs
1661	11,75 talirs	1673–74	7,0–7,5 talirs
1662	11,75 talirs		

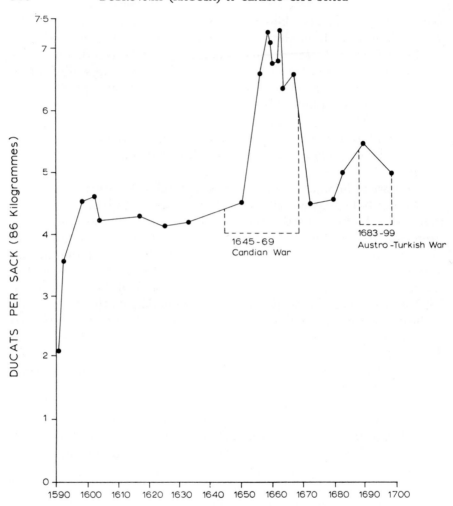

FIG. 81. Price of wool, paid by Dubrovnik merchants in Sofia, 1590–1700. Source: Dubrovnik Archives, (1590–1700). *Diversa Cancellariae*; *Debita Notaria*; *Privata* (Resti); *Testamenta, Diversa di Foris.*

Price information on salt is also forthcoming for there is extensive material on Dubrovnik's salt trade. Much correspondence exists on the selling price of salt in the Turkish hinterland often in relation to the standard weight measure. In 1482 the Turks conquered Herce-govina and three years later an agreement with Dubrovnik stated that salt was to be sold at 13 akçe a müzür[93] which was divided

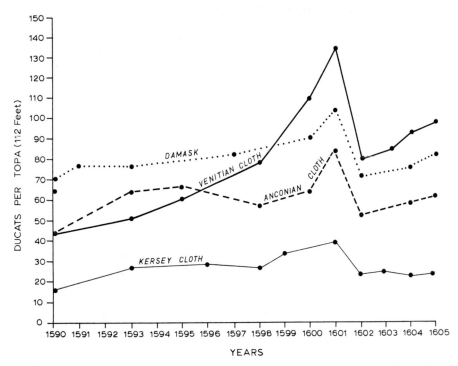

FIG. 82.   Cloth prices sold by B. Resti in Sofia, 1590–1605. Source: Dubrovnik Archives (1590–1605). *Privata* (Resti).

equally between Dubrovnik and the Turkish treasury. At Gabela (formerly Drijeva) it was sold for 12 akçe. In 1559 Dubrovnik traders, claiming the high cost of transportation, managed to amend the original agreement so that two-thirds of the price paid went to Dubrovnik and one-third into the Sultan's treasury. The price was raised to 15 akçe per müzür in 1574, Dubrovnik merchants undertaking to keep Gabela continually supplied with salt. By 1591 Dubrovnik's traders once again concentrated on raising the selling price of salt to offset the devaluation of the akçe; the outcome was seen in the increase of salt prices to 24 akçe in 1593.[94] Even this price proved to be insufficient for Dubrovnik's merchants believed it should be raised to at least 40 akçe[95] and by 1595 they had independently increased the price at Gabela to 36 akçe, whilst comparative prices for other ports (Novi, Risan, Makarska) showed that they had already risen to 40 akçe and over.[96]

Tertiary Activity: Shipping

After 1500 internal competition arose from the home traders. These people were Bosnian merchants who wished to exclude Dubrovnik's middlemen, and trade directly with markets in western Europe and the Levant.[97] In the sixteenth century their influence was mainly confined to west-central Bosnia but in the following century their trading network stretched eastwards into Serbia and northward beyond the Sava River into Hungary.

Coupled with this growth of Bosnian home traders was the development of the new ports.

In the second half of the sixteenth century Turkish traders were becoming increasingly dissatisfied with the lack of harbour facilities in Dubrovnik, the lower Neretva valley and Split for trade to Italy. They wished to find a trading point on the east Adriatic coast, by which goods from the whole of their Empire, especially Thrace, Serbia, Bosnia and Macedonia could go to Italy[98] and they could import commodities in the opposite direction. In 1590 a new harbour and quarantine house were built in Split to act as a link between the Balkan interior and Venice.[99] Split had certain advantages over Dubrovnik. First, the land route from Sarajevo and Banja Luka to Split was shorter than to Dubrovnik so that transport costs were much less. This greatly helped the Bosnian home traders who wished to export goods to the Italian markets. Second, danger from piracy, along the coast near Split was removed with the Venetian occupation of Omiš, the main pirate centre of mid-Dalmatia, in 1444, making it much safer to transport goods through Split. Third, Split harbour was much more spacious, cheaper and safer than that of Dubrovnik.[100] Fourth, a swift galley service from Split to Venice meant that goods were quickly transported to the Italian markets, and not allowed to stand long periods in Split's warehouses.[101] Split therefore set the precedent for the new harbours, followed in the seventeenth century by others along the east Adriatic coast. After the Austro-Turkish War, as Austria's ally, Venice gained considerable territory along the Adriatic coast and then began to build the new harbours of Gabela and Počitelj (circa 1700) to serve the Bosnian markets which together with Kastelnuovo, Omiš and Makarska resulted in the expansion of Sarajevo at the expense of Dubrovnik.

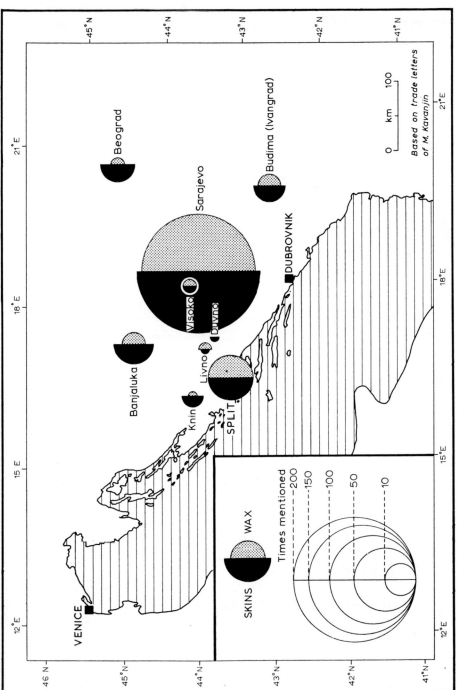

Fig. 83. Skins and wax imported by Venice through Split (1637–1659).

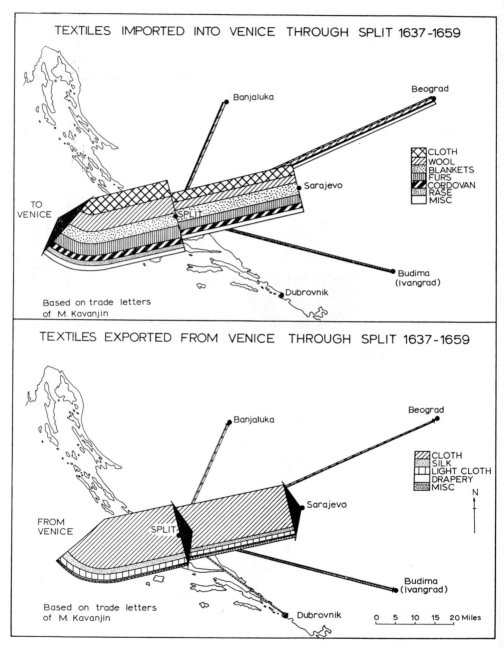

TEXTILES IMPORTED INTO VENICE THROUGH SPLIT 1637-1659

Banjaluka

Beograd

CLOTH
WOOL
BLANKETS
FURS
CORDOVAN
RASE
MISC

Sarajevo

TO
VENICE

SPLIT

Dubrovnik

Budima
(Ivangrad)

Based on trade letters
of M. Kavanjin

TEXTILES EXPORTED FROM VENICE THROUGH SPLIT 1637-1659

Banjaluka

Beograd

CLOTH
SILK
LIGHT CLOTH
DRAPERY
MISC

N

Sarajevo

FROM
VENICE

SPLIT

Budima
(Ivangrad)

Based on trade letters
of M. Kavanjin

Dubrovnik

0   5   10   15   20 Miles

FIG. 84.

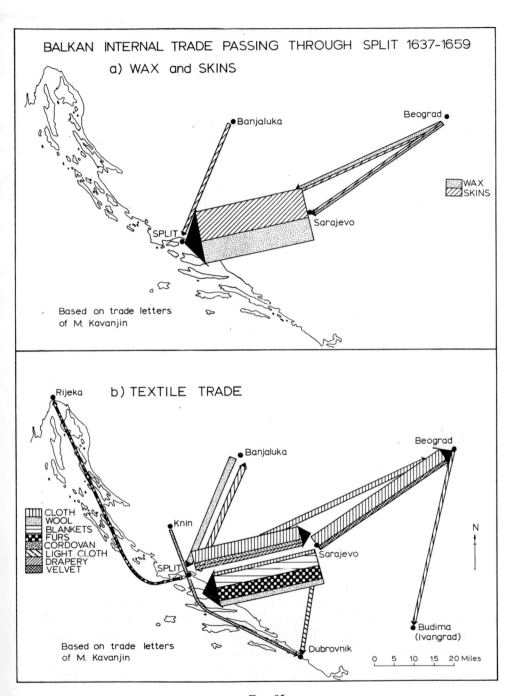

BALKAN INTERNAL TRADE PASSING THROUGH SPLIT 1637-1659

a) WAX and SKINS

Banjaluka

Beograd

WAX
SKINS

SPLIT

Sarajevo

Based on trade letters
of M. Kavanjin

b) TEXTILE TRADE

Rijeka

Banjaluka

Beograd

CLOTH
WOOL
BLANKETS
FURS
CORDOVAN
LIGHT CLOTH
DRAPERY
VELVET

Knin

SPLIT

Sarajevo

N

Budima
(Ivangrad)

Dubrovnik

Based on trade letters
of M. Kavanjin

0   5   10   15   20 Miles

FIG. 85.

Some of the disappointments which faced Dubrovnik were partially offset by the development of tertiary activities, in the form of providing ships and seamen for the service of other nations. Despite Dubrovnik's early importance as an outlet for Bosnia and Serbia, it did not, until the fifteenth century, build ships capable of carrying 100 tons of wheat. However, by 1530 the republic had built up her merchant fleet to 180 ships,[102] and was one of the most powerful navies of the time. Even by 1574 its fleet was still the largest in the Adriatic[103] and its merchants had contacts in all the important towns of the Mediterranean and contrary to trends in some other ports (e.g. Marseilles) the size of Dubrovnik shipping was increasing.[104] Trade was not only with the Adriatic ports of Italy but also to a wider sphere beyond. Dubrovnik's ships took wine, spices and raisins to London in return for cloth and metal goods, and sailed regularly to eastern Spain and the Levant. It is interesting to compare the English and Dubrovnik fleets at this time. As Davis states

'In 1560 England ranked low among the maritime states; her merchant fleet was by European standards an insignificant one. It stood far behind that of the Dutch . . . behind Venice or even *Ragusa* and Genoa'.[105]

By 1582 English merchant shipping totalled 76,000 tons, whilst that of Dubrovnik was about 40,000 tons. According to Mirković[106] Dubrovnik had the third largest fleet of big ocean-going vessels (above 300 tons) in the period between the Spanish conquest of Portugal (1580) and 1610 or 1618 (the naval expedition of Pedro Giron into the Adriatic Sea). Only Spain and the Netherlands maintained a larger fleet of big ships but Dubrovnik's ships were usually in the employment of some foreign state. They covered the waters between England and Flanders in the north, Alexandria, Tripolis, Ormuz and Goa in the east, and Brazil and the Caribbean in the west.

The great Spanish Empire of the sixteenth and seventeenth centuries offered a wide field of maritime activity to the more enterprising merchants of Dubrovnik, of which they were not slow to avail themselves. Dalmatian merchants in other towns were under Venetian rule, and therefore precluded to a great extent from these expeditions. Throughout the seventeenth century, therefore, Dubrovnik's ships, manned by her own personnel, accumulated large

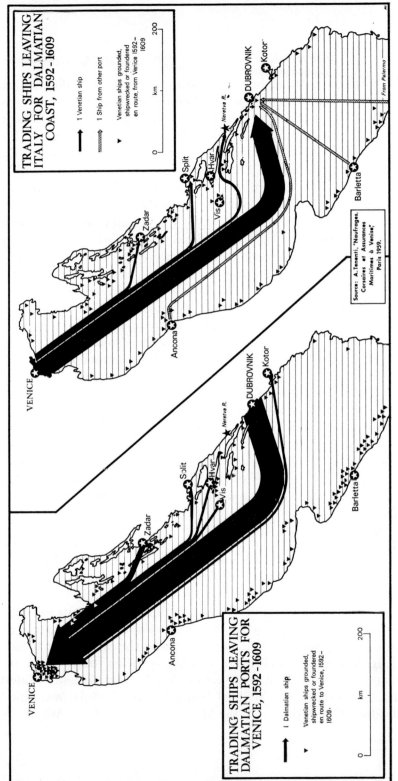

Fig. 86.

fortunes taking part not only in Spain's commercial traffic but also
in her naval expeditions. Much of Dubrovnik's carrying trade, particularly between states other than her own, was centred on Messina
in Sicily, then under Spanish rule. The station at Messina enabled
Dubrovnik's merchants to distribute goods brought from the East
without having to call at Dubrovnik first. From Messina, with its
nodal position in the Mediterranean, Dubrovnik boats were then in a
good position to supply much of southern Italy and the north
African coast, together with this station being an important base for
Dubrovnik's fleets serving the England route. Tadić has calculated
that Dubrovnik's merchants obtained a yearly income of 180 to
260,000 ducats from the hiring of boats and their services to other
countries, during the sixteenth century,[107] and the crews earned about
100,000 ducats annually.[108] Nevertheless, it must also be remembered
that the heavy lossess endured in the many unsuccessful enterprises
of Spain[109] were a severe drain on Dubrovnik's resources, and was one
of the contributory factors in the ruining of her commerce.

The naval activity of Dubrovnik reached its climax during the
sixteenth century despite the discovery of America and the resulting
consequences. One of the main causes of its decline was the presence
of the French, Dutch and English navies in the Mediterranean Sea
and the ensuing competition. This is seen from a letter from the Count
of Tuhelj, Admiral of Naples, to the Dubrovnik Senate dated March
4th, 1643. In it he mentions the fact that there had been at one time
from 70 to 80 large ships manned by 5,000 sailors under the Dubrovnik flag

'employed in traffic throughout the Adriatic and Mediterranean,
voyaging even as far as Lisbon, Flanders and England. These vessels were well armed with artillery and ammunition, and manned
by excellent officers and crew who were always ready to withstand
enemy action, which induced many European merchants to employ
them for the transport of goods. They were constantly in use and
made large profits, so that not only were the ships kept in good
repair, but new vessels were constantly being built. As a consequence of the recent truce concluded by His Catholic Majesty
with the Netherlands, Michael Waez, Count of Mola, was able to
introduce Dutch ships into the Mediterranean and the Adriatic for

the purposes of commerce, and these vessels, not being exposed to the attacks of the Turks, the Moors, the English and other enemies of Spain, were under no necessity to defend themselves. They were therefore able to sail small crews at small expense, and charge lower freights. The only remedy for this woeful decline is that His Catholic Majesty, in the interests of your most excellent Republic, should grant to all those who build large ships special exemptions and privileges throughout his kingdoms of Spain, Naples, Sicily and Sardinia, and that preference should be given to those designed for the transport of grain, salt, wool and other similar goods'.[110]

Little notice seems to have been taken of this advice for the seventeenth century was a period of increasing decline of the Dubrovnik merchant navy. By the middle of the century there were 114 ocean going ships flying the Dubrovnik flag. Between 1650 and 1667 (year of the earthquake) eighty of these ships had a loading capacity of about 7,000 carrs, and between 1667 and 1700 seventy-five of them with a capacity of 6,100 carrs, were paying taxes to the Senate.[111]

The main reason for the decline of Dubrovnik's merchant navy was the invasion of the Mediterranean by northern shipping. Towards the end of the sixteenth and in the seventeenth centuries the insecurity of overland routes, the growing efficiency of maritime trade notably as a result of Dutch shipbuilding and organization, and the advantages of an unbroken journey all tended to give a greater advantage to the all-sea route around the European peninsula. Unfortunately it was now northern European shipping, not the Mediterranean fleets, which were making the journey, with the net effect of making places, like Dubrovnik, the termini of sea-routes, not the vital and strategic transit points between long-distance land and sea routes that they had once been. The size of Dubrovnik's merchant fleet decreased,[112] yet in comparison,[113] English merchant shipping grew from 115,000 tons in 1629 to 340,000 tons by 1686, of which 39,000 tons was serving in the Mediterranean.[114]

Conclusion

Commercial relations during the period 1500–1700 saw Dubrovnik trying to adapt herself to the changing conditions of the time, and this was particularly discernible between 1500–1700. The Turkish occupation of the Balkan peninsula meant an end to her mineral exports together with increased competition from Bosnian traders and harbours causing a decline in her inland salt markets. Added to this the Portuguese in India and the Far East harassed the town's former prosperity from the spice trade. All this led to a gradual re-orientation of Dubrovnik's trading sphere with greater emphasis now being placed on cheaper raw materials from the central and eastern Balkans. Manufactured products were also affected, particularly textiles, for competition in the Levantian markets from the English, French and Dutch, meant a greater concentration on Balkan demands, even on occasions reaching as far as Persia.

Only during war-time could Dubrovnik benefit on a large scale from her trading connections. With all her competitors in either the Christian or Muslim camp, neutral Dubrovnik was the only avenue through which east-west trade could flow, but unfortunately for her, wars were either too infrequent or did not last over a long enough period.

The annual customs duty from imports gives some indication of their importance; the annual revenue gradually rose from 1500 to 1531 (– the peak year of textile imports), and is followed by a rapid decline until the short war of 1537–1540. It then remained steady at 20,000 ducats up to the Candian War (except for the Cyprus War of 1570–1573) with a rise in annual revenue from 20,000 to 500,000 ducats in the peak year of 1666, only to be followed by an equally rapid descent to 60,000 ducats four years later. The Austro-Turkish War, from 1683–1699, again saw a rise but to a much lesser extent than the previous war. This illustrates how a small commercial city-state like Dubrovnik could gain financially from a policy of neutrality during wartime periods but unfortunately the decline, both politically and militarily, of Venice, and the end of Turkish expansion in the Mediterranean, meant less opportunity for such a policy. A partial answer to her problems was found in the development of tertiary activities, in which Dubrovnik's fleet was employed in the carrying trade of other countries, particularly Spain. But the incursion of the English, French and Dutch into the ports of the Levant all contributed to Dubrovnik's problems, to which no permanent answer was found and after 1700 the town slowly moved towards her impending decline.

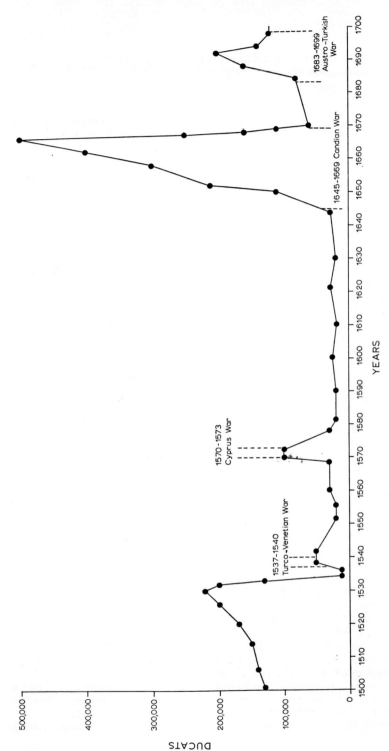

Fig. 87. Dubrovnik's annual revenue from import customs duty (1500–1700). Source: Dubrovnik Archives (1500–1700). *Diversa Cancellariae; Debita Notaria; Registro de debitori per titolo di guimruccho del' anno 1531–1534: Diversa di Foris; R. Samardžić, Borba Dubrovnika Protiv Mletačkih pokušaja da unište njegovu nezavisnost u XVII Veku: Dubrovačko Pomorstvo*, Dubrovnik (1952), p. 376.

9. Notes

1. N. Mirković, 'Ragusa and the Portuguese spice trade', *Slavonic and East European Review*, Vol. 21, American Series March (1943), p. 175.
2. N. Mirković, *op. cit.*, p. 175.
3. N. Mirković, *op. cit.*, pp. 174–187.
4. F. C. Lane, 'The Mediterranean spice trade', *American Historical Review*, Volume XLV No. 3, April (1940), pp. 581–590.
5. A. H. Lybyer, 'The Ottoman Turks and the routes of oriental trade', *Economic History Review*, Volume XXX, London (1915), pp. 577–588.
6. F. C. Lane, 'Venetian shipping' . . . *op. cit.*, p. 228.
7. N. Mirković, *op. cit.*, pp. 174–187.
8. L. S. Stavrianos, *The Balkans Since 1453*, New York (1963), p. 71.
9. Dubrovnik Archives, (21/II/1519). *Diversa Cancellariae*, 104, folders 1–1'.
10. F. C. Lane, 'The Mediterranean spice trade', *op. cit.*, p. 587.
11. *Ibid.*, p. 586.
12. *Ibid.*, p. 582.
13. Dubrovnik Archives, (21/VII/1572). *Diversa Cancellariae*, 157, folders 160–161';
    (16/V/1574). *Diversa Notaria*, 119, folder 84';
    (26/V/1574). *Diversa Notaria*, 119, folder 85;
    (February 1576). *Diversa Cancellariae*, 163, folder 40'. All mention spices being exported to Italy, which had come from the Levant.
14. Dubrovnik Archives, (28/IV/1583). *Lettere di Levante*. Salt imported by Dubrovnik from Sicily;
    ibid, (20/I/1580). Salt imported by Dubrovnik from Spain 'et altri luoghi lontanissimi'.
15. J. Tadić, 'Le port de Raguse et sa Flotte au XXIᵉ Sìecle', *Travaux du Second Colloque International d'Histoire Maritime*, Paris (1959), p. 25.
16. Zadar Archives, Document 18/a, Book III. *Dragomanski Archives*.
17. A. Handžić, 'Uvoz soli u Bosnu u XVI vijeku', *Prilozi za Orijentalnu Filologiju*, Vol. X–XI, Sarajevo (1960–61).
18. Dubrovnik Archives, (20/I/1580). *Lettere di Levante*. Mentions a complaint by Dubrovnik Government about the local Turkish 'emin' at Gabela permitting the sale of 'foreign' salt for he had made a deal with a certain Don Mattheo di Lesina for 30,000 moggio (1 moggio = 43,00 kg).
19. E. Nikolić, 'La contesa del sale fra Venezia e Ragusa 1645–1769', *Scintille*, Godina (1890), Broj. 6, Zadar., p. 10.
20. A. Vucetić, *Dubrovnik za Kandijskog rata*, Č. K. Velikoga Državnoga Gimnazija, Dubrovnik (1895), p. 42;
    Dubrovnik Archives, (1659). *Diversa di Foris*, 97, folders 79'–80. Twelve 'Kola' of salt (about 8,150 kg) sent from Dubrovnik to Prokuplje.
21. B. Hrabak, 'Dubrovački trgovci u Beogradu pod Turcima 1521–1551 g,' *Godišnjak grada Beograda*, Vol. 13, Belgrade (1966), pp. 29–47.
22. T. Lewicki, 'Osadnictwo słowiańskie i niewolnicy słowiańscy w krajach muzułmanskjch według średniowiecznych pisarzy arabskich', *Przegląd Historyczny*, Vol. XLIII, Warsaw (1952), fasc. 3/4, pp. 473–91;
    Ch. Verlinden *L'Esclavage dans l'Europe Médiévale*, Tome I, Bruges (1955), pp. 211–25.

23. Zadar Archives, (16/XII/1523). Document 34, Book IV, *Dragomanski Archives*;
S. Rizaj, 'Rudarstvoto vo Makedonija od XV do XVIII Vek', *Glasnik na Institutot za Nacionalna Istorija*, God. XIV, Broj 2–3, Skopje (1970), pp. 91–111.

24. Zadar Archives, (30/V/1538). Document 25/I, Book IV, *Dragomanski Archives*.

25. Dubrovnik Archives, (1499). *Diversa Notaria*, 78, folder 129. A Dubrovnik merchant sold his one-third right to a silver mine at Fojnica.

26. A. H. Lybyer, *op. cit.*, p. 582.

27. A. H. Lybyer, *op. cit.*, pp. 587–588.

28. M. Akdag, 'Osmanli Imperatorluğunum kuruluş ve inkişafi devrinde Türkiye' nin iktisadî vaziyeti', *Belleten*, Vol. 51, Constantinople (1949), p. 512.

29. V. Makušev, *op. cit.*, Tome I, p. 213.

30. K. Jireček, 'Stari putošestrija po Blgarijo ot 15–18 stoleča', *Istorija Blgarijo*, Kniga IV, Odessa (1878), p. 103.

31. V. Vinaver, 'Bosna i Dubrovnik 1595–1645', *Godišnjak Društva Istoričara Bosnei Hercegovine*, Godina XIII Sarajevo (1962), p. 222.

32. Dubrovnik Archives, (1630). *Diversa di Foris*, 50, folders 230–231. From Prokuplje to Dubrovnik, 276 buffalo skins, 170 cattle skins and about 240 sacks (20,880 kg) of wool.

33. P. Matković, 'Prilozi k trgovačko-političko historija republike Dubrovačke', *Rad. J.A.*, Kniga 136, Belgrade (1925), p. 51.

34. P. Earle, 'The commercial development of Ancona 1479–1551', *The Economic History Review*, Second Series, Vol. XXII, No. 1 April (1969), pp. 28–44.

35. Dr. I. Sakazov, *Stopanskite vrzki mezdu Dubrovnik i Blgarskit zemi prez 16 i 17 stolitija*, Sofia (1930), p. 138.

36. Dubrovnik Archives, (1934). *Diversa de Foris*, 51, folders 135–142. In 1634, during the month of August alone three ships left Dubrovnik for Ancona loaded with 3,400 cattle skins, 584 bundles (58–60 kg per bundle) of red and white goat skins, 80 ram skins, 70 of buffalo and twelve sheets of copper. In fairness this was probably a seasonal peak, for in November of that year only 10 bundles of goat skins are recorded as being sent to Ancona, (Dubrovnik Archives, (November 1634). *Procurae Cancellaria*, 39, folder 117′).

37. Dubrovnik Archives, (1699). *Lettere degli mercanti e ambassatori*, Facsimile 37, No. 1784. This is seen from a letter by the Dubrovnik ambassador in Constantinople Luksa Barka, dated 1699. He states that one trading house in Constantinople with considerable capital, bought skins and other raw materials from the region around the Black Sea and sent them in the first place to Venice, then Ancona and Dubrovnik.

38. In the commercial correspondence at Genoa Archives from 1560–1580 only two letters were found referring to trade with Bulgaria. One of these was connected with the purchase of skins. Genoa Archives, (8/V/1556). *Lettere detti agente Ferrari alla Ferari alta S^{mo} Rep^{ca} di G (enov) a Busta No. 2170, folder 3*, 'abiano nolegiatto sopra di essa quora sechi fonj 243 et XXI di bufalo et XII bulgorini'.

39. Pegolotti, an Italian traveller and writer in his section on trade in the lands of the Black and Mediterranean Seas, confirmed that wax exported from Bulgaria was the best in the whole Balkans. [L. Pegolotti, *Della Mercatura*,

Firenze (1766), p. 26.' . . . cera Zagore e la migliore cera che descenda in Romonia . . .'].

This quality is corroborated from earlier sources: Enrico Bensa, *Francesco di Marco da Prato. Notizie e documenti sulla mercatura italiana del. Sec. XIV*, Milano (1928), p. 406;

Genoa Archives, *Massoria, tome I a. 1340*, folders 23v°, 77v°, 127, 132. However, 1590 is the first time it is recorded in Dubrovnik documents. [Dubrovnik Archives, *Resti*, folder 8. 'Cera giala deve dare adi ultimo Decembre (1590) aspri 17,544 . . .'].

40. In 1625 the Dubrovnik ambassador in Constantinople complained about this to the Sultan [Dubrovnik Archives, (1625). *Lettere degli mercanti e ambassatori*, 44, No. 1818]. Further in 1676 the Turkish Beg (a Turkish governor of a town, province or district) of Vidin forbad merchants from Dubrovnik to transport wax, because it was to be used in Italian Christian churches. Dubrovnik Archives, (20/VI/1676). *Lettere degli mercanti e ambassatori*, 51, No. 1914.

41. Dimitrejević has estimated that 'there were ten thousand Italian churches dependant on Serbian wax supplies,' but one suspects this to be a little high seeing that he gives no statistical proof for his estimate, and his general approach is aimed at extolling the virtues of the Serbian economy. S. Dimitrejević, '*Dubrovački karavani u Južnoj Srbiji u XVII Veku*', S.A.N. Posebna Izdanja Kniga CCCIV Istoriski Institut Kniga 10, Belgrade (1958), p. 23.

42. I. Božić, *Dubrovnik i Turska aXVI i XV veku*, S.A.N. Belgrade (1952), pp. 303–304.

43. Vittorio Emannele Archives, Rome. *Fondo gesuitico* No. 402, folder 232 v°.

44. Dubrovnik Archives, (23/VII/1619). *Lettere e commissioni di Levante* 43, folders 168, 168'.

45. The Dubrovnik ambassador in Constantinople wrote in a letter dated 1625, to one of his merchants in Sofia—'you can freely transport wool, skins and wax from Bulgaria to our city'. Dubrovnik Archives, (1625). *Lettere degli mercanti e ambassatori*, 44, No. 1818.

A footnote to a document of 1646 states that Dubrovnik's merchants have the export of wool, like that of skins completely in their hands. Dubrovnik Archives, (August 1646). *Lettere degli mercanti e ambassatori*, 90, No. 2219.

46. A Dubrovnik colony at Prokuplje was first mentioned in 1631 [Dubrovnik Archives, (29/XI/1631). *Lettere di Levante*, 45, folder 234] and according to Dimitrejević [S. Dimitrejević, *Dubrovačka Trgovina u Leskovcu i Okolina*, Leskovac (1955), p. 11] a total of 493 documents refer to this town in Dubrovnik Archives, many of which are concerned with the wool trade.

47. According to the insurance books, they sent in 1626, 1,276 sacks (i.e. 110,000 kilogrammes) of wool to Italy, more than a fifth i.e. 21.5% of the total Dubrovnik exports in wool for that year. (Dubrovnik Archives, *Securtà di notaria*, Book 55; *Securtà i nolli cancellariae*, Books 54 and 56).

48. In 1627 these brothers sent from Prokuplje—one delivery in March, two in April, two in May, thirteen in June, five in July and two in August. Dubrovnik Archives, (1627). *Diversa di Foris*, 48, folders 76'–77.

49. This is seen from a comment by Des Hayes de Courmenin, ambassador in Serbia to the French King in the mid-seventeenth century. 'All the commerce

in this town (Prokuplje), as at Novi Pazar, is found to be in the hands of the Dubrovnik merchants, who buy here skins, wool and wax which they send to Italy.' Dr. N. Vulić, 'Antički Spomenici u Srbiji', *Spomenik*, S.A.N. No. 37, Belgrade (1905), pp. 95–99.

50. F. W. Carter, 'An analysis of the medieval Serbian oecumene: a theoretical approach.' *Geografiska Annaler*, Vol. 51, Series B, Stockholm (1969), No. 1, pp. 39–56.

51. Out of an average annual export of 600,000 kilogrammes of wool sent from Dubrovnik to Italy between 1620 and 1640. V. Vinaver, 'Trëgtoret ë Raguzës ne Kosove-Metohi', *Perporini* No. 3 (Priština) 1961, p. 150.

52. One document of 1612 illustrates this point. The largest batches of wool which Dubrovnik exported, rarely exceeded 100 sacks (8,600 kilogrammes), but in this year 119 sacks (10,234 kilogrammes) of Bulgarian wool were sent via Dubrovnik to Venice in only one load. Dubrovnik Archives, (1612). *Testamenta* 55, folder 82; I. Sakazov, *op. cit.*, p. 151.

53. M. Aymard, '*Venise, Raguse et le commerce du blé pendant la second moité du XVIᵉ siècle*', Paris (1966).

54. H. İnalcik, 'Osmanli Imperatorluğunun kuruluş ve inkişafi devrinde Türkiye' nin iktisadî vaziyeti üzerinde bir tetkik munasebetiyle', *Belleten*, Vol. XV, Constantinople (1951), pp. 629–690 (caused by a decrease of the acreage seeded with corn during that period).

55. V. Vinaver, 'Dubrovačko-albanski ekonomiski odnosi krajem XVI veka', *Anali Historiskog Instituta Jugoslovenske Akademije Znanosti i Umjetnosti u Dubrovniku*, Vol. I Dubrovnik (1952), svezak I, pp. 207–232.

56. These imports were divided as follows: 643 pieces from London; 297 pieces from Carcassone; 2,359 pieces from Venice; 21 pieces from Florence; 78 pieces from Verona; 16 pieces from Brescia; 19 pieces from Padova; 4 pieces from Perpignon; 870 pieces from Constantinople; 587 pieces from Drinoplje; 213 pieces from Rhodes; 26,404 pieces of cloth of varied origin, not specified; total 31,407. Dubrovnik Archives, *Registro de 'debitori per titolo di guimruccho del' anna 1531–1534*.

57. F. W. Carter, 'The trading organization of the Dubrovnik Republic' *Historická Geografie*, Vol. 3, Prague (1969), ČSAV, pp. 33–50.

58. 'boats had come from England laden with 9,000 pieces of cloth worth 85,000 ducats, besides tin and various kind of stuff valued at 13,000 ducats, all belonging to Dubrovnik citizens'. G. Valentinelli, *Exposizione dei Rapporti fra la Republica Veneta e gli Slavi Meridionali. Brani tratti dai Diarj di Marin Sanudo*, Vol. I, Venice (1863), p. 297.

59. The ship was laden with English cloth, and mistakenly thought to be English property. A Theinen, *Vetera Monumenta Slavorum Meridionalium historiam illustrantia*, Vol. I, Zagreb (1875), p. 805. Part of the cargo was recovered, but the loss amounted to 70,000 ducats, which caused a number of bankruptcies at Dubrovnik. (N. Ragnina, *op. cit.*, p. 42); also from the Dubrovnik import list of 1531, it is interesting to note that 2,359 pieces came from Venice. According to Sella, the number of cloths produced in Venice in 1531 totalled 4,537 pieces, of which presumably 52% were exported to Dubrovnik. (D. Sella, *op. cit.*)

60. J. Tadić, *Jevreji u Dubrovniku do polovine XVII stoljeća*, Sarajevo (1937), p. 137.
61. *Annuario Dalmatico*, Vol. I, Split (1884), p. 131.
62. Venetian State Archives, (30/IV/1621). *Deliberazioni*, (Senato Secreta) No. 111·
63. Venetian State Archives, (15/X/1626). *Deliberazioni*, (Senato Secreta) No. 128.
64. J. Tadić, *Jevreji . . . op. cit.*, p. 160.
65. The French traveller Recault noticed that Dubrovnik was very poor during the period prior to the Candian War but when the war began 'this town was a canal in which the manufactured products from Venice and the whole of Italy went to Turkey.' H. Recault, *Histoire de l'état de l'empire Ottoman*, Amsterdam (1670), p. 164.
66. Dubrovnik Archives, (1547). *Diversa Cancelloriae*, 132, folder 235.
67. Dubrovnik Archives, (1593). *Resti*, folder 54'.
68. Dubrovnik Archives, (1591). *Resti*, folder 41.
69. I. Sakazov, *Stopanskite vrzki . . . op. cit.*, p. 178.
70. Dubrovnik Archives, (1568). *Lettere e commissioni di Levante*, 35, folder 145; (1586). *ibid.*, 35, folder 158.
71. Dubrovnik Archives, (24/II/1522). *Consilium Rogatorum*, 36, folder 172.
72. H. Hausmer, *Deschichte des osmanischen Reiches*, Vol. III, Budapest (1828), p. 7.
73. Dubrovnik Archives, (28/VIII/1535). *Consilium Rogatorum*, 42, folder 211'. The Sultan wrote to Dubrovnik's government recording his successes in Persia.
74. Dubrovnik Archives, (1592). *Naula et Securitates*, 28, folders 63'–64. One Persian merchant mentioned amongst 13 Turkish traders who arrived in Dubrovnik with silk.
75. Istanbul Archives, (11/II/1572). *Basnekâlet arşivi Mühimme*, defteri 28, No. 27, p. 25.
76. Dubrovnik Archives, (1524). *Consilium Rogatorum*, 37, folder 69';
(1530). *ibid.*, 40, folder 94';
(1532). *ibid.*, 41, folders 34 and 161';
(1534). *ibid.*, 42, folders 101'–2;
(1543). *ibid.*, 46, folder 201';
(1574). *ibid.*, 62, folder 108;
(1572). *Diversa Cancellaria*, 158, folder 46;
(1571). *Naula et Securitas*, 38, folders 63'–4.
77. Dubrovnic Archives, (19/XII/1525). *Consilium Rogatorum*, 38, folder 69'.
78. Istanbul Archives, (1572). *Basnekâlet arşivi Mühimme*, defteri 12, p. 545 No. 1038.
79. Dubrovnik Archives, (February 1536). *Consilium Rogatorum*, 42, folder 258.
80. Dubrovnik Archives, (1525). *Consilium Rogatorum*, 38, folder 39';
(1528). *ibid.*, 39, folder 34;
(1530). *ibid.*, 40, folder 117;
(1533). *ibid.*, 41, folder 112.
81. Dubrovnik Archives, (1567). *Letterae Ponentes*, I, p. 67.
82. B. Hrabak, 'Trgovina Persijanaca preko Dubrovnika u XVI veku', *Zbornik Filozofskog Fakulteta*, Knj. V–I Belgrade (1960), pp. 257–267.
83. P. Masson, *Histoire du Commerce Français dans le Levant 17ᵉ siècle*, Paris (1911), pp. 356–365.

84. Dubrovnik Archives, (September 1582). *Diversa Notaria*, 122, folder 114′; (December 1586). *Diversa Cancellaria*, 174, folder 126.
85. Dubrovnik Archives, (1642). *Testamenta*, 63, folder 25.
86. Dubrovnik Archives, (1555). *Testamenta*, 41, folder 20′.
87. News of the expectation of peace between Venice and the Turks in 1540 pushed up the price in Antwerp of those cloths which were popular in the Ottoman Empire and at the same time lowered the price of spices because it assumed that Venice would soon be able to pick up supplies in Aleppo and Alexandria once more and compete with Lisbon. H. Heaton, *Economic History of Europe*, New York (1948), p. 250.
88. B. H. Slicher van Bath, *The Agrarian History of Western Europe (A.D. 500–1850)* (Arnold, ed.), London (1963), p. 196.
89. Dubrovnik Archives, (1596). *Resti*, folder 87.
90. Venetian Archives, *Inquisitorato alle Arti*, busta 45; *Senato Rettori*, filza 72, sub 4/1/1669; D. Sella, 'Les mouvements longs de l'industrie lainière a Venise aux XVI et XVII siècles', *Annales: Economies, Societes Civilisations*, Vol. XII, Paris (1957), No. 1, pp. 29–45.
91. V. Vinaver, 'Dubrovačka Trgovina u Srbiji i Bugarskoj krajem XVII veka (1660–1700)', *Istoriski Časopis*, Vol. XII–XIII, Belgrade (1963), p. 205.
92. Dubrovnik Archives, (1651). *Diversa di Foris*, 81, folder 206.
93. Derived from the Italian 'misura'; also referred to as 'moggio' and weighed 42 kg.
94. Dubrovnik Archives, (22/V/1593). *Lettere di Levante*, 38, folder 286.
95. Dubrovnik Archives, (26/III/1594). *Ibid.*
96. Dubrovnik Archives, (7/I/1595). *Ibid.*
97. Prior to the Turkish occupation, Dubrovnik had arranged with the Bosnian feudal lords that home traders who possessed such ideas were gaoled. Once the Turks had consolidated their power in Bosnia, many were freed by the Pashas and Sandjakbegs of Bosnia-Hercegovina who saw these traders as a possible means of winning their way to the Adriatic seaboard and a lever against Dubrovnik's grip on hinterland commerce.
98. Padua Biblioteca seminora *Citirani Documenti* (Senato Secreto) p. 365, edt. Solitro.
99. G. Novak, *Povijest Splita*, Vol. II, Split (1957), p. 40.
100. Venetian State Archives, (3/VI/1600). *Relatione di ne Leonardo Bollani ritornato di Conte et cop di Spalato presentata ne 'E. Cons. Relazione Collegio V Secreta* Fasc. 72.
101. Venetian State Archives, (23/IX/1602). *Relazione del N.H. Andrea Renier letta in Collo. Relazione Collegio V Secreta* Fasc. 72.
102. J. Tadić, 'O Pomorstvu Dubrovnika u XVI i XVII veku' *Dubrovačko Pomorstvo*, Dubrovnik (1952), p. 169.
103. E. Cléray, 'Le voyage de Pierre Lescalopier Parisien de Venise à Constantinople l'an 1574', *Revue d'Histoire diplomatique*, Paris (1921), p. 26.
104. Between 1570 and 1585 Dubrovnik had more than 180 boats with twice the tonnage of the average ship of that port of thirty years earlier. It had more than 36,000 tons, 5,500 crew members and was worth approximately 700,000 ducats. (*Enciklopedija Jugoslavije, op. cit.*, p. 140.)

105. R. Davis, *The Rise of the English Shipping Industry in the Seventeenth and Eighteenth Centuries*, Macmillan, London (1962), p. 2.
106. N. Mirković, *op. cit.*, p. 175.
107. J. Tadić, *op. cit.*, p. 172.
108. J. Luetić, 'Povijest Pomorstva Dubrovačke Republike', *Pomorski Zbornik*, Vol. II, Zagreb (1962), p. 1,710.
109. Over 10% of the armed vessels in the Spanish Armada were from Dubrovnik (33 out of 130). V. Novak, 'Učešće dubrovačke flote u španskoj Nepobedivoj armadi', *Zgodovinski Časopis, Kosov Zbornik*, Ljubljana (1953), p. 604.
110. G. Gelcich, *I Conti di Truhelj*, Dubrovnik (1889), p. 104.
111. J. Luetić, 'Nekoliko vijesti o dubrovačkim brodovima zadnjih decenija XVII st', *Dubrovačko Pomorstvo*, Dubrovnik (1952), pp. 196–204.
112. It totalled only about 120 boats by 1650, with an average carrying capacity of 100 tons. Thus the total carrying power was no more than 12,000 tons, in other words only a third of the second half of the sixteenth century, but even worse it did not carry a third of the former revenue. During the second half of the seventeenth century the number of boats fell below 100 with a total carrying capacity of about 8,000 tons. B. Kojić, 'Brodogradnja na Istočnom Jadranu Kroz Vijekove', *Pomorski Zbornik*, Vol. 1, Zagreb (1962), pp. 87–94.
113. T. Guiard Larrauri, *Historia del consulado y Casa de Contratacion de Bilbao y del comercio de la villa (1511–1880)*, 2 vols. Bilbao (1913–1914), Vol. I, p. 531, where a similar decline is recorded.
114. R. Davis, *op. cit.*, pp. 15–17.

10
The Decline of the Dubrovnik City-state

Owing to her position between east and west Europe, and her connections with Spain and Italy and with the Turks, Dubrovnik became subject to the general pattern of economic and political events which occurred during the eighteenth century. In that century the dramatic rise of east European powers, such as Russia (after 1709) and Prussia (after 1740), and the growing economic influence of the colonial powers, caused a radical change in the political and economic framework within which the Dubrovnik merchants had to operate.

The decline of the sea-state in Europe was due to two happenings which separated medieval from modern times. The overseas discoveries, by reducing to comparative insignificance the economic importance of inland seas destroyed the natural foundations of the states which surrounded their shores. This transformation was further marked by a legal controversy, for, in connection with the vast size of the outer oceans, there arose a new conception, the *mare liberum,* directly opposed to that of the *mare clausum.* The new seas were much too immense and too complex to be controlled by one power. 'Can the vast, the boundless sea be the appanage of one kingdom alone?'[1] asked the thinkers of the early seventeenth century, and the idea of the freedom of the seas they propounded with reference to the greater seas was extended to include the smaller basins. The new political theory still needed to be defended towards the end of the seventeenth century, but about that time it was formally enunciated by lawyers like Salmasius and Grotius. At present, by international agreement, political domain extends only to one marine league beyond the coastline, and this fact indicates the disappearance of the sea-state as a feature of the political map.

The second revolution occurred within the continent itself; communication by land greatly improved. The improvement was both a physical one which resulted from better roads, and also an economic one due to the abolition of tolls over larger areas. This in turn was partly the cause and partly the consequence of the consolidation of the Western nation-states around some inland centre. It is significant that it was not until the beginning of the modern period that a system of public posts was founded in Europe, when relays of horses, with the necessary officials, were established by various countries to ensure regular communication for official purposes. The hinterlands of the coasts were asserting themselves and the sea-state did not benefit by this change.[2]

The erosion of traditional lines of division between classes and the erection of new ones, the decay of some social groups and the rise of others, none the less proceeded more rapidly than the growth of factories and the modernization of agriculture. Even before the industrial revolution had got properly under way the growth of trade and towns had gone some distance, at least in the more advanced parts of Europe, towards replacing a society of communities, 'orders' and traditionally organized groups by a more modern social structure based mainly though by no means entirely on wealth.

Dubrovnik's Decline 1700-1750

Political Considerations

Always of importance were the events and attitudes of the Ottoman Empire. During the eighteenth century the Turkish Empire started, at first slowly and intermittently, eventually catastrophically, to decline. This decline had become unmistakable in the struggles of the Turks with Austria, Poland and Venice, which were ended by the Treaty of Karlovitz in 1699; it was already giving rise, at the beginning of the eighteenth century to projects for a partition of the decaying bulk of the Empire. The belief that Turkey was on the verge of collapse seemed justified by the unmistakable and fundamental defects from which she suffered.

Turkey's internal difficulties and military campaigns had indirect effects on the Dubrovnik republic. The small republic suffered economic eclipse in the years 1699 to 1740. With the conclusion of the Austro–Turkish War in 1699 Dubrovnik had hoped to regain some, at least, of her former trade, but this was not to materialize. As Austria's ally Venice had gained considerable territory along the Adriatic coast in the Karlovitz Peace. Now she too, like Turkey opened up 'new' harbours to serve the Bosnian markets with the result that Sarajevo expanded at the expense of Dubrovnik. In 1714 war between Venice and the Turks broke out once more, the Sultan desiring above all to reconquer the Morea; he succeeded in his purpose very quickly, for the Venetians, relying on the peace of Karlovitz, which was to last for twenty-five years (the Turks never concluded treaties of perpetual peace), had made no adequate pre-parations for defence. The Venetians allied themselves with the Austrian Emperor and an army entered southern Hungary. The Turks were defeated ending with the capture, by the Imperialists, of Bel-grade. In 1718 the representatives of the various powers met at Passarovitz (Požarovac) in Serbia and by the peace treaty the Em-peror retained all his conquests, but the capture of the Morea by the Turks was confirmed, the Venetians having lost their last possessions in the Levant save for the Ionian Islands, now intensified their trading and political interests within the Adriatic Sea. On the other hand some of the arrangements of the Karlovitz peace were reconfirmed; for example Venice gave up the posts of Popovo, Zarina and Subzi on the Dubrovnik border.

The composition and policies of the Turkish government were extremely unstable, above all in the early decades of the century. The chief minister of state (Grand Vizier) was liable to lose his position and even his life as the result of some temporary setback in war or diplomacy or some whim of the Sultan. Even the Sultan himself was not safe from deposition, for Mustapha II was removed in this way in 1703 and Ahmad III in 1730. Moreover the Empire lacked any real administrative unity or military efficiency. The emer-gence of powerful and virtually independent war lords who were sometimes able to transmit their power to descendants seemed both to illustrate and to intensify the incompetence of its rulers. The development of its economic life was impeded by a number of factors; misgovernment, religious conservatism and not least the devastating epidemics from which the area continued to suffer. Intellectual life was backward in the extreme, but above all the definiteness of the distinction between Muslim rulers and Christian ruled, a distinction which was often strengthened by differences of language, increasingly

FIG. 88. Firmān of Sultan Ahmed III, dated 1707, which allowed Dubrovnik to pay her tribute every three years.

undermined the foundations of the European parts of the Empire as time went on.

The fate of the Balkan peoples under Ottoman rule varied very considerably : in a few areas, notably in Bosnia and much of Albania. the population had been converted *en masse* to Islam. The position of the peasantry was deteriorating in many areas as the 'timar' system of land tenure (under which the peasant had enjoyed some security and fiefs had not been hereditary) gave way to the 'chiflik' system (under which fiefs were hereditary and the peasants virtually serfs).[3] At the same time the slow growth of trade tended to produce, especially in some seaports such as Salonika, a commercial middle class which was anti-Turkish in outlook. All these factors were either directly or indirectly affecting Dubrovnik's commercial prosperity. The small republic suffered economic eclipse in the years 1699 to 1740 resulting from Turkey's internal difficulties and military campaigns. With the conclusion of the Austro-Turkish War in 1699 Dubrovnik had hoped to regain some, at least, of her former trade. The Turkish authorities allowed the development of new ports along the Adriatic coast, under their control, such as Novi (present-day Hercegnovi), Budva, Bar and Ulcinj. As a result Sarajevo expanded at the expense of Dubrovnik. Further the tribute to the Sultan was now 12,500 ducats a year, and with gifts and bribes amounted to 16,000; Dubrovnik's government also paid blackmail to the Barbary States and a tribute at irregular intervals to Austria. Every year a present was sent to the Pope, and twelve 'astori' (falcons) to the King of Naples.[4] Even so despite this dismal situation there were signs that at least some political events were advantageous for Dubrovnik. Trade, which had been apparently in a hopeless condition, began to show signs of improving. In 1727 Dubrovnik's ships once more extended their voyages beyond the limits of the Adriatic; in that year a vessel went to Smyrna for the first time for many years. The wars between England, France and Spain in 1739–1750 and in 1756–1763 (the Seven Years War), proved advantageous to Dubrovnik shipping, and much of the commerce of the Mediterranean once more passed into their hands as neutrals.

Dubrovnik's Land Trade

In the western Balkans. During the first half of the eighteenth century Dubrovnik's hinterland commerce was in a very depressed condition. In 1712 the Dubrovnik Ambassador wrote to the Bosnian Vizier:

> 'Today, in the Turkish Empire, we have fewer traders than we used to have colonies ... In a year as many goods arrive in Dubrovnik as used to be sent in a month'.[5]

Dubrovnik therefore waged a continual diplomatic struggle between 1699 and 1740 to get the new harbours closed, but increasing Turkish apathy in the affairs of Dubrovnik led to little success. The effects of these new harbours were keenly felt in the salt trade. Dubrovnik still had one pan at Ston, but merchants from Bosnia no longer arrived with orders. The Venetians undercut Dubrovnik's salt prices gradually eliminating her share of the Bosnian market. In 1726 the Dubrovnik government wrote to the Turkish Pasha in Bosnia complaining about the decline of Dubrovnik's salt trade and the need for the town's merchants to stifle new competitors in Novi Pazar.[6]

Another problem, which faced Dubrovnik at this time was increased taxes on goods. The Turks, in order to promote their own Bosnian traders and at the same time gain revenue to finance their intermittent wars with Austria, put heavy taxes on all goods going through Dubrovnik. In August 1721 the Dubrovnik ambassador stated in a letter to the Bosnian Pasha

> 'the heavy taxes you place on foreign traders who come to our harbour have caused them to desert us. Now they are going to Split, Novi, Risan and Makarska, where no Turkish customs have to be paid'.[7]

Throughout the twenties, the decline continued, so that by 1730 the Dubrovnik government was writing 'that now trade was very badly developed on all sides'.[8] This was even further accentuated in 1731 when the Turkish government opened up Nikšič (formerly Onogošt) as a collecting centre for livestock products, which were sent to Kotor in exchange for salt. Final humiliation for Dubrovnik, came during the Austro-Turkish War in 1736–39 which involved Bosnia, for Austrian troops invaded part of her territory. This seemed an excellent opportunity for goods to be channelled once more through neutral Dubrovnik, but French boats blockaded her port on the pretence of Dubrovnik's sympathies with Austria, and goods from the inland Balkans were taken to Novi. It should be remembered that eighteenth-century France inherited a well-established tradition of political interest and activity in the Near East tracing back from

FIG. 89. Oil painting of Dubrovnik in 1736. (In Dubrovnik museum).

Francis I (1515–1547). Her activity was inspired in this period as in the past above all by her desire to use the Turks as a weapon against Austria and thus divert the attention and resources of the Hapsburgs away from the politics of western Europe to a struggle against the Ottomans in the Balkans. Consequently, Dubrovnik, whilst only a pawn in the political game, suffered commercially from the French intrusion[9] and thus the new harbour of Novi profited at the expense of the small republic.

In the eastern Balkans.   In the eastern Balkans Dubrovnik's merchants also saw their commerce declining. By the beginning of the eighteenth century the period of her intensive trade in Bulgaria and Serbia was over. Two main reasons may be forwarded to explain this situation. Firstly, there was increasing competition from foreign traders who managed to infiltrate into the Balkan markets. From the landward side Austrian traders came down the Danube and through Serbia into markets which were formerly Dubrovnik's monopoly. Added to these were the Cincars (Arumuni), a small group of people who came to Serbia in the seventeenth and eighteenth centuries and achieved commercial predominence for

> 'practically the entire wholesale and retail trade of the Near East and central Europe was in their hands'.[10]

They used every method from the most primitive barter exchange to the most complex monetary and financial affairs. In certain kinds of business they were unrivalled and often they were able to monopolize certain commodities like textiles and wax trading in Hungary, Transylvania, Rumania, Bukovina and the Turkish Empire with ever-increasing profits.[11] Also by sea, west European traders, especially the French were beginning to enter Balkan commerce through Solun (as the Black Sea was still closed to western merchants). This intrusion of western traders again has its roots in the attitudes of the Turks. The contempt which most Turks felt for commerce, their ignorance and mental inflexibility and the essentially military character they had given their empire made it impossible for them to play any real part in foreign trade. The result was that west Europeans came to the Ottoman Empire, above all Frenchmen, through their close political contacts with Turkey, and that in many Turkish ports small but very important colonies of western merchants were to be found. For example after 1700 few merchants from Dubrovnik entered Bulgaria

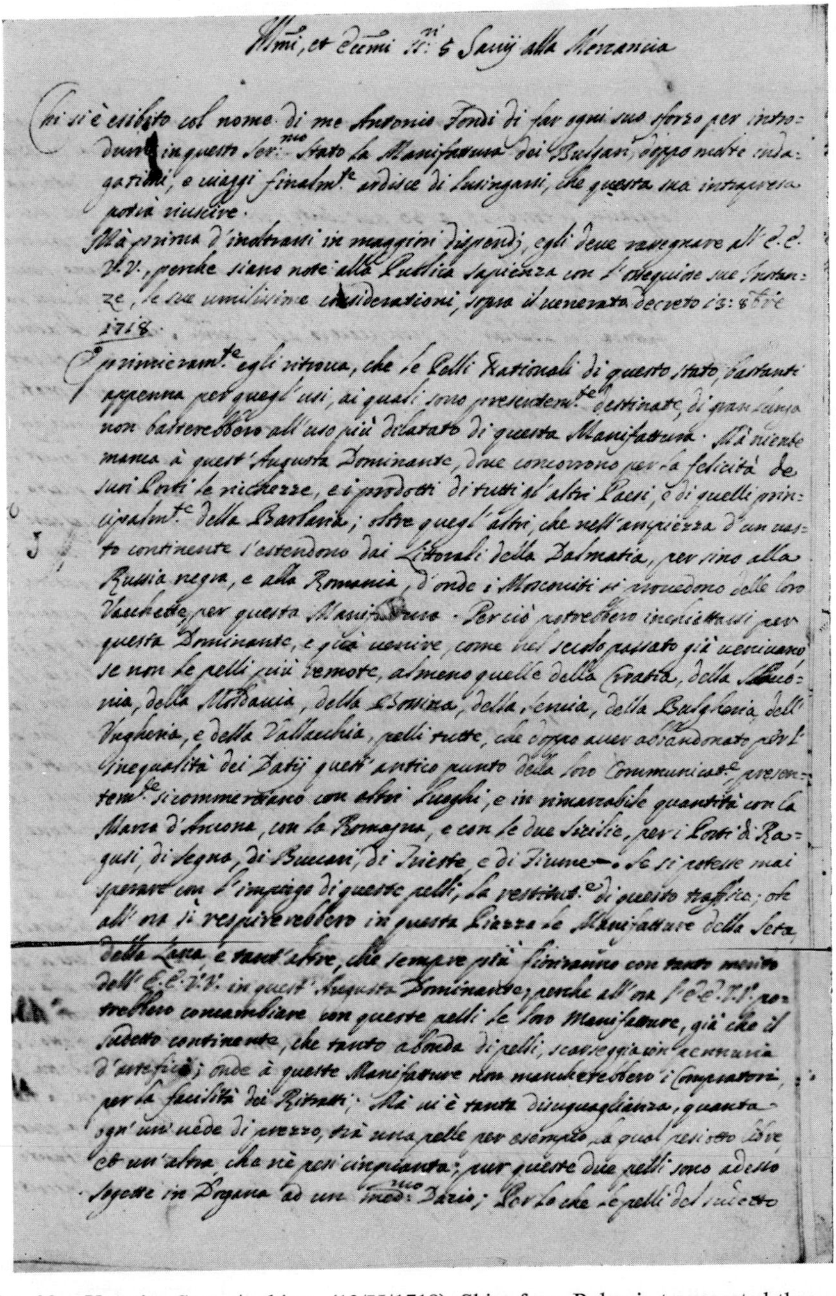

Ill.mi, et Ecc.mi S.ri 5 Savij alla Mercanzia

Chi si è esibito col nome di me Antonio Fondi di far ogni suo sforzo per intro=durre in questo Ser.mo Stato la Manifattura dei Bulgari, doppo molte inda=gationi, e viaggi finalm.te ardisce di lusingarsi, che questa sua intrapresa potrà riuscire.

Mà prima d'inoltrarsi in maggiori dispendi, egli deve rassegnare all'E.E. V.V., perche siano note alla Publica Sapienza con l'ossequiose sue Instan=ze, le sue umilissime considerationi, sopra il venerato decreto 13: 8bre 1718.

Primieramente egli ritroua, che le Pelli Nationali di questo stato, bastanti appena per quegl'usi, ai quali sono presentem.te destinate, di gran lunga non basterebbero all'uso più dilatato di questa Manifattura. Mà niente manca à quest'Augusta Dominante, dove concorrono per la felicità de suoi Porti le ricchezze, e i prodotti di tutti gl'altri Paesi, e di quelli prin=cipalm.te della Barbaria; oltre quegl'altri, che nell'ampiezza d'un vas=to continente s'estendono dai Litorali della Dalmatia, per sino alla Russia negra, e alla Romania, d'onde i Moscoviti si provedono delle loro Vacchette per questa Manifattura. Perciò potrebbero incamminarsi per questa Dominante, e già venire, come nel secolo passato già venivano se non le pelli più remote, almeno quelle della Croatia, della Schiavo=nia, della Moldavia, della Bossina, della Servia, della Bulgheria, dell'Vngheria, e della Vallacchia, pelli tutte, che doppo aver abbandonato per l'inegualità dei Datij quest'antico punto della loro Communicat.e presen=tem.te si commerciano con altri Luoghi; e in rimarcabile quantità con la Marca d'Ancona, con la Romagna, e con le due Sicilie, per i Porti di Ra=gusi, di Segna, di Buccari, di Triette, e di Fiume. Se si potesse mai sperare con l'impiego di queste pelli, la restitut.e di questo traffico; ora all'ora si respirerebbero in questa Piazza le Manifatture della Seta, della Lana, e tant'altre, che sempre più fioriranno con tanto merito dell'E.E. V.V. in quest'Augusta Dominante, perche all'ora V.V. po=trebbero concambiare con queste pelli le loro Manifatture, già che il sudetto continente, che tanto abonda di pelli, scarseggia in general d'artefici; onde à queste Manifatture non mancherebbero i Compratori, per la facilità dei Ritratti. Mà vi è tanta disuguaglianza, quanta ogn'un vede di prezzo, tra una pelle per esempio da quel prezzo lire et un'altra che ne val cinquanta; pur queste due pelli sono adesso soggette in Dogana ad un med.mo Dario; Porto che le pelli del sudetto

FIG. 90. Venetian State Archives, (13/X/1718). Skins from Bulgaria transported through Dubrovnik for Venice. *Cinque Savi alla Mercanzia* (*Serie Diversorum*) B.355, N.3391: carte 'autentiche' relative all 'introduzione nello Stato veneto della manifattura dei cuoi bulgari, con documentazione retrospettiva sul commercio dei medesimi anche con la Bulgharia ed anche via Ragusa (= Dubrovnik) (9.III.1720).

with Italian cloths, yet German agents in Dubrovnik were exporting Venetian cloth and other German goods through the town for Belgrade, Sofia and Constantinople.[12]

Secondly the devastation brought about by the Austro-Turkish War (1683–1699) disrupted commercial relations in Bulgaria and Serbia, coupled with the general decline of the Ottoman Empire. Attacks on Turkish garrison towns like Sofia and Plovdiv ruined trade with a consequent decrease in the number of Dubrovnik's traders in these towns. A Dubrovnik trader writing from Sofia in 1704, states that none of her merchants were in the town in 1700, nor in 1703. He describes how the churches had been plundered and all the houses in the neighbourhood of the town were in ruins.[13] In 1705 Dubrovnik's government was worried over the losses in her Sofian colony, where shops had been abandoned by her traders and constant distress was suffered by those few who had remained.[14]

With the restoration of peace in the Balkans with the Treaty of Passarovitz 1718 Dubrovnik's merchants reappeared in the main trading towns, but in nothing like their previous strength as Table VII illustrates:[15]

Table VII

Place	1670–1680	1680–1690	1720–1730	1730–1750
	Dubrovnik Merchants			
Sofia	36	12	6	6
Plovdiv	24	—	8	10
Prokuplje	42	10	7	9
Total	102	22	21	25

An analysis of the figures shows that by the mid-eighteenth century there were only a quarter as many Dubrovnik merchants in these three important trading centres as there had been for the decade 1670–1680, whilst even during the warring period of 1680–1690, there were more traders on average than the decade 1720–1730.

The Danubian colonies of Ruščuk and Vidin[16] appeared to be more important for Dubrovnik during the first half of the eighteenth century having 35 of her traders in each place between 1727 and 1755.

FIG. 91. Dubrovnik Merchant—from an eighteenth century engraving.

Registered Voyages of Dubrovnik Boats 1701-1763

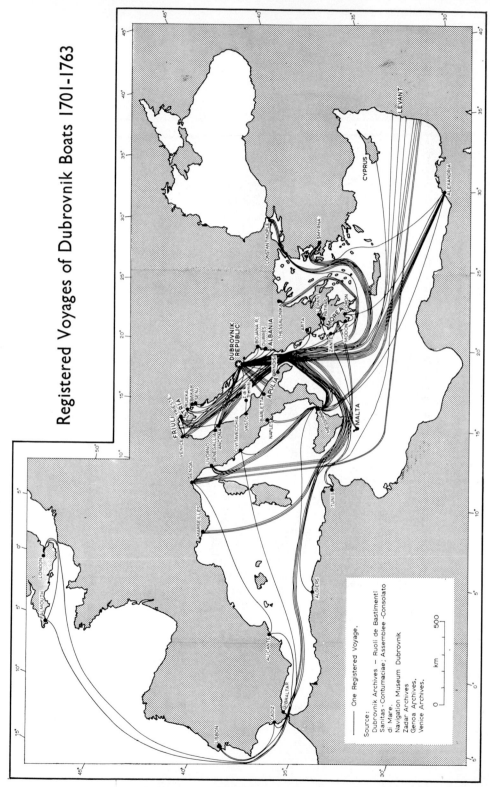

FIG. 92.

Even so, one comment from this period noted that 'the main part of the goods which our (Dubrovnik) traders work with are only wax, wool and skins'.[17] The main commodity of interest to Dubrovnik in the first half of the eighteenth century was wax. Much of the wax was collected in Wallachia and Moldavia, which according to the Dubrovnik Consul in Constantinople were the only places in the whole of the Balkans where Dubrovnik traders remained in any strength.[18] This shows that her merchants were now having to go greater distances and to regions which they had previously ignored as being uneconomical. Wax collected from Wallachia was sent to warehouses in Ruščuk and Vidin to be later transported to Dubrovnik. The Turks, in need of finance at this time, placed extortionate taxes on wax exports which considerably reduced the profit margin for Dubrovnik merchants.

Changes in Maritime Trade

Decline of Venice. In the Mediterranean, Venice formerly so important in the commercial life of Europe, was now sinking into irreparable decay.[19] Nevertheless, the city was still a trading centre of some significance. In 1703 it was claimed that it earned 10 million ducats a year through its activity in marine insurance, whilst in 1759 nearly 1,800 ships touched there.[20] However its own merchant marine was small and declining; and its growth was hampered by the rapidly-growing competition of Trieste and Ancona and by the hostility which existed for much of the century between Venice and the Barbary States of North Africa. Leghorn, in the Grand Duchy of Tuscany, was by contrast one of the greatest commercial centres of Europe during this period. The city was a free port with admirable quarantine arrangements, and considerable colonies of Greeks, Jews and Armenians who played so large a part in the commercial life of the eastern and even western Mediterranean. The Tuscan merchant marine nevertheless was completely negligible and Leghorn depended for its importance entirely on the British, French, Dutch and Genoese ships which called there. The kingdom of Naples, the largest of the Italian states was also of minor importance in the trade of Europe. The salt, grain and other commodities she exported, the manufactured goods she imported, were carried in French, British, Genoese and other foreign ships not her own. T. G. Jackson noticed that

Q

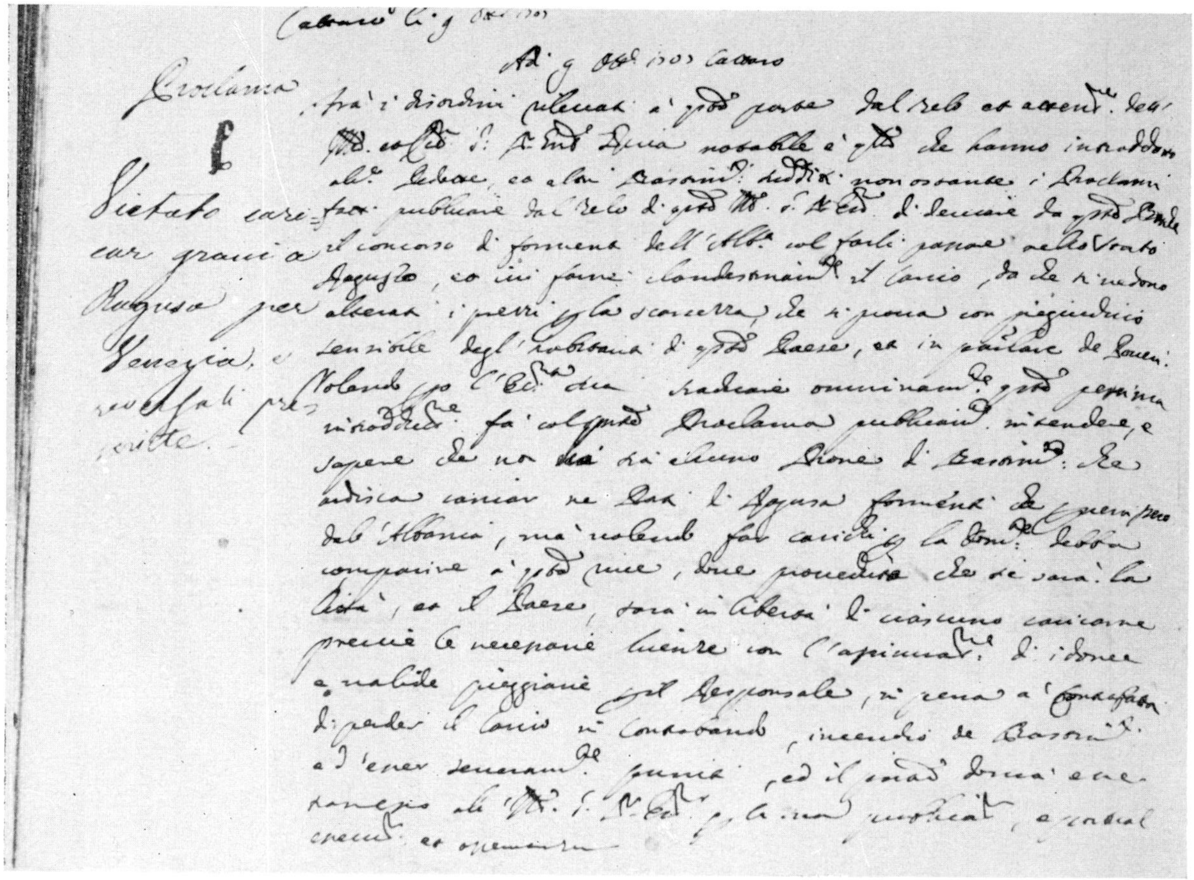
Cattaro li 9 Ott. 1707

Adì 9 Ott. 1707 Cattaro

Proclama

Vietato caricar grani a Ragusa per Venezia, e revensali prescritte.

FIG. 93. Document relating to a ban on the loading of Albanian grain bound for Venice at Dubrovnik under pain of destruction of the cargo and of the ships together with severe punishment for those involved. Dated 9/X/1707, Zadar Archives (Archivo Antico Luogotenenzale di Zara) Guistan da Riva (1705–08) Libro 11 Carte 161 (Vietato caricar grani a Ragusa per Venezia, e revensali presscritte).

'as the commercial greatness of Venice declined towards the end of her career, the prosperity of her dependencies naturally passed away at the same time. Decay and torpor set in, shipbuilding declined, the ports were deserted and the trade came nearly to a standstill . . . except at Dubrovnik, which still preserved its liberties and some remains of its former prosperity'.[21]

In fact in international trade Dubrovnik had to face increasing competition from the west European nations.

West European Competition.   In this competition for trade Britain was on the whole decidedly more successful than her rivals. The growth of her overseas trade is reflected in that of her merchant fleet. From 3,300 ships with a total tonnage of 260,000 in 1702, it grew to over 8,100 with a tonnage of 590,000 in 1764.[22] French commercial influences remained very important throughout the century particularly with Spain, encouraged by geographical proximity and political alliance. Italy also proved a fertile field for French trade, but the most striking expansion of French commerce in Europe during this period was seen in the Levant.[23] The activity of the Marseilles merchants and the encouragement given them by the French government made France a dominant force in Europe's commerce with the Near East. The Dutch were also important in Mediterranean trade, even during the first decade of the eighteenth century, but were gradually losing the dominant position they had occupied in the commercial life of seventeenth century Europe.

Nevertheless, all this increased competition in seaborne trade affected Dubrovnik's maritime commerce. The number of new ships built at Dubrovnik decreased to an alarming extent at the turn of the century, and soon even the Spanish merchant navy began to decline owing to English and Dutch competition.

All this increased competition in seaborne trade affected Dubrovnik's maritime commerce, and most of Dubrovnik's ships began to fall into disrepair and were not renovated. The Dutch, French and English monopolized the carrying trade of the Mediterranean, and it became cheaper not only to obtain northern products but even eastern spices in Amsterdam or Marseilles, where they arrived by the Cape route, than directly overland and distributed by Italian or Dalmatian ships.

The first half of the eighteenth century had proved to be a disast-

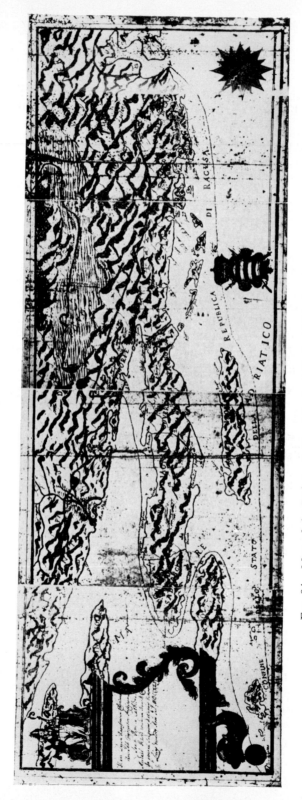

Fig. 94. Map of the Dubrovnik Republic, by Mihajlo Pešić, dated 1746 (Original in Dubrovnik Archives.)

rous one for Dubrovnik. Not only her land trade but also her maritime commerce suffered decline due to the growth of foreign traders, particularly from western Europe, continued war between Austria and Turkey and the lack of opportunities during wartime for Dubrovnik to exploit her neutral position.

Dubrovnik's Decline 1750–1800

Political Events and Consequences

In the second half of the eighteenth century two political events affected the course of Dubrovnik's trade. Firstly, the war between England, France and Spain in 1756–1763 proved advantageous to Dubrovnik's shipping, and much of the commerce of the Mediterranean passed into their hands as neutrals; for it was during the Seven Years War that Dubrovnik took greatest advantage of her neutrality. This war involved Anglo-French rivalry in North America,[24] during which time France dominated trade in the Mediterranean. The French controlled Livorna (Leghorn) which had previously become the funnel through which the Turkey trade of the British, French and Dutch all ran. Alexandria was the other prominent port in the Mediterranean and between these two ports, the main line of maritime trade existed. Dubrovnik seeing the decline of her own harbour, used the town's maritime fleet to convey trade in the Mediterranean and thus once more to increase her tertiary activities.

The second important event for Dubrovnik was the Russo-Turkish War of 1768–1774 and its consequences on trade. During the course of the war a Russian fleet entered the Mediterranean and sailed up the Adriatic. Finding that a number of Dubrovnik's ships were carrying foodstuffs from Alexandria and other Levantine ports to Constantinople, the Russians treated these and all other Dubrovnik ships as enemies. They summoned the republic to renounce Turkish suzerainty, and to place itself under the protection of a Christian power, together with a demand that all the larger Dubrovnik ships should be sold to Russia. The government first thought of resisting and tried to place Dubrovnik in a state of defence, but reserves in the town arsenal were poor. For example on examination it was found that of the 400 cannons on the forts only 40 were mounted while ammunition consisted of less than 2,000 lb of powder and about

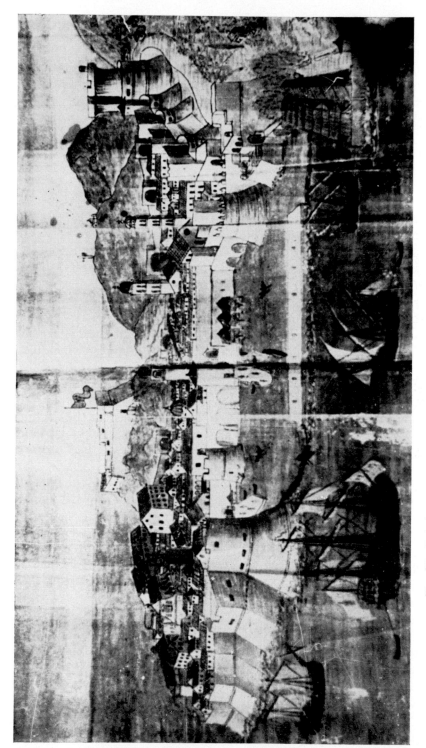

Fig. 95. Painting of Dubrovnik in the second half of the eighteenth century. (Date and artist unknown.)

5,000 cannon balls. The republic then resorted to bribery and the storm was for a moment averted,[25] but the Russian fleet continued to harry Dubrovnik's trade. Finally in 1774 the Russian army advanced across the Danube and compelled the Grand Vizier to agree to peace terms at the Bulgarian village of Kutchuk-Kainardji. Dubrovnik felt two main effects from this event. Firstly, in the long run, Bulgaria would be open to even more foreign traders than before, now that the Black Sea was no longer a *mare clausum*. Secondly, in the short run, fighting over the Danubian frontier, coupled with plague, had ruined her main colony of Ruščuk. Also by the 1780's Dubrovnik saw Russian influence in the Levant at the highest pitch it had hitherto reached.

Dubrovnik's Land Trade

Thus throughout the eastern Balkans Dubrovnik was having to face a situation which could contribute to her decline. The situation in Bulgaria had worsened during the second half of the eighteenth century. Improved relations between Austria and Turkey meant that Dubrovnik's merchants were no longer needed as middlemen. A Dubrovnik government official wrote in 1767 that

'some ferries have been opened on the Danube by Austria, which did not exist earlier; therefore our warehouses and traders are now only one of many alternatives'.[26]

All goods from Hungary, Wallachia and northern Bulgaria, which used to go through Dubrovnik were now being taken by Austrian traders using the Danube and more northerly routes to western Europe, thus benefiting such ports as Trieste and Rijeka at the expense of Dubrovnik. In 1770 the Dubrovnik government stated that only Ruščuk of her Bulgarian colonies, was frequented by her traders, complimenting a statement made three years earlier that

'only one or two of our colonies remain in the whole of the Sultan's Empire, because our traders no longer find it possible to make a living from existing trade'.[27]

The effects of the Russo-Turkish War are clearly seen from one Dubrovnik merchant who went by boat to Ruščuk in 1772 to obtain wax and skins and complained about the trouble he had leaving the town.[28]

After the war there were still some Dubrovnik traders in Ruščuk (1794)[29] but their presence was only a shadow of former times.

In Serbia, Dubrovnik met with similar problems. Although the Serbian lands were at peace from 1739 to 1788, the condition of the Serbian peasantry had greatly deteriorated. As the central authority of Turkey grew weaker, the rapacity of its local officials grew greater. Serbia, too had now become a frontier province of the Turkish Empire, and the social and economic condition of the Serbian people grew ever worse because of its frontier position. A contemporary writer[30] states that

> 'we crossed the deserts of Serbia, almost quite overgrown with wood, through a country naturally fertile. The inhabitants are industrious but the oppression of the peasants is so great they are forced to abandon their house and neglect their village'.

This statement is borne out by the almost complete abandonment of Dubrovnik colonies in Serbia in the second half of the eighteenth century. The small number of Dubrovnik merchants visiting Serbia with, or without, goods for three five-year periods in the eighteenth century clearly points to decline (Table VIII):[31]

Table VIII

Years	Novi Pazar	Prokup-lje	Prije-polje	Novi Varoš	Užice	Belgrade
	Dubrovnik Merchants					
1717–21	25	2	2	3	3	7
1748–52	24	—	1	1	—	3
1776–80	14	—	—	—	1	1
Total	63	2	3	4	4	11

Despite these five year periods all being during peace-time, only Novi Pazar seems to have had any real importance at all. Belgrade suffered from the influx of Austrian and Cincar traders whilst the other four towns declined due to the poor economic state of central Serbia.

Faced with the loss of Levantine, Bulgarian and Serbian markets, Dubrovnik's land trade now concentrated on two areas contiguous to her own frontiers – south-east Bosnia and Hercegovina together with Montenegro. Bosnia and Hercegovina were traditionally areas of interest for Dubrovnik's commerce. In the fourteenth and fifteenth centuries her traders had gone there to find markets for western goods and to buy raw materials. Now, Bosnian and Hercegovinian traders came to Dubrovnik to use her port as a collecting and exchange centre for their goods. Dubrovnik's desertion of her Bosnian markets is mentioned in a census on traders from the middle of the eighteenth century –

'there are very few Dubrovnik traders in Bosnia, and those that exist restrict themselves to buying cordovan and rough wool'.[32]

Only rarely did merchants from Dubrovnik visit Sarajevo, therefore Sarajevo traders arrived at Dubrovnik in large numbers as they did at Split and other new harbours. The Turks did not suppress Bosnia, as they did Serbia but encouraged this growth in home traders, seeing them as an important source of revenue.

From an analysis of documents a comparison can be made of goods arriving in Dubrovnik from its hinterland in any one year for the following periods.[33]

The increase in importance of Bosnian trade through Dubrovnik

Table IX

Circa 1600–1645 From All Dubrovnik Colonies		Circa 1750 From Bosnia	
Average number by weight of skins	24 tons	Average number by weight of skins	137 tons
Average number by weight of cordovan	82 tons	Average number by weight for wax	120 tons
Average number by weight for wax	31 tons	Average number by weight for iron (40% were manufactured goods)	94 tons
Average number by weight for wool	5 tons		

Q*

even allowing for inflationary tendencies, can be seen by comparing the value of Bosnian exports through the port: [34]

Table X

1618	1750
Bosnian exports through Dubrovnik valued at 10,200 cekinas (3,400 ducats).	Bosnian exports through Dubrovnik valued at 165,000 cekinas (55,000 ducats).

If Sarajevo and its traders were the most important part of Dubrovnik's commerce with Bosnia, then Trebinje and its merchants were the same for Hercegovina. There were many traders from Hercegovina in Dubrovnik as shown by the number of such traders in Dubrovnik quarantine between 1746 and 1752:

Table XI

Trader	1746	1747	1748	1749	1750	1751	1752
Sarajevo	53	50	53	75	60	80	74
Mostar	31	27	32	53	36	63	102
Trebinje	100	140	171	230	93	120	128
Rest of Hercegovina	14	33	25	8	15	30	35
Total	198	250	281	366	204	293	339

This meant, of the total Hercegovinian traders who went to Dubrovnik for the seven year period (1,586 traders), Trebinje had 1,082 or 71%. Trebinje was an important communication centre at the southern end of Popovo Polje and lay on the main caravan route to Bosnia. It was the collecting centre and focal point of Hercegovinian trade. Wax, skins, wool, and often live cattle also were the main exports from Hercegovina, trade remaining lively up to about 1760.[35] After this date both south east Bosnia and Hercegovina deserted Dubrovnik harbour, its traders directing their goods to the wealthier Austrian and Danubian lands, or to other Dalmatian ports including

Trieste, which was now becoming the main collecting centre for the central and west European markets.

The region of present day Montenegro experienced a growth in trade relations with Dubrovnik *circa* 1750, simultaneously with south east Bosnia and Hercegovina. Montenegro, itself, was then a much smaller territory than it is today having expanded later at the expense of Serbia and Hercegovina. The whole barren limestone region, centred around Cetinje was an inaccessible fortress, and its caves and rocks gave ample opportunity for guerilla warfare, and remained the only corner of the Balkan lands to escape the domination of the Turk from the fourteenth century onwards. When the other markets were more easily accessible for Dubrovnik's merchants this difficult terrain had little attraction before the eighteenth century. Such was the plight of Dubrovnik's trading life in this century that she had to turn to poorer markets, to maintain her existence and identity.[36]

Podgorica (present-day Titograd) is mentioned several times in Dubrovnik's documents particularly in the second half of the century. It was an important communication centre near the northern end of Lake Skadar, where the shepherds from the mountain areas brought their products down to market. Wool, wax and skins (including buffalo and bear) together with the recently introduced tobacco, formed the major part of Montenegran trade. Merchants from the town did not go automatically to Dubrovnik, as there were several outlets (i.e. the new harbours) for their products. Only when Dubrovnik's prices were higher than elsewhere, are merchants from Podgorica mentioned in archival material.

Bijelo Polje on the upper reaches of the Lim valley, became important for Dubrovnik after the destruction of Budimlje (present-day Ivangrad) by Austrian and Turkish soldiers during the first half of the eighteenth century. Wool was the main export from the town much of it going via Dubrovnik to Ancona and Senegalia. Other towns mentioned as sending livestock products to Dubrovnik were Sjenica, Plevlje and Kolašin, all small collecting centres for their respective local areas. None of the markets in Montenegro could be said to have been sure and reliable ones for Dubrovnik, but with the loss of so many of her former markets in Southern Pomoravlje and Kossovo – Metohija to the Austrians, and parts of Bosnia to the Venetians and 'home' traders, the town was forced to rely on what few areas she could trade in to maintain her livelihood.

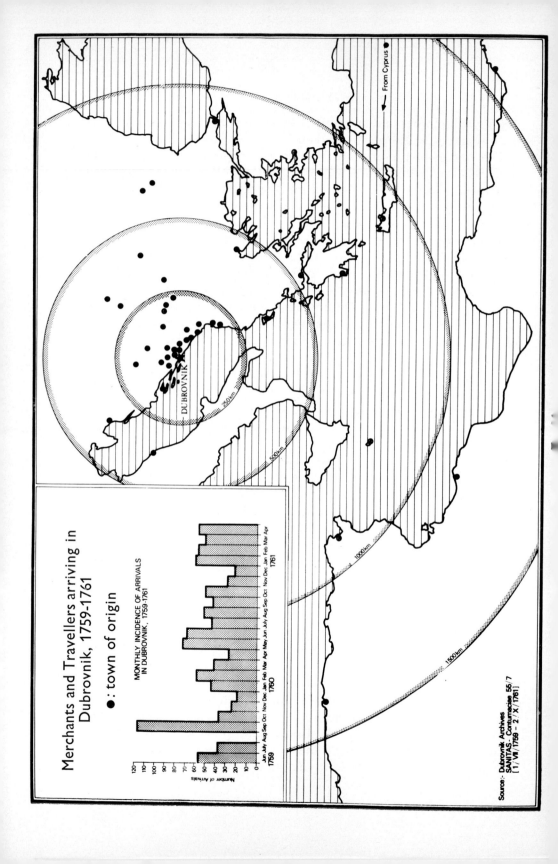

Merchants and Travellers arriving in
Dubrovnik, 1759-1761

●: town of origin

MONTHLY INCIDENCE OF ARRIVALS
IN DUBROVNIK, 1759-1761

From Cyprus ●

DUBROVNIK

250km

500km

1000km

1500km

Source:- Dubrovnik Archives
SANITAS:- Contumaciae 55/7
[1 / VII/1759 – 2 / X /1761]

Dubrovnik's Maritime Trade

Commercial Revival. In the second half of the eighteenth century Dubrovnik's maritime fleet had little traffic outside the Adriatic, except as a carrier for other nations. In the Levant[37] and North Africa[38] Dubrovnik's maritime service took increasing interest in the carrying trade from Alexandria, which consisted mainly of flax, cotton, wool, silk, varied textiles, skins, saffron, wax, salt, ammonia and medicinal plants. The importance of this trade after the Seven Years War is seen from Table XII.[39]

Table XII

Place	1766	1767	1768	1769	Total 4 years
Livorno	20	18	13	7	58
Constantinople	9	9	12	18	48
Smyrna	6	6	13	12	37
Other places in E.	8	12	4	8	32
North Africa	8	7	8	4	27
Crete	7	5	4	6	22
Solun	2	1	6	5	14
Dubrovnik	2	1	—	2	5
Other places in W.	1	—	—	1	2
Total—Year	63	59	60	63	245

From these statistics certain facts emerge. Firstly, Livorno[40] appears to have been the main port of call for Dubrovnik's boats leaving Alexandria. Secondly, the resurgence of the Levantian trade for Dubrovnik, is seen in the times Constantinople, Smyrna, Solun and Crete are mentioned. Trading consuls at Constantinople,[41] Smyrna and Sidon, were strengthened for these eastern ports were important for their supplies of raw materials, foodstuffs, drugs and even some spices which could still find markets in western Europe even at this late date. Thirdly, the table emphasizes the insignificance of Dubrovnik's own port as a trading centre in the Levantian trade receiving only 5 boats (2%) of the total 245 boats over the four year period. Fourthly, the yearly total seems to have been fairly stable over the four year period with about 60 Dubrovnik boats leaving Alexandria each year, indicating the constancy of this carrying trade.

Fig. 97. Painting of Dubrovnik dated 1772 (on wood, measuring 12·9 cm × 7·9 cm).

Within the Adriatic Dubrovnik's merchants were mainly concerned with transporting varied raw materials including wool, various skins and wax to the harbours of Apulia, Abruzzi and Venice. Wheat, beans, salt and oil still remained the main commodities from southern Italy, for despite strong competition from France, Dubrovnik's traders never let them have complete domination in the south Italian markets.[42] Occasionally quarrels arose between the Dubrovnik Republic and the kingdom of Naples as for example in 1782. The Neapolitan government, for some unknown reason suddenly claimed to revive its old rights over Dubrovnik, dating back to 1081–1085 when the town was under the Norman rule of southern Italy. This request was refused, so it tried to enforce the idea by placing an embargo on Dubrovnik ships in the ports of the kingdom of Naples and seizing all Dubrovnik property in the kingdom. Eventually a compromise was arrived at, the embargo was removed, the confiscated property restored and an Italian official appointed in the city provided he refrained from interfering with the affairs of the republic.[43] Much of the commerce with the north Adriatic was in manufactured goods,[44] but the impetus of former centuries had been lost. Therefore although occasional difficulties arose Dubrovnik's citizens realized that as their trading sphere in the Balkans and Levant was continually shrinking, efforts must be made to preserve at least some of her overseas markets, particularly those that were in closer proximity to the town.

Towards the end of the eighteenth century there was some improvement in the general condition of the small republic. During the protracted wars between England and France, and between England and America, Dubrovnik's trade revived to an unexpected extent and by 1779, Dubrovnik's fleet totalled 189 ships. The land trade also flourished with the widespread cultivation of the new colonial products, cotton and maize, which were exported to western Europe, where there was a steady and growing demand. The development of new export crops in turn contributed to the growth of a class of native Balkan merchants and mariners. Foreign merchants and shipping companies handled much of the export business but a considerable proportion fell to the new entrepreneurs.[45] The result was a rapid growth of the Dubrovnik, Ulcinj, and Greek merchant fleets, and also the enrichment of the Greek and Macedonian merchants who controlled much of the overland trade up the Danube valley into central Europe. Finally, the Anglo-French Wars disrupted commerce in the Mediterranean and ruined the western

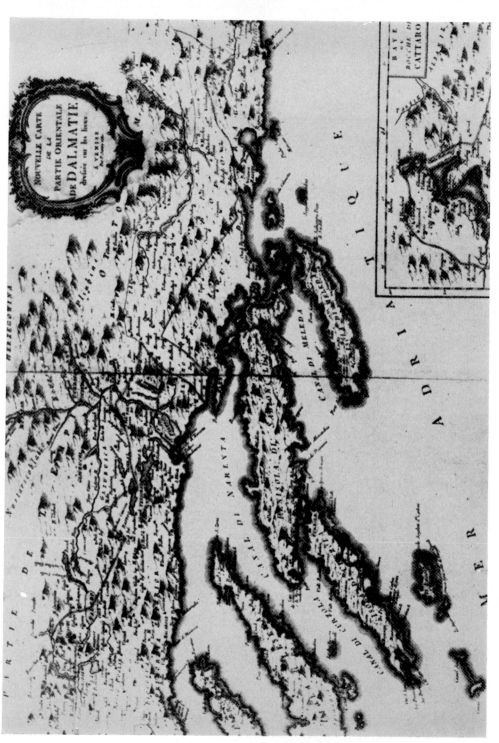

FIG. 98. Map of the Dubrovnik Republic 1780. (Original in the Naval Museum, Dubrovnik.)

merchants who had established themselves in various Balkan ports, like Solun, and had monopolized the overseas trade. Local merchants promptly took the place of the westerners and exported Balkan products to central Europe.[46]

These developments enormously increased the volume of Balkan commerce, both foreign and domestic. Trade was carried along transversal and longitudinal routes. The transversal routes began in the Adriatic ports like Dubrovnik, Split,[47] Dürres and Arta and ended in Novi Pazar, Belgrade, Solun, Sërres, Varna and Constantinople. The longitudinal routes began in Budapest and Cernauti and ended in Solun and Constantinople. Thus Dubrovnik was again part of a Balkan commercial revival.

The expansion of trade in turn stimulated the demand and output of handicraft products.[48] Important manufacturing centres appeared in various parts of the peninsula, frequently in isolated mountain areas where the artisans could practice their crafts with a minimum of Turkish interference. But the degree of industrial expansion can be easily exaggerated. It never approached western proportions for various reasons, including lack of security, the competition of western manufactured goods, the active opposition of western consuls and the absence of a persistent mercantilist policy on the part of the Ottoman government. Nevertheless, the fact remains that industrial output in the Balkans rose sharply during the latter part of the eighteenth century.

Dubrovnik's Merchant Fleet. The rise of commerce and industry stimulated the growth of a merchant marine. Dubrovnik again became one of the important maritime centres along the Dalmatian coast together with Zadar, Trogir, Split and Kotor, for shipbuilding revived during the middle of the eighteenth century and increased towards its end. The famous shipbuilders from Korčula were once more in great demand. It became one of the most important industrial branches of the republic's economy whilst the merchant fleet, according to Luetić employed a total of over 2,380 seamen, shipowners and carat holders, an impressive figure when compared with the total population of the republic estimated at about 25,000 inhabitants.[49] Dubrovnik's larger ships mainly operated outside the Adriatic, tramping between the Levantine ports and the west, the Mediterranean and the Atlantic Ocean. The merchant navy was com-

FIG. 99. Letter from the Shari, a judge in Alexandria's harbour, concerning the carrying of Mohammedan pilgrims in a Dubrovnik boat to Tripoli, but who were not the Sultan's subjects, dated 11/VII/1780. (Dubrovnik Archives, *Acta Turcarum*, 1396).

pletely independent of its home port, only returning there when obliged to by the government's maritime regulations. Between 1787 and 1793 shipowners (carat holders) had to pay a special tax for ships with a total loading capacity of 15,000 carrs or more for there were 190 ships taking part in the long (non-Adriatic) voyages. During this period most of Dubrovnik's merchant fleet outside the Adriatic consisted of sailing ships weighing between fifty and 100 carrs. This growth in the fleet's size meant that by the end of the century the number of Dubrovnik's seamen rose to over 3,000.[50]

Occasionally serious trouble arose for Dubrovnik's fleet as, for example, in 1792 when war was declared by the European Coalition against the French Republic. The Court of Vienna complained that Dubrovnik's ships were carrying grain to French ports. Dubrovnik's Senate protested that such acts had been done against its orders and no objection was raised to punishment of those responsible, which was a familiar story – Dubrovnik's seamen profiting by foreign wars, while the government cast off all responsibility. Nevertheless by 1797 Dubrovnik's fleet had increased to 363 ships of over fifteen tons, only eighty of which were employed on coastwise trade, the others presumably used for longer distance traffic. Most of their trade was in the export of Balkan products such as cotton, maize and other grains, dyeing materials, wine, oil and various fruits, especially currants. In return they brought back mostly manufactured goods and colonial products, particularly spices, sugar, woollens, glass, watches, guns and gunpowder.[51]

Consular Services. The development of Dubrovnik's commerce and shipping in the middle of the eighteenth century encouraged the government to establish a whole series of new consular offices in many towns and cities throughout the Mediterranean. Nearly all the more important ports in the Mediterranean and even some on the Adriatic seaboard[52] contained representatives from the small republic.[53] During the second half of the eighteenth century there was a total of 60 consulates, of which half of them were located in towns and ports in the western Mediterranean, and were maintained until the fall of the republic in 1808.[54] Geographically the distribution of the consulates could be divided into two main areas. First, those active in the eastern Mediterranean (Levant) which really meant the Turkish Empire, and secondly those in the western Mediterranean (Ponent) which included the North African states of Tripolis, Tunis,

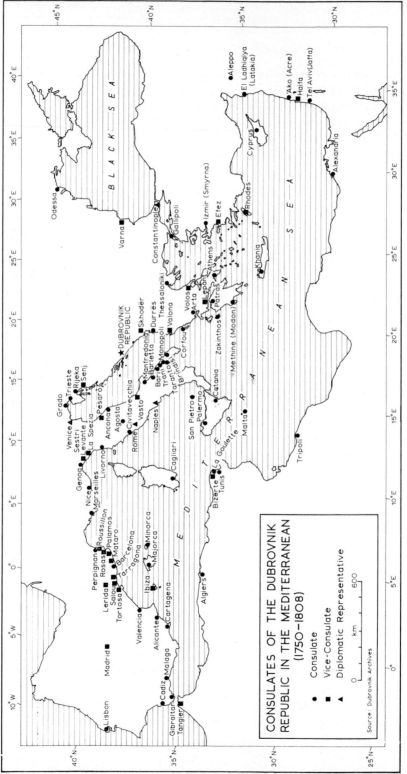

FIG. 100.

Algeria and Morocco. This was a basic division also applied by the Dubrovnik government for appointments, terms of office, salary etc.[55]

It is interesting to note that in neither the Levant nor Ponent did the Dubrovnik Republic employ professional consuls, i.e. people of Dubrovnik nationality, who were solely employed in the consular service. In the Ponent honorary consuls were used, whose only financial reward came from the collection of consular fees. They were permanent residents of the consuls' location and usually of that country's nationality. One exception to this general rule was Dubrovnik's representatives in North Africa (mostly Dutch consuls).[56] Although they despatched Dubrovnik's business transactions as any other Dubrovnik consul, they did not, for political reasons, bear a consular title, only Consular Administrator ('amministratore del consulato'). In the Levant (i.e. Turkish territory),[57] Dubrovnik appointed her consuls from amongst her own citizens, based on the approval and confirmation of the Turkish authorities in Constantinople. They were employed for a fixed period lasting between three and five years, and on a fixed salary. On completion of the terms of office these consuls returned to Dubrovnik to resume their former employment, indicating that they were specially chosen to fulfill the needs of the republic in the East and capable of maintaining the specific relationship which Dubrovnik enjoyed with the Turkish Empire.

Dubrovnik's consular representatives performed the same duties in both the Levant and Ponent. The main tasks were to protect the interests of Dubrovnik's shipping, promote trade relations, inform the Dubrovnik Senate of all political events, the state of the harvest, any military manoeuvres, and of contemporary financial and legal developments in their country of residence. Further duties involved the issuing of receipts and legalizing transactions with a consular stamp, and mediation in disputes between captains and crews, all performed within the boundaries of a certain consular area. This meant that Dubrovnik's government always had accurate information on the movement and sailings of its own shipping and conversely the consuls were kept up to date with the latest political, economic and social changes which may effect their merchant fleet. In cases of emergency the various consuls could communicate between themselves, without informing Dubrovnik and such direct communication often saved the republic's shipping from serious loss or damage.[58] In summary one may say that little direct material benefit accrued from

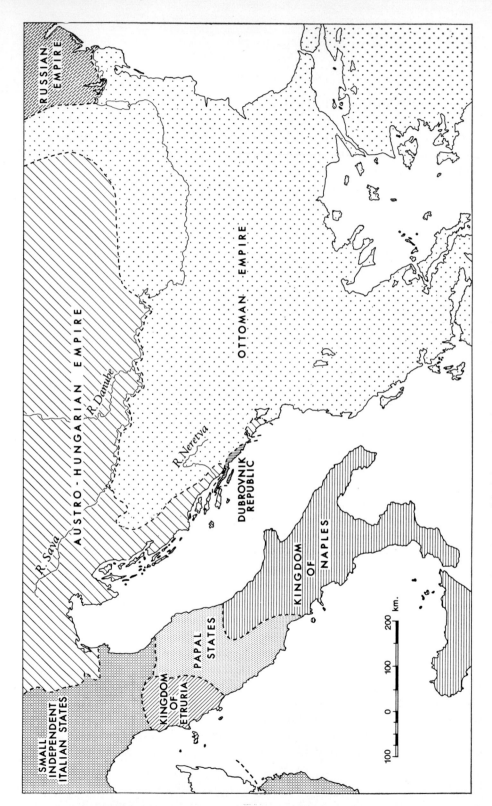

Fig. 101.   Political situation in the Balkans and Italy *circa* 1800 AD

these consuls in either the Levant or Ponent, but the real advantages came from Dubrovnik's merchant fleet being able to pursue its commercial functions undisturbed which in turn helped increase the republic's national revenue.[59]

Dubrovnik's Revival 1800–1806

In 1797 the French armies occupied Venice, put an end to the republic and annexed its possessions while a French fleet seized the Ionian Islands. Meanwhile Austrian troops were advancing into Dalmatia, which, as part of Venetian territory, in theory belonged to France, and warships of all nations began to appear in the Adriatic. What might have been a serious situation was averted in the Peace of Campoformio, when Istria, Dalmatia and Kotor, as well as Venice and her mainland possessions, were ceded to Austria (October 18, 1797).[60]

The fall of Venice was on the whole satisfactory for the people of Dubrovnik, but the close proximity of the Austrians, who were useful so long as they remained at a safe distance, was regarded as a danger. The Austrian Emperor, however, expressed his intention of protecting the republic in every way. These immediate troubles and dangers having been warded off, there follows a period of five years (1800–1805) which is perhaps the most prosperous in the whole history of the republic. All the other states of the Mediterranean, large or small, were involved in war; Dubrovnik alone remained neutral, and therefore enjoyed almost a monopoly of the carrying trade. Her ships were more numerous than they had ever been before,[61] and her income enormous. English privateers harried French commerce, and French ones that of England; Venice was no longer of any mercantile importance; the Turks plundered all Christian ships except those of Dubrovnik. The Dubrovnik Senate, with its traditional diplomacy, kept on good terms with everybody, especially with the Turks. A few frontier incidents with Austria occurred, but they were settled amicably. The Austrian consul in Dubrovnik had instructions to protect Austrian commercial interest, and to assure the Dubrovnik Senate that the Emperor intended to protect the republic and guarantee the integrity of its territory.

One area of particular interest was the Crimea. The opening up of the Black Sea after 1774 proved a filip for Mediterranean commerce and attracted Dubrovnik's shipping during the first five years of the

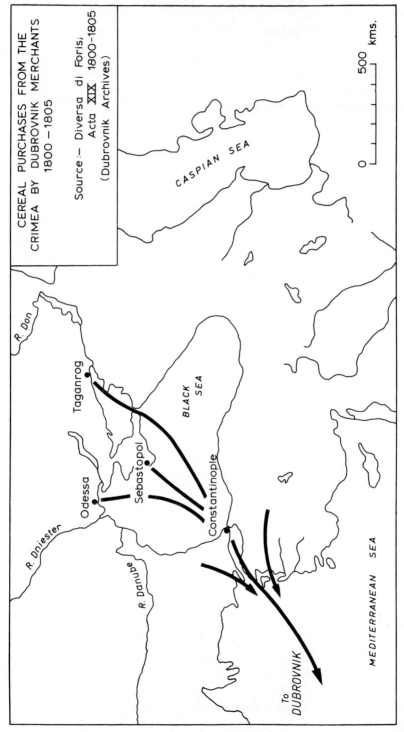

CEREAL PURCHASES FROM THE
CRIMEA BY DUBROVNIK MERCHANTS
1800 – 1805

Source:– Diversa di Foris;
Acta XIX 1800-1805
(Dubrovnik Archives)

500 kms.

CASPIAN SEA

R. Don

Taganrog

BLACK SEA

Odessa

Sebastopol

Constantinople

R. Dniester

R. Danube

MEDITERRANEAN SEA

To
DUBROVNIK

Fig. 102.

nineteenth century. In the 1790's Taganrog, which lies to the west of the Don estuary, was the chief Black Sea outlet; it derived goods, especially wheat, not only from the Don basin but also from the Volga. Odessa was opened up as a port in 1795 serving the wide hinterland of the Ukraine. Sebastopol with its excellent harbourage became an important port after 1804.

The surplus commodities of Russia attracted merchant ships from Dubrovnik. These products were for the most part those which had figured in Russia's medieval trade, timber, furs, honey, hemp, tar, linen and flax, but for Dubrovnik's merchants it was the cereals, especially rye and wheat which drew their attention. Wheat from Taganrog and Sebastopol are regularly mentioned at the beginning of the nineteenth century[62] often *en route* for Italy. For example in 1801, 130 boats of wheat left the Crimea for Italy in Dubrovnik ships;[63] whilst in the month of June 1804 alone, ten boats of wheat were transported from Odessa to Livorno.[64]

Unfortunately Dubrovnik's idyllic commercial position could not last. In 1805 war broke out between France and Austria but Dubrovnik refused to commit herself. The Austrian consul in Dubrovnik wrote in that year

'it appears that this government, of which the apathy, indolence and venality are at their height, will undergo the fate for which it is destined. . . . I am convinced that if peace be not concluded, the French will try to get possession of this republic and form a body of troops here with whom to attack Kotor'.[65]

Unfortunately his prophecy turned out to be true.

Conclusion

The eighteenth century proved to be a declining period for Dubrovnik. Political events and economic factors beyond her control had adverse effects on the town's commerce. But she was not alone. Both Venice and Turkey were falling into irreparable decay whilst new competitors both in land and maritime trade were gradually taking over the commerce of the eastern and western Mediterranean. The growth of Russia in the Black Sea area, the rise of Austria at the expense of the Turks, the increase of British, French and Dutch merchants in Italy, Spain and the Levant all helped to decrease

Dubrovnik's former trading role making her more dependent on regions of closer geographical proximity like Bosnia-Hercegovina, Montenegro and Apulia.

By the end of the eighteenth century Dubrovnik found herself isolated from trade, for the new ports, like Trieste and Rijeka, were nearer to the newly developed Pannonian Plain and to the western capitals. Dubrovnik found herself off the main shipping routes of the Adriatic and away from the new avenues of trade in the Balkan hinterland. Yet, she could still benefit by a policy of neutrality. This was demonstrated during the Seven Years War and for a short period at the beginning of the nineteenth century, but it was always a risky position as she found to her expense when Napoleonic troops occupied the town in 1806 and finally liquidated the small republic. Therefore her strength as an entrepôt port lay in an earlier period when a certain combination of factors had contributed to her success. Once this combination of factors was radically altered then her position lost its impetus and her ability to continue successfully declined.

10 Notes

1. H. van Groot Grotius, *Freedom of the Seas*, Paris (1608), p. 4.
2. H. C. Darby, 'The Medieval sea-state', *Scottish Geographical Magazine*, Vol. XLVIII, No. 3 Edinburgh (1932), 148.
3. L. S. Stavrianos, *The Balkans Since 1453* London, New York (1863), pp. 138–139.
4. P. Pisani *La Dalmatie de 1797 à 1815* Paris (1893) p. 12.
5. V. Vinaver 'Trgovina Bara Bijolog Polje Podgorice sa Dubrovnikom (1720–1760)' *Istoriski Zapisi* Kniga IV–2 Cetinje (1953) p. 458.
6. Dubrovnik Archives (1726). *Lettere di Levante* 72 folder 96.
7. V. Vinaver *op. cit.* p. 470.
8. Dubrovnik Archives (1730). *Copia Lettere* 2 folder 10.
9. M. le Comte de Saint-Priest *Memoires sur l'Ambassade de France en Turquie* Paris (1877) pp. 402 419. Already by 1597 the French had obtained permission to buy leather cordovan (better quality leather) and cotton yarn. In 1604 this permission was extended to include wax.
10. F. Kanitz *Das Königreich Serbien* Leipzig (1868) p. 336.
11. D. J. Popović *O Cincarima* Belgrade (1937), 2nd edition, pp. 114–117; (D. Warriner, ed.) *Contrasts in Emerging Societies*, London (1965), p. 317.
12. Dubrovnik Archives (1699). *Lettere degli mercanti e ambassatori*, Facsimile 37, No. 1784.
13. Dubrovnik Archives (1704). *Consilium Rogatorum*, 139, folder 163.

14. Dubrovnik Archives (1705). *Lettere di Levante*, 68, folder 140.
15. L. Voinovitch, *La monarchie francaise dans l'Adriatique*, Paris (1917), p. 104;
    I. Sakazov, *op. cit.*, p. 104;
    V. Vinaver, *Dubrovnik i Turska u XVIII veku*, S.A.N. Posebna Izdanza
    CCCXXI, Kniga II, Belgrade (1960), p. 55;
    V. Vinaver, Dubrovačka Trgovina u Srbiji i Bugarskoj Krajem XVII veka
    (1660–1700)', *Istoriski Časopis*, Vol. XII–XIII, Belgrade (1963), pp. 189–235.
16. Ruščuk was known particularly for its skins especially ox and buffalo amongst
    the domestic varieties and skins of wolf, bear and fox of the wild animals.
    Foreign textiles were imported through Dubrovnik. Dubrovnik Archives
    (1712), *Diversa di Foris*, 140, folder 232. From Vidin furs and skins were sent
    to Dubrovnik as well as barrelled caviar from fish caught in the Danube.
17. Dubrovnik Archives (1728). *Lettere di Levante*, 72, folder 118.
18. Dubrovnik Archives, (20/IV/1726). *Acta XVIII*, 124/3163.
19. M. Berengo, 'Problemi Economico-Sociali della Dalmazia Veneta alla fine
    del '700', *Revista Storica Italiana*, No. 4, Rome (1954), pp. 469–510.
20. M. S. Anderson, *Europe in the Eighteenth Century 1713–1783*, London (1963),
    p. 59.
21. T. G. Jackson, *Dalmatia, The Quarnero and Istria*, Vol. 1, Oxford (1887),
    p. 181.
22. M. S. Anderson, *op. cit.*, p. 54.
23. Dubrovnik's government in 1703 sent a commission to Alexandria to explore
    the possibilities of augmenting her trade in the Levant but the venture failed,
    and a further attempt in 1719 had no success. Dubrovnik Archives (1703).
    Consilium Rogatorium, 138, folder 78; (1719), *ibid.*, 149, folder 56.
    Between 1730 and 1740 many letters from Constantinople mention the
    absence of Dubrovnik's boats, and traders there,
    e.g. Dubrovnik Archives, (8/IV/1734). *Acta Sancta Mariae Maoris*, 124/3163;
    ibid., (16/X/1742), letter from Constantinople 'Although in earlier centuries
    we had over 400 traders here bringing velvet, cloths, etc., we now only have
    a few merchants remaining'. In the discussion the letter blames this situation
    on the new trade with America and India.
24. Z. Muljačić, 'Američka revolucija i dubrovačka pomorska trgovina', *Pomorski
    Zbornik*, Vol. 6, Zadar (1968), pp. 521–530.
25. F. C. H. L. Pouqueville, *Voyage dans la Grèce*, Vol. I, Paris (1826), p. 24;
    J. C. von Engel, *op. cit.*, p. 56.
26. Dubrovnik Archives (1767). *Lettere di Levante*, 88, folder 160.
27. Dubrovnik Archives (1770). *Lettere di Levante*, 91, folder 164;
    (1767), *ibid.*, 88, folder 160.
28. Dubrovnik Archives (1772). *Diversa di Foris*, 194, folders 186′–189;
    (1772), *ibid*, 195, folder 115′.
29. Dubrovnik Archives (1794). *Proclamentum Consiliensis*, 82 b, folder 74′.
30. *Letters of the Right Honourable Lady Mary Wortley Montague*, Vol. I, London
    (1763), p. 152.
31. Dubrovnik Archives. Based on *Sanitas*, the book recording all merchants
    who went from Dubrovnik to Turkey, for quarantine purposes.
32. V. Vinaver, 'Sarajevski Trgovci u Dubrovniku sredinom XVIII veku',
    Godišnjak Istoriskog Društva Bosne i Hercegovine, Godina VI, Sarajevo (1954)
    p. 255.

33. Dubrovnik Archives, series *Nola i securita* 50 onwards from which these figures have been calculated;
V. Vinaver, 'Bosna i Dubrovnik 1595–1645' *Godišnjak Društva Istoričara Bosne i Hercegovone*, God. XIII, Sarajevo (1962), pp. 199–232. V. Vinaver, *Dubrovnik i Turska u XVIII veku*, S.A.N. Belgrade (1960), Ch. IV, pp. 66–86.

34. S. Traljić, 'Trgovina Bosne i Hercegovine s Lukama Dalmacije i Dubrovnika u XVII i XVIII Stoljeća' *Pomorski Zbornik* Zagreb 1962, p. 341–372.

35. V. Vinaver, 'Hercegovačka Trgovina sa Dubrovnikom početkom 18 veka', *Istoriski Zapisis*, Knj. XI, 1–2. Cetinje (1955), pp. 65–94;
H. Kapidžić, *Veze Dubrovnika i Hercegovina u XVIII vijeku*, Sarajevo (1939), pp. 1–27;
V. Ćorovic, 'Bosansko-Hercegovački Trgovci u Dalmaciji', *Godišnjica Nikole Čupića*, Kniga. XXXV, Belgrade (1923), pp. 212–223.

36. V. Vinaver, 'Trgovina Bara, Bijelog Polija, Podgorica sa Dubrovnikom (1720–1760)', *Istoriski Časopis*, Knj. IV, 1–2, Cetinje (1953), pp. 458–480; *ibid.*, 'Skadar i Dubrovnik krajem XVIII veka' *Istoriski Časopis* Knj. XII (1956), pp. 42–77.

37. Dubrovnik Archives 1753 Corals sent from Dubrovnik to the Levant. *Consilium Rogatorum* 167, fol. 105, 195; V. Ivančević 'Dubrovački Brodovi za prvog Rusko-Turskog Rata (1768–1774) *Pomorski Zbornik*, Vol. II., Zagreb 1962, pp. 1725–1732.

38. Dubrovnik Archives 1754 Building wood taken from Dubrovnik to Tripoli. *Consilium Rogatorum* 168, folder 88; 1753 Dubrovnik boat took arms to Tunis *ibid.*, 167, folders 201, 204, 205, *ibid.* 168 folder 134.

39. M. Popović-Radenković 'Dubrovački Konzulat u Alexandriji od šestdesetih do osam desetihgodina XVIII veka'. *Istoriski Glasnik*, Kniga 4, Belgrade 1954, p. 61.

40. V. Ivančević, 'Luka Livorna i dubrovački brodovi (1760–1808), *Gradja za pomorsku povijest Dubrovnika*, J.A.Z.U. Knj. 4, Dubrovnik (1968), pp. 1–145.

41. I. Mitić, 'Konzulat Dubrovačke Republike u Carigradu', *Pomorski Zbornik*' Vol. 6, Zadar, pp. 455–474.

42. This is borne out by documentary evidence from Naples Archives. A document dated 1760 states that the traffic with Dubrovnik brought in treasure for the kingdom of Naples amounting to 30,000 ducats a year from customs duties alone. Naples Archives, (14/V/1760). *Estere* No. 4388. *Memoire de Sarino Maria Zamagna*; even later, in 1784, one piece of information records that Dubrovnik merchants frequently came to the ports of the Napulian kingdom and bought textiles including cotton cloth, soap, salt and other merchandise, whilst bringing skins and all sorts of wax for sale. Naples Archives, (16/IX/1784). *Estere* No. 974 *Consulta del Supremo magistrato di Commercio*.

43. F. C. H. L. Pouqueville, *op. cit.*, p. 30.

44. J. Luetić, 'Nekoliko Vijesti o Dubrovačkim Brodovima zadnjih decenija XVIII stoljeća', *Dubrovačko Pomorstvo*, *op. cit.*, p. 194;
V. Ivančević, 'Osvrt na pomorske i trgovačko-kulturne veze Dubrovačke Republike z Ankonom i 18 i 19 stoljeće', *Dubrovnik*, Vol. XII, No. 1 (1969), pp. 115–127.

45. L. S. Stavrianos, *op. cit.*, p. 142.

46. V. Popović, 'Trgovina Budimlića u prvoj polovini XIX stoleća', *Narodna Starina*, Vol. VI, No. 1, Zagreb (1927), pp. 59–70; Arhiv S. R. Bosne i Hercegovine, Sarajevo *Fond porodice Budimlića* (Knjiga J. Budimlića); V. Vinaver, 'Dubrovnik i Turska', *op. cit.*, pp. 43, 73, 113, 129, 130, 152, 153; V. Skarić, *Srpski pravoslavni narod i crkva u Sarajevu u 17.i 18 vijeku*, Sarajevo (1928), pp. 65–66.
47. G. Novak, *Split u svjetskom prometu*, Split (1921), pp. 153–154.
48. L. Grdić-Bjelokosić, *Mostar nekad i sad*, Belgrade (1901), p. 27; H. Kreševljaković, *Esnafi i obrti u Bosni i Hercegovini*, Sarajevo (1961), p. 104.
49. J. Luetić, 'Povijest Pomorstva Dubrovačke Republike', *Pomorski Zbornik* Zagreb (1962), p. 1715.
50. *Ibid.*, p. 1718.
51. L. S. Stavrianos, *op. cit.*, p. 143.
52. Ž. Muljačić, 'Odnisi Dubrovnika i Sjedinjenih Dršava', *Naše More*, Dubrovnik (1958), br. 1.
53. Dubrovnik Archives, *Acta Sanctae Mariae Maioris, Lettere di Ponente. Lettere di Levante, Consilium Rogatorum, Consolati nazionali* (Ser. XXXVIII),
54. B. Krizman, 'O Dubrovačkoj Diplomacijij' Zagreb (1951), p. 133; *ibid.*, *Diplomati i konzuli u starom Dubrovniku*, Zagreb (1957).
55. J. Andrassy, *Međunarodno pravo*, Zagreb (1949), pp. 125–128.
56. Dubrovnik Archives, *Lettere di Ponente XVIII st.*, pp. 103–107.
57. V. Ivančević, 'Dubrovački konzulat u Odesi', *Naše More*, br. 5–6 Dubrovnik (1956); Z. Šundrica, 'Dubrovački konzulat u Ateni', *Naše More*, br. 2 Dubrovnik (1959).
58. Dubrovnik Archives *Acta Sanctae Mariae Maioris XVIII st.* ser. 91.3130, p. 26–28.
59. J. Luetić, 'Konzulati Dubrovačke Republike u XVIII i u početku XIX stoljeća' *Narodni Kalendar za 1960* Zadar, 1959, pp. 102–105; I. Mitić 'O Konzularnoj Službi Dubrovačke Republike' *Pomorski Zbornik*, Vol. ll, Zagreb 1962, pp. 1733–1745.
60. P. Pisani, *op. cit.*, pp. 33 sqq.
61. I. Rusko, 'Stanje dubrovačke trg. mornarice pred samu propast Dubrovačke Republike početkom XIX st.', *Dubrovačke Pomorstvo*, Dubrovnik (1952), p. 205; Dubrovnik Archives (1805), *Arboraggi*, 56—3/16, folder 150 (Indice di nomi dei Capitani). In 1805 Dubrovnik's merchant navy totalled at least 278 various types of vessels sailing outside the Adriatic with a total loading capacity of 24,000 carrs.
62. Dubrovnik Archives (1805), *Diversa di Foris*, 234, folders 142, 182, 186; (1806), *op. cit.*, 237, folders 160, 187, 188', 190, 235, 241.
63. Dubrovnik Archives, (23/IX/1801). *Acta Sanctae Mariae Maioris XIX*, No. 17/599–3, 8.
64. Dubrovnik Archives, (I/VI/1804). *Acta Sanctae Mariae Maioris XIX*, No. 17/599–3, 22.
65. P. Pisani, *op. cit.*, pp. 135–136.

11
Cultural Life of the Dubrovnik Republic

Owing to Dubrovnik's position between the Italian and Slavonic elements, and her connections with Venice and with the Serb states, her cultural development was subject to many varied influences. Just as Bohemia under German influence became the most advanced of all the Slavic nations of central Europe, so Dubrovnik evidently owed her civilization to her position on the shores of the Adriatic, opposite, and of easy access to, the Italian peninsula. The city came to be known as the 'Slavonic Athens', a name acquired during the seventeenth century, but the Ferrara of a hundred years previous comes within the limits of a more just parallel. The prosperity gained from great commercial achievement enabled the small republic to plough back some of the profits into the cultural development of the area. Also, while the neighbouring Slav territories were under the Turks in deep obscurity and poverty, and the whole of Dalmatia under Venetian rule was economically exploited and culturally backward, Dubrovnik remained an oasis of material and spiritual progress. This was seen in the various aspects of the town's development and it is proposed to examine more closely the architecture, sculpture and contribution of Dubrovnik's citizens to the world of literature, painting and science.

Architecture and Sculpture

The oldest known core of Dubrovnik's settlements was thought to have been built by refugees from Epidaurus at the beginning of the seventh century on the former islet of Lava, today included in the most southerly part of the old town. This islet, with its steep cliff, already possessed a partially complete stone fortification by the end of the eighth century AD which by the mid-tenth century at the very latest, surrounded the whole settlement. Inside these oldest known fortifications, Constantine Porphyrogenitus, mentioned one particular object of architectural interest, the church of St. Stjepan (Stephen). Recent excavations have revealed the church's foundations which are thought, probably to date from the seventh or eighth centuries AD and of early Christian origin. Nearby, various fragments of wicker material have been found, dating from the late prehistoric to the early Roman period. On the other hand, other interesting finds have been located on Lava, along its northern coast, in the area of present-day Prijeko, showing evidence of early Slavic settlers. Here the foundations of two sites (St. James and St. Nikola) have been discovered, falling typologically into the category known as 'old Croatian' architecture developed between the ninth and mid-eleventh centuries AD.

Between the tenth and twelfth centuries the two separate parts of the town were gradually joined together, the canal dividing them having been filled in; this former channel was to become Stradun (Corso), the main street of the town and the basis for further urban development. During the Venetian period, with the increasing wealth and consequence of Dubrovnik, the city itself was beautified by the erection of numerous handsome buildings, both lay and ecclesiastical, and by 1358 the city was almost entirely reconstructed. Already in 1272 the town statutes announced a building programme for part of the town, whilst during the thirteenth and fourteenth centuries, when the importance of Dubrovnik in maritime trade increased beyond all expectations, an intensive period of construction took place. In its early days the walls, the castle, and one or two stone churches were the only stone edifices; all the rest of the town was of timber. Much of the new building was on top of remains of other Romanesque remnants like the church of St. Stjepan, and the oldest part of the Mala brača (Franciscan) monastery, whilst a small number of preserved fragments of Romanesque architecture and a few sculptured details were included in the new masonry.

After the departure of the last Venetian Count from Dubrovnik in 1358, although Hungarian political supremacy succeeded to that of Venice, the artistic and civilizing influence of the Venetian Republic survived, and its impress in the town is unmistakable to this day. The pointed arches in the Venetian Gothic style, the carved balconies, the two-light and three-light windows, the general character of the stonework and sculpture, in spite of certain distinctive features, bear witness to the strength of the Venetian example. Venice was the nearest centre of civilization to Dubrovnik, and the fountain-head of art. In spite of the jealousy and suspicion which the little republic always felt towards its powerful neighbour, many of Dubrovnik's artists received their training in Venice, while many Venetians came to execute work on the public and private buildings of Dubrovnik.

FIG. 103. Rector's Palace built according to the design of Onofrio di Giordana della Cava, on the site of an earlier fortified palace, which was destroyed by an explosion in 1435. The arcaded portico on the ground floor was reconstructed by Salvi di Michiele (Michelozzi) in Renaissance style after a second explosion in 1463.

Venice was not the only city which influenced Dubrovnik; other towns, such as Ancona, Florence, Padua and Naples, contributed towards her artistic development, in which even Hungary had some small share.

The most important and interesting building in the town is undoubtedly the Rector's Palace (Knežev Dvor), which is to Dubrovnik what the Ducal Palace is to Venice. It was commenced by architects inspired by Venetian ideas, and completed by others devoted to Renaissance art. The site of the existing edifice was originally occupied, in the days when the whole town was confined to the seaward ridge, and separated from the mainland by a marshy channel where the Stradun (Corso) now runs, by a castle as a defence against the Vlach settlements on the opposite side. When this was absorbed, and the marshy channel filled in, the castle was enlarged and strengthened, and later became the seat of the government and residence of the Count. Beyond the fact that it was protected by four towers[1] nothing is known about this early building. Already, in 1272, it was spoken of as a very ancient edifice,[2] and in 1349 the Great Council decided 'quod sala veteris palatii ubi dominus Comes habitat reaptetur et altius elevetur'[3] which seems to show that it had been allowed to fall into disrepair. In 1388 it was demolished, and on its site the foundations of a larger and more commodius building were laid. The new palace was not completed until 1420, and of this also little is known, as fifteen years later, in 1435 it was destroyed by fire caused by an explosion of gun-powder. Thus ended

'the spacious palace of Dubrovnik, which was in ancient times the castle, together with certain towers, and nearly all the ammunition and arms which were kept for the defence of the city and the armament of the galleys'.[4]

Further,

'then the Dubrovnik government decided that the palace should be rebuilt with more magnificent construction, sparing no expense, and that the greater part of the former castle which the fiery flame had not consumed should be levelled to the ground, the architect being a certain Onofrio di Giordano della Cava in the kingdom of Naples'.

The walls are made of ashlar stones,[5] finely wrought and very ornamentally carved, with great vaults resting on tall, stout columns

R

brought from Korčula. (Korčula has always been well-known for its building stone, which is almost marble, and acquires a rich yellow patina with age.) The capitals, or upper parts of these columns, are carved with great finesse. There are five large full columns, but two other half-columns, each attached to the two towers; on the first was carved Æsculapius, the restorer of medical art, at the instigation of that remarkable poet and learned man of letters, Niccolo de Lazina (Larina or Laziri), a noble of Cremona. Lazina had found out from his literary studies that Æsculapius was born in Edipaurus, which is now called (Cavtat) Ragusavecchia, and so great effort was made to carve his image on the building, and a metrical epitaph was composed to him, which was affixed to the wall. On a central column at the entrance to the palace there is a sculpture of the first righteous judgement of Solomon. In an angle of the principal door is a carving of the Rector hearing offences, whilst at the entrance to the Small Council, is a sculpture of Justice holding a scroll, on which is written 'Jussi summa mei sua vos cuicumque tueri'.[6]

It was not long before this second palace was overtaken by a fate similar to that which befell the first. On August 8th 1462, a fire broke out, followed by the explosion of the powder magazine in the arsenal, which for some strange reason the Dubrovnik officials persisted in keeping close to their principal buildings, and the greater part of the Rector's Palace was destroyed, only the ground floor escaping from the general ruin. Other buildings were also destroyed, or partly damaged, including the Palace of the Great Council. Steps were at once taken by the Great Council to repair the damage, the new plans being drawn up by the architect to the Dubrovnik Republic, the Florentian Michelozzo Michelozzi (Salvi di Michiele).[7]

He was one of the early masters of the early Renaissance, and his influence may probably be seen in the adoption of the new style for the alterations and repairs in the palace. It appears that he was in Dubrovnik in March 1463, superintending the construction of the city walls; on February 11th 1464, the Council of Appeal (Consiglio dei Rogati) ordered that the palace be rebuilt to the design and advice of 'Michelotio ingeniaro'. His commitments elsewhere perhaps prevented his staying to complete the work at Dubrovnik, and it was left to local experts to carry out the reconstruction, no doubt according to the general instruction and plans of Michelozzi. The following June, Giorgi Orsini was appointed to complete the work.[8] He was a descendant of the great Roman family of that name, which had settled in Dalmatia before coming to Dubrovnik, and he had helped to rebuild the cathedral at Šibenik.

These two architects laid the basis for the Rector's Palace, in the form which has existed with few alterations, up to the present, for although the building was damaged in the earthquake of 1667, and then underwent extensive repairs, no details of much architectural importance were added later than 1464. Such is the history of the palace based on documentary evidence, and it is now possible to compare the written accounts with the actual building, and in doing so to try and distinguish the work of Onofrio di Giordano della Cava (1435) from that of Michelozzi and Orsini in 1464. It is interesting to note that the style of Orsini's early work had been Gothic, but even while at Šibenik he was half converted to Renaissance ideas. When he came to Dubrovnik he had adopted them completely, and his work on the palace shows no traces of Gothic. Thus parts of the building are in the Gothic style by Onofrio, and parts in that of the Renaissance by Orsini and Michelozzi; comparison with the cathedral in Šibenik shows that both buildings had different architects at work at a short interval of time, and during that interval the architecture began to pass into a new phase.

The facade towards the main square is two stories high, the lower consisting of an arcade of six round arches between two solid structures which contain windows, while the upper floor is pierced by eight two-light Venetian Gothic windows. The reason why the arcade is not continued to either end of the building, is probably explained by the fact that there was probably a tower at each end of the front, which would of course need a solid substructure. These towers may also explain the tradition that there was a third storey to the palace (i.e. ground, first and second floors) and that the second floor was destroyed in the 1667 earthquake and never replaced. Also evidence from a small silver model of the palace shows a low tower at either end of the facade, raised only by one extra storey above the rest of the two storey building. The main facade of the Rector's Palace began to be restored in 1468. The capitals in the arcade are partly Gothic and partly Renaissance work. A closer examination of the capitals reveals an elaborate half column adorned with the figure of Æsculapius devised by the Cremonese chancellor[9] and obviously the work of Onofrio, as are the three outer capitals. They are bolder in design and more perfect in execution than the three classical ones in the centre. Nevertheless, an alternative viewpoint is put forward by Eitelberger who believed that the main capital is a relic of the older building, but that the

> 'other capitals with angels, festoons, and foliage, have the decided character of the Renaissance, like the whole structure of the pillars'.[10]

It seems that the problem is not so easily solved; on the one hand the arcade contains much more of Onofrio's work than the one Æsculapius capital, whilst on the other it obviously has work that is later than his time, and in a style different from that of Onofrio. The Æsculapius represents an old man seated with an open book in his hand, a number of distilling apparatuses, retorts and other scientific instruments by his side, and two men standing beyond, one with a bird in his hand. It is evidently intended to represent an alchemist or physician giving advice. The capital next to this is considered by some to be better:

> 'The tender rigidity of the foliage, the delicate pencilling of the fibres, and the just proportioning of light and shade in this lovely piece of sculpture can hardly be surpassed'.[11]

The four outside capitals are all by Onofrio, and the wall belongs to the same period, as is proved by an inscription recording the erection of the palace in 1435. The three middle capitals, with their heavy abaci, and round arches which support them, are by the later architects of 1464 including the work of Orsini. It is probable that the original arches of Onofrio were pointed, but that they and the middle capitals were badly injured by fire to such an extent that new ones had to be provided, and Orsini wishing to give the building a more Renaissance character, provided round arches to replace the pointed ones. Unfortunately the original abaci on the older capitals by Onofrio were very shallow and decorated by a band of running leaves. These had to be replaced by heavier abaci so as to make the arches high enough to support the vaultings.

From all this various information it is now possible to piece together the development of the arcade. The four extreme capitals are Onofrio's work, together with his five columns of Korčulan stone, and the two half columns at the ends. Also the interior walls of the arcade are his work, together with the brackets, or consoles, that carry the vaulting, the ground floor and mezzanine windows, and the magnificent door in the back wall that gives access to the interior cortile. All this was preserved by later architects when they took over reconstruction. Three of the old capitals, in the centre of the row were so damaged that they had to be replaced by new ones. On all seven, Orsini then placed his massive abaci without spoiling the architectural effect and then made the round arches with their classic festoons and ribands.

New problems arise with the upper storey, because although it is above the restored Renaissance arches of the arcade, it belongs to the earlier period. The carved stringcourse at the first floor level and the eight windows above are all genuine Gothic work of 1435, although they stand above the Renaissance work of 1464. The end windows provide no problem; they were under the towers and have windows of the same date below them, probably never having been disturbed. The critical part is the central six windows over the portico. The most plausible explanation[12] lies in the fact that during restoration old materials (columns and other adornments) which had fallen without being greatly damaged, were utilized again. This supposition is supported by a council minute of 1464, from which it seems that the front was not actually thrown down by the explosion, but had partly been taken down and reconstructed, and this would account for the well-preserved state of the windows,[13] whilst the capitals of these upper windows are small but excellent in design. Their chief motif is foliage intertwined with faces of human beings and lions.

The doorway leading into the courtyard of the palace from the arcade is really magnificent. It is decorated with a scroll of foliage round the pointed arch, from which emerge small half-length figures, while the capitals and imposts are richly carved with groups of figures full of movement. The impost to the right bears on the front face four small boys with wings and nimbus; one plays the organ, a second blows the bellows for him and the other two are blowing trumpets, quite in the style of Michelozzi probably by Salvi di Michiele. On the return face there is a group of three naked men with javelins and shields, who are advancing as if to disturb the harmony. On the left hand impost the front face is adorned with a peaceful theme of a man embracing his wife, and a winged boy by their side; conversely the return face has a disorderly theme with a riotous troop of figures, one blowing a horn, and the others dancing, struggling or racing, all in a curious type of perspective, but all are admirably carved and full of life and fancy. The small brackets from where the vaulting springs are also well carved with groups of men and animals. The best of these is the one with a shepherd boy and a dragon, both full of movement and grace, and similarly interesting in perspective. This doorway is part of Onofrio's building, and so is the Porta della Carità, to the right at the southern end of the arcade, otherwise called the 'Porta e l'Officio del Fondico'. Here in times of famine the poor assembled to receive grain, sold below cost price, or on easy credit,[14] as well as the other small door near it which led by a private staircase to the hall of the Small Council on the mezzanine floor. To the right and left of the main entrance are rows of carved marble benches running along the back of the wall, where 'Sotto i volti' as the old documents phrase it, the Rector and the Ground Council sat in state. The ones on the right are in double tiers, and here on particularly important occasions the Rector would sit with the Small Council, the Archbishop, and in later times, the Imperial Resident. The lower single-tier seats to the left were for the Great Council.[15]

On passing through the great gateway, one's attention is drawn to the bronze knockers on the double door, one of which, a fine Byzantine lion's head, may possibly have survived from the palace of 1388, or from the still older castle. Once inside the courtyard, the interior cortile consists of a square enclosed by two tiers of round arches enclosing two arcades. Both the upper and lower arches are vaulted, but the iron ties, so common in Italian architecture have not been used here. The arches on the upper storey are twice as numerous as those of the lower, whilst the lower arcade rests on plain cylindrical columns with square plinths. The capitals are of a well-known Renaissance type with shallow abaci, and the width of the impost of the arches is confined, classic in design, to the top diameter of the shaft. The mouldings are rather clumsily distorted, and the foliage is so simple as to recall Romanesque work. All the mouldings are stopped on square stoolings. The arches are plain and without mouldings. The upper arcade has twin columns, one behind the other, and this part of the buildings is the work of Orsini. The carving is coarse, and the details commonplace. These arcades are not earlier than the fire of 1464, but on the wall behind the arcades there are doors with pointed tympanum, and windows of Venetian Gothic in the pointed style of the earlier edifice, which all belonged to Onofrio's palace.

Two open stone staircases of no great age, lead from the courtyard to the upper storey. The main one, to the left of the entrance, is poorly designed but the general effect is large and stately; to the right, a smaller flight leads to the mezzanine floor and the hall of the Small Council. This latter staircase has low rounded arches, but the balustrade is adorned with a Gothic frieze, similar to the seats of stone used by the Rector and Great Council. Beside the door of this hall, at the head of the stairs is a sculptured capital representing the Rector administering justice (the officer is wearing the traditional 'opankas', or sandals still common in Dalmatia); and opposite is a symbolical female figure of Justice, the 'Quaedam justitiae sculptura' of de Diversis, holding a scroll, or 'breve', with the words now scarcely legible 'Jussi summa mei'. She is carved on a bracket, or console, and from behind the flowing drapery the mutilated figures of two lions peep out, keeping guard, one each side of her. The two lions' heads and part of the scrollwork have been rather clumsily restored, but again this was originally Onofrio's work. Here too, the capital of the Rector administering justice is just as described by de Diversis, but it does not appear to be in its original place. It serves as part of the capital of a detached square shaft, although at some previous time it was once fitted with a round attached shaft, and has been rudely adapted to the square pier by a cut leaf which eases off the inconvenient angle. The style of the figures, although on a somewhat smaller scale correspond exactly with those of the Æsculapius and Solomon capitals, and the Rector wears here the coif of a Doctor of Law, just as Solomon's principal law officer does. The culprit brought up for sentence has a dogged look, and the satisfied, complacent air of the officer who arrested him is very amusingly expressed. On the return face is the secretary seated at a desk with a prisoner before him in custody of another officer.

The interior of the palace contains little of interest, having been completely restored and modernized. There is, however, one small room on the ground floor, with a wooden ceiling charmingly painted with arabesque designs and gilding, dating probably from the sixteenth or early seventeenth century. Below the small arcade is the entrance to the state prisons, with their very gloomy dungeons, where some prisoners were walled up alive; the worst cells are found under the theatre, below sea level and flooded during periods of high tide. Finally, in the centre of the atrium there stands a green bronze bust of a figure with a pointed beard and dressed in the style of the early seventeenth century. It is in honour of Miho Pracatović, benefactor to the republic and below the statue on a pedestal is inscribed: *Michaeli Prazatto, bene merito civi, 1638.* He was one of the merchants of Dubrovnik, who left 200,000 gold zechins[16] for charitable purposes invested in the bank of San Giorgio in Genoa, but on a closer inspection it is possible to see a slightly concave skull, and another face on the pedestal containing the inscription: *Conlapsa maximo terraemutu, 1667* – a reminder of the dreadful earthquake of that year, which destroyed all but the strongest buildings. Repairs on the Rector's Palace after 1667 until 1739 were carried out by the Korčulan builder Jerolim Škarpa.

On the whole, the Rector's Palace is one of the most interesting and beautiful buildings in Dalmatia, along with the Romanesque cathedral at Trogir. Its graceful design, perfect proportions and its many charming details of stone work make the palace a worthy rival of many of the famous 'palazzi pubblici' of some Italian towns. It bears strong resemblance to the Loggia dei Mercanti at Ancona, on which some of the same artists were employed. Unfortunately the Korčulan stone, although admirable for building purposes, for columns, and plain adornments, is not quite hard enough for elaborate sculpture, so that the designs of the artists, although worthy, sometimes have a rough and unfinished appearance, and lacks the accurate and finished work of the Florentines. Nevertheless, the Rector's Palace in Dubrovnik is in its way a small masterpiece and one of those fine edifices produced on the eve of the 'Cinque Cento', the massive Roman arches, the curious medieval sculptures, that spirit of Gothic detail render it a most picturesque building and denote the transition of taste when the beauties of antique art were observed and admired but approached from a different viewpoint.

In the past the churches and other religious buildings formed an integral part of the city. In former times the town and her suburbs had more than 150 churches and private chapels. There the religious orders for men and women had their great monasteries and convents. Very few traces remain of the catholic churches mentioned in old legends during the first few centuries of the city's existence, but amongst the oldest ones are the two little churches of Prijeko: St. Nikola, built probably in the twelfth century, and St. James, beneath the ramparts (1222). The church of St. James (St. Jakov, San Giacomo) formerly belonged to the Benedictine Order, is still complete (first recorded in 1225) and now occasionally used for service. Externally there is nothing which gives it the appearance of a church but it is the only remaining purely Romanesque building in Dubrovnik. Inside it consists of a nave about three metres wide and three bays long, each measuring nearly two metres in length and it ends eastward with an apse. The vault is a compromise between groined and barrel construction, for there are lateral arches, though they are very low and the groins are very slightly developed; but the building suffered from the earthquake in 1667, and possibly the vault is not in its original state. There is a fourteenth century painting of the Madonna over the altar. The other churches of the Byzantine period, St. Maria (1206–1250) the cathedral church, and St. Nikola in Prijeko have been rebuilt, and Dubrovnik contains nothing more of the Byzantine period, except probably a fine early doorway near the cathedral which could be twelfth century. Eitelberger maintains that

'of eastern Byzantine buildings no vestige remains and only the names of Mount Sergio (Mount Srđ) and some saints remind one of the East and the Eastern Church'[17]

and although this is not absolutely true, he was not far wrong. Most of the architectural remains of Dubrovnik do date from the period of Venetian rule, or the time of independence and much of the earlier evidence has vanished without trace.

One of the great losses sustained by Dubrovnik in the earthquake of 1667, was the destruction of the ancient cathedral (Duomo). It was built during the first half of the thirteenth century (1206–1250) and the only existing evidence of its appearance is the confused account of de Diversis.[18] Although in places it is extremely incomprehensible, his description is one of mosaic floors, vaulted roofs on lofty and massive columns, figures of animals inserted in the masonry, wall pictures with stories from the Old and New Testaments, marble thrones for the archbishop and the rector, a ciborium over the high altar resting on four columns, a silver 'pala' or reredos, a pulpit, or ambo, on columns of marvellous workmanship, and coloured glass in every window, casting a dim light on all the sacred objects. It appears it was a church with a nave for the men and side aisles for the women. With the additional help of a model of Dubrovnik from a later date it seems that the cathedral had a cupola mounted on a drum pierced with windows, and that the nave had a low clerestory; there is also reason to believe from de Diversis' description that it had a triforium. One of the most individual parts of the design must have been the covered ambulatory, or cloister, decorated with carvings of various animals, which surrounded the church, reached to more than half the height of the aisle walls, and was covered by a leaden roof. Further details can only be imagined by making analogies with other Dalmatian churches. Comparison of coevality place it with the naves of Lincoln and Wells Cathedrals in England, or the duomo of Lucca, with which it must have had a similar round-arched shape, but unlike the Lombard buildings it no doubt retained the Byzantine detail, with the crisply curved and sharply raffled leaves, and flat shallow surface carving which is found throughout Dalmatia, even in buildings dated from post-Byzantine rule.

The history of the original foundation of the cathedral has unexpected interest, according to local tradition, in its connection with the fate and fortunes of Richard Coeur-de-Lion, King of England. On returning from a crusade in the Holy Land, so the tale goes, he encountered a terrible storm off the island of Corfu, and made a vow that he would build a church to the Virgin in the place where he first landed safely. After several days at sea he was finally able to land on Lokrum Island, opposite Dubrovnik. In fulfilment of his vow the church was begun, at the request of Dubrovnik's citizens in the city itself, with funds which Richard endowed, out of gratitude of his deliverance, as well as a small chapel on Lokrum itself. There is, however, no evidence of the validity of this story, and none of the contemporary accounts of Richard's even mention Dubrovnik, while entries in the Dubrovnik Archives maintain that the church was built with contributions from the local nobility. Nevertheless, the subsequent adventures of Richard, Coeur-de-Lion are comparatively well-known. It is definitely stated in the chronicles of Zadar, that it was at that city he disembarked, and commenced in disguise on his journey to Vienna, no doubt through Croatia.

The old cathedral was destroyed during the earthquake in 1667 (a year after St. Paul's was burned down in London) and a plan for the new edifice was made by Andria Buffalini, sent from Rome on the recommendation of the Dubrovnik diplomat there, Gradić, in 1671. The Great Council approved the project in 1672 and the work of rebuilding began under Paulo Andrietti. It was completed by Angelo Bianchi in 1713 (the same year as St. Paul's was finished). The new cathedral is a fine spacious edifice, in mainly classical style with baroque ornamentation, built in cream coloured, almost marble stone. Although it cannot compete with the splendour of the ancient cathedral, its tall cupola and decorated front give it a certain character, but its real attraction is the contents of the treasury. The treasury is famous for the value and beauty of the precious objects and art pieces (ancient pictures, and relics framed in gold) all enclosed behind massive doors. The principal object of interest in the

Fig. 104.   The Baroque church of St. Blaize (Sv. Vlah), built by Marino Gropelli (1706–1714). Photo J. Cruise.

collection is the crown-shaped casket of enamelled work, containing part of the skull of their patron saint, St. Vlah (San Biagio, St. Blaize, or St. Blasius) and possibly brought to Dubrovnik from the Levant as early as 1026.[19] Among the other treasures of the cathedral is a fine ostensorio, or monstrance, surmounted by a crucifix, a fine cross with ornate silver work, and other examples of the silversmith's art including a water-pitcher and basin probably a product of local craftsmen.

The original church of St. Vlah was built resulting from a vow made during the visitation of the plague in 1348, and was completed by local craftsmen, Anđelo Lorrin, Butko and Mihajlo Petrović, within three years, in 1352.[20] From the description left by de Diversis it was very similar to the cathedral, but on a smaller scale. Within the church there is a silver statuette of St. Vlah, which besides its artistic merit is important because in his hand he holds a model of Dubrovnik, which shows buildings later destroyed in the earthquake. The original church, according to the model, had an eastern apse, a nave with aisles, and apparently a low outer aisle, which may have been part of an ambulatory. Further information on the church can be obtained from a picture in the Dominican church, showing an apse, like the cathedrals at Trogir and Šibenik, and both the nave and aisles were covered, like Lombard churches, with several tiers of arcading. Today the church still stands in Luža Square, but although suffering little damage from the earthquake of 1667, it was burned in 1706. Nevertheless the Great Council decided to have it repaired, under the plan and leadership of the Venetian builder Marino Gropelli, and it was completed in its present form in 1715. From the dedicatory inscription on the modern church it appears that it was rebuilt on a larger scale than the old one. Though Baroque in style it is very cleverly and effectively planned, and the general interior view is pleasing. Built in a stone of a rich mellow tone, the outer walls enclose a square, which is brought by four columns into a cruciform plan with a central cupola, and the only irregularity is an extension of one arm for the chancel.

During the Renaissance period a number of new churches and chapels were built at Dubrovnik, the majority of them quite small. At the entrance to the main street near the Pile Gate, is the most beautiful of these, the small consecrated church of the Holy Saviour (San Salvatore or Sv. Spas). It was founded, as the inscription on the door states, as a result of a vow made by the government of the time, to commemorate those who suffered in the great earthquake of 1520, the first of the fatal series from which Dubrovnik has suffered.

FIG. 105.   Church of the Holy Saviour (Sveti Spas) built in the style of the Lombardic Renaissance (1520–28), by Petar Andrijić.

'This shock caused much spiritual benefit, for many people confessed their sins, said prayers, and gave alms. Each Sunday the government with all the people went in procession to implore the Divine mercy, and vowed to build a church in honour of the Saviour, on which it was decided to spend 1,500 ducats ... For the building of it, certain nobles were appointed (Provveditori) to regulate the expense, but they raised the cost to more than 2,500 ducats, and the building proceeded so slowly that it was not finished for sixteen years. Nevertheless the nobles carried stones for the building barefooted and even noble matrons lent a hand to the work'.[21]

The delay may have been caused, some suspect, by the three Provveditori, who employed the masons for their own private houses as well. The Church in the style of the Lombardic Renaissance (1520–28) is built in a north-south direction and consists of a nave about 12 metres long and 7 metres wide, with an apse at the northern end and a choir of about four metres. Classic pilasters divide it into three bays, but the vaulting is of a Gothic construction, as are the side windows, with their narrow lights and plain tracery (similar to the church of St. Francis, at Hvar). The cornice is arcaded in Gothic fashion, but like a similar church on Korčula Island each arch is filled with a Renaissance shell. The facade is a simple but very beautiful specimen of Renaissance architecture, recalling that of the Lombardi's church of the Madonna dei Miracoli in Venice. The front has a semicircular gable between two quadrants like churches at Hvar and Starigrad, whilst the facade and the roof are built in the same manner as those of Šibenik Cathedral, where, however, the rounded gables actually close and are generated by the constructive form of the vaulting behind them. Like other buildings in Dalmatia, this church is an example of the tenacity with which local architecture clung to the older forms when elsewhere artistic development was moving away from them into newer forms. It was built by Petar Andrijić but the architect may probably have been Bartolommeo da Mestre, for the acts of the Great Council mention architects being summoned from Italy in 1520,[22] but unfortunately their names are not given; they do however refer to one Paduan working at Šibenik, who was there between 1517 and 1523, but absent in 1520, the year in which this church was begun in Dubrovnik.[23] This would also help to explain the similar roof construction in San Salvatore and Šibenik cathedral, where de Mestre was described by the local notary as 'protomagister fabricae Santi Jacobi'.

Among the other churches and chapels that of Santissima Annunziata (Blagovijesti, Nuncijata) deserves mention. The front is unadorned, but in the tympanum of the Gothic doorway is a group of three figures in high relief, representing St. John the Baptist and two other saints. There is much dignity about the figures, but the execution of the work is as usual somewhat rough. This chapel contains an interesting sixteenth century doorway built by Petar Andrijić in 1536 and is situated under the lee of the town walls, which at this point make an abrupt outward curve, so as to include the Dominican monastery. Close by is the church of St. Luke, with some good Renaissance decorations and an elaborate tympanum. More important perhaps, is the church of the Rozarijo (Confraternità del Rosario), built in 1594 and reconstructed between 1642 and 1659, but unfortunately desecrated and at some time in the past used as a military storehouse. The interior consists of two naves with a colonnade of three arches, and a low, dark storey above. The capitals are of a handsome classical design with attractive mouldings, but the proportions are bad, the church being too high for its length. In the upper part of the town is the little early Croatian chapel of the Sikurata (or Transfigurata), its facade on a tiny piazza, which is almost a courtyard. St. Nikola, in Prijeko, previously mentioned as probably having Byzantine connections, has a Renaissance doorway with Ionic columns and a classical pediment, the adornments being very pure and sober; the rosette window has a wheel pattern common in Dubrovnik architecture. The belfry is adorned with excellent mouldings and a twisted stringcourse. The date 1607 over the door refers to the restoration, the building itself being at least 80–100 years older, while the little figure over the door is even more ancient. Outside the walls, near the Pile Gate, is the tiny 'chiesa alle Danče' on the verge of a low cliff near the sea (Danče promontory) a chapel begun by public decree in 1457 to provide a resting place for the poor. The church contains a polyptych, and a triptych which has arched and cusped heads, with a frieze and cornice above, surmounted by a lunette. Each compartment holds paintings with religious themes. The west door is a handsome piece of Venetian Gothic with mouldings and a sculptured group of the Virgin and Child in the tympanum. In front of the church a platform spreads out, where a portico must formerly have been, as there are the bases of six large piers.

The immediate locality around Dubrovnik also has many ancient churches, important either for their style or works of art. Most of them are now preserved and declared monuments of historical value. One of these, with its own churchyard belonged to members of the Serbian Orthodox faith, but in 1877 a larger place of worship was built for them, in the Byzantine style near the centre of the city. A

Jewish Synagogue formerly existed in Dubrovnik, in Židovska ulice (street of the Jews), centre of the Jewish colony founded in 1352. The interior furniture from this synagogue, dates back to the seventeenth century. The synagogue is one of the oldest surviving in the Balkan peninsula. More recently members of the Islamic faith have founded a mosque in the city.

Of the remaining religious buildings mention should be made of the four monasteries, three within the city walls, the fourth on Lokrum Island. The two monasteries inside the wall were constructed alongside the two main entrances to the city, the Franciscan monastery at the Pile, and the Dominican at the Ploča Gates. The Dominicans (White monks, Bijeli Fratri) first established themselves in the small church of St. James, and did not move to their later site until between 1245 and 1253, their new church being opened for divine worship in 1306.[24] The church and monastery originally formed the southern bulwark of the city, the monks being entrusted, like the Franciscans, with the defence of the gate; later a second wall was built outside the monastery. The convent and cloister seem to have been completed in 1348, whilst the campanile was begun in 1424,[25] but according to de Diversis still incomplete in 1440.[26] Although built in the fifteenth century the campanile has rounded arches, and shafts set back to the centre of the wall, as if it had been constructed in the eleventh or twelfth century. The church consists of a vast single nave, which is crossed towards the eastern end by a triple arch separating the polygonal choir and two lateral chapels. The style is transitional between Romanesque and Gothic, but earthquakes and repeated repairs have left only a little of the original building. The choir is probably very old but extremely simple in design having hardly any architectural character. The only feature of any interest is the south doorway with a round arch of German Gothic style, which is increased by the tall moulded bases of the jamb shafts.[27] There are several pointed windows of extreme simplicity, one decorated with an outside frill of small Venetian arches.

The cloister was constructed by local builders according to a modified design of Maso di Bartolomeo and bears no trace of north European influence. It is an irregular square, with five bays on each side, individual bays being divided by three lights. The style is a curious medley

'of Gothic and Renaissance, of forms understood and otherwise, as indeed could only occur in a land which, being on the borders of Eastern and Western culture, did not possess the power to create and execute the various styles correctly'.[28]

The arches of the bays are round, but the inside work has more the character of Venetian Gothic, especially in the foliage. The shield of the semicircular head is pierced by quatrefoil lights encircled alternately with an ornament of interlacing circles almost Byzantine in character. The Dalmatian architects including Utišenović, Grubačević and Vlatković, had doubtless seen Gothic work in Italy, but

'had failed to grasp the idea of receding orders in the arch, or consistent mouldings in the tracery'.[29]

Classic traditions are seen in the columns with their Attic base and square capital. In spite of its deviations from architectural orthodoxy this cloister, with its Venetian well in the centre bearing the date 1623, is part of one of the loveliest monastic buildings in Dalmatia.

The Minorites first arrived in Dubrovnik in 1235 and lived outside the Pile Gate, not moving inside the city walls until after the destruction of the first Franciscan house. Serbians under Uroš II (1282–1321) repeatedly harassed Dubrovnik with constant invasions and the abandoned convent provided adequate shelter for his troops. The republic seeing this danger destroyed the convent and built the friars a new one inside the walls at public expense in 1317.[30] The church and convent of the Franciscan Order (Mala Brača) were seriously damaged during the great earthquake of 1667, mainly by the ensuing fire, which amongst other things reduced 6,500 volumes of precious manuscripts to ashes.[31] The church built in French Gothic style and a large part of the monastery have been rebuilt since the earthquake, although a few earlier interesting details remain. The fine campanile for example, forms one of the main ornaments of the Stradun and marks the transition from the Romanesque to the Gothic. The top stage with its cupola is later than the earthquake, but the rest of the building is fourteenth century, the round arch still being used even at that date, although mixed with pointed architecture. There is also a handsome doorway in the Venetian Gothic style on the south side opening on to the Stradun. It is surmounted by a 'pieta' in a central niche, an interesting piece of sculpture probably dating from the fifteenth century. This richly ornamental portal was probably made by Leonard and Peter Petrović. The chief interest of the building lies in the cloister, which has been described as 'one of the most singular pieces of architecture ever seen'.[32] Here is one of the most notable features of Dalmatian architecture, for although it dates from later than 1319 it is thoroughly Romanesque in character, and all its arches are round. Each bay consists of a group of six roundheaded lights divided by coupled octagonal shafts, above which the tympanum of the round including the arch is pierced with a large circle. Most of the circles are cusped into a quatrefoil, but the central one on each side of the cloister is not cusped but ornamented by a rich border of acanthus leaves laid on the waved section of the splay and radiating from the centre outwards. The coupled octagonal shafts stand one behind the other, and have a common base and abacus, the latter being long enough to receive the full thickness of the wall above. The separate capitals serve as mullions to the arches, and recall the wildest and most grotesque fancies of early Romanesque work, full of grinning faces, masks, animals, monsters, dragons and winged beasts, all mixed into conventional foliage, spiral volutes and block leaves that are very primitive in design. They give the appearance of belonging to the twelfth or thirteenth centuries, but in fact are of a later date. These early forms were preserved much longer in the monasteries of the East when they had already given place to the Gothic style in western Europe. Fortunately the name of the architect has been preserved in an inscription in the cloister itself. He was an Albanian, called Mihaje Brajkov from Antivari (Bar), a town where Byzantine influence was stronger than at Dubrovnik. Although the inscription is without a date, it is close to two others of 1363 and 1428, whilst the style of lettering could be even earlier than 1363, the cloister having probably been built shortly after the foundation of the new convent in 1317. Already in 1440 de Diversis described the cloister with its orange trees, shrubs, and fountain, which appears to have changed little over the ensuing centuries.[33] In the sacristy there is a beautiful monstrance, attributed to the work of the goldsmiths of Mezzo (Mljet). Finally, the monastery has a chemist's shop, one of the oldest in Europe, founded in 1317.[34]

Two other monasteries deserve some mention. The first is inside the city walls and concerns the baroque church and monastery of the Jesuit order. This building was started before the earthquake of 1667 but not completed till after 1715. The resumption of the building after 1667 was carried out according to the plans of the Jesuit architect, Andrea Pocco. The most notable feature is the large Baroque staircase which leads from the Gundulićeva Poljana to the Poljana Ruđera Boškovića, and completed in 1738 by the Italian architect Padalequae based on plans of the Trinità dei Monti in Rome. The neighbouring building was constructed about 1735 and was previously known as the 'Collegium Ragusinum'. The second monastery is outside the city walls on the island of Lokrum, and belonged to the Benedictine Order who also had another on the island of Mljet. Benedictine monks settled on Lokrum during the first half of the eleventh century, and at the beginning of the fourteenth the church of St. Mihajla and adjoining monastery were constructed by the architect and builder, Radin. It is situated in a sheltered part of the island in a small valley and its origin is connected with the legend of Richard Coeur-de-Lion. In the fifteenth century the church was extended and what is left of the ruined remains indicates that it was of considerable size, of Byzantine form, and evidence of Gothic details amongst the preserved remnants.

Dubrovnik also contains two large convents, now desecrated, which were used to lodge two religious orders for women; one was that of St. Claire (founded 1290) with its orphanage, and the other St. Catherine. They have both been restored and preserved as historical monuments, but today the former is the trade union headquarters (Ivan Morđin-Črni House), whilst the latter is a College of Music; reconstruction work here revealed the foundations and crypt of the first cathedral in Dubrovnik, the church of St. Peter the Great (Sv. Petar Veliki).

Of the lay buildings in Dubrovnik the most striking after the Rector's Palace, is undoubtedly the Sponza[35] (or Divona, from the Italian word 'dogona'), the ancient customs-house and mint of the republic. The secular buildings in Dubrovnik all belong to a much later period than this edifice for much of it was constructed in the early fourteenth century. It stands at the end of Stradun, opposite the open space that corresponds to the Venetian Piazzetta, on one side of which is situated the Rectorial Palace. The Sponza is a three-storied building, surrounding a courtyard, which was probably the result of work done in two, or perhaps three different periods. The original building most likely only contained the ground floor, with its arcades and warehouses, and was already an ancient edifice in 1440 when de Diversis described it,[36] and it is certain that a Sponza was standing in 1312, because the government ordered its completion in that year.[37] If the ground floor is older than that date the work then ordered to be finished was probably the first floor surrounding the interior cortile with an upper order of arches. Nevertheless, there could have been little difference in the date. Both have the same square soffits to the arches, the details of their mouldings are very similar, and although there is some discrepancy in the long sides of the oblong court (the upper tier of the arches are pointed while those below are round) at the narrow ends of the court the arches are round both on the ground and first floor. Thus the oblong courtyard is surrounded on the lower storey by vaulted arches, supported on short plain solid octagonal columns, without bases, (like those of the Ducal Palace at Venice) and short capitals opening into a square abaci.

The ground floor was occupied by the customs-house where the public scales were found for weighing merchandise, which hung in the arch at the end of the court. The first floor was devoted to social gatherings and literary assemblies of the nobility and men of learning. The third storey, or second floor, was the mint, and belongs apparently to the date of the inscription on the end wall 1520. This part of the building is based on a model devised by the Dubrovnik builder Paskoje Miličević, dated 1516, and helped by the Andrijić brothers, stone-masons from Korčula. It is transitive between the Gothic and Renaissance styles of architecture, with the monogram I.H.S., found on so many houses in Dubrovnik to commemorate the earthquake of that year (1520). The doors of the warehouses opening from the lower cloister have the names of saints over them, whilst inside the warehouses are covered with plain cross vaulting without ribs. The facade towards the main square has a very handsome Renaissance arcade in front of it, and this like the third floor was probably added in 1520. Behind this, on the ground floor, are the windows and doors of the customs-house, while the first floor above has a row of windows, with tracery and ogeed head, in the purest Venetian style of the fifteenth century. The central window is a three light aperture, the two side ones are of a single light; the windows of the third storey are square like those looking on the courtyard. In the centre is a niche for the statue of St. Vlah, while the row of pinnacles on the roof are similar to those found on a Venetian palazzo (e.g. Ca d'oro in Venice).

FIG. 106.   Sponza Palace built between 1516–22 in the Gothic-Renaissance transitional style according to designs by Paskoje Miličević. The building was used as a customs house, mint, state treasury, bank and office for the valuation of goods, while the upper two floors served as a granary, and today house the Dubrovnik State Archives.

The Sponza has many interesting associations with Dubrovnik's history. It was here that the caravans formed up at the start of their journey into the Balkan interior, and those which arrived in Dubrovnik made their customary stop. Every bale of goods arriving, or departing from, the city, by land or sea, had first to be examined at the Sponza, where the proper amount of duty was assessed and paid. All business was transacted at, or around this building, and in 1277 the statutes of the Dogana were compiled by the then Count of Dubrovnik, Marco Giustiniani. He found the numerous rules of preceding Counts confused and inadequate.[38] They dealt with export dues on Dubrovnik's manufactures, or articles sold from the city to foreigners, with duty on the purchase of slaves (until 1417), or their removal from Dubrovnik's territory, with duty on purchase of land, houses, or other real estate, and on the export of hawks (Venetians exempted), with duty on the sale of fresh and salt meat in the public market, with the excise on wine and oil, and duty on goldsmith's work. Other ordinances by subsequent Counts and Rectors followed, and after 1332, for the first time, the Italian language begins to appear instead of Latin, though only occasionally. The Sponza was still being used as a customs-house at the beginning of the twentieth century but today the ground floor houses the Museum of the Socialist Revolution 1941–45 and the upper floors contain the State Archives of the Dubrovnik Republic.

The efficient management of all public affairs required the existence of public buildings, as lodgings for state officials and foreign diplomats as well as other travellers, together with different health and community services. Yet the buildings so far described were mainly the stone edifices in the town. Prior to the thirteenth century all the buildings, with the exception of the Rector's Palace, and the Castello (supplanted by another building in 1388), were of timber.[39] Dubrovnik was in great part destroyed by fire in 1292, and rebuilt shortly afterwards, mostly of wood as before. In a 'Reformatio' of 1310 the government published a decree against the excessive use of timber in construction, but already the city was improving in various ways. The streets had been widened and made more regular and stone steps were built on either side of the Stradun to make the higher quarters more accessible. Elaborate rules were issued to ensure the solidity of the roofs and chimneys, and by 1355 the town was paved with brick.[40] The steep streets on the seaward ridge and on the slopes of Mount Srđ began to assume their present aspect, although few details of fourteenth century architecture have remained. There are several houses in the Venetian Gothic style, but these were built during the Hungarian occupation, for the artistic influence of Venice outlasted her political sovereignty. The great earthquake in the seventeenth century destroyed most public buildings. In the harbour behind large outlets in the walls, there was an arsenal (first recorded in 1272 and extended in 1535) for boat repairs, but today this no longer exists. At the inner side of the arsenal there was the Palace of the Great Council, built in 1344 and connected to the Rector's Palace, but this again was destroyed, this time by fire in 1816. In its place the City Hall (Gradska Općina) was built in the Lombardic style of early neo-Renaissance between 1863–64, according to a design by Emilio Vecchietti and now includes the National Theatre (Bondino Kazalište) and town cafe. Although the requirements of this building are now very different it is still possible to see traces of the old architectural framework. Other important public buildings still preserved include the Rupe (the

holes) in the south-west part of the city built in the sixteenth century
(1542–1590) as a warehouse for cereals (total capacity 30,000 bushels)
whilst outside the ramparts along the coast stretch the buildings of the
Lazaretto (Lazaret, Tabor or quarantine house) dated 1590. This
building was mainly concerned with commercial traffic and the pre-
vention of epidemics which may have been brought into the town
by merchants, or their goods. The Lazaretto remained in ruins for a
long time, but has recently been restored as a place of interest for
tourists.

Other public monuments in Dubrovnik include various statues,
steeples, a clock-tower, fountains and an aqueduct. Quite a number

FIG. 107.   Coat of arms of the Dubrovnik Republic.

of stone statues representing St. Vlah (Saint Blaise), protector of the city, are placed in niches, in prominent parts of the ramparts, and above the gates of Dubrovnik. They are the work of different artists as far back as the thirteenth century, and the saint is presented in various ways, sometimes only in profile, but usually with a model of the town in his arms. To the east of Placa at Luža, stands the Orlando (Roland) statue with the figure of a warrior, the medieval symbol of a free merchant city and of Dubrovnik's independence, erected in 1418, and was the work of a local man Antun Dubrovčanin. Here the state decrees were proclaimed in public, and on more solemn occasions the flag of the republic flew from its mast. The warrior's right forearm was the standard measure of length (lakat = elbow = 78 cm) in the Dubrovnik Republic. The statue was blown over by a hurricane in 1825 and restored in 1878. It is interesting to note that the republic did not erect statues itself, not even to those of her sons who had deserved this honour, the only exception being the one to Miho Pracatović (1522–1607) in the courtyard of the Rector's Palace. After

FIG. 108. View of the harbour with the Lazaret (quarantine house) in the foreground.

FIG. 109. Dubrovnik's main street, Placa (Stradun), with the City Tower at the far end. Photo J. Cruise.

the fall of the republic in 1808 several statues were erected in the city. One of these was to the great poet Ivan Gundulić (1588–1638) by Ivan Rendić, its inauguration in 1893 leading to a national demonstration throughout Yugoslavia against foreign domination and oppression. More recently the sculptor Ivan Meštrović created several monuments for the city including a statue of Sv. Vlah at Pile Gate, the relief and balustrade at the entrance to the town. Others include the statue of Marin Držić, the comedist and the bust of the scholar Ruđer Bošković. In 1954 a monument in honour of the dead from the Word War II was executed by the sculptor Fran Kršinić.

The two high steeples and the clock-tower add a special charm to the general view of the town. The highest steeple is the one on the church of the Franciscans (44 metres), built during the fifteenth century in Gothic style; the other steeple belongs to the Dominican church (41 metres high) and was built between the end of the fourteenth and third decade of the fifteenth century, containing the craftsmanship of such local builders as Radinović, Bogančić and Radončić. Baroque elements were introduced on restoration after the earthquake of 1667. The clock tower (Gradski Zvonik) is thirty-one metres high, and has at the top two small statues of green men (Zelenci) who strike the hours. It was first erected in 1445, but completely rebuilt in its present form in 1929, again the work of local craftsmen. The Bell Loggia (Loža Zvonara) was built in 1463, pulled down in mid-nineteenth century to make room for an apartment for the local Austrian commander, and reconstructed in 1962. The most interesting of the fountains in Dubrovnik is at the entrance to the city through the Pile Gate. It was constructed in 1438 and is polygonal in form, the work of Onofrio di Giordiano della Cava. The upper part was destroyed during the earthquake of 1667. Another, smaller fountain of his (Onofrijeva Česma) is found at Luža near the town cafe (Gradska Kafana), and is famous for its ornaments and figurines. It is the work of the stone mason Pietro di Martino da Milano and dates from the same period as its larger counterpart at the other end of the town. Other fountains exist in the city including the one already referred to in the courtyard of the Rector's Palace. In 1900 a fountain was erected at Pile, adorned with figures of a nymph and satyr, the work of the sculptor Rendić, and given as a gift to the town by the Amerling brothers. Finally mention should be made of the town aqueduct. This was built between 1436 and 1438, and the story of its origin is rather curious. Prior to 1438 the city was supplied with water from cisterns, but in 1437 the government decided to look for springs in the Gionchetto hills (present-day Šumet), and invited Onofrio, who was a noted hydraulic engineer as well as an architect, to construct it. The sum of 8,000 ducats was devoted to the purpose, but before its completion 12,000 were spent. Many people began to think Onofrio's project was impossible and he was summoned before the magistrates as an impostor. Fortunately the evidence of the experts was in his favour, and Onofrio succeeded in completing the

FIG. 110. Large fountain by Onofrio di Giordano della Cava, a 16-sided reservoir surmounted by a cupola, one of the terminal points of the old water-supply system completed 1444.

work in the prescribed time. Nothing now remained to be done but to erect a fountain (Onofrijeva velika česma), a sixteen-sided reservoir surmounted by a cupola, and one of the terminal points of the water supply system, all provided for by funds collected by public subscription.

A conspicuous architectural feature of the city is its defences. The greater part of the old town is surrounded by the city walls which were built according to plans drawn up in 1272 and 1296, but parts date back to the eighth and tenth centuries. The main part of the city walls and their fortifications were built, strengthened and recon-

Fig. 111. View of part of the city walls and Minćeta Tower.

structed over a period from the twelfth to the second half of the seventeenth century and included many prominent builders and architects involved in the various projects.[41] The main wall is 1,940 metres long and up to twenty-five metres high; towards the mainland it is 4–6 metres wide and seaward it is 1·5–3 metres. It is strengthened by three circular and twelve rectangular towers, five bastions, two corner fortresses and a large fort (St. John, Sv. Ivan). The most impressive tower is Minčeta (Torre Menze) in the north-west corner, one of the most beautiful features of the city. Its erection was decreed on July 3, 1319, but it was entirely rebuilt in the fifteenth century and considerably altered in the sixteenth. It stands on one of the highest points of the old town on the slopes of Mount Srđ (Sergio), on the site of an old square tower. The outer wall which runs along the main wall on the landward side, is strengthened by one large and nine small semi-circular bastions together with the casemated Bokar Tower, the oldest surviving fortification of its kind in Europe. The town was also protected by two free standing fortresses: in the eastern part of the town Fort Revelin is an impressive construction first dating from 1463, but later rebuilt according to the plans of A. Ferramolino (between 1539–1551). Its main function was to protect Dubrovnik from possible Turkish attack; to the west lies the other fortress, Lovrjenac, on a cliff rising forty-six metres above sea level.

FIG. 112.   View of part of the city walls and Pile Gate. Photo. J. Cruise.

It was designed, according to the chronicles, in 1050, but the earliest records of it date from 1301. It was later reconstructed in 1418, 1464 and 1571. It bears the inscription 'liberty is not for sale, for all the

gold in the world'. Lovrjenac and Revelin are the two strongest con-
structions in the whole fortification system, mainly due to their position, dimensions and interior design. During the Dubrovnik summer
festival, they are both often used as open air stages. The oldest of the
defences on the wings of the ramparts is Fort St. John (San Giovanni,
Sv. Ivan or Forte Molo) a huge round bastion, considerably altered
in later times. It was originally built at the end of the eighth century
to defend the entrance to the port, but during the fourteenth was
enlarged, its present shape and size dating from the sixteenth century. Of the tower called 'Campana Morta' (the dead bell), few traces
survive. It was so named because its bell tolled to announce an execution of a criminal, a proclamation of exile, or the approach of a
hostile fleet.[42] These towers were garrisoned by the town guard of
127 men, who were chosen by lot from the citizens every month, and
increased at times of danger. In 1346, for example, forty additional
sentries were conscripted and distributed among the posts, and an
extra body of archers was enrolled,[43] a year when Venice was constantly trying to prevent many Dalmatian towns from acknowledg-
ing the protection of Hungary. Of course when military expeditions
were organized, a much larger levy was made both in the city and
throughout the territory of the republic. Other towers were built
along the walls, and their defence was entrusted to the private
families whose houses they adjoined. The building of the city's Main
Guard (Glavna Straža) was constructed between 1706–08 by Marino
Gropelli on the site of an earlier building. This had been in the form
of an open arcade adjoining the old church of St. Vlah and destroyed
by fire in 1706.

The walls are pierced by four gates, Pile (Porta Pile), the Ploče
Customs (Porta Ploce) (Porta Dogana), and Ponta (Vrata od Ponta).
At Pile Gate there is a double circuit of walls; the outer gate is a
round arch in a semi-circular outwork, with embrasures on either
side. The gate has over the city's moat a drawbridge, with a well-
preserved mechanism for lifting the bridge. Similarly, Ploče Gate
has its own drawbridge, forming part of the main eastern entrance
into the town. The street leading from the city centre to Ploče Gate
opens out on to the quays of the harbour (Gradska Luka). It is sheltered by the fort of St. John and other towers, while the pier built
by Pasquale di Michele juts out into the sea. Large walled-up arches
led to the shelters for the galleys.[44]

Dubrovnik also has still standing a few of the private houses and

FIG. 113.   View of Pile Gate from outside the walls.

palaces of former wealthy inhabitants which have architectural pretensions. Many along the Stradun were destroyed by the 1667 earthquake, but this street (292 metres long), still links the Pile and Ploče
Gates, and remains the main thoroughfare of the city. A thirteenth
century statute on sanitary measures decreed that the city's main
sewerage system flowed under this street towards the harbour, a
system still operative today. Both sides of the Placa were lined with
shops, the former wooden buildings in the eastern part of the north
side being replaced by stone houses with porticos about the middle
of the fourteenth century. In 1468 the Placa was provided with a

FIG. 114.　View of Ploče Gate from outside the walls.

pavement and completely reconstructed after the earthquake of 1667, with Baroque style fronts based on designs made by Ceruti of Rome. Some of the houses have retained the old type of shop entrance on the ground floor. Parallel to the Stradun on the slope of Mount Srđ, lies Prijeko Street, where several picturesque old palaces may be found. This thoroughfare is very narrow and the houses are of great height, many of them adorned with charming Venetian balconies and fragments of sculpture. One of these houses (No. 170) has a fine doorway, with a rectangular entablature enclosing a pointed arch. In the corners thus formed are two centaurs, very spirited and

Fig. 115. Dubrovnik from the air.

full of movement, though not quite perfectly executed. The balcony above, which is exceptionally wide in proportion to its length, is supported by three carved brackets. A veritable gem of Venetian work is found on the palace (No. 316) with a beautiful little balcony supported by a marble collonade. On several other houses there are similar fragments, as in other streets, especially near the cathedral. Many of the houses are plain and unadorned, but the rich yellow hue of the Korčulan stone give them a harmonious appearance.

The patrician families built their houses, and the rich citizens followed as did the mariners and merchants. Among the palaces under preservation, three are worthy of special mention. They all belonged to the mariner and commoner, Škočibuha. One of his houses stands in the city behind the cathedral and built by Josip and Ivan Andrijić between 1549 and 1553, according to the plans of Antun di Padua. It is the best preserved example of a private building prior to the 1667 earthquake together with the Gothic Zamanja Palace. The second one is a summer residence of the Škočibuha-Bonda family (1657–88) at Boninovo. During the siege of Dubrovnik in 1806 the building was destroyed by a powder-keg explosion, but was reconstructed in 1938 and more recently has been adapted as the Yugoslav National Army Hall. The third is at Lapad. Many other residential houses were built along the coast of rich architectural design, often surrounded by gardens, out-houses and farm buildings. The water front at Gruž is full of former summer residences of the Dubrovnik noble families. The house of the Bunić-Pucić-Gradić families has a Renaissance ground floor, a Gothic upper storey, and a Gothic-Renaissance chapel on a large terrace. In the nineteenth century the Renaissance residence of the Bunić family was reconstructed with a boat house (orsan) and a terrace. The Gundulić family also had a summer residence here, constructed in the Renaissance style by Korčulan builders in the sixteenth century, with a chapel and summer house over the 'orsan'. There are two old summer residences of Dubrovnik families at Batali: those of Majstorović, a house with a Renaissance ground floor and Gothic upper storey, and of Getaldić-Gundulić with a chapel and boat house. Farther on near the sea lies the residence of Petar Sorkočević dated 1521, with Renaissance arcades on the ground floor and Gothic windows (single and triple lights) in the upper storey. The large grounds contain a chapel, large terrace and fish pond. The reconstructed building now houses the Historical Institute of the Yugoslav Academy of Science and Art.

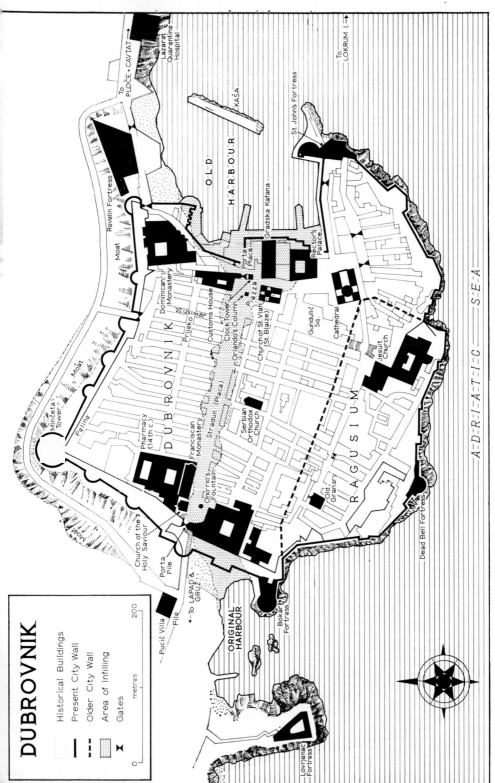

Fig. 116 Map of present-day Dubrovnik

Table XIII
Principal Buildings in Dubrovnik

Foundation	Name of building	History: Remarks
	BYZANTINE PERIOD	
9th/10th C.	St. Stephan's Church	Ruined by earthquake in 1667. Four walls and fragments remain.
9th/11th C.	Sikurata chapel	Exists.
1050	Lovrjenac Fort begun	Exists, reconstructed 1418, 1464, 1571.
9th/11th C.	Church of St. James	Exists, first recorded 1225.
11th/12th C.	Doorway on hill near Cathedral.	Exists.
	VENETIAN PERIOD	
1222	St. James Church (Višnjice)	Exists.
1200–50	Cathedral	Destroyed by earthquake in 1667.
1245	Church of St. Luke	Exists. Extended 1787.
13th C.	Arsenal	Reconstructed 1489. Extended 1535. Converted into café in 1933.
1290	Nunnery of St. Claire	Exists. Reconstructed in 19th C.
1290	Church of St. Michael (Lapad)	Exists. Contains graves of Dubrovnik noblemen.
1303	Palace of the Great Council	Enlarged in 1489, destroyed by fire in 1817.
1306	Dominican Church opened	Exists, though modernized in 1883. South doorway and choir stalls very ancient.
1306	Chapel of St. Lazarus	Exists. Contained old leprosarium.
1312	Sponza ground and first floors of Cortile (date uncertain).	Exists.
1317–60	Franciscan Church, Convent and Cloister (M. Brajkov)	Cloister perfect. Church and Convent modernized.
1348	Dominican Convent begun	Cloister perfect, Cloister well-preserved.
1348	Church of St. Vlah	Destroyed by fire in 1706 and rebuilt.
	HUNGARIAN PERIOD	
1388	Rector's Palace, on site of ancient castle.	Destroyed by fire 1435.
1395	Baptistery	Destroyed in 19th C.
	PERIOD OF INDEPENDENT REPUBLIC	
1424	Tower of Dominican Convent by Fra. Stefano	Exists. Top stage modern.

Table XIII—continued
Principal Buildings in Dubrovnik

Foundation	Name of building	History: Remarks
1435	New Rector's Palace begun by Onofrio di Giordano	Ruined by fire in 1463, but a large part incorporated in present building.
15th C.	Synagogue	Exists.
1437	Fountains of Onofrio di Giordano	The larger ruined, but the smaller one perfect.
1444	Town Resevoir	Exists.
1444	Clock Tower	Completely reconstructed 1929.
1457	Votive Church at Danče	Exists, but altered.
1463	Bell Loggia built	Demolished mid-19th C., reconstructed 1962.
1463	Revelin Fort begun	Exists, reconstructed 1538
1464	Rector's Palace repaired and partly rebuilt by Michelozzi and Giorgio Orsinin.	Exists.
1464	Minčeta Tower by Orsini	Exists.
1507	Church of St. Nikola	Exists. Extended 1607.
1520–28	Church of the Holy Saviour	Exists.
1521	Summer Residence of Petar Sorkočević.	Exists.
1516–22	Sponza, upper storey and portico	Exists.
1536	Church of the Annunciation	Exists, Renovated 1910.
1542–90	Rupe Granary	Exists.
1549–53	Skočibuha Palace	Exists.
1590	Lazaret	Exists, Recently renovated.
1594	Church of the Rozario	Exists, reconstructed 1642 after fire, and again in 1962.
1671–1713	Cathedral rebuilt	Exists.
1675–88	Skočibuha-Bonda Summer Residence	Exists. Destroyed by explosion 1806, reconstructed 1938.
1699–1725	Jesuits' Church	Exists.
1706–15	Church of St. Vlah rebuilt.	Exists.
1735	Collegium Ragusinum	Exists.
1738	Stairs to Jesuits' Church	Exists.
	PERIOD AFTER INDEPENDENCE	
1852	Nautical School	Exists.
1863–64	City Hall	Exists.
1863–64	National Theatre	Exists.
1875	Dubrovnik's Lighthouse on Daksa islet	Exists.
1877	Serbian Orthodox Church	Exists.

Other noted families with summer villas included the Kabužić and Staje residences at Batala, and that of Luka Pucić with a Renaissance ground floor, Gothic windows in the upper storey and a collonade at the rear.

In conclusion, evidence has shown that Dubrovnik's architecture and sculpture was strongly, indeed prevalently, inspired by Venetian example, both in the work which is known as Venetian Gothic and in that of the Renaissance period. Although, as a rule, the earlier artistic forms survived much longer in Dalmatia than in Italy, the Dalmatians exhibited 'a natural almost precocious liking for the Renaissance style'.[45] Giorgi Orsini's work at Šibenik actually preceded that of Leon Battista Alberti in Rimini by nine years. Another characteristic of Dubrovnik's architecture and sculpture is that the names of so few of the artists are preserved, and most of those who are remembered were foreigners. Doubtless there were many local artists, but Dubrovnik talent seems to have been of a collective rather than an individual character and much of the work was probably done by master masons, stone cutters and similar craftsmen, and may have been the outcome of the general artistic feeling of the people rather than the conception of great masters.

Painting

The Dalmatians seem to have been less conspicuous in painting than in architecture but more recent research has proved some of the earlier opinions to have been unfair in their judgements.

'With regard to Dubrovnik there are a few specimens of native art, but hardly a record of the life of any painter'.[46]

Another authority

'did not know of any Dubrovnik painter earlier than the fifteenth century, but found it possible that some of the pictures in the Dominican monastery, which are of an earlier date, to be by native brush'.[47]

Yet again

'In the field of art Dubrovnik has been less distinguished (than in science and literature), for native artists were not wanting among the Dubrovnik citizens . . . caring very little for anything but commerce and very little for literature; and the number of Dubrovnik

artists who worked at Florence, at Rome and at the court of
Hungary, and earned for themselves both bread and fame in
foreign countries, proves that they had little prospect of winning
either at home'.[48]

Nevertheless one of them admits that a guild of painters did exist
in the sixteenth century with nineteen members, all so poor that they
had to be subsidized by the state.[49]

It is true that there is very little evidence of paintings from the
twelfth to the fourteenth centuries, but according to de Diversis
there were paintings on the walls of Dubrovnik's old cathedral. The
old votive church had murals, whilst the windows contained figures
of saints painted on the glass. From archival documents it appears it
was the work of Michael from Bologne, who is mentioned as living
in the city between 1313 and 1341. Pale traces of wall paintings are
also found in the apses of the Romanesque church on Lokrum Island,
together with further examples on the walls of the church at Jezera
on Mljet Island. During the fourteenth century several Italian and
Greek artists worked in Dubrovnik. Archival material mentions the
two distinct groups. The Italian masters included Bernado (1345),
Durantea (1348), Marco from Apulia (1351), Giovannio from Rimini
(1367–71), Francesco from Bologne (1371–1405), the Venetian master
Augustine (1376), Zanina (1389) and Antonio (1390–91). The Greek
contribution included Emanuala (1367–68), Joana from Dürres
(1388–89) and Georgija (1377–86); they were collectively known as
'pictures gracci' who were famous throughout Dalmatia in the fourteenth century. During the first half of the same century, local artists'
names began to appear; these included Stanče (1302–13), Marko
Vlahov (1313) and Mihovil from Zadar (1348), whilst in the second
half of the fourteenth century the name of Stojko Drušković (1371–
1420) appears, the first important person in the Dubrovnik branch
of the Dalmatian school of painters.

From the end of the fourteenth to the first half of the sixteenth
century there is evidence of a native Dubrovnik school of painters
who modelled their style on that of Italy, though painting in Dalmatia, like architecture, lagged behind the more advanced countries
of Europe. Between 1421–1426, the painter Blaž Trogiranin worked
in Dubrovnik and in the church of St. Georgia (Sv. Đurda) at Boninovo one of his pictures, together with others, now in Split Gallery,
of Dubrovnik's noble families, show distinct characteristics of the

Dubrovnik school of painting. Other examples of this earlier period of the school are seen in the work of Ivan Ugrinović, in his polyptych at the church of St. Anthony (Sv. Ante) in Koločep dated 1434, and of Matej Junčić in the church of Our Lady at Šunja, on Lopud, from 1452. They all possess an element of composition similar in character to the Venetian school of the late thirteenth century mixed with some Byzantine influences.

The first real evidence of exact dating for the Dubrovnik school is the well-preserved polyptych by Lovro Marinov Dobričević, (from Kotor) in the votive church of Our Lady at Danče. This picture is on the main altar, contains figures of the Virgin and Child, St. Nicholas, St. George, St. Vlah and St. Francis, and bears the date 1465, nine years after the church was built. His earlier work, the figures of Mary and John the Evangelist, around the painted Gothic cross (14th century) in the Dominican church, (alternatively attributed to Paolo Veneziano), still contain the true thirteenth century form and feeling; the polyptych at Danče is beginning to portray a new spirit of line, blend of colours and rhythmic composition in the character of the faces. Other similar works of the school can be roughly dated from this period, and comparative analysis gives some insight into their specific gravity. Archival documents and extant works from the fifteenth century have made it possible to discover the names of some early painters in the Dubrovnik school; these include Ivan Ognjanović and his sons, Petar and Pavl, Stjepan Zorno and Božidar Vlatković, father of the greatest painter in the Dubrovnik school, Nikola Božidarović.[50]

Nikola Božidarović (alias Nicolaus Rhagusinus, Nikola Dubrovčanin, Božidarević) died in Dubrovnik in 1517 but his birthplace remains unknown. Nevertheless he is one of the Dubrovnik artists whose works are preserved and whose name at least is recorded, despite the fact that his style was as archaic as that of Crivelli sixty or seventy years earlier.[51] Several of his paintings may be seen in the Dominican monastery and in the votive church at Danče. From the date on the Danče triptych it appears that he flourished at the beginning of the sixteenth century, and it is fairly certain that he must have studied in Italy. His style shows traces of Crivelli's school, and in this, as in other arts, the Dalmatians continued to work in the older manner long after it had been abandoned in Italy. Some argue that maybe this painter was not really a native of Dubrovnik at all, for if he had been, there was no reason to be called Rhagusinus in his own city.⁵² It is of course unusual, though not unheard of, for an artist to call himself by the name of his own city while actually living in it; but in this case he may have done so because the citizens of Dubrovnik were so used to having their pictures painted by foreigners, that when a local artist actually painted them the fact was worthy of special mention. Another authority thinks that these pictures

> 'bear some resemblance to certain paintings in the Marca of Ancona; it is not impossible, however, that even from Apulia some influence may have reached the Dubrovnik painters, but we have too little information to enable us to express an opinion as to the connection between the Dubrovnik school and that of Italy'.⁵³

Some even fail to mention him, although describe work of other local artists whose works are nearly all lost.⁵⁴

According to documentary evidence Božidarović worked on several paintings within the republic; at the Franciscan church at Cavtat (1495), the Franciscan monastery in Dubrovnik (1502), the church of St. Mary (Sv. Marija) in Dubrovnik (1504, 1510), for wealthy individuals, (1494, 1508, 1514), and in the Great and Small Councils (1510, 1517), but unfortunately none of these pictures exist today. In fact only four works which are undoubtedly by Božidarović can at present be located; one is an unsigned triptych on the left side altar in the Dominican church, another is 'Blagovijest' (The Annunciation) in the sacristy, a third is the altar picture dedicated to the Đorđić family (1513) at the same church and finally the triptych at Dance. The church of St. Maria at Dance contains a triptych by him of very considerable merit, with a predella and lunette. The middle panel is a group of the Virgin and Child surrounded by cherubs. The Madonna wears a red robe with a cloak of rich cloth-of-gold, on which an elaborate pattern is picked out in dark blue. This design is not adapted to the folds, but drawn as though on a flat surface. The Child is holding some fruit; the cherubs have scarlet wings, and in the background there is a gilt nimbus. At the feet of the Virgin kneels the infant St. John with a scroll in his hands. In the right hand panel is St. Martin on horseback cutting off half his cloak to give to a beggar. He is attired in a green tunic, over which is a golden coat with a design picked out in red lines; the cloak being cut is of a bright scarlet. In the left hand panel St. Gregory is seen with a crucifix in his hand, and a dove on his shoulder; he is dressed in pontifical robes

S*

— a richly embroidered cape adorned with a red pattern in cloth-of-gold, and figures of saints in niches along the border. Above is a lunette representing the Crucifixion, with the Virgin, St. Mary Magdalen, St. John, and other figures at the foot of the Cross, with some cherubs. The robe of the Virgin is of a rich deep blue, those of the others red, or green. The background is of gold. The predella is divided into three panels; the centre panel contains St. George and the Dragon, very spirited in composition, with a charming pale blue landscape in the background and a glimpse of the sea. In the right hand division there is a saint receiving a mitre from two bishops, and surrounded by other bishops, monks and choir-boys. To the left a pope in a golden robe is being crowned by two cardinals; all round is a host of cardinals, bishops, Dominicans, Franciscans, and behind a landscape with smaller figures. The faces are all very pale, and somewhat northern in character but those of the Virgin and Child in the principal panel are of great tenderness and feeling. The chief merit lies in the colouring of the picture; it is indeed exceptionally rich and brilliant, especially in the robes, which are characteristic of the painter's work. The whole composition is enclosed in a handsome carved frame, divided into compartments by pillars. The background of this frame is dark blue, with designs picked out in gold, and adorned with arabesques of a solid Renaissance pattern.

In the Dominican church there are quite a number of early pictures, but it is the one on the left hand side of the high altar that is the work of Božidarović. This is entitled 'The Annunciation' with seven scenes from the history of the Dubrovnik Dominicans, signed in 1513. This triptych has in the centre panel the Virgin and Child, the former with a lily in her hand and the moon lying at her feet, surrounded by cherubs; St. Paul and St. Vlah are to the right and St. Thomas Aquinas and St. Augustine to the left. St. Vlah holds an interesting model of Dubrovnik in which one can make out three large towers and several smaller ones. The gold background has been restored, and is rather too garish. Two other possible works by Božidarović are found in the Dominican monastery; one is to the left of the sanctuary, in the chapel of the Gundulić family (designed by the architect Luka Paskojev in 1536) in the form of a triptych painted sometime after 1485, and the second is in the chapter house with an altar piece dated 1513. These, with the possible exception of one or two more paintings on the island of Mljet, are the only known works of this artist, but he managed to inspire a wide circle of collaborators,

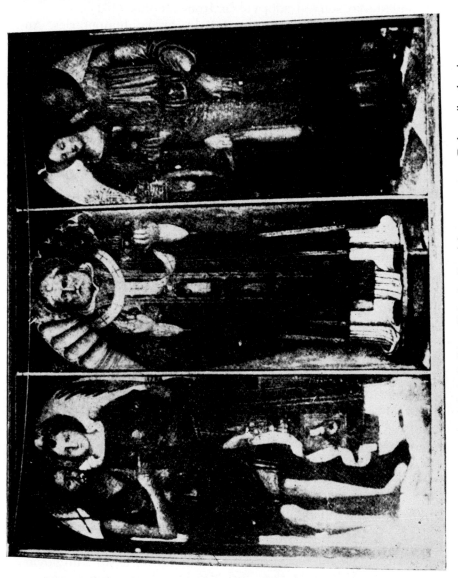

Fig. 117. Triptych by Nikola Božidarović in the Dominican monastery, Dubrovnik, showing St. John the Baptist, St. Nicholas, St. Stephen, St. Mary Magdalen and St. James (left to right).

including Ivan Nikolić from Železnik, Petar Marković from Konavle (1511) and Marko, son of Radoj Vakčić from Trebinje (1517).

Božidarović's influence was also felt by his contemporaries. An early example is Pietro Grgurić-Ohmučević, who painted some pictures at Sutjeska in Herzegovina and flourished about 1482; Mihajlo Hamžić, a pupil of Mantegna, who painted the 'Krštenja Kristova' (Baptism of Our Lord) in the Rector's Palace in 1509. The picture contains the three figures of Christ, an angel and St. John. The faces are very beautiful, and the figures though lean and severe are well drawn but the water is treated conventionally, and stands in a heap as in Gothic sculptures. The triptych of St. Nicholas (Sv. Nikola) in the Dominican monastery, to the right of the sanctuary (chapel of the Lukarević family, fifteenth century) is also by Hamžić and dated 1512; Biagio Darsa, author of a pictorial globe and some studies of perspective; and Vicko, son of Lovro Dobričević, whose polyptych at the Franciscan monastery in Cavat, dated 1509 gives evidence of the new wave of development in the Dubrovnik school. In 1510 he also decorated a church and monastery at Trebinje. This change of style is also reflected by two foreigners working in Dubrovnik at this time; Pier di Giovanni from Venice and Pier Antonio from Urbino. The former painted a large polyptych in the church of Our Lady (Spilica) on Lopud in 1523, and the latter provided the most notable painting in the church of the Holy Saviour (Sv. Spas) in Dubrovnik. The 'Ascension' (Uzašašća) is dated 1527, but Pier Antonio also painted the front of a cabinet (Resurrection of Christ) in the sacristy of the Franciscan church in 1528. The arrival of large imported paintings at this time, particularly from Venice, placed before the local masters of the Dubrovnik school a further challenge to their ability. This proved to be a turning-point in the history of the school causing the formation of several sub-groups. The older artists were in favour of retaining the earlier style and heritage and just adapting it to the new developments. Others were in favour of completely returning to the Byzantine style, whilst a third group began to imitate Venetian works of the 'Cinque cento'. Of this latter branch one may single out the works of Marin Županović, Krsto Antunović Nikolin, Franjo Milović Matkov and Blaž Drižić, as being representative of this phase from about the middle of the sixteenth century.

The seventeenth and eighteenth centuries only saw the production of mediocre works by the Dubrovnik school, much of it under the strong influence of the Italian Later Renaissance and Baroque styles. The most important artists during this very modest period of development were the Dubrovnik Baroque painters Benko Stay-Stojić (1650–87) and Petar Mattei-Matejević (*circa* 1670–1726). The paintings on the balustrade of the organ loft in the church of St. Vlah, are believed to be the work of this latter artist. Much of the work done by the Dubrovnik school in the eighteenth century is very bad, such that it is suffice to mention only Petar Katušić and Rafo Martini, both greatly influenced by the Sicillian painter Carmelo Reggio.

From the fifteenth to the eighteenth century a large number of foreign paintings were imported into Dubrovnik. In the church of Our Lady of Carmel (Gospa od Karmena) the altar-pieces are by A. Canini (main altar 1641), A. Vaccaro (St. John's altar, seventeenth century) and the altar painting of 'Our Lady of Carmel', probably by S. Ricci. One of the paintings believed to be by C. Reggio includes a view of the summer residence of the Sorkočević family in Lapad. The cathedral has four pictures of second rate interest by Padovanino together with a head of Christ by Pordenone, a head of St. Catherine by J. Palma the Elder (Palma Vecchio) and works by C. G. Savoldo, G. Salviati, C. Caliari, L. Cambiaso, N. Bacciacca, Konstantin Zane Parmigianino, propably a spurious Andrea del Sarto, an equally spurious Raphael and a large polyptych of the Assumption of the Virgin on the main altar attributed to Titian but probably by one of his assistants, painted after 1552. There are several other works by unknown artists. Amongst the church's collection is an interesting triptych undoubtedly of the Flemish school, and according to Eitelberger,[55] reminiscent of Memling. The subject is the Adoration of the Magi. In the centre panel the Virgin is seated with the Child on her lap. He is kneeling and extending His right hand to the oldest of the kings, who has placed his sceptre and gifts at the feet of the Saviour; behind Him is another king also offering gifts, and through the arches at the back a landscape is painted. On the left hand wing stands the third king, a Moor, and behind him is a group of figures and another landscape. On the right stands a bald-headed man wearing a richly decorated robe, with a castle in the background, probably the donor. The technique Eitelberger maintains is extraordinarily careful, and the picture, in spite of having been damaged by wax candles, is yet so well-preserved that it needs only the hand of a good restorer for it to make a great impression even on the uninitiated. The head of the Virgin has an expression of lovingness and purity such as is peculiar to the Flemish school alone. It obviously did impress the people of Dubrovnik for this small triptych was carried as a portable altar by emissaries of the republic when they went to Constantinople to pay the annual tribute to the Sultan. As to how it found its way originally to Dubrovnik is not known. Eitelberger conjectures that it must have come from Naples, as the republic was in constant commercial intercourse with that city, which in turn had its connections with Flanders, and the Neapolitan painters were greatly under the influence of Flemish art. Conversely, it is quite possible that it came direct from the Low Countries, for there was a colony of Flemish merchants at Dubrovnik. The remaining paintings in the cathedral are by Dalmatian artists, Petar Mattei-Matejević did the St. Bernard altar in 1721, Benko Stay-Stojić worked on the altar of 'The Annunciation' at the end of the seventeenth century, and it is probable that the early sixteenth century altar of 'Our Lady of Porat' was done by Nikola Božidarović. The altar to 'The Martyrs of Boka Kotorska' was painted by C. Reggio in 1803.

In the Dominican church there is further evidence of foreign artists. Over the first altar to the left of the church is a picture attributed to Titian, and probably that master's genuine work. It is still in good condition, dated 1554, and entitled 'St. Mary Magdalene between St. Vlah and the Archangel Raphael' and includes the donor's figure, a member of the Pucić family. Magdalene with hands clasped and tresses flowing, has St. Vlah to her right in white mitre and crimson velvet robe, his pastoral staff in his right hand, and a model of the city in his left. To her left in the corner kneels the donor with a little child, over whom bends a youthful angel wearing a dark blue dress, a very graceful and attractive figure. The two latter forms are Tobit and the archangel Raphael – probably Raffaelle and Maddalena were the names of the donor and his wife. Other foreign paintings in the church include two altar pieces by Francesco di Maria from the second half of the seventeenth century; a picture of the 'Assumption of Maria' showing a panorama of Dubrovnik signed by an unknown master A.B.D. between 1648 and 1658; a portrait of Skočibuha, the donor, incorporated into 'The Descent of the Holy Spirit' by A. Vaccaro from the first half of the seventeenth century; a painting of 'Our Lady' by A. Bizamano commissioned by a religious fraternity in Rijeka Dubrovačka in 1518; and two works by unknown artists, one on the main altar 'Our Lady of the Rosary' (Gospe od Krunice) from the seventeenth century, and the second a polyptych in the chapel by someone of the Dubrovnik school in the early sixteenth century. The treasury contains a diptych 'Christ and Mary' by Enguerrand Charonton from the fifteenth century, and a sixteenth century work 'The Holy Family' after the style of Lorenzo di Credi.

Other paintings worthy of mention include several Baroque works by unknown masters in the church of St. Joseph (Sv. Josip); the altars of the Domino Church by A. Vaccaro and B. Linterino ('The Annunciation'); a fifteenth century painting by a local master in the church of St. Nicholas; and another example of the Dubrovnik school (second half of fifteenth century) in St. James Church (Sv. Jakov na Pelinama) called 'The Virgin', together with two smaller Baroque paintings by unknown artists. The Sikurata chapel has an embroidery representing the 'Washing of the Feet' designed by Niccolà di Pietro from the fifteenth century, whilst in the Franciscan monastery the altars and paintings belong to the post-Baroque era; only the work by F. Francia, 'Christ at the Martyrs Pillar', is from the Renaissance period. The Rector's Palace contains a picture which Jackson noted 'is easily recognized by an Englishman as a duplicate of the "Daphnis and Chloe" by Paris Bardone in our National Gallery'.[56] Other works include the 'Sacra conversazione' by J. Palma the Elder on Lopud, and Vasarijev's 'Descent of the Holy Spirit' (Silizak sv. Duha) at the Dominican monastery, but they are of minor interest. Examples of the Flemish masters can be found in the cathedral at Lopud, whilst Dubrovnik's cathedral has paintings belonging to the Raspijeva group (named after its owner) which are Italian dating from the High Renaissance. Despite all this import of foreign paintings into Dubrovnik over the period from the fifteenth to the eighteenth centuries, remarkably little is known of the exports from the Dubrovnik school abroad. One exception is Francesca da Ragusa, one of whose works is said to be in Rome, and another at Brescia (1600–1620).

In the nineteenth century the only well-known Dubrovnik artist was the engraver Petar Mančun (1803–1888), but he had little direct influence in his native city for he lived and worked most of his life in Rome. Towards the end of the century several new painters emerged and were closely connected with the new nationalist revival movement. Two painters played an important role in the initial development of modern Croatian art, Vlaho Bukovac (1855–1922) from Cavtat and Celestin Medović (1859–1931) from Kuna. An example of Bukovac's work is found in the Dominican church, with 'The miracle of St. Dominic' on one of the altars, dated 1912. Another artist of this generation is Marko Murat (1864–1944) from Luka Šipanska, a specialist on local Dubrovnik landscapes, portraits, historical and biblical compositions. One of the most original personalities in modern Croatian painting during the first half of the twentieth century was Ignjat Job, born in Dubrovnik in 1895 and died, 1936. He gathered around him an interesting group of contemporary Dubrovnik painters including, Gabro Rajčević (1912–43), Ivo Dulčić (1915–), Antun Masle (1919–), Duro Pulitika (1922–) and Ivan Vojvodić (1923–). In 1945 the city's art gallery (Umjetnička galerija) was established in a large new building at Ploče. It serves two main purposes, the first to exhibit the works of contemporary Yugoslav artists, and secondly to collect, protect and study the older paintings still to be found within the Dubrovnik region.

Finally, a discussion of Dubrovnik's art would not be complete without some mention of the gold and silversmith's work which flourished in the city. The goldsmiths and silversmiths of Dalmatia were famous, and many of the church treasuries in this region are very rich and splendid. That of the cathedral in Dubrovnik is one of the finest, in spite of the earthquake and the depredations of the freebooters after that calamity. Its two most amazing pieces, however, are not by natives of Dubrovnik. One is an enamelled casket enclosing the 'skull' of St. Vlah. The copper back is concealed by twenty-four metal plaques on which enamel and filigree work are laid; each of them contains a medallion, the name written in Lombardic letters with the head of a saint in the centre, except four triangular plaques on the top. The surface not covered by the plaques is filled in with the most delicate enamels of flowers, fruit, leaves, pearls, insects and scroll work. This reliquary is said by Resti to have been brought to Dubrovnik in 1026, but de Diversis does not mention it in his account of the treasures in the cathedral. Eitelberger merely observes that it has lost some of its value by the addition of saints' names in the thirteenth, fourteenth centuries or even later.[57] Jackson believed that it belonged to two widely differing periods, maintaining that the medallions are Byzantine work of the eleventh or twelfth century, whereas the intervening scrolls of flowers etc. are of a much later date. His discovery of an inscription in a corner of the lower edge, dated 1694, seems to bear out his assumptions.[58]

Another treasure is the curious silver-gilt basin and ewer attributed to Giovanni Progonović, a jeweller of the fifteenth century, but more probably foreign work, as the plate mark – an N within a circle – is not that of Dubrovnik.[59] The ewer contains imitations of bunches of dried leaves and grasses in silver, whilst the basin is strewn with ferns and leaves. In the midst of these creep lizards, snakes, eels, and animals all wrought in silver, and enamelled and tinted so as to deceive one into believing them real. It is an extraordinary piece of work, but more strange than beautiful. It is probably not older than the early seventeenth century, though it has been suggested as the work of W. Jamnitzer about 1550. There are many other specimens of the jeweller's art in this collection, which totals 138 gold and silver reliquaries of various shapes, chalices and cups, mostly by local craftsmen, some of them very handsome. Notable specimens include the reliquary containing 'St Vlah's hand' (thirteenth century?), 'St. Lawrence's hand' (attributed to Guglielmus in the fourteenth century), 'St. Vlah's leg' (work done by Dubrovnik's goldsmiths from 1684),

Table XIV
List of Local and Foreign Artists in Dubrovnik

Dalmatian and Local Artists		Foreign Artists	
Name and date (if known)	Known or Existing work	Name and date (if known)	Known or Existing work
PRIOR TO THE FIFTEENTH CENTURY			
Stanče 1302–13		Michael from Bologne 1313–41	Murals in old Cathedral
Marko Vlahov 1313		Bernado 1345	
Mihovil from Zadar 1348		Durantea 1348	
Stojko Drušković 1371–1420		Marko of Apulia 1351	
		Giovanni from Rimini 1367–71	
		Francesca from Bologne 1371–1405	
		Augustina 1376	
		Zanina 1389	
		Antonio 1390–91	
		Emanuala 1367–89	'Pictures graeci'
		Joana from Dürres 1388–89	
		Gorgija 1377–86	
		Guglielmus	Reliquary, in Cathedral

Table XIV—continued
List of Local and Foreign Artists in Dubrovnik

Dalmatian and Local Artists		Foreign Artists	
Name and date (if known)	Known or Existing work	Name and date (if known)	Known or Existing work
FIFTEENTH TO EIGHTEENTH CENTURIES			
Blaž Trogiranin 1421–26	Church of Sv. Durda at Boni- nova and Split Gallery	Enguerrand Charonton A. Bizamano 1518	Dominican Church Dominican Church
Ivan Ugrinović 1434	Church of Sv. Ante at Koločep	Beltrandus Gallicus 1521	Sponza Palace
Giovanni Progonović	Basin and ewer at Cathedral	Pier di Giovanni from Venice 1523	Church of Gospa od Spilica (Lopud)
Matej Junčić 1452	Church of Gospe od Šunja, Lopud	Pier di Antonio from Urbino 1527–28	Sv. Spas and Franciscan monastery
Lovro M. Dobričević 1465	Votive Church, Dance	W. Jamnitzer 1550	Basin and ewer (?) at Cathedral
Jerolim Matov	Cross relief, at Cathedral	Niccolà di Pietro A. Vaccaro	Sikurata chapel Church of Gospa od
Ivan Ognjanović Petar Ognjanović Pavl Ognjanović Stjepan Zarno Božidar Vlatković Pietro Grgurić- Ohmučevic 1482	Sutjeska, Hercegovina	S. Ricci	Karmina, Domino Church, and Dominican Church Church of Gospa od Karmina
Nikola Božidarović 1485–1517	Dominican monastery and votive church at Dance	Padovanino Pordenone J. Palma, The Elder. (Palma Vecchio)	The Cathedral The Cathedral The Cathedral and Lopud Cathedral
Biagio Darsa Mihajlo Hamžić 1509–12	Rector's Palace, Dominican monastery	C. G. Savoldo G. Salviati C. Caliari L. Cambiaso N. Bacciacca	The Cathedral The Cathedral The Cathedral The Cathedral The Cathedral
Vicko Lovrin 1509–10	Franciscan monas- tery at Cavtat, Church and monastery at Trebinje	Konstantin Zane Parmigianino Andrea del Sarto Titian School 1552	The Cathedral The Cathedral The Cathedral The Cathedral
Ivan Nikolić Petar Marković		Raphael (?)	The Cathedral

Table XIV—continued
List of Local and Foreign Artists in Dubrovnik

Dalmatian and Local Artists		Foreign Artists	
Name and date (if known)	Known or Existing work	Name and date (if known)	Known or Existing work
1511 Marko Vukčić		Memling (?)	The Cathedral
1517		Titian (1554)	Dominican Church
Petar Bogdanović	Wooden figure in	Francesco di	Dominican Church
1550	Domino Church	Maria	
Marin Županović		P. P. Jacometti 1637	Rector's Palace
B. Krsto Nikolin	*circa* 1550	A. Canini 1641	Church of Gospa od Karmina
F. M. Matkov			
Blaž Držić		A.B.D.(?) 1648–58	Dominican Church
Francesco da	Rome and Brescia	B. Linterino	Dominican Church
Ragusa 1600–20		F. Francia	Franciscan monastery
B. Stay-Stojić	The Cathedral	Paris Bordone (?)	Rector's Palace
1650–87	(c.1600)	Vasarijev	Dominican monastery
P. Mattei-Matejević (c.1670–1726)	Church of St. Vlah and the Cathedral (1721)	Flemish School Raspijeva (Italian School)	Cathedral at Lopud The Cathedral
Petar Katušić Rafo Martini			
NINETEENTH AND TWENTIETH CENTURIES			
Petar Mančun 1803–88	Rome	Carmelo Reggio from Sicily	The Cathedral (1803), and the Church of Gospa od Karmena
Vlaho Bukovac 1855–1922			
Celestin Medović 1859–1931			
Marko Murat 1864–1944	Dominican Church (1912)		
Ignjat Job 1895–1936			
Gabro Rajčević 1912–43			
Ivo Dulcic 1915–?	Modern Croatian School		
Antun Masle 1919–?			
Duro Pulitika 1922–?			
Ivan Vojvodić 1923–?			

and a late Gothic cross with relief of saints by Jerolim Matov (sixteenth century).

The little silver statuette of Sv. Vlah in the church of that saint is interesting historically as well as artistically, because the figure bears a model of Dubrovnik before the earthquake. The head is excellent both in expression and workmanship, and the exquisitely chased chasuble reminds one of the robes in Božidarović's paintings. The original figure is, according to Jackson,[60] as old as the church (about 1360), but it has been restored at various times. The mitre, crook, pastoral staff and dalmatic have been renewed, while the lower part of the statuette has evidently been cut away. The model shows that fourteenth and fifteenth century Dubrovnik was not all that different from today, except for the cathedral and the church of St. Vlah which have have been rebuilt, and the little church of the Three Martyrs of Kotor in the Stradun, which has disappeared. Many of the houses in that street have gabled fronts and some have projecting pents to shelter the shops. The Orlando column supports a huge standard. (See Fig. 54).

Some church plate is preserved at Mljet, of which the most beautiful piece is a large silver-gilt chalice. On the foot is a figure of Sv. Vlah in relief, and on the lower part of the cup are the emblems of the four Evangelists. The handles are formed by two graceful little angels poised with one foot on the top and the other hanging in the air, their hands clinging on to the edge of the cup. The hall-mark – a bishop's head – is that of Dubrovnik, and the chalice is probably Mljet work, the island having been famous for its goldsmiths. Many other specimens of this art exist in the various churches of Dubrovnik and the neighbourhood, together with other old monasteries in Bosnia-Hercegovina, Albania and Dalmatia.

Literature

Dubrovnik's literature was of a threefold nature; some of her citizens wrote in Latin, others in Italian and yet a third group used the Slavonic language, but so mixed was the character of the people that in many instances the same author composed works in all the three languages. This has already been noted by others for 'Dalmatia, and especially Dubrovnik which represents the highest degree of Slavonic culture, shows at the end of the Middle Ages a peculiar and characteristic blend of Italian and Slavonic elements, which even today is a remarkable trait of this people'.[61] As in architecture, sculpture and painting, again Venetian influence is strong, in this case strengthening the original Latin elements of the population. Most of the nobles had Italian names, although later these were given an alternative Slavonic form. The collapse of Venetian power in Dalmatia in 1358 opened the way to Slavonic influences, for Hungary was too alien to the Dalmatians to impress more than her political sovereignty on them; also Latin and Italian culture was maintained side by side with that of the Slavic, and indeed the Slavonic literature at Dubrovnik was wholly inspired by that of Italy.

The literary movements and forms of Italy were all reflected at Dubrovnik. The city had no connection with the old Slavonic tradition or the Serbian popular songs, but was based almost exclusively on Italian influences. Thus one finds specimens of Latin ecclesiastical literature, of the Provençal troubadours, of Renaissance culture and the revival of learning.

'Under the influence of peculiar historical conditions there arose in the Serbo–Croatian littoral an important poetical literature, of which Dubrovnik was the centre, and the pure vernacular of the organ'.[62]

In the Dubrovnik epic, Italian influence is conspicuous, and also in the native lyric poetry, which is mainly inspired by Petrarch's 'Canzoni'; the Dubrovnik dramas are imitated from medieval mystery plays, the pastoral plays of Tasso, and the Italian comedies. Even the so-called 'macaronic' verses (verses of burlesque form containing Latin, or other foreign words and vernacular words with Latin and other terminations) were adopted at Dubrovnik using a medley of dog-Latin and Slavonic. The outward forms of Italian literary life were copied in other ways, for learned literary academics were established at Dubrovnik, where men of culture met to discuss their favourite topics, and in this way the city came to be known as the 'Slavonic Athens'. Italians of learning were invited to lecture at Dubrovnik, for the Senate had maintained Chairs of Italian and Latin literature since the early fifteenth century. Owing to Byzantine tradition, the study of Greek was to some extent maintained, and further promoted by the influx of learned Greeks who took refuge at Dubrovnik after the fall of Constantinople in 1453. Conversely, many Dubrovnik citizens went abroad, especially to Italy, for study purposes, and some of them achieved considerable fame in various spheres of life.

The poetry of Dubrovnik was of two types, that written in Latin, and that written in the Slavonic language but Italian in character. The Dubrovnik poets who wrote in Latin were of little importance. The most celebrated of them was Elio (Cerva) Zrieva, who went to Rome in 1476, at the age of sixteen where he studied the humanities and joined the Quirinal Academy. He latinized his name, as was the fashion of the time, into Ælius Lampridius Cervinus, and was later crowned Poet-Laureate. He soon returned to Dubrovnik, married, and was determined to devote his life to public service, but on the death of his wife took Holy Orders and spent most of his time at Ombla (Rijeka Dubrovačka). He died in 1520. Cerva was much appreciated by his contemporaries, especially Sabellico and Palladius Fuscus, and his chief compositions are an elegy on his retreat at Ombla, on the tomb of Cicero's daughter, and a number of odes, epigrams, and hymns. Another Latin poet of some reputation was Ivan Gučetić (Giovanni Gozze) 1451–1502. He was employed by the republic in various embassies, in the course of which he made acquaintance with a number of statesmen and men of letters, among them the celebrated Agnolo Poliziano. Gozze sent some of his works to Poliziano, who in his return letter of thanks expressed admiration for the poems. Gozze later published this letter together with his other epistles. Three other Latin poets from Dubrovnik are worthy of mention in the context: Jakov Bunić (Giovanni Bona), the author of several poems of a religious character, who died in 1534; Niccolò Brattuti (1564–1632) from Mljet, who became Bishop of Sarsina in Italy, but was later imprisoned. He wrote several religious poems whilst in prison and these were published in 1630 under the title of 'Martyrologium Poeticum Sanctorum Totius Italiæ'; finally the name of Stjepan Gradić (Stefano Gradi)[63] may also be included as the author of sundry works in Latin[64] on philosophy, epistles and poems. He was born in Dubrovnik in 1613 and in 1629 went to Italy to study in Rome. He did much for the relief of his fellow Dubrovnik citizens at the time of the earthquake, writing to most parts of Europe for help. His correspondence on this matter (332 letters) are preserved, and Gradić was also instrumental in obtaining aid from the Pope and other foreign potentates for the grief stricken city. He died in Rome in 1683.

Far more important is the Slavonic literature of Dubrovnik. The first person from Dubrovnik to write verse in the vernacular was Siško Menčetic (Sigismondo Menze),[65] born in 1457 and died 1527.

He may be called the father of Dubrovnik poetry, writing over 500 love lyrics of the Provençal troubadour character, a form introduced in Dubrovnik through the republic's connection with the Spanish Court of Naples. His best known canzoniere (like a madrigal) is entitled 'Pjesni Ljuvesne'. Of a similar character are the poems of Džore (Gjore) Držić,[66] born in Dubrovnik in 1461 and died there in 1501. His poems, together with those of Menčetić and other contemporaries were preserved in the original manuscript entitled 'Zbornika Nikša Ranjina' dated 1507 and kept in Zadar; unfortunately these were destroyed by bombing in the World War II. Držić remained under the influence of the Italian poets from the end of the fifteenth century, although evidence of local feelings are evident in his writing as for example 'Djevojka je podranila', 'Odiljam se' and others; his lyrics also were far more intimate than those of Menčetić. Another contemporary was Hanibal Lučić (or Lucio)[67] born at Hvar about 1485 and died in 1553. Although not a native of Dubrovnik, he was under the influence of Menčetić and Držić and in fact wrote his most famous ode about the city 'U pohvalu grada Dubrovnika' (In praise of Dubrovnik) of which the following is a translated extract:

'My songs cannot in any way tell of all the lands with which the famous Dubrovnik trades. Over mountains through forests, all the world over, does she send her merchants without let or hindrance, through lands where the sun shines from afar, where it burns moderately, and where it blazes too much. All receive the wares which they peacefully bring, and what is given in exchange they peacefully carry away. Worthy is the city that she should everywhere be praised, that God and men should bless her!'

His early writing came under the influence of Ovid, Petrarch and later by Držić and others. His best known play called 'Robinja' (*The Slave Girl*) concerns an episode of the Turkish Wars and is a dialogue between the daughter of an enslaved Turk and the grand-daughter of a local prince, set in the Dubrovnik slave market. It is interesting to note that in this as with other works by Dubrovnik writers, no animosity is shown against the Turks. The Turk was regarded by the citizens of Dubrovnik as a law of nature rather than as an enemy, and a wholesome fear made them careful to avoid doing, or even saying, anything to offend him.

Another much admired poet was Nikola Vetranić-Čavčić (1482–

1576), a member of a Dubrovnik noble family, and Abbot of a local monastery. Later in life he retired to a hermitage on a small island off the coast, where he continued to write poetry and keep up contacts with his literary friends. His 'Sacrifice of Abraham' is considered one of the best of the Slavonic mystery plays, for it contains really artistic presentations of characters and situations, while some of the episodes begin to resemble popular Serbian poetry. In a poem called 'Remeta' (*The Hermit*), he describes his island retreat, and in the 'Putnik' (*The Wanderer*) the beauty of Dubrovnik's scenery. 'Italija' is an ode to Italy in which he demonstrates how the citizens of Dubrovnik considered themselves to be almost Italians, and the hope he had that the ancient glory of Italy may return. Further he expresses the wish that Dubrovnik will remain independent of the heathen (The Turks) and that neither the Eagle nor the Cock (the Empire and France) will do her any harm, wishing only for freedom and unity. Vetranić-Čavčić is also the author of a translation of *Hecuba of Euripides*.

Unlike all the previous poets mentioned Andrija Čubranović[68] (Andrija Zlatar), who died about 1550, was a man of the people. His best known poem is the 'Jeđupka' (*The Gypsy*) a masquerette published posthumously in Venice in 1599. (Jeđupka gospodina Andrie Civbranovichia Dubrovcianina. In Vinegia, MDXCIX). It seems to have been a carnival song, and recalls some of the Italian 'Canti Carnascialeschi', but is a mixture of the conventional troubador and personal Renaissance-carnival tones. It is said to have been publicly recited at Dubrovnik in 1527, and is considered remarkable for the purity of its language. Besides Jeđupka, Čubranović contributed a number of poems to the 'Zbornik Nikša Ranjina'.

A form of literature much in vogue at Dubrovnik was the pastoral play or idyll, based on Italian models. The Slavonic pastoral play is of two types, that of Dubrovnik, which is comic, and that represented by Hvar (Lesina), which is more purely idyllic. The mathematician and astronomer Nikola Nalješković,[69] (born in Dubrovnik, 1510 and died there 1587) achieved some poetic fame as a writer of plays of the former type, together with a total of 178 poems. Much of his work was in the conventional manner of the day, under the influence of such writers as Menčetić, Držić and Vetranović. Nevertheless as a pupil of the Latinist, Ilija Crijević he was well versed with Plato. This is seen in the setting of his plays, one in which the shepherd falls in love, not as expected with the classical nymph, but with the

'Vila' fairy of the South Slavonic popular legend. His 'Dialogo sopra sfera del monde' was published in Venice in 1579. Another writer of such plays was Marin (Marino) Držić,[70] born in Dubrovnik, 1508, and a man who enjoyed the fruits of a varied career. After religious offices in Dubrovnik, he won a scholarship to Sienna (1538) and in 1541 became chancellor of its university. He returned to Dubrovnik (1545), but then went as a count's valet to Venice in 1546, and later to Constantinople. He again returned to Dubrovnik (1548) became a deacon and in 1550 a priest, but his travels were not over for in 1562 he went to Venice, and was in Florence (1566), returning to Venice in 1567 where he died. His Italian contemporaries praised Držić's plays for 'il puro vago e dolce canto'. The principal works of Držić are 'Tirena' (5 acts) published in Venice (1549), and noted for its sentimental, idyllic motives with realistic yet rustic charm', 'Dundo Maroje' (Venice, 1550) in five acts, and 'Novela od Stanea' (Stanac's tale) a one act farce written in 1551. He also wrote sacred poems.

The most famous Dubrovnik poet of the sixteenth century was Dinko Ranjina[71] (Domenico Ragnina), born in Dubrovnik, 1536, and died there in 1607. His grave is in the chapter house of the Dominican monastery to the east of the cloister. Ranjina was born into one of the noblest families in the city, and after schooling in Dubrovnik, spent some years in Italy (Messina) attending to his father's business interests. It was here that he studied Greek and Roman classic works and those of contemporary Italian poets. Later in Florence Ranjina entered the Duke Cosima Medici's circle of friends, a fact partly responsible for the publication of his 'Pjesni razlike' (*Different Poems*) written in 1563. Subsequently he returned home and entered the service of the republic as a lawyer, in 1588 becoming a member of the 'Council of Requests' (Vijeća Umoljenijeh), followed by seven times Rector of the city. His poems are chiefly love lyrics, but he also wrote epistles, didactic poems, and idylls in the classical Renaissance manner, as well as translations from Tibullus, Propertius, and Martial. Amongst his preserved manuscripts there is one Italian anthology (1563) and 27 Italian sonnets, three of which were translated in to French by Philippe Desportes (1546–1606). Ranjina's close friend Nikola Gučetić (1549–1610) was also important at this time as a leading writer on philosophy.

Another Dubrovnik nobleman from this period was Dinko Zlatarić (1556–1610), who studied in Padua. At the age of 23 he was appointed Rector of the university gymnasium, later moving to Zagreb and then home to Dubrovnik. He translated Tasso's 'Aminta' under the title of 'Ljubomir', the 'Electra' of Sophocles, and the episode of Pyramus and Thisbe from Ovid, as well as being the author of several love idylls and didactic poems. His name is often coupled with that of Floria Zuzzeri, a lady from Dubrovnik renowned for her beauty, virtue and as a poetess of distinction, whom Zlatarić adored. She had been the centre of a little circle of literary ladies at Dubrovnik until her father took her to Ancona on business. There in 1577 she married Bartolomeo Pescioni, a wealthy Florentine. She settled in Florence and kept a salon frequented by many famous Italian authors and dilettanti, but also by people from Dubrovnik, such as the aforesaid Zlatarić, Ranjina and Ivan Gundulić. Some of her sonnets, became famous throughout Italy although she wrote both in the Italian and Slavonic languages. She died in 1600.

The most celebrated of all the Dubrovnik poets is Ivan (Divo Franov) Gundulić[72] (Giovanni Gondola) born in Dubrovnik, 1589 (?) and died there, 1638. He was born into the noble Gundulić-Gondola family and received his first schooling in Dubrovnik, where amongst the teachers there were Camillo Camilli, who continued the Tasso epic, and Peter Palikuća. Gundulić entered the service of the republic, becoming a senator in 1636, and two years later a member of the Small Council (Malo Vijeća). He began publishing early and in 1621 produced his 'Pjesni pokorne kralja Davida' (*Poems of the Vanquished King David*) in Rome. Gundulić was a great admirer of Italian literature, based on his study of the classics, philosophy and law, wanting to introduce the harmony of Italian verse into the local Slavonic tongue and purify the language. He preferred the style of Tasso, particularly his 'Gerusalemme' which he closely imitated, but his first youthful essays were pastoral dramas of no extraordinary merit. It is interesting, however, that he followed Tasso rather than Petrarch, till then the favourite model for Dubrovnik's poets. Instead of a line of eleven, twelve or thirteen syllables, he adopted that of eight, in rhymed strophes, which he deemed more fluid and vigorous, capable of expressing feelings with greater power, and more in accordance with the genius of the local language. His first essay was a translation of Tasso's 'Gerusalemme', after which he devoted himself to dramas, composing or translating from the Italian a number of plays, which he and a circle of literary friends produced for the stage. The most important of these were 'Dubravka'; Arijadna', 'Armida' and 'Galatea', whilst his 'Suze sina razmetnoga' (*The Tears of the Prodigal Son*) was published in Venice in 1622.

The work on which most of Gundulić's fame mainly rests, and regarded as the most important composition in the Serbo-Croat language, is 'Osman' an epic in twenty cantos. The subject the fall of Sultan Osman after his defeat in the war between Turkey and Poland. The choice of Gundulić's subject seems a strange one, if viewed without reference to the political situation of Dubrovnik, in the very century in which the Turks were the most hated of people. It is only at Dubrovnik that a Christian writer would have made a Turkish Sultan his hero, and it is only here and there that a few passages are introduced reflecting unfavourably on the Turks. A great deal of it is simply an adaption of Tasso, and whole passages are translated from that work. It is full of repetitions and exaggerations and useless accessories, but it also contains many passages of real beauty and feeling, such as the address to Dubrovnik:

'O mayest thou ever live peaceful and free as thou art now, O white city of Dubrovnik, famous throughout the world, pleasing to the heavens . . . Bondmen are they neighbours, oppressive violence grinds them all down, thy power alone sits on the throne of freedom'

(Canto viii). Gundulić also apostrophizes Stefan Dušan, the Nemenjas, Marko Kraljević, and other Serbian heroes. Cantos xiv and xv have been lost and rewritten by other poets.

The interest is divided between the two heroes. Osman and Ladislas, and a great deal of the work is lyrical rather than epic in character. The Polish victory of Koczim in 1621 forced the Turks to make peace, and the action of the poem begins at this moment. After the defeat of the Turks, Osman deplores the disaster and attributes it to the decadence of the Ottomans, and proposes a number of reforms. He orders the arrest of his uncle Mustafa, who has already usurped the throne once. The Sultan sends Ali to Warsaw to sue for peace, and Cislar to the provinces to find a number of fair damsels, from among whom he will choose the Sultana. He also orders that the Polish prisoner, Prince Koreski, immured in the Castle of the Seven Towers, shall be carefully watched. Ali goes through Moldavia, where he finds Kronoslava, Koreski's wife, attired as a warrior, and tells of her husband's imprisonment. She resolves to go in disguise to Constantinople and obtain his ransom. The Poles are celebrating the anniversary of the victory at Koczim, when Prince Ladislas of Poland meets Sokolica, daughter of the Grand Mogul, and her amazons; Ladislas captures them, but out of admiration for their courage sets them free, and they return to Constantinople. Meanwhile Ali has reached Warsaw and enters the Royal Palace, where he notes the splendour of the Court and sees the tapestries representing the battle of Koczim, which are described in great detail. He concludes the peace treaty and returns home. By now Cislar has collected the required number of maidens from Greece, Macedonia and the Archipelago, and goes to the borders of Moldavia to capture Danica, the daughter of Prince Ljubidrag. The Prince is living in a rural retreat having lost his estates and, while he and his friends are performing rustic games, Cislar and his companions arrive and carry off Danica. Satan, enraged at the victories of Christians summons his demons and flies with them to Constantinople to create trouble. There Kronoslava has arrived too in search of her husband; she is told that he is in love with the daughter of the prison governor, and, although not quite convinced, begins to feel jealous. Only through bribery does she manage to see Prince Koreski, is convinced of his fidelity, and falls into his arms. The Sultan soon afterwards sets him free and Koreski returns home with his wife. Cislar appears with his fair captives but Osman seeing Danica's despair and hearing her story, sends her back to her father, Prince Ljubidrag. Sokolica, too, comes to Constantinople, and Osman chooses her as first Sultana but also marries two Greek maidens. The Sultan then prepares for an expedition to Asia against some rebels, but the Janissaries revolt. They demand the heads of Dilaver Pasha (the Grand Vizir), the Aodja and the chief eunuch. The rebellion spreads, the Grand Vizir is murdered, and Osman's uncle Mustafa freed and proclaimed Sultan. While Osman is deploring his misfortunes and recalling the glories of his ancestors, he too is assassinated on Mustafa's orders.

The war with Poland in 1621, the captivity of Koreski as hostage in Constantinople, the disguise of his wife as a Hungarian boy to deliver him, the condition of all these countries and the variety of episodes and adventures, concluding with the Sultan's death, thus form the staple part of the work. Thus, just as Milton's subject was often too remote from the daily existence of the poet, that of Gundulić was too near; and party-spirit, rather than strict historic justice, inspires the portrait of the hero. The same objection to the introduction of contemporary subjects may apply to Dante, only he was not a spectator to the action of his poem, but part and parcel of it; the adventures of Osman in the political history of Turkey fail to awaken ones interest. Yet while the remains of this Turk are scarcely known, the poetry of Gundulić will preserve the events of Osman's life when greater names are forgotten. Although Gundulić died at only 51 years of age he was survived by three able sons, two fought in the Thirty Years War under Wallenstein and the yougest died in 1682, whilst holding the supreme office of Rector of the Republic. Today Gundulić is still remembered in Dubrovnik with a square dedicated in his name (Gundulićeva Poljana) containing his statue, the work of Ivan Rendić in 1893.

Of the prose writers from this period, the one most deserving notice is Mavro (Mauro) Orbini,[73] born in Dubrovnik sometime during the middle of the sixteenth century and died there, 1611. His chief work, written in Italian, is entitled 'Il regno degli Slavi', and published in Pesaro in 1601. It is of no great historic value, but is the first attempt to deal comprehensively with the history of all Slavs as a whole. The work is an uncritical, enthusiastic piece of writing which includes several Germanic and other tribes amongst the Slavic people. According to Orbini Slavs were found in all three continents of the then known world. Later works concentrated on Dubrovnik's own locality giving much previously unknown information for the fourteenth and fifteenth centuries. It was published in Rome in 1603. Other historians include Niccolò Ragnina, author of 'Annali di Ragusa', Giacomo Luccari, whose 'Copioso Ristretto degli Annali di Ragusa' contains much interesting information about the constitution of the republic, and Giunio Resti, author of the very detailed 'Cronaca Ragusina', in thirteen volumes, a most unreliable work. None of these writers have shown any conspicuous qualities as historians of their native city, being inspired by a strong political bias, and are only to be consulted with caution.

Between the second half of the eighteenth century and mid-nineteenth, three important writers were associated with Dubrovnik. The first was Đuro Ferić,[74] born in the city, 1739 and died there 1820. He was a pupil of the Dubrovnik Jesuits and, after completing his studies in philosophy and theology, he entered the church. Ferić is one of the last known writers to publish mainly in Latin, beginning when he was over fifty years of age, with 'Paraphrasis psalmorum poetica' (Dubrovnik 1791), and followed by 'Fabulae ab illyricis adagiis desumptae' (Dubrovnik 1794) of which 113 copies were printed and a further 346 were by hand. The second author, Đuro Hiđa (Hidža),[75] was born in Dubrovnik in 1752, finished medical studies in Bologna, and returned to his city to practice. Hiđa is best remembered for his translated works of Horace (Quinta Horacia Flaka piesni liricke', Dubrovnik 1849) and Virgil into the Croatian language, and the conversion of the classical metre to fit more closely the spirit of the local tongue. Thirdly, there is Marc René Bruère Desrivaux,[76] (known locally as Marko Bruerević, or Bruerović) who was born in Lyon, France before 1770(?) and died in Cyprus (1823). He came to Dubrovnik as a child and finished his schooling there, while his father was the French consul in the city (his first teacher was Đuro Ferić). Like his father, he entered the consular service and spent several years at Travnik (Bosnia), Skadar, Dubrovnik, later in Tripoli and Syria, finally dying en route to Tripoli in Cyprus. His early training in the local language and customs can be seen from his poems, which contain elements of folklore, local traditions and above all a feeling for the local populace ('Mala puka'). His best known works are 'Zvjedoznanci' (*The Astronomers*) in 1805, 'Ćupe' (*Tousled Hair*), 'Spravljenice' (*Preparation*), and his comedy 'Vjera iznenada' (*Sudden Persuasion*), written in the Dubrovnik dialect.

The mid-nineteenth century saw an interesting literary venture established in Dubrovnik. It was in the form of a 'literary almanac' ('književni almanah') and attracted several influential writers to edit and submit poems, essays and other scholarly work. It first appeared in 1849 under the editorship of Matija Ban[77] (born near Dubrovnik, 1818, died Belgrade 1903). He began publishing in 1834, first in Italian, and later in Serbian, producing two volumes of 'Različnih pjesama' (*Different Poems*) appearing in Belgrade in 1853 and 1861. Ban was a writer deeply involved in ideas on Panslavism, besides writing dramas and tragedies, fourteen of which are known to be preserved. It was in the spirit of this identity with nationalist feeling that he helped found the Dubrovnik 'literary almanac' and remain its editor for the first critical years, 1849–1852. Amongst the contributors was Medo Pučić,[78] born in Dubrovnik, 1821 and died in his native city, 1882. He attended schools in Dubrovnik, Venice, Padua and Vienna, finally completing his studies in law. While in Venice he was exposed to many liberal ideas of the Risorgimento, and in 1844 published his 'Slavjansku antologiju iz rukopisa dubrovačkih pjesnikah (*Celebrated Anthologies of Dubrovnik Poets*) in Vienna. Five years later he returned to Dubrvonik to help Ban found the almanac. His interest in the political events of Europe and the need to free the Southern Slavs from the Turkish yoke, prompted him later to write 'La Serbia e l'impero d'Oriente', 'Nuova Antologia' (Florence 1867), together with other works of a nationalistic flavour. Finally, mention should be made of Petar Budmani[79] (born in Dubrovnik, 1835, died Ancona 1914), philologist, and one of Yugoslavia's greatest polyglots. Having finished his schooling in Dubrovnik he went to Vienna, graduating first in medicine and then in law. He later travelled to Italy where, like Pučić, he experienced the ideas of the Italian Risorgimento, which influenced his future attitudes on the political subjugation of the Southern Slavs. His contributions to some of the later issues of the Dubrovnik almanac include five stories translated from Sanskrit, and 'Nebožiju komediju' (*The Ungodly Comedy*) by Krasińsky. He also published a grammar of the Russian language and four books on early writers.

Dubrovnik was therefore the birthplace of many scholars who have contributed to Yugoslavia's present-day literary heritage. These range from the early Latin poets of the fifteenth century, to the Romantics of the nineteenth century, and more recently to the modern Croatian school of contemporary literature.

Table XV
Dubrovnik's Writers and Men of Science

Name	Details	Remarks
	WRITERS IN LATIN	
Elio Zrieva	b. Dubrovnik 1450 d. „ 1520	Poems, became poet-laureate, Used latinized name, Ælius Lampridius Cervinus, brother of historian Ludovic (Tubero) Cerva (Zrieva).
Ivan Gučetić	b. Dubrovnik 1451 d. „ 1502	One of early generation of Dubrovnik Humanists. Poems, prose, best work 'Delphinus'.
Jakov Bunić	b. Dubrovnik 1469 d. „ 1534	Religious poems best work 'De vita et gestis Christi'.
Nikola Gučetić	b. Dubrovnik 1549 d. „ 1610	Philosophical works, best book 'Dello stato delle Repubbliche'.
Niccolò Brattuti	b. Mljet Island 1564 d. „ „ 1632	Religious poems, was Bishop of Sarsian, Italy.

Table XV—continued
Dubrovnik's Writers and Men of Science

Name	Details	Remarks
Stjepan Gradić	b. Dubrovnik 1613 d. Rome 1683	Epistles, poems, helped organize earthquake relief.
Đuro Ferić	b. Dubrovnik 1739 d. ,, 1820	Religious poems.

WRITERS IN SLAVONIC

Name	Details	Remarks
Siško Menčetić	b. Dubrovnik 1457 d. ,, 1527	'Father of Dubrovnik poetry' love lyrics, madrigals.
Džɔre Držić	b. Dubrovnik 1461 d. ,, 1501	Poems show Italian influence, love lyrics.
Hanibal Lucić	b. Hvar 1485 d. ,, 1553	Early influence of classical writers, later of Menčetić and Držić. Best play 'Robinja'.
Nikola Vetrančić-Čavčić	b. Dubrovnik 1482 d. ,, 1576	Mystery plays, odes, chauvenistic poems.
Andrija Čubranović	b. Sixteenth century d. details uncertain	Masquerades, poems. Best work 'Jeđupka'.
Nikola Nalješković	b. Dubrovnik 1510 d. ,, 1587	Pastoral plays, poems.
Marin Držić	b. Dubrovnik 1508 d. Venice 1567	Pastoral plays of idyllic character and rustic charm. Sacred poems.
Dinko Ranjina	b. Dubrovnik 1536 d. ,, 1607	Love lyrics, epistles, didactic poems and idylls, sonnets.
Dinko Zlatarić	b. Dubrovnik 1556 d. ,, 1610	Translation of classics, love lyrics, idylls, didactic poems.
Floria Zuzzeri	b. Dubrovnik, circa 1556 d. Florence 1600	Sonnets in Italian and Slavonic languages.
Mavro Urbini	d. Dubrovnik circa 1550 d. ,, 1611	Prose writer; best work on first history of Slavs.

Table XV—continued
Dubrovnik's Writers and Men of Science

Name	Details	Remarks
Ivan Gundulić	b. Dubrovnik 1589? d. „ 1638	Strong influence of Tasso, introduced Italian verse into Slavonic language, dramas, poems, plays. Best work 'Osman' epic.
Đuro Hiđa	b. Dubrovnik 1752 d. Zaton 1833	Translation of classics, adopted classical metre to local language.
Marc R. Desrivaux	b. Lyon (France) circa 1770 d. Cyprus 1823	Poems and plays in Dubrovnik dialect.
Matija Ban	b. Dubrovnik 1818 d. Belgrade 1903	First editor of literary almanac, dramas, tragedies of nationalistic character.
Medo Pučić	b. Dubrovnik 1821 d. „ 1882	Helped found literary almanac, anthologies of political nature.
Petar Budmani	b. Dubrovnik 1835 d. Ancona 1914	Philology, translations from Sanskrit, contributed to literary almanac.
	SCIENCE	
Marin Getaldić	b. Dubrovnik 1568 d. „ 1626	Mathematician applied geometry to algebra and discovered equations of fourth degree.
Ruder J. Bošković	b. Dubrovnik 1711 d. Milan 1787	Mathematician, physicist, astronomer and philosopher. Molecular theory of matter, measured meridians. Best work 'Theoria Philosophiae Naturalis'.

Science

Dubrovnik was the birth place of several men of science, two of whom deserve to be remembered – Marin Getaldić (Marino Ghetaldi) and Ruđer Bošković (Ruggerio Boscović, or Boscovich). At the same time as Gundulić was preparing and writing his 'Osman' epic, Getaldić was pursuing those experiments in natural science which gained him a European reputation. Even so the Dubrovnik peasantry thought him an enchanter and dreaded to approach the cave which served him for a laboratory. In the eighteenth century the achieve-

T

ments of Bošković as a mathematician and natural philosopher also shed lustre on his native city. It is interesting that both men travelled to England. Getaldić stayed for two years, whilst Bošković was made a Fellow of the Royal Society. Boswell, Dr. Johnson's biographer, mentions him on several occasions; Bošković met Dr. Johnson at dinner in the houses of Sir Joshua Reynolds and Dr. Douglas (later Bishop of Salisbury), where 'that celebrated foreigner expressed his astonishment at Johnson's Latin conversation' (*The Life of Dr. Johnson*, ch.li).

Marin Getaldić[80] was born in 1568, into an old and respected Dubrovnik family. After his early education in the city he travelled widely, much of it with his close friend Marino Gučetić (Gozze) the writer. Together they visited much of Europe over a six year period including travels through Germany, Belgium, England, France and Italy. He met several interesting scientists of the day, including François Viète, the founder of algebra, in Paris, Christopher Clavius and Galileo, in Rome. During his travels he held the professorship of mathematics at Louvain, but subsequently returned to Dubrovnik, and served in several government offices. He was accepted as a member of the Great Council (Velika Vijeća) in 1588, was on the Council of Requests (Vijeća Umoljenih) between 1618 and 1622, and a member of the Small Council (Mala Vijeća) in 1625. In summer he would retire to his villa by the sea to meditate and make experiments in a cave on his estate. Getaldić was regarded as a magician by local people and his experiments in setting fire to boats out at sea by means of mirrors and burning-glasses were considered quite diabolical. Nevertheless he was one of the first astronomers and natural philosophers in Europe; his 'Promotus Archimedes seu de Variis corporum generibus gravitate et magnitudine comparatis' (Rome 1603) gave the first definite specific weight of seven metals and five liquids, showing a dim perception of the coming discoveries of Newton. His basic work was 'Appollonius redivivus seu restituta Apollonii Pergaei Inclinationum geometra' (Venice 1607) in which he solved forty-two geometrical problems connected with the conic sections of Apollonius (*circa* 220 B.C.). Other mathematical works included 'Variorum problematum Collectio', with solutions to a further forty-seven problems, and 'De resolutione et compositione Mathematica, Opus posthumum' (Rome 1630). He has also been credited with applying geometry to algebra before Des Cartes, and to have been the first to discover equations of the fourth degree.

FIG. 118.   Oil painting of Ruđer Bošković (1711–1787) by Robert Edge Pine. (Original in the Franciscan monastery, Dubrovnik.)

Ruđer Josip Bošković[81] was born in Dubrovnik, 1711, and at an early age became a Jesuit. In 1725 he joined their 'Collegium Romanum' in Rome where he studied philosophy, mathematics and physics, and came under the influence of contemporary French mathematicians. By 1736 he had published his first essays ('dissertationes') covering the fields of mathematics, physics, astronomy and geodesy, and in 1740 was appointed to a professorship in mathematics in Rome (publicus matheseos professor). Whilst in Rome he worked on the problem of cracks in the cupola of St. Peter's basilica (1742) and the construction in the same building of strong, firm, apses (1743). Maria Theresa called upon his expertise for the court library in Vienna, whilst in Paris he helped to work out the carrying capacity of pillars in St. Génève's church. Bošković next turned his attention to the measuring of meridians, and began in 1750 to calculate the meridian between Rome and Rimini with the Englishman, Charles Le Maire. The work took two and a half years finally being published in Rome (1755) as 'De litteraria expeditione per pontificiam ditionem ad dimentiendos meridiani gradus et corrigendam mappam geograficam', with a French translation appearing in 1770. In 1759 he was sent to England on a diplomatic mission, and helped with the compilation of measurements for North America which had recently been completed in Pennsylvania. Whilst in London he was made a Fellow of the Royal Society, to whom he dedicated his poem 'De Solis et Lunae Defectibus' written in elegant Latin style on his theory of the eclipse. He visited Greenwich, Oxford and Cambridge and at the beginning of 1761 worked with the astronomers J. Bradley, N. Maskelyne and other members of the Royal Society.

Later in 1761 he decided to travel to Turkey for further scientific work, leaving London via Belgium, Holland, Lorraine, Germany and Venice en route to Constantinople, where he stayed seven months. Once again he was on the move this time through Bulgaria and Moldavia to Poland recording his experiences and in consequence published his 'Giornale di un viaggio da Constantinopoli in Polonia', published in Bassano, 1784. He left Cracow for Rome. During the following year, 1762, he became professor of mathematics at Pavia and Director of the Brera Observatory, but his vanity and egoism made him many enemies. In 1770 he left Italy for Paris, where he was made Director of Optics in the Ministry of Marine, an office held for ten years. By 1783 he returned to Italy to publish the rest of his works, but failing health and a reputation now on the wane, led to increasing melancholia and death in Milan, from pneumonia in 1787.

Bošković's work was very comprehensive and diverse. In mathematics, most of it was of an applied rather than pure nature. On the other hand his philosophical criticism included discussions of very basic problems such as the concept of continuity, and the definition of infinity. Probably his most important work was 'Theoria Philophiae Naturalis redacta ad unicam Legem Virium in Natura existentium' published in Venice in 1763, which was concerned with the molecular theory of matter. Cartographically, he is best known for his map of the Papal States dated 1741. The name of Bošković stands deservedly high among the mathematicians and astronomers of the eighteenth century, but the more recent progress of science has meant that his works, like those of Getaldić, are today unread and forgotten.

The cultural life of the Dubrovnik Republic and beyond up to the present day has been proved to be far greater than one would have expected for such a small city-state. The architecture of Dubrovnik, like that of Dalmatia, as a whole, has so much in it that is peculiar and distinctive that it is entitled to rank as a style by itself among the various national styles of medieval Europe. The history of Dalmatia is in fact the history of the maritime towns, and it was in them that art and letters found a congenial soil and took root. In the field of art Dubrovnik has been less distinguished probably than in the sphere of literature and science. Nevertheless, native artists were not wanting among Dubrovnik's citizens, although they have been indebted to strangers, particularly from Italy, for their principal buildings. Maybe the Dubrovnik people were contented to carry on with the problems of commerce and leave any artistic work to people more able than themselves. During periods of political and commercial tranquility as in the eighteenth century, Dubrovnik's citizens had more leisure for domestic matters, seen in the completion of the Jesuit church, and the grand flight of stairs by which it is approached, but designed by an eminent Roman architect. In fact, as the commercial greatness of Venice declined towards the end of her career, the prosperity of her dependencies naturally passed away at the same time. The arts were neglected, and the series of architectural works was closed, except at Dubrovnik, which still preserved its liberties and some remains of its former prosperity. Even so Dubrovnik herself was gradually drawn into the vortex of the Napoleonic Wars, in which she, like her great rival Venice and many another still more powerful state, was to disappear.

11 Notes

1. G. Gelcich, *Delle Instituzioni Marittime e Secritarie delle Republica di Ragusa*' Trieste (1892), p. 42.
2. G. Gelcich, *op. cit.*, p. 42.
3. Dubrovnik Archives, (3/X/1349). *Reformationes* II.
4. Filippo de Diversi de Quartigiani wrote an account of the buildings and customs of Dubrovnik, dated 1440. The original manuscript is in the Franciscan monastery in Dubrovnik, and later published in part by Professor Brunelli, (ed). *Philippus de Diversis de Quartigianis, Situs Aedificiorum Ragusii*, Zadar (1882).
5. Lapidibus vivis, de Diversis later explains 'lapidibus non terreis sed ut communi nomine utar vivis' Brunelli (ed.) *op. cit.*, p. 29.
6. de Diversis was a witness both of the fire and reconstruction of the Rector's Palace. Brunelli, *op. cit.*, p. 39.
7. Michelozzi was a pupil of Donatello, and earned considerable reputation as a sculptor. In 1430 he worked on the palace for Cosimo de Medici (now called the Palazzo Riccardi) in Florence, and in 1433 the Library of S. Giorgio Maggiore in Venice. It is thought that he died in 1478.
8. Dubrovnik Archives, (2/XII/1464), *Acta Consilii Maioris* XII.
9. 'Mvnera diva patris q sol'apolis artes, invenit medicas ọ secl'a qnq' sepl'ltas, et docvit gramen q d vsv̄q̄qvaleret, hic escvlapivs coelatvs gloria nostra, Ragvsii genitvs volvit qv̄ē grata relatv̄, esse deos inter vetervm sapīa patrvm, hvmanas laudes svọaret rata q'ommes, qvo melivs toti nemo qvasi profvit orbi,' is the Cremonese chancellor's metrical 'epitaph', on a wall nearby.
10. T. G. Jackson, *Dalmatia, the Quarno, and Istria*, Oxford (1887), p. 336.
11. R. von Eitelberger von Edelberg, 'Kunstdenkmale Dalmatiens', Vol. IV of his *Gesammelte kunsthistorische Schriften*, Vienna (1884), p. 320.
12. T. G. Jackson, *op. cit.*, p. 338.
13. Dubrovnik Archives, (11/XII/1464). *Acta Consilii Maioris XII.*
14. G. Gelcich, *op. cit.*, p. 63.
15. These have been incorrectly drawn with two tiers by Eitelberger, *op. cit.*, (plate XXIII), and in Freeman's book (E. Freeman, *Sketches from the Subject and Neighbour Lands of Venice*, London (1881), p. 245.
16. One zechin (cekin) = 52·5—60 Dubrovnik dinars.
17. R. von Eitelberger, *op. cit.*, p. 314.
18. F. de Diversis, (ed. Brunelli) *op. cit.*, pp. 28–29.
19. G. Resti, *Chronica Ragusina*, South Slavonic Academy, Zagreb (1884).
20. N. Ragnina, *Annali di Ragusa*, South Slavonic Academy Zagreb (1890).
21. Anonymous account of Dubrovnik, quoted by G. Gelcich, *op. cit.*, p. 76.
22. Dubrovnik Archives, (1520). *Acta Consilii Maioris.*
23. G. Gelcich, *op. cit.*, p. 77.

24. *Ibid.*, pp. 17, 23.
25. *Ibid.*, p. 23.
26. 'Campanile nondum completum in dies crescit' de Diversis, Brunelli (ed.), *op. cit.*, p. 35.
27. R. von Eitelberger, *op. cit.*, p. 336, gives an elevation of this doorway, and p. 333 a plan of church and convent.
28. *Ibid.*, p. 334.
29. T. G. Jackson, *op. cit.*, p. 364.
30. F. de Diversis (Brunelli, ed.), *op. cit.*, p. 40.
31. P. Evang, Cusmich, quoted by J. Fabianich, *Storia dei Frat. Min. in Dalmazia'e Bossina*, Vol. II, Zara, (1895), p. 186.
32. T. G. Jackson, *op. cit.*, p. 372.
33. F. de Diversis, (Brunelli, ed.), *op. cit.*, 'the fountain and "lauri et aranciorum arbores" '.
34. H. Tartalja, 'Kulturna uloga ljekarne "Male brače" u Dubrovniku'. *Dubrovnik* Vol. 11, No. 1 (1968), pp. 63–72.
35. Derived from the word 'spongia' meaning deposited matter. The name also applied to open arcades, built on the borders of the republic as resting places for caravans. (loggie), G. Gelcich, *op. cit.*, p. 73.
36. F. de Diversis (Brunelli, ed.), *op. cit.*, p. 42.
37. G. Gelcich, *op. cit.*, p. 73, 'Quod sponzia compleatur'.
38. Dubrovnik Archives (1277). *Liber Statutorum doane.* Quoted by R. von Eitelberger, *op. cit.*, p. 357.
39. G. Gelcich, *op. cit.*, p. 19;
    L. Beritić, *Urbanistički Razvitak Dubrovnika*, Dubrovnik (1962), 46 pp.
40. G. Gelcich, *op. cit.*, p. 20;
    Monumenta Ragusina, libri reformationum, Vol. II, p. 294; Vol. III, p. 48, Jugoslovenska akademija znanosti i umjetnosti, Zagreb, (1879–1897).
41. Nićifor Ranjina (1319), Johannes di Siena (1397), Johannes di Vienna (1381–87), M. Michelozzi (1461–64), Juraj Dalmatinac (1465–66), Paskoje Miličević (1466–1516), Antonio Ferramolina (1538), Saporoso Matteucci (1570–71), Giovani Battista Zanchi di Pesaro (1571–73), Mihajlo Hranjac (1617), Marin Držić (1645-60), Marcantonio Bettaci (1658–60), Ivan Giorgi (1668–71) and Marchione Perroni (1676–78).
42. G. Gelcich, *op. cit.*, p. 278.
43. Dubrovnik Archives, (24/III/1346). *Liber Reformationes* I.
44. F. de Diversis (Brunelli, ed.), *op. cit.*, p. 42; 'arsenatus galearum domus, in qua triremes pulchræ et biremes resident quibus armatis, cum opus fuerit, utuntur Ragusini'.
45. T. G. Jackson, *op. cit.*
46. F. M. Appendini, *Notizie Istorico-Critiche de Ragusei*, Vol. II, Dubrovnik (1803), p. 170.
47. L. Villari, *op. cit.*, p. 361.
48. T. G. Jackson, *op. cit.*, p. 313.
49. G. Gelcich, *op. cit.*, who also gives a considerable list of Dubrovnik artists, pp. 78–82.
50. I. Kukuljević, *Slovnik umjetnijak jugoslovenskih*, Zagreb (1958);
    K. Kovać, 'Nikolaus Ragusinus und seine Zeit, *Beiblatt zum Jährbuch des Kunsthistorichen Instituts der k.k. Zentralkommission für Denkmalpflege*, Vol. XI, Vienna (1917);

Lj. Karaman 'Notes sur l'art byzantin et les Slavs catholiques de Dalmatie', *Recueils Uspenskij*, Paris (1932), Vol. II, p. 2; *ibid.*, *Umjetnost u Dalmaciji*, XV i, XVI vijek, Zagreb (1933); D. Westphal, 'Malo poznata slikarska djela XIV do XVIII stoljeća u Dalmaciji', *Rad. J.A.* (1937), p. 258; J. Tadić, 'Grada o slikarskoj školi u Dubrovniku XIII–XVI vijek', *Grada S.N.A.*, Vol. IV (1952); Lj. Karaman, 'O staroj slikarskoj školi u Dubrovniku', *Anali Historijskog Instituta u Dubrovniku*, Vol. II, Dubrovnik (1953), pp. 101–123.

51. T. G. Jackson, *op. cit.*, p. 385.
52. G. Gelcich, *op. cit.*, p. 80.
53. R. von Eitelberger, *op. cit.*, Vol. IV, p. 357.
54. F. M. Appendini, *op. cit.*
55. R. von Eitelberger, *op. cit.*, Vol. IV, p. 317.
56. T. G. Jackson, *op. cit.*, p. 345.
57. R. von Eitelberger, *op. cit.*, p. 329 and Plate XXVI.
58. T. G. Jackson, *op. cit.*, p. 354, 'Franco Ferro Veneto F.A. 1694'.
59. *Ibid.*, p. 356.
60. T. G. Jackson, *op. cit.*, p. 376.
61. A. N. Puipin and W. Spasowicz, *Geschichte der Slavischen Literature*, Vol. II, Leipzig (1880), p. 224.
62. *Ibid.*
63. F. Ambrosoli, 'Stefano Gradi', *Galleria di Ragusei illustri*, Dubrovnik (1841), pp. 1–4;
V. Bogošić, 'Dvije riječi o Stepanu Gradiću i njegovim pismima Dubrovačkoj republici', '*Dubrovnik zabavnik Narodne Stionice dubrovačke*', Split (1867), pp. 303–321;
D. Korbler, 'Gradičéva proslava', *Savremenik* Zagreb (1913), No. 4;
A. Liepopili, 'Una causa di Stefano Gradi col Capitolo di Ragusa', *Rešetarov zbornik*, Dubrovnik (1931), pp. 139–142;
F. Banfi, 'Christina di Svezia e Stefano Gradi di Ragusa', *Archivio storico per la Dalmazia*, Vol. XXVI, Split (1939), pp. 363–394.
64. His works include *Peripateticae philosophiae pronuntiata disputationibus proposita* (no date or place of publication);
Oratio de eligendo summo pontifice sede vacante post obitum Alexandri VII, Rome (1667);
De laudibus serenissimae reipublicae Venetae et cladibus Patriae suae carmen, Venice (1675); and
Disputatio de opinione probabili cum, P. Honorato Fabri, Rome (1678).
65. V. Jagić, 'Trubadur i najstariji hrvatski lirici', *Rad. J.A.* (1869), p. 9;
F. Dujmušić, *Jezik Menčetićev i Držićev prema Marulićeva*, Vijenac (1896);
M. Murko, 'Nekokliko riječi o prvim dubrovačkim pjesnicama', *Rešetarov zbornik* (1931), pp. 233–244;
J. Torbarina, *Italian influence on the poets of the Ragusan Republic*, London (1931);
M. Rešetar, 'Život i rad Š. Menčeta i Dz. Držića, '*Stari pisci hrvatski J.A.* (1937), p. 2. (Second edition).
66. M. Medini, 'Prvi dubrovački pjesnici i Zbornik Nikole Ranjine', *Rad. J.A.* (1903), p. 153;
B. Vodnik, *Povijest hrvatski književnosti*, Vol. I, Zagreb (1913), pp. 90–95;

P. Popović, *Pregled srpske književnosti*, (Third edition) Belgrade (1919), pp. 127–129, 131, 132, 136 and 167.

67. F. Maixner, 'O Hrvatskom prievodu XV(XVI) Ovidijeve heroide Paris Helenae od Hanibala Lucića', *Rad. J.A.* (1888), No. XCI;

A. Gavrilović, 'Lucićeva, Robinja i narodna poezija', *Nastavnik*, Zagreb (1898), pp. 7–8;

A. Dobroncic, 'Robinja Hanibala Lucića i muzičko-dramska pučka gluma u Pagu', *Vjesnik Etnografskog muzeja u Zagrebu*, Zagreb (1936);

M. Franičević, 'Uz stihove Hanibala Lucića', *Književnost jučer i danas*, Zagreb (1959).

68. L. Zore, 'O Jegjupci Andrije Čubranovića', *Rad. J.A.* (1874), p. 27;

M. Medini, 'Dubrovačke poklade u XVI i XVII vijeku i Čubranovićevi nasljednici', *Program dubrovačke gimnazije*, Dubrovnik (1898);

M. Rešetar 'Nachtrag zu Dr. M. Medini's Aufsatz über Čubranović', *Archiv. für slavische Philogie*, Leipzig (1900), p. 22;

P. Kolendić, 'Sakupljanja grade za proučavanje književika: Andrije Čubranović, Ignajata Dordevića, marine Držića i Nikole Nalješkovića', *Godišnjak S.A.*, Belgrade (1925), No. 34;

M. A. Petković, Dubrovačke maskerate, *Posebna izdanja S.A.*, Belgrade (1950), No. CLXVI.

69. M. Rešetar, 'Ispravci i dodaci tekstu starieh pisaca dubrovačkijeh', *Rad. J.A.* (1894), p. 119;

M. Pantić 'Nalješkovićeva komedija "aresitana u Mara Klaričića na pivu" ', *Zbornik M.S.*, Belgrade (1955);

R. Bogišić, *Dvije pjesme Nikole Nalješkoviáa Krugovi* (1958);

M. Simonović, 'O godini rođenja Nikole Nalješkovića', *Prilozi* (1959).

70. J. Dayre, *Dubrovačke studije*, Zagreb (1938), 211 pp.;

M. Rešetar, 'Jezik M. Držića', *Rad. J.A.* (1933), No. 248, p. 99–240;

M. Krleža, 'O našem dramskom repertoiru', *Djelo*, Zagreb (1948), No. 1;

J. Tadić, *Dubrovački portreti*, Belgrade (1948);

M. Finci, 'Marin Držić', *Književnost*, Zagreb (1948);

M. Matković, '*Dramaturški eseji*', Zagreb (1949);

Ž. Jeličić, 'Marin Držić, pjesnik dubrovačke sirotinje', *Hrvatsko kolo*, Zagreb (1949).

71. G. Gagliuffi, 'Domenico Ragnina', *Galleria di Ragusei illustri*, Zagreb (1841);

F. Maixner, 'Prijevodi Ranjine Dinka iz latinishkih i grčkih klasika', *Rad. J.A.* (1884), No. 70;

I. Kasumović, 'Utjecaj grčkih i rimskih pjesnika na dubrovačju liričku poezija', *Rad. J.A.* (1914), Nos. 201, 203, 205;

Š. Urlić, 'Nekoliko priloga biografiji Dinka Ranjine', *Grada J.A.* (1927);

J. Dayre, 'Dinko Ranjina i njegov životopis', *Dubrovačke studije*, Zagreb (1938);

V. Marinović, 'Dinko Ranjina i njegovo doba', *Republika*, Zagreb (1957).

72. J. Tadić, 'Dubrovnik za vreme Điva Gundulića', *Srpski književni glasnik*, Belgrade (1939), No. 4, pp. 257–282;

A. Haler, 'O Gundulićevim Suzama sina razmetnoga' *Gunduličev zbornik*, Zagreb (1938);

F. Fotez, 'Ivan Gundulić i njegov Dubravka', *Scena*, Belgrade (1938), No. 8;

J. Ravlić, 'Gundulić i njegov Dubravka', *Anali Historijskog instituta J.A. u Dubrovniku* (1956);

A. Pavić, *Estetična ocjena Gundulićeva Osmana, Zagreb 1879*;

A. Jensen, 'Gundulić und sein Osman', Goteborg (1900);

A. Cronia, 'L'Influenza della Gerusalemme liberata del Tasso sull' Osman di Giovanni Gondola *L'Europa Orientale*, Rome (1925);

V. Setschkareff, *Die Dichtungen Gundulic's und ihr poetischer Stil*, Bonn (1952);

M. Ratković, *Predgovor zagrebačkom izdanju Osmana*, Zagreb (1955);

F. Šveleč, 'O Gunduliceva Osmana', *Republika*, Zagreb (1954), No. 11–12;

N. Ivanisin, 'Iskre iz Gundulićeva Osmana', *Republika*, Zagreb (1955), No. 7;

V. K. Zaitčev, 'Istoricheskaja osnova i ideinoe soderžanie poem', Ivana Gundulića 'Osman' *Literatyra slavjanskih narodov*, No. 2 Moscow (1957).

73. V. Makušev, *Issledovanija ob istoričeskih pamjatnikah i bitopisateljah Dubrovnovnika*, St. Petersburg (1867);

L. Rava, *Mavro Orbini, primo storico dei popoli slavi*, Bologna (1913);

N. Radojčić, *Srpska istorija Mavra Orbinija*, Belgrade (1950).

74. T. Chersa, *Della vita e delle opere di monsignore Giorgio Ferich*, Dubrovnik (1824);

I. Kasumović, 'Ferićeva Perijegeza i rimski pjesnici', *Nastavni vjesnik*, Zagreb (1900);

D. Grubor, ' "Ferić, Ilir iz Dubrovnika" u Gajevoj "Danici Ilirskoj" g. 1836 i Ivan Mažuranić' *Nastavni vjesnik*, Zagreb (1909);

S. Kastropil, *Rukopisi Naučne biblioteke u Dubrovniku*, Vol. I, Zagreb (1954).

75. I. A. Kaznačić, 'Gjuro Hidža', *Slovinac*, Zagreb (1882), No. 4, pp. 62–63;

J. Bersa, *Dubrovačke slike i prilike*, Zagreb (1941).

76. M. Pučić, *Marko Bruère Desrivaux, pešnik slovinski, Dubrovnik*, Zagreb (1852);

J. Nagy, 'Marko Bruère Desrivaux als ragusanischer Dichter', *Archiv für slavische Philologie*, Vienna (1906), No. 28, pp. 52–76;

R. Warnier, 'Comment un consul de France décrit au Directoire la civilisation ragusaine', *Zbornik iz Dubrovačke prošlosti Milanu Rešetaru*, Dubrovnik (1931) pp. 157–164;

J. Dayre, 'Marc Bruère Desrivaux', *Hrvatsko kolo*, Zagreb (1941), pp. 48–63.

77. S. Pjerotić, *Sulla vita e sulle opere di Mattia Ban*, Zagreb (1881);

J. Bošković, 'Govor o proslavi 50 godišnjice književnog rada Matije Bana', *Glasnik Srpskog učenog društva*, Vol. LXV, Belgrade (1886), pp. 12–39;

K. Lucerna, 'U spomen Matije Bana, Dubovčanina', *Ljetopis J.A.*, Vol. 21, Zagreb (1907), pp. 120–168;

J. Skerlić, *Istorija nove srpske književnosti*, Belgrade (1921), pp. 199–201.

78. F. Marković, 'Knez Medo Pučić', *Rad. J.A.* (1883), No. 67;

A. Fabris, 'Medo Pučić', *kalendar Dubrovnik* (1897);

K. Milutinović, 'Medo Pučić i narodni preporod u Dubrovniku', *Dubrovnik* (1962).

79. S. Brusina, 'Pero Budmani', *Prosvjeta*, Zagreb (1905), No. 22;

I. Krnić, 'Stari Budmani. Intimne uspomene', *Savremnik*, Zagreb (1915), pp. 169–175;

M. Rešetar, 'Pero Budmani', *Ljetopis J.A.*, Vol. 36, Zagreb (1926), pp. 91–111.

80. O. Kučera, 'O Marinu Getaldiću, patriciju dubrovačkom, znamenitom matematiku i fiziku na početku XVII vijaka, *Rad. J.A.* (1893), No. 117;

H. Wieleitner, 'Marino Ghetaldi und die Anfange der Koordinatengeometrie', *Bibliotheca Mathematica*, Berlin (1912–13), pp. 242–247;

A. Favaro, 'Amici e corrispondenti di Galileo, Marino Ghetaldi', *Atti dell Instituto Veneto*, Venice (1910), No. 2, pp. 303–310;

N. Saltykow, 'Souvenirs concernant le Géomètre yougoslave Marinus Ghetaldi, conservés à Doubrovnik en Dalmatie', *Isis*, Paris (1938), No. 38, pp. 1–22;

J. Klein, 'Die griechische Logistik und die Entstehung der Algebra II, Quellen und Studien zur Geschichte der Mathematik, Astronomie und Physik', *Abt.B: Studien*, Berlin (1936), No. 3, pp. 122–235;

M. Petrović, *Godišnjak Srpske kralevske Akademije*, Vol. XLVII, Belgrade (1937), pp. 277–280.

81. J. Todhunter, *A History of the Mathematical Theories of Attraction and the Figure of the Earth*, London (1873), pp. 305–334;

M. Oster, *Roger Joseph Boscovich als Naturphilosoph*, Cologne (1909), 164 pp.;

D. Nedelkovitch, *La Philosophie Naturelle et Relative de R. J. Boscovich*, Paris (1922), 201 pp.;

P. Popović, 'Ruđer Bošković i Dr. Džonson', *Prilozi za književnost, jezik, istoriju i folkor*, Zagreb (1929), No. 1–2, pp. 194–200;

S. Ristić, 'Bošković and Faraday', *The Anglo-Yugoslav Review*, London (1937), No. 7–8, pp. 74–79;

H. V. Gill, *Roger Boscovich, S.I. (1711–1787). Forerunner of Modern Physical Theories*, Dublin (1941), 183 pp.;

J. Torbarina, 'Bošković u krugu engelskih književnika', *Almanah Bošković za 1950*, Dubrovnik (1950), pp. 53–90;

J. Smolka, 'Ohlas díla R. J. Boškoviče v Českych Zemích, *Sborník Pro Dějiný Přírodních Věd a Techniký*, Vol. II, Prague (1967), pp. 117–123.

12
The Final Fall of the Dubrovnik Republic

The impact of the French Revolution of 1789 on the history of eastern Europe remains a matter of dispute among historians. This is partly because of lack of agreement over the nature of the societies of eastern Europe that were exposed to revolutionary ideas and, subsequently, to military action.[1] The message of the French Revolution in south-east Europe may not be so easy to measure, but in more practical terms it meant that Dubrovnik was now forced to enter into the vortex of the Napoleonic Wars in which she, like her great rival Venice, both with their particular brand of aristocratic government, was to disappear along with many other still more powerful states. Further, the plans of both Russia and Austria for eastern expansion were interrupted by the French Revolution and the Napoleonic Wars. For the next few years the attention of Europe was turned towards combatting French power and the political influences of the French Revolution.

Two aspects of the complicated diplomatic manoeuvring of the period are of significance for Balkan history in general, and Dubrovnik in particular. First, in 1805 and 1809 France took from Austria and Venice the lands of Istria, Slovenia, Dalmatia, and parts of Croatia – all of which were inhabited by South Slavs – and formed from these the so-called 'Illyrian Provinces'. The reforms associated with the French Revolution were incorporated into the government. This state, the first modern political union of the South Slavs, lasted only for a short time, but it inspired later movements for unity in the area. The second event of significance was the conclusion of the treaties of Vienna in 1815, which ended the long years of warfare in Europe. Austria received the former Venetian possessions in Dal-

matia and further increased the number of South Slav peoples within
her boundaries.

The Napoleonic Episode

When war broke out between France and Austria in 1805 Dubrovnik
refused to commit herself, but Timoni the Austrian consul at Dubrovnik informed his government that the sympathies of the citizens
were with the French.

> 'It appears, that this Government, of which the apathy, indolence
> and venality are at their height, will undergo the fate for which it
> is destined.... I am convinced that if peace be not concluded,
> the French will try to get possession of this republic, and form a
> body of troops here with whom to attack Cattaro (Kotor). The
> only means by which this could be avoided, and which I venture
> to submit to the superior intelligence of your Excellency, is that in
> case hostilities should recommence you should place a garrison in
> the town until peace is declared, without, however, interfering in
> the affairs of the government'.[2]

By the Peace of Pressburg, France regained Venice and consequently Istria and Dalmatia. To this last possession Napoleon
attached great importance, as it formed an excellent base for operations in the Balkans and in the East. In February 1806 French troops
under General Molitor occupied the country as far as Makarska, and
preparations were made for an attack on Kotor, where resistance was
expected on the part of the Montenegrins and Albanians, supported
by the Russians.

The Russians had long desired to establish a footing in the Mediterranean, so as to attack Constantinople from both sides, and during
the war of 1805 Russia had sent a fleet of forty-two ships and trans-
ports, under Admiral Siniavin, into the Adriatic. After the battle of
Austerlitz it concentrated at Corfu. The consequent treaty of Pressburg compelled Austria to hand over Dalmatia to France, putting
Dubrovnik in a novel dilemma. Kotor held by the Venetians against
the Turks, was always accessible to Venice, which was a naval power.
But while France held the land, England and Russia held the sea;
and while France was marching her troops from Austerlitz to Dalmatia, eleven Russian sail of the line entered the Bay of Kotor and
landed 6,000 men, and the Admiral was invited by the Montenegrins

to occupy Kotor. This he did, obliging the Austrian garrison to retire. On hearing the news the French were furious, and declared
Austria responsible for the Russian occupation of Kotor, which they
would now have to attack in force. The Russian occupation of Kotor
had two main effects. In the short run it intensified the struggle over
the possession of south Dalmatia; in the long term it meant that Napoleon's plan of connections across the Balkans and an agreement with
the Turks, could no longer be realized. These events disturbed
Dubrovnik, for its citizens feared lest the passage of French troops
through their territory should end in a permanent occupation. As
5,000 Frenchmen under Marshal Molitor marched southwards, and
took pacific possession, one after another, of the fortresses of Dalmatia, the Russians pressed the senators of Dubrovnik to allow them
to occupy their city, as it was an important fortress, thus anticipating
France might block the further progress to Kotor. Unfortunately for
Dubrovnik at this time there was no way from Dalmatia to Kotor,
but through its city. The Senate sent conciliatory letters to Napoleon,
congratulating 'the most glorious of Emperors' on his victories, and
to Talleyrand, 'the most virtuous of Ministers'. They offered to transport the French army by sea from Ston to Cavtat thus avoiding the
passage through the town of Dubrovnik, and voted 30,000 piastres
for the purpose. Unfortunately, Sankovski, the Russian Commissary,
heard of the offer, and threatened that if these were the republic's
intentions he would order the occupation of Cavtat, adding that the
garrison would be a Montenegrin one, well knowing how the Dubrovnik citizens hated and feared those lawless mountaineers. Another Russian agent came to Dubrovnik on board a frigate, insisted
that all arrangements with the French should be cancelled, and
ordered the Senate to inform the Russians as to the movements of
the French troops. The Senate instructed Bassegli and Zlatarić, their
agents in the French camp, to do everything to hinder Molitor's advance, by describing the strength of the Russians and the risks of
the march. This they did, and Molitor was so impressed by their
statements that he gave up the plan for the moment. His demand
for a further loan of 300,000 francs was refused on the plea that the
treasury was empty, although as a matter of fact it was not. Also
Marshal Molitor was equally abundant in friendly professions, pressing instances, and solem pledges, to respect the integrity of the
republic, in his passage to Kotor. Dubrovnik felt herself without the
power of causing her neutrality to be respected, and long and anxious

were the debates that ensued. Siniavin now proposed to attack Dubrovnik and occupy it, but the Senate's protestations of loyalty to the
Csar, and possibly its bribes, induced him to desist from a move
which would have secured him from all fear of a French attack.[3]

Now the French General Lauriston came on the scene, and prepared to advance; he concentrated a force at Makarska, and then
moved on to Slano in Dubrovnik's territory. The senators were at
their wits' end; the old diplomacy had broken down in the clash of
the Napoleonic Wars; they could no longer temporize, and were
under the necessity of calling in either the French or the Russians.
The latter seemed the more dangerous, especially on account of their
allies, the Montenegrins. Moreover, the French consul had made
many friends, while his Russian colleague was deservedly hated.
Count Caboga's proposal that the population should emigrate en
masse to Corfu or Turkish territory was rejected, and the majority
decided in favour of the French.

Count John Caboga said,

'Dear as this land is to me, consecrated as it is to our affections by
its venerable institutions, its wise laws, and the memory of illustrious ancestors, it will henceforth cease to deserve the name of
patria, if its independence be subverted. With our large fleet of
merchantmen, let us embark our wives and our children, our
state treasures and our laws, and ask of the Sultan an island in the
Archipelago, which may become a new Epidaurus, and the
sanctuary of our time-honoured institutions'.

Serious as the dilemma was, the senators were unprepared for so
desperate a remedy. A large majority were for opening the gates to
Russia; but the echoes of Austerlitz had scarce died away, and such
an act would have at once exposed them to the vengeance of
Napoleon, then in the zenith of his lawless ambition and military
power. So the occupation of the city was assigned to the French
under General Lauriston. On the evening of May 26, 1806 Lauriston,
with 800 men, reached Dubrovnik after a forced march of twenty
hours. He found the gates closed and the drawbridge up; two senators
met him and requested him not to enter the town, but this was a mere
formality. He went to the Palace, where the Small Council was
assembled, and declared that his orders were to occupy the fortified
points of the state of Dubrovnik, but to respect the liberty of the
republic and the persons and property of the inhabitants. He offered

them the protection of Napoleon, and said that as the Austrian Emperor had closed all his ports to the Anglo-Russian fleets, it was important that Dubrovnik should not remain the only harbour in the Adriatic open to the enemies of France. Meanwhile Colonel Teste with the troops had entered the town and seized the forts: Dubrovnik was thus occupied for the first time in her history by uninvited foreign troops. Great consternation ensued, and the Russians at once seized all Dubrovnik's ships in the harbour at Gruž.

No sooner did this take place than the Russian force moved towards the siege of the city, and unhappily for Dubrovnik

'a barbarous and undisciplined horde of Montenegrins accompanied the regular Russian troops; and such a scene of horror had not been seen since the Huns and the Avars swept round Aquileia. The environs were studded thickly with villas, the results of a long prosperity; and the inhuman scenes of rapine with which the wars of the Montenegrines with the Turks were accompanied were transferred to these abodes of ease and luxury. Accustomed to the poverty of their own mountains, these invaders could scarce believe their own eyes when, passing Ragusa Vecchia (Cavtat), the smiling villas and well-filled store-houses of Breno Ombla and Pille were presented to their cupidity, and the siege of Dubrovnik commenced by the burning and plundering of the villas, involving the irretrievable loss of above half a million sterling'.[4]

On May 29 Lauriston issued the following proclamation:[5]

'1) Repeated concessions to the enemies of France have placed the Republic of Dubrovnik in a state of hostility, all the more dangerous inasmuch as it was disguised under the appearance of neutrality and friendship. The entry of the French troops into Dalmatia, far from putting an end to such conduct, has only given occasion to our enemies to exercise their influence on the State of Dubrovnik still further, and whatever may have been the motives of the condescension shown by the magistrates of this State, the Emperor could not fail to be aware of them; he desired to put an end to intrigues so contrary to the laws of neutrality.

'2) Consequently, in the name and by the authority of His Majesty the Emperor and King of Italy, I take possession of the town and territory of Dubrovnik.

'3) I declare, however, that it is the intention of His Imperial and

Royal Majesty to recognise the independence and neutrality of this state as soon as the Russians evacuate Albania, Corfu, and the other former Venetian possessions, and the Russian fleet ceases to disturb the coasts of Dalmatia.

'4) I promise succour and protection to all Dubrovnik's citizens; I shall see that the existing laws and customs and the rights of property be respected; in a word, I shall so act that, according to the behaviour of the inhabitants, they will be satisfied with the residence of the French troops in the country.

'5) The existing government is maintained; it will fulfil the same functions and have the same attributions as before; its relations with states friendly to France or neutral will remain on the same footing.

'6) M. Bruère, commissioner of commercial relations (consul), will act as Imperial Commissary to the Senate.

ALEX. LAURISTON.'

Dubrovnik, May 28, 1806.

This coup de main was most successful, but Lauriston did not execute the rest of his programme by attacking Kotor, for he was himself beseiged in Dubrovnik instead.

His forces amounted to about 800 men but he sent to Molitor at Zadar for reinforcements and supplies, which arrived from Split soon after; the garrison was thus raised to 2,000. Dubrovnik was put in a state of defence, the guns in the arsenal were mounted, a cargo of powder for the Turks seized, and the Cavtat-Obod line held by 200 Frenchmen. Thus the city was in the utmost straits; General Molitor, who had advanced within a few days' march of Dubrovnik, made an appeal to the Dalmatians to rise and expel the Russians and Montenegrins, which met with a feeble response, for only three hundred men joined his standard; but a strategem made up for his deficiency of numbers. A few days later the Montenegrins and Orthodox Kotorians, instigated by the Russians, advanced into Konavle, which they proceeded to pillage, while 500 more landed from Russian ships near Cavtat. The French drove them back, but fearing to be cut off if the Russians landed at Srebreno, they withdrew to that point, and then to Brgat where they were joined by reinforcements under General Delgorgue. The Russian squadron sailed up and landed a force at Srebreno, which encouraged the Montenegrins to attack Delgorgue. He was hard pressed by the enemy, who availed themselves of every inch of cover. On June 17 he attempted a bayonet charge, which failed, and he himself was killed in the mêlée; the retreat became a rout, Brgat was abandoned, and the Russians seized Mt. Srđ and Gruž. Dubrovnik was filled with refugees fleeing before the Montenegrins, and from that day was closely invested. A Russian attack on Lokrum was repulsed, but on June 19 the bombardment commenced. The battery on Mt. Srđ discharged 3,374 shells in seventeen days, but only twenty-three people were killed. All the houses round the town were razed to the ground; the villas of the rich nobles were plundered, the more valuable contents being seized by the Russian officers, and the rest left to the Montenegrins, Kotorians, Konavlese, Bosnians, and even Turks, who had swarmed down in the hope of loot. The inhabitants who did not get away in time were murdered and even tortured. On June 22 there was a suspension of hostilities, and the nobles tried to induce Lauriston to surrender, which he refused to do. On the 28th Admiral Siniavin summoned him to capitulate without success; the bombardment recommenced, but without much vigour, and the siege by Siniavin became a blockade.

Suddenly on July 6 a body of French troops appeared before the Ploče Gate and soon after Molitor himself arrived, drove off the Russians, and entered the town. When the news of the defeat at Brgat reached Zadar, he had quickly collected 2,000 men and advanced on Dubrovnik. He sent a message to Lauriston which was designed to fall into the hands of the Russians, announcing his arrival at the head of 10,000 men. This letter, seemingly confidential, was despatched to General Lauriston in Dubrovnik, announcing his approximate arrival to raise the siege with such a force of Dalmatians as must overwhelm the Russians and Montenegrins; this letter was, as intended by Molitor, intercepted and believed by the besieging Russians. With his force thinly scattered, to make up a show, Molitor now advanced towards Dubrovnik and turning the Montenegrin position in the valley behind, threatened to surround the Russians who occupied the summit of the hill between him and the city; he also made a small body of troops march several times past a spot near Ombla (Dubrovačke Rijeka) whence they could be seen by the enemy. The Russians, thus deceived as to the strength of the French, abandoned Mt. Srđ, and together with the Montenegrins fled to the coast and embarked on board ship, and retreated to Kotor. The French were received at Dubrovnik with much show of enthusiasm, for although a large part of the population had no sympathy with them, they rejoiced that the siege was at an end, and the fear of a sack of the town by the Montenegrins removed.

Molitor returned to Zadar, Lauriston remaining behind to organize the French protectorate at Dubrovnik. He discovered that the Senate had sent an agent to Constantinople with a report bitterly reviling the French, another to Vienna and St. Petersburg (Leningrad) asking for intervention in favour of Dubrovnik, and a third to Paris with a humble letter to Napoleon, and instructions to ask the Turkish ambassador to protest against the occupation of a state tributary to the Porte. He also learned that the republic had deposited 700,000 florins in Schuller's bank at Vienna, of which a part had been withdrawn in March and June. The French Commissary thereupon declared that henceforth all affairs dealt with by the Senate and the Small Council should be first communicated to him, and that no payments were to be made without his authority.

Although Lauriston in his proclamation of May 29, 1806, had promised that Dubrovnik would be evacuated when peace was declared, the French had no intention of doing so, and on July 21st Napoleon wrote to Eugene Beauharnais

'You will make General Lauriston observe that, if I have said in the treaty (Peace of Ouvril) that I recognize the independence of Dubrovnik, that does not mean that I shall evacuate it; on the contrary, when the Montenegrins have gone home, I intend to organize the country, and then abandon it if necessary, retaining only Ston'.

The citizens of Dubrovnik did not know of this, and believed that they would soon be free, but their hopes were dashed on August 24, when war broke out again.

The French paid the indemnities for the siege very liberally – 13,000,000 francs – as the money was to be provided for by Austria, whom they held responsible for all the consequences of the Russian occupation of Kotor. On the strength of this generosity the Senate tried once more through Count Sorgo, a Dubrovnik citizen resident in Paris, to get another loan of 600,000 francs refunded, but without success.

The French reinforced by 4,000–5,000 men, were now commanded in chief by General Marmont, the newly appointed civil and military Governor of Dalmatia, who, with 9,000 sabres and bayonets, boldly advanced to the gulf of Kotor. They defeated the Russians and

Montenegrins again, at Sutorina with great loss, the battle of
Friedland taking place in 1807.

At last, on July 8, 1807, the Peace of Tilsit was signed, by which
Russia gave up Kotor to the French. Berthier, in a letter to General
Marmont, who was now in command of Dalmatia, wrote:

> 'Dubrovnik must certainly be united to Dalmatia; you must there-
> fore continue to fortify it'

for under the treaty of Tilsit, France was left in undisputed possession of the coast. On August 13 Marmont stopped at Dubrovnik on
his way to Kotor and received the Senators very affably; but in the
course of conversation he said to one of them: 'Vous allez être des
nôtres'. On being asked for an explanation of these ominous words,
he added

> 'that in the present circumstances they could not remain free: the
> delegates having said that without merchant shipping the state
> could not exist, Marmont replied that by belonging to the great
> Emperor, His Majesty would find means of compensating them.
> The next day the General told the delegates who had called on
> him that he was instructed to inform them of their future destiny,
> and that pending the arrival of those to whom the organization
> of the new government was entrusted, that of Dubrovnik might
> continue in its functions'.[6]

The declaration seemed the death-knell of Dubrovnik's independence, and Timoni describes the condition of the State in consequence
of the French occupation:

> 'Agriculture ruined, the merchant navy reduced to inaction,[7]
> public finances dilapidated, private citizens crushed down by re-
> quisitions, the monasteries converted into barracks, the invasion
> of the Jews as army contractors, the establishment of a masonic
> lodge and a club, and on the top of all this the blindness of the
> people and the bourgeoisie who receive the French with open
> arms'.

As Timoni observes, the French party was still strong among the
middle and lower classes, who were tired of the oligarchic rule of
the nobles.

As soon as Marmont had departed a secret meeting of the Senate
was held, and it was decided to send a disguised messenger to Vienna

with a petition to the Emperor of Austria. As usual insufficient secrecy was observed, and Marmont heard of their action, but did nothing for the moment. On November 4 a demand was made for 300 sailors for the French-Venetian fleet, to which the Senate replied that there was always an insufficiency of seamen in Dubrovnik, that a third of the crews were foreigners, and that many of their ships had been captured by the Russians or were abroad. Instructions were sent to Kiriko, the Dubrovnik consul at Constantinople, to try to obtain Turkish intervention. But the French ambassador, General Sebastiani, had so much influence with the Porte that Kiriko had been obliged to remove the Dubrovnik arms from his house, and to request the Dubrovnik ship-captains to substitute the tricolor for the banner of St. Blaize (Sv. Vlah). For this the republic dismissed him from his office, and sent Antonio Natali to inform the Sultan of the dangers which menaced 'the oldest and most faithful tributary of the Porte'. On December 21, Lauriston informed the Small Council that Dubrovnik's ships must take out Italian patents within three days or be seized on leaving the port. The Senate replied that it could not take such a step without consulting the Ottoman government. Two days later Lauriston left Dubrovnik and on the 26th, Colonel Godart put up a notice declaring that any captain who did not hoist the Italian colours at once would be imprisoned. On January 2, 1808, General Clauzel took command of Dubrovnik, and on the 6th the tricolor was hoisted on the flagstaff in the Placa. The Senate tried to send Count Caboga to the Emperor of Austria but Clauzel prevented his departure. Urgent messages were despatched to Constantinople, and overtures were even made to Timoni. The Pasha of Bosnia was also approached, but he was friendly to the French, and informed them of all Dubrovnik's communications. On January 31, 1808, Marmont returned to Dubrovnik and summoned the Senate saying that he had a declaration to make. Timoni writes,

'The Council gathered together in less than an hour, and Colonel Delort repaired to the Palace, followed by the Consul Bruère, the war commissary, the commander of the garrison, the interpreter Vernazza, and two other officers. The Colonel sat down beside the Rector, and read out to the Senate a document in which the government of Dubrovnik was accused of disloyalty, of having set the Pasha of Bosnia against the French, of having tried to raise an agitation among the people; the intimation made by Marmont the preceding August not having had any effect, it was now necessary to take further measures. He then drew another paper from his pocket, and read as follows: "The General Commander-in-Chief in Dalmatia orders: The Republic of Dubrovnik has ceased to exist; the Government and the Senate, as well as the lawcourts, are dissolved. M. Bruère is appointed provisional administrator of the State of Dubrovnik".

'The Senators were silent for a while; then Count Biagio Bernardo Caboga arose, and informed the Colonel that neither the moment nor the circumstances permitted him to enter into a long justification; that, as far as concerned himself, his conscience was pure and clear, and that he could answer for the loyalty of his colleagues. The Senate was ready to submit to the Divine Will as manifested through the organ of His Majesty Napoleon the Great'.

Meanwhile troops seized the Palace, the chancellor's office, and the custom house, on which seals were affixed. That night the burghers of Dubrovnik gave a ball to celebrate the end of the oligarchy! But though resistance might now seem indeed hopeless, the Senate continued to intrigue for a little while longer. Napoleon then ordered Marmont to arrest ten of the chief agitators and send them to Venice as hostages, and to threaten to shoot all who were found to be in correspondence with foreign governments. The nobles ceased to agitate openly, but they did not yet renounce all hope of regaining their independence. Thus freed from Russians and Montenegrins, Napoleon soon forgot the pledges of neutrality given by his lieutenants; and in January, 1808, as the senators met, an adjutant of General Marmont announced to them that the independence of Dubrovnik had ceased to exist, and that all administrative functions had devolved on the French commander. Thus ended the Republic of Dubrovnik: after a municipal existence that filled up the whole period from the fall of the Empire of the West to the nineteenth century; and a virtual independence that, in spite of conflicting claims for nominal superiority by the Byzantine Czars and the Venetian Republic, had been preserved in the same political forms for eight centuries.

Under French Rule (1808–1815)

The French occupation is of considerable importance in the history of Dalmatia, despite its brief duration. By the Treaty of Vienna

(October 14, 1809) France gained western Croatia and its seaboard so that it now possessed a large strip of territory stretching from Carinthia in the north to Dubrovnik in the south and known collectively as the 'Illyrian Provinces'. Under the direction of Marshal Marmont the material condition of the province was greatly improved, for new roads were constructed, agriculture developed, commerce rejuvenated and brigandage suppressed.

In March, 1808, Marmont was created Duke of Dubrovnik, a title of which, according to Pisani, he was not very proud, for in his memoirs he mentions it as having been conferred on him in 1807, perhaps because he did not like to be reminded of the fact that it was a reward for his services in the suppression of a free republic.

Napoleon had appointed the Venetian Dandolo, Provveditore of Dalmatia, while General Marmont retained the supreme military command. But Dubrovnik and Kotor were given a separate administration under G. D. Garagnin, who was independent of Dandolo, and responsible only to Marmont. The territory of the republic was divided into three districts: Dubrovnik, Ston, and the Islands. Dubrovnik was given a council of eighteen members (six nobles, six burghers, and six plebeians), with Count Sorgo as mayor, and four adjoints. The state's finances proved still to be in good condition in spite of all the troubles and the requisitions, and large sums were invested in foreign banks.

Nevertheless the position of the 'Illyrian Provinces' was a precarious one, situated as it was between the Austro-Hungarian and Turkish Empires to the east and Italy to the west. With the withdrawal of the Russian Adriatic fleet the British navy (allies of Austria) began to prey upon French and Dalmatian shipping in Adriatic waters. They also prevented the French from maintaining secure communication links between Italy and Dalmatia and in January 1812 Sir Duncan Robertson, commander of the already occupied island of Vis, also took control over Lastovo. The British were determined to occupy the other Dubrovnik islands. On February 18 an attack was made on Lopud but repulsed. The island was then blockaded; part of the garrison deserted, and the rest under Lieutenant Tock retired; a British force landed, seized the main fort and placed a battery on a hill commanding Tock's position. Unable to hold out any longer, the French surrendered with the honours of war. Šipan and Koločep were also captured, and the Dubrovnik Count Natali was appointed Governor of the Archipelago under

FIG. 119. Painting of Dubrovnik in 1812. (Original in the cathedral on the altar of St. Peter, St. Lawrence, and St. Andrew.)

British protection. An attack on Cavtat was repulsed by a Croatian battalion on October 11; but two days later that same battalion deserted from the French to the English side, and Count Biagio Bernado Caboga was appointed Governor of the town. The same day another Croatian detachment abandoned the island of Daksa at the entrance to Gruž harbour, and a British force occupied Ston. Thus Dubrovnik was blockaded from the sea on all sides.

A provisional government was set up under Dubrovnik's nobles, and the old city's laws were revived. With the capture of Ston the whole country west of the Ombla rose in favour of the Anglo-Austrians, and Captain Lowen issued a proclamation to Dubrovnik citizens from Lopud, declaring that

'the English and Austrian forces were advancing towards this country to give it back its liberty ... Remember that you bear a glorious name, and fight as the Spaniards and the Russians have fought to restore your independence'.

The Austrian proclamation issued by General Hiller contained no mention of the word independence.

In the meantime Dubrovnik's Count Caboga and Marchese Bona raised a force of 3,000 Konavlese; as this was not sufficient to recapture Dubrovnik, it became necessary to apply for British assistance. But no one wished to be the first to ask for it, as it was feared that if the British did seize Dubrovnik they might end by retaining it; while if they failed, the French would show no mercy on the rebels. At last it was agreed to send a popular deputation of twenty-five peasants to Captain Hoste, who was in command of the squadron at Kotor asking for help from the Allies to re-establish the republic.

On October 28, 1813, a small British detachment under Lieutenant Macdonald landed at Cavtat, raised the British flag, and declared that the ancient laws of Dubrovnik were revived in the place of the French ones, and Count Caboga was made commandant of the town *pro tempore*. The raising of the British flag and the appointment of Caboga displeased the Dubrovnik nobles, who regarded these acts as infringements of their own rights. They met in council, and proposed to send an agent to Constantinople to notify the restoration of the republic to the Sultan and place it once more under his suzerainty. Caboga spoke against the proposal as constituting a slight to the English, whereupon he was at once accused of having sold himself to them. Lowen was then asked for permission to raise Dubrovnik's standard, but he said that he had no authority, and that application must be made to Admiral Fremantle, who held the chief command in the Adriatic. But when Hoste arrived at Cavtat on November 15, he at once had the standard of St. Blaize (Sv. Vlah) hoisted, saluted it with twenty-one guns from his frigate, and proclaimed the independence of the republic.

Caboga was then determined to begin the attack on Dubrovnik with his insurgents. The town was at that time a first-class fortress. The Ploče Gate was defended by the Revelin Tower, and the Pile Gate by the Lovrjenac Tower; while on Mt. Srđ the imperial fort had been erected the previous year. An assault on the latter having failed, the blockade was commenced. At first the operations were not very successful, for although Bona raised some of the people from the Primorije, the chiefs of the villages beyond Slano told him that they had been ordered by General Tomasić to swear fealty to Austria alone – a proof of that Power's intentions with regard to Dubrovnik. Captain Hoste also refused to provide a landing party or a siege train.

On January 3, 1814, the Austrian General Milutinović arrived before Dubrovnik at the head of two battalions, bringing letters from Baron Tomasić, who thanked Caboga and Bona for their services. His first act, however, was to attempt to disband the local volunteers, to which Caboga refused to agree, demanding the recognition of the insurgents as independent belligerents. This Milutinović granted, as he was not strong enough to refuse, and he left Caboga in command of the besiegers during his own absence at Kotor. The General pretended to acquiesce, as he was not in a position to do otherwise. Hoste agreed to supply Milutinović with artillery and on January 21, 1814, the bombardment of Dubrovnik began but did little damage at first. An attack on the imperial fort failed, but a few days later another battery was raised at Sv. Jakob, and armed with ten British guns, brought into position by a difficult and circuitous route; it opened fire at once on the imperial fort and Lokrum. On January 27 a capitulation was finally agreed upon, by which the Anglo-Austrians were to enter the town at midday on the 28th, but the insurgents were not to be admitted until disarmed. The French and Italian troops were to be shipped to Ancona without the honours of war. When Caboga heard the terms of the capitulation he was most indignant, because a few days previously Milutinović had promised that on the surrender of the town 200 armed insurgents should enter it together with the troops, that the Dubrovnik flag should be raised on the forts with that of Austria and Great Britain, and that the civil government should be carried on by Caboga and a commission of nobles.

Milutinović dissolved the National Guard organized by the French, and the Austrian troops seized all the posts. On the 29th the Austrian standard was raised on the Orlando (Roland's) column, and Austrian and English detachments occupied the forts. The French garrison left, and a few days later the British fleet set sail.

The party of nobles did not yet abandon all hope although it was obvious that the republic was no more, especially after the departure of the English. On February 15 the civil officials swore fealty to the Emperor of Austria as King of Dalmatia, Dubrovnik and Kotor and on March 2 the clergy did the same. Nevertheless the nobles continued in their opposition, and assailed all the magistrates who did not belong to their own order. General Tomasić, to please them, dismissed three officials who were of the bourgeoisie and put nobles in their places. Emboldened by this concession, they went about declaring that the Congress of Vienna was going to proclaim the independence of Dubrovnik, like that of the Republic of Cracow. Pisani writes

> 'Dubrovnik citizens had but too much reason to compare their own fate to that of Poland, and in seeking the causes of their misfortunes one may find more than one feature of resemblance between them and the Poles'.[8]

At last General Milutinović lost patience, and when a deputation of nobles came to propose a series of administrative reforms which would have prepared the way for the restoration of the Constitution, he threatened to imprison all who took part in secret conclaves, and in his report of April 4 he denounced the nobles for their correspondence with the Turks. Finally on July 13, 1814, Milutinović made the following proclamation:

> 'The Imperial and Royal Chancery has been pleased to inform me by a Note of January 3 that, in consequence of an agreement between the allied Powers, the territory included under the name of Illyria during the rule of Napoleon, and consequently the State of Dubrovnik, the islands depending from it, and the Bay of Kotor are definitely made over to the Imperial and Royal Court of Austria.

'I notify this decision so that the inhabitants of the said provinces may learn their fate, and try to deserve, by a prompt and loyal submission, the effects of the benevolence of Our august Sovereign the Emperor and King Francis I.

'By the Civil and Military Government of Dalmatia, Dubrovnik and Kotor.

Baron Tomasić, Feldmarschall-Lieutenant.

By authentic copy.

Milutinović, General-Major   Zadar, July 7.'

This proclamation was received respectfully and in silence.

Even so the nobles were still not finished in their efforts to resume control. Early September 1814 found forty of them signing a protest in which they declared they had 'the sole authority to speak in the name of our country'. Most of them were arrested the following day, but in an amnesty dated September 15 an assembly of the people elected a deputation to go to Zadar and swear fealty in the name of all. Milutinović then addressed a very severe admonition to the nobles, and all of that order who occupied judicial positions were dismissed.[9]

The Austrian Period 1815–1918

Attempts to revive the Republic of Dubrovnik at the Congress of Vienna in 1815 were not taken seriously by any of the major powers. By the treaties of 1814–1815, Dalmatia (with Dubrovnik) was assigned to Austria which acquired the whole of the east Adriatic coast from Soča to Budva, and the western coast from Soča to the mouth of the River Po.

The Dubrovnik archipelago remained under British protection until July 16, 1815. On August 3, 1816, Dalmatia and Dubrovnik received a definite organization by imperial rescript, and Baron Tomasić was appointed Statthalter or Military and Civil Governor, the Emperor assumed the title of Duke of Dubrovnik, and Milutinović departed from Dubrovnik.

By the middle of the nineteenth century an eyewitness account of the town stated that

'Dubrovnik is still the port of Hercegovina, whence its raw products are exported, and whither its manufactures are imported; the Turkish bazaar outside the town is sequestered, for sanitary reasons, off the main southern road, by two stone fences which permit commerce and conversation without contact; and the excellent macadamized road to Hercegovina is seen forming a red-brown zigzag line on the face of the hill above; on the other side of the barrier mules were loading and unloading, while bags of wool and grain were being weighed and delivered. The Moslem merchants and dealers from Hercegovina sat smoking on stone benches within, coolly ordering their servants to bring this bale or that bale, while the Greeks of Dubrovnik outside were full of agility, and perpetually on the move to turn a penny. The Moslem beyond the barrier, whether he bought or sold, acted the master; the Greek on this side, whether he bought produce off the Moslem, or sold him manufactures, seemed his servant'.[10]

Further the author maintains that

'Ever since the destruction of her mercantile navy, in consequence of the French occupation, Dubrovnik has ceased to possess any maritime importance in the Adriatic. Once exclude a place from trade for a few years, and disperse its capital, and it is very difficult to restore it again; one of the drawbacks to the town can scarcely be remedied; the old port under the walls was sufficiently large for the galleys of the middle ages, but unfit for vessels of long course. After the great earthquake it was proposed to build the new city at Gruž, but the circumstance of the solid walls of the old town remaining almost uninjured, determined the re-edification on the old spot. Now that lofty ramparts, in the style of the Middle Ages are of no value, this resolution is regretted; as Gruž, which could contain all the largest ships of the Adriatic, is a mile off, and this undoubtedly keeps down the value of house-property in the town.

With a university and no Customs tariff, I think that Dubrovnik might bloom forth anew, if the inhabitants chose to second these measures by putting forth their own energies. It was by self-reliance that their forefathers laid the foundation of that wealth which is passed away. It is by the same qualities that the Greeks of Hercegovina, now established in Dubrovnik, have almost a monopoly of the internal trade. And it is by accommodating their position to their means that they have any chance of retrieving their past splendour. In the meantime, it is an unquestionable advantage for the whole coast, that the Steam Navigation of the

Table XVI
Events of Importance to Dubrovnik 1300–1806

Year	1300–1400	1400–1500	1500–1600	1600–1700	1700–1800
0	1301–02 War with Serbia		1500 Turks control whole of Balkans. 1502–1503 Famine in Dubrovnik. 1503 Lisbon receives first spices by Cape Route.		1705 Leopold I consolidated Austria's position in N. Adriatic at expense of Turkey. 1714–18 War. Venice v Turkey Dubrovnik neutral. 1718 Treaty of Požarevec— Venice gains land in Dalmatia.
20	1317 War with Serbia	1409 Venice bought whole of Dalmatia, Zeta and Albania from Ladislas of Naples. 1416 Dubrovnik merchants forbidden to sell slaves in town. 1420 Venice has complete control of Dalmatia (except Dubrovnik).			
20	1323 War with Serbia. 1330 War with Serbia. 1330 Dušan, King of Serbia.	1422, 25, 31–33, Venice forbids Dalmatian goods to go anywhere but Venice. 1430 Turks take Solun. 1431 As neutral power, Dubrovnik had trade treaty with Greek Despot of Morea. 1432 Pope Eugene IV allows Dubrovnik to trade with Infidels. 1439 Further Venetian restrictions on Dalmatian trade.	1522 First Persian traders in Dubrovnik. 1523 Turkish Sultan forbids Dubrovnik to export minerals. 1526 Hungarians defeated by Turks at Mohaćs. Dubrovnik becomes protectorate of Turks.	1618–48 Thirty Years War.	
40			1537–40 War. Venice v. Turkey. Famine in Dubrovnik.		1737–40 War. Austria v. Turkey. Dubrovnik neutral.
40		1444 Pirate centre of Omiš-surrenders to Venice. 1446 Venice forbids import of slaves from Dubrovnik. 1452 Further Venetian restriction on Dalmatian trade. 1453 Fall of Constantinople.	1540 Hungary under the Turks. 1549 Famine in Dubrovnik.	1645–69 War. Venice v. Turkey. (Candian) Dubrovnik neutral.	1740 French textiles in Balkans. 1741–48 War of Austrian Succession. Dubrovnik neutral.
60	1348 Plague in Dubrovnik. 1355 Death of Dušan—decline of Serbia. 1358 Dubrovnik's break with Venice, under protection of Hungary. 1359 Venetian trade concessions to Dubrovnik cancelled.	1459 Turks occupy Serbia— Dubrovnik treaty with Turks.			1750 Dubrovnik in conflict with French fleets in Levant. 1756–63 Seven Years War— Dubrovnik neutral.

1377–81. War. Venice v. Genoa —Dubrovnik expelled Venice from Kotor. Corn now bought from Asia Minor.	1460 Turks control Peloponnesus. 1463 Turks occupy Bosnia. 1464, 67, 77. Important trade treaties with Kingdom of Naples.			
	1479 Turks take Albania.			1767 Opening of ferries on Danube. Important for N. Adriatic ports. 1768–74 War. Russia v. Turkey. 1774 Treaty of Kutchuk-Kainardji.
1389 Serbs defeated at Kossovo-Polje.	1482 Turks take Hercegovina.	1570–73 War. Venice v. Turkey, Dubrovnik neutral.	1667 Earthquake in Dubrovnik.	1787–97 Freer trade in Dalmatia—less Venetian control.
1391 Death of Tvrtko I. Bosnia declines. 1392 Dubrovnik 1st official relations with Turks. 1393 Fall of 2nd Bulgarian Empire.	1490 Ferdinand & Isabella of Spain restrict Dubrovnik trade with Kingdom of Naples.	1590 Opening of Split harbour by Venetians.	1683–99 War. Austria v. Turkey. Dubrovnik neutral. 1684 Dubrovnik under protection of Leopold of Austria, trade with Trieste and Rikeja.	
1397 Turks give Dubrovnik guarantee of free trade in Balkans.	1496 Vasco da Gama finds Cape Route.		1969 Peace of Karlovac. Venice had control of Lower Neretva.	1797 Venice captured by Napoleonic forces. Dalmatia to Austria.
				1806 Dubrovnik under Napoleon.

60

80

80

100

Austrian Lloyd's Company now extends along all the eastern shore of the Adriatic'.[11]

Dubrovnik remained under Austrian rule up to 1918 when in that year it became part of the new Yugoslav state.

Conclusion

Thus ends after more than twelve hundred years the history of Dubrovnik. It illustrates very well the importance of the perfect appreciation that can be gained from the potentialities of space and their skilful exploitation. Further, as Roglić has stated,

> 'the Napoleonic conquest and the industrial revolution, interrupted the life of this small state. The railroad and the steamship did not follow the routes of the caravans and the galleys. The railroad followed the valleys that had previously been avoided, and the shepherds' paths of the mountainous plateaux and the caravan stations were soon abandoned. The steamship led to the growth of maritime centres at the head of the Adriatic. The experienced Dubrovnik citizens continued to use their maritime and commercial skills, especially their role of middleman, but the change meant a radical break with the centuries of commercial tradition'.[12]

Finally, it has been shown how Dubrovnik, in the same way as her great rival Venice, was occupied by foreign troops for the first time in her long history. In 1808, Napoleon's General Marmont decreed the end of the republic, but he in turn had to surrender to a couple of Austrian battalions. The Congress of Vienna awarded the city to Austria and it remained a Hapsburg possession until 1918, and then became part of the modern Yugoslav state.

12 Notes

1. S. Fischer-Galati (ed.), *Man, State and Society in East European Society.* Pall Mall Press, London (1971), p. 127.
2. P. Pisani, *La Dalmatie de 1797 a 1815*, Paris (1893), pp. 135–136.
3. *Ibid.*, pp. 135–136.
4. A. A. Paton, *Highlands and Islands of the Adriatic*, London (1849), Book II, pp. 229–230.

5. *Enciklopedija Jugoslavije*, Vol. 3 Zagreb (1962), p. 151.
6. *P. Pisani*, *op. cit.*, pp. 299–300 includes dispatches sent by Timoni to the Austrian Chancery.
7. Already by August 1806 the Dubrovnik Senate had sent out a circular to its consulates stating 'Order your country's boats to give up the garrison, leaving only the most necessary arms in the vessels; and so wherever they are located please await our further orders. The remaining property in your boats can be sold.' Some of the boat owners contacted the Porte for their interjection but the French merely insisted on it being carried out, despite fear of disrupting relations between Dubrovnik, the Turks and themselves. *Enciklopedija Jugoslavije*, *op. cit.*, p. 151.
8. P. Pisani, *op. cit.*, pp. 457–458.
9. *Loc. cit.*
10. A. A. Paton, *op. cit.*, p. 255.
11. *Ibid.*, pp. 256–257.
12. J. Roglić, 'The geographical setting of medieval Dubrovnik', in *Geographical Essay on Eastern Europe*, (N. J. G. Pounds, ed.), The Hague (1961), p. 157.

13
Conclusion

Thus came to an end, after more than twelve hundred years, the changing fortunes of Dubrovnik and its small republic. Its government and citizens may have had their defects, but they were full of a real, if somewhat narrow, patriotism. The state gave a prosperity and happiness to its inhabitants which have fallen to the lot of few peoples during that long and troubled period. The peculiar, almost unique, position occupied in European history and policy by the tiny republic is in itself a subject of great interest. Dubrovnik was at the same time a city-state and a sea-state and it is therefore necessary to define and determine what these concepts stood for as political units.

The Concept of the City-state

From the beginning of Greek history to its climax in the fifth and fourth centuries BC, the Greeks were organized in autonomous neighbourhoods now known as city-states. The term 'city' as the translation of the Greek πόλis or Latin 'civitas' involves the ancient conception of the state or 'city-state'. This has been defined as

> 'of the state as not too large to prevent its government through the assembled body of the citizens, and is applied not to the place but to the whole body republic'.[1]

The object of the Greek State was 'the good life' for the individual; that state, they held, must

> 'not be so large that the individual could not be known and utilized. Since the city-state was autonomous, different states and the same state at different times varied through all degrees from the absolute monarchy to pure democracy; the state might be ruled as it wished

and might change at will. Economic self-sufficiency was an ideal, though some states, as Athens, had relatively large commercial interests; in Sparta, commerce was forbidden. Households commonly were supported directly by their little farms. Unemployment was unknown, and the extremes of wealth and poverty were exceptional and speedily remedied. The good life was held to be hindered by excess in material possessions as by other excess'.[2]

More simply a city-state has been defined as 'a city that is also an independent sovereign state'.[3]

The city-state was the characteristic unit of political organization in classical Greece, though not peculiar to that country.[4] City-states had grown up in Sumeria, and the Phoenician towns and colonies were city-states. The institution was derived partly from the geographical environment, particularly the small and isolated coastal plains, but also partly from the evolution of social institutions, the fusion of separate village settlements into regional units, with each focussing itself for defence and commerce on a single town. Unfortunately the city-state was usually small, and its agricultural resources were limited. If there was an increase in population beyond a certain point, some of their number had to emigrate which in turn provided the motive for Greek colonization. Newly founded colonies often tapped new resources, which in turn increased the commercial prosperity of the mother city, but once established, the colony became an independent unit, bound to its parent city only by sentimental ties.

The Concept of the Sea-state

Another type of territorial division also of importance is that effected by arms and gulfs of the sea. The significance of such 'sea-states' was formerly much greater than it it today and has been defined by Darby as those which

> 'By establishing trading posts and strategic colonies at convenient points around the shore(s) . . . combined the uses of economic and political power, and united its ports to one another by the strong persuasions of trading facilities . . . such a (sea) state could therefore govern without excessive decentralization, and to this extent it was stronger than the feudal land-state of the age.'[5]

Many of the city-states of classical Greece formed an alliance which lay around the coasts of the Aegean. Similarly the early medieval Danish sea-state was partly in England, partly in Denmark, and later covered not only the Danish peninsula and islands but also southern Sweden. Further, the Anglo-Norman sea-state covered southern England and northern France, and medieval Aragon included many western Mediterranean islands and also for a time Sicily.

This rise of the sea-state is not difficult to comprehend, for they developed at a time when movement, especially of merchandise, was difficult by land but relatively easy by sea. Their economy was based on seaborne trade; their political expansion was by sea and their culture and civilization was carried by their ships. The sea which so often was regarded a highly desirable frontier, thus became a bond of union and East[6] describing the Byzantine Empire states that it was 'characteristically a sea-state, in the sense that the unity of its possessions could be preserved only by its fleet'. Later he notes that Genoa and Venice 'were easily the greatest sea-states in the last years of the Middle Ages'.[7] There were two very different types of unit – the large-scale unit such as the Byzantine Empire which covered the anciently civilized lands of Greece, the Aegean islands, Asia Minor, Syria, Cyprus, Egypt and Cyrenaica, as well as Dacia, Thrace to the south of the Danube, and the Chersonesus in the Crimean peninsula; and the small-scale unit consisting of a port and its immediate hinterland, such as Venice or Genoa. Darby's definition could apply to both types.

More recently, Sweden came to dominate the Baltic Sea, and during the twentieth century the island state of Japan expanded in a similar way to control the opposite coasts of Korea and China and turned the intervening sea into a Japanese lake. Nevertheless, the sea-state in Europe has long been in decline. The French expelled the English from their foothold in northern France, the Germans and Russians drove the Swedes from their bases along the eastern and southern shores of the Baltic and more recently Japan has lost all possessions on the Asiatic mainland. Therefore many of the states today which spread over an island group, e.g. Denmark, Phillipines, are under considerable stress from costly transport facilities which are always liable to interruptions and the sea now forms a sort of social barrier in their development.

The Role of Dubrovnik as a Maritime City-state

Dubrovnik has been considered by some[8] as a typical example of a medieval sea-state which prolonged its form of political and commercial organization until long after the close of the Middle Ages. Rochefort[9] calls Dubrovnik a 'city-state' and likens it to Tyre, Miletus, Genoa, Pisa and Venice. All these, however, lay on the sea coast, whereas a 'city-state' such as Milan, Parma and Modena could equally exist inland. A different approach is that of Febvre[10] who asserts that 'states are usually formed by methods which imply the existence of routes and communications' and so 'routes play a necessary and sovereign part in the life of political units'. Routes were for Dubrovnik vital for its commercial role and therefore also for its existence as a political unit. The city of Dubrovnik formed, in the words of Vidal de la Blache[11]

'a solid nucleus around which the parts annexed have grouped themselves by a sort of crystallization'

for in the sixteenth century it controlled about 1,092 kilometres of territory and 80,000 people.[12] Even during the Middle Ages Dubrovnik was commonly referred to as the 'city' by its hinterland peoples, and was as Rochefort says a 'city-state'. But is this precise enough? According to Darby's definition Dubrovnik may also have been a sea-state, but not according to East, for as Dubrovnik had many land ties in the forming of trading colonies it was not dependent on 'the unity of its possessions being preserved only by its fleet'. Alternatively Dubrovnik could be defined as a 'maritime city-state'. This interpretation does not confine Dubrovnik solely to sea trade, but allows for the overland trade relationship, which the city maintained with a large part of the Balkan peninsula.

Unfortunately, the case of Dubrovnik does not appear to support the view put forward by Shaudys that 'one of the reasons small states are created and continue to exist is because they function as buffer states'.[13] His study on the external aspects of the political geography of five diminutive European states tends towards this conclusion, but certainly Dubrovnik was never looked upon by outsiders or by itself as an effective buffer state between East and West or Christian and Islam. In fact it proved to be the reverse of a buffer state in that it was always dependant on one side or the other for protection, as it proved throughout its history. What appears nearer to the truth is that one of the reasons small states are created and continue to exist is because they function as intermediaries particularly during wartime as a means of effective political and economic communication between two or more opposing parties.

Value of the Study

The characteristic civic outlook and patriotism of the city-state exists in its most enlightened form in a republic. This study has shown how a small republic with few natural advantages could grow and develop mainly through her function as a trade and political mediator between the underdeveloped regions of the Balkans and the Levant, and the more developed regions of western Europe. Dubrovnik relied on the profits made from her entrepôt trade and the shrewdness of her diplomats in preserving a neutralist policy during wartime; it also managed to develop and prosper as a trading city for her citizens were their own politicians, legislators and officials and their loyalties were more fully involved than when their role was a subordinate one. The destiny of their city was

'their own work, the success or otherwise of its affairs not merely all-important for their own welfare but the outcome of their endeavours'.[14]

To this may also be added the fact that almost all its citizens, and especially those of conventional and conservative temperaments, felt towards what was familiar, the appearance of the same daily surroundings and customary ways of speech.

Documentary evidence has proved that the trading sphere of Dubrovnik (Fig 120) was much larger than would have been expected from a second class Adriatic port (i.e. compared to Venice). However, Dubrovnik's success was only part of a general development in the Mediterranean in the Middle Ages. With Florence as the financial and Venice as the commercial capital, the Mediterranean became again the centre from which trade routes radiated throughout Europe, North Africa and Asia. The

'search for markets, the exchange of commodities and the protection of lines of communication broke down barriers of ignorance and indifference and restored something of the old unity of civilization lost with the Roman Empire'.[15]

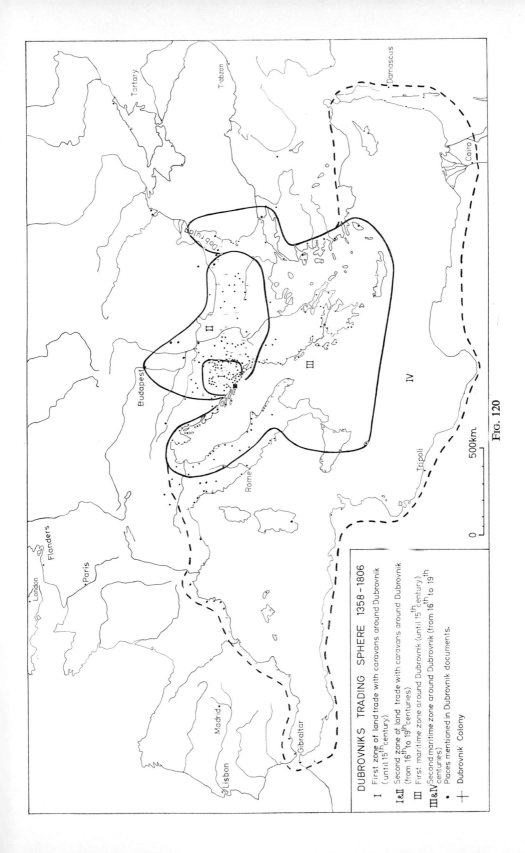

DUBROVNIK'S TRADING SPHERE 1358 – 1806

I   First zone of land trade with caravans around Dubrovnik (until 15th century).

I & II   Second zone of land trade with caravans around Dubrovnik (from 16th to 19th centuries).

III   First maritime zone around Dubrovnik (until 15th century).

III & IV   Second maritime zone around Dubrovnik (from 16th to 19th centuries).

• Places mentioned in Dubrovnik documents.

✝   Dubrovnik Colony

Fig. 120

Gradually Dubrovnik's merchants extended their influence from within the Adriatic and in Bosnia-Hercegovina during the twelfth and thirteenth centuries, to Hungary, Roumania, Bulgaria, Persia, the Near East, North Africa, Spain, northern Europe and even the New World and India by the sixteenth century. Within this trading sphere the city's merchants were providing a valuable middleman's service, supplying the more advanced western countries particularly Italy, with much needed raw materials whilst in the reverse direction selling manufactured goods to the less developed regions of south-eastern Europe and the Near East. Moreover the city's merchant fleet gave staunch service to other countries notably in the carrying trade of Spain, and it was in the Spanish Service that Dubrovnik ships ventured into the New World and the Far East.

Work on Mediterranean trade in medieval and modern Europe has been largely done by historians, economic historians or economists often in microscopic detail, but little has been done by geographers in trying to put into perspective the chronological emphasis placed on it by other disciplines, and to examine trade more in its spatial concepts. To place two centuries of trade, in a particular commodity on a map, and compare it with other centuries may seem hypocritical to some methods of thought, but to a geographer it shows quickly, the general pattern of distribution and what spatial changes have taken place, giving him greater ability to see things as a whole rather than in the minutae.

Such a geographical application as this could be done for other ports besides Dubrovnik. For example, the trading spheres of Venice, or Alexandria could be studied geographically and probably compare what real spatial effects the new discoveries and the changing of trade routes had on Mediterranean commerce. It may also help to answer the question as to whether the Turks were as great a stumbling block to trade as past history has made them out to be. Unfortunately these problems cannot be properly answered from a study of just one port, however large, or important, it may have been, therefore there is a need for several specialist studies in the historical geography of Mediterranean trade and only when a full integration of the results has been achieved can an attempt be made to resolve some of these problems.

The ideas put forward here can only be regarded as very tentative. Work on markets and trade in all parts of the Balkans is only just beginning and the need for more detailed field studies and comparative work in other parts of the Mediterranean world is clearly necessary. The whole problem, however, is not simply a matter of collecting more and more data. Many of the data are not quantifiable or, if so, not subject to manipulation to any clear interpretive purpose.[16] It is also a question of trying to construct some general conceptual framework within which to consider such complex and little understood phenomena as market institutions. Without some such framework the study of these and similar features of the landscape can never develop beyond the presentation of a series of discrete descriptions.

Finally, Dubrovnik was a victim to external influence. By the end of the eighteenth century the city found itself isolated from trade, for the new ports, like Trieste and Rijeka, were nearer to the newly developed Pannonian Plain and to the west European capitals. Dubrovnik found herself off the main shipping routes of the Adriatic, away from the new avenues of trade in the Balkan hinterland, and by 1806 under the occupation of a foreign power. Therefore her strength as an entrepôt port lay in an earlier period when a certain combination of factors had contributed to her success. Once this combination of factors was radically altered then her position lost its impetus and ability to continue successfully declined.

In the seventeenth century, Samuel Purchas called the attention to the talk among historians of geographical understanding:

'History without that so much neglected study of Geography is sick of half-dead palsy'.[17]

In recent years the corollary of this dictum has received greater attention and emphasis, and geographers have come increasingly to stress the development of present conditions. Yet today, visually considered, Dubrovnik is an enigma. It can be understood only in terms of the spatial and economic relations existing at the time when it originated and developed. Apart from Venice, there is probably no similar example of man's adaption and use of space as Dubrovnik.[18] Thus the contribution which the geographer may offer towards a greater knowledge of our present European civilization is one which takes account of development throughout historical time, since residuary features from the past survive, though in varying degrees, in different parts of the present stage. It is hoped that by a study of the Dubrovnik Republic some knowledge has been added to that stage.

U*

13 Notes

1. *Encyclopedia Britannica*, Vol. 5, London (1932), p. 729.
2. *The Columbia Encyclopedia*, (15th printing), New York (1958), p. 396.
3. *The Concise Oxford Dictionary*, (Fourth Edition) Oxford (1959), p. 215.
4. A. E. Zimmern, *The Greek Commonwealth: Politics and Economics in Fifth-century Athens*, Oxford (1911), (5th ed. 1931);
   G. Glotz, *The Greek City and its Institutions*, (N. Mallinson, ed.), Oxford (1930);
   P. J. Jones, 'Communes and despots: the city-state in late medieval Italy; *Transactions of the Royal Historical Society*, 5th series, Vol. XV, (1965).
5. H. C. Darby, 'The medieval sea-state', *Scottish Geographical Magazine*, Vol. 16 (1932), p. 138.
6. W. G. East, *An Historical Geography of Europe*, London (Fourth Edition) (1959), p. 164.
7. W. G. East, *op. cit.*, p. 321.
8. K. Jireček, 'Važnost Dubrovnika . . . ', *op. cit.*, p. 10;
   J. Roglić, 'The Geographical Setting . . . ' *op. cit.*, p. 144;
   M. Dinić, 'Dubrovačka srednjevekovna . . . ', *op. cit.*, p. 20.
9. R. Rochefort, 'Une cite-état en Mediteranée. Dubrovnik-Raguse', *Revue de Geographie de Lyon*, Vol. XXXVI, No. 3. Lyon (1961), p. 231.
10. L. Febvre, *A Geographical Introduction to History*, London (1932), p. 316.
11. P. Vidal de la Blache, 'La Géographie politique d'apres les écrits de M. Fr. Ratzel.' *Annales de Geographie*, Vol. VII, Paris (1898), p. 108.
12. J. Roglić, *op. cit.*, p. 144.
13. V. K. Shaudys, *op. cit.*, p. 29.
14. D. Waley, *The Italian City-Republics*, McGraw-Hill Book Co., New York (1969), p. 8.
15. M. V. Clarke, *The Medieval City State: An Essay on Tyranny and Federation in the Later Middle Ages*, London (1926), p. 26.
16. A. H. Clark, 'Geographical change: A theme for economic history', *Journal of Economic History*, Vol. 20 (1960), p. 609.
17. Cited by E. G. R. Taylor, *Late Tudor and Early Stuart Geography*, London (1921), p. 56.
18. J. Roglić, 'The Geographical Setting . . . ', *op. cit.*, p. 158.

Appendix 1
Money, Prices and Weights

Money

One of the commonest documents in the Dubrovnik Archives is the Merchants' Agreement. It proves of interest to the monetary historian because it indicates routes taken by the merchants, and to the numismatist for comparing the types and values of one currency against others. Metcalf has made a close study of Balkan currencies for the period 820–1355,[1] and evidence from the peace treaty of 1189 between Dubrovnik and the Grand Župan Kulin[2] indicates that there was already a localized currency circulation in evidence and may in fact have dominated the monetary affairs of the coastlands. Metcalf further maintains that

'The question of connexions between the Adriatic coast and its hinterland further to the south focuses on Dubrovnik. Merchants from that city were trading in Bosnia by the end of the twelfth century, and were to maintain special links there for many years. The Ragusan grosi (grossi) are first mentioned in 1301; the date of their introduction may have been somewhat earlier, but it almost certainly falls between 1301 and 1284, since their obverse design would seem to derive from that of the Venetian zecchini first struck in that year. Already in 1282, however, Serbian groši were of sufficient importance in Dubrovnik for the citizens to have a vested interest in them: the first Venetian embargo on the circulation of Serbian coins specifically excluded Dubrovnik. Before that, various coins and moneys of account are mentioned in documents referring to Dubrovnik. One quite clear reference to a coinage which seems not to have survived to find its way into the cabinets of modern collections speaks of 'folaros qui dicuntur capuciae, et generaliter omnes folaros factor et facturos in formam veteram'. The caputiae

FIG. 121. Dubrovnik currency. (1) Minca or Mjed (Follaro); (2) The New Vižlin (Tallero Rettorale); (3) Follari; (4) Perpera (Perpero); (5) Poluškuda (half škuda or scudo); (6) Poludinar (half dinar); (7) Talir, Bradan; (8) Dinarić (Grossettus, Grosetto); (9) Škuda (Scudo); (10) Dukat (Ducato); (11) The Old Vižlin (Ragusino or Tallero Rettorale).

Table XVII
Dubrovnik Coinage

Name of coin	Date of issue	Value
COPPER COINS		
Minca, mjed (or follaro)	1294–1612	Smallest coin
Solad (solidus, soldo)	1678–1797	5 minca or 5 Venetian bagattini
Poludinarić, medzalin (mezzanino)	1785–1796	3 soldi or 15 minca
SILVER COINS		
Dinar (grossus, grosso)	1337–1621	6 soldi or 30 minca
Dinarić (grossettus, grosetto)	1626–1761	6 soldi or 30 minca
Poludinar (medzalin or mezzanin d'Argento)	1370–1626	3 soldi or 15 minca
Artiluk (artiluccas, altiluccus, artilucco)	1627–1701	3 dinarić (grossetti)
Perpera (perpero)	1683–1750	12 dinarić or 72 soldi
Poluperpera	1801	6 dinarić or 36 soldi
Škuda (scudo)	1708–1750	3 perperas or 36 dinarić
Poluškuda	1708–09 and 1748–50	1½ perperas or 18 dinarić
Dukat (ducato, ducat)	1722 and 1723	40 dinarić
Talir (bradan)	1725–1743	1½ ducats, 5 perperas, or 60 dinarić
Old vižlin (ragusino, or tallero rettorale)	1743–1779	as above
New vižlin (tallero rettorale)	1790–1803	as above

Table XVII—continued
Dubrovnik Coinage

Name of coin	Date of issue	Value
Polutalir (i) Polubradan (mezzo tallero di san biagio) (ii) Poluvižlin (mezzotallero rettorale)	1731 and 1735 1747 and 1748	30 dinarić as above
Old libertina	1791	2 ducats or 80 dinarić
New libertina	1792–1795	as above

GOLD COINS

Perpera	1618 and 1683	12 dinarić or 72 soldi (never in circulation)

were prescribed in 1294, in which year measures were also taken against false grossi. These legal decisions are perhaps an echo from the date of introduction of the groši of St. Blasius (Sv. Vlah)'.[3]

The Dubrovnik mint was in production from 1337 to 1803, and made a large quantity of copper and silver coins. It is known, for example, to have produced fifteen different sorts of silver coins of various types with variations within them.

Coinage Description[4]

Copper Coins

The Minca or Mjed, (Follaro).   This is the smallest coin used in the Republic of Dubrovnik, was struck from 1294–1612. 'Mjed' is the Serbo-Croat word for brass. Follaro, a copper coin, was common to a large number of Italian states. The name 'follaro' is derived from the Latin 'follis aeris' ('follis' means purse or bag containing money and 'aeris' means copper). It was an ancient custom to count money by the number of bags of gold (follis aurii), bags of silver (follis argentei) and bags of copper (follis aeris). The obverse of the early minca or follaro resembles the obverse of the late Roman Imperial coins. In old Latin records the minca or mjed was also called 'parvulos', 'bagatinus' and 'abolus'. There are two types: (i) the older coins have a bust of a man on the obverse side crowned with laurel, facing right and wearing the Roman toga. The reverse has in the centre a large ornamented letter R (RAGUSII) in Gothic style, surrounded by four stars. Diameter: 14–20 mm; weight 0·63–2·8 grammes; (ii) the follari struck at a later date the obverse containing a woman's head, crowned with laurel, facing left and the legend *MONETA RAGUSII*. On the reverse is a view of a city gate with three towers, and on its perimeter a legend which reads: *CIVITAS RAGVSII*. Diameter: 17 mm; weight 1·614 grammes.

The Solad, (Solidus, Soldo). This was struck from 1678 to 1797. 'Solad' or 'soldo' is probably derived from 'solidus', a gold coin of the Byzantine Empire, first issued by Constantine the Great. The same name was retained to some extent for silver coins issued by the Teutonic Order in Poland and various Baltic provinces as late as the sixteenth century. The same name is also given to copper coins of Livonia from c. 1550 to 1750. Its value was equivalent to five follari (minca) or in the Venetian monetary system to five bagattini. The coin's obverse has a bust of St. Blaize (Sv. Vlah), the Patron Saint of Dubrovnik, shown above the city's walls. The Saint's right hand is raised in benediction, while his left is holding a crosier. Around the circumference is the legend: *CIVITA–RACVSII*, and, at the bottom is the date of the year when the coin was issued. On the reverse side there is the figure of Christ, standing with his right hand held up in blessing, and the left hand holding the globe. His figure is surrounded by eleven stars, and on each side there is a small coat of arms of Dubrovnik. Diameter: 20–23 mm; weight 1·44–2·73 grammes.

The Poludinarić or Medzalin, (Mezzanino). This was struck in 1785 and 1796. 'Poludinarić' means in Serbo-Croat half a small dinar. 'Mezzanino' is a known Italian coin, half the value of the grosso and it was first issued under the Doge F. Dandolo of Venice. The Dubrovnik mezzanino is, of course, a copper coin. Its value was 3 soldi or 15 follari (minca). On the obverse there is a figure of St. Blaize standing with his right hand in blessing and left hand holding a crosier. The figure is surrounded by the legend: *PROT* (ector) *REIP* (ublicae) *RHACVSINE*, and in the field the date of issue. On the reverse side there is the figure of Christ standing with his right hand in blessing and the left holding a globe. The legend around Christ reads: DEVS REFVG (ium) ET VIRTVS. Diameter: 24–25 mm; weight 3·95 grammes.

Silver Coins

The Dinar, (*Grossus, Grosso*).   This was struck from 1337 to 1621. The word 'dinar' is derived from the Roman 'denarius', the most important silver coin of ancient Rome. 'Denarius' (from Latin 'deni' — ten times) originally equalled ten bronze coins called 'aes' or 'asses'. The denarius, first issued about 190 BC, was used during the periods of the Republic and the Empire. The obverse side of the Dubrovnik dinar remained unchanged for about three centuries. Value of a dinar was 6 soldi or 30 follari. The coin was not dated. On the obverse side St. Blaize (Sv. Vlah) is shown in Greek vestments, standing, his right hand held up in blessing and his left holding a crosier, encircled by the legend *S. BLASIVS-RACVSII.* On the reverse is the figure of Christ standing with his right hand held up in blessing. Christ's initials (*IC–XC*) are on the right and left side of the figure which is in the middle of an elliptical pearl frame. Diameter: 17–22 mm; weight: 0·64–1·85 grammes. Rešetar's outstandingly fine catalogue of the series of groši (grosso) was not able to overcome the uncertainty which still surrounds the chronology of the coins before 1350. It seems that they were not carried inland very much in that period, for they have not been recorded in the hoards from Serbia and Bosnia. Nevertheless, it is doubtless correct that the group of coins without secret-marks below the saint's right hand is the earliest. Their weight-standard, *c.* 1·84 grammes, corresponds convincingly with a reduced Serbian weight-standard. Rešetar catalogues 151 specimens that he considers to be before 1356 in date, and among them there are thirteen instances of obverse die-linkage, of which one is uncertain, and one uncertain instance of duplication.

The Dinarić, (*Grossettus, Grosetto*). This, (diminutives of dinar and grosso respectively) was struck between 1626–1761. It is similar to the dinar (grosso) and had the same value: 6 soldi or 30 follari. On the obverse side St. Blaize is shown in Latin liturgical garments, with his right hand in blessing, and in his left a model of the city and a

crosier. Around his figure is the legend: *S. BLASIVS-RACUSIL.*
The date is in the field.

On the reverse side is the figure of Christ standing in the middle of
an elliptical frame of stars with his right hand raised in blessing and
left hand holding the globe. The surrounding legend reads: *TVTA
SALVS* (certain salvation). Diameter: 18–20 mm; weight 0·43–0·66
grammes.

The Poludinar – half a dinar, or Medzalin, (Mezzanin d'argento).
This was struck from 1370–1626. Its value totalled 3 soldi or 15 follari
(minca).

The obverse side bears the head of St. Blaize inside a circle with
the legend *S. BLASIVS RACVSII* around it. On the reverse side there
is a bust of Christ with the legend *IESVS CRISTVS.* Diameter: 17–
18 mm; weight 0·31–0·66 grammes.

The Artiluk (Artiluccus, Altiluccus, Artilucco). This was issued
from 1627–1701. The name artiluk apparently had its origin in the
Turkish word 'alty' for six, because in the Ottoman Empire the coin's
value was equivalent to 6 'paras'. Artiluk is similar to a Polish coin of
three 'groszy' (Dreigröscher) issued in Riga in the sixteenth and
seventeenth centuries. Its value was 3 grossetti (dinarićs), 18 solda, or
19 minca. On the obverse side is a short bust of St. Blaize, facing to the
right, wearing a mitre. The bust is surrounded by the legend *S.
BLASIVS RAGVSII.*

On the upper half of the reverso the coin's value is indicated with
the Roman numeral III – for three grossetti. The Arabic numerals on
each side of the Roman numeral stand for the year when the coin
was issued. Thus, the inscription on the first artiluk issued 1627
reads: *16.III.27.* Below these numbers a city gate is shown with
towers and a small crowned coat-of-arms on each side. In the upper
half a city gate with towers and a small crowned coat-of-arms on
either side is also shown. The lower half has a three line inscription
GROS(us) *ARGE*(ntus) *TRIP*(lex) *CIVI*(tatis) *RAGV*(sii). Diameter:
19 mm; weight: 1·15–1·90 grammes.

The Perpera (Perpero). This was struck from 1683–1750 and from
1801–1803. The word 'perpera' is of Greek origin. The same name
was used for centuries in Europe for golden Byzantine coins. Its

value was equivalent to 12 grossetti (dinar) or 72 soldi. The Perpera is considered a typical coin of the Baroque style. On the obverse side there is a full figure of St. Blaize standing in richly decorated bishop's robes. His right hand is held up in blessing, his left holds a model of the city and a crosier. Around the figure is the legend, *PROT*(ector) *RAEIP*(ublicae) *RHAGUSINAE*. In the field, between the letters of his monogram *S.B.* (Sanctus Blasius), is printed the year when the coin was issued. On the reverse side is the full figure of Christ in the middle of an ellipse made of stars. Christ's right hand is held up in blessing, and his left hand holds a globe. The surrounding legend reads: *TVTA-SALVS*. Diameter 26–29 mm and 24 mm (1801–03), weight: 3·98–6·42 grammes.

The Poluperpera.   This coin, half a perpera, was struck only in 1801, and its value was 6 grossetti or 36 soldi.

On the obverse side there is again the figure of St. Blaize standing, with his right hand raised in blessing and his left holding a model of the city and a crosier. The legend around it reads: *PROT*(ector) *REIP*(ublicae) *RHACUSI*(nae) 1801.

On the reverse side there is a three lined legend *GROSSETTI VI*, surrounded on each side by a leafy branch. Diameter: 20 mm; weight: 2·0 grammes.

The Škuda, the silver Scudo.   This was struck from 1708–1750. The 'Škuda', 'scudo' or 'scudo d'argento' of the Papal States was introduced at the end of the sixteenth century. It was divided into ten paoli or one hundred baiocchi. 'Scudo' means a shield; coins having a shield in their design became known as 'scudos'. It value was equivalent to 3 perperas or 36 grossetti. On the obverse side there is a figure of St. Blaize standing in ornate bishop's robes, his right hand raised in blessing; his left hand is holding a crosier. The letters *S.B.* and date are in the field. For the first time this central design is inside a circle of pearls whilst outside the circle, around the coin's edge, is the legend: *PROTECTOR REIPVBLICAE RHACUSINAE* with a star at top centre. The reverse side has the figure of Christ standing, right hand raised in blessing, left hand holding a globe, surrounded by 20 stars. The legend *TVTA SALUS SPES ET PRESIDIVM* is between a circle surrounding the central design and the edge of the coin, with a star at top centre. Diameter: 37 mm; weight: 16·68–17·68 grammes.

decorated crowned coat-of-arms of the Republic of Dubrovnik and with it the legend *DVCE DEO-FIDE ET IVST* (itia). Below the coat-of-arms is the date and again the engraver's initials *G.A.* Diameter: 41–43 mm; weight: 28·88 grammes.

The Libertina struck from 1792–1795 has the same obverse as the *Libertina* of 1791, but a new reverse side. The Rector's crown is above a shield with the inscription *LI-BER-TAS*, within a wreath of flowers. At the bottom is the date and the engraver's initials *G.A.* The surrounding legend reads: *DUCE DEO -FIDE ET IUST*(itia).

Gold Coins

A *gold perpera* was first minted in 1618 and engraved by a Frenchman Barnaba Tortelle; the obverse and reverse sides are similar to the silver perpera, except that all designs are more richly and carefully executed. A second golden perpera, minted in 1683, is similar to the silver one of the same date, but again is more richly decorated and much better executed. However, the 1618 issue is by far the better coin of the two. The golden perpera was never in circulation as a means of payment.

The Mint

The republic's mint was in the customs-house building which was called 'divona'. In Latin a customs-house is called 'sponza' and this name for the mint has survived to this day and it is called the Sponza Palace. The directors of the mint were elected from among the senators for a three year term by the Small Council (Malo Vijeće), with the Knez (Rector) presiding. At first there were three directors and later five. The last elected directors before the republic's fall were: Franjo Gučetić, Djuro Menčetic, Nikša Gradić, Miše Bunić and Niko Sorkočević. Engravers are mentioned for the first time on November 8, 1346, with the death of Marko, the engraver of the dinar and son of Angeli the goldsmith. Later engravers deserving mention include the following masters: Pava Lonciares 1706–1709; Niko Matov Fišević 1730–1749; Ivo Bettinelli (G.B.) 1730–1749; Domo Menitto (D.M.) 1765–1779; Domenico Bendetto (D.B.) 1791–1797; Ivo Karlo Angeli (G.A.) 1766–1809 and the last one Antun Obad (A.O.) 1794–1803.

Conclusion

Coins from the Dubrovnik Republic listed above constitute the most important ones of their kind. However, an almost endless array of all sorts of coins are extant, especially those of the earlier period. There is also a great differential to be found in the fall in value of Dubrovnik's money.[5] In 1337, Dubrovnik's government decided that a grossi contained 916·67 miligrammes of silver. It is reported as having been changed in 1452 when it fell to 874 miligrammes, a measure which lasted until 1594 when it rose to 900 miligrammes. Fresh falls followed with 800 miligrammes in 1675 dropping even lower to 750 miligrammes, so that by the end of the seventeenth century the grossi contained only 600 miligrammes of silver. By 1723 the silver content was down to 566·66 miligrammes, and despite an

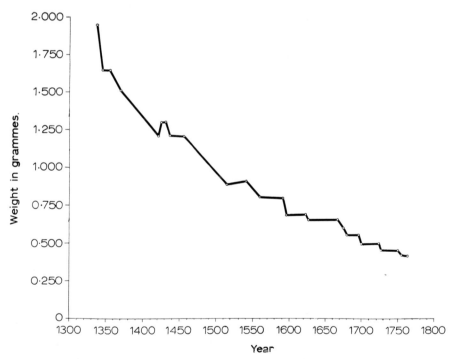

FIG. 122. Weight of the Dubrovnik grossi (groši) 1337–1761. Source: *Annales Econ. Soc. Civ.* No. 6, Paris (1961), p. 1170. (After Tadić.)

increase between 601–613 miligrammes by 1791, it fell ten years later to 469·41 miligrammes. The weight of the grossi naturally varied accordingly. Up to the seventeenth century in Dubrovnik, as elsewhere, coins were struck by hand. When a metal blank was placed between the dies, the master smith would strike the dies with his hammer so that the metal would be impressed on the inner sides of both dies. In the seventeenth century mints began to use machines with the result that coins became finer and more precise. Dubrovnik's coinage remained in circulation after the fall of the republic, in fact up to August 31, 1817, when the Austrian government issued an order stating they were no longer legal tender.

Prices

This review of prices is by no means complete but is based on the work of such historians as Dinić, Manken, Tadić and Vinaver (see bibliography) together with various pieces of information collected in my notes during work on archival material. The three *Diversa* series are invaluable for a study of prices as they give precise information on the trade and price of merchandise. Some of the more important commodities and their price in Dubrovnik are given below, not necessarily covering the whole six centuries but for periods when information is most reliable and forthcoming.

Commodity Prices

Cereals

One good example is the price of corn. In the first half of the fourteenth century, corn was sold in Dubrovnik at 15 to 28 grossi for one 'starium' (nearly a hectolitre). Even so this varied according to some routes taken as seen from a document dated 1329, when 31½ grossi per starium were charged for wheat brought via Drijeva.[6] Another document dated March 1320 shows that wheat was sold to the Dubrovnik commune for 18 grossi per starium, which had previously been bought for 17 grossi.[7] During the Great Plague of 1348 the price rose almost 100% to 37 grossi. Immediately afterwards it fell to a lower level and then gradually tended to rise until after 1370. Between 1380 and 1390 it reached 50 grossi (35% increase).

For example, in June 1381, wheat was sold for 10 grossi per copellum (i.e. 60 grossi per starium), whilst in March 1383 a document refers to wheat at 36 grossi per starium.[8] The cost of grinding corn seems to have been about one grossus per starium, depending on the season of the year.[9]

At the end of the fourteenth century corn prices fell from 42 to 32 grossi (i.e. 36% to 16%). The price then remained fairly stable, despite slight oscillations up to the middle of the sixteenth century. In 1555 a noticeable price increase was seen, for a starium of corn rose to 60 grossi (43% increase) followed by new rises between 72–90 grossi (20%–50%) during the period 1569 and 1574. Finally between 1587 and 1609 the price was fixed between 102 and 156 grossi. Corn prices then fell by 50% but in 1623 new rises amounted to 54% (120 grossi). This level was maintained for a long time until the second half of the eighteenth century, when prices began to oscillate between 180 and 200 grossi, showing a rise of 50% to 60%[10] Vinaver found similar trends for the eighteenth century[11] and there followed a period of continued price rises up to the first years of the nineteenth century i.e. 360 grossi between 1790 and 1800, (480 grossi in 1796) and 900 grossi in 1801. Thus corn prices on average were over fifty times greater in 1801 than in 1350.

Price changes can also be followed for other cereals but in lesser detail. This is particularly so for those regions where Dubrovnik gained her wheat supplies, namely Apulia, Albania, Sicily, Greece etc. Manken found that the price of barley in the fourteenth century was just over half the price of wheat, whilst millet was a little higher in price than barley.[12] In the eighteenth century both rye and rice saw an increase in price, the latter costing about half as much as rye up to about 1760 when rye suffered similar inflationary tendencies as wheat.

Minerals

In the fourteenth and fifteenth centuries Dubrovnik was a very important centre for commerce in certain metals, particularly silver and lead. Between 1300 and 1310 a 'librarium' (328 grammes) of Dubrovnik silver cost 145–170 grossi. The value then rose 41%–65% and by the end of the fourteenth century cost nearly 240 grossi per pound. This coincided with the greatest period of development in the Bosnian and Serbian mineral industry, and large quantities of

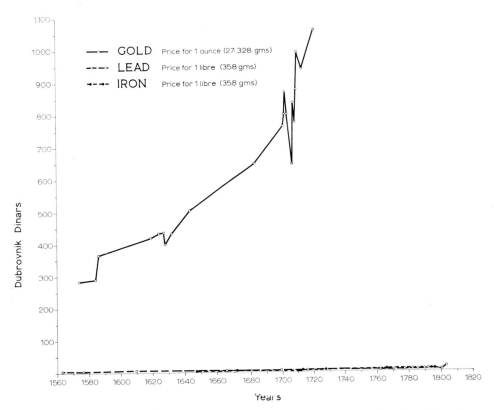

FIG. 123.   Source: Dubrovnik Archives, *Detta; Consilium Rogatorum; Consilium Minoris; Diversa Foris.*

its lead and silver arrived in the Venetian, Sicilian, Levantian, and Hungarian markets. In 1430 the Bosnian King sent 30,000 ducats worth of silver to Dubrovnik and this meant that a further 1·2 tons was now in the government's possession.[13] At the end of the fifteenth century the value of silver rose, with certain years attracting a price of 260 grossi per pound and recording an 8% rise. After 1450 the price rose a further 4% (270 grossi) and towards the end of the century to 11%, or 300 grossi. This indicates that the price of Dubrovnik's silver rose over 100% between 1300 and 1500.

Lead prices ranged between ten and eleven ducats per librarium (358 grammes) in Dubrovnik from 1370 to 1390,[14] whilst Vinaver quotes similar figures (1372, 11·5 ducats; 1383–85; 10 ducats; 1390,

7 ducats).[15] By 1470 the price had doubled to 15 ducats per librarium only to drop again to 12 ducats in 1480 and 8·5 ducats by 1503. According to Božić one Dubrovnik trader alone carried about 634,000 litres of lead from Bosnia to the republic.[17] Further analysis of lead prices by Vinaver as with iron show a similar price range. They have a decided increase after 1790 resulting from continental wars. Gold prices rose from about 280 dinars per ounce in 1580 to over 1,000 dinars by 1720, a fourfold increase in 140 years.

Meat

Meat is another commodity whose price changes can be traced. During the fourteenth century this rose nearly 60% and then re-

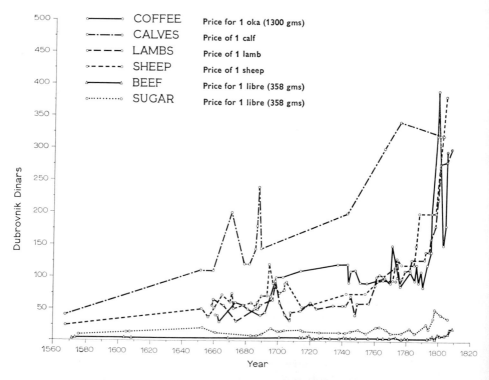

FIG. 124.   Sources Dubrovnik Archives, *Detta; Consilium Rogatorum; Consilium Minoris; Diversa Foris.*

mained fairly stable for the next two centuries. At the beginning of the fourteenth century it was slightly higher in price than 1272, the time of the Statute Book. All prices seemed to be compared with that of mutton. Beef and goat meat was 20% cheaper, whilst pork appeared more expensive. Between 1300–1310 mutton cost about 5 follari per librarium (358 grammes), by 1360, up to 8 follari, and after 1380 from 8–10 follari. In March 1380 'carnes castrate' cost 10 follari per librarium, 'carnes salite porcine cum ossibus' fetched 15 follari and 'carne salite porcine sine ossibus', 20 follari. Lamb's meat was slightly higher priced than mutton and usually sold in ¼ librarium cuts.[18] At the end of the sixteenth century it again rose briskly by almost 100% and indicates the changes that were taking place in Dubrovnik's hinterland, the main cattle source. It appears that during the fourteenth century the independent states of Bosnia and Serbia did not develop the pasture land to its full extent compared with the ensuing two centuries under Turkish domination. Meat prices continued to rise for much of the remaining period under review, with sharp increases during war time at the end of the seventeenth century and the inflationary period at the end of the eighteenth.

Livestock

Information on prices is less forthcoming for the earlier period. One commercial treaty dated 1393, shows that 30 sheep cost a total of 30 perpera, 3 cows, 15 perpera, 1 ox for 8 perpera, and 1 donkey for 6 perpera.[19] *Circa* 1380 a horse cost between 8 and 30 ducats, whilst in 1392 6 mares fetched a total of 110 perpera.[20] By the end of the sixteenth century the change in meat prices is also reflected in other livestock commodities such as skins, wool etc. During the fourteenth and fifteenth centuries Italy and other western European countries made great use of the Balkan raw material base and despite price rises in these goods they do not appear to have been as great as in the West. The more developed western countries obviously profited from the price differential of certain commodities and continued to exploit the two principal branches of the Turkish economy, namely agriculture and animal production. Prices for most livestock continued to rise up to the nineteenth century, particularly calves, which on average fetched much higher prices than lambs.

Other Livestock Products

In this category one may include such goods as cheese, wax and tallow. After wheat and meat, cheese was one of the main victuals consumed in Dubrovnik, and as such was under strict governmental control. The two main types were 'caseus salsus' and the more expensive 'caseus vlashescus'. Between 1300 and 1310 a librarium of the latter cost up to 10 follari, whilst the former varied between 8–9 follari. Both varieties were cheaper in summer than during the winter months. By 1380 each type was fetching about 12 follari,[21] and like other livestock products continued to rise in price during the ensuing centuries. Wax ('Cera Munda') seems to have had a fairly constant price up to about 1350 of between 19 and 21 perpera per librarium. This rose to 24 perpera during the second half of that

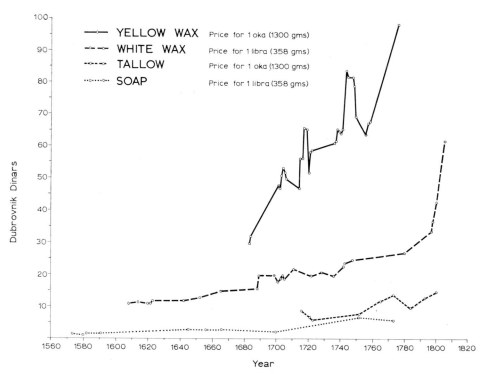

FIG. 125.   Source: Dubrovnik Archives, *Detta; Consilium Rogatorum; Consilium Minoris; Diversa Foris.*

century.[22] The price of white wax is typical of goods coming from the hinterland. It remained fairly steady until the great earthquake of 1667. There then followed the problems of war and quick price acceleration up to 1790, together with rapid inflation at the end of the eighteenth century. Yellow wax, much of which was processed in Dubrovnik's own factories fetched higher prices, and had an even greater tendency to inflationary conditions. Tallow for candles ('Candelas de sepo') had a price of about 16 follari per librarium during the first half of the fourteenth century. In 1352 the city council forbad two merchants selling their candles for more than 24 follari per librarium, so that halfway through the fourteenth century candles in Dubrovnik fetched on average about 18 follari per librarium. By 1380 'candelarum de sepo' were being sold at 24 to 26 follari per librarium,[23] but an order from the city council of September 31, 1381, stated that tallow candles must not be sold for more than 22 follari per librarium. In later centuries both tallow and soap saw a gradual increase in price.

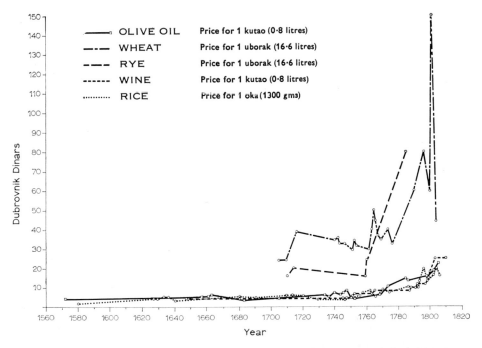

FIG. 126.   Source: Dubrovnik Archives, *Detta; Consilium Rogatorum; Consilium Minoris; Diversa Foris.*

Wine

Like wheat and olive oil another of the traditional Mediterranean crops, wine, remained a cheap local commodity compared with some of the imported hinterland products. According to Čremosnik, one 'quinquo' (21 litres) of wine cost ¼ perpera in about 1300, which doubled in price by the middle of that century.[24] Data from the mid-seventeenth to early nineteenth centuries for malvasy wine showed a sixfold price increase. (4–24 dinars per kutao = 0·8 litres.)

Olive Oil

Information on prices between 1366 and 1375 show an increase from 24 to 36 ducats per 'milliarium' (358 kg).[25] In 1390 a 'quartoço' of oil (0·405 kg, or 0·4 litres) cost between 20 and 25 follari.[26] Later information shows that olive oil prices were eight times greater in 1803 than in 1580.

Salt

Documentary information on salt prices is numerous in the archives, and some of it has already been referred to in the main text. It is sufficient here to point out the early price trends. From about 1300 onwards the price of salt in Dubrovnik seems to have been rising. At this time the city council was buying salt at between 12 and 18 perpera per 'modiorum' (42 kg).[27] By 1363 it had risen to 19 perpera,[28] and in 1380 to 66 perpera per modiorum[29] – a fourfold increase in 80 years. Further information on salt prices is given in Chapters 6 and 9.

Overseas Products

Two products of particular interest are coffee and sugar. They both showed a distinct increase in price towards the end of the eighteenth century when inflation in Dubrovnik was quite severe due to the effect of wars in Europe and beyond. For example the American War of Independence against the English greatly affected coffee prices, for one of the two types of coffee sold in Dubrovnik in the eighteenth century was American, the other was Arabian. The price of coffee

conditions of work, artisan salaries, and even those of agricultural labourers. Further it is possible to follow the movement of state appointments, such as chancellors, solicitors, doctors, teachers, registrars etc. from about 1300 right up to the first decade of the nineteenth century. Workers' wages appear to have been stable during the fifteenth century, but the following century saw a rise of over 100%. A similar percentage rise was experienced during the first years of the next century, which continued even after the disastrous earthquake of 1667. Towards the end of the seventeenth century wages rose between 60% and 80%, accompanied by even greater increases in the first few decades of the eighteenth century. Almost all the rises were accompanied by a fall in money value, so that the real value of salaries and their purchasing power had not undergone, in fact, any great change.

Table XVIII

Interest Rates received by Dubrovnik citizens, etc., from Italian Banks[30]

Year	Bank	Interest Rates
1575	(Average Interest Rates between 7%–10%)	
	Genoa (Banco di San Giorgio)	3%–4%
	Naples (Partite con Sua Maesta)	16%
	Venice (Zecca)	8%–10% (once 14%)
1581	(Average Interest Rates between $6\frac{1}{2}$%–9%)	
	Rome	$5\frac{1}{2}$%
	Naples	5%
1621	(Average Interest Rates between 6%–9%)	
	Rome	$4\frac{1}{2}$%–7%
	Naples	$5\frac{1}{2}$%–7%
	Venice	no evidence
1635	(Average Interest Rates between 5%–7%)	
	Rome	5%–6% (also $10\frac{1}{2}$%)
	Naples	$2\frac{1}{2}$%–7%

Investments Abroad

Some mention should be made of the various money deposits of Dubrovnik's private individuals and public institutions in the different 'monti' ('monte' – capital of a merchant or mercantile partnership, used to trade with for a common profit – F. Edler, *op. cit.*, p. 188) at Naples, Rome, Venice, Genoa and other Italian cities. Much of this material is found in the series *Acta et Diplomata*, whilst one specialist section called 'Monti' exists from 1575 to 1790 and contains 14 volumes. Within it all deposits belonging both to Dubrovnik citizens and people from abroad are recorded. The documents always record the name of the owner, the value of the deposit, the monti, the interest rate received, and any overcharges involved. In 1575 for example Dubrovnik citizens had 262,140 ducats in deposit which by the end of the seventeenth century had reached more than 600,000 ducats (40·3% increase). In Rome money was deposited in 14 monti, Naples in 20 monti, Genoa in the Banco di San Georgio, Venice in the Zecca, etc. (See Table XVIII.)

Conclusion

Council reports in the Dubrovnik Archives contain interesting information on prices and price movements in the republic for certain periods of time and for particular commodities. Furthermore the reports convey numerous information on prices in other countries, resulting from Dubrovnik's trading activity. This is seen even more clearly in the official governmental correspondence. Here information is recorded on harvests, commerce and prices in other Mediterranean countries together with transport costs, port taxes and other public expenses. As a result it is possible to a certain extent to follow in detail the price movements of some commodities from the end of the thirteenth right up to the first years of the nineteenth century.

Weights and Measures

In 1875 a convention in Paris finally agreed on standard metric measurements (Convention internationale du metre). Prior to this date each European country had maintained its own system of measurement, which had that state's own names and sizes. France had already adopted the metric system by the end of the eighteenth century; Austria passed a law on July 23, 1871, ordering the use of the metric system which was first applied in 1876. Serbia also adopted this system in a law of December 1, 1875, and came into effect on January 1, 1883. There was a need in Dalmatia for a similar standardization, but the problem was complicated by the fact that each major town, or port, along the coast including Dubrovnik, had its own measurements for weight, surface area etc. Even today some of the old measures still persist in Dalmatia, particularly for surface area in vineyards, e.g. 'motikama', 'gonjajima' and 'vritima': many of these measures for various areas refer to the amount of land that could be cultivated in a day. The name 'motika' originates from an old agricultural implement used for tilling a vineyard whilst both 'gonjaj' and 'vrit' are very old names for specific surface areas. During the nineteenth and early twentieth centuries some attempt was made to compare and classify the various measures which then existed in Dalmatia.[31]

Linear Measurement

There was no one set of measurements in Dubrovnik for length. There were separate measures for land and for commerce.

Areal Measurement

Dubrovnik and Cavtat had their own separate measures for length. In the fourteenth century land was usually measured in 'zlaticama' (soldo, solidus) with paša (passus) as a sub-unit.

1 soldi = 400 passus.

One soldo appears to have covered between 14 and 19·5 ara, whilst one hectare contained between 5–7 zlatica (soldi). Even in the eighteenth and nineteenth centuries this land unit was still in operation with the zlatica equalling 400 paša (i.e. 20 × 20 or 1681·7052 m²).

Measurements of Length

Evidence here is found particularly with reference to textiles. In the fourteenth century cloth was measured in lakats ('lakat' – Serbo-Croat for 'elbow) with an Italian equivalent 'braccio' and English 'ell'.

1 lakat = 2 palmas = 24 digita,

There appears to have been a difference between the Dubrovnik and Venetian lakat. Rešetar[32] maintains that a Dubrovnik lakat equalled 0·55 cm and in the eighteenth century measured 0·512 cm whilst a palma equalled 27·5 cm. The Venetian lakat (braccio) differentiated between woollen and silk material so that in the fourteenth century the measure was as follows:

100 Venetian lakats of woollen cloth = 124 Dubrovnik lakats
100 Venetian lakats of silk cloth = 115–116 Dubrovnik lakats

The other measure (for width, height of house etc.) was the 'passus' or 'paša', which was divided likewise into 'palmas':

1 Dubrovnik paša = 8 Dubrovnik palmas.[33]

Rešetar states that a paša was about 2·20 metres. Other writers appear more precise for Madirazza says it was 2·050043 metres and Lago maintains it was divided into 4 Dubrovnik lakats. It was particularly in evidence in Dubrovnik, Cavtat and Ston, and is still referred to in the local dialect as 'sežanj' but there are no names for the sub-units, although divisible into ½, ¼, ⅛, $^1/_{16}$, $^1/_{32}$ paša.

The island of Lastovo had its own measure – the Lastovian 'palac' ('palac'–Serbo–Croat for thumb) which was 1·02413 metres and like the Dubrovnik paša was based on a series of halving. Madirazza gives the length as 1·025 metres, whilst Lago says it was half a Dubrovnik paša.

Customary Weights and Measures

In Dubrovnik these could be divided into three main sections.

Basic Weights

The basic weight measurement was the librarium (libra). In the fourteenth century this was divided into two classes:

(i) 'ad pondus subtile', and only used for weighing gold, silver and pearls. 1 libra = about 328 grammes.
(ii) 'ad pondus grossum' for all other goods. 1 libra = about 358 grammes. The libra could be broken down into sub-units as follows:
1 libra = 12 unca
    1 unca = 6 exagia
       1 exagium = 24 karata.

larger measures included:

100 libra = 1 centenarium
10 centenaria = 1milliarium = 1,000 libra.

In present day measures this would be as follows.

Table XIX

Dubrovnik weights	For gold, silver, pearls	Other goods
	about	about
1 libra	328 grammes	358 grammes
1 unca	27⅓ grammes	30 grammes
1 exagium	4½ grammes	5 grammes
1 centenarium	32,8 kg	35,8 kg
1 milliarium	328 kg	358 kg

Later evidence states that a Dubrovnik 'libra' equalled 0·3770 kg divided into 12 'unca' (0·031417 kg). The book *Istruzione* . . . gives it as 0·376 9665 kg, whilst Rossetti[34] states that a Dubrovnik libra was 0·377 03 kg. However after Napoleon the value of the libra totalled 0·3770 kg.

Other Dubrovnik measures included the 'oka' and 'kantar'. The Dubrovnik oka weighed 1·30330 kg. Madirazza gave a value of 1·312 kg and Rossetti 1·300 kg which is substantiated in the *Istruzione* . . . The Dubrovnik kantar was equal to 55 oka so that it had a weight of 71·6815 kg. Madirazza gives a value of 71·694 kg but Lago states that a kantar was 42 oka and was only used for measuring timber. Vinaver[35] writing on trade relations *circa* 1600 says that a kantar was 56 kg. A measure prevalent in the Middle Ages was the 'salma', or horse load. One Dubrovnik salma (of wax, flax, skins etc.) weighed 400 libra, or about 140 kg. However this varied according to commodity, for example a load of salt weighed 354 libra or 127 kg.[36]

Cereal Measures

The main cereal measure was the 'star' (starium) for freight transport. Rešetar states that it equalled 99 libra, but evidence from 1361 suggests that it measured up to 200 libra.[37] Manken maintains that from documentary sources in the fourteenth century she believes a Dubrovnik star to be between 180 and 198·5 Dubrovnik libra.[38] A further breakdown of the star was as follows:

1 star = 6 copelli[39] = about 180 – 200 libra (today 64·5 – 71·5 kg)
1 copellus = 30 libra (today 10·740 – 11·9 kg).

Later evidence shows that within Dubrovnik's territory and on Lastovo Island cereals were measured by Dubrovnik 'staj' which equalled 111·0907 litres, and was divided into 4 'uborak' (27·7727 litres), 6 'kupela' (18·5–151 litres), 16 'bagaša' or 'starića' (6·9432 litres). Neither Lago nor Madirazza mention uborak, but state that a staj was divided into 6 kupela, 16 bagaša or starića. The *Istruzione* . . . does not mention either of the latter terms. Vinaver states that a Dubrovnik star in 1600 equalled one hectolitre, divided into 6 uboraks (kupelas) of 16·6 litres each.

Salt Measures

The main salt measure was the 'modia' (modium, modius; in Serbo-Croat – 'mjerica', 'spud'). The earliest information on the actual weight of a modia is 1670, for according to Rešetar it then equalled 42 kg (33 oka) although the term 'ad mensuram subtilem salis Ragusii' is found much earlier.[40] Salt was transported in sacks (vreća) and loads usually weighed about 3 mjerica.[41] Occasionally, however, salt was measured in litres.[42] Kovačević has calculated that if the average load was 3 mjerica, then in present day values this equalled 136 kg.[43] Later information from the eighteenth century, according to Rešetar, states that 1 modia was equal to half a star. The problem of exact weight definition for the modia has also caused difficulty for other parts of the Mediterranean.[44]

Liquid Measures

These measures may be understood from a particular study of documentary evidence on wine and olive oil.

Wine. In the fourteenth century wine was measured in 'quinqua'. This was divided into small (quinqua picolo) and large (quinqua grande) sizes, the latter being 3 'terceria' more than the former. The small quinqua was subdivided as follows:

$$1 \text{ quinquum} = 2 \text{ media quinqua} = 8 \text{ dimidia quarta}$$
$$= 24 \text{ terceria} = 48 \text{ media tercia}.$$

In 1386 wine measures were correctly equated with silver libras[45] as follows:

1 dimidia quinqua = 29 libra, 3 unca, 4,5 exagia.
1 dimidia quarta = 8 libra, 3 unca, 1 exagium, 15 karata.
1 tercerium = 2 libra, 5 unca, 1 exagium, 21 karata.
1 medium tercium = 1 libra, 2 unca, 3 exagia, 22 karata.

In present day measures these would equal:

1 quinqua grande = about 21 litres
1 quinquo piçolo = about 18·75 litres
1 tercerium = about 0·78 litres (after 1460 even less)

Olive Oil. As with wine, olive oil had its own set of measures in the fourteenth century. The main units were the 'staria d'oio' and the 'libra d'oio'. Again these were correctly standardized in 1386 as follows:

1 star of oil = 3 libra d'oio = 24 quartoçe = 48 meçe quartoçe.

These were then equated as follows:

Table XX

Weight	Silver Measure			Kilogrammes	Litres
	libra	unca	exagium		about
1 starium d'oio	29	8	0	9·730	9·5
1 libra d'oio	9	6	4	3·243	3·0
1 quartoço	1	2	2	0·405	0·4
1 meça quartoça	–	7	1	0·203	0·2

Later centuries saw both of these commodities converted into the same standard measurements usually based on the Venetian 'baril', which totalled 64·387 litres. Various parts of the Dubrovnik Republic had their own measures. For example the Pelješac peninsula and Lastovo Island used the Venetian baril divided into 6 sića or 84 kutlja (0·788 litres). Dubrovnik had its own baril with a liquid capacity of 64·3880 litres and divided into 7 staro (9·1938 litres) or further into 84 kutlja (0·766 litres). According to Madirazza the Dubrovnik staro had a liquid capacity of 9·200 litres and a kutlo one of 0·7667 litres. Further, the town of Ston had its own liquid measure based on the Venetian baril but divided into 104 'small kutlja' totalling 0·619 litres, and both Lago and Madirazza state that this same system was used at Slano.

Conclusion

The complexity of weights and measures within Dalmatia meant that values varied with locality, and even within political units. For example, in the Dubrovnik Republic there was no evidence of a single system in force. This makes comparative work very difficult, but an attempt has been made to equate most of the units involved, with the present-day metric system.

Appendix 1. Notes

1. D. M. Metcalf, *Coinage in the Balkans, 820–1355*, Institute of Balkan Studies No. 80, Thessaloniki (1965), 286 pp.
2. G. Wenzel, *Codex Diplomaticus Arpadianus Continuatus*, Vol. VI, (890–1235), *Monumenta Hungariae Historica Ser. Diplomataria, Vol. XI*) Budapest (1867), No. 105;
S. Ljubić, *Listine o Odnošajih izmedju Južnoga Slavenstva i Mletačke Republike*, Vol. I, Zagreb (1968), No. XVII.
3. D. M. Metcalf, *op. cit.*, p. 192.
4. In this description the local names of Dubrovnik coins are given first. The Latin or Italian names by which the coin is known internationally are in parentheses.
5. Information on money values may be gleaned from A. Evans, 'Some coinage systems of the fourteenth century', *Journal of Economic and Business History*, Vol. III (1931), pp. 481–496;
J. Colich, 'Coins of Dubrovnik', *Journal of Croatian Studies*, Vols. IX–X, New York (1968–69), pp. 160–173;
V. Kopać, 'Pregled Dubrovačkog novca', *Bilten Numizmatickog Društva u Zagrebu*, Vol. III, Zagreb, pp. 18–42;
I. Rendjeo, *Corpus der mittelalterlichen Munzen von Kroatien, Slavonien. Dalmatien und Bosnien.* (Graz) Akademische Druck-und Verlagsanstalt (1959), 306 pp.;
M. Rešetar, *Dubrovačka numizmatika*, Vol. I, 'Povjesni dio', Sremski Karlovci (1924) and Vol. II, 'Opisni dio', Belgrade-Zemun (1925).

6. I. Manken, *Dubrovački Patricijat u XIV veku*, S.A.N. Knj. CCCXL, (Od Društ. Nauka) Knj. 36, Belgrade (1960), p. 107.
7. *Monumenta Ragusina*, Vol. V, Zagreb (1897), p. 165.
8. M. Dinić, 'Odluke veča dubrovačke republike', Vol. I, Belgrade (1951), *Zbornik za I.J.K.*, III Odelj. Knj. 15.
9. Dubrovnik Archives (1359). *Reformationes*, Vol. XVII, folder 137; (1364); *ibid.*, 22, folder 143.
10. J. Tadić,'Les archives économiques de Raguse', *Annales Économies, Sociétiés, Civilisations*, No. 6. Paris (Nov.–Dec. 1961), pp. 1169–1170.
11. V. Vinaver, 'Cene i Nadnice u Dubrovniku XVIII Veka', *Istoriski Časopis*, S.A.N., Vols. IX–X, Belgrade (1959), pp. 315–325.
12. I. Manken, *op. cit.*, p. 107.
13. M. Dinić, 'Prilošci za istoriju srednjeg veka', *Prilozi*, Vol. XIII, Belgrade (1933), p. 70.
14. V. Vinaver, *Problem Proizvodnje Srebra u Srednjovekovnoj Srbiji*, Titograd (1960)
15 Dubrovnik Archives (1371). *Diversa Cancellariae*, 23, folder 106';
    (1375). *ibid.*, 24, folders 13', 171';
    (1377). *Reformationes*, 24, folder 154;
    (1385). *Diversa Cancellaria*, 26, folders 102', 124;
    (1390). *ibid.*, 28, folder 23.
16. V. Vinaver, *Problem . . . op. cit.*, p. 20.
17. I. Božić, *Dubrovnik i Turska u XIV i XV veku*, S.A.N. Knj. CC, 1st. Inst. kniga. 3, Belgrade (1952), pp. 22, 292, 297, 305.
18. *Monumenta Ragusina*, *op. cit.*, Vol. IV, p. 100, Vol. V, pp. 240, 310; M. Dinić, *op. cit.*, pp. 23, 26.
19. Dubrovnik Archives (1393), *Diversa Cancellaria*, 30, folder 83'.
20. M. Dinić, *op. cit.*, pp. 23, 220, 313, 329; (1392). *Diversa Cancellariae*, 30, folder 151.
21. *Monumenta Ragusina*, *op. cit.*, Vol. IV, p. 100, Vol. V, pp. 183, 222, 253; M. Dinić, *op. cit.*, pp. 25, 36, 74, 132, 179, 208, 358. Dubrovnik Archives (1335). *Diversa Cancellaria*, 12, folder 207; (1367). *ibid.*, 21, folder 53, 138; (1340). *Diversa Notaria*, 6, folder 150.
22. *Monumenta Ragusina*, *op. cit.*, Vol. V, pp. 122, 335.
23. *Ibid*, Vol. II, pp. 155, 197, 243; Vol. IV, p. 5; M. Dinić, *op. cit.*, pp. 74, 80–82.
24. G. Čremosnik, 'Vinogradarstvo i vino u Dalmaciji srednjega veka; *Glasnik Zemaljskog Muzeja*, Vol. XLV, Sarajevo (1933), p. 27.
25. Dubrovnik Archives (1366). *Diversa Cancellaria*, 20, folder 102; (1368). *ibid.*, 21, folder 135; (1375). *ibid.*, 24, folder 76.
26. Dubrovnik Archives (1364). *Reformationes*, 22, folder 91; (1385), *ibid.*, 26, folder 69'; (1396), *ibid.*, 30, folder 22; (1398), *ibid.*, 31, folders 37', 39, 49, 57.
27. Dubrovnik Archives (1333). *Diversa Cancellaria*, 10, folders 66, 193; *Monumenta Ragusina*, Vol. V, pp. 92, 137.
28. Dubrovnik Archives (1363). *Reformationes*, 20, folder 32.

X*

29. M. Dinić, *op. cit.*, p. 52;
    M. Gečić, 'Dubrovačka trgovina solju u XIV veku', *Zbornik Filozofskog Fakulteta*, Knj. III, Belgrade (1955), pp. 116, 150.
30. J. Tadić, *op. cit.*, p. 1175.
31. *Istruzione popolare sui pesi e sulle misure in Dalmazia*, Zadar (1858);
    V. Lago, *Memorie sulla Dalmazia*, Venice (1869);
    F. Madirazza, *Storia e constitzione dei comuni dalmati*, Split (1911).
32. M. Rešetar, *Dubrovačka Numizmatika*, Vol. I, Sremska Karlovac (1924), pp. 90–100.
33. Dubrovnik Archives (1367). *Diversa Cancellaria*, 21, folder 151; (1375), *ibid.*, folder 15.
34. A. Rossetti, *Ragguaglio universale dei pesi*, Trieste (1829).
35. V. Vinaver, 'Dubrovačko-Albanski Ekonomski Odnosi krajem XVI veka', *Anali Historiskog Instituta u Dubrovniku*, Vol. I, No. 1 (1952), p. 230.
36. I. Manken, *Dubrovački Patricijat u XIV Veku*, S.A.N.U. Knj. CCCXL, Odelj. Druš. Nauka' Kniga. 36, Belgrade (1960), p. 103.
37. Monumenta Ragusina, *op. cit.*, Vol. III, p. 136.
38. I. Manken, *op. cit.*, p. 104.
39. Dubrovnik Archives (1383). *Reformationes*, 25, folder 49′.
40. Dubrovnik Archives, (11/VI/1404). *Diversa Cancellaria*, 35, folder 76′.
41. Dubrovnik Archives, (21/V/1390). *Diversa Cancellaria*, 29, folder 98. ('100 salmas salis de tribus modiis prosingula salma').
42. Dubrovnik Archives, (22/VI/1390). *Diversa Cancellaria*, 29, folder 108′. Vlahs carried 46 loads of salt to Prača, each weighing 390 litres; (11/VI/1404). *Diversa Cancellaria*, 35, folder 78′. Vlahs transported to Deževica or Podvisoki 'sexaginta salmas salis ponderis qualibet salma librarum 436'.
43. D. Kovačević, *Trgovina u Srednjovjekovnoj Bosni*, Naučno Društvo N.R. B.i H. Djela Knj. XVIII Odjel. 1st Fil. Nauka Knj. 13 Sarajevo (1961), p. 180.
44. D. Jenness, *The Economics of Cyprus: A Survey to 1914*, McGill University Press, Montreal (1962), p. 48, footnote 10—'The word "moza" comes from the old Roman measure of capacity, *modius*, which spread widely throughout Italy and the eastern Mediterranean, but, in the Middle Ages at least, varied greatly in value from one region to another. If Mas Latrie, who reckoned the Cyprus moza at 73 litres, meant litres of the metric system, then it would equal about two English bushels; but if he meant Cyprus litres, each of which equals 24/5 English quarts, then it would be equivalent to over six bushels. Since a bushel of wheat weighs around 21 okes, the latter value would coincide with De Vezin's, who wrote in 1790: "The moza contains eight caffisis (Persian Kafiz, a bushel-measure) and each caffisi weighs between 16 and 17 okes (taken at 44½ lb English) according as the weigher is more or less tired, or the grains are heavier." '
45. R. Eitelberger von Edelberg, *Die mittelalterlichen Kunstdenkmale Dalmatiens*, Vienna (1884), (Gesammelte kunsthistorische Schriften Bd. IV)—*Statut doane*, pp. 384–385.

Appendix 2
The Dubrovnik Archives

In 1955 R. S. Lopez and I. W. Raymond[1] wrote that they had

'explored, so far as the scanty documentation permitted, the non-'Romance countries of the eastern (and southern) Mediterranean'

and add in a footnote that

'the number of documents from each town, is not always in proportion to the importance of the town'.

For example, Piacenza, Bologna, Ragusa (Dubrovnik), Ibiza and Almira do not receive adequate representation (in their book) because few private commercial documents from these cities had so far appeared in print. More recently, both Tadić and Krekič have drawn attention to the Dubrovnik Archives with works published in French,[2] whilst Biegman used them as a basis for his book in English.[3] All three have drawn attention to the archives for two main reasons. Firstly as a source for foreign historians, particularly those interested in the Mediterranean region, and the complex economic and historical problems of that region, and secondly as a source base for economic historians engaged in analyzing monetary affairs in the Balkans and eastern Mediterranean. It may also be argued that the archives provide ample evidence for a geographical study based on the spatial differention of trade using documentary sources. Thus the archives are not only a rich collection of material for a study of the town's history but also the vast regions with which Dubrovnik had political and commercial relations, covering a period of more than five centuries for much of the Mediterranean region and beyond.

History of the Archives

The Dubrovnik Archives have experienced a varied history. The year 1272 is a very important one in Dubrovnik's annals, as it is the date of the promulgation of the Statute Book by the Count Marco Giustiniani, although the original is unfortunately lost. The oldest extant copies date from the fourteenth and fifteenth centuries. Prior to 1272 the constitution and laws of Dubrovnik had been based on custom, altered and modified by statutes. Giustiniani codified all the existing sources of Dubrovnik's jurisprudence into a corpus called the *Liber Statutorum*. Dalmatian law was based on a Roman substratum, with additions from local statutes, Slavonic customs, and certain commercial and maritime statutes. The contents of the new code may be summed up in the following mnemonic distich:

'Elligit officia comes civitatis in *primo*,
Officiis fides datur sacrata *secundo*,
Causa litis sequitur *terno* sub ordine libri,
Conjugis inscripsit *quarto* dotalia bona,
Ordo datur domibus *quinto* plateasque divisit,
Judicis officum crimen exposit in *sexto*,
Septimo navigii additur, et mercium ordo,
Octavo in codice diversa colligit auctor.'

The introduction, which is full of generalities and abstract ideas, after the manner of the time, states that the object of the code was to collect the statutes of the Dubrovnik Republic,

'to harmonize the discrepancies, suppress superfluities, supply omissions, explain obscurities, so that nothing superfluous, obscure, of captious should remain in them'.

The first book defines the position, rights, and duties of the count and of the other chief functionaries of the republic, and deals with sundry financial matters. The second book contains the formulae and oaths of each officer of state, and in cap. xxiv the salaries of the Dubrovnik envoys to foreign countries were fixed. The third embodies the law of procedure and the judicial system, and sets forth the rules for the stanico, or international court of arbitration. The fourth book deals with marriage, wills, and family affairs. The fifth deals with municipal regulations, building laws and contracts, land tenure, etc. The sixth is the criminal code, and also contains fiscal enactments and smuggling laws. The seventh regulates shipping, the relations between officers and crew, agreements for voyages, marine insurance, responsibilities and risks and the last book contains enactments on diverse matters. It became law on May 9, 1272.

This code, although it is imperfect and not altogether well constructed, marks a great improvement on previous legislation, and compares favourably with the statutes of many of the more famous Italian republics. The shipping and commercial enactments are often excellent, and parts of the code, especially those relating to land tenure and certain forms of contract were valid at Dubrovnik up to the nineteenth century. The Liber Statutorum was afterwards added to and enlarged, and numbers of new laws were enacted.

All this activity could have suggested the need to found the city's archives, which were established in 1277. Unfortunately documents stored there often led to embarrassment, which in turn help create the archives varied history. This was partly the result of the Dubrovnik government's deliberate attempt to destroy documents on several occasions. For example when Dubrovnik passed from Venetian domination to Hungarian protection, many documents which may have proved dangerous or embarrassing, were burnt. This same reason led to the large scale destruction of documents in 1807 after the French occupation (1806) and before the republic's final liquidation in 1808. The secret discussions of the Senate were the largest section to be destroyed. After the Austrian occupation in 1814–15 a large number of documents became scattered or just disappeared and a portion of the archives were transported to Vienna in 1818 and 1833 after the annexation. Further confusion was added in 1820 when the Austrian authorities decided to re-classify documents into three categories, namely, judicial, financial and maritime-sanitary sections, which again led to the loss of numerous documents. A little later on the Austrians had about five thousand varied documents transported to Venice, particularly charters written in ancient slavic and cyrillic scripts. Fortunately in 1895 the Austrians agreed to return all documents they had confiscated from various institutions in Dubrovnik. Much of the credit for this action must go to the celebrated Czech historian K. Jireček, himself a great expert on Dubrovnik's archives, who intervened on the town's behalf. By 1918 the Austrians had returned a large part of the 5,000 documents, which had previously been sent to Venice, but unfortunately they were not shipped to Dubrovnik itself but to Belgrade (Serbian Academy of Sciences). These documents were not finally returned to Dubrovnik until after 1945.

In spite of these detrimental events the material preserved in the present archives is still very rich. The documents include about 7,000 registers and about 100,000 separate acts, all divided into ninety-two series. They cover varying periods of time. Some commence in 1280 just after the foundation of the archives, and follow through till the fall of the republic. Other series start later some even in the eighteenth century, whilst others terminate long before the fall of the republic. Various languages are used in the documents. Official languages in Dubrovnik were Latin (the accounts of the Council's sessions were written in that language until 1780) and Italian (in which, among other things, the correspondence with the envoys was conducted). There were three chanceries: one handling Latin and Italian, one Slavonic, and one Turkish material. Many of the earlier Slavonic examples were written in the cyrillic alphabet, but later equally in the Latin characters with Italian spelling. Acts in Greek, French, Spanish etc. are rarely found but there are several thousand such acts in Turkish.

Main Documentary Groups

The oldest series is *Acta Sancta Maria Maioris*, which contains various documents dating from the eleventh to the nineteenth centuries. This series also contains the oldest of the town's legal acts. For example there is a Papal Bull preserved in the original, dated 1022, signed by Benedict VIII, in which the bishopric of Dubrovnik was instituted. Only one other authentic act exists from the eleventh century but this is preserved in a thirteenth century copy. Two other extant documents from the eleventh century are to be found but these are thought to be false, whilst two others from the pontifical chancellory are not to be found in Dubrovnik. Documents from the twelfth century are more numerous, including international agreements (with other coastal towns in Dalmatia, Italian cities and Balkan noblemen from Serbia, Bosnia and Hum), pontifical bulls, together with other documents concerned purely with local affairs. The thirteenth century has an increasing number of original charters from the Bosnian and Serbian rulers written in Slavonic cyrillic script. It is during the second half of this century that the first registers begin, and the oldest register preserved in the original is *Liber Statutorum Doane* dated 1277 concerned with customs duty. It is quite probable that registers existed long before this date but there is no evidence to prove it. Documents in the present modern archives in Dubrovnik

were reorganized in 1920 into three main sections: (a) those belonging to the period of the republic, (b) documents concerned with the
French occupation, and (c) finally those from the nineteenth and
twentieth centuries. The archives provide interesting information for
a study of the Middle Ages, but naturally are not so numerous as for
the later periods. The earliest information dates back to c. 1277–78
and some of these early acts provide interesting data on the early
history of the town, besides coinciding with the foundation of the
archives there.

Documents from the Republic (1277–1808)

All the documents in Dubrovnik Archives can be divided into four
parts.
   The first is based on the minutes of the three councils of the commune. They dealt with two main aspects – the internal politics of
the various merchant class factions in the town, and the international
political relations of the Dubrovnik Republic. This group contains
two large series. These are, firstly the register of the three councils,
dating from 1301 to 1808 which contains 434 volumes, and secondly
the minutes and correspondence of the Dubrovnik Republic from
1359 to 1808 (244 volumes). Acts related to the political and diplomatic life of Dubrovnik are mainly found in government council
decisions. These help form the series *Reformationes* (thirty-four
volumes) which began in 1301 and include discussions of the three
main councils – *Consilium Maius* (Great Council), *Consilium Minus*
(Small Council) and *Consilium Rogatorum* (Council of Appeal), all
recorded up to 1415. After this date the decisions were recorded in
Acta Consilii Rogatorum (Transactions of the Court of Appeal) with
211 volumes, *Secreta Rogatorum* (Confidential appeals), with seven
volumes, *Acta Consilii Minoris* (Transactions of the Small Council)
with 117 volumes, and *Acta Consilii Maioris* (Transactions of the
Great Council) with sixty-seven volumes. The *Consilium Rogatorum*
is a very copious series which contains the resolutions of the Senate.
For example one period alone (1575–1595) consists of 6,000 pages
written in Latin and bound in thirteen volumes whilst the series
covers the whole of Dubrovnik's internal and external politics.
   The *Litterae et Commissiones Levantis*, or *Lettere di Levante*, is
a very important series for the study of political life. It contains
copies of the Senate's instructions which have been preserved in 110

volumes covering the period 1359–1566 for all parts of the then known world and 1566–1802 for the eastern half, especially Turkey. Thus scholars are abundantly supplied with material from the correspondence between Dubrovnik's Senate and its envoys abroad. This is supplemented by 137 volumes of the *Lettere di Ponente*, addressed to Dubrovnik envoys in western countries between 1566 and 1802. For the period covering 1575–1595, there are six volumes of *Lettere di Levante* (Volumes 33–38), together with more than 3,000 folio pages written in Italian. Both series form a valuable basis not only for Dubrovnik's own politics but that of other Italian and Balkan powers, together with information on the varying attitudes of other European countries. Unfortunately, the *Lettere di Levante* as well as *di Ponente* are as yet unbound for the years 1802–1808. Of equal importance is the correspondence which the republic received from abroad and from its overseas possessions. The counterpart of the *Lettere* consists of the *Acta Sanctae Mariae Maioris*, also called *Acta et Diplomata*, which include letters and reports written to the Dubrovnik authorities by their own and foreign envoys as well as by private individuals. Unfortunately, some of this material has been lost, making it incomplete for the whole period going only as far as the end of the sixteenth century. However it is almost completely preserved and comprises 247 volumes for the period after 1600. Fortunately, many incoming letters from envoys are recapitulated in the Senate's replies, copies of which are to be found in the *Lettere*. Since the instructions are strictly chronologically entered into the *Lettere di Levante* and *Ponente* they are cited by their date and not by volume and page; in some places this supplies additional information. The same applies to the *Consilium Rogatorum*. The *Acta et Diplomata* series is not chronologically arranged, and therefore quoted by serial number, in addition to the date.

The second group refers to Dubrovnik's financial affairs and includes port tax returns, expenditure on armaments, the guard service, navigation and food supplies, the maintenance of salt pans, revenue from customs duties and the cost of public works. The council reports are a precious source for the history of prices, particularly for food. In Dubrovnik the councils were always authorized to fix the maximum price of food products and to regulate the buying of provisions, both decisions obviously very significant for price movements.

The abundance of case book series makes it possible to compare prices of other merchandise, such as the cost of different textile imports from Italy, France, Flanders and England. More locally, salt prices are recorded in the collection known as *Salinaria* which is in three parts dated 1443, 1453 and 1473, together with other documents from 1546 to 1800 covering purchases bought in Apulia, Sicily, Sardinia and the Balearic Islands together with areas of sale. Case books also exist giving details of Dubrovnik's annual budget. For example, thirteen years ago a table was discovered in the series *Bilanciae* for 1622, which gave a general list of receipts and expenses incurred by Dubrovnik in the sixteenth and seventeenth centuries. This series has further enabled the analysis of customs duties for each month and year from 1534 to 1800. Two other series in this financial group give information on food purchase and sales, namely *Grassia* from 1500–1809 (fifty-four volumes) and the *Libra di Cassa pubblica* containing forty-six volumes covering a slightly shorter period. These large books contain various definitions, often in great detail, for weights which are included in Dubrovnik's expenses and receipts. Further these two series contain not only food prices converted from foreign currency, into grossi, but also embarking costs in the port of origin, disembarking prices at Dubrovnik, transport costs, port taxes, tips, and also figures given on the course of different Mediterranean currencies. Two sections are particularly concerned with the navy and maritime economy, namely *Naula et securitates* in sixty-nine volumes (1563–1755) and *Liber navigiorum* (1578–1806). Within these volumes information is included on the value of boats, salaries, assurances, profits from boat-building, insurance for voyages etc. There are also rules for claiming boat damages, an inventory on naval freight and the values of registered cargo. The amount of detail recorded is seen from the following example of a ship which travelled from England to Messina, Sicily, in 1523. Although a Dubrovnik vessel it was attached to Messina and carried 8,017 different cloths, 7,377 of which were kersey (92%); 4,365 and 119 other cloths of the ship's total belonged to Dubrovnik merchants; the freight had a total value of 66,000 ducats. In the same year three other Dubrovnik vessels carried English cloth to other Mediterranean harbours as well as to the home port. Further the Dubrovnik merchant navy in 1534 transported another load on the same route (England–Messina) which totalled 6,522 different cloths, 5,045 of which were kersey (77%) and total freight was estimated at 82,100 ducats. It is therefore possible to follow the price of different merchandise, together with transport costs over diverse distances by the skilful use of documentary evidence. The oldest account book in the archives dates from 1277 and is concerned with customs duties – *Liber statutorum doane*. This is part of the series *Dogana* containing sixty-five volumes and continuing till after the fall of the republic. Further information may be gleaned from the series *Fabbriche* beginning in 1519 and totalling 145 volumes. It contains all expenses incurred for work done throughout the whole republic and is partly substantiated by the less important series *Detta* which gives further information on state expenses (ninety-two volumes).

The third group refers to public law including reports on court cases over public property, tribunal sentences, books on contraband, cadastral surveys in the fourteenth century, and information on the chancellery of the Dubrovnik commune. The town statutes are found in three principal books, the first being *Liber Omnium reformationum* (dated from 1335 with additions up to 1410). Until 1357 many laws were incorporated in the Statute Book, but after the last Venetian Count left in that year a new code was begun, called the *Liber Viridis* or Green Book. This book is mainly concerned with the fifteenth century but contains laws from 1357–1408 not included in the previous book together with new laws up to 1460. Then the *Liber Croceus* or Yellow Book was begun, and continued down to 1791. The last laws of the republic, from 1791 to its fall in 1808, are preserved in the *Parti dei Pregadi*. The deliberations and enactments of the various assemblies are contained in the *Liber Reformationum*, which was begun in 1306. Of all these collections of enactments, only the last has been published, but not in a complete form (see Bibliography). Judicial matters began to be recorded by the middle of the fourteenth century with *Sententiae Cancellariae* (260 volumes). Others included *Lamenta de Foris* (138 volumes) and *Lamenta de intus* (136 volumes), and dealt exclusively with judicial affairs to be followed in the following century by *Lamenta de criminale* (247 volumes) and *Lamenta de intus et de foris* (74 volumes). Lastly the archives also contain acts which refer specifically to the various small possessions within the republic such as the town of Ston and the islands of Mljet and Lastovo.

The fourth group is a collection of documents referring to civil contracts. These include wills made between 1282 and 1815, con-

tracts of sale, marriage and dowry contracts, debtors books, a large
number of solicitors' writs and the actions of different chancellors.
This last group is the richest and most varied.

Between 1278 and 1282 several series were started which are
invaluable for studying Dubrovnik's economic life. These include
Diversa Cancellariae (235 volumes), *Diversa Notaria* (147 volumes)
and *Diversa de Foris* (256 volumes). All three series exist until the
fall of the republic but each with different dates of origin, 1282, 1310
and 1593 respectively, together with *Debita Notaria* (116 volumes)
and *Testamenta* (94 volumes) both beginning in 1280–82. The sources
for all five series are the same. They consist of acts brought forward
by private individuals and include contracts of purchase and sale, of
hire, mutual agreements between parties, business liquidations, lists
of merchandise, inventories with prices included etc. Besides these
there are extracts from commercial handbooks, private correspondence, commercial letters and business interest reports all providing
a suitable base for comparison with other Dalmatian and foreign
archives. Some less important documents often fill in the smaller
details and these have been inserted at the end of the *Diversa* reports.
Similarly other later series are to be found including *Liber dotium
notaria* (22 volumes) (Solicitor's Dowry Books), and *Venditae
Cancellariae* (9 volumes) begining in the fourteenth century and
Pacta Matrimonialia (14 volumes) dating from 1447. Thus these series
are able to provide large amounts of often small incidental information which is invaluable today in the understanding of the daily
economic life of a small community, which many of the larger, richer
European archives fail to provide as they were more involved in the
problems of 'grande politique' and the larger contemporary
economic questions of the time.

Although the majority of the *Diversa* documents refer to commerce, there is also information on particular financial affairs. The
collection *Debita notariae*, records private debts which were contracted between 1280 and 1810. Other parts of the *Diversa* series
contain letters of exchange in different currencies, a large number of
rules for joint accounts and often a breakdown of exchange rates
between various currencies, together with the expenses incurred for
each financial transaction. Thus money from England, Spain and even
as far away as Constantinople, Syria and Alexandria are mentioned.
Yet another fundamental source is the series *Privata* covering the
period 1420 to 1829, containing over thirty volumes of merchants

books and business transactions. The oldest are the books of the
Kabozić brothers (*Caboga*) dating from 1426 to 1433. They
specialized in the export of various raw materials from Dubrovnik to
Venice and the rest of Italy, particularly Bosnian and Serbian silver,
lead and wax, together with the import of manufactured goods,
especially textiles in the reverse direction. The Caboga books also
make reference to the separation of gold and silver, a problem of
particular interest to historians. Other commercial books in this
series include those of *merchants at Novo Brdo mine* (1432–1440),
those of the great merchant-ship-owner *Vice Stjepović-Skočibuha*
(1585–1588) who personally recorded all business accounts, expenses
and individual prices; yet again the books of *Nikola Miosa* a
Dubrovnik merchant who lived and worked in Venice (1581–1586).
Finally mention should be made of *Benedikt Resti,* resident in Sofia
who registered all his commercial transactions, for a large part of
Bulgaria from 1590 to 1605. Numerous such books exist from the
seventeenth and eighteenth centuries and give precise information
on trade, owners reports, prices and daily domestic expenses.

Turkish Sources

Finally something should be said about the Turkish material in the
archives as it is of sufficient importance to warrant special mention, although it does not constitute a separate group. Turkish
material in Dubrovnik's archives exceeds over 10,000 documents and
consist mainly of *firmāns* (Turkish: fermān) which were a Sultan's
orders issued and addressed to Ottoman officials and tributary rulers.

The firmāns in Dubrovnik's Archives may be divided into two series
the *K group,* consisting of those documents returned by Vienna, and
the *A, B and C groups,* which have always remained in Dubrovnik;
and in which various other Turkish documents are also to be found.
In addition there is the *Carte Turche* series, a collection of about 800
Turkish documents which were given to Zadar Archives in 1836, and
only recovered after World War II. They still bear the signature of the
Zadar Archives (Državni Archiv Zadar). Neither date, subject-matter,
nor addresses, seem of any help in determining why some documents
should have been collected in the *K series* and others elsewhere for
this division already existed in the eighteenth century.

Eighteenth century Italian translations of *K* firmāns, form a hand-
written volume entitled *Traduzioni di Capitulazioni e di Firmani*

containing firmāns from the time of Mehmed II until Selīm III (1451–1807). They are often very inexact when compared with the actual firmāns. Such discrepancies are found both in the contents and the date quoted at the end of the firmāns. The same applies to the notices written primarily in Italian on the back or cover of the firmāns. The *Traduzioni* do contain, however, translations of a number of firmāns which have subsequently been lost but should be used with the utmost caution.

Since Dubrovnik sent its representatives as circumstances required to all imaginable Turkish governors and other authorities the *Lettere* contain a wealth of information about conditions prevailing in Turkey and personalities involved. Apart from the daily routine of commercial and other matters, the *Lettere* (and *Acta*) also deal with the advent of officials. Very often, the *Consilium Rogatorum* and *Lettere* are concerned with the maximum to be spent for the goodwill of Turkish officials, whilst it may be said that all in all, the *Consilium Rogatorum, Lettere* and *Acta* give a vivid picture of Dubrovnik's dealings with local, provincial and the central Turkish authorities. They are often also very helpful in understanding the background of a firmān. Other non-Turkish sources in the Dubrovnik Archives such as the *Diversa Cancellariae, Diversa Notariae, Sententiae Cancellariae, Lamenta* with *de Foris* etc. do not have such a direct bearing on the firmāns.

Documents from the French Occupation (1808–1814)

The French regime which was installed after the fall of the republic, had completely different administrative principles than those of the former republic. This meant the adoption of a system of registering detached documents in a formal treaty, each with its own current number. These acts, cover the period of the French occupation from 1808 to 1814, and total about 180 voluminous dossiers.

Documents from the Nineteenth and Twentieth Centuries

Documents from the nineteenth and twentieth centuries are extremely numerous and for the most part are not yet included in the archival lists as many are still being checked, catalogued and classified.

Inventories

Inventories of the Dubrovnik Archives are very inadequate. Probably the earliest inventory dated from 1830, which has been largely superceded by more recent work in the archives. In 1910 Josip Gelčić actually classified and published an inventory (*Dubrovački Archiv,* Separatni Otisak iz *Glasnika Zemaljskog Muzeja u Bosni i Hercegovini,* Vol. XXIL, No. 4, Sarajevo 1910, pp. 537–588) which is by no means perfect, but in the absence of anything better is reproduced in the following pages (Appendix 3).

Other Source Collections

Although documents from Dubrovnik Archives serve as a base for this work other source collections little known or difficult of access have also been utilized. These include :

T. Smičiklas, *Codex diplomaticus regni Croatiae, Dalmatiae et Slavoniae,* J.A.Z.U. Zagreb (1903–1934). 15 volumes;
F. Miklosić, *Monumenta Serbica Substantia Historium Serbiae, Bosniae, Ragusii,* Vienna (1858);
V. Makuščev, *Monumenta Historica Slavorium Meridionalium,* Warsaw (1874);
S. Ljubić, *Historia o odnošajih između Juznoga Slavenstva i mletačke republike,* J.A.Z.U. Zagreb (1868–1891), 10 volumes;
N. Jorga, *Notes et extraites pour servir a l'histoire des croissades au XVe siècle,* Paris (1899);
A. Theiner, *Vetera Monumenta Slavorum Meridionalium Historium spectantia,* Rome (1863);
Venice Archives (Senato Misti and Senato Secreta);
Zadar Archives (*Ducali e Terminazioni*);
Genoa, Istanbul and Padua Archives.

Various interesting works on Dalmatia have also been written in English:

A. A. Paton, *Highlands and Islands of the Adriatic,* London (1849);
Sir John Gardener Wilkinson, *Dalmatia and Montenegro,* London (1848);
W. F. Wingfield, *A Tour in Dalmatia, Albania and Montenegro with a Historical Sketch of the Republic of Ragusa,* London (1859).

Many of these include a historical survey of Dubrovnik, but the only special history of the town itself in English is by the Italian political historian, Luigi Villari: L. Villari, *The Republic of Ragusa, an Episode of the Turkish Conquest,* London (1904). This book provides a mine of information but deals principally with the internal development, the archaeology and the architecture of the town and does not dwell enough on its international position. Special histories also exist in German and Italian, but these are by no means complete. The best is probably Guiseppe Gelcich's *Dello Sviluppo Civile di Ragusa,* Dubrovnik (1884), but this suffers similar criticism to Villari's work; mention should also be made of J. C. von Engel. *Geschichte des Freystaates Ragusa,* Vienna (1807) for this is useful and fairly accurate, but is more in the nature of a chronicle of events than a real history. The works of local historians and chroniclers, below, although containing some interesting details and picturesque descriptions, traditions, etc. are written without historical accuracy and are inspired by a strong bias which admits no facts unfavourable to Dubrovnik:

G. Resti, *Chronica Ragusina,* South Slavonic Academy, Zagreb (1884);
N. Ragnina, *Annali di Ragusa* and *Annali Anonimi di Ragusa,* South Slavonic Academy, Zagreb (1890);
G. Luccari, *Copioso Histretto degli Annali di Ragusa,* Dubrovnik 1790);
G. Gondola, *Chronica Ragusina,* South Slavonic Academy, Zagreb (1887).

Finally, that of the Tuscan, Rozzi, (S. Rozzi, *La Storia de Raugia,* Lucca, 1588) is more reliable, but by no means wholly to be depended on, and it only brings us down to the end of the sixteenth century.

Conclusion

This brief description of Dubrovnik's archives shows why they serve as a base for this work. The four documentary groups are invaluable for a study of the commerce, and particularly the history of the republic. Due to the difficult physical conditions of the surrounding karstic area, Dubrovnik led a continual struggle against economic hardship in order to create suitable living standards for its citizens.

Combined with this fact is the apparent independent character of the Dubrovnik citizens, who cared little for others, or their politics. This is seen from their self-government over six centuries and the lack of interference in the politics of other states. Nevertheless in the course of this period they succeeded in establishing a most important economic centre not only in the Balkans but for much of the Mediterranean. For this reason all the documentary series in the archives form a rich source for a closer analysis of Dubrovnik and its republic.

Appendix 2. Notes

1. R. S. Lopez and I. W. Raymond, *Medieval Trade in the Mediterranean World*, London (1955), p. 8.
2. J. Tadić, 'Les Archives économiques de Raguse', *Annales, Économiques, Sociétés Civilisations*, Paris (Nov.–Dec. 1961), pp. 1168–1175;
   B. Krekić, *Dubrovnik (Ragusa) et le Levant au Moyen Age*, Paris (1961), pp. 161–165 (Note sur les Archives d'État de Raguse).
3. N. H. Biegman, *The Turco-Ragusan Relationship*, The Hague-Paris (1967), 203 pp.

Appendix 3
Catalogue of the Dubrovnik Archives (after Gelčić)

I. Acta Consiliorum. (Proceedings of the Council)

I. Praecepta Rectoris. (Rectors' Instructions)
(Vol. 15.)

1. Factus tempore Marci Geno comitis Ragusii a. 1279–1280 per manum Thomasini de Savere sacri palatii et com. Ragusii scrib. et notarii, folder 106, 106, scripta. (Cod. Chart.).
2. Tempore Andreac Dauro com. Ragusii a. 1299–1301, folder 170 ser.
3. 1387–1390, folder 356.
4. 1390–1392, folder 191.
5. 1420–1423, folder 281.—Pracceptor. extraord. 1–9.
6. 1420–1426, folder 314 + 9.
7. 1455 folder 133 + 166.
8. 1474, folder 1 − 199 = 1 − 266.
9. 1613–1618, folder 210.
10. 1621–1630, folder 136 + 7, 146, 98.
11. 1630–1652, folder 194, 97, 72 (4–76), 70(20–90) + 7.
12. 1552–1563, folder 87, 93, 92 + 2.
13. 1648–1649, folder 20 (fragm.).
14. 1664–1682, folder 79 + 2, 89, 88.
15. 1682–1762, folder 41, 71, add. et Intentiones 1682–1727, folder 11. (Vide infra 'Acta Rogatorum', Vols. 6, 7, 8, 9, 11, 15, 16).

II. Reformationes. (Reforms)
(Vol. 34.)

(Vols. 1-30 edidit accademia Zagrabriensis, sub titulo Monumenta I-V.)

1. Tempore Marci Danduli comitis Ragusii 1301–1303, folder 95, ser.
2. Tempore Martini Bodoarii comitis Ragusii 1303–1305, folder 53, ser.
3. Tempore Bellecti Fallerii comitis Ragusii 1306, folder 10+1.
4. Tempore Petri Michaelis comitis Ragusii 1311–1312, folder 15.
   Add. 'Litterae pracceptoriae et de bandis praeconicatis' (tempore quo s.), folder 6.

5. Tempore Bartholomei Gradonigi comitis Ragusii 1312–1315, folder 36.
   Add. 'Litterae citatorie et de praeconicationibus' (tempore quo supra), folder 16.
6. Tempore Ugholini Iustiniani comitis Ragusii 1318–1320, folder. 83, per manum Pone can cellarii com. Rag.
7. Tempore Lodoici Mauroceni comitis Ragusii 1322–1324, folder 80.
   Add. 'Lictere pracceptorie et citatorie, et de praeconicationibus' (tempore u.s.), folder 16.
8. Tempore Pauli Trivisani comitis Ragusii 1325–1327, folder 101.
   Add. 'Liber de praeconicationibus et de licteris citatoriis' (tempore u.s.), folder 11.
9. Tempore Baldavni Dalphyni comitis Ragusii 1328–1330, folder 73.
   Add. 'Capitulum de licteris citatoriis et de praeconicationibus' (tempore u.s.), folder 21.
10. Tempore Lodoici Mauroceni comitis Ragusii 1330–1333, folder 123.
    Add. 'Capitulum de citatoriis et de praeconicationibus' (tempore u.s.), folder 27.
11. Tempore Nicolai Falletri comitis Ragusii 1336, folder 23.
    Add. 'Capitulum de praeconicationibus', tempore u.s. ann. 1334–1336, folder 33.
12. Tempore Marci Mauroceni comitis Ragusii 1343–1345, folder 52.
    Add. 'Capitulum literarum citatoriarum', tempose u.s., folder 9.
13. Tempore Leonardi Mocenigi comitis Ragusii 1345–1347, folder 81.
    Add. 'Capitulum bannorum et licterarum citatoriarum' (tempore u.s.), folder 21.
14. Tempore Phylippi Aurio comitis Ragusii 1347–1348, folder 62.
    Add. 'Capitulum et supra', folder 10: Add. 'Capitulum Racionum cuiuslibet measis', folder 2.
15. Tempore Petri Instiniani comitis Rafusii 1348–1360, folder 101.
    Add. 'Capitulum bapnorum et citatoriarum', folder 14.
16. Tempore Marci Superantii comitis Ragusii 1350–1352, folder 72.
    Add. 'Capitulum gridatarum', folder 5; Add. 'Capitulum gridatarum', folder 8.
17. Tempore Marci Superantio comitis Ragusii 1356–1358, folder 1–50.
    Tempore Triumvirorum 1358–1359, folder 50–101.
    Add. 'Capitulum gridatarum et citatoriarum', folder 26.
18. Tempore Rectorum comunis Ragusii 1359–1362, folder 123.
    Add. 'Capitulum gridatarum et citatoriarum', folder 13.
19. Tempore Rectorum comunis Ragusii 1361–1363, folder 148.
20. Tempore Rectorum comunis Ragusii 1363–1364, folder 1–46.
    Add. 'Deseni in Bielen, Breno, Gredec. S. Lazzaro, Concheto', folder 15–60.
    Add. 'Possessiones', folder 93–139.
21. Tempore Rectorum comunis Ragusii 1354, folder 5.
    Add. 'Capitulum citatoriarum' 1362–1364, folder 12.
22. Tempore Rectorum comunis Ragusii 1364–1366, folder 1–16, 33–43, 53–58, 103–104.
    Add. 'Staciones comunis incantatae' a. 1364, folder 28–29.
    Add. 'Capitulum citatoriarum', folder 44–52, 60–102, 105–152.
23. Tempore Rectorum comunis Ragusii 1366–1367, folder 65.
24. Tempore Rectorum comunis Ragusii 1378–1381, folder 252.
25. Tempore Rectorum comunis Ragusii 1382–1384, folder 284.

26. Tempore Rectorum comunis Ragusii 1384–1486, folder 150.
27. Tempore Rectorum comunis Ragusii 1386–1388, folder 135.
28. Tempore Rectorum comunis Ragusii 1388–1390, folder 143.
    Ordene sovra fare de Navilii; de carnibas poreinis; de nanlicamentis, folder 1
    IV De mensuris, ad ev. folder 149.
29. Tempore Rectorum comunis Ragusii 1390–1392, folder 141.
30. Tempore Rectorum comunis Ragusii 1395–1397, folder 154 (folder I
                                                    Rectores).
31. Tempore Rectorum comunis Ragusii 1397–1399, folder 199.
32. Tempore Rectorum comunis Ragusii 1401–1404, folder 222.
33. Tempore Rectorum comunis Ragusii 1407–1411, folder 294.
34. Tempore Rectorum comunis Ragusii 1412–1414, folder 318.

III. Acta Consilii Rogatorum. (Trans. of the Court of Appeal) (Vol. 211.)

1. Annorum 1415–1418, folder 138.
2. Annorum 1418–1420, folder 147.
3. Annorum 1420–1426, folder 301.
4. Annorum 1427–1431, folder 287.
5. Annorum 1431–1435, folder 296.
6. Annorum 1435–1438, folder 244.
   Add. Praecepta ann. 1437–1438, folder 6.
7. Annorum 1438–1441, folder 366.
   Add. Praecepta ann. 1338–1341, folder 16.
8. Annorum 1441–1443, folder 264.
   Add. Praecepta ann. 1441–1443, folder 25.
9. Annorum 1444–1446, folder 261.
   Add. Praecepta ann. 1444–1446, folder 247.
10. Annorum 1446–1448, folder 217.
    Add. Praecepta ann. 1446–1448, folder 30.
11. Annorum 1448–1454, folder 280.
    Add. praecepta ann. 1448 et 1450.
12. Annorum 1451–1452, folder 289.
13. Annorum 1452–1453, folder 269.
14. Annorum 1454–1456, folder 296.
15. Annorum 1468–1556, folder 277.
    Add. Praecepta ann. 1438.
16. Annorum 1450–1461, folder 283.
    Add. Praecepta ann. 1459 et 1461, folder 2.
17. Annorum 1451–1463, folder 299, Index I.
    Add. Salariati del Comun, folder 1.
18. Annorum 1463–1466, folder 285.
19. Annorum 1466–1457, folder 297.
20. Annorum 1468–1470, folder 298, Index I.
21. Annorum 1470–1472, folder 281, Index I.
22. Annorum 1473–1476, folder 27–312.
23. Annorum 1476–1478, folder 291.
24. Annorum 1481–1485, folder 289.
    Add. Denunciaciones 1481–1482, folder 2.

25. Annorum 1485–1488, folder 289, Index I.
26. Annorum 1489–1492, folder 296, Index I.
    Add. Process. de argento 1489.
27. Annorum 1492–1496, folder 298, Index I, II.
28. Annorum 1497–1501, folder 8–291.
29. Annorum 1501–1504, folder 293, Index I–III.
30. Annorum 1504–1508, folder 298, Index I–IV.
31. Annorum 1508–1514, folder 296, Index I–III.
32. Annorum 1511–1513, folder 297, Index I–III.
33. Annorum 1513–1516, folder 297, Index I–II.
34. Annorum 1516–1518, folder 22–296, Index I.
35. Annorum 1518–1520, folder 306, Index I–II.
    Add. Per la via alli maestri delli coppi a Cupari, 307–408.
36. Annorum 1521–1522, folder 288, Index I–II.
37. Annorum 1523–1525, folder 294, Index I–IV.
38. Annorum 1525–1527, folder 9–292.
39. Annorum 1527–1529, folder 288.
    Add. Supplicatio pro rebus obtinendis a Sede Apostolica circa congreg.
    Melitensem f.1.—Providimentum salinarum Stagni.
40. Annorum 1530–1531, folder 266, Index I–VI.
41. Annorum 1531–1534, folder 286.
42. Annorum 1534–1536, folder 282, Index I–VI.
43. Annorum 1536–1538, folder 257.
            Index alfab. 19, gon. I–IV.
44. Annorum 1538–1540 folder 2–326.
            Index gen. I–III.
45. Annorum 1540–1542, folder 15–277, Index I–VII.
46. Annorum 1542–1544, folder 272, Index II.
47. Annorum 1544–1546, folder 269, Index I.
48. Annorum 1547–1549, folder 272, Index VIII.
49. Annorum 1549–1550, folder 269, Index X.
50. Annorum 1551–1552, folder 203, Index X.
51. Annorum 1552–1553, folder 269, Index XI.
52. Annorum 1553–1550, folder 262, Index XII.
53. Annorum 1555–1557, folder 2–331, Index XII.
54. Annorum 1557–1559, folder 2–301, Index XIII.
55. Annorum 1559–1564, folder 284, Index XIV.
56. Annorum 1563–1564, folder 288, Index XV.
57. Annorum 1563–1566, folder 268, Index XXL.
58. Annorum 1566–1568, folder 269, Index XXII.
59. Annorum 1568–1570, folder 251, Index XXII.
60. Annorum 1570–1572, folder 248, Index III.
61. Annorum 1572, folder 180, Index XVI.
62. Annorum 1573–1575, folder 362, Index XXVI.
63. Annorum 1575–1576, folder 287, Index
64. Annorum 1577–1578, folder 295, Index XXVII.
65. Annorum 1579–1580, folder 272, Index XXII.
66. Annorum 1581–1582, folder 245, Index XXIII.
67. Annorum 1582–1583, folder 249, Index XII.
68. Annorum 1584–1586, folder 338, Index XII.

69. Annorum 1586–1588, folder 356. Index
70. Annorum 1589–1590, folder 314, Index VIII.
71. Annorum 1591–1592, folder 224. Index
72. Annorum 1592–1593, folder 281. Index
73. Annorum 1593–1594, folder 262. Index
74. Annorum 1595–1596, folder 282. Index
75. Annorum 1596–1598, folder 246. Index
76. Annorum 1598–1599, folder 267. Index
77. Annorum 1600–1601, folder 273. Index
78. Annorum 1602–1603, folder 146, Signatum.
79. Annorum 1603–1605, folder 212, Index XXXI.
80. Annorum 1605–1606, folder 274, Index XXIV.
81. Annorum 1697–1698, folder, 250, Index XXIV.
82. Annorum 1609–1611, folder 302, Index XXIV.
83. Annorum 1611–1613, folder 253, Index XXIV.
84. Annorum 1613–1615, folder 258, Index XXIV.
85. Annorum 1615–1617, folder 259, Index XXII.
86. Annorum 1617–1619, folder 257, Index XXII.
87. Annorum 1619–1621, folder 254, Index XXII.
88. Annorum 1622–1624, folder 266, Index XXII.
89. Annorum 1624–1626, folder 265, Index XXII.
90. Annorum 1626–1628, folder 257, Index XXII.
91. Annorum 1628–1629, folder 167, Index XXII.
92. Annorum 1629–1631, folder 269, Index XXII.
93. Annorum 1631–1633, folder 255, Index XXII.
94. Annorum 1634–1636, folder 252, Index V.
95. Annorum 1636–1638, folder 239, Index XXII.
96. Annorum 1639–1640, folder 249, Index XLIII, Alph.
97. Annorum 1640–1643, folder 216, Index LVIII, Alph.
98. Annorum 1643–1645, folder 229. Index XXII. Alph incompl.
99. Annorum 1645–1646, folder 221. Index XXIV, Alph incomph.
100. Annorum 1646–1648, folder 210, Index XX, Alph. incomph.
101. Annorum 1648–1650, folder 217, Index XXII, Alph. incompl.
102. Annorum 1649–1651, folder 215, Index XXII, Alph. incompl.
103. Annorum 1652–1654, folder, 226, Index, XXII, Alph. incompl.
104. Annorum 1652–1653, folder 205, Index XXII, Alph. incompl.
105. Annorum 1653–1654, folder 225.
106. Annorum 1655–1656, folder 222.
107. Annorum 1656–1657, folder 240.
108. Annorum 1657–1658, folder 219.
109. Annorum 1658–1660, folder 275.
110. Annorum, 1660–1662, folder 273.
111. Annorum 1662–1663, folder 234.
112. Annorum, 1663–1665, folder 206.
113. Annorum 1665–1666, folder 216.
114. Annorum 1666–1667, folder 174.
115. Annorum Libro delli providimenti et terminazioni 1667, 11–28 Aprilis folder 8.
116. Annorum 1668–1669, folder 213.
117. Annorum 1669–1670, folder 219.

118. Annorum 1670–1671, folder 208.
119. Annorum 1671–1672, folder 197.
120. Annorum 1673–1674, folder 242.
121. Annorum 1674–1675, folder 240.
122. Annorum 1675–1677, folder 260, Index —
123. Annorum 1677–1679, folder 245, Index —
124. Annorum 1679–1680, folder 226, Index —
125. Annorum 1681–1682, folder 305, Index —
126. Annorum 1683–1684, folder 258, Index —
127. Annorum 1684–1685, folder 309, Index —
128. Annorum 1686–1687, folder 250, Index —
129. Annorum 1687–1688, folder 314, Index —
130. Annorum 1689–1690, folder 239, Index —
131. Annorum 1590–1692, folder 264, Index —
132. Annorum 1692–1693, folder 253, Index —
133. Annorum 1693–1694, folder 218, Index —
134. Annorum 1695–1696, folder 228, Index —
135. Annorum 1696–1698, folder 259, Index —
136. Annorum 1698–1700, folder 256, Index —
137. Annorum 1700–1702, folder 255, Index —
138. Annorum 1702–1704, folder 243, Index —
139. Annorum 1704–1705, folder 232, Index —
140. Annorum 1706–1707, folder 226, Index —
141. Annorum 1707–1709, folder 252, Index —
142. Annorum 1709–1710, folder 260, Index —
143. Annorum 1710–1712, folder 225, Index —
144. Annorum 1712–1713, folder 226, Index —
145. Annorum 1713–1715, folder 217, Index —
146. Annorum 1715–1716, folder 207, Index —
147. Annorum 1716–1717, folder 223, Index —
148. Annorum 1717–1718, folder 205, Index —
149. Annorum 1719–1720, folder 223, Index —
150. Annorum 1720–1722, folder 214, Index —
151. Annorum 1722–1724, folder 230, Index —
152. Annorum 1724–1726, folder 232, Index —
153. Annorum 1725–1728, folder 231, Index —
154. Annorum 1728–1730, folder 244, Index —
155. Annorum 1730–1732, folder 228, Index —
156. Annorum 1732–1735, folder 244, Index —
157. Annorum 1735–1737, folder 229, Index —
158. Annorum 1737–1739, folder 229, Index —
159. Annorum 1739–1741, folder 233, Index —
160. Annorum 1711–1743, folder 228, Index —
161. Annorum 1743–1744, folder 227, Index —
162. Annorum 1745–1746, folder 219, Index —
163. Annorum 1746–1748, folder 224, Index —
164. Annorum 1748–1750, folder 224, Index —
165. Annorum 1750–1751, folder 232, Index —
166. Annorum 1751–1752, folder 227, Index —
167. Annorum 1752–1754, folder 221, Index —

169. Annorum 1755–1756, folder 226, Index —
170. Annorum 1756–1758, folder 223, Index —
171. Annorum 1758–1759, folder 222, Index —
    Add. Suppliche: Pesca del Corallo 1758.
        Suppliche: Ampliamento parrocchiale di
        Slano 1758.
172. Annorum 1759–1760, folder 246, Index —
173. Annorum 1760–1762, folder 221, Index —
174. Annorum 1762–1763, folder 219, Index —
175. Annorum 1763–1764, folder 228, Index —
176. Annorum 1764–1765, folder 234, Index —
177. Annorum 1765–1766, folder 229, Index —
178. Annorum 1766–1762, folder 239, Index —
179. Annorum 1768–1769, folder 225, Index —
180. Annorum 1769–1771, folder 221, Index —
181. Annorum 1771–1772, folder 226, Index —
182. Annorum 1772–1773, folder 226, Index —
183. Annorum 1774, folder 80, Index —
184. Annorum 1775, folder 224, Index —
185. Annorum 1775–1776, folder 233, Index —
186. Annorum 1777, folder 160, Index —
187. Annorum 1778–1779, folder 217, Index —
188. Annorum 1779–1780, folder 227, Index —
189. Annorum 1780–1781, folder 252, Index —
190. Annorum 1782, folder 294, Index —
191. Annorum 1783, folder 205, Index —
192. Annorum 1784, folder 227, Index —
193. Annorum 1784–1786, folder 223, Index —
194. Annorum 1786–1787, folder 224, Index —
195. Annorum 1787–1788, folder 230, Index —
196. Annorum 1788–1789, folder 203, Index —
197. Annorum 1790, folder 174, Index —
198. Annorum 1791, folder 230, Index —
199. Annorum 1792–1793, folder 236, Index —
200. Annorum 1793, folder 178, Index —
201. Annorum 1794, folder 143, Index —
202. Annorum 1795, folder 66, Index —
203. Annorum 1796, folder 181, Index —
204. Annorum 1797, folder 173, Index —
205. Annorum 1798–1799, folder 233, Index —
206. Annorum 1799, folder 107, Index —
207. Annorum 1800, folder 186, Index —
208. Annorum 1801–1802, folder 233, Index —
209. Annorum 1802–1803, folder 76, Index —
210. Annorum 1801–1898, Quad, 17, Index —
211. Repertorium Alph. 1603–1808, folder 37.
    Additur: Ex lib. Rog. 1762–1763, soprr.
    le elezioni.
    Additur: Ex lib. Rog. 1791. sopra le elezioni.

IV. Secreta Rogatorum. (Confidential Appeals) (Vol. 7.)

1. Annorum 1497–1537, fragm., folder 13.
   Add. Lettere e Commissioni 1498–1550.
2. Annorum 1555–1569, folder 182.
   Add. Giuramento dei Cap. marittimi nella guerra del 1569, folder 1.
   Add. Lettere e Comm. 1559–1563, folder 5.
3. Annorum 1604–1605, fragm., folder 13.
4. Annorum 1624–1658, folder 284.
   Add. Banni 1624–1636, folder 9.
5. Annorum 1659–1698, fragm., folder 62.
6. Annorum 1421–1495, Excerpta, folder 11.
7. Annorum Diverse Commission, 1777–1787, folder 20.

V. Acta Minoris Consilii. (Trans. of the Small Council) (Vol. 117.)

1. Annorum 1418–1445, folder 211.
2. Annorum 1418–1422, folder 259.
3. Annorum 1422–1426, folder 299.
4. Annorum 1426–1429, folder 284.
5. Annorum 1430–1432, folder 229.
6. Annorum 1432–1435, folder 296.
7. Annorum 1435–1438, folder 266.
   Add. Praecepta 1436–1438, folder 7.
8. Annorum 1438–1441, folder 264.
   Add. Praecepta 1438–1444, folder 9.
9. Annorum 1441–1443, folder 221.
   Add. Praecepta 1441–1443, folder 22.
10. Annorum 1444–1446, folder 247.
    Add. Praecepta 1444–1446, folder 17.
11. Annorum 1446–1448, folder 233.
    Add. Praecepta 1446, folder 12.
12. Annorum 1351–1448, folder 260.
    Add. Praecepta 1448, folder 26.
13. Annorum 1451–1455, folder 262.
    Add. Praecepta 1451, folder 22.
14. Annorum 1455–1459, folder 268.
    Add. Praecepta 1455–1459, folder 23.
15. Annorum. 1459–1462, folder 246. And. Alph.
    Add. Praecepta 1459–1462, folder 24.
16. Annorum 1462–1466, folder 258.
17. Annorum 1466–1469, folder 274.
    Add. Praecepta 1466–1469, folder 274.
18. Annorum 1470–1472, folder 267.
    Add. Praecepta 1470–1472, folder 11.
    Add. div. cedule alligate, folder 18.

19. Annorum 1473–1475, folder 277.
    Add. Praecepta 1473–1475, folder 48.
20. Annorum 1475–1478, folder 292.
    Add. Praecepta 1475–1478, folder 11.
21. Annorum 1478–1481, folder 11.
    Add. Praecepta 1478–1481, folder 11.
22. Annorum 1482–1486, folder 294.
    Add. Praecepta 1482–1486, folder 5.
23. Annorum 1486–1490, folder 276.
    Add. Matricula Beretariourm 1487, folder 3.
    Add. Praecepta 1488, folder 4–5.
    Add. Lettere di cambio Giac. Doni di Fi renze e relative gestioni, folder 6-12.
    Add. Praecepta 1489–1490, folder 13–14.
24. Annorum 1490–1493, folder 297.
25. Annorum 1493–1496, folder 295.
26. Annorum 1497–1500, folder 300.
    Add. Capitoli dei Tintior, folders 291–293.
27. Annorum 1500–1503, folder 293.
28. Annorum 1503–1506, folder 303.
29. Annorum 1506–1508, folder 312.
30. Annorum 1508–1511, folder 297.
31. Annorum 1511–1514, folder 297.
32. Annorum 1514–1517, folder 291.
33. Annorum 1517–1520, folder 291.
    Add. Citationi et praecepta 1518–1520, folder 5.
34. Annorum 1520–1524, folder 294.
35. Annorum 1524–1528, folder 289.
    Add. Examina 1526–1528, folder 4.
36. Annorum 1528–1532, folder 296.
37. Annorum 1532–1536, folder 293.
38. Annorum 1536–1540, folder 327.
    Add. Acceptat. et Extracciones 1537, folder 14.
39. Annorum 1540–1543, folder 273.
    Add. Accept. et Extracciones 1540, folder 15.
40. Annorum 1543–1547, folder 270.
    Add. Accept. et Extr. 1543–1547, folder 12.
41. Annorum 1547–1550, folder 293.
    Add. Accept. et Extr. 1547–1550, folder 6.
42. Annorum 1550–1552, folder 292,
    Add. Accept. et Extr. 1550–1652, folder 5.
43. Annorum 1553–1555, folder 283.
    Add. Accept. et Extr. 1553–1555, folder 7.
44. Annorum 1555–1557, folder 275.
    Add. Accept. et Extr. 1555–1557, folder 7.
45. Annorum 1557–1560, folder 269.
    Add. Accept. et Extr. 1556–1560, folder 4.
46. Annorum 1560–1563, folder 266.
    Add. Matrieula Confraternitatis S. Mariae de Pachlina de Iupana, folder 20.
47. Annorum 1563–1565, folder 273.
    Add. Fedi, folder 2.

48. Annorum 1666–1668, folder 285.
    Add. Fedi, folder 6.
49. Annorum 1568–1570, folder 270.
    Add. Vlegi, folder 11.
    Add. Matrieula Contraternitatis Juppane de Lueea, folder 3.
50. Annorum 1570–1572, folder 185.
    Add. Fedi, folder 1.
51. Annorum 1572–1573, folder 231.
52. Annorum 1573–1575, folder 321.
    Add. Cap. Fraternitatis Aurifieum, folder 2.
    Add. Cap. Citationes, folder 2.
53. Annorum 1575–1577, folder 210.
    Add. Fedi. X, folder 2.
54. Annorum 1577–1579, folder 223.
55. Annorum 1580–1581, folder 270.
56. Annorum 1582–1583, folder 233.
57. Annorum 1583–1585, folder 250.
58. Annorum 1585–1586, folder 273.
59. Annorum 1587–1588, folder 201.
60. Annorum 1589–1590, folder 315.
61. Annorum 1591–1592, folder 275.
62. Annorum 1592–1594, folder 271.
63. Annorum 1594–1596, folder 275.
64. Annorum 1596–1598, folder 260.
65. Annorum 1599–1601, folder 272.
66. Annorum 1602–1604, folder 290.
67. Annorum 1605–1606, folder (46–258) 212.
68. Annorum 1607–1609, folder 276.
69. Annorum 1610–1612, folder 316.
70. Annorum 1612–1614, nee non 1615–1618.
71. Annorum 1618–1621, folder 279.
72. Annorum 1622–1624, folder 266.
73. Annorum 1625–1628, folder 282.
74. Annorum 1628–1631, folder 291.
75. Annorum 1632–1635, folder 288.
76. Annorum 1635–1639, folder 272.
77. Annorum 1630–1644, folder 278.
78. Annorum 1644–1648, folder 273.
79. Annorum 1648–1652, folder 277.
80. Annorum 1656–1659, folder 270.
81. Annorum 1656–1658, folder 270.
82. Annorum 1664–1667, folder 259.
83. Annorum 1668–1671, folder 221.
    Gabella vini lieitata pro 1671 folder 1.
84. Annorum 1672–1676, folder 217.
85. Annorum 1677–1685, folder 279.
86. Annorum 1686–1603, folder 259.
87. Annorum 1694–1700, folder 245.
88. Annorum 1701–1708, folder 265.
89. Annorum 1708–1714, folder 279.

90. Annorum 1710–1721, folder 267.
91. Annorum 1721–1726, folder 272.
92. Annorum 1726–1732, folder 274.
93. Annorum 1732–1737, folder 271.
94. Annorum 1737–1741, folder 289.
95. Annorum 1741–1745, folder 276.
96. Annorum 1716–1719, folder 290.
97. Annorum 1750–1751, folder 278.
98. Annorum 1754–1758, folder 324.
99. Annorum 1758–1761, folder 275.
100. Annorum 1761–1765, folder 275.
101. Annorum 1765–1768, folder 279.
102. Annorum 1768–1771, folder 211.
103. Annorum 1771–1774, folder 270.
104. Annorum 1774–1777, folder 228.
105. Annorum 1777–1780, folder 279.
106. Annorum 1780–1741, folder 271.
107. Annorum 1784–1786, folder 274.
108. Annorum 1787–1789, folder 286.
109. Annorum 1790–1792, folder 277.
110. Annorum 1792–1795, folder 268.
111. Annorum 1795–1797, folder 275.
112. Annorum 1797–1800, folder 278.
113. Annorum 1800–1802, folder 374.
114. Annorum 1802–1805, folder 294.
115. Annorum 1805–1808, 28/8, folder 266.
116. Index partium Minoris Consilii ab. a 1783 (d.2. Junii) ad a 1790.
117. Recordanze dei Signori dell' Eccmo Minor
    Consiglio dell 'anno 1608 a quelli dell anno 1609, et seq asque ad a 1685–1686,
    folder 66.

VI. Detta. (Decrees.)
(Vol. 92.)

1. Annorum 1543–1549, folder 201.
    Add. Spese de'astori 1543–1549, folder 7.
2. Annorum 1459, folder 16.
3. Annorum 1575–1576, folder 42.
4. Annorum 1575–1580, folder 406.
5. Annorum 1577, folder 36.
6. Annorum 1583, folder 4.
7. Annorum 1583, folder 4.
8. Annorum 1589, folder 45.
9. Annorum 1618–1622, folder 47.
10. Annorum 1688–1621, folder 20/17.
11. Annorum 1623–1628, folder 16.
12. Annorum 1630–1640, folder 259/7.
    Add. Spese falconi 1640–1651.
13. Annorum 1653–1665, folder 169/7.
    Add. Spese falconi 1652–1665.

14. Annorum 1657–1660, folder 122/9.
    Add. Spese astori 1658–1659.
15. Annorum 1661–1667, folder 93/7.
    Add. Spese falconi 1660–1666.
16. Annorum 1670–1657, folder 152/7.
    Add. Spese falconi 1670–1674.
17. Annorum 1676–1679, folder 86/6.
    Add. Spese diverse 1676–1678.
18. Annorum 1680–1682, folder 80/5.
    Add. Spese falconi 1680–1682.
19. Annorum 1684–1688, folder 118/7.
    Add. Spese falconi 1684–1688.
20. Annorum 1689–1696, folder 181/7/14.
    Add. Spese falconi 1680–1696.
    Add. Spese Corrieri 1616.
21. Annorum 1696, folder 76.
22. Annorum 1697–1704, folder 168/6.
    Add. Spese falconi 1697–1704.
23. Annorum 1669, folder 14.
24. Annorum 1705–1712, folder 153/7.
    Add. Spese falconi 1705–1712.
25. Annorum 1713–1717, folder 114.
26. Annorum 1718, folder 20/1.
    Add. Spese falconi 1718.
27. Annorum 1719, folder 20/1.
    Add. Spese falconi 1719.
28. Annorum 1721, folder 19.
29. Annorum 1722, folder 16/1
30. Annorum 1723, folder 21/1.
    Add. Spese falconi 1723.
31. Annorum 1724, folder 18.
32. Annorum 1725, folder 19/1.
    Add. Spese falconi 1725.
33. Annorum 1726, folder 21/1.
    Add. Spese falconi 1726.
34. Annorum 1726, folder 26/1.
    Add. Spese falconi 1727.
35. Annorum 1728, folder 18/1.
    Add. Spese falconi 1728.
36. Annorum 1729, folder 21/1.
    Add. Spese falconi 1729.
37. Annorum 1730, folder 20/1.
    Add. Spese falconi 1730.
38. Annorum 1731, folder 25/1.
    Add. Spese falconi 1734.
39. Annorum 1732, folder 19/1.
    Add. Spese falconi 1732.
40. Annorum 1733, folder 18/1.
    Add. Spese falconi 1733.

41. Annorum 1734, folder 24/2.
    Add. Spese falconi 1734.
42. Annorum 1735, folder 20/1.
    Add. Spese falconi 1735.
43. Annorum 1736, folder 23/1.
    Add. Spese falconi 1736.
44. Annorum 1737, folder 23/1.
    Add. Spese falconi 1737.
45. Annorum 1738, folder 35/1.
    Add. Spese falconi 1738.
46. Annorum 1739, folder 25/1.
    Add. Spese falconi 1739.
47. Annorum 1740, folder 31/1.
    Add. Spese falconi 1740.
48. Annorum 1741, folder 30/1.
    Add. Spese falconi 1741.
49. Annorum 1742, folder 31/2.
    Add. Spese falconi 1742.
50. Annorum 1743, folder 26/2.
    Add. Spese falconi 1743.
51. Annorum 1744, folder 20/2.
    Add. Spese falconi 1744.
52. Annorum 1745–1746, folder 28/3.
    Add. Spese falconi 1745.
53. Annorum 1746, folder 21/3.
    Add. Spese falconi 1746.
54. Annorum 1747, folder 20/4.
    Add. Spese astori 1747.
55. Annorum 1748, folder 31/3.
    Add. Spese astori 1748.
56. Annorum 1749, folder 27/2.
    Add. Spese falconi ed astori 1749.
57. Annorum 1745–1788, folder 282.
58. Annorum 1750, folder 28.
    Add. Spese falconi ed astori 1750.
59. Annorum 1751, folder 26.
    Add. Spese falconi ed astori 1751.
60. Annorum 1752, folder 28/8.
    Add. Spese falconi ed astori 1752.
61. Annorum 1752–1776, folder 283.
62. Annorum 1753, folder 26/2.
    Add. Spese falconi ed astori 1753.
63. Annorum 1754, folder 28.
64. Annorum 1765, folder 30.
65. Annorum 1736, folder 25.
66. Annorum 1757, folder 25.
67. Annorum 1760, folder 28.
68. Annorum 1761, folder 38.
69. Annorum 1763, folder 35.

70. Annorum 1765, folder 44.
71. Annorum 1766, folder 40.
72. Annorum 1767, folder 36.
73. Annorum 1768, folder 46.
74. Annorum 1769, folder 45.
75. Annorum 1776, folder 45.
76. Annorum 1771, folder 17.
77. Annorum 1773, folder 15.
78. Annorum 1774, folder 19.
79. Annorum 1776, folder 17.
80. Annorum 1777, folder 50.
81. Annorum 1779, folder 53.
82. Annorum 1782, folder 39/2.
   Add. Spese falconi ed astori 1782.
83. Annorum 1788–1793, folder 247.
84. Annorum 1783–1787, folder 228.
85. Annorum 1757, folder 50.
86. Annorum 1777–1800, folder 281.
87. Annorum 1793–1799, folder 252.
88. Annorum 1785–1807, folder 6.
89. Annorum 1800–1801, folder 252.
90. Annorum 1801, folder 130.
91. Annorum 1808, folder 1.
92. Annorum 1808, folder 1.

VII. Fabbriche. (Manufactures) (Vol. 143.)

1. Lo primo actobre 1519 presentato per officiali de far condur acqua chiamada Chnesica in lo canal de la fontana, folder 41/1.
2. Lavorieri del Comun 1564, folder 13.
3. Lavorieri del Comun 1562, folder 26.
4. La via di salixe de la citta 1557, folders 2, 64/8.
5. Reverino a le Ploce 1574, folder 58/3.
6. Lavorieri del Comun 1576, folder 21.
7. Lavorieri del Comun 1577, folder 31.
8. Officiali della fabricha de la Mencetta 1577, folder 21/13.
   Sala del Conseglio 1563, folder 2.
9. Casse 1663, folder 8
10. Lavori del Comun 1587, folder 27.
11. Lavori del Comun 1388–1389, folders 25, 8.
12. Lavori del Comun 1590, folder 12/3.
13. Lavori del Comun 1590, folder 15/8.
14. Fabticha dela Chiesa noua de Santo Giorgio a le Pille. Anno 1590, folder 24.
15. Lauoreri del Comun 1592, folder 22.
16. Lauoreri del Comun 1598, folder 7.
17. Repizio 1592, folder 7.
18. Spese per restaurare li molini de Tarsteno 1594, folder 8.
19. Fabricha di Santa Maria di Castello 1598, folder 11.

20. Lavorieri de Comun 1699, folder 16.
21. Spese molini di Breno 1597, folder 14.
22. Lavorieri de Comune 1600 folder 12.
23. Fabrica del muro al bersaglio della Pile 1600, folder 9.
24. L'acquedotto 1601, folder 10.
25. Lavoreri de Comune, 1602, folder 20/2.
26. Repizio e altre spese 1602, folder 22.
27. Fabrica de Castello de S. Lorenzo 1603, folder 11.
28. Lavorieri de Comun 1603, folder 9, 4/19.
29. Fabricha di Sta Clara 1602, folder 5.
30. Fabricha di Sta Pietro 1601, folder 1.
31. Lavorieri del comune 1691, folder 13/2.
32. Spese di Dacsa 1603, folder 7.
33. Lanori del Comun 1606, folder 7/2.
34. Fabrica di Sto Biagio di Grauosa 1606, folder 13.
35. Fabrica delle casse 1606, folder 5.
36. Spese ordinarie 1608, folder 19, 1, 1.
37. Fabrica de Fossato 1608, folder 9/1.
38. Lavorieri 1611, folder 3/1.
39. Spese ordinarie 1614, folder 21, 3, 3.
40. Restaurazione del monastero di S. Francesco 1614, folder 3.
41. Fabrica de le casse del Porto 1618, folder 2.
42. Lavorieri del Comune 1618, folder 5.
43. Fabricha alla Ponta 1616, folder 2.
44. Repizio 1618, folder 5.
45. Fabricha di Stagno 1617, folder 4.
46. Lavorieri di Comon 1617, folder 10, 1.
47. Fabrica del Monastero di Sta Maria 1620.
48. Ripeza la Saplunaria 1618, folder 0/4.
49. Lavorieri del Comun 1618, folder 7.
50. Palazzo d'areivescono 1602, folder 9.
51. Lavorieri de Comone 1620, folder 4.
52. Fabrica della Carnasaria 1620, folder 13.
53. Fabricha delle palate di beccaria 1620, folder 12.
54. Fabricha e molini d'Ombola 1620, folder 1.
55. Spese ordinarie 1620, folders 4, 19, 2, 4.
56. Condotti di Castello Sto Giovanni 1621, folder 3.
57. Spese di Stagno Grande 1621, folder 22.
    Spese di Providitori 1621, folder 5/1.
    Spese di sale 1621, folder 7.
    Mandata a Narente 1621, folder 11/2.
58. Monastero di Sto Simeone 1622, folder 2.
59. Lavorieri del Comone 1623, folder 5.
60. Lavorieri del Comone 1621, folder 8.
61. Spese di Purchi 1624, folder 37/22.
62. Ripezare li molini 1625, folder 1.
63. Lavorieri 1625, folder 13.
64. Lavorieri del Comune 1623, folder 1.
65. Fabrica di Saneto Petrilaurenti 1631, folder 3.
66. Fabrica di Muraglia e Fossato alle Pille 1625, folder 7, 4/3.

67. Fabrica dell 'aquedotto 1625, folder 26.
68. Lavorieri del Comon 1626, folder 10.
69. Monasterio di S. Francesco di Ragosa 1626, folder 4.
70. Fabrica del Lazaretto 1627, folder 90.
71. Lavorieri del Comone 1627, folder 6.1.
72. Lavorieri del Comone 1629, folder 19/1.
73. Fabrieha di Sto Clara 1629, folder 2.
74. Lavori eell'aquidotto 1629, folder 32.
75. Lavorieri del Cooon 1630, folder 6.
76. Spese delle saline 1630, folder 3.
77. Molini d'Ombla 1631, folder 1.
78. Lavorieri di Comone 1631, folder 12.
79. Lavorieri di Comone 1633, folder 5.
80. Polize dello aquedotto 1631, folder 23.
81. Condotti di Postierna 1634, folder 3.
82. Lavorieri del Comone 1634, folder 1.
83. Fabrica di molinimd'Ombla 1636, folder 6.
84. Fabrica di Herzegonina 1636, folder 21.
85. Lavorieri di Com, 1637, folder 3.
86. Lavorieri del Comone 1638, folder 6.
87. Lavorieri del Coman 1638, folder 16.
88. Monastero di Sto Biagio di Canal, 1638, folder 3.
89. Monastero di Sto Francesco di Ragnsa 1539, folder 5.
90. Spese del Asacho 1639, folder 3, 8, 3.
91. Lauorieri del Comone 1639, folder 3.
92. Sto Francesco di Stagno 1640, folder 3.
93. Polize di Aquedotto 1610, folder 12.
94. Lauori del Comono 1611, folder 1.
95. Monasterio Sto Chiara 1642, folder 11.
96. Fabrica di Santo Andrea 1611, folder 9.
97. Fabrica delle easse 1620, folder 11.
98. Fabrica di S. Biagio in Gravosa 1645, folder 3.
99. Fabrica del campanile dell' orologio 1645, folder 6.
100. Spese della Munitione et Fonditoria 1646, folders 16, 34.
101. Fabriche in accomodare il totto di San Francesco in Ragusa 1646, folder 1.
102. Infermeria di Sto Chiara 1648, folder 2.
103. Fabrica della eisterna del monastero delle monache di S. Andrea 1619, folder 1.
104. Spese nella infirmaria del Monastero di Sto Chiara 1651, folder 7.
105. Fabrica del convento di Sta Maria 1659, folder 1.
106. Fabrica del coavento di Sto francesco di Ragusa 1652, folder 3.
107. Debito 1653, folder 3/4.
108. Fabrica di Becharia 1655, folder 2.
109. Fabrica del connento di S. Biagio di conali 1655, folder 3.
110. Fabrica di casa in piazza 1658, folder 9.
111. Spese nell'accomodare il monasterio di santa Chiara 1661, folder 4.
112. Repezo delle casse del Comone 1662, folder 5.
113. Spese nel accomodare pla difetti e mancamenti nel conuento di Daxa 1664, folder 2.
114. Nel ristaurar le chiese in Canali 1658, folder 1.

115. Per nettare la citta delle rovine 1667, folder 6.
116. Fabrica delle mura della citta, e d'altro 1667, folder 3.
117. Fabrica di San Biagio 1667, folder 31.
118. Acconci 1667, folder 4.
119. Spese del companile d'orologio 1663, folder 12.
120. Seconda case del publico 1670, folder 34.
121. Fabbrica del castello di S. Giovanni detto Molo 1675, folder 4.
122. La caleina 1671, folder 6.
123. Spese di acquedotto 1676, folder 10.
124. Fabbrica del palazzo publico 1686, folder 67.
125. Pollize di casa nuova di S. Chiara 1696, folder 3.
126. Spese d'aquedotto 1680, folder 4.
127. Per la Fabbrica della slaniza di Commercio 1675, folder 16.
128. Fabbrica di casa nuova a sciroca ulizza delli signori cinque di ragioni 1678, folder 12.
129. Fabbrica della casa delli signori cinque legioni, posta a strada larga in piazza 1671, folder 7/3.
130. Spese di calcina 1670, folder 12, 1/10.
131. Fabbrica della casa in piazza apresso il Ghetto 1687, folder 20.
132. Spese fatte nel periezionare la casa avanti S. Francesco, doue habita il sig. Residente 1637, folder 1.
133. Fabbrica della chiesa di S. Clemente 1697, folder 5.
134. Fabbrica delle case in piazza grande 1719, folder 11.
135. Spese dell' Acquidotto 1755, folder 3.
136. Spese nella fabbrica del Dome 1706, folder 6.
137. Fabbrica di arsenale 1721, folder 31.
138. Fabbrica di Sta Cattarina 1733, folder 1.
139. Spese per la barca nanfragata 1718, folder 5/1.
140. Spese di molini 1773, folder 1.
141. Polize di riparare le mura 1751, folder 3.
142. Spese d'acquidotto 1799, folder 2.
143. Spese che occorrono nella fabbrica di due camere in monasterio di Stc Maria 1785, folder 5.

VIII. Acta Consilii Maioris. (Trans. of the Great Council) (Vol. 67.)

1. Annorum 1416–1419, folder 194.
   Add. Rubriche, folder 1.
   Add. Rectores 1415–1419, folder 1.
2. Annorum 1419–1423, folder 144.
   Add. Rectores 1419–1423, folder 1.
3. Annorum 1423–1428, folder 234.
4. Annorum 1428–1433, folder 310.
   Add. Rectores 1428–1433, folder 1.
5. Annorum 1434–1435, folder 230.
   Add. Regimen et officinalis 1437, folder 4.
6. Annorum 1440–1442, folder 174, fragm.
7. Annorum 1442–1445, folder 276.
   Add. Rubriche, folder 1.

Y*

8. Annorum 1445, folder 15, fragm.
9. Annorum 1449–1453, folder 218.
10. Annorum 1453–1456, folder 247.
11. Annorum 1457–1460, folder 206.
    Add. Rubr. Alfab.
12. Annorum 1460–1466, folder 242.
    Add. Firme, folder 40.
13. Annorum 1473–1477, deest.
14. Annorum 1477–1483, folder 258.
    Add. Firme, folder 41.
    Annorum—deest.
15. Annorum 1485–1491, folders 40–291.
    (1484 deest de h. v.
    Add. Firme 1484–1491, folder 27.
16. Annorum 1491–1498, folder 271.
    Add. Firme 1491, folder 25.
17. Add. Firme 1498–1506, folder 270.
    Add. Firme 1502, folder 25.
18. Annorum 1506–1513, folders 17, 37–272.
19. Annorum 1513–1522, folder 279.
    Add. Firme 1513–1522, folder 18.
20. Annorum 1522–1534, folder 286.
    Add. Firme 1522–1523, folder 10.
21. Annorum 1534–1542, folder 315.
    Add. Firme 1536–1544, folder 2.
22. Annorum 1543–1551, folder 279.
    Add. Firme 1545–1550, folder 2.
23. Annorum 1551–1559, folder 277.
24. Annorum 1559–1570, folder 288.
25. Annorum, 1570–1576, folder 233.
26. Annorum 1577–1581, folder 226.
27. Annorum 1582–1586, folder 269.
28. Annorum 1577–1591, folder 407.
29. Annorum 1592–1598, folder 344 (f.1–20 des.)
30. Annorum 1599–1604, folder 305.
31. Annorum 1595–1610, folder 280.
32. Annorum 1610–1615, folder 287 (f.1–2 des.)
34. Annorum 1621–1626, folder 294.
35. Annorum 1626–1633, folder 284.
36. Annorum 1633–1637, folder 271.
37. Annorum 1637–1642, folder 284.
38. Annorum 1642–1647, folder 278.
39. Annorum 1646–1650, folder 245.
40. Annorum 1650–1653, folder 264.
41. Annorum 1653–1657, folder 311.
42. Annorum 1658–1661, folder 277.
43. Annorum 1661–1665, folder 235.
44. Annorum 1665–1668, folder 256.
45. Annorum 1668–1672, folder 187.
46. Annorum 1672–1676, folder 252.

47. Annorum 1676–1680, folder 278.
48. Annorum 1680–1684, folder 259.
49. Annorum 1684–1690, folder 281.
50. Annorum 1600–1626, foldes 290.
51. Annorum 1697–1704, folder 235.
52. Annorum 1701–1710, folder 312.
53. Annorum 1711–1717, folder 272.
54. Annorum 1717–1723, folder 267.
55. Annorum 1723–1728, folder 207.
56. Annorum 1729–1734, folder 271.
57. Annorum 1734–1738, folder 265.
58. Annorum 1739–1754, folder 282.
59. Annorum 1746–1754, folder 265.
60. Annorum 1754–1761, folder 278.
61. Annorum 1761–1768, folder 261.
62. Annorum 1769–1776, folder 276.
63. Annorum 1776–1782, folder 278.
64. Annorum 1782–1790, folder 271.
65. Annorum 1790–1796, folder 279.
66. Annorum 1797–1805, folder 322.
67. Annorum 1806–1808 (28/2.), folder 12.

IX. Guardie ed armamento. (Guards and Armaments) (Vol. 115.)

1. Vacchetta Armamento 1523, folder 77, perg.
2. Inventarii delle armi e munizioni dell'armento 1614' folder 87.
3. Salari dei soldati e guardie del' 1617, folder 221.
4. Libro delli pagamenti de soldati di Sopragionta 1618, folder 216.
5. Libro delli pagamenti de 'soldati 1526, folder 15.
6. Libro Seritta dell' Armamento 1554, folder 49.
7. Libro Seritta dell' Armamento 1566, folder 38.
8. Libro Seritta dell' Armamento 1570, folder 50.
9. Libro Seritta dell' Armamento 1573, folder 46.
10. Libro Seritta dell' Armamento 1573, folder 48.
11. Libro Seritta dell' Armamento 1574, folder 76.
12. Libro Acconcio Armamento 1575, folder 82.
13. Libro Biscotti Armamento 1581, folder 5.
14. Libro Condennati al vogar 1595, folder 9.
15. Libro Condennati del Comonale 1506, folder 20.
16. Libro Acconcio 1592, folder 2.
17. Libro Scritta dell' Armamento 1585, folder 23.
18. Libro Officiali della fregatta 1581, folder 8.
19. Libro Metalli che si trovano in fondaria dopo la fuga di Francesco fonditore, 1583, folder 10.
20. Libro Scritta dell' Armamento 1588, folder 34.
21. Libro dell' Armamento 1589, folder 8.

22. Libro dei soldati e pagamenti 1593, folder 25.
23. Libro dell' Armamento 1594, folder 11.
24. Libro dell' Armamento 1595, folder 13.
25. Libro dell' Armamento 1595, folder 22.
26. Libro Giornale di Francesco protto della piatta 1598, folder 32.
27. Libro dell' Armamento 1599, folder 19.
28. Serivano dell 'Armamento dell 'anno 1603, folder 18.
29. Officiali dell 'Armamento dell 'anno 1601, folder 40.
30. Serivano dei Soldati dell 'anno 1606, folder 28.
31. Provveditori delle Guardie e Puntature dell 'anno 1607, folder 10.
32. Spese dell 'Armamento dell 'anno 1608, folder 68.
33. Di Lorenzo Basso serivano della galeotta grande armata dell 'anno 1608, folder 17.
34. Memoriale di spese e altro nel disiare la lave 1609, folder 13.
35. Pagamento ai soldati della barea longa 1608–1609, folder 36.
    Visto et Acconcio 1609, folder 36.
36. Armamento 1611, folder 9.
37. Guardie e Barabana 1612, folder 43.
38. Sopragionta dell 'anno 1612 folder 43.
39. Pagamenti dei Soldati 1613, folder 28.
40. Libro delli Condannati 1613, folder 28.
41. Libro delli soldati che hanno vogato nella galera armata dell 'anno 1613, folder 80.
42. Della Galera, Aconcio 1613, folder 7/4.
43. Originale dei Armamenti et Arsenale 1614, folder 169.
44. Soldati di Sopragionta di Castello grande 1614, folder 94.
45. Pagamenti dei Provveditori alle Guardie 1614, folder 214.
46. Libro della galera grande armata del 1608, folder 75.
47. Libro delle Navi e Navigli 1605, folder 6.
48. Libro spese Condennati delle galeotte 1605, folder 26.
49. Libro pagamento della gente delle due galeotte 1605, folder 30.
50. Libro spese delle galeotte 1597, folder 16.
51. Libro dell 'Armamento 1612, folder 7.
52. Libro dei Barabanti 1612–1617, folder 54.
53. Libro Salari delle guardie 1617, folders 15–222.
54. Libro Condennati alla Galiota 1620, folder 20.
55. Libro Spese della Galiota 1620, folder 3.
56. Libro Pagamenti degli assentati di fuori.
57. Libro della Galiotta 1622, folder 17.
    Constituto delli Famegli 1642/44, folder 14/4.
58. Polizze dell 'Arsenale 1532, folder 5.
59. Libretto del funditore 1627, folder 3.
60. Libretto dell 'Armemento 1627, folder 21.
61. Polize dell 'Armemento 1632, folder 9.
62. Libro del burchio 1635, folder 11.
63. Libro del burchio 1637, folder 11.
64. Libro del burchio 1639, folder 7.
65. Libro del burchio 1642, folder 9.
66. Libro del burchio 1644, folder 9.
67. Spese della Gallera 1648, folder 4.

68. Riscossione del biscotto 1650, folder 9.
69. Polize del Burchio 1650, folder 3.
70. Giornale dell' Armamento 1651, folder 12.
71. Libro remiganti 1554, folder 7.
72. Polize dell' Armamento 1659, folder 11.
73. Soldati che lavorano il Terrapieno 1657, folder 7.
74. Pagamento alli soldati ordinarii, 1665, folder 7.
75. Polizze dell' Armamento, 1666, folder 4.
76. Resarcimento delli Arsenali grandi 1668, folder 10.
77. Polizze dell' Armamento 1670, folder 10.
78. Polizze dell' Arsenale 1670, folder 7.
79. Inventario delle robbe del Castol grande di Stagno 1678, folder 12.
80. Pragamenti di Stagno 1708, 1727, folder.
81. Polizze dell' Armamento 1728, folder.
82. Libro dei Salarii 1759, folder 1.
83. Libro Salariati 1725–1748, folder.
84. Piani di difesa e osservasioni sulle fortificazioni 1785, folder.
    Inventario Artiglierie ecc. all' Armamento 1786, folder 8.
85. Soldati, 1810, folder 14.
86. Salariati pagati dal Scrivano di loggia, folder 4.
87. Ordo Stagni 1470, folder 3.
88. Soldati di Stagno s.d., folder 6.
89. Soldati di Stagno 1529, folder 1.
90. Soldati di Sopragionta 1528, 1529, folder 12.
91. Soldati di Sopragionta 1529–1536, folder 16.
91. Soldati di Sopragionta 1529–1536, folder 16.
92. Soldati di Sopragionta 1532, folder 14.
93. Soldati di Sopragionta 1528–1537, folder 14.
94. Soldati di Stagno 1591, folder 14.
95. Soldati di Stagno 1595, folder 16.
96. Soldati di Stagno 1596, folder 2.
97. Soldati di Stagno alla giornata 1516–1570, folder 18.
98. Soldati di Stagno alla giornata 1576, folder 17.
99. Arsenale di Stagno 1609, folder 7.
100. Salarii di Stagno 1614, folder 12.
101. Salarii di Stagno 1614, folder 28.
102. Salarii di Stagno 1628, folder 64.
103. Salarii di Stagno 1663, folder 11.
104. Salarii di Stagno 1670, fragm.
105. Paghe soldati di Stagno 1663–70, fragm.
106. Paghe soldati di Stagno 1673, folder.
107. Paghe soldati di Stagno 1677–1683, folder.
108. Paghe soldati di Stagno 1677–1685, folder
109. Salarii 1631, fragm.
110. Paghe dei Soldati di Stagno 1683.
111. Paghe dei Soldati di Stagno 1678–1685,
112. Paghe dei Soldati di Stagno 1684–1685, folder 12.
113. Paghe dei Soldati di Stagno 1688, folder 12.
114. Armamento 1786, folder 12.
115. Soldati di Stagno 1801, folder 56.

X. Testamenta. (Wills)

1. Testamenta de Notaria. (Advocates' Wills) (Vol. 94.)

1. Annorum 1282–1283, folder 28.
2. Annorum 1295–1324, folder 63.
3. Annorum, 1324–1348, folder 82.
4. Annorum 1347–1365, folder 84.
5. Annorum 1345–1365, folders 141, 162–180, 214–310.
6. Annorum 1365–1379, folder 141.
7. Annorum 1381–1391, folder 250.
8. Annorum 1391–1402, folder 283.
9. Annorum 1402–1414, folder 222.
10. Annorum 1416–1418, folder 241.
11. Annorum 1418–1429, folder 242.
12. Annorum 1430–1437, folder 210.
13. Annorum 1437–1445, folder 222.
14. Annorum 1445–1451, folder 196/2.
15. Annorum 1451–1456, folder 179, Index.
16. Annorum 1456–1458, folder 182, Index.
17. Annorum 1458–1462, folder 175/3.
18. Annorum 1462–1465, folder 179.
19. Annorum 1465–1467, folder 182.
20. Annorum 1467–1471, folder 177/2.
21. Annorum 1471–1473, folder 175/2.
22. Annorum 1473, folder 63.
23. Annorum 1476–1481, folder 176/3.
24. Annorum 1481–1493, folder 180.
25. Annorum 1483–1486, folder 135.
26. Annorum 1486–1494, folder 181.
27. Annorum 1494–1497, folder 199.
28. Annorum 1498–1503, folder 199.
29. Annorum 1503–1506, folder 201.
30. Annorum 1506–1511, folder 198.
31. Annorum 1512–1516, folder 200.
32. Annorum 1517–1510, folder 198.
33. Annorum 1519–1524, folder 230.
34. Annorum 1525–1527, folder 220.
35. Annorum 1528–1533, folder 209.
36. Annorum 1533–1536, folder 150, 1, 1–2.
37. Annorum 1536–1539, folder 224.
38. Annorum 1539–1543, folder 260.
39. Annorum 1543–1549, folder 211.
40. Annorum 1549–1555, folder 285.
41. Annorum 1555–1562, folder 264.
42. Annorum 1562–1568, folder 251.
43. Annorum 1568–1572, folder 218.

44. Annorum 1573–1577, folder 218.
45. Annorum 1577–1581, folder 223.
46. Annorum 1582–1585, folder 254.
47. Annorum 1585–1588, folder 266.
48. Annorum 1588–1592, folder 258.
49. Annorum 1592–1595, folder 259, Index.
50. Annorum 1595–1599, folder 197.
51. Annorum 1599–1602, folder 223, 2.
52. Annorum 1503–1607, folder 249.
53. Annorum 1607–1608, folder 225.
54. Annorum 1609–1613, folder 256, 10.
55. Annorum 1613–1619, folder 253.
56. Annorum 1620–1624, folder 175.
57. Excerpta testamentorum 1620–1640.
58. Annorum 1625–1628, folder 168.
59. Annorum 1628–1630, folder 109, Index.
60. Annorum 1630–1633, folder 105, Index.
61. Annorum 1633–1642, folder 190, Index.
62. Annorum 1638–1642, folder 169, Index.
63. Annorum 1642–1646, folder 150, Index.
64. Annorum 1615–1650, folder 250, Index.
65. Annorum 1651–1657, folder 249, Index.
66. Annorum 1658–1653, folder 129, Index.
67. Annorum 1663–1666, folder 133, Index.
68. Annorum 1666–1667, folder 116, Index.
69. Annorum 1667–1672, folder 125, Index.
70. Annorum 1673–1686, folder 216, Index.
71. Annorum 1686–1693, folder 188/1, Index.
72. Annorum 1693–1702, folder 169, Index.
73. Annorum 1702–1713, folder 226, Index.
74. Annorum 1714–1720, folder 176, Index.
75. Annorum 1721–1731, folder 200, Index.
76. Annorum 1731–1738, folder 195, Index.
77. Annorum 1738–1746, folder 227, Index.
78. Annorum 1746–1753, folder 230, Index.
79. Annorum 1754–1759, folder 216, Index.
80. Annorum 1760–1767, folder 240, Index.
81. Annorum 1767–1772, folder 242, Index.
82. Annorum 1772–1774, folder 179, Index.
83. Annorum 1775–1782, folder 218, Index.
84. Annorum 1782–1787, folder 206, Index.
85. Annorum 1786–1789, folder 161, Index.
86. Annorum 1790–1793, folder 94, Index.
87. Annorum 1793–1797, folder 192, Index.
88. Annorum 1797–1800, folder 188, Index.
89. Annorum 1800–1801, folder 184, Index.
90. Annorum 1804–1808, folder 214, Index.
91. Annorum 1808–1811, folder 116, Index.
92. Annorum 1812–1815, folder 12, Index.
93. Alfabeto de Testamenti de speciali persone scripte in libro di Signori Thesorieri

de S. Maria, scripti per me Antonio de Marco in MDXI. Adi XII Lnio Index XIII.

(ab. a 1297—ad. 1511 —et prosecutio ad a. 1793—Membr.

94. Testamenta ab. a. 1793 ad. a. 1891 Incompletum.

Sunt etiam litterae ab. a. 1772.

Vide etiam 'Debita Notarie', Vol. 1, 6, uon Div. et al. passim.

2. Distributiones testamentorum. (Distribution of Wills.) (Vol. 33.)

1. Annorum 1349 ad 1354, folder 160.
2. Annorum 1364 ad 1368, folder 197–14.
   Add. Diversa Cancelarie, folder 14.
3. Annorum 1371 ad 1372, folders 82–11.
4. Annorum 1374 ad 1384, folder 190.
5. Annorum 1385, folder 169.
6. Annorum 1395 ad 1405, folder 198.
7. Annorum 1604 ad 2416, folder 232.
8. Annorum 1419 ad 1427, folder 273.
9. Annorum 1427 ad 1432, folder 218.
10. Annorum 1433 ad 1437, folder 272.
11. Annorum 1437 ad 1440, folder 264.
12. Annorum 1440 ad 1443, folder 267.
13. Annorum 1443 ad 1447, folder 262.
14. Annorum 1448 ad 1453, folder 263.
15. Annorum 1453 ad 1457, folder 259.
16. Annorum 1458 ad 1462, folder 266.
17. Annorum 1462 ad 1466, folder 273.
18. Annorum 1468 ad 1475, folder 355.
19. Annorum 1475 ad 1481, folder 277.
20. Annorum 1481 ad 1484, folder 279.
21. Annorum 1484 ad 1489, folder 373.
22. Annorum 1490 ad 1494, folder 329.
23. Annorum 1495 ad 1499, folder 274.
24. Annorum 1500 ad 1502, folder 269.
25. Annorum 1503 ad 1506, folder 282.
26. Annorum 1506 ad 1510, folder 277.
27. Annorum 1509 ad 1515, folder 272.
28. Annorum 1515 ad 1518, folder 272.
29. Annorum 1518 ad 1522, folder 272.
30. Annorum 1522 ad 1528, folder 290.
31. Annorum 1528 ad 1530, folder 310.
32. Annorum 1530 ad 1534, folder 282.
33. Annorum 1558 ad 1581, folder 155.

3. Tutores Notarie. (Deeds of Attorney) (Vol. 15.)

1. Annorum 1534 ad 1547, folder 179.
2. Annorum 1552 ad 1572, folder 256.
3. Annorum 1573 ad 1583, folder 168.

4. Annorum 1584 ad 1598, folder 241.
5. Annorum 1599 ad 1618, folder 215.
6. Annorum 1619 ad 1650, folder 231.
7. Annorum 1650 ad 1671, folder 165.
8. Annorum 1671 ad 1709, folder 279.
9. Annorum 1709 ad 1740, folder 276.
10. Annorum 1741 ad 1762, folder 267.
11. Annorum 1762 ad 1773, folder 226, Index.
12. Annorum 1773 ad 1785, folder 249.
13. Annorum 1785 ad 1794, folder 238.
14. Annorum 1794 ad 1801, folder 234.
15. Annorum 1801 ad 1809, folder 242.

XI. Lamenti politici. (Political Complaints) (Vol. 7.)

1. De Maleficiis et dampnis tempore Barth. Gradonigi 1312–1313, folder 47.
2. Liber maleficiorum incepto a. d. MCCCCXVII. Die XXVI Junii. Usque 1419, folder 341.
3. Lamenti politici dell' anno 1441, folder 283.
4. Lamenti dinnanzi il Minor Consiglio 1537–1544, folder 431.
5. Lamenti politici 1547–1551, folder 282.
6. Processus secreti Minoris Consilii 1547–1563, folder 142.
7. Lamenti criminali in affari marittimi e degli Uscocchi 1570, folder 90.

XII. Cathasthicum. (Codastres) (Vol. 11.)

1. Liber de introitibus stacionum et terrenorum communis 1286, membr. folder 19.
2. Deseni e sentencie de Stagno. Ponique, Cernagora, Janina, Dubrave, Terstenica 1323 (fragm. membr.)
3. Case del Comune de Ragusi e terreni e affitti 1481, folder 162.
4. Libro rosso—nune 'Matica sed non reete dictus partem ultimam scripsit Nicolans filius Antonii Cancellarii, folder 463.
5. Verifica delle terre della Comune poste nello stato 1525, folder 17.
6. Verificazioni e divisioni delle terre dello stato 1440 (accopiavit Joh. Laur. Reginus de Feltre.)
7. Liber de custodiis per decenas in Punta fiendis 1562, folder 37.
8. Sentenze e dissegni—(recte: Determinationes. sententie et desegni de Stagne et de la Ponta.) Ann. 1396, folder 271.
9. Sententiae et vendiciones Terrarum communis Stagni et Puncte XI Augusti 1505, Ind. VIII. Estesi dalli officiales et indices super occupationibus quos rendam iurium et terrenorum comunis, oppressorum per speciales et diversas personas in Stagno et Puneta. Annorum 1505–1562, folder 139.
10. Case del Comun de Ragusa, terreni e fitti 1417, folder 87/8.
11. Case del Comun de Ragusa, terreni e (duplo) 1417, folder 85. (Vide etiam II. 23.)

XIII. Giustizieria. (Justice)
(Vol. 15.)

1. Ad consilium rogatorum. Cause, 1467–1481, folder 197.
2. Processum matrimoniale Marusse relicte olim Antonii Bratossaglich 1480, folder 103.
3. Libro dell e sentenze de'Giudici civili dell 'anno 1488, membr. (fragm. Indicis.) folder 244.
4. Lamenti dinnanzi ai gindici del Criminale 1493–1495, folder 127.
5. Pene e diverse scritture 1499–1506, folder 147.
6. Libro delli Instizieri dal 19 giugno 1506–23 Apr. 1509, folder 195.
7. Lamenta Notarie 1519–1524, folder 199.
8. Lamenti delli Signori Giustizieri 1667–1670, folder 50.
9. Lamenti di Giusticieria 1670–1671, folder 45.
10. Sententie de Giustizieri 1509–1512, folder 299.
11. Sententie de Giustizieri 1514–1517, folder 173.
12. Sententie de Giustizieri 1520–1522, folder 180.
13. Sententie de Giustizieri 1522–1525, folder 297.
14. Sententie Insticiariorum 1531, folder 112.
15. Sententie Insticiariorum 1531–1532, folder 153.

XIV. Chiese e Monasteri. (Churches and Monastries)
(Vol. 32.)

1. Beliquiae s.s. corporum repertae in Ecclesia Cathedrali S. Mariae Maioris 1335, folder 1.
2. Diversa pro collegio Societatis Jesu erigendo 1659, folder 60, vol. 2.
3. Diversa PP. ord. S. Benedieti (S. Andrea, Lagosta, Gravosa. Ragusa, S. Giacome Breno Bergatto, Gionchetto, Place, Mezzo)—(fragmentariae a.n.).
4. Alla Sacra Congregazione dei Vescovi. Memoriale-Terremoto 1667.
5. II Cardinal del Carpo. Indulgenza 1555 (copia).
6. Indulto 1616 (de affictibus).
7. Indulgenza 18 Settembre 1749. Ai vescovi.
8. Indulto Dalmazia. Sui digiuni 2 Ottobre 1833.
9. Indalgenza 5 Aprile 1786.
10. Lieenza per la monacazione 1504–1811, folder 30; 1557–1755, folder 28.
11. Vacehetta Monastero Rv. Monache di Santa Chiara 1695–1789, folder 212.
12. Vacehetta generale di S. Giacomo (Exactiones) 1795–1803, folder 179.
13. Capitoli incorporazione Monastero S. Maria de Lacroma con la Congregazione di S. Giustina di Padova (Copie sacc. XVII). 1466, folder 5.
14. Indices livellorum Monasteri La Cromae 1631–1633, folder 12.
15. Liber Curiae Archiepiscopalis Ragusinae 1471, folder 142; 1472, folder 20 (fragm.)
16. Liber Curiae Archiepiscopalis inceptum per Ieronimum Antonini cancell. Curiae 1477.
17. Acta Archiepiscopalis per D. Hieronymum Faventinum die 21 Madii 1493, folder 37/12.

18. Processus Tribunalis Consistorii Sacrae S. Conseientiae, et in Curia causarum delegatarum 1586, folder 85.
19. Miscellanca Ecclesistica 1746–1761, folder 39/5.
20. Scripturae 1483 ad Nutum Rmi. Domini Viearii, folder 11.
21. Super facto beneficii S. Redentoris de Paludo. Sententia.
22. Epidaurensis inspatronatus. Votum pro veritate Testamentum Mathei Androvich, folder 11.
23. Visitaciones (fragm. sine datum), folder 9.
24. Diversa Curiae Archiepiscopalis 1482, fragm., folder 19.
25. Alla congregazione dei Vescovi, sulle Monache di Santa Chiara, A. 1667, folder 3.
26. Versio latina ciusdem, nee non partes captae Caroli de Ferriis Adv. et Nicolai de Augustinis.
27. Robbe trovate a Stagno piccolo in casa di Mr. Vescovo 17 Settembre 1652, folder 1.
28. Res et bona reperta in Monasterio Melitensi 9 Aug. 1458.
29. (Copia saec. XIX.) Bulla Zachariae Papae, folder 1.
30. Diversa super immunitate 1724, 1726, 1730, 1736, folder 4.
31. Fideicommissi reintregrationis causa ad Curiam romanam (s.d.), folder 8.
32. Benedetto XIII alla rp. di Venozia 1724, folder 3.

XV. Appellationes. (Appeals)
(Vol. 11.)

1. Liber preceptorum causarum appellat, diffinendarum in consilio rogatorum 1118–1167, folder 108.
2. Appellazioni di cause al Minor Consiglio 1547–1720, folder 222.
3. Appellazioni di cause civili 1557–1573, folder 137.
4. Appellationes Rogatorum 1553–1586, folder 270.
5. Part del Collegio 1573–1599, folder 179.
6. Appellationes Collegii et Rogatorum 1580–1598, folder 284
7. Appellationes Collegii et Rogatorum 1599–1618, folder 236.
8. Appellationes Collegii et Rogatorum 1618–1642, folder 246.
9. Libro dello terminazioni delli arbitri nel fallimento Rogoglianni 1623, folder 5.
10. Appellationes Rogatorum et Collegii, 1642–1734, folder 296.
11. Estrationi delle Appellazioni ossia supplimento 1685–1734, folder 114.

XVI. Criminalia. (Criminal)
(Vol. 27.)

1. Indice (alfabetico) condemnationi scritte in quaderno ab a. 1427, folder 12.
2. Libro delle condempnationi vecchie ab a. 1481 ad 1521, membr., folder 321.
3. Registro pegni dovati per appellazioni di sentenze a 1496, folder 210 (folders 1–19).
4. Registro pegni ut supra ab a. 1556 ad a. 1581, folder 179.
5. Registro sentenze criminali 1708–1752, folder 245.
6. Sentenze de li condannati a morte, e di membro 1551–1667, folder 58/143.
7. Sentenze de criminale in civile 1574–1811, folder 363.

8. Alfabeto del libro delle sentenze del criminale 1655, folder 66.
9. Libro de li stridati, banditi e tormenti, e sententiati a morte de 1520–1657, folder 79.
10. Penale de 1556–1560, folder 109/31.
11. Terminationi del criminale; cretenus 1778 in 1811, folder 261.
12. Terminazioni Tribunale di Prima istanza del 1814, folder 119.
13. Alfabeto sentenze criminale del 1793.
14. Alfabeto sentenze criminale del 1627.
15. Alfabeto sentenze criminale del 175(?)
16. Alfabeto sentenze criminale del sine dato.
17. Registro Terminazioni appartenenti ai gindiei dei governo Provvisorio 1808–1809, folder 125–130.
18. Pene de Criminale 1560–1566, folder 170/33. Criminale, diversa de 1560.
19. Sentenze del Criminale 1586–1591, folder 158/33.
20. Libro delli stridati 1657–1719 (Alphabet), /3, Esempi diversi.
21. Sentenze promulgate dalli signori gindiei del Criminale 1679–1720, folder 287.
22. Libri sentenze Criminali 1627–1655, folder 277.
23. Libro Criminale (folder 1–30 desunt) de 1562–1602.
24. Libro delle sentenze criminali de 1655–1701, folder 300.
25. Libro at supra 1751 in 1775, folder 273.
26. Libro at supra 1775 in 1792, folder 244.
27. Libro at supra 1793 in 1812, folder 129.

XVII. Vigne. (Vines)
(Vol. 56.)

1. Contrabbandi del vino 1512–1520, folder 239.
2. Libro de le vigne tagliate in Terrenove, piantade contra li erdeni 1514, folder 38.
3. Liber offitialium Contrabanni Vini 1533–1539, folder 128.
4. Vigne tagliati in Terrenove 1546, folder 53.
5. Libro Offitiali de Contrabando del Vine 1550–1553, folder 273.
6. Contrabando de Vini 1554–1562, folder 257.
7. Libro de li condemnati per li officiali de tagliar le vite de 1553–1554, folder 91.
8. Executione de li officiali de desra dicar le vigne in Slano 1553, folder 44.
9. Cabella de'Vini, folder 57.
10. Libro de li offitiali di Canali del 1554, folder 26.
11. Introito de'vini nuovi dello stato 1554, folder 102.
12. Officiali per tagliar le vigne piantate in Canale 1568, folder 46.
13. Contrabandi de 'Vini 1573–1754, folder 92.
14. Officiali di tagliar la vigna 1577, folder 44.
15. Officiali di tagliar la vigna in Primorie 1577, folder 21.
16. Officiali di tagliar la vigna in Terrenove 1583, folder 57.
17. Officiali di tagliar la vigna 1579 in folder 172.
18. Vino nuvo 1580, folder 45.
19. De tagliar le vite da Slano a Imotiza 1583, 1606, 1612, 1626, 1642, folder 105.
20. Vino nuvo 1599–1731, folder 159.
21. Registro introito vini nuovi dello stato 1603, folder 64.
22. Registro introito vini nuovi delle stato 1612, folder 46.
23. Libro della gabella dei vini 1613, folder 11.

24. Libro delli vini 1614, folder 45.
25. Officiali dazio della citta del 1633, folder 13.
26. Officiali dazio della citta del 1639, folder 21.
27. Descrizione delli Vini di Ponta, 1611, folder 11.
28. Libro de li Signari offitiali di tagliar le viti di Slano e Petrovoselo 1612, folder 15.
29. Acconeio delli vini vini 1647, folder 14.
30. Acconeio delli vini 1651, folder 11.
31. Nota delle botte mesurate 1646, folder 20.
32. Vini novi 1626, folder 49.
33. Malvasie (Indice Alfab.) s.d. folder 60.
34. Vini novi 1638, folder 32.
35. Gaidel Comone nel territ. di Slano 1637, folder 12.
36. Vini novi 1662, folder 12.
37. Vini novi 1662, folder 12.
38. Indice Dazi del Vino 1480, folder 33.
39. Stragni 1498, folder 68.
40. Vini di Vendemmie 1501, folder 107.
41. Vini di Vendemmie 1520, folder 146.
42. Vini di Vendemmie 1529, folder 103.
43. Vini di Vendemmie 1583, folder 53.
44. Vini di Vendemmie 1647–1755, folder 68.
45. Vini di Vendemmie 1644, folder 129.
46. Spoglio Dazio Vino della eitta 1691, folder 4.
47. Contralettere 1732–1764, folder 135.
48. Indice Dazii Vini 1733–1735, folder 136.
49. Riassanto statistico Vini.
50. Polovije Vini 1743–1744, folder 7.
51. Copia lettere Stagno 1762–1786, folder 189.
52. Gabella Vini 1763–1764, folder 58.
53. Gabella Vini 1763–1764, folder 13.
54. Gabella Vini 1763–1764, folder 9.
55. Copia lettere Stagno e Ponta 1787–1788.
56. Contralettere 1787, folder 77.

XVIII. Officiales Rationum. (Public Rations) (Vol. 23.)

1. Istruzioni per l'uffizio delle Razioni, folder 53.
2. Sentenze de l'offizio delli 5 delle razioni 1419–1502, 1419 6/2–1502 14/11, folder 201.
3. Casnacine della Contrada di Canali 29 Ag. 1588, folder 121.
4. Ricordi dello Offitio delle razioni 1585–1633, folder 82.
5. Pontadure e Paghe morte de Soldati 1585, folder 22.
6. Pontadure e Paghe morte de Soldati 1604, folder 35.
7. Registro dell 'Uffizio delle Razioni 1618–1622, folder 116.
8. Ricordanze 1637–1725, folder 76.
9. Per le Monache 1644, folder 142.
10. Licenze ai Conti di fuori 1703–1727, folder 79.

11. Riscossioni dell 'Officio 1711–1724, folder 139.
12. Riscossioni dell 'Officio 1728–1740, folder 192.
13. Partite accettate 1734–1796, folder 591.
14. Partite ributtate 1738–1797, folder 132.
15. Memorie di quello ogni anno si deve dare 1753, folder 104.
16. Libretto delli Officiali 1765, folder 7.
17. Partite ributtate 1796–1807, folder 61.
18. Partite accettate 1796–1807, folder 135.
19. Contrabbandi delle razioni 1722–1796, folder 195.
20. Vacchetta Officiali 1556–1559, folder 130.
21. Spese dello ufficio 1796–1807, folder 31
22. Lasciti da Testamenti 1444–1481, folder 88.
23. Specchio delli Testamenti 1520, folder 19.

XIX. Privata. (Private Affairs) (Vol. 58.)

1. Dare ed Avere Polo de Pozza 1446, folder 4.
2. Dare ed Avere Jacobo de Gondola 1457, folder 37.
3. Memorie Maroie Milutinovich 1473–1474, folder 70.
4. Dare ed Avere Marcovich 1475–1479.
5. Beni Radulovich 1524–1562, folder 16.
6. Strazza (incerto) 1528, folder 12.
7. Indico. d.A. (n.n.) 1541, Alf.
8. Libro di Negozio N.N. 1558, folder 87.
9. Libro di Negozio Francesco Sorgo 1563.
10. Amminist. Nicolo e Marusena di Gozze 1569–1599.
11. Indice n.n. 1582–1677.
12. Memorie di spese n.n. 1591.
13. Dare ed Avere Michele Dobrotich 1594, folder 46.
14. Dare ed Avere Savino de Sorgo 1595, folder 70.
15. Strazza Zanobi Cinli 1599–1601.
16. Strazza n.n. 1611–1615.
17. Atti Martolossi 1628–1629, folder 11.
18. Indice Dare ed Avere Amadis de Ganla 1669. All.
19. Epitropia Luca Michele de Giamagna 1676–1692, folder 70.
20. D. & A. u.n. 1661–1664.
21. Inventario Asse Biagio Cr. Milli 1753, folder 7.
22. D. & A. Antonio Cingria 1756–1781, folder 13.
23. Pitropia Campos, folder 70.
24. Casa e servita di un Console ragusen 1782.
25. Giornaletto n.n. 1784–1785, folder 41.
26. Lite Tudisi 1785, folder 63.
27. Pitropia n.n. 1422–1450.
28. Libro di negozio Nicolo Luca Caboga 1426, folder 142.
29. Libro di negozio Andr. Luca di Sorgo 1526, folder 86.
30. Pitropia di Volco 1576, folder 117.
31. Libro Maestro di Stefano di Polo Radognich 1585, folder 49.
32. Libro di Negozio di Vencenzo Stefani d'Ancona 1585–1688, folder 189.

33. Epitropia Biagio Luchei 1596, folder 23.
34. Descrizione Assicurazioni grani nove di Marin di Francesco 1596, folder 43.
35. Libro di negozio n.n. 1598, folder 204.
36. Epotropia q^m Michele Francesco barbiere 1665, folder 89.
37. Giornale del libro della Compagnia di Nicolo e Lucha de Chaboga et comenca nell' Anne 1437–1438 (coroso), folder 8.
38. Libro Giornale di Stefano di Polo Radognichi dello libro segnato L. ciose le partite di questo giornale si reguagliano a libro maestro, segnato come se detto, 1585, folder 19.
39. Libro giornale (Frammento 1570–1572) di ignoto, folder 6.
40. Quadernuccio dell' Epitropia del q^m Biagio Luchei 1596, folder 29.
41. Indice alfab. estratto dal libro Rosso di Raffaelle Naldini segn. A. 1578, folder 18.
42. Quaderno A. dell' amministrazione di Nicolo Miossa stabilito in Venezia, dell'anno 1571, folder 222.
43. Libro A. dell'Amministrazione di Benedetto Marino di Resti, dimorante in Sofia, dell'auno 1590–1605, folder 204, Indice allegato.
44. Quaderno di debitori e creditori C. di Martolo de Georgi in Venezia 1580–1583, folder 115.
45. Libro di negozio N.N. frammento, Mancano folders 1, 2/1, 43, 79 e seg. ann., folder 78.
46. Controversie Ohmuchievich.
    1. Libello di Pietro Ohmuchievich contra Petricevich, folder 2.
    2. Ragusina Fideicommissi.
    3. Appunti caso si ottenesserole spedizioni da Roma, folder 1.
    4. Hisco tamen, folder 3.
    5. Extratto fflobile 1658, folder 130, folder 1.
    6. Extratti ex L° Venditionum 1661–1695, folder 57.
    7. Procura Catterina Parisan al March. Carlo Pierizzi 1693, folder 2.
    8. 18 atti da parte Cifuentes, folder 18.
    9. Consulta del Colleggio di Lecce in causa Ohmuchievich 1712, folder 17.
    10. Processus fratrum Ohmuchievich contra Fratres Ord. Seraphiei Conventus Posgeghe, folder 3.
    11. Libellum contra Societatem Jesu 1714, folder 1.
    12. Revisione differenze fra Ohmuchievich-Cifuente 1721, folder 10.
    13. Copia della risposta dei Senatori 1721, folder 2.
    14. Intenzione da parte dei fratelli Ohmuchievich 1722, folder 6.
    15. Vendite G. Darsa a Mokosciza. Estratti 1722, folder 27.
    16. Extractum Diversorium 1675 a 1722, folder 2.
    17. Extractum ex Statuto VIII, 47, folder 2.
    18. Processo liti in Ragusa D. Ohmuchievich-Cifuentes 1722, folder 32.
    19. Specificazione legati e debiti de D^na Paula 1722, folder 1.
    20. Specificazione debiti di Masibradi 1722, folder 1.
    21. Extract. Rogatorum, 18 Febr. 1483–1722, folder 1.
    22. Extract. Div. de Foris 1722, folder 1.
    23. Editto Giudiziario 1678, folder 1.
    24. Debito Paula Masibradi Ex Div. de F.—1722, folder 1.
    25. Extract Sententie Cancellarie 1634, folder 82, folder 6.
    26. Informaz. delle possessioni in Mokosiza 1722, folder 2.
    27. Extract, Venditionum Cane. 1650, folder 2.

28. Extract, Diversor. Cancell. 1628, folder 1.
29. Extract Diversor. Sentent. 1648, folder 1.
30. Extract Regatorum 1672, 17 Juii, 1722, folder 2.
31. Attestazione Regitano, 1725, folder 1.
32. Formula jurandi, folder 5.
33. Decretum liberatorium imperiale 1722, folder 1.
34. Probationes contra Comitem Cifontani 1723, folder 9.
35. Decretum Cesareum. Copia 1724, folder 1.
36. Protesto contra D.G. Chiros procur. del Cifuentes 1722, folder 7.
37. Extract, e libro Sententiarum 1653, folder 4.
38. Extract, Statutorum VIII, 1722, 95, folder 1.
39. Copie de lettere, 1722, folder 4.
40. Extract, Diversor. Cancellarie 1708, folder 1.
41. Esame con Cifuentes 1723, folder 2.
42. Certificato Regitano 1724, folder 1.
43. Extract, Sententiarum supra possessionem Omble, folder 8.
44. Duplica enm allegatis. 1728, folder 51.
45. Duplica (sine allegatis.), 1724, folder 19.
46. Appelatio ad Cesarem 1724, folder 17.
47. Replica ad Imperatorem 1724, folder 47.
48. Stato dell'eredita di Paolo Giganti, folder 7.
49. Estratti diversi Sentenze 1725, folder 17.
50. Sinopsis 1726, folder 1.
51. Schema familiae Masibradi, folder 1.
52. Acta Ragusii 1726, folder 44.
53. Acta Ragusii 1726, folder 44.
54. Inventarium Scripturarum 1726, folder 10.
55. Acta Ragusii 1726, folder 31.
56. Acta Ragusii 1726, folder 36.
57. Acta Ragusii 1726, folder 69.
58. Fragm. questionarii, folder 6.

XX. Privilegi. (Special Rights) (Vol. 6.)

1. Privilegi in slavico. Vol. membr. contenente le copie di privileg. e rescritti de principe balcanici, e dei Sultani (1226–1495). Mal conservato, folder 121. (Edid. Miklosich—'Monumenta Serbica').
2. Traduzioni di capitolazione e firmani (1784). 1459–1756, folder 1115.
3. Traduzioni di Capitulationi e firmani di Sultan Mustafa III, Abdulhamid-Selim III (1785), folder 254.
4. Materie coll'indice 1785, folder 271.
5. Registro di Comandamenti imperiali, Hatiscerifi e Capitulazioni, 1781, folder 418.
6. Diverse tradozioni e memorie:
    1. Traduz. del commandamento della Sublime Porta ai gindier ecc. del litorale di Europa Asia ed Arcipelago 1224—Trad. del passaporto imp. ott a Reis Manoli Pandel. teniotto 1224—Ricevuta dell'esattore di Galata —Trad. del commandamento della Sublime Porta per Reiis Manoli Pandeli, folder 12.

2. Diploma imperiale ad Sangiaenm Heregovine et ad indices civitatis Mostar—Latin ed Ital.
3. Comand. di Abdul-Hamid al Passa di Bosna, folder 2.
4. Firmano 1708, luca architetto, folder 1.
7. Copia privilegiorum regnum Hungariae—libertatem ragusinis mercandi concedditor 1387, 1439, 1454, 1455, 1470, 1474, 1477, 1488, 1492. Additur regestum privilegiorum ab. a 1438—usq. ad. a 1562.
8. Copia ut s. privilegiorum a regibus ungaricis Ragusinis coicessis ab. a. 1358, usq. ad. a. 1465.
9. Repertorio de Privilegi concessi a la repubbl. in Napoli Sicilia etc, ab. a. 1429, usq. ad. a. 1600.
10. Copia ut supra Stephani Thomae Servie regis Bosnae etc. 1458, Dec. 18.
11. Copia ut supra de Privilegi per li regni di S.M. Cattolica e specialmente in Messina ab. a. 1535—ad. a. 1580—Additur: Conferme de li privilegi di Filippo re etc. 1623, Febbr.
12. Copia ut supra de la scriptura de li privilegi, de 1628.
13. Copia e traduzione Firmano Murad III tributo di Ragusa 1577.
14. Lettere di Principi e primi ministri in affari di Barberia 1750-1753.
15. Copia—Ahmed Pascia, Buiurulti a favore di Ragusa 24 Ginguo 1728.
16. Copia u.s. Tvartko Ban di Bosna ammette i mercanti Ragusei alla sua protezione 1356.
17. Copia u.s. Ferdinando re d'Ungheria.—Privilegio 1471, 27 Julii.
18. Copia u.s. Privilegi Carlo re delle due Sicilie, 1671.
19. Copia u.s. Privilegi re di Aragona. Estratta 22 Ag. 1748.
20. Copia u.s. Privilegi consulatus subditorum regis catholici, 1510.
21. Copia u.s. Privilegi Ferdinandi regis. 1472, 18 Aprilis.
22. Copia u.s. Privilegi e traducione Firmani (Mehmed II, 1473; Suleiman I, 1560, Mehmet IV. 1594, Mustafa I. 1591. Mustafa gr. vezir 1754 = folder 7).
23. Copia u.s. Privilegii re di Aragona—regesto ed Executoriali 1455-1491.
24. Copia u.s. Privilegii Ferdinando—e Carlo V. 1459, 1535.
25. Copia u.s. Comandamento ad Achmet pascia e Mustafa Tefterd. di Bosna (s.d.).
26. Traduzione u.s. di privilegi turchi 1716, 1747, 1795, 1730, 1775, 1798.
27. Nota di Privilegii exsistenti in Tesoreria nel armaro grande. (Privileg. Pontificia.)

XXI. Manuali practici del Cancelliere.
(Chancellors' Practical Handbooks)

1. Leggi e Istruzioni. (Laws and Instructions)
(Vol. 29.)

1. Indice Magistrature ed officiali (nune Specchio del Magior Cousiglio dictum) 1440-1492, vol. 2. (Cum ... sepissime vidissem occurrere, quod multum laboreretur in querendo qui poterant eligi ad regimina et officia, et qui non poterant ... ego Johannes de Arimino civis patavinus immeritus, Ragusii cancellarius ... coaduuavi et descripsi in presenti libro ut plurimum omnia officia et regimina ab intra et extra que fiunt in majori consilio, ut puta comitatus, capitaneatus, castellanatus et diversa officia civitatis et procura-

tiones monasteriorum. Addidi etiam, etsi non esse multum necesse, ambassiates et armatas galearum, ponens primo per alphabetum tabullam quandam, aperientum summatim totius libri continentiam … Et ut sine nomine minime transeat ipse liber guam merito possit appellari 'semicronica dignitatum nobilium Raquseorum' tamen non voce bitur nisi 'Speculum officialium", ab usu speculi, inceptum de 1440.

N.B. Premittitar:

(a) Prohemium.

(b) Queste sono le casade de li Centilomi de la magnifica Citade de Ragusi qui descrite per alphabeto de ba, be, bi, bo, bu secondo apar per ordene.

(c) Index alphabet.

(d) Speculum officialium.

(e) In fine: Consegieri de gran conseio.

2. Indice Magistrature ed officiali (nune Specchio del Maggior Consiglio dectum: 1500–1599.

3. Indice Magistrature ed officiali (nune Specchio del Maggior Consiglio dictum: 1606–1699.

4. Indice Magistrature ed officiali (nune Specchio del Maggior Consiglio dictum: 1700–1799.

5. Indice Magistrature ed officiali (nune Specchio del Maggior Consiglio dictum: 1800–1808, vol. 2.

6. Specchietto della Nobilta 1786–1808, folder 3.

7. Titolario per la Corrispondenza coi principi.

8. Ceremeniale, vol. 2.

9. Statutum Ragusinum (Cod. Fr. Gondola) 1777.

10. Compendio dei Libri degli Statuti di quelli del Maggior Consiglio.

11. Liber Viridis.

12. Liber Croseus.

13. Ordinamenti di Stagne.

14. Index Reformationum all. ord. dispositus.

15. Indice delli Statuti e leggi concernenti all'eletioni, creazioni e vacanze delli Magistrati et offitii.—Duplicate tantum litt. A.C.

16. Istruzioni per i magistrati per procedere a norma degli statuti e delle antiche consuetndini.

17. Praxis Judiciaria juxta stilum curiae Ragusine Nicolai Jo de Bona—Mss.

18. Indice alf. delle sentenze.

19. Capitulare et quaedam notabiles materiae extractae ex libris octo Statutorum. Reformationum libro Viridi, Crocco, Legum et ordinum Ragusinae civitatis

20. Elezioni di Capitani di notte.

21. Libro della Scorovaita 1644.

22. Libro della Scorovaita 1673.

23. Esattissimo Indice di tutte le divisioni occorse tra tutti gli ordini di persone dall anno 1600 in 700, nelli Div, di Cancell, e Div, de Foris, raccolto e compendiato da Antonio Damiano Ohmuchievich Cancell. nel 1693, folders 11, 24, 4.

24. Indice di tutte le doti e patti matrimonia e contratti dotali in Div. di Notaria, raccolti da Ant. Dam. Ohmuchievich Cancell. nel 1693, folder 3/20.

25. Indice locali ecclesiastiche e secolari ecc. dello stesso, folder 36.

26. Index sive regestum Partium Consilii Rogatorum Rpbl. Ragusanae ab. a. 1400 usq. ad. a. 1700 folder 239.

27. Diverse Commissioni Ecc. Consiglio de' Pregati ab. a. 1777 ad 1787, folder 20.
28. Providimenti del Senato super navibus et sale, folder 27.
29. Parti dell'Ecc. Consiglio di Pregati per la cassa dal 1784, folder 26.

2. Memoriae (Memoirs)
Cronache.—Diarii.—Manuscripta diversa.—Curiosa.
(Vol. 22.)

1. Memorie scarse di Ragusa cavate dall'istoria di don Mauro Orbini, ms. 32, p. 283.
2. Bibliographia racusina Baldovini Bizarro (desumpta ab opere Vallentinelliano —De in. labeatide), fasc. 2.
3. Matricula Congregationis presbiterorum S. Petri in Cathedra, folders 1–15.
   Estratti pensieri filosofici ecc., folders 46–55.
   Del Blasone, Degli ordini cavallereschi, folder 56.
   Squarei del Metastasio, folders 57–64.
   Massime e sentenze, folder 65.
   Libri statutorum reip. Ragusine, folders 66–69.
   Ex libro Indicis sententiarum, folders 70–82.
   Brevi compendi della S. Scrittura, folders 88–89.
   Proverbi illirici, folder 90.
   I Papi per nazionalita, folder 91.
4. Giorgi Ignazio. Ab. di Meleda, ad istanza dell'Arcid. Capor—'L'onore della venuta di S. Paolo Ap. restituito a Melita illiricana.
5. Ludovici Heliani—de bello adversus Venetianos. (Lat. et ital.), folder 43.
6. Fragmentum Chronacae Ragusinae (Cabogae?).
7. Sulla vita e sugli scritti di Gian Francesco Gondola del P.F.M. Appendini, folder 29.
8. Brevi notizie sulla fondazione di Ragusa estratte da un antico anonimo (Usque a. 1771), folder 57.
9. A di ll Luglio 1800, Brevi notizie della fondazione e lungamento della citta di Ragusa raccelte dell'anticho anonimo manuscritto. De 1790, folder 56.
10. Ignazio Giorgi. Apocrise alle opposizioni di certi favoreggiatori di Malta, all'Areiv. Giusto Fontanini, folder 15.
11. Iscrizioni (ragusee) diverse, folder 11.
12. Delle donne pubbliche. (Fragm. di una Disertazione medica) del Dr. Stulli, folder 20.
13. Tudisi Tom. Parere sul ristauro del palazzo dei rettori, folder 10.
14. Saggio alfabetico di Bibliografia ragusea dei Dr. G. A. Casnacich.
15. In morte di alcuni Ragusei. Inscrizioni, folder 6.
16. Sulla repubbl. di Ragusa, Discorso di L. di L. Stulli, folder 12.
17. Vita ed opere di Gioacchino Stulli, folder 1.
18. Origine della citta di Ragusa, estratta da certe scritture antichissime, cou agginuta di aleune cose piu memorabili costumate in Ragusa.—I. Giorgi Ab. Melitense, 1507, p. 255.
19. Copia di una lettera del P.G.R. Boscovich al Card. Valenti del 28. Maggio 1756, folder 12.
20. Miscellanea di Marco Marinovich. (Tomo VIII, p. 366.)
    Arrivo a Ragusa del Gov. Gdn. de Lilieuberg.
    Esercizio letterario del gimnasio di Ragusa del 1833.

Sermone del Missirini.
Poesie del Tomasini.
In morte del P.U. Appendini.
Per il Natalizio dell' Imperatore.
In lode del celebre giovane Pugliesi.
Sur la mort d'un enfant.
Negrologia di Caterina Tren-Nani.
Dell'amicizia.
Natalizio di Francesco I festeggiato a Ragusa, Zara, Spalato, Milano,
Venezia, Trieste.
De Caesaris (Ferdinandi II) Clementia.
Berta filava.
In morte di M. Miglcovich.
Natalizio di Ferdinando I a Ragusa, Zara, Spalato, Milano.
A Nina Somaglia.
Sa Usviscegnje Knesa od Lilienberg.
Natalizio Ferdinando I a Milano.

21. Relazione della Corte e monarchia di Spagna, 1671, dell'ill, ed Ece. Sign.
    Girolame de Bonda al P. Vladislao Luca di Gozze.
22. Statuto fondazionale del Monte di pieta di Ragusa del 1835.
23. Appendini Urbano.—Poesie (ms. orig.)
24. Dell'origine della citta di Ragusa. ms.
25. Catalog libreria Raf. Androvich.
26. Ferrich G.—Tassoni Ragusine cessionis navis 1805.
27. Socolovich.—Copia lettere ad areivescovi ragusei—(dell' epoca froncese).
28. Zlatarich M. Osman. Canto XIII.—ms.
29. Zlatarich della vita di Plinio, di G. d'Orvey.
30. Tusbe Marunkove.
31. Ferrich.—Epigrammata (autogr).
32. Trattato. Origine di Ragusa.—snec. XVI.—ms.
33. Boscovich Bartol. Poesie ital, e latine.
34. —preghiere e componimenti poetiel diversi.
35. Fragmenta. Dizionario geogr. storico universale. ms.
36. Fragmenta. Storia della letteratura italiana. ms.
37. Kopitari Appendinio, et Dobrovsky Kopitario epistole.
39. Discours par l'abbe Melch. Cessarotti, envoye a l'academic des Archades de
    Roma, trad. par M.A. Chersa ms., 8° p. 35.
40. Lettera del P. Andriasci M.o.a. Diodoro Bosdari in Ancona dd. 16 Aprile
    1667, folder gr. 4 pag.
41. Hyer. Avaictins ver. nobilissimo viro ac Poctae ill. Aclio Lamp. Cervino
    Ragusaee S.P. (cop. del. sec XVIII.—Additamenta et notae de Partenio.
    Francovitz. Georgio Ragusano, Cervario, Dolcio, etc., folder, page 4.
42. Jacobi Flavii Eborensis Seu Didaci Pyrri de Ragusinae urbis laudibus carmen.
    Cop. Chersae folder, page 24.
43. Cuiusdam testamenti slavici copia—dd. Curzolae 1435, Memorie Sorga de a.
    1825 Arrivo dell' imperatore a Milano vel 1838.
44. Stephani Gradii de cladibus patriae suae (nec non alia carmina ciusdem).
    16° p. 10.
45. Ludov. Cervarius Tubero: Cenni biografici Recensione delle opere, folder,
    p. 8 additamenta Holstein, Gradi, Lucio.

46. Ant. Chersa carmi al Rosaver ed allo Scacoz, con note Mezzofanti e Trivulzio, folder, p. 2.
47. Fragmentum ms. Seraph. Cervae, ex Bullario Dominicano, Series regum serblorum 4 p. 20.
48. Adnotationes ad librum Fraternitatis S. Lazari, folder, p. 1.
49. (Copia) Resiripto senatoria a Catherina delle Russie, sec XVIII. 4° p. 1.
50. Monitum Auctoris ad. Monumenta Historica Seb. Dolci.—Notae. 4° p. 1.
51. Memorie Johannis Gazuli O.P., folder, p. 2.
52. (Stampa) Specchio del Consiglio pro 1779.
53. Carmina Bern, Zamagnae—Napoleonis I allocutio in Campis Sarmatiae—Ad. L. Stulli, folder, p. 2.
54. Aelius Lampr. Cervarius P. L. Sigismundo Giorgio 4° p. 12.
55. Bibliotheca ragusina Serafino Cervae O.P. conscripta 4° gr. p. 12.
56. Marci Faustini Gagliuffi Ragusini. Libellus III, folder, p. 7.
57. Sorgo, Ode al Vescovo Giuriceo-Gagliufii Epigramma, folder, p. 3.
58. Bernardi Zamagne Epigramata, ad. Dom. Garagninum, de Napoleonis in bellis infelietate De Britannis in Hispania. Cur Galli semper vincant, folder, p. 4.
59. Marci Faust. Gagliuff: Carmina folder, p. 11.
60. M. N. Sorgo. In funere P. de Sorgo, folder, p. 2.
61. Extractum ex monumentis congregacionis S. Dominici de Ragussio, editis a P. Serapdi. Cerva, folder, p. 25.
62. Enrico Petrovich. Appunti stor. riguardanti i domenicani de Ragusa.
63. Appunti per l'istoria sacra di Ragusa 4° p. 4.
64. Appunti per l'istoria francescana di Ragusa folder, p. 2.
65. F. Gaglinfii. Elegia de Lod. J. Planae et Alexandrillae Lagrangiae, folder, p. 2.
66. Fr. Ant. Aghich. G.B. Spagnoletti. Cenni biografici, folder, p. 10.
67. Prospetto e apunti litterati ragusei (1493–1518).
68. Biografie succinte di alcuni (1700–1800) scrittori ragusei, folder, p. 2.
69. De Didache Pirro, Appunti, estratte ex folder, p. 4.
70. Sonetti del Conzo e del Petrarca trad. dal Gagliuffi, folder, p. 2.
71. In morte del Gagliuffi, folder, p. 4.
72. Cerva Seraph. (mss. orig.) Marcellus Tarchaniota, 4° p. 1.
73. Appunti biogr. crit. su scrittori e letterati che hanno qualche attinenza con la storia e letter ragusa, folder, p. 4.
74. Appunti (autogr.) del P. Cerva per la storia della metrop. Ragusina, folder, p. 4.
75. Breve di PP. Innocenza VIII. (Braccio di San Giovanni Batt. a. Ragusa. 4, p. 2.)
76. Appunti ai P.S. Cerva, 1° p. 2.
77. Liepopilli, Innocentio Chiulich et Raph. Radegliae, Carmina, folder, p. 2.
78. Ex Epistolario senatus rag. ad Capitulum S. Justinae—nee non adnotata diversa (Dolci), folder, p. 19.
79. Monumenta ragusanorum scriptorum P. Ser. Cervae, folder, p. 10. (Additur Mentio brevis loci O. M. Ragusini.)
80. Monumenta ex Bibliotheca P. Scraph. Cervae O.P. folder, p. 15. (? pro Coleto.)
81. Marulus. Haelius. Crotius, Benignus 4° p. 2.
82. Ad Ragusanam Historiam. Extractum. 8° p.
83. De Hist. ordinis Minor. Ragusii. Memorie 4° p. 6.

84. P. Fr. Antonius Aghich—Eruditis lectoribus, folder, p. 1.
85. Aelii Lampr. Cervini Carmina ex Cod. Vaticano, folder, p. 3.
86. Damiano-Benessa-Cenni biogr., folder, p. 1.
87. Aelii Lampridii Cervini.—Ex Cod. Mantovano, folder, p. 1.
88. Notae autobiograph. Mat. Joh. Mattei, 4° p. 4.
89. Confutazione dell' elogio di T. Chersa di Ant. Cesari 1° p. 4.
90. Notae hist. nonnulle Seraphini Cervae.
91. Opuscula tres.—Excerpta ex Carminibus Aelii L. Cervini—4° p. 86.
92. Aghich. In Aelii L. Cervini vitam, folder, p. 19.
93. Vita di M. Beccadelli vesc. die Ragusa, folder, p. 14.
94. A perpetua onoranza di Luca Stulli.
95. T. Chersae de Didaci Pirri Commentario, folder, p. 4.
96. Satira a M. Lazzari vesc. di Ragusa. folder, p. 2.
97. Varie poesie di Ragusi al Governatore Lilienberg, folder, p. 6.
98. Per le nozze di Giov. Mar. Gozze, folder, p. 5.
99. Maestri e rettori del Collegio dei gesuiti di Ragusa, folder, p. 4.
100. De mandato Aloysii Spagnoletti Archiep. Ragusani, folder, p. 1.
101. Aelii Lampridii Cervini Carmina nonnulla 1° p. 15. (mb. Higgia).
102. Fragmenta ex Seb. Dolci.

XXII. Fratrie. (Fraternities)

1. Matricole. (Registers)
(Vol. 16.)

1. Di S. Maria dell'Isola di Mezzo (membr. del 1416 die 14 mensis Octobris), folder, ser 12.
2. Di Sta Anna di Bergatto 2 Decembre 1611, membr. folder scr. 5.
3. Di S. Luca de'Bottegai di Ragusa 28 Gennaio 1450, membr, folder 12.
4. Degli Orefici di Ragusa, ms, sec. XVII, folder 48.
5. Di S. Giorgio alle tre Chiese e di S. Michele di Gravosa, ms. ser. XVII, folder 29.
6. Di S. Pietro in Catedra dei Preti di Stagno, ms. XVII, folder 12/15.
7. Della Immacolata concezione dei mobili di Ragusa, ms. s. XVIII, folder 12.
8. Della Immacolata concezione dei mobili di Ragusa, ms. s. XIX, folder 12.
9. Di San Michiele di Mercine superiore in Canali, 10 Giugno 1754, folder 4.
10. Di San Giovanni di Vatassi, 1 Junii 1755, folder 3.
10b. Di San Giovanni di Vatassi 2 Decembre 1760, folder 3.
11. Dei Preti di Ragusa San Pietro, 23 Giugno 1766, folder 2.—(Vide et XX. 2 No. 3).
12. Dei Pellizari di Ragusa 1697, Lulio 17, folder 11.
13. Confraternita dei Barrettari, 25 Ottobr. 1487, folder 3.
14. Specchio della Matricola degli Artusti 1758–1799, Alf.
15. Matricola della confraternita di S. Lazzaro 1536, folder 96.
16. Statuta et Decreta Congregationis Sacerdotun S. Petri in Cathedra instit. A.D. 1399, di 11 Augusti, folder 66.
17. Matricola della confraternita de ferrari e calderari 1 Febbr. 1696.
    Matricula Confrat. S.M. de Paclina. (Vide V, No. 46.)
    Matricula Confrat. Jupanae de Luca. (Vide V, No. 52.)

2. Capitoli e Parti. (Chapters and Sections) (Vol. 13.)

1. Libro delle Parti Confr. dei Fabbri 1661–1810, folder 90/21.
2. Libro delle Parti Confr. dei Muratori 1669–1806, folder 50/1.
3. Libro Capitolo Maggiore. Confr. di S. Lazzaro 1672–1811, folder 193/1.
4. Libro delle Parti Confr. de Satori 1674–1809, folder 87.
4a. Capellani della nostra scola dopo il terremoto 1667–1811, folder 11.
5. Capellani delle Parti nostra degli Orefici 1774–1810, folder 10.
6. Capellani delle Parti (frg.) nostra del Domino 1634–1811, folder 14.
7. Capellani officiali senatori all'arte degli Scarpari 1792–1796, folder 14/3.
8. Capellani delle Parti senatori dei Preti di Stagno 1732–1778, folder 79.
8a. Capellani delle Parti senatori dei Preti di Stagno 1779–1811, folder 44.
8b. Capellani officiali senatori dei Preti di Stagno 1740–1778, folder 9.
9. Capellani delle Parti senatori dei Barbieri Stagno 1709–1811, folder 16.
11. Terminazioni e note dell'offizio Servo della Confr. Macellari 1784–1786, folder 9.
12. Terminazioni e note del Senato sul Sevo della Confr. Macellari 1785–1791, folder 13.
13. Diverse terminazioni senatorie sulle arti, (fragm.,) 1747–1787.

3. Amministrazione. (Administration) Ricevute.—Spese.—Affitti. (Vol. 20.)

1. Ricevute de'Mansionari della Confraternita de'Preti 1631, folder 5. Ricevute Preti Ammalati 1631, folder 3.
2. Libretto di Tabacaria d. Confr. Pellipari 1657, folder 3.
3. Libretto Affitti della Confr. S. Antonio 1672–1684, folder 16.
4. Libretto delle Pontazioni della Confr. Preti di Stagno 1672–1684, Alf.
5. Libretto del'Escita della Confr. Orefici 1689–1732, folder 18.
6. Libretto Esacioni della Confr. Sant'Antonio 1692–1741, folder 87.
7. Libretto Spese della Confr. Beccari 1719–1738, folder 61.
8a. Libretto Spese della Confr. Barbieri 1728–1810, folder 37.
8b. Libretto Entrata della Confr. Barbieri 1728–1810, folder 49.
9. Libretto Ricevate Spese, malati della Confr. Preti Ragusa 1734, folder 82.
10. Libretto dell'Escita della Confr. Orefici 1734–1807, folder 67.
11. Libretto dell'Entrate della Confr. de'Fabri 1745–1811, folder 66. Spese della Amministrazione 1786–1811, folder 26.
12. Libretto Vendite, testamenti della Confr. Preti di Stagno 1776–1810, folder 148.
13. Libretto Confrati che devono pagare della Confr. Orefici 1772–1775, Alf.
14. Libretto Capitoli e loro pesi della Confr. Preti Stagno 1629–1811, folder 53.
15. Libretto Entrata ed Esito della Confr. Muratori 1781, folder 43.
16. Libretto Entrata ed Esito della Confr. Bottegai 1785–1811, folder 24/27.
17. Libretto Ricevute della Confr. di S. Lazzaro 1785–1811, folder 14.
18. Libretto Messe annuali della Confr. di S. Luca 1800–1811, folder 14.
19. Libretto Messe annuali della Confr. Preti 1718, folder 10.
20. Libretto Messe annuali della Confr. Preti 1718, folder 14.

4. Vacchette. (Leather)
(Vol. 14.)

1. Vacchetta dei Soldati 1588–1598, folder 27.
2. Vacchetta di Mokoscizza 1651–1679, folder 10.
3. Vacchetta parrocchiale di Ombla 1610–1714, folder 25.
4. Di Malfi, Verbizza, Ombla, Breno, Skalocce e Giupana 1742–1773, folder 45.
5. Dei Conti della Confr. dei Sartori 1746–1711, folder 85.
6. Della Confr. dei Beccari di S. Nicolo di Prieki 1763–1811, folder 40.
   Scossione dei debiti di S. Nicolo di Prieki 1742–1811, folder 33.
7. Vacchetta dei Soldati 1778–1787, folder 3.
8. Vacchetta della Confr. di S. Lazzaro 1792–1811, folder 28.
9. Vacchetta della Concezione 1787–1811, folder 62.
10. Vacchetta della del Carmine 1783–1811, folder 62.
11. Vacchetta della S. Rocco 1785–1811, folder 10.
12. Vacchetta della Rosario 1783–1811, folder 32.
13. Vacchetta della degli Orefici 1802–1803, folder 25.
14. Vacchetta della degli Scarpari 1811, folder 1.

5. Testamenti (Wills)
(Vol. 3.)

1. Alfabeto dei Specchi di Testamenti 1572, Alf.
2. Libretto dei Testamenti della Confr. S. Maria di Bison 1577–1656, folder 38.
3. Libretto dei Testamenti della Confr. di S. Lazzaro 1607–1772, folder 21.

6. Giornali e Libri. (Journals and Books)
(Vol. 35.)

1. Giornale vecchio della Confr. di Sta Maria del Bisson 1610–1634, folder 121.
2. Maestro vecchio della Confr. di Sta Maria del Bisson 1610–1634, folder 107.
3. Dare ed avere della Confr. dei Sacerdoti di Stagno 1647–1731, folder 94.
4. Maestro vecchio della Confr. di S. Rocco 1648–1774, folder 609.
5. Giornale vecchio della Confr. di S. Rocco 1648–1774, folder 731.
6. Maestro vecchio della Confr. di Rosgiatto 1661–1739, folder 282.
7. Giornale vecchio della Confr. di Rosario 1661–1740, folder 412.
8. Libro vecchio della Confr. di S. Rocco 1667–1773, folder 94.
9. Croceus della Confr. Preti di Stagno 1684–1743, folder 85.
10. Giornale della Confr. della Concezione 1684–1786, folder 634.
11. Giornale vecchio della Confr. del Carmine 1689–1780, folder 288.
12. Maestro della Confr. del Carmine 1689–1778, folder 205.
13. Giornale della Confr. Preti di Ragusa 1689–1730, folder 333.
14. Maestro della Confr. Sacerdoti di Stagno 1713–1786, folder 117.
15. Giornale della Confr. Sacerdoti di Stagno 1713–1788, folder 195.
16. Maestro della Confr. S. Lazzaro 1724–1810, folder 257.
17. Giornale della Confr. S. Lazzaro 1724–1811, folder 372.

18. Dare ed Avere della Confr. Sacerdoti di Ragusa 1732–1795, folder 127.
19. Maestro Nuovo della Confr. Rosgiatto 1740–1809, folder 351.
20. Giornale della Confr. Rosario 1740–1811, folder 514.
21. Maestro della Confr. S. MAria d. Bissone 1759–1809, folder 155.
22. Maestro della Confr S. Rocco 1774–1809, folder 168.
23. Giornale della Confr. S. Rocco 1774–1810, folder 280.
24. Giornale della Confr. S. Maria del Bisson 1760–1810, folder 219.
25. Giornale della Confr. S. Antonio 1779–1810, folder 241.
26. Giornale della Confr. Carmine 1781–1811, folder 157.
27. Maestro della Confr. Carmine 1781–1808, folder 97.
28. Maestro della Confr. Carmine 1785–1809, folder 130.
29. Giornale della Confr. Concezione 1785–1811, folder 199.
30. Specchietto Esito della Confr. Falegnami 1794–1810, folder 10/7.
31. Dare ed Avere della Confr. Preti di Stagno 1795–1811, folder 18.
32. Indice dei Libri Vecchi della Confr. del Rosario.
33. Indice dei Libri Vecchi della Confr. del St' Antonio.
34. Indice dei Libri Vecchi della Confr. del S. Rocco.
35. Indice dei Libri Vecchi della Confr. del Concezione.

7. Lanae. (Wool)
(Vol. 7.)

1. Vacchetta dell'arte delle Lane 1437–1477, folder 31/6.
2. Officiali dell'arte della Lana 1358–1563, folder 94.
3. Libro partite delle Lane 1571, folder 43.
4. Vacchetta delle Lane spagnole 1575–1590, folder 76.
5. Amministrazione delle Lane 1568–1604, folder 229.
6. Dare e Avere 1637–1641, folder 58.
7. Officiali dell'arte della Lana 1661, folder 30.

XXIII. Puntature. (Proceedings)
(Vol. 14.)

1. Dell'a. 1534–1540 (Ord. alph.), folder 142.
2. Dell'a. 1541–1577 (Ord. alph.), folder 193.
3. Dell'a. 1576–1602 (Ord. alph.), folder 187.
4. Dell'a. 1591–1592 (fragment.), folder 79.
5. Dell'a. 1599–1632 (Ord. alph.), folder 250.
6. Dell'a. 1619 in (Ord. alph.), folder 28.
7. Puntature Ecc. Minor Consiglio de anni 1573–1685, folder 7.
8. anni 1694–1732, folder 88.
9. anni 1732–1753, folder 139.
10. anni 1753–1772, folder 141.
11. anni 1772–1786, folder 143.
12. anni 1786–1797, folder 133.
13. anni 1797–1807. folder ?
14. Puntature dei Nobili de 1652 in 1740 folder 223.

z

XXIV. Sentenze di Cancellaria.
(Chancellory Decrees)
(Vol. 260.)

1. Annorum 1352.
2. Annorum 1376.
3. 4. Annorum 1388–1406.
5.–86. Annorum 1414–1434.
9.–47. Annorum 1436–1487.
48.–258. Annorum 1489–1811.
259. Annorum 1814.
260. Annorum 1815.

XXV. Diversa Cancellariae.
(Various Chancellory Documents)
(Vol. 235.)

1. (a) 1282. (XV Julii) ad 1284 (18 Januarii).
   (b) 1282. Liber in quo abreviate sunt omnes notariae, exceptis testamentis et sententiis tempare nobilis viri D. Johannis Georgii comitis Ragusii, scriptus per me Thomasinum de Savere, sacri palatii et com. Ragusii notarium. 1282 (19 Julii ad 1283 2 Novembr.).
   (c) 1283. Liber in quo abreviate sunt carthe notarie factus per me Thomasinum not, com. Ragusii. exceptis cartis debitorum, et sententiarum. Tempore dom. Johannis Georgii Comitis Ragusii, 1283. (3 Nov.)—ad 1284 (18 Januari).
   N.B. Partes (b), (c) huic volumini allegate, ad Diversa Notarie pertinent.
2. (a) 1284. Liber de procurationibus, testificationibus et aliis actibus omnibus, exceptis malefitiis . . . tempore nob. viri domini Michaelis Manroceni comitis honorab. Ragusii, per me Thomasinum de Savere, sacri palatii et comunis Ragusii notarium existentibus iuratis indicibus Dimitrio de Mence, Andreas de Benessa, . . . de Bincola et Ursacio de Villiarico. Anno Domini MCCLXXXIIII, Ind. XII.—Qui Dominus Comes predictus, die ultimo mensis iunii (1284) applicuit Ragusiam.
      Anno Domini MCCLXXXV, Ind. XIII.
      Anno Domini MCCLXXXVI, Ind. XIIII.
   (b) Diversa Cancellarie ab anno MCCLXXIIII (17 Julii)—ad MCCLXXXVI 15 Jan.)
   Diversa Cancellarie ab anno MCCLXXIIII (8 Julii)—ad MCCLXXXVI (17 Martii).
   Diversa Cancellarie ab anno MCCLXXIIII (16 Martii) ad MCCLXXXVI (19 Jan.).
   N.B. Pars (a) huius voluminis, ad Diversa Notarie adscribenda est.
3. (a) 1295. Quaternus de induciis datis in curia maiori per nobilem virum dom. Marinum Maurocenum honorabilem comitem Ragusii, et iuratos indices Andream Benexe Vitalem Bincole, Martolum Cereve . . . currente anno Domini MCCLXXXXV,—halictione VIII (a die XXIIII Madii—ad diem III Julii MCCLXXXXVII).

(b) Capitulum de possessionibus venditis et praeconicatis (a die XI Junii—ad diem XVI Junii.

(c) Venditiones, debita, maleficia etc., a die XVI Septembr. ad ann. MCCLXXXXVII d. XXX Martii.

N.B. Pars (a) ad seriem etiam Notariorum pertinet partes nulem (b), (c) Venditionibus, Debitis alque Maleficiis, adscribuntue.

4. 1305 Liber generalis diversarum scripturarum ad memoriam et cautclam tempore nobiis viri domini Bellecti Falletro comitis Ragusii, currente anno domini MCCCV, Indiet III scriptus per me Ricardum notarium et comunis Ragusii iuratum cancellarium. Qui dominus (Comes) applicuit Ragusii et iuravit regim. Ragusii die domiaieo XXII ineunte mense Augusti—(a die XXII Augusti 1305—ad diem XVIIII Augusti 1306).

5. 1312–1314.
(a) Liber generalis diversarum scripturarum etc., tempore nobilis viri (Bartholomei Gradonigo comitis, in sue secundo regimine, sub anno domini (1312) die XX Julii).
(b) Capitulum de venditionibus, usque ad d. XXI Julii (1314).
N.B. Pars (b) ad seriem 'de venditionibus' adscribenda est.

6. 1320–1322.
(a) Liber pactorum, snetentiarum et venditionum rerum stbilium et emnium aliarum diversarum scripturarum . . . tempore egregii et potentis viri Domini Bartholomei Gradonigo, honorab. comitis, per me Ponem de Stamberto, iur. cancell, comunis Ragusii in anno dom. MCCCXX. Indict. III (a die XXII Junii 1320—ad diem V Aprilis 1322).
(b) Capitulum de Venditonibus etc., a die VIIII Julii 1321—ad diem 1 Aprilis 1322.
N.B. Pars (b) ad seriem 'de Vendicionibus' pertinet.

7. 1323—a die XVII Junii, usq. ad. d. II Decembris.

8. 1325–1327.
(a) Liber diversarum factus tempore potentis viri domini Pauli Trivixani, honorab comitis Ragusii, per me Ponem Stamberto inratum cancellarium, in Anuo Domini MCCCXXV. Indict. VII. (A die XXVII Junii, ad d. XXVII Augusti 1327).
(b) Capitulum de Venditionibus eee. (a die XXVIII Junii 1325, ad d. XVIII Junii 1327).
N.B. Capitulum sub b ad seriem 'de venditionibus' pertinet.

9. 1328–1330.
Liber de sententiis et aliis diversis scripturis, et de possessionibus venditis et alienatis, scriptus per me Ponem de Stamiberto ecc. tempore nob, et potent, viri dom. Balduyni Dalphyno hon. com. Ragusii, bus anno Domnii MCCCXXVIII—a die XIIII Octobris 1328—usque ad d. XVII Sept. 1330).

10. 1333–1334.
Liber sententiarum, pactorum et aliarum diversarum scripturarum, factus tempore nob. et potent. viri domini Marchi Iustiniani honorab. comitis Ragusii sub MCCCXXXIII Ind. 1—(a die XVII mensis Marcii 1333—usq. ad. d. III Novembr. 1334.

11. 1334–1336.
(a) Capitulum lamentationum facturum tam per mare quam per terram, dampnorum, datorum tam per insulas, quam per Astaream et testium examinatorum, scriptum tempore egregi et potent. viri domini Nicolay Faletro, honor,

comitis Ragusii. Anno dni. MCCCXXXIIII. Ind. II die IIII Novembris—
(usque ad d. 4 Decembris 1336.
(b) Capitulum dampnorum datorum in possessionibus per insulas. Anno Dni.
MCCCXXXIIII. (a die 6 Novembr. usque ad d. 8 Novembr. 1336).
(c) Capitulum testium examinatorum (eiasdem temporis).
(d) Die XIIII Novembr. MCCCCLXXXIIII 'Vendiciones et fines' (folder 1).
N.B. (a), (b), (c) ad 'Lamenta'; d.) per accidens alligatum ad 'Vendinones'
pertinent.

12. (a) 1334–1337. (a die VIII Novembr.—ad. d. Kal. Maii 1337).
(b) 1350–1351. Capitulum diversarum scripturarum factarum nobilis et
potentis Domini Marchi Superantio, honor, com. Lagusii MCCCL Ind. III—
die VIIII mensis Octobris (usq. ad. d. 20 Octobris 1351.

13. 1341–1351. Liber in quo scripte sunt omnes diverse scripture, pacta et con-
ventiones, tempore nobilis et potentis viri domini Johannis Fuscareni honor.
Com. Ragusii, sub a. MCCCXLI. Ind. VIIII die primo mensis Martii applicuit
regimini civitatis Ragusii—(a die 2 Aprilis 1341—usq. ad d. Decembris
1342).

14. (a) 1328–1329 (a die 15 ineunte mense octobris 1328—usq. ad. d. 1 Decembr.
1320).
(b) 1343–1345 (a.d. Kal. Maii 1343—a d. 22 Madii 1345).
(c) adduntur. Gride de ann. 1343 (a d. 16 Junii—)—1345 (usq. ad d. 12
Februarii).

15. 1345–1348 (a die 8 Junii usq. ad d. 9 Octobr. 1348).

16. 1348–1350 (a die 14 Octobris 1348 usq. ad d. 30 Maii 1350).

17. 1351–1352 (a die 26 Octobr. 1354 usq. ad d. 19 Januarii 1352).

18. 1354–1356. Liberdiversarum scripturarum factus tempore domini Nicolai
Barbarige honor. Cpmiti Ragusii (a d. 23 Martii 1354 usq. ad. d. 5 Novembr.
1356).

19. 1362–1371 (a d. 20 Novemb. 1362 usq. ad. d. 22 Junii 1365) (a d. 22 Octobr.
1364 usq. ad. d. 15 Februar 1371). (Everso: 26 Junii 1364 usq. ad d. 25 Septemb.
1364).

20. 1365–1366 (a d. 18 Martii 1365 usq. ad. d. 1 Decemb. 1366).

21. 1366–1368 (Vide et Div. Canc. vol. 2) (a d. 11 Novembr. 1366 usq. ad d.
27 Maii 1368).

22. 1369–1370 (a d. 18 Junii 1369 usq. ad d. 27 Februar. 1370).

23. 1371–1372. (a) (a die 2 Januar. 1371 usq. ad d. 30 Decemb. 1372).
(b) Everso—Distributiones testamentorum 1372, Decembr., folder 2.

24. 1375–1376 (a die 1 Januarii 1375 usq. ad d. 31 Decemb. 1376) additur. Div.
Cane. 1 Jan. 1377, additur. Parzogna quedam c a. 1376 d. d. 18 Augusti.

25. 1381–1383—In Christi nomine. Amen. Liber Diversarum scripturarum
comunis Ragusii. hic est inceptus sub ann. dom. nativ. MCCCLXXXI. Ind.
IIII die XXII m. Septembris (— usq. ad d. 4 Octobr. 1383).

26. 1385–1387 (a die 17 Novembr. 1385 ad d. 27 Maii 1387).

27. 1387–1389 (a d. 2 Junii 1387 usq. ad d. 30 Julii 1389).

28. 1388–1395 (a die 3 Octobr. 1388 usq. ad. d. 12 Decembr. 1396). Gride, b) 1436
(a die 27 Februari 1436 usq. ad d. 29. Martii 1436).

29. 1389–1391. Liber diversarum scripturarum cancellarie in millesimo CCC
LXXXVIIII. Ind. XII. die I mensis Aug.—usq. ad d. 29 Decembr. 1391.

30. 1392–1394. r. (a die VIII Maii 1392—usq. ad d. 11 Martii 1393). Ev. (a die
11 Martii 1393—usq. ad d. 16 Febr. 1394).

31. 1391–1396. (a d. 7 Nombr. 1391—usq. ad d. 3 Martii 1396).
32. 1306–1399. Liber diversarum scripturarum Cancellarie Ragusii inchoatus in MCCCLXXXVI Indict IIII. de mense Novembris. (a. d. 27 Novembr. 1396—ad. d. 18 Junii 1399).
33. 1396–1402. (a die IIII Februari 1396—ad d. 31 Januari 1402.)
34. 1401–1403. Liber diversar. scripturarum Chancellarie Ragusii, inchoatus in MCCCC I. Ind. VIIII. die primo mensis Julii 1401. (usque ad d. 23 Maii 1403).
35. 1403–1405. Liber diversar. scripturar. Cancellarie Ragusii in MCCCCIII. Ind. XI die VIIII mensis Junii 1403. (usq. ad d. 30 Novembr. 1405).
36. 1405–1408. (a d. 12 Decembr. 1405. usq. ad. d. 8 Januari 1408).
37. 1408–1409. Liber diversarum scripturar. cancelarie inchoatus in MCCCCVIII. Ind. I. die VII Februari (1408) (usq. ad d. 31 Augusti 1409).
38. 1408–1443. (a d. 1 Maii 1408—ad d. 2 Novembr. 1413).
39. 1411–1414. Liber diversar. scripturar. cancellarie comunis Ragusii in MCCCCXI. Ind. IIII. die VI Decembris. (usq. ad 13 Januarii 1413).
40. 1414–1416. (a d. 7 Maii 1414 usq. ad 31 Marcii 1416).
41. 1416–1418. (a d. 1 Aprilis 1416 usq. ad 21 Septembr. 1418).
42. 1422–1424. (a d. 25 Januari 1422 usq. ad 16 Julii 1424).
43. 1424–1426. (a d. 17 Julii 1424 usq. ad Kal. April 1426)
44. (a) 1426–1428. (a d. 24 Marcii 1426 usq. ad 18 Junii 1428).
    (b) Sententie misse et facte de foris s. d. 27 Februarii 1428.—In Srebernica.
45. (a) 1428–1429. (a d. 16 Junii 1428—usq. ad 13 Augusti 1429).
    (b) Cautela sententiarum de foris. Acta in Rudnicho (d. d. 2 Zugno 1428).
46. 1429–1431. (a die 13 Augusti 1429 usq. ad. d. 28 Februari 1431).
47. 1432–1433. (a die 6 Decembris 1432 ad d. 25 Maii 1433).
48. 1433–1435. (a die 23 Novembr. 1433 ad. d. 16 Mareii 1435). Ev.) Copia cuiusdam sentente arbitralia d. d 29 Decembr. 1434 in Srebernica.—Screbernica.—Compromissum d.d 7 Zugno 1434.
49. 1435–1436. Liber diversarum scripturarum canzelarie incheatus die XVI Marcii MCCCCXXXV (usq. ad d. 18 Novembr. 1437).
50. 1436–1437. (a) Liber diversarum etc. inchoatus die primo Junii MCCCCXXXVI Indict. XIIII. (usq. ad d. 18 Novembr. 1437). (b) Ev.: Sententia lata per Capitaneum de la Punta d.d. 31 Decembris 1434.
51. 1437. (a die 13 Augusti 1437 usq. ad d. 17 Septm. 1437).
52. 1437–1438. (a die 19 Decembr. 1437 usq. ad d. 31. Decembr. 1438).
53. 1438–1439. (a die 16 Septmbr. 1438 usq. ad d. 1 Novembr. 1439).
54. 1439–1440. (a die 2 Novembr. 1439 usq. ad d. 10 Septmbr. 1440).
55. 1440–1442. (a die 11 Septmbr. 1440 usq. ad d. 30 Januari 1442).
56. 1442. (a die 6 Februari 1442 usq. ad d. 28 Octobr. 1442).
57. 1442–1443. (a die 26 Octobris 1442 usq. ad d. 6 Julii 1443).
58. 1443–1444. (a die 6 Julii 1443 usq. ad d. 29 Maii 1444).
59. 1445–1446. (a die 20 Junii 1445 usq. ad d. 30 Julii 1446.
60. 1446–1447. (a die 1 Augusti 1446 usq. ad. d. 21 Novembr. 1447).
61. 1447–1449. (a die 22 Novembr. 1447—ad d. 3 Januari 1449).
62. 1450–1451. (a die 18 Januari 1450—ad d. 21 Julii 1451).
63. 1451–1452. (a die 23 Juli 1451—ad d. 31 Decembr. 1452).
64. 1454. (a) (a die 4 Gluglo 1454—ad d. 30 Decembre 1454).
    (b) Chontra lettere 4 gluglo ad 9 gluglo 1454. Per chomandamento de Signori Chazamorti dd. 16 Augusto.

Z*

65. 1455–1456. (a) (a die 3 Marcii 1455—ad diem 2 April 1456).
    (b) cautela: Litteratum Episcopi Merchanensis ad Archiep. et clerum ragusinum de mandato Calixti Pont. dd. 14 Julii. 1455. Gravaminis Marini qui. Viti Goze, 15 Julii.
66. 1456–1457. (a die 31 Maii 1456 usq. ad d. 11 Octobr. 1457).
67. 1457–1458. (a die 10 Octobr. 1457 usq. ad d. 20 Octobr. 1458). Registrum alphabeticam.
68. 1458–1459. (a die 19 October. 1458 usq. ad d. 25 Septembr. 1459).
69. 1459–1460. (a die 20 Septembr. 1459 usq. ad d. 29 Novmbr. 1460. nee non 3 Decembr. 1460). Registrum alphabet.
70. 1460–1461. (a die 11 Decembr. 1460 usq. ad d. 23 Novembr. 1461). Registrum imperfectum. (—1461–1463 Hic vide Diversa Notarie Nr. 45. huius temporis.
71. 1463–1464. (a die 9 Februarii 1463 usq. ad d. 26 Junii 1464).
72. 1464–1465. (a die 26 Juni 1464 usq. ad d. 3 Decembr. 1465).—1465–1467, addas Nr. 50 'Diversorum Notarie'.
73. 1466–1467. Liber diversarum actionum que aguntur per Selavos contra Raguseos, inceptus die XX Januarii MCCCCLXVI.
    N.B. Hoc loco vide vol. 52 'Div de Notaria'.
74. 1469–1471. (a die 28 Julii 1469—usq. ad d. 1 Junii 1471).
75. 1471–1473. (a) (a die p° Junii 1471 usq. ad d. 4 Augusti 1473).
    (b) Collegantia dd. 18 Sept. 1471. Jacobi velutarii et Johannis Januensis.
76. 1473–1474 (a die 6 Augusti 1473 usq. ad d. 29 Decembr. 1474).
77. 1475–1476. (a die 4 Januarii 1475 usq. ad d. 20 Aprilis 1476). 1476–1477. Hoc loca adde 'Diversa Notarie' huius temporis Nr. 62.
78. 1477–1478. (a) (a die 17 Maii 1477—usq. ad d. 20 Junii 1478).
    (b) cautele diverse.
79. 1478–1479. (a) (a die 1 Julii 1478. usq. ad d. 19 Novembr. 1479).
80. 1479–1481. (a die 27 Novembr. 1479 usq. ad 30 Januarii 1481).
81. 1481–1482. (a die 1 Februari 1481 usq. ad 4 Maii 1482).
82. 1482–1483. (a) (a die 5 Maii 1482 usq. ad 14 Decembr. 1483).
    (b) Creatio tabeliouis per Barth. de Sfondatis d. d. 28 Decembr. 1482. Cautela libelli Joh. B., Ragnina 22 Oct.
    1481. Presentatio abadis—6 Martii 1482. Protectum Naulizati. 12 Decembr. 1484.
83. 1483–1485. (a) (a die 20 Novmbr. 1483 usq. ad. d. 28 Februari 1485).
    (b) Cautele U.S.
84. 1485–1486. (a die p° Martii 1485 usq. ad 3 Junii 1486).
85. 1486–1487. (a die 10 Junii 1486 asq. ad 24 Octobr. 1487).
86. 1487–1489. (a) (a die 25 Octobr. 1487 usq. ad 7 Septmb. 1489).
    (b) Cautele u.s.
87. 1489–1491 (a die 7 Septmbr. 1489 usq. ad d. 7 Februarii 1491).
88. 1491–1492 (a die 28 Februar 1491 usq. ad d. 4 Augusti 1492).
89. 1492–1493. (a) (a die 4 Augusti 1492 usq. ad d. 28 Decmbr. 1493).
    (b) Cautela.
90. 1494–1495. (a) (a die 30 Decembr. 1494 usq. ad d. 18 Augusti 1495).
    (b) Sequestratum: 8 Juli 1495.
91. 1495–1497 (a die 18 Augusti 1495 usq. ad d. 29 Aprilis 1497).
92. 1497–1498. (a) (a die 6 Februarii 1497 usq. ad. d. 14 Maii 1498).
    (b) Inventarium bonorum defuneti 25 Sept. 1497).

92. 1497–1498. (a) (a die 13 Octobr. 1497 ad d. 14 Augusti 1498.
    (b) Cautela 14 Novembr. 1497. (Volumen hoc addes ad seriem Diversarum Notarie ad Nr. 72).
93. 1498–1499. (a die 15 Maii 1498 usq. ad d. 12 Octobr. 1499).
94. 1499–1500. (a) (a die 12 Octobr. 1499 usq. ad d. 18 Decembr. 1500).
    (b) Cautela u.s.
95. 1500–1502. (a die 22 Decembr. 1500 usq. ad d. 1 April 1502).
96. 1502–1503. (a) (a die 1 Aprilis 1502 usq. ad d. 18 Julii 1503).
    (b) Cautela sententie 5 Januari 1503.
97. 1503–1505. (a) (a die 18 Julii 1503 usq. ad d. 31 Januari 1505).
    (b) Cautele u.s.
98. 1505–1506. (a) (a die prima Februarii 1505 usq. ad d. 11 Aprilis 1506).
    (b) Cautela ut supra.
99. 1506–1507. (a) (a die 11 Aprilis 1506 usq. ad d. 12 Junii 1507).
    (b) Cautele u.s.
100. 1507–1508. (a) (a die 1 Julii 1507 usq. ad d. 21 Novembr. 1508).
    (b) Cautele u.s.
101. 1508–1509. (a) (a die 21 Novembr 1508 usq. ad d. 2 Decembris 1509).
    (b) Cautele u.s.
102. 1509–1511. (a) (a die 29 Novembr. 1509 usq. ad d. 28 Aprilis 1511).
    (b) Cautele u.s.
103. 1511–1512. (a) (a die 29 Aprilis 1511 usq. ad d. 30 Septmbr.
    (b) Cautele u.s.
104. 1512–1514. (a) (a d. 29 Septembr. 1512 usq. ad 27 Februarii 1514).
    (b) Cautele u.s.
105. 1514–1515. (a) (a d. Martii 1514 usq. ad d. 30 Juli 1515).
    (b) Cautele u.s.
106. 1515–1516. (a) (a d. 31 Julii 1515 usq. ad d. 21 Novembr. 1516).
    (b) Cautele u.s.
107. 1517–1518. (a) (a d. 21 Martii 1517 usq. ad d. 1 Julii 1518).
    (b) Cautele u.s.
108. 1518–1519. (a) (a d. p^a Julii 1518 usq. ad d. 30 Junii 1519).
    (b) Cautele u.s.
109. 1519–1522. (a) (a d. 1 Julii 1519 usq. ad d. 26 Novembr. 1520).
    (b) Cautele u.s.
110. 1520–1522. (a) (a d. 27 Novmbr. 1520 usq. ad d. 6 Januarii 1522).
111. 1522–1523. (a) (a d. 22 Martii 1522 usq. ad d. 17 Junii 1523).
    (b) Cautele u.s.
112. 1523–1524. (a) (a d. 18 Junii 1523 usq. ad d. 23 Augusti 1524).
    (b) Cautele u.s.
113. 1524–1525. (a) (a d. 18 Augusti 1524 usq. ad d. 14 Junii 1525).
    (b) Cautele u.s.
114. 1525–1526. (a) (a d. 13 Junii 1525 usq. ad d. 12 Augusti 1526).
    (b) Cautele u.s.
115. 1526–1527. (a) (a d. 14 Augusti 1526 ad d. 17 Aprilis 1527).
    (b) Cautele u.s.
116. 1528–1529. (a) (a d. 18 Aprilis 1528 ad d. 14 Aprilis 1529).
    (b) Cautele u.s.
117. 1529–1530. (a) (a d. 18 Aprilis 1529 ad d. 26 Februarii 1530).
    (b) Cautele u.s.

118. 1530. (a) (a d. 26 Februarii a d. 28 Novembr. 1530).
     (b) Cautele u.s.
119. 1530–1531. (a) (a d. 29 Novembr. 1530 ad d. 26 Octobr. 1531).
     (b) u.s.
120. 1531–1533. (a) (a d. 26 Octobr. 1531 ad d. 15 Januarii 1533).
     (b) Cautele u.s.
121. 1533–1534. (a) (a d. 18 Januarii 1533 ad d. 11 Augusti 1534).
     (b) Cautele u.s.
122. 1534–1535. (a) (a d. 27 Augusti 1534 ad d. 28 Octobr. 1535).
     (b) Cautele u.s.
123. 1535–1537. (a) (a d. Novembr. 1535 ad d. 23 Januarii 1537).
     (b) u.s.
124. 1537–1538. (a) (a d. 23 Januarii 1537 ad d. 13 Augusti 1538).
     (b) u.s.
125. 1538–1539. (a) (a d. 13 Augusti 1538 ad d. 23 Septembr. 1539).
     (b) u.s.
126. 1539–1540. (a) (a d. 24 Septembr. 1539 ad die 12 Novembr. 1540).
     (b) u.s.
127. 1540–1541. (a) (a d. Novembr. 1540 ad d. 22 Novembr. 1541).
     (b) u.s.
128. 1541–1542. (a) (a d. 23 Novembris 1541 ad diem 29 Novmb. 1542).
     (b) u.s.
129. 1542–1544. (a) (a d. 29 Novmbr. 1542 ad diem 19 Aprilis 1544).
     (b) u.s.
130. 1544–1545. (a) (a d. 22 ad diem 3 Septembr. 1545) .
     (b) Cantela u.s.
131. 1545–1546. (a) (d. 29 Augusti 1545 ad diem 19 Novembr. 1654 a).
     (b) u.s.
132. 1546–1548. (a) (a d. 19 Novembr. 1546 ad diem 9 Januari 1548).
     (b) u.s.
133. 1548–1549. (a) (a d. 10 Januarii 1548 ad diem 12 Martii 1549).
     (b) u.s.
134. 1549–1550. (a) (a d. 12 Februarii 1549 ad diem 28 Martii 1550).
     (b) u.s.
135. 1550–1551. (a) (a d. 29 Martii 1550 ad diem 21 Maii 1551).
     (b) u.s.
136. 1550–1552. (a) (a d. 20 Maii 1551 ad diem 11 Maii 1552).
     (b) u.s.
137. 1552–1553. (a) (a d. 13 Maii 1552 ad diem p^a. Aprilis 1553).
     (b) u.s.
138. 1553–1554. (a) (a d. 6 Aprilis 1553 ad diem p^a. Februarii 1554).
     (b) u.s.
139. 1554. (a) (a d. p^a Februarii 1554 ad diem 3 Novembr. 1554).
     (b) u.s.
140. 1554–1555. (a) (a a. 15 Novembr. 1554 ad diem ult^a Maii 1555).
     (b) u.s.
141. 1555–1556. (a) (a d. 30 Maii 1555 ad diem 12 Martii 1556).
     (b) u.s.
142. 1556–1557 a d. 13 Martii ad 26 Jan. 1557 Cautelae Divisio Tabacchariae.

143. 1557 a d. 26 Jan. and 9 Octobr. Litt. Comitis Iusulae de medio—Scripturae ex Messana et Missina.
144. 1557–1558. a d. a dic 9 Octobr. ad 25 Junii 1558 Cautelae—Recordia Computaque nonnulla.
145. 1559–1560. a d. 27 April. ad 16 Febr. 1560 Cautelae n. u. Actr ex Messana et Baro.
146. 1560–1561. a d. 20 Febr. ad 21 Januar. 1561 Cautelae n. u. Scripturae ex Neapoli Yanua, Messana, Florentia, Ancona, et Chio Epistolae Episcopi tribuniensis n. a. Archiep. Ragusini.
147. 1561. a d. 23 Januarii ad 17 Octobr. Cautelae.
148. 1561–1562. a d. 17 Octobr. ad 24 Julii 1562 Cantele. Acta ex Ancona, Curzola, Yanua, Messana, Venetiis, Barulo, Syracusis, Cautelae.
149. 1562–1563, a d. 24 Julii ad Aug. 1563 Cantelae n. u. Acta Curiae Archiepiscopalis.
150. 1563–1574. a d. 7 Aug. ad 18 Januar. 1564. Cautelae u.s.
151. 1565–1566. a d. 19 Januarii ad 27 Aprilis 1566 Cantelae Sorgo, Nenchovich, Gradii, Menze, Sumicich, Milerii, de Pasqualious, de Primo, Milatovich, Bonaccorsi, Pardi, Gondola, Giorga, Bolizae, Elorio, Chiolich, de Gentilibus.
152. 1566–1567, a d. Maii ad 9 Augusti 1567 Cautelae Bisia, Cerva, Allegretti, Gondola, Yesusovich, Conssessina, Miniate, Menge, Gualberucci, Caloscevich, Bonda, Drago Polo, Marini, Acta e Messana.
153. 1567–1568. a d. 11 Augusti ad 15 Julii 1568 Cautelae Jerro, Zuzzovi, Ruscinovich, Jelich, Draceviza, Sorgo, Cerva, Gondola, Gozze, Bonda, Pozza, Radulovich, Herges, de Stephanis, Lucari, Dobrich, Nascinbeni, Angeli, Sassin, Tudisio, de Antichiis Bersica.
154. 196. Cautelae ab anno 1568 u. a. a. 1608.
197. Cautelae annor. 1610–1611.
198–209. Cautelae annor. 1614–1644.
210–212. Cautele annor. 1650–1665.
213–234. Cautelae annor. 1669–1815.

XXVI. Diversa Notariae. (Various Solicitors Documents) (Vol. 147.)

1. Annor. 1310–1313 a die Kal. Febr. MCCCX ad d. primam Junii MCCCXIII.
2. Annor. 1314–1317 a die XVIII Intr. Novembr. MCCCXIII ad d. XXII Madii MCCCXVII.
3. Annor. 1318–1320 a d. XXII Madii MCCCXVIII ad d. XXVII Julii MCCCXX
4. Annor. 1324–1325 Liber de sentenciis et vendicionibus possessionum et aliarum diversarum scripturarum, compositus tempore egregii et potent. viri Domini Hugolini Justiniani honorab. Comitis Raugii et scriptus per me Ponem de Stamberto imp ant. notaret nune Communis Raugii iuratum cancel. in anno dni millesimo tercentesimo vigesimo quarto. ind. VII A die II Mai MCCCXXIIII ad d. XVIIII Septembris MCCCXXV.
5. Annor, 1324–1330. a die X Septemb. MCCCXXIIII ad d. XXIII Febr. MCCCXXX Adduntur: (a) Fiuccii et Sauellae procura de mena frumenti. (b) Fhilippi de Florentia proc. mandatum. XVIIII Junii. (c) De Domini episcopi catharensis electione et procesc. II Dec. MCCCXXVIIII. (d) De

libris XI e. gross. venetor, acceptis Petro Magistri Antonii de Yadra XXVI Aprilis MCCCXXX. (e) Electio Abatis s. Transfigurati per Archiep. Bonaventuram (s.d.). (f) Sindicatus de rebus frumentariis XV Julii MCCCXVIIII. (g) Solutio debiti Jacobelli de Barulo MCCCXXVIIII d. XV Augusti. (h) Charta debitorialis Demetrii presbiteri XXIIII. Junii MCCCXXXIII. (i) Usurpatio possessiouis Milieni Stoiani de Lagusta per Vlacoe de Curzola e. d.). (k) Permutatio inter italicos mercatores. XV Martii MCCCXXVIIII. (l) Debita communis Ragusii V Augusti MCCCXXVIIII (m) Syndicatus frumentorum. V Augusti MCCCXXVIII. (n) Jadratini salem et res aliquasad mercata regis Raxie ducere nequant. Augusti (s. a) (o) Marcata Jadratini Cathari exercere nequcant XIIII. Aug. (s.a). (p) Hominos de la Crayna ad portum Juliane marinarios iadertinos interficiunt. (s.d). (q) Johannes pp. Fratribus Minoris Observatiae licentian, ecclesiam, conventumque erigendi in civitate concedit (22 Sept. 1317). (r) Ragusani ab Anchonitanis pacem ac concordium petunt. (s. d.). (s) Naves frumento Acarallorum onustae e partibus Apuleae, consentientibus magistris portulanis, Ragusium applicuerunt a M. de Ranina ductae (9 Nov. ?). (t) Tarrida u.s., fabis onusta et a Fr. Thinduysio ducta, ibidem applicuit (5 Nov. ?) (u) Ragusani a Veneciarum duce franchigiam mercibus e Romania evectis, petunt (10 Nov. ?). (v) Debiti solutionis pattialis per commune Ragusii mandatum (s.d.). (w) De lite inter Thomam Archiep. ragusanum et Aclitum Saraca Canpnicum vertente coram legato apostolico. (s.d.). (x) (N. 24) deficiens (s.d.). (x) Debita Michaelis Ranina (s.d.). (y) Fragmentum procurae cuiusdam s.d.) (x) De lite inter Archiepiscopum et canonicum quemdam, germanum num suum (forsitan ut supra de Aclio Saraca), solutio et absolutionis protestum.

6. Diversa notarial ab anno 1339–1341.
7. Diversa notariae ab anno 1352–1358.
8. Diversa notariae ab anno 1362–1370.
9. Diversa notariae ab anno 1370–1379.
10. Diversa notariae ab anno 1387–1391.
11. Diversa notariae ab anno 1402–1408.
12–65. Diversa notariae ab anno 1413–1481.
66–101. Diversa notariae ab anno 1485–1530.
102–116. Diversa notariae ab anno 1533–1559.
117–135. Diversa notariae ab anno 1563–1619.
235. Diversa notariae ab anno 1617–1658.
138–140. Diversa notariae ab anno 1618–1681.
141–144. Diversa notariae ab anno 1686–1781.
145. Diversa notariae ab anno 1772–1773.
146–147. Diversa notariae ab anno 1783–1811.

XXVII. Lettere e Commissioni.
(Letters and Commissions)

1. Lettere di Levante. (Letters from the Levant) (Vol. 110.)

1. Annorum 1395, ad. 1425, folder 130 Littere sclavicae, edite ab Urso e comitib. Pozza cubtitulo Cpnckn Cnomehnlln y beorpary 1858.
2. Annorum 1359, ad. 1380, folder 148, n. n. Citatoriae 1376–1379, 1380.

3. Annorum 1382, ad. 1383, folder 165. n. n. 1419–1422, 1442–1443, 1419–1420, 1420 intenciones 1382, 1383: lamenta a 1442–1444.

4. Annorum 1403, ad. 1410, folder 167. u. n. cilaciones et consulatus.

5. Annorum 1403, ad. 1410, folder 211, n. n. 1411, 1413, 1473–1492, 1501, 1568–1570, 1595—item. Cautelae et citatoriales;—cautela testamenti d. d. 28 Dec. 1400: Regestum e diversi notariae, maior, et minor, consilii ad usum cancellarie notar.—Receptio bonorum Dionisii de Victoriis Faventini notarii Ragusii: Cautela balle Innocentii VIII. d. d. 10 Julii 1490.

6. Annorum 1411 ad. 1522, folder 169, n. n. Relationes consulum et mercatorum in Sreberniza ad Senatum. Citaciones et appellaciones passim.

7. Annorum 1411–1416, folder 161. Citaciones passim.

8. Annorum 1420, ad. 1423, folder 183, n. n. 1446–1447, item Citationes et Peticiones.

9. Annorum 1423, ad. 1427, folder 200. nonnullae sec. XVI item. Citationes.

10. Annorum 1427, ad. 1430, n. n. 1426, 1431, 1433–1435, item Citationes.

11. Annorum 1430, ad. 1435, folder 282, n. n. Appellationes.

12. Annorum 1435, ad. 1440, folder 231, n. n. Appellationes, Citationes.

13. Annorum 1440, ad. 1448, folder 286, n. n. Citationes.

14. Annorum 1448, ad. 1462, folder 238, n. n. 1464–1466, 1468, 1470, 1472–1479–1481–1483, 1485–1490, 1492–1494, 1496, 1546. Item Citationes et Lamenta passim.

15. Annorum 1449, ad. 1453, folder 188.

16. Annorum 1454, ad. 1460, folder 266.

17. Annorum 1493, ad. 1568, folder 178, n. n. 1569, 1575, 1574–1593, 1596, 1606–1607, 1612, 1623, 1635, 1654, 1656, 1664. Lamenta et Citationes passim.

18. Annorum 1511, ad. 1519, folder 113–2, n. n. 1526.

19. Annorum 1504, ad. 1505, n. n. 1416 ad. 1526, folder 255–1.

20. Annorum 1526, ad. 1535, folder 274, n. n. 1541–1542.

21. Annorum 1535, ad. 1538, folders 140–150. Bulla pom. d. a. 1534.

22. Annorum 1538, ad. 1542, folders 289–17.

23. Annorum 1542, ad. 1548, folder 281.

24. Annorum 1548, ad. 1551, folders 280–1.

25. Annorum 1551, ad. 1555, folder 318.

26. Annorum 1555, ad. 1558, folder 262.

27. Annorum 1558, ad. 1560, folder 275.

28. Annorum 1560, ad. 1562, folder 293.

29. Annorum 1562, ad. 1565, folder 294, fol. 1, 2 et 95 desid.

30. Annorum 1565, ad. 1569, folder 280, Index.

31. Annorum 1571, ad. 1573, folder 325.

32. Annorum 1572, ad. 1575, folder 231.

33. Annorum 1575, ad. 1580, folder 286.

34. Annorum 1580, ad. 1583, folder 276.

35. Annorum 1583, ad. 1587, folder 197.

36. Annorum 1587, ad. 1590, folder 161.

37. Annorum 1590, ad. 1592, folder 373.

38. Annorum 1592, ad. 1595, folder 286.

39. Annorum 1595, ad. 1600, folder 209.

40. Annorum 1600, ad. 1604, folder 225.

41. Annorum 1604, ad. 1608, folder 237.

42. Annorum 1608, ad. 1614, folder 279.

43. Annorum 1615, ad. 1622, folder 285–2. Cautele ecclesiasticae, 2.
44. Annorum 1622, ad. 1629, folder 269.
45. Annorum 1629, ad. 1632, folder 286.
46. Annorum 1632, ad. 1635, folder 288.
47. Annorum 1635, ad. 1640, folder 277.
48. Annorum 1640, ad. 1645, folder 276.
49. Annorum 1645, ad. 1649, folder 285.
50. Annorum 1649, ad. 1652, folder 280, folder 1 desid.—folder 2 erosum.
51. Lettere ed istruzioni per inviati a Parigi. Venezia. Napoli e Dalmazia (Arm. Nr. 9 suec XVII. Nr. 1748–1753.—A. S. M.M.).
52. (a) Lettere e Commissioni per vari ambasciatori a Costantinopoli (ibid. Nr. 1751–1761).
   (b) Lettere u.s. (ibid. Nr. 1762–1772).
   (c) Lettere e commissioni per vari ambase di Adrianapoli e Costantinopoli (ibid. Nr. 1772–1778).
53. Lettere u.s. di Belgrado e Adrianapoli (ibid. Nr. 1785–1795).
54. (a) Lettere e Commiss. di Levante (ibid. N. 1796–1792).
   (b) Lettere e Commiss. di Levante (ibid. Nr. 1803–1806).
55–60. Annorum 1652–1667.
61. Annorum 1670–1671.
62–63. Annorum 1673–1687.
64–107. Annorum 1692–1794.
108–110. Annorum 1697–1802.

2. Copia lettere diverse. (Copies of Various Letters) (Di Turchia.) (from Turkey)

1. Annorum 1712–1740.
2–4. Annorum 1729–1763.
5. Annorum 1780–1782.
6. Lettere e forumlari di corrispondenza turea per il Dragomanno Vernazza.

3. Minute di Lettere vecchie. (Minutes of Old Letters)

1. Annorum 1656–1699.
2. Annorum 1700–1708.
3. Annorum 1708–1714.
4. Annorum 1715–1720.
5. Annorum 1721–1729.
6. Annorum 1730–1739.
7. Annorum 1740–1743, 1745, 1747–1749.
8. Annorum 1750–1753.
9. Annorum 1753–1762.

4. Lettere e Relazioni. (Letters and Reports)

1. Annorum 1740–1767 Di officiali ed incaricati dellp stato in affari coi Turchi.
2. Annorum 1760–1773 in affari commerciali coi Turchi.

5. Lettere e Relazioni di Conti e Capitani del territorio.
(Letters of Counts and Captains of the Territory)

1. Annorum 1705–1706.
2. Annorum 1709.
3. Annorum 1710.
4. Annorum 1716–1717.
5. Annorum 1717.
6. Annorum 1718.
7. Annorum 1718.
8. Annorum 1719–1720.
9. Annorum 1720–1721.
10. Annorum 1736.
11. Annorum 1737–1738.
12. Annorum 1737–1738.
13. Annorum 1739–1740.
14. Annorum 1741.
15. Annorum 1742.
16. Annorum 1744.
17. Annorum 1700–1799.
18. Lettere di Conti e Capitani de 1711. Lettere di Conti e Capitani de 1712–1713.

6. Lettere e Commissioni di Ponente. (Letters and Commissions from the West.)
(Vol. 137.)

1, 2. Annorum 1566–1571.
3–38. Annorum 1575–1689.
39–64. Annorum 1691–1754.
65. Annorum 1755–1766.
66–137. Annorum 1756–1802.

7. Minute di Lettere per Ponente.
(Minutes of Letters for the West)

1–11. Annorum 1665–1723.
12–20. Annorum 1727–1753.
21. Annorum 1755–1758.
    Addas hie et vol. huius sectionis XXVI. ad seriem 1, sub. Nr. 54.

XXVIII. Lettere e Relazioni Corrispondenze, etc.
(Letters and Reports, Correspondence, etc.)
(Videbis seriem ad Acta Sanctae Mariae Maioris.)

XXIX. Procure di Cancellaria. (Chancellors' agreements)
(Vol. 90.)

1. Annorum 1470–1473.
2. Annorum 1580–1581.
3–4. Annorum 1583–1585.

5–6. Annorum 1589–1593.
7–40. Annorum 1595–1636.
41–78. Annorum 1640–1784.
79. De foris et de manimorte 1784–1787.
80–81. Annorum 1784–1790.
82–90. Annorum 1794–1815.

XXX. Procurae de Notaria. (Solicitors' authorizations) (Vol. 37.)

1. Annorum 1434–1438.
2. Annorum 1446–1449.
3. Annorum 1459–1463.
4–9. Annorum 1467–1497.
10–28. Annorum 1502–1569.
24–28. Annorum 1573–1590.
29–31. Annorum 1592–1595.
32. Annorum 1600–1602.
33–34. Annorum 1607–1627.
35. Annorum 1629–1650.
36. Annorum 1662–1802.
37. Annorum 1802–1814.

XXXI.

(a) Vendite Cancelarie. (Chancellors' Sales)

1. Capitulum Venditionum factarum tempore nob. et pot. viri domini Nic. Volpe honor. Com. Ragusii MCCCLII Ind. V.a die 12 Oct. ad 23 Martii 1354. Liber Summarum factus tempore nob. et pot. v. Domini Nicolay Barbarigo hon. Com. Rag. in MCCCLIIII Ind. VII die XXIII Marcii a die XX(IIII) m. Marcii ad. d. altiman Marcii MCCCLVI (folder 136), a die XXI Maii MCCCLVI (folder 146) ad d. 9 Julii 1356; a die 22 Marcii 1360 (folia 194–205 desiderantur) usque ad 24 febr. 1360.
2. Quaternus vendicionum factus Anno dni MCCCLXV ... a Francisco et Theodoro Cancellariis ragusinis—a die 23 Marcii 1365 (folder 1)—ad d. Jan. 1380.
3. A die sec. Jan. 1371 (folder 1) ad d. 3 Maii 1282 (usq. ad folder 187 fragment).
4. In X nom. A. Anno Nat. eiusdem MCCCLXXXII Ind. V. Liber Vendicionum possessionum bonorum secundum consuetudinem Ragusii prout infrapatet. Inceptus die XXVIII mens. Octobris (folder 1), ad d. XVI April 1384. Capitulum Venditionum—a die 27 Febr. 1384 ad 11 Jan. 1386.

(b) Proclamationes Venditionum Cancellariae. (Proclamations of Chancellors' Sales) (Vol. 5.)

1. Ann. 1508–1527 folder 146. Laudationes 1509–1521 folder 43.
2. Proclamationes Ann. 1594–1656 folder 209.
3. Ann. 1659–1686 folder 141.
4. Ann. 1685–1713 folder 130.
5. Ann. 1786–1809 folder 282.

XXXII. Liber dotium Notariae.
(Solicitors Dowry Books)
(Vol. 22.)

1. (a) 1348. 10 Nov. ad 31 Dec. folder 5. (b) Hic sunt in brevitate descripte et notate per me Johannem de Pergamo not. Com. Ragusii iur. not. in A.D. MCCCXXXXVIIII Sec. Ind. mensibus et diebus infrascriptis, ita et co modo ut infra (folder 5-15). (c) a.d. VII. Nov. MCCCXXXXVII ad d. XXI Dec. (folder 38-45) (d) a.d. 1 Jan. MCCCXXXXVIIII ad d. XVI. Augusti (folder 45-74). (e) Testamenta MCCCXXXXVIIII (folder 82-89).

2. Annorum 1380, 3 Nov.—1391 2 Octobr. (folder 155).

3. (a) Capitulum Dotium omnium mei Adree ... olim ... de Bononia, receptorum in MCCCXXXXVI Ind. IIII a die 17 Apr. ad d. 17 Junii MCCCLXXXXVIIII (folder 1-6). (b) Liber dotium catastici Notariae Rag. inchoatus in MCCCLXXXV de mense Januarii ad d. 4 Febr. 1412 (folder 6-89). (c) E verso folder 1-12 fragmentaria folder 12-89 Venditiones.

4. (a) folder 1-4 fragm. a die 2 Julii 1412 ad d. 2 Jan. 1420. (b) Venditiones u.s. 1412-1419.

5. (a) Dotium a d. 3 Januar 1420 ad 25 Nov. 1439. (b) Venditiones u.s. ad 4 Jan. 1420 ad 24 Nov. 1439.

6. Dotium a. d. 8 Decemb. 1439 ad 24 Jan. 1450. (b) Venditiones u.s. a d. 3 Decembr. 1439 ad 21 Jan. 1450.

7. (a) Dotium a.d. 10 Jul. 1460. ad d. 30 Martii 1472. (b) Venditiones u.s. a d. 10 Juli. 1460 ad d. 18 Apr. 1472.

8. (a) Dotium a. 16 Junii 1472 ad d. 16 Nov. 1485. (b) Venditiones u.s. a d. 12 Apr. 1473 ad d. 73 Nov. 1495.

9. (a) Dotium a d. 19 Nov. 1495 ad d. 13 Nov. 1496. (b) Venditiones u.s. a d. 19 Decembr. 1495 ad d. 23 Decembr. 1496.

10. (a) Dotium a d. 30 Decembr. 1496 ad d. 14 Sept. 1506. (b) Venditiones u.s. a d. 23 Decembr. 1496 ad d. 29 Sept. 1506.

11. (a) Dotium a d. 11 Octobr. 1506 a d. 24 1507. (b) Venditiones u.s. a d. 21 Sept. 1506 ad d. 6 Augusti 1507.

12. (Folder 1-10 desid.) (a) Dotium a d. 21 Januarii 1519 ad d. 25 Januarii 1530. (b) Venditiones u.s. (folder 1-21 desid.) a d. 8 Octobr. 1521 ad d. 8 Febr. 1530.

13. (a) Dotium a d. 5 Martii 1530 ad d. 11 Febr. 1559. (b) Venditiones u.s. a d. Februarii 1530 ad d. 14 Decembr. 1558.

14. (a) Dotium a d. 23 Jan. 1154 ad d. 4 Januar. 1560. (b) Ordo limitationis dotium (folder 1-5). (c) Limitatio dotis d. d. 20 Augusti 1558 folder.

15. (a) Dotium a d. 7 Martii 1559 ad d. 20 Octobr. 1617. (b) Venditiones u.s. a d. 30 Martii 1559 ad d. 31 Mart 1617.

16. (a) Dotium a d. 12 Decembr. 1617 ad d. 20 April 1654. (b) Venditiones u.s. a d. 20 Julii 1617 a d d. 11 Januar 1649.

17. (a) Dotium a d. 28 Januar 1654 ad d. 11 Nov. 1689. (b) Venditiones u.s. a d. 27 Octobr. 1654 ad d. 24 Jan. 1678.

18. (a) Dotium a d. 10 Apr. 1700 ad d. 5 Jan. 1747. (b) Venditiones a d. 17 Januar 270) ad d. 19 Maii 1743.

19. (a) Dotium a d. 5 Maii 1747 ad d. 2 Sept. 1769. (b) Monti, frutti cambi a d. Julii 1748 ad d. 9 Julii 1763 Index.

20. (a) Dotium a d. 30 Novmbr. 1769 ad d. 2 Decemb. 1799. (b) Cantela, Monti, Cambi a d. 7 Januar. 1764 ad d. 5 Sept. 1789.
21. (a) Dotium a d. 22 Febr. 1790 ad d 12 Junii 1862. (b) Venditiones a d. 13 Aprilis 1790 ad 7 Sept. 1902 Index.
22. (a) Dotium a d. 20 Decembr. 1802 ad 28 Sept. 1811. (b) Venditiones a d. 20 Novembr. 1802 ad d. 14 Jan. 1812 Index.

XXXIII. Pacta matrimonialia. (Marriage Settlements) (Vol. 14.)

1–2. Annor. 1447–1464.
3–13. Annor. 1495–1703.
14. Annor. (a) 1704–1754. (b) Cautela cuiusdam pacti navalis de 1801.

XXXIV. Diversa de Foris. (Various Public Papers)

Volumen 1–254 ab anno 1593 usque ad annum 1815.

XXXV. Dogana. (Customs) (Vol. 65.)

1. (a) Liber statutorum doane, compilatus tempore nobilis et egregii viri domini Marci Justiniani Comitis honorabilis Ragusii, cum voluntate maioris et minoris consilii, et cum laude populi, publica concione adunati, per sonum campane, ut moris est, anno domini MCCLXXVII. Indict, quinta, die penultimo septembris (folder 1–12 = Capit. 1–XXXVIIII).
   (b) Additamenta (folder 12–19 = Capit. XXXX–LV.)
   (c) Adnotata (folder 19–24).
   (d) Additamenta (folder 24–30 = Capit. LVI–LXXXIIII.)
   (e) De li libri—De la moneta (ordinamenta—folder 35–36. (membrau.)
        (*N.B. Edidit Eitelberger Knustdenkmáler Dalmatiens.*)
2. 1577. Tariffa de la Doana fatta in tempo delli cinque officiali delle Ragioni P. s. Gozee, B. M. Gondola, D. M. Pozza, St. Cr. Zamagna, Mart. Dr. Cerva (Membr.—Alphabetice.)
   (Sunt in fine imagines polichrome Crucifixi cum quatuor evangelistis, ac S. Blasii.)
3. Registro de la Dohana de 1380 in 1381.
4. Registro de la Dohana de 1482.
5. Registro debitori Dohana de 1534.
6. Registro debitori Dohana de 1569.
7. Registro debitori Dohana de 1572–1588.
8. Registro debitori Dohana de 1572–1577.
9. Registro debitori Dohana de 1575. (Fragmentum).
10. Libro della Doana granda 1575–1577.
11. Registro Doana granda 1578–1579.
12. Registro Doana granda 1579.

13. Registro Doana granda 1581.
14. Debiti de la dohana grande de 1581–1582.
15. Gabella di Carne 1580.
16. Dohana grande 1592–1593.
17. Registro dohana grande de 1587–1594.
*18. Registro dohana grande de 1597–1667.
19. Gabella de Carne dohana grande de 1596.
20. Registro dohana grande 1597–1598.
21. Libro dohana grande 1607–1608.
22. Peso dohana grande 1600.
23. Registro dohana grande 1609–1610.
24. Peso dohana grande 1611–1614.
25. Libro dohana grande 1612–1613.
26. Libro dohana grande 1613–1614.
27. Debitori dohana grande 1617–1618.
28. Copia delle lettere missive delli Signori Dohanieri 1628–1632.
29. Libro delle polize che li Signori officiali si sono imborsati dalle taverne 1614.
30. Gabella di carne 1643.
31. Libro che tiene il scrivano, che si rimborsano li officiali delle tavernare 1616.
32. Gavala di Carne 1648.
33. Libro di un terzo per cento de 1651–1656.
34. (a) Diversi di Dogana de 1652–1679.
    (b) Diversi comandamenti de 1652–1679.
35. Nota di tutti li cori de 1653–1655.
36. Debitori della dogana de 1673–1674.
37. (a) Cristiani de 1674—(alphabet).
    (b) Ebrei e Turchi de 1674—(alphabet.)
38. Copia delle lettere de 1686–1701.
39. Indice dell'officio doganale (Tariffa doganale) riassunto alphab. 1276–1711 (alphabet).
40. Libro delle pieggiarie de 1740–1749.
41. (a) Libro ordini delli doganieri de 1746–1752.
    (b) Libro processi di dogana de 1742–1748.
42. (a) Libro diversi di dogana de 1752–1763.
    (b) Libro processi e terminazioni de 1752–1770.
43. Debitori del dazio delle caldaro de 1703–1756.
44. Ordine della stima de 1655.
45. Debitori della dogana de 1778–1779.
46. (a) Diversi di dogana de 1692–1730.
    (b) Processi e terminazioni della Dogana de 1682–1730.
47, 48, 49. Indici alfabetici sine titulo ac sine dato.)
50. Dazio delle alienazioni dei caratti de 1782–1810.
51. (a) Libro dei piegi de 1432–1740.
    (b) Libro debiti de 1432–1740.
52. (a) Libro debiti (sine data).
53. Libro debiti de 1670.
54. Debitori per gabele ordinarie et di nove importe de 1632–1647.
55. Libretto dei vini di Terre vove de 1613.
56. Debitori di Dogana de 1636.
57. Diversi conti di danari pubblici de 1612–1682.

58. Doganieri e specchio.
59. Doganieri di dogana grande-Crediti de 1658–1680.
60. Debitori di dogana grande-Crediti de 1753–1789.
61. Debitori di dogana grande-Crediti de 1585–1588–1589.

XXXVI.

(a) Debita Notarie. (Solicitors' Debts)
(Vol. 98.)

1. In hoc libro abreviate sunt charte notarie facte tempore nobilis et egregii viri domini Nicolai Mauroceni honor. comitis Ragusini. Scriptus est per me Thomasinum de Savere, sacri palatii et comunis Ragusii Notar. iurat. 1280. usque 1282. In hoc libro sunt alique testamenta de 1280 in 1282.
2. Liber debitorum notarie de 1334 in 1339.
3. Liber debitorum notarie de 1352 in 1356.
4. Quaternus debitorum et instrumentorum MCCCXLVIII usq. LX. Liber instrumentorum omnium scripturarum factarum tempore egreg. et potenti viri Petri Justiniani honorab. Comit. Ragusii de anno domini MCCCXIX. Indict secunda de 1358 in 1360.
5. Debitorum A. MCCCLX usque MCCCLSV. In hoc libro non sunt societates de 1360 in 1365.
6. Debita Notarie de 1362 in 1364. Testamentum Unue de Bonda d. d. 12 februari 1364.
7. Debita Notarie de 1365 in 1370.
8. Liber diversarum scripturarum inceptus MCCCMXXVII. die primo Januarii. Oblighi di debitori, recezioni, contratti ecc. de 1377 in 1379.
9. Liber debitorum, securitatum protestacionum, inceptus in a. d. MCCCLXXX. Indict III—die XXI Januarii de 1380 in 1383.
10. Liber debitorum de MCCCLIIXXIX Indict. XII. Protestationum. societatum Notarie inceptus XII Junii—usque in 1382 de 1389 in 1392.
11. Fragmentum libri debitorum de 1393.
12. Liber debitorum Notarie de 1400 in 1405.
13. Liber debitotum Notarie de 1417 in 1422.
14–20. Libri debit. notar, ab anno 1426–1441.
21. Liber debitorum potestatum et societatum inceptus a.d. MCCCCXLI die nono augusti (1441–1443).
22–34. Libri debitorum notarie ab. anno 1444–1460.
35–37. Idem ab. anno 1462–1467.
38–91. Idem ab. anno 1469–1574.
92–98. Idem. ab. anno 1576–1810.

(b) Debita notarie pro comuni.
(Solicitors' Public Debts)
(Vol. 5.)

1. Liber factus pro rebus communis vigore partis captae in minori cousilio sub die VI. junii 1449, in quo scribuntur que scribebautur in Diversis Notariae et in debtis. Amor. 1440–1522.
2–5. Idem ab anno 1523 u. a. a. 1617.

(c) Citationes. (Charges) (Vol. 19.)

1–19. Ab anno 1432 u.a.a. 1811.

XXXVII. Diversi e Possesso de Criminali. (Various Criminal Affairs) (Vol. 90.)

1–2. Annorum 1512–1526.
3. Annorum 1543–1550.
4. Annorum 1570–1577.
5. Annorum 1581–1586.
6. Annorum 1592–1595.
7. Annorum 1609–1611.
88–90. Annorum 1615–1815.

XXXVIII. Consolati. (Consulates) (Vol. 67.)

1. Libro delli officiali del quarto delly sensali presentato per Natale Gondola qresto di XI de Marzo 1575, folder 72.
2. Consolati nazionali 1752–1796, folder 96.
3. Parti di Pregati relative ai Consulati di Levante de ann. 1751 in 1805, folder 74.
4. Consolati fuorestieri in Ragusa de 1757 in 1804, folder 20.
5. Conto del Consolato de 1768–1771, folder 14.
6. Conti del Consolato et altre de 1780, folder 64. Porto delle lettere ed altre spese de 1803 in 1806, folder 6.
7. Lettere dell' offizio della navigazione de 1794 e 1794, folder 100.
8. Conto Ambassadori al Gran Signore, in Belgradi 1697.
9. Conto Ambassadori in Belgradi de 1604, folder 1.
10. Conto Ambassadori al Signor Bassa de 1606, folder 1.
11. Partite ributtate dall' offizio delli Consolati di Levante, de 1762 in 1807, folder 173.
12. Partite accetate dall. offizio delli Consolati di Levante, de 1762 in 1807, folder 95.
13. Riassunto de titoli dati alla repubblica di Ragusa che si notano seconde L' Ordine dei tempi (1677–1763), folder 1.
14. Copia lettere scritte al pubblico dei consoli ragusei (1742–1745), folder 52.
15. Copia lettere dei Consoli al pubblico 1747 in 1749, folder 65.
16. Conto di Marino Tudisi da Vienna alta patria (4 Maggio 1772), folder 7.
17. Giornale del viaggio a Constantinapoli, fatto dagli ambasciatori della Rp. di Ragusa alla Sublime Porta l'anno 1792, folder 6.

XXXVIIII. Registrum Citationum de Foris.
(Register of Civil Charges)
(Vol. 13.)

1. Inceptus de MCCCXXXIII a 17 dicembr. 1433 ad 29 dec. 1437, folder 220.
   Registrum literarum ex parte dominii per Cancellarium 1431–1433, folder 14.
2. 1617–1630, folder 188.
3. 1642–1649, folder 90.
4. 1649–1654. folder 98.
5. 1662–1674, folder 92.
6. 1674–1685, folder 93.
7. 1685–1697, folder 95.
8. 1697–1714, folder 103.
9. 1714–1721, folder 122.
10. 1721–1744, folder 165.
11. 1745–1772, folder 281.
12. 1772–1797, folder 277.
13. 1797–1816, folio 120.
    N.B. Vide etiam citationes sub II. 1–10, 12, 13, 15, 17, 18, 21, 22, IV. 33.
    XXXIII. 2–5, 8–10, 13, 14, 17.

XXXX. Sequestra. (Sequestration)
(Vol. 4.)

1766–1775 (folder 323); 1775–1782 (folder 261); 1482–1491 (212); 1791–1807 (272).

XXXXI	Dona Turcarum. (Vol. 2.) 1566–91; 1594–1617.
XXXXII.	Giumruch. (Vol. 7.) 1531–1535; 1550; 1593: 1609–1618; 1635; 1641; 1637.
XXXXIII.	Legata. (Vol. 66.) 1486–1807.
XXXXIIII.	Grassia. (Vol. 75.) 1428 ad 1805.
XXXXV.	Zecca. (Vol. 7.)
XXXXVI.	Misericordia. (Vol. 39.) 1599–1803.
XXXXVII.	Affitti. (Vol. 94.)
XXXXVIII.	Aptaj de Misericordia. (Vol. 20.) 1362–1802.
XXXXVIIII.	Tesorieri Santa Maria. (Vol. 5.) Saec. XVI–XVIII. Diversa de Tesorieri vol. 39. Repizo vol. 35—ab a. 1554.
L.	Lamenti de Criminale Sive Liber Maleficiorum. (Vol. 247). 1407–1816.
LI.	Lamenta de Intus. (Vol. 136.) 1348–1598.
LII.	Lamenta de Foris. (Vol. 138) 1348–1598.
LIII.	Lamenta de Lutus et de Foris. (Vol. 74.) 1464–1695.
LIIII.	Intentiones de Cancellaria. (Vol. 63.) 1380–1802.
LV.	Scale, Marina e Sanita, Arboraggi. (Vol. 133.) 1660–1802.
LVI.	Noli e Sicurta. (Vol. 69.) 1313–1614.
LVII.	Stabile Ordinario. (Vol. 259). 1415–1804.
LVIII.	Mobile Ordinario. (Vol. 210.) 1448–1865.

LVIIII.	Cassa del Comune. (Vol. 51.) Saec. XVI–XVIII.
LX.	Offizio de Stagno (Sali). (Vol. 81.) 1536–1864.
LXI.	Monti. (Vol. 63.) 1488–1800.
LXII.	Salinaria. (Vol. 77.) 1443–1860.
LXIII.	Aministrazione Domaniale Francese. (Vol. 163.) 1806–1815.
LXIIII.	Aptay de Stagne. (Vol. 63.) 1474–1866.
LXV.	Lamenta de Jagnina de 1653 in 1804 (Vol. 14.)
LXVI.	Lamenta de Breno de 1608 in 1805. (Vol. 20).
LXVII.	Diversa de Terstenizza de 1766–1770. (Vol. 1.)
LXVIII.	Diversa de Mezzo (Vol. 8.)
LXVIIII.	Lamenta de Stagno. (Vol. III.)
LXX.	Procurae de Stagno. (Vol. 23.)
LXXI.	Debita de Stagno. (Vol. 20.)
LXXII.	Diversa de Stagno. (Vol. 90.)
LXXIII.	Diversa et Lamenta de Slano. (Vol. 79.)
LXXIIII.	Diversa, Lamenta Depita et Cancellaria de Meleda. (Vol. 161.)
LXXV.	Diversa Turcharum sunt fascicula CCLXXV, quae ad Archivum Dohanae Maioris pertinebant, et saculis, more Turchorum, parieti appensis scrvabantur. Expectant ad historiam quotidianao actionis nundinariae inter Ragusanos et finitimos ultramontanos, Turcorum imperio subiectos.

(Proceedings of Acta Sanctae Mariae Maioris, Great St. Mary)

Bullae pontificiae, regum ac principum rescripta, privilegia, tractata, indulgentiae etc. quae antiquis temporibus in aede Cathedrali (reliquias) sub vocabulo Sanetae Mariae Maioris. Ibidem vero saeculo XVIIII et Lettere e relationi, lamenta diversa, arringhe etc. commixta fuerunt.

Acta Gallica (Dealings with France)
quae historiam Francigenarum dominationis illustrant ab al 1801 ad a 1815.

Appendix 4
Catalogue Index of the Dubrovnik Archives (according to Gelčić)

I	Acta Consiliorum (Praecepta Rectoris)
II	Reformationes
III	Acta Consilii Rogatorum
IV	Secreta Rogatorum
V	Acta Minoris Consilii
VI	Detta
VII	Fabbriche
VIII	Acta Consilii Maioris
IX	Guardie ed armamento
X	Testamenta (Testamenta de Notaria, Distributiones testamentorum, Tutores Notarie)
XI	Lamenti politici
XII	Cathasthicum
XIII	Giustizieria
XIV	Chiese e Monasteri
XV	Appellationes
XVI	Criminalia
XVII	Vigne
XVIII	Officiales Rationum
XIX	Privata
XX	Privilegi
XXI	Manuali practici del Cancelliere (Leggi e Istruzioni, Memoriae)
XXII	Fratrie (Matricole, Capitoli e Parti, Amministrazione, Vacchette, Testamenti, Giornali e Libri, Lanae)
XXIII	Puntature

XXIV	Sentenze di Cancellaria
XXV	Diversa Cancellariae
XXVI	Diversa Notariae
XXVII	Lettere e Commissioni (Lettere di Levante, Copia lettere diverse, Minute di Lettere vecchie, Lettere e Relazioni, Lettere e Relazioni di Conti e Capitani del territorio, Lettere e Commissioni di Ponente, Minute di Lettere per Ponente)
XXVIII	Lettere e Relazioni Corrispondenze
XXIX	Procura di Cancellaria
XXX	Procurae de Notaria
XXXI	Vendite Cancelarie
XXXII	Liber dotium Notariae
XXXIII	Pacta matrimonialia
XXXIV	Diversa de Foris
XXXV	Dogana
XXXVI	Debita Notarie
XXXVII	Diversi e Possesso de Criminali
XXXVIII	Consolati
XXXIX	Registrum Citationum de Foris
XL	Sequestra
–	Acta Sanctae Mariae Maioris
–	Acta Gallica

Suggested Further Reading

Geography

Alfier, D., 'Deset godina poslijeratnog dubrovačkog turizma', *Turistički pregled*, Zagreb (1955), pp. 5–6.

Carter, F. W., 'Dubrovnik: the early development of a pre-industrial city', *Slavonic and East European Review*, Vol. XLVII, no. 109, (1969), pp. 355–368.

Carter, F. W., 'Balkan exports through Dubrovnik 1358–1500: a geographical analysis', *Journal of Croatian Studies*, Vols. IX–X, New York (1968–1969), pp. 133–159.

Carter, F. W., 'The trading organization of the Dubrovnik Republic', *Historická Geografie*, no. 3, Prague (1969), pp. 12–24.

Carter, F. W., 'The decline of the Dubrovnik City-State', *Balkan Studies*, Vol. 9, no. 1, Thessaloniki (1968), pp. 127–138.

Carter, F. W., 'An analysis of the medieval Serbian Oecumene: a theoretical approach', *Geografiska Annaler*, Vol. 51, series B, no. 1, Stockholm (1969), pp. 39–56.

Carter, F. W., 'The commerce of the Dubrovnik Republic 1500–1700', *The Economic History Review*, Second Series, Vol. XXIV, no. 3 (August 1971), pp. 370–394.

Carter, F. W., 'The woollen industry of Ragusa (Dubrovnik) 1450–1550: problems of a Balkan textile centre', *Textile History*, Vol. 2, no. 1, Newton Abbot (December 1971), pp. 3–27.

Chataigneau, Y., 'Le Bassin de Sarajevo', *Annales de Géographie*, Vol. XXXVII, Paris (1928), pp. 306–327.

de Couremenin, D.-H., 'Voyage de Lévant', Paris (1649).

Cvijić, J., *La Péninsule Balkanique*, Géographie Humaine, Paris (1918), 528 pp.

Cvijić, J., 'Les migrations dans les pays yougoslaves: l'adaptation au milieu', *Revue des Études Slaves* III, (1923), pp. 5–25; 254–267.

Ćulibrk, S., 'Cvijić's sociological research into society in the Balkans', *The British Journal of Sociology*, Vol. XXII, no. 4, London (December 1971), pp. 423–440.

Darby, H. C., 'The medieval sea-state', *Scottish Geographical Magazine*, Vol. XLVII, no. 3 (July 1932), pp. 136–149.

Dedijer, J., 'La transhumance dans le Pays Dinaric', *Annales de Géographie*, Vol. XXV, (1912).

East, W. G., *An Historical Geography of Europe*, London (1935).

Evans, A. J., *Through Bosnia and the Herzegovina on Foot, . . . with an Historical Review of Bosnia*, London (1876).

Evans, A. 'The Adriatic Slavs and the overland route to Constantinople', *Geographical Journal*, London (April 1916), pp. 241–265.

Hoffman, G. W., *The Balkans in Transition* (Searchlight Series), New York, London (1963), 124 pp.

Jireček, C., 'Die Bedeutung von Ragusa in der Handelsgeschichte des Mittelalters', *Almanach der Kaiserlichen Akademie der Wissenschaften*, Wien (1899).

Marčić, L., *Dubrovnik i Okolina*, Belgrade (1937); *Godišnji Izveštaj Turističkog Saveza u Dubrovniku*, Dubrovnik (1940); *Dubrovačko Pomorstvo*, (*Spomenici Stogodišnjici Nautičke Škole u Dubrovniku*), Dubrovnik (1952).

Milojević, B., 'The Kingdom of the Serbs, Croats and Slovenes', *Geographical Review*, New York (1925), Vol. 15, pp. 70–83.

Neigebauer, J. D. F., *Die Süd-Slaven und deren Länder*, Leipzig (1815).

de Nicolay, N., *Les Navigations et Pérégrinations et Voyages faicts en la Turquie*, Anvers (1576).

Paton, A., *Highlands and Islands of the Adriatic*, London (1849).

Pouqueville, F. C. H. L., *Voyage dans la Grèce*, Paris (1826).

Ramberti, B., *Libri Tre delle Cose dei Turchi*, (1539).

Rochefort, R., 'Une cité- état en Méditerranée: Dubrovnik-Ragusa', *Revue de Géographie de Lyon*, Vol. XXXVI, no. 3, Lyon (1961), pp. 231–242.

Roglić, J., 'The geographical setting of medieval Dubrovnik', *Geographical Essays on Eastern Europe* (N. J. G. Pounds, ed.), The Hague (1961).

Roglić, J., 'The Yugoslav littoral', in *The Western Mediterranean World* (J. M. Houston, ed.), Longmans London (1964), pp. 546–580.

Rogić, V., *Geografski Osnovi Razvoja Našeg Pomorstva*, Zagreb (1961), 10 pp.

Rubić, I. 'Zadar-Split-Dubrovnik', *Geografski Horizont*, God. VII, Br. 1–2, Zagreb (1961), pp. 3–30.

Shaundy, V. K., 'The external aspects of the political geography of five diminutive European states', *The Journal of Geography*, Vol. LXI, Chicago (1962), pp. 20–31.

Simić, V. *Istoriski Razvoj Našeg Rudarstva*, Belgrade (1951), 438 pp.

Sindik, I., 'Dubrovnik i okolica naselja i porijeklo stanovništva', *Srpski Etnografski Zbornik*, Knjiga 38, Belgrade (1926).

Sindik, I., 'Dubrovnik i okolica, Vođa puta III', *Kongresa Slav Geografa i Etnografa* Belgrade (1930).

Škrivanić, G., *Atlas Srednjovekovne Srbije, Bosne i Dubrovnika*, Istorski Institut, S.A.N., Belgrade (1957).

Turrill, W., *The Plant Life of the Balkan Peninsula*, Oxford (1929).

Watkins, T., *Travels through Swisserland, Italy . . . to Constantinople*, London (1794).

Wilkinson, J. G., *Dalmatia and Montenegro*, London (1848).

Wingfield, W. F., *A Tour in Dalmatia, Albania and Montenegro, with a Historical Sketch of the Republic of Ragusa*, London (1859).

Wray, D. A., 'The Karstlands of Western Yugoslavia', *Geographical Magazine*, Vol. 59, London (1922), pp. 392–409.

'Caterino Zen's journey to Constantinople', *Starine*, Vol. X, the South-Slavonic Academy, Zagreb (1878).

History: Sources

'Annales Ragusini Anonymi item Nicolai de Ragnina', (N. Nodile, ed.), *Monumenta Spectantia Historiam Slavorum Meridionalium*, 14, Scriptures I, Zagreb (1883).

Besta, E., and Predelli, R., 'Gli statuti civili di Venezia anteriori al 1242', *Nuovo Archivio Veneto, Nuova Serie*, Anno I, tomo I, (1901), pp. 205–300.

Biegman, N. H., *The Turco-Ragusan Relationship*, The Hague-Paris (1967), 203 pp.

Bogišic, B. B., and Jireček, C., 'Liber statutorum civitatis Ragusii . . . ', *Monumenta Historico-Juridica Slavorum Meridionalium JA*, Vol. 9, (1904); *Codex Diplomaticus Regni Croatiae, Dalmatiae et Slavoniae JA*, Vols. 2–15 (1904–1934).

'Chronica ragusina Junii Restii (ab origine urbis usque ad annum 1451), item Joannis Gundulae (1451–1484)', (N. Nodile, ed.), *Monumenta Spectantia Historiam Slavorum Meridionalium*, 25, Scriptores II, Zagreb (1893).

'Commissiones et relationes venetae', Collegit et digessit Simeon Ljubić, Vols. I–III (1433–1571), *Monumenta Spectantia Historiam Slavorum Meridionalium*, Vols. 6, 8, 11, Zagreb (1876–1880).

Čremošnik, G., 'Nekoliko dubrovačkih listina iz XII. i XIII stoljeća', *Glasnik Zemaljskog Muzeja u Bosni i Hercegnovi*, Vol. XLIII, no. 2, pp. 25–54.

Čremošnik, G., 'Kancelariski i notarski spisi 1278–1301', *Zbornik za Istoriju, Jezik i Književnost Srpskog Naroda SA*. XXXI, Belgrade (1932).

Čremošnik, G., 'Dubrovački Liber de introitibus stacionum et territoriorum communis', *Glasnik Zemaljskog Muzeja u Bosne i Hercegnovi*, Vol. XLVI (1934) pp. 43–67.

Čremošnik, G., 'Notarske listine sa Lastova', *Spomenik SKAN*, Vol. XCI, no. 70, Belgrade (1939).

Čremošnik, G., Извори за историју робља и сервицијалних односа у нашим земљама средњега вијека, *Историско-правник Зборник*, год. I, св. 1, pp. 148—162, Сарајево (1949).

Čremošnik, G., 'Spisi dubrovačke kancelarije', *Monumenta Historica Ragusina JA.*, Vol. I (1951).

Dinić, M., 'Odluke veća Dubrovačke Republike I', *Zbornik za Istoriju, Jezik Književnost Srpskog Naroda SAN.*, Vol. XV, Belgrade (1951).

de Diversis de Quartgianis de Lucca, P., *Situs aedificiorum, politiae et laudabilium consuetudinum inclytae civitatis Ragusii* (Brunelli, ed.), Zara (1882). (Estratto dai programmi del Ginnasio superiore di Zara degli anni 1880–1882.)

Dujčev, I., *Avvisi di Ragusa*, Roma (1935).

Dusanov, Z., preveo 'Nikola Radojčić' *Naučna Izdanja Matice Srpske*, Knjiga III, Novi Sad (1950).

Eitelberger von Edelberg, R., *Die mittelalterlichen Kunstdenkmale Dalmatiens*, (Gesammelte Schriften IV), Wien (1884).

Elezović, G., 'Turski spomenici', *Zbornik za Istočnjačku Istorisku i Književnu Građu* SA, Vol. I, Belgrade (1940); Vol. II, Belgrade (1952).

Elezović, G., 'Nekretna dobra Ahmed paše Hercegovića u Dubrovniku izvor za pljačku Dubrovačke Republike', *Prilozi*, I, Belgrade (1950).

Foretić, V., 'Dvije isprave zahumskog kneza Dese o Mljetu iz 1151 god', *Anali Historijskog Instituta u Dubrovniku*, Dubrovnik (1952), pp. 63–72.

Gelcich, G., *Delle Istituzioni Marittime e Sanitarie della Republica di Ragusa*, Trieste (1882).

Gelcich, G., and Thallóczy, L., *Diplomatarium Relationum Reipublicae Ragusanae cum Regno Hungariae*, Budapest (1887).

Giese, F., 'Die osmanisch-türkischen Urkunden im Archive des Rektorenpalastes (Ragusa)', *Festschrift Georg Jacob*, Leipzig (1932).

Jelavić, V. J., 'Iz prepiske Nikole Bourdina francuskoga residenta u Dubrovniku', *Starine JA.*, Vol. 34, (1913).

Jelić, L. 'Zadarski bilježnicki arhiv', *Vjestnik Kr. Hrvatsko-Slavonko-Dalmatinskog Zemaljskog Arihiva*, Zagreb (1899–1901), God. I, 162–192; 252–261; God. II, 12–19; 114–120; God. III, 42–46; 134–146; 240, 262.

Jireček, C., 'Spomenici srpski', *Spomenik, SKAN*, Vol. XI, Belgrade (1892).

'Kancelariski i notarski spisi 1278–1301', svezka 1, *Zbornik za Istoriju, Jezik i Knijževnost Srpskog Naroda SKAN*, Belgrade (1939).

Körbler, Dj., and Bogišić, B., 'Abbatis Stephani Gradii Ragusini ad Consilium Rogatorum reipublicae Ragusinae epistolae scriptae', *Monumenta Spectantia Historiam Slavorum Meridionalium JA.*, Vol. 37 (1915).

Korkut, B., *Arapski Dokumenti u Državnom Arhivu u Dubrovniku*, I Sarajevo (1960); II, Sarajevo (1961).

Kraelitz, F., 'Osmanische Urkunden in türkischer Sprache aus der zweiten Hälfte des 15. Jahrhunderts. Ein Beitrag zur osmanischen Diplomatik', *Sitzungsberichte der Akademie der Wissenschaften in Wien, Phil.-Hist. Kl.*, Bd. 197, 3. Abh. Wien (1922).

Kukuljević-Sakčinski, I., 'Regesta documentorum Regni Croatiae, Slavoniae et Dalmatiae saeculi XIII', *Starine* XXI, XXII, XXIII, XXIV, XXVII, XXVIII, Zagreb (1889–1896).

'La chronique des Veniciens de Maistre Martin da Canal', *Archivio Storico Italiano*, tomo VIII, Firenze (1845), pp. 268–766.

'Liber Statutorum civitatis Ragusii compositus anno 1272 cum legibus aetate posteriore insertis atque cum summariis, adnotationibus et scholiis a veteribus iuris consultis ragusinis additis', (V. Bogišić and C. Jireček, eds.), *Monumenta Historico-Juridica Slavorum Meridionalium*, Vol. IX, Zagreb (1904).

'Libro delli ordinamenti e delle usance della universitade et dello commun della isola de Lagusta (Knjiga o uredbama i običajima skupštine i obćine otoka Lastova)', (Fr. Rački, ed.), *Monumenta Historico-Juridica Slavorum Meridionalium*, Vol. VIII, Zagreb (1901).

'L'Italia descritta nel Libro del Re Ruggero' compilato da Edrisi. Testo arabo pubblicato con versione e note da M. Amari e C. Schiaparelli, Roma (1883). *Atti della Reale Accademia dei Lincei, Anno CCLXXIV* (1876–1877), Serie seconda, Vol. VIII.

Lubić, S., 'Listine o odnošajih između južnoga Slavenstva i Mletačke republike', *Monumenta Spectantia Historiam Slavorum Meridionalium JA*, nos. 1–5, 9, 12, 17, 21, 22, 24 (1868–1893).

Ljubić, S., 'Izvještaj gosp. la Maire francezkoga konsula u Korunu o Dubrovačkoj republici', *Starine JA.*, Vol. 13 (1881).

Ljubić, S., 'Poslanice dubrovačke na mletačku republiku', *Starine JA.*, Vol. 15 (1883).

Lopašić, R., 'Hrvatski izvještaj o velikom dubrovačkom potresu', *Starine JA.*, Vol. 25 (1892).

Макушев, В., Итальянские архивы и хранящиеся в них материалы для славянской истории, I: Флорентинский государственный архив, II: Неаполь и Палермо, III: Неаполь, Бари, Анкона, *Записки Имп. Акад. Наук*, Т. XVI, приложение 5, Т. XIX, приложения 3 и 4 С.-Петербург (1870–71).

Makušev, V., *Istorijski Spomenici Južnih Slavena i Okolnih Naroda* II, Belgrade (1882).

Makušev, V., *Monumenta Historica Slavorum Meridionalium Vicinorumque Populorum e Tabulariis et Bibliothecis Italicis Deprompta*, Vol. 1, (Ancona, Bononia, Florentia), Warsaw (1874); Vol. 2, (Genoa, Mantua, Mediolamum, Panormus et Taurinum), Belgrade (1882).

Makušev, V., and Šufflay, M., 'Isprave za odnošaj Dubrovnika prema Veneciji', *Starine JA*, Vol. 30, Zagreb (1902); Vol. 31, Zagreb (1905).

Marković, M., 'Vizantinske povelje Dubrovačkog arhiva, *Zbornik Radova Vizanto-loškog Instituta SAN*, Vol. XXI, Belgrade (1952), pp. 205–262.

Matković, P., 'Spomenici za dubrovačku povjest u vrijeme ugarsko-hrvatske zaštite, *Starine*, I, Zagreb (1869), pp. 41–210.

Miklosich, F., *Monumenta Serbica Spectantia Historiam Serbiae, Bosnae, Ragusii*, Wien (1858).

Miklosich, F., and Müller, J., *Acta et Diplomata Graeca Medii Aevi, Sacra et Profana*, III, IV, (1865–1871).

Milić, V., 'Ex libro Viridi Com. Ragusii', *Bulletino di Archeologia e Storia Dalmata*, XV (1892), pp. 207–210; XVI (1893), pp. 120–127; Split (1892–1893).

Monumenta Catarensia, Vol. I, (A. Mayer) *Kotorski Spomenici. Prva Knjiga Kotorskih Notara od God.* 1326–1335, Zagreb (1951).

Monumenta Historico-Juridica, I: Дубровачки закони и уредбе, (Ед А. Соловјев и М. Петерковић,) Београд (1936), (Зборник за ИЈК, III одељ. књ. 6).

Monumenta Historica Ragusina, Vol. I: (Gr. Čremošnik), *Spisi Dubrovačke Kancelarije*, књ. 1, *Zapisi Notara Thomazina de Savere* 1278–1282, Zagreb (1951).

Monumenta Ragusina, Vols. I–V, (*Monumenta Spectantia Historiam Slavorum Meridionalium*, 10, 13, 27, 28, 29.) (contains Libri Reformationum 1301–1397), Zagreb (1879–1897).

Monumenta Traguriensia, Pars prima: *Notae Seu Abbreviaturae Cancellariae Communis Tragurii*, (Miho Barada, ed.), I (1263–1273); II (1274–1294); (*Monumenta Spectantia Historiam Slavorum Meridionalium*, 44, 45). Zagreb (1950).

Monumenta Traguriensia, Pars secunda: *Acta Curiae Comunis Tragurii*, (Miho Barada, ed.), I (1266–1299): (*Monumenta Spectantia Historiam Slavorum Meridionalium*, 46). Zagreb (1951).

Morozzo dela Rocca, M., and Lombardo, A., *Documenti del Commercio Veneziano nei Secoli XI–XIII*, I, II, Roma (1940).

Notae et Acta Cancellariae Ragusinae, Vol. I, *Monumenta Historica Ragusina*, Vol. I, Zagrabiae (1951).

Pucić, N., *Statut Oli Zakoni od Otoka od Mljeta*, Dubrovnik cvet narodnog Knižestva za Godina 1851, sv. III, Zagreb (1852).

Pucić, M., *Spomenici Srbski*, I–II, Belgrade (1858–1862).

Rački, Fr., *Monumenta Historica Slavorum Meridionalium*, I. *Acta Croatica*, Zagreb (1863).

Rački, F., 'Dubrovački spomenici o odnošaju dubrovačke obćine naprama Bosni i Turskoj', *Starine JA.*, Vol. 6 (1874).

Rački, F. 'Documenta historiae croaticae periodum antiquam illustrantia', *Monumenta Spectantia Historiam Slavorum Meridionalium JA.*, Vol. 7, Zagreb (1887); *Monumenta Ragusina, ibid.*, 10 (1879); 13 (1882); 27 (1895); 28 (1896); 29 (1897), Zagreb.

Radić, F., 'Knjiga o uredbama i običajima skupštine i obćine otoka Lastova', *Monumenta Historico-Juridica Slavorum Meridionalium JA.*, Vol. 8 (1901).

Radonić, J., 'Dubrovačka akta i povelje', *Zbornik za Istoriju, Jezik i Knji* ž *evnost*, Belgrade, Vol. II (1934); Vol. IV (1935); Vol. VIII, Vols. IX, X (1939); Vol. XI (1941); Vol. XII (1942); Vol. XVII (1951).

Rešetar, M., 'Dva izvještaja o velikoj dubrovačkoj trešnji', *Starine JA.*, Vol. 26 (1893).

Smičiklas, T., *Codex Diplomaticus Croatiae, Dalmatiae et Slavoniae*, II–XV, Zagreb (1904–1934).

Соловјев, Александар *Одабрани споменици српског права,* (*од XII до краја XV века*), Београд (1926).

Solovjev, A., and Peterkovič, M., 'Dubrovački zakoni i uredbe', *Zbornik za Istoriju Jezik i Knjževnost,* Vol. VI (1936).

Saffet, 'Raguza (Dobrovnik) Cumhurluğu', *Ta'rih-i Osmānī Encümeni Mecmū'asi,* III, Constantinople (1328).

'Statuta confraternitatum et corporationum Ragusinarum (ab aevo XIII–XVIII); I. 'Bratovštine dubrovačke; (K. Vojnović, ed.); II. 'Dubrovačke obrtne korporacije' (K. Vojnović, ed.), *Monumenta Historico-Juridica Slavorum Meridionalium,* VII, Zagreb (1899–1900).

'Statuta et leges civitatis Buduae, civitatis Scardonae et civitatis et insulae Lesinae', (S. Ljubić, ed.), *Monumenta Historico-Juridica Slavorum Meridionalium,* pars I, Vol. 3, Zagreb (1882–1883).

'Statuta et leges civitatis et insulae Curzulae (1214–1558), (J. J. Hanel, ed.), *Monumenta Historico-Juridica Slavorum Meridionalium,* pars I, Vol. 1, Zagreb (1877).

'Statuta et leges civitatis Spalati', (J. J. Hanel, ed.), *Monumenta Historico-Juridica Slavorum Meridionalium,* pars I, Vol. 2, Zagreb (1878).

'Statuta lingua croatica conscripta. Vinodolski, poljički, vrbanski a donekle i svega krčkoga otoka, kastavski, veprinački i trsatski', (Fr. Rački, V. Jagić and I Črnčić, ed.), *Monumenta Historico-Juridica Slavorum Meridionalium,* pars I, Vol. 4, Zagreb (1890).

Stojanović, LJ., 'Stare srpske povelje i pisma', *Zbornik za Istoriju, Jezik i Knjževnost Srpskog Naroda SKAN,* Vol. XIX (1929); Vol. XXIV (1934), Belgrade-Sr. Karlovac.

Šabanović, H., 'Turski diplomatski izvori za istoriju naših naroda', *Prilozi,* I Belgrade (1950).

Šabonović, H., 'Izrazi eva'il, evāsit i evāḫir u datumima turskih spomenika', *Prilozi,* II, Belgrade (1951).

Šabanović, H., (Čeviren Ismail Eren). 'Dubrovnik Devlet arsivindeki türk vesikalari', *Belleten* No. 119, Ankara (1966), pp. 391–437.

Škrivanić, G., 'Dnevnik Dubrovčanina Mihajla Pešića o požarevačkom mirovnom kongresu 1718 godine', *Građa Istoriskog Instituta SAN,* Vol. VII (1952).

Surmin, Dj. 'Hrvatski spomenici (Acta croatica)', sv.l (od god. 1100–1499), *Monumenta Historico-Juridica Slavorum Meridionalium,* Vol 6, Zagreb (1898).

Tadić, J., 'Pisma i uputstva Dubrovačke Republike', *Zbornik za Istoriju, Jezik i Knjževnost Srpskog Naroda, SKAN,* Vol. IV, Belgrade (1935).

Tadić, J., 'Грађа о сликарској школи у дубровнику,' *XII–XVI* в., I. II., *Грађа САН,* књ. 4, 5., *Историски институт* књ. 3, 4, Београд (1952).

Tadić, J., 'Les archives économiques de Raguse', Annales Economiques Sociétés Civilisations, pp. 968–1175, Paris (Nov.–Dec. 1961).

Tafel R. and Thomas, G. 'Griechische Originalurkunden zur Geschichte des Freistaates Ragusa', *Sitzungsberichte der Kaiserlichen Akademie der Wissenschaften in Wien Phil.-Hist. Klasse,* Wien (1851).

Tafel R. and Thomas G., 'Urkunden zur älteren Handels-und staatsgeschichte der Rupublik Venedig, mit besonderer beziehung auf Byzanz und die Levante', I–III, *Fontes Rerum Austriacarum,* XII–XIV, Wien (1856–1857).

Thallóczy, L., Jireček, C., and Sufflay. Em. *Acta et Diplomata Res Albaniae Mediae Aetatis Illustrantia,* I, II, Vindobonae (1913–1918).

Theiner, A., *Vetera Monumenta Slavorum Meridionalium Historiam Spectantia* Rome (1863).

670   DUBROVNIK (RAGUSA) A CLASSIC CITY-STATE

Truhelka, Ć., 'Tursko-slovjenski spomenici dubrovačke arhive', *Glasnik Zemaljskog Muzeja* (1911).

Valentinelli, G., *Bibliografia della Dalmazia e del Montenegro*, Zagreb (1855–1856).

Valentinelli, G., *Esposizione dei Rapporti fra la Repubblica Veneta e gli Slavi Meridionali. Brani tratti dai Diarj di Marin Sanudo*, Venice (1863).

Vojnović, K., 'Bratovštine i obrtne korporacije u republici dubrovačkoj od XIII. do konca XVIII. vijeka', *Monumenta Historico-Juridica Slavorum Meridionalium JA*, Vol. 7 (1899).

Vukasović-Vuletić, V., 'Narodni sud, sudije . . . na ostrvu Mljetu s početka XV.' vijeka, *Spomenik SKAN*, Vol. XLIX, Belgrade (1910).

Wenzel, G., 'Der "liber de ordinamenti et dele usance" der Insel Meleda', *Archiv für Kunde österreichischenscher Geschichts-Quellen*, Zweiter Band, Wien (1849).

History: Important Works and Treatise

Adamović, V., 'O trešnjama grada Dubrovnika', *Biblioteka za Povjest Dalmatinsku Upravlijana*, od J. Gelčića, Knjiga, 7, Dubrovnik (1884).

Anerssen, W., 'Verfassungsgeschichte von Ragusa', *Zeitschrift fur Vergleichende Rechtswissenschaft*, Bd. L., Stuttgart (1936).

Андреева, М. А., 'Торговый договор Византии и Дубровника и история его подготовки,' *Byzantinoslavica* VI, стр. 110–165, Praha (1935–1936).

Anselmi S., 'Venezia, Ragusa, Ancona tra cinque e seicento, deputazione di storia patria per le marche', *Atti e Memorie*, Serie VIII, Vol. VI, Ancona (1969), 75 pp.

Antolak, S., 'Prilog proučavanju trgovačkih veza između Dubrovnika i Skopja u XV i XVI stoljeću', *Godišnik Zbornik*. (Ed. Filozofski fakultet na Univerzitetot Skopje), Vols X, XI (1959), pp. 57–74.

Appendini, F., *Notiziae Istorico–Critiche Sulle Antichità, Storia e Litterature de Ragusei*, Vols I–11, Dubrovnik (1802–1803).

Appendini, F.m., *Ratovanje oko Dubrovnika Godine 1806*, Dubrovnik (1906).

Barada, M., 'Dalmatia superior', *Rad JA*, No. 2070 (1949).

Bartoli, M., 'Das Dalmatische, Altromanische Sprachreste von Veglia bis Ragusa und ihre Stellung in der Appennino-Balkanischen Romania', I, II, *Schriften der Balkankommission der Kaiserlichen Akademie der Wissenschaften in Wien, Linguist*, Abt. Bd. 4, 5. Wien (1906).

Belić, A., 'Misli o dubrovačkom književnom i narodnom jeziku; *Zbornik iz Dubrovačke Prošlosti Milanu Rešetaru o 70-oj Godišnjici Života*, Dubrovnik (1931), pp. 445–448.

Beritić, L., 'Izgradnja i utvrđivanje gradske luke', *Dubrovačko Pomorstvo* (U spomen sto godina nautičke škole u Dubrovniku), Dubrovnik (1952), pp. 285–292.

Beritić, L. 'Stonske utvrđe', *Anali Historijskog Instituta u Dubrovniku*, God. III, Dubrovnik (1954), pp. 297–354.

Beritić, L., 'Utvrđenja grada Dubrovnika', *Odjel za Likovne Umjetnosti JA* (1955).

Beritić, L., 'Dubrovački arsenali', *Mornarički Glasnik*, Vol. 5, Split (1956).

Bersa, I., 'La questione colonica ragusea innanzi al Reichsrath', *Nazionale*, supplemento al No. 85, Zara (1874).

Bersa, J., 'Dubrovačke slike i prilike (1800–1880)', *Izdanje Matice Hrvatske*, Zagreb (1941).

Besta, E., 'Gli statuti civili di Venezia anteriori al 1242', *Nuovo archivio veneto, Nuova serie*, tomo I, pp. 1–117.

Biegman, N. H., 'Ragusan spying for the Ottoman Empire', *Belleten*, 106, Constantinople (1963).

Bjelovučić, N. Z., *Povijest Poluotoka Rata (Pelješac)*, Split (1921).

Bjelovučić, N. Z., 'Poluostrov Rat (Pelješac), Naselja i poreklo stanovništva', Knjiga II, *Srpski Etnografski Zbornik SKAN*, Belgrade (1922).

Bjelovučić, N. Z., 'Dubrovačka vlastela bijahu feudalni gospodari na teritoriju dubrovačke republike', *Rad.*, br. 133, od. 15, VI, Dubrovnik (1922).

Bjelovučič, N. Z., *Rješenje Dubrovačkog Kmetstva i Polovništva sa Nacrtom Novog Agrarnog Zakona za Dalmaciju*, Dubrovnik (1924).

Bjelovučič, N. Z., 'Od kojih vladara kupi ili dobi dubrovačka republika pojedine svoje krajeve, Kalendar', *Napredak*, Sarajevo (1930).

Birimiša, V., *Dubrovačko Kmetstvo*, *Dubrovački List*, br. 6–13 (1924).

Bettera, B., *Zapisci o Političkoj i Građanskoj Uredbi Bivše Republike Dubrovačke, Ponašio s Francuskoga Nikola Putica*, Dubrovnik, *Zabavnik, Narodne Štionice Dubrovačke za* 1867., Split (1866), pp. 182–209.

Bogišić, B., 'Glavnije crte obiteljskog pisanoga prava u starom Dubrovniku', *Rad JA*, Vol. 5 (1868), pp. 123–149.

Bogišić, B., *Le Statut de Raguse. Codification Inédite du XIII° Siecle*, Paris (1894).

Božić, I., 'Ekonomski i društveni razvitak Dubrovnika u XIV i XV veku', *Istoriski Glasnik*, Vols. 1–2, Belgrade (1948).

Božić, I., *Dubrovnik i Turska u XIV i XV veku*. (Posebna izdanja SAN), Vol. CC, Belgrade (1952).

Brajković, V., 'Dubrovački edikt za plovidbu 1794', *Dubrovačko Pomorstvo* (1952).

Bulić, A., 'Necropoli antica cristiana a Slano di Ragusa', *Bull. Arch. Bulić*, Nos. 6–7 (1901).

Cornaro, C., 'Relazione dell'horribile terremoto seguito nella città di Ragusa ed altre della Dalmazia ed Albania, il giorno delli 6 Aprile 1667', published by *Ivana Petra Pinellia*, Venezia (1667).

Cornaro, C., 'Raconto dela navigazione di Monsignor Arcivescovo colle Monache di Ragusa, del loro ricevimento in Ancona il 2 maggio 1667, e di altri successi del già narrato Terremoto', *In Ancona Nella Stamperia Camerale con licenca de S.S. Super*, Ancona (MDCLXVII).

Cornaro, C., 'Realizione del terremoto seguito a Ragusa il 6 Aprile 1667'; data dall' Eccmo Sig. Catt. Cornaro Provveditore Generale in Dalmazia al Serenissimo Principe di Venezia, *Starine*, Knjiga 14, 15, Zagreb (1882).

Crijević, S., (Cerva) 'Pisma o potresu arčiđakona Brnje Đordica i nekih drugih Dubrovčana opatu Stj. Gradiću', *Starine*, Knjiga 15, Zagreb (1882).

Cusmich, G. E. O. M., *Cenni Storici sui Minori Osservanti di Ragusa*, Trieste (1864).

Cvjetković, B., *Dubrovnik i Ljudevit Veliki* (1358–1382), Dubrovnik (1913).

Cvjetković, B., *Uvod u Povijest Dubrovačke Republike*, Vol. I, Dubrovnik (1916).

Cvjetković, B., *Povijest Dubrovačke Republike*, Vol. I, Dubrovnik (1917).

Cvjetković, B., *Dubrovačka Diplomacija*, Dubrovnik (1923).

Cvjetković, B., 'Dubrovnik i Petar Veliki', *Bulićev Zbornik*, Zbornik, Zagreb (1924).

Čičin-Šain, Ć., 'Pisma Marka Kavanjina splitskog trgovca iz prve polovine XVII stoljeća', *J.A.Z.U.*, *Starine*, Knjiga 49, Zagreb (1959), pp. 105–226.

Ćorović, V., 'Teritorialni razvoj Bosanske države u Srednjem Vijeku', *Glas SKAN*, CLXVII, drugi razred 85, Belgrade (1935).

Ћоровић, Вл., 'Како је војвода Радослав Павловић продавао Дубровчанима Конавле 1425–1427,' *Годишњица Николе Чупића* XXXVI (1927).

Čremošnik, G., 'Naša trgovačka društva u srednjem veku, *Glasnik Zemaljskog Muzeja*, XXXVI (1924), pp. 69–81.

Čremošnik, G., 'Dubrovački gramatik Ozren', *Naradna Starina* IV, Zagreb (1925), pp. 329.

Čremošnik, G., 'Novčarstvo u starom Dubrovniku', *Jugosl. Njiva* IX (1925), pp. 16–24.

Čremošnik, G., 'Увозна трговина Србије год. 1282 и 1283,' *Споменик САН* LXII, (1925), pp. 61–69.

Čremošnik, G., 'Dubrovačke kancelarije od god. 1300 i najstarije kniige dubrovačke arhive', *Glasnik Zemaljskog Muzeja*, Vol. XXXIX (1927), pp. 231–253.

Čremošnik, G., 'Prodaja bosanskog Primorja Dubrovniku God. 1399 i kralj Ostoja', *Glasnik Zemaljskog Muzeja*, Vol. XL (1928), p. 126.

Čremošnik, G., 'Notarske listine za Lastova', *Spomenik SKAN* br. XCI, drugi razred 70, Belgrade (1929).

Čremošnik, G., Dubrovački konzulati u Srbiji do Dušanovog vremena', *Glasnik Zemaljskog Muzeja*, XLI, sv. 2, Sarajevo (1929), pp. 81–94.

Čremošnik, G., 'Vrednost dubrovačkog izvoza u Srbiju i Bosnu', *Glasnik Zemaljskog Muzeja*, XLI, sv. 2, Sarajevo (1929), pp. 57–61.

Čremošnik, G., 'Dodatak članku, Dubrovačka kancelarija do god. 1300', *Glasnik Zemaljskog Muzeja*, XLI, II sv. (za historiju i etnografiju), Sarajevo (1929), pp. 121–132.

Čremošnik, G., 'Nekoliko ljekarskih ugovora iz Dubrovnika', *Zbornik iz Dubro vačke Prošlosti Milanu Rešetaru o 70-oj godišnjici Života*, Dubrovnik (1931), pp. 43–45.

Čremošnik, G., 'Odnos Dubrovnika prema Mlecima do god. 1358', *Narodna Starina*, Zagreb (1933), pp. 169–178.

Čremošnik, G., 'Vinogradarstvo i vino u Dalmaciji srednjega veka', *Glasnik Zemaljskog Muzeja*, XLV (1933), pp. 15–38.

Čremošnik, G., 'Dubrovački notar prezbiter Johanes (1284–1293)', *Glas SA* Vol. CLXXI, Belgrade (1936), pp. 87–119.

Čremošnik, G., 'O dubrovačkom notaru Paskalu', *Glasnik Zemaljskog Muzeja*, L., sv. 2 (1938), pp. 129–132.

Čremošnik, G., 'Notarijat Lastovo u srednjem veku', *Jugoslovenski Istoriski Časopis*, Vol. V, Belgrade (1939).

Čremošnik, G., 'Ugovor između kralja Tvrtka I i Dubrovnika od 9 aprila 1387', *Glasnik Zemaljskog Muzeja, Nova serija*, društvene nauke I (1947), pp. 69–73.

Čremošnik, G., 'Postanak i razvoj srpske ili hrvatske kancelarije u Dubrovniku', *Anali Historijskog Instituta JA u Dubrovniku*, Vol. I (1952), pp. 73–84.

Čremošnik, G., 'Isprave zahumskog kneza Dese,' *Anali Historijskog Instituta JA u Dubrovniku*, Vol. III (1954).

Dalsar, F., 'Selīm I'in Dobrovnik cumhuriyeti ile yaptiği muahede', *Tarih Vesikalari cilt*, II, sayī 12, Constantinople (nisan 1943).

Damm von, J., (Damma), *Alter und Neuer Staat des Königreichs Dalmatiens*, II, Nürnberg (1718).

Danilović, J., 'Dubrovnik' *Istorija Država i Prava Jugoslavenskih Naroda do 1918, godine*, Ch. V, Belgrade (1962).

Dayre, J., *Dubrovačke Studije*, Zagreb (1938).

Decaris, A., 'Die Agrarfrage Dalmatiens', Inaugural-Disertatien an der Philosophischen Fakultät der Universität Basel, Split (1928).

Deanović, M., 'Frano Dživa Gundulić i njegov put u Moskvu 1655. godine', *Starine JA*, Vol. 41 (1948).

Deanović, M., *Anciens Contacts entre la France et Raguse* (Bibliothèque de l'Institut francais de Zagreb, III) Zagreb (1948).

Degl'Ivellio, A., *Saggio d'uno Studio Storico-critico Sulla Colonia e Sul Contadinaggio nel Territorio di Ragusa*, Ragusa (1873).

Devliegher, L., 'Een Vijftiendeeuwse Brugse Edelsmid in Joegoslavie', *Annales de la Société d'Emulation de Bruges*, Vol. XCVIII, Bruges (1961), (Oorkonden en Mededelingen), pp. 117–121.

Dimitrijević, S., *Dubrovačka Trgovina u Leskovcu i Okolina, Seperat Časopis 'Naše Stvaranje'*, Leskovac (1955), 151 pp.

Dimitrijević, S., 'Dubrovački Karavani u Južnoj Srbiji u XVII veku S.A.N.' *Posebna Izdanja*, Knjiga CCCIV. Istoriski Institut, Knjiga 10, Belgrade (1958), 306 pp.

Dinić, M. J., 'О Николи Алтомановићу', *Посебна Издања Српске Краљ. Акад. XC, Друштвени и историски списи* књ. 40, Belgrade (1932).

Dinić, M. J., 'Dubrovački tributi. (Mogoriš, Svetodimitarski i Konavoski dohodak, Provižun braće Vlatkovića'), *Glasnik Srpske Kr. Akademije*, Vol. CLXVIIII, Belgrade (1935), pp. 203–257.

Dinić, M. J., 'Dubrovačka srednjevekovna karavanska trgovina; *Jugoslovenski Istoriski Časopis*, Vol. III, Belgrade (1937), pp. 119–146.

Dinić, M. J., 'О крунисању Твртка I за краља,' *Глас Српске Краљ. Акад. CLXVII*, Belgrade (1937).

Dinić, M. J., 'Trg Drijeva i okolina u Srednjem veku', *Godišnjica Nikole Čupića*, Vol. XLVII, Belgrade (1938).

Dinić, M. J., 'Крсташки грошеви,' *Зборник Радова САН XXI, Византолошки Институт* књ. 1, Belgrade (1952), pp. 86–112.

Dinić, M. J., 'Западна Србија у Средњем веку,' *Издања Археолошког института САН* књ. II, Belgrade (1953), pp. 23–30.

Dinić, M. J., 'Растислалићи,' *Зборник Радова САН, XXXVI, Византолошки Институт* књ. 2, Belgrade (1953), pp. 139–144.

Dinić, M. J., 'За историју рударства у средњевековној Србији и Босни,' I део, *Посебна Издања САН, CCXL, Одељ Друштв. Наука* књ. 14, Belgrade (1955).

Dinić-Knežević, D., 'Trgovina vinom u Dubrovniku u XIV veku', *Godišnjak Filozofskog Fakulteta u Novom Sadu*, Vol. 9 (1966), pp. 39–85.

Dinić-Knežević, D., 'Prilog proučavanju mjera za vino u Dubrovniku u XIV vijeku', *Historijski Zbornik*, Vols. 19–20, Zagreb (1966–1967), pp. 419–427.

Dinić-Knežević, D., 'Trgovina žitom u Dubrovniku u XIV veku', *Godisnjak Filozofskog Fakulteta u Novom Sadu*, Vol. 10 (1967), pp. 79–131.

Diversis, de F., *Situs Aedificiorum, Politiae et Laudabilium Consuetudinum Inclytae Civitatis Ragusii* (V. Brunelli, ed.), Zadar (1882).

Efendić, F., *Dragomani i Kanelarija Turska u Dubrovniku*, Sarajevo (1939).

'Ein Gedenkbuch der Erhebung Ragusas in den Jahren 1813–1814', (G. Gelcich, ed.), *Archiv für Österreichische Geschichte*, Vol. LXIV, Wien (1882).

Engel, von, J. C., *Geschichte des Freistaates Ragusa*, Wien (1807).

Engel, von, J. C., and Stojanović, I., *Povjest Dubrovačke Republike*, Dubrovnik (1922).

Farlati, D., *Illyricum Sacrum*, Vol. VI: 'Ecclesia ragusina', Venezia (1800).

Forenbacher, A., 'Otok Lastovo', *Rad JA Akademije*, Knjiga 185, Zagreb (1911).

674　　　DUBROVNIK (RAGUSA) A CLASSIC CITY-STATE

Foretić, V., 'Ugovor Dubrovnika sa srpskim velikim županom Stefanom Nemanjom i stara dubrovačka djedina', *Rad JA*, No. 283 (1951) pp. 51-118.

Foretić, V., 'Dvije isprave zahumskog kneza Dese o Mljetu iz 1151. godine', *Anali Historijskog Instituta JA u Dubrovniku*, Vol. I (1952) pp. 117-164.

Foretić, V., 'Nekoliko pogleda na pomorsku trgovinu Dubrovnika u srednjem vijeku' *Dubrovačko Pomorstvo*, Dubrovnik (1952).

Fortunić, V., *Crtice o Ribarstvu Uopće, a Nadasve u Području Bivše Republike, Dubrovačke*, Dubrovnik (1930).

Galleria dei Ragusei Illustri, Ragusa (1841).

Гавриловић, М., 'Земљотрес у Дубровнику 1667,' *Писмо Hardena из Млетака, Који је Био у Дубровнику на дан Потреса. Писмо је Било Упућено Банкару Charpentier-у. —Из Мазареnове Библиотеке.—„Срп. Књиж. Гласник*, Belgrade (1903).

Gečić, M., 'Dubrovačka trgovina solju u XIV veku', *Zbornik Filozofskog Fakulteta*, Belgrade (1955).

Gelcich, G., *Dello Sviluppo Civile di Ragusa*, Ragusa (1884).

Gelcich, I., *Conti di Tuhelj*, Dubrovnik (1890).

Giesberger, H., 'Das Ragusanische Erdbeben von 1667', *Münch. Geographische Studien, Herausgegeben von S. Günther*, 28, München (1913).

Grujić, R., 'Župa Konavle pod raznim gospodarima od XII do XV veka', *Spomenik SA*, Vol. LXVI, Zemun (1926).

Grujić, R., 'Kaznačine u Konavlima XVI veka', *Rešetarov Zbornik*, Dubrovnik (1931).

Gušić, B., 'Kako je Mljet pripao Dubrovačkoj Republici', *Rešetarov Zbornik*, Dubrovnik (1931).

Hrabak, B., 'Pirot i Dubiča u Dubrovačkim dokumentima od kraja XV do početka XVII veka', *Istoriski Glasnik*, Vols. 1–2, Belgrade (1951), pp. 114–118.

Hrabak B., 'Uticaj primorskih privrednih centara na društveno-ekonomsku istoriju Bosne i Hercegovine u srednjem veku', *Pregled*, Sarajevo (1953).

Hrabak, B., 'Trgovina Persijanaca Preko Dubrovnika u XVI veku', *Zbornik Filozofskog Fakulteta*, Knjiga V, No. 1, Belgrade (1960), pp. 257–267.

Hrabak, B., 'Dubrovački trgovci u Beogradu pod Turcima 1521–1551', *Godišnjak Grada Beograda*, Vol. 13 (1966), pp. 29–47.

Ivančević, V., 'O brodogradnji u Dubrovniku potkraj Republike', *Anali Historijskog Instituta JA u Dubrovniku*, Vol. III, Dubrovnik (1955).

Ivančević, V., 'Luka Livorno i dubrovački brodovi (1760–1808)', *Gradja za Pomorsku Povijest Dubrovnika, knj, JAZU*, Knjiga 4, Dubrovnik (1968), pp. 1–145.

Ivančević, V., 'Osvrt na pomorske i trgovačko-kulturne veze Dubrovačke Republike s Ankonom i 18 i 19 stoljeću', *Dubrovnik*, Vol. XII, no. 1 (1969), pp. 115–127.

Ivanović, I., *Pravovjerstvo Starijeh Mladijem Dubrovčanom na Izgled*, Dubrovnik (1804).

Ivanović, M., 'Prilozi za istoriju carina u srednjevekovnim srpskim državama', *Spomenik SAN*, Vol. XCVII (1948).

Jagić, J., 'Einige Bedenken aus Anlass der vorhergehenden Abhandlung', *Archiv für Slavische Philologie*, Vol. XIII, Wien (1891), pp. 388–400.

Jelavich, C., and Jelavich, B., *The Balkans*, New Jersey (1965), 148 pp.

Jeremić R., and Tadić, J., *Prilozi za Istoriju Zdravstvene Kulture Starog Dubrovnika*, Vols. I–III, Belgrade (1938–1940).

Jireček, C., 'Die Handelsstrassen und Bergwerke von Serbien und Bosnien während des Mittelalters', *Abhandlungen der Kgl. Böhm. Gesellschaft der Wissenschaften in Prag*, Vol. 6, Bd. 10, Prag. (1879).

Jireček, C., 'Nastojanje starih Dubrovčana oko raširenja granica', *Slovinac*, Vol. II, br. 4, 5, Dubrovnik (1879), pp. 58–59; 75–76.

Jireček, C., 'Die Wlachen und Maurowlachen in den Denkmälern von Ragusa', *Sitzungsberichte der Kgl. Böhm. Gesellschaft der Wissenschaften in Prag.*, Jg. (1879); Prag, (1800), pp. 109–125.

Jireček, C., 'Srbský cář Uroš, král Vikašin a Dubrovčane', *Časopis Musea Královstvi Českého*, Ročník LX Prague (1886), pp. 3–26; 241–276.

Jireček, C., 'Die beziehungen der Ragusaner zu Serbien unter Car Uroš und König Vlkašin (1335–1371)', *Sitzungsberichte der Kgl. Böhm. Gesellschaft der Wissenschaften in Prag, Hist-Phil. Classe*, Jg (1885); Prag. (1886).

Jireček, C., Тољен, Син Кнеза Мирослава Хумског, *Глас САН XXXV, Други Разред* 21, Belgrade (1892).

Jireček, C., *Poselstvi Republiky Dubrovnické k Císarovne Katerine II.* 1771–1775, Prag. (1893).

Jireček, C., 'Dubrovnik', *Ottův Slovník Naučny VIII*, Prag. (1894).

Jireček, C., 'Der ragusanische Dichter Siško Menćetić (1457–1527)', *Archiv für Slavische Philologie*, Vol. XIX (1897), pp. 22–89. (Naročito je važno I poglavje: Ragusa in der 2. Hälfte des 15. Jhs.)

Jireček, C., 'Die Romanen in den Städten Dalmatiens während des Mittelalters, I–III', *Denkschriften der Kais. Akademie der Wissenschaften in Wien, Phil.-Hist. Klasse*, Bd. 48, 49, Wien (1902).

Jireček, C., 'Die mittelalteriche Kanzlei der Ragusaner', *Archiv für Slavische Philologie*, Vol. XXV, pp. 501–521; Vol. XXVI, pp. 161–214, Wien (1904).

Jireček, C., 'Skutari und sein Gebiet im Mittelalter', *Illyrische-Albanische Forschungen*, Vol. I, pp. 94–124, München-Leipzig (1916); (in Serbo-Croat *Glasniku Geogr. društva* III, pp. 149–171, Belgrade, 1914).

Jireček, C., 'Valona im Mittelalter', *Illyrisch-Albanische Forschungen*, Vol. I, pp. 168–187, München-Leipzig (1916).

Jireček, C., 'Die Lage und Vergangenheit der Städt Durazzo in Albanien', *Illyrisch-Albanische Forschungen*, Vol. I, pp. 152–167, München-Leipzig (1916).

Jireček, C., *Geschichte der Serben*, I, II, I, Gotha (1911).

Jireček, C., 'Staat und Gesellschaft im mittelalterlichen Serbien. Studien zur Kulturgeschichte des 13–15. Jahrhunderts', *Denkschriften der Kaiserlichen Akademie der Wissenschaften in Wien, Phil-Hist. Klasse*, Bd. 56, 58, 64, Wien (1913; 1915; 1920).

Jireček, C., *Историја Срба*, Превео Јован Радонић, Прва књига до 1537 године (*Политичка историја*), Друга књига (*Културна историја*), 2. исправљено и допуњено издање, Belgrade (1952).

Jireček, C., and Cvjetković, B., *Važnost Dubrovnika u Trgovačkoj Povijesti Srednjeg Vijeka*, Dubrovnik (1915).

Jireček, C., and Pejanović, D., *Trgovački Drumovi i Rudnici Srbije i Bosne u Srednjem Vijeku*, Sarajevo (1915), 146 pp.

Kadlec, K., *Introduction à l'Étude Comparative de l'Histoire du Droit Public des Peuples Slaves*, Paris (1933).

Kapidžic, H., 'Veze Dubrovnika i Hercegovine u XVIII Vijeku', *Bosanska Pošta*, Sarajevo (1939), 27 pp.

Kapidžić, H., 'Postupak s Dužnicima u Dubrovniku (XVIII stoljecé)', *Inst. Prav. Zbornik*, Vol. I, Sarajevo (1949).

Kindersley, A., 'The Battle of Kossovo', *History Today*, Vol. XX, No. 5 (May 1970), pp. 348–355.

Kišpatić, M., 'Potresi u Hrvatskoj', *Rad JAZU*. Knjiga CVII, Zagreb (1891).

Klaić, V., *Poviest Bosne do Propasti Kraljevstva*, Zagreb (1882).

Klaić, V., 'Trešnja u Dubrovniku god. 1667', (*Čitanka za II raz. Gimn*), Zagreb (1901).

Klaić, V., 'Dubrovačka vlastela Zunjevići u Senju i Vindolu 1477–1502', *Vjestnik Kr. Hrvatsko-Slavonsko-Dalmatinskog Zemaljskog Arkiva*, God. III, Zagreb (1901), pp. 237–239.

Колендић, П. 'Биографска дела Игњата Ђурђевића,' *Зборник за ИЈК*, II одељ., књ. 7, Belgrade (1935).

Колендић, П. 'Крунисање Илије Цријевића у академији Пемпонија Лета, *Зборник радова* X, Институт за проучавање књижевности, књ. 1, Belgrade (1951), pp. 65–95.

Körbler, Dj., 'Jakov Bunić, Dubrovčanin, latinski pjesnik (1469–1534)', *Rad*, Vol. CLXXX (1910), pp. 58–145.

Körbler, Dj., ' "Zanovićeva škola" u Dubrovniku', *Grada za Povijest Književnost Hrvatske JA*, Vol. 7 (1912).

Körbler, Dj., 'Iz mladih dana triju humanista Dubrovčana XV vijeka (Karlo Pavlov Pucić, Ilija Lampričin Crievié i Damjan Paskojev Benešić)', *Rad*, Vol. CCVI, Zagreb (1915), pp. 218–252.

Körbler, Dj., 'Pisma Stjepana Gradića Dubrovčanina senatu republike dubrovačke', *Monumenta Spectantia Historiam Slavorum Meridionalium*, Vol. XXXVII, Zagreb (1915).

Körbler, Dj., 'Talijansko pjesništvo u Dalmaciji XVI vijeka, napose u Kotoru i u Dubrovniku', *Rad*, Vol. CCXII, Zagreb (1916), pp. 1–109.

Körbler, Dj., 'Dubrovačka republika i zapadne evropske države. Veze Dubrovnika s Napuljem, Sicilijom, Francuskom i Španjolskom', *Rad*, Vol. CCXIV, Zagreb (1916), pp. 165–252.

Kos, M., 'Dubrovačko-srpski ugovori do sredine 13-og veka', *Glasnik SKAN*, Vol. 123, Belgrade (1927), 65 pp.

Kos, M., 'Listine bana Stevana Kotromanića za Dubrovnik', *Rešetarov Zbornik*, Dubrovnik (1931).

Костић, К. Н., *Трговински центри и друмови по српској Земљи у Средњем и Новом веку*, Belgrade (1899).

Košćak, V., 'Dubrovačka republika prema Rijeci Senjskoj do osnutka konsulata', *Dubrovačko Pomorstvo*, Dubrovnik (1952), pp. 351-364.

Košćak, V., 'Travnički sporazum', *Republika*, Vol. 3, (1956).

Kovač, K., 'Crtice o statistici i o vojničkim ustanovama u repulici dubrovačkoj', *Glasnik Zemaljskog Muzeja u Bosni*, god. 28, Sarajevo (1916).

Kovačević, D., 'Trgovačka knjiga Nikole i Luke Kabužića', *Istorijski Pregled*, Vol. I, Zagreb (1954), pp. 46–48.

Ковачевић, Д., 'О Јањеву у доба средњевековне српске државе,' *Историски Гласник*, год. 1952, Belgrade (1952), pp. 121–126.

Krekić, B., 'Курирски саобраћај са Цариградом и Солуном у првој половини XIV века,' *Зборник Радова САН XXI, Византолошки Институт*, књ. 1 Belgrade (1952), pp. 113–120.

Krekić, B., 'Prilozi unutrašnoj istoriji Dubrovnika početkom XV veka', *Istoriski Glasnik*, Vols. 1–2, Belgrade (1953), pp. 63-70.

Krekić, B. 'Вук Бобаљевић,' *Зборник Радова САН XLIX, Византолошки Инст.*, књ. 4, Belgrade (1956), pp. 115–140.

Krekić, B., 'Dubrovnik i Levant (1280–1460)', *Posebna Izdanja SAN*, Vol. CCLVI, Belgrade (1956).

Krekić, B., *Dubrovnik (Ragusa) et le Levant au Moyen Age*, Paris (1961), 306 pp.

Krekić, B., 'Trois fragments concernant les relations entre Dubrovnik (Raguse) et l'Italie au XIVᵉ siècle, *Godišnjak Filozofskog Fakulteta u N. Sadu*, (1966), p. 1937.

Krizman, B., *O Dubrovačkoj Diplomaciji*, Zagreb (1951).

Krizman, B., 'Dubrovački propisi o konzulima iz XIV stoljeća', *Historijski Zbornik* god. IV, Zagreb (1951), pp. 141–149.

Krizman, B., ' "Memoire" Bara Bettere aust. generalu T. Milutinoviću o dubrovačkoj republici iz 1815 godine', *Anali Historijskog Instituta JA u Dubrovniku*, Vol. I (1952).

Krizman, B., *Diplomati i konzuli u starom Dubrovniku*, Zagreb (1957).

Leicht, P. S., *Storia del Diritto Italiano. Il Diritto Privato*. Part I: 'Diritto delle persone e di Famiglia', Milano (1941).

Leontovič, I. T., 'Gosudarstvenoje ustroistvo starovo Dubrovnika', *Žurnal Ministarstva Narodnovo Prosvjaščenija*, Vol. XII (1868).

Liepopili, A. 'Agrarno pitanje u Dubrovačkoj Republici', *Narodna Svijest*, br. 4, 5, 8, 11, Dubrovnik (1924).

Лопичић, Ст. Л., 'Биљешке из обичајнога права у старој Црној Гори,' *Зборник за Народни Живот и обичаје Јужних Словена*, XXIV, Загреб (1919), pp. 273–294.

Ljubić, S., *Dizionario degli Uomini Illustri della Dalmazia*, Zara-Vienna (1856).

Ljubić, S., 'Ob odnošajih dubrovačke sa mletačkom republikom tja do god. 1358', *Rad, JA*, Vol. 5 (1868), pp. 44–122.

Ljubić, S., 'Ob odnošajih među Dubrovačani i Mletčani za ugarsko-hrvatskog vladanja u Dubrovniku', *Rad*, Vol. XVII (1871), pp. 1–69.

Ljubić, S., 'Ob odnošajih medu republikom mletačkom i dubrovackom od početka XVI stoljeća do njihove propasti', *Rad JA*, Vols. 53, 54 (1880), pp. 94–185, 62–159.

Ljubić, S., 'Pisma o potresu', *Rad JA Akademije Znanosti i Imjetnosti*, Knjiga 53, Zagreb (1880).

Luccari, J., *Copioso Ristretto degli Annali di Ragusa, Libri Quattro*, Venezia (1605).

Lucianović, M., 'Lastovo u sklopu Dubrovačke republike', *Anali Historijskog Instituta JA u Dubrovniku*, Vol. III (1954), pp. 253–295.

Lučić, J., 'Prilog brodogradnji u Dubrovniku u 2 polovini XIV stoljeća, *Historiski Zbornik*, God. IV, Zagreb (1951), pp. 133–140.

Lučić, J., 'Agrarno-proizvodni odnosi u okolici Dubrovnika (od polovine XIV st.)', *Zgodovinski Časopis*, Vol. 22, No. 1–2 (1968), pp. 61–96.

Luetić, J., 'Pomorac i diplomat Vice Bune', *Anali Historijskog Instituta JAZU u Dubrovniku*, Vol. I, (1952). pp. 255-267.

Luetić, J., 'Nekoliko vijesti o dubrovačkim brodovima zadnjih decenija XVII st.', *Dubrovačko Pomorstvo*, Dubrovnik (1952), pp. 189-204.

Luetić, J., *Pomorac i diplomat Ivan Kaznačić s osvrtom na dubrovačko pomorstvo 18 i početka 19 stoljeća*, Dubrovnik (1954).

Luetić, J., 'Još o državnoj zastavi Dubrovačke Republike', *Dubrovnik*, Vol. 11, No. 1 (1968), pp. 90–92.

Lukić, B., 'Diplomatski odnosi i sukob između Dubrovačke republike i Maroka u XVIII stoljeću', *Anali Historijskog Instituta JAZU u Dubrovniku*, Vol. III (1954).

Łatusazynska, J., 'Siedemnastowieczny Dubrownik w oczach cudzoziemców', *Pamietnik słowanski* (Kraków), Vol. XVI, (1966), pp. 116–157.

Макушев, В., 'Исследования об исторических памятниках и бытописателях Дубровника,' *Записки Имп. Академии Наук*, Т. XI, приложение 5, С.-Петербург (1867).

Mahken, I., Dubrovački patricijat u XIV veku', SANU, knjiga 340, Belgrade (1960), 562 pp.

Marinović, A., 'Prilog poznavanju dubrovačkih bratovština', *Anali Historjskog Instituta u Dubrovniku*, Vol. I, Dubrovnik (1952), pp. 233–245.

Marinović, A., 'Lopudska universitos (Pravni položaj otoka Lopuda u Dubrovačkoj republici)', *Anali Historijskog Instituta u Dubrovniku*, God. III, Dubrovnik (1954), pp. 181–235.

Marinović, A., 'Stari dubrovački zakon o pomorskom osiguranju' *Osiguranje i Privreda*, Vol. 9, No. 6, Zagreb (1968), pp. 21–28.

Марковић, М., 'Један грчки ферман Султана Мехмеда II Ел Фатиха, *Историски Часопис*, IV, (1952–53), Belgrade (1954), pp. 1–7.

Марковић, М., 'О хоризми бугарског цара Јована Асена додељеној Дубровнику, *Историски Часопис*, IV (1952–53), Belgrade (1954), pp. 9–12.

Matas, A. K., *Miletii Versus, Biblioteka za Povijest Dalmatinsku*, Dubrovnik (1882).

Matić, T., 'Izvještaj austrijskoga političkoga emisara o Dubrovniku i njegovu balkanskom zaleđu iz god. 1805', *Starine JA*, Vol. 37 (1934).

Matković, P., Trgovinski odnošaji izmedju Dubrovnika i Srednje Italije', *RAD Jugoslavenske Akademije Znanosti i Umjetnosti*, Zagreb (1871), knjiga XV.

Matković, P., 'Prilozi k trgovačko-političkoj historiji republike dubrovačke, I, II, *RAD*, Vol. VII (1869), pp. 180–266; Vol. XV (1871), pp. 1–69.

Matković, P., 'Putovanja po balkanskom poluotoku za srednjega vieka', *RAD*, Vol. XLII (1878), pp. 56–184.

Matković, P., 'Putovanja po balkanskom poluotoku XVI vieka', II. 'Putovanja B. Kuripešića, L. Nogarola i B. Ramberta', *RAD*, Vol. LVI (1881), pp. 141–232; IV. 'Putovanje Jean-a-Chesnau-a', *Rad*. Vol. LXII (1882), pp. 67–87; XIV. 'Dnevnici o putovanju mletačkih poslanstva u Carigrad: osobito Jakova Sorance od g. 1575 i 1581, i Pavle Kontarina od g. 1580', *RAD*, Vol. CXXIV, (1895), pp. 1–102.

Matković, P., 'Vicko D., Volčić, Dubrovčanin, kartograf XVI, vieka', *RAD JA*, Vol. 130 (1897).

Mažuranić, V., 'Melik "Jesa Dubrovačanin", u Indiji godine 1480–1528 i njegovi prethodnici u Islamu prije deset stoljeća', *Zbornik Kralja Tomislava*, Zagreb (1925).

Medini, M., '*O Postanku*: *Razvitku kmetskih i težačkih odnošaja u Dalmaciji*, Zadar (1920).

Medini, M., *Starine Dubrovačke*, Dubrovnik (1935).

Miklosich, F., *Die Bildung der Slavischen Personen- und Ortsnamen*, Heidelberg (1927).

Milosavljević, S., 'Izvozne carine koje su Dubrovčani plaćali turcima za robu izvezenu iz Turske u vremenu 1481 do 1520 godine', *Istoriski Glasnik*, Vols. 1–2, Belgrade (1953), pp. 70–77.

Mirković, M., 'Ragusa and the Portuguese spice trade', *The Slavonic and East European Review*, American Series, Vol. II (1939).

Mitić, I., 'Konzulat Dubrovačke Republike u Carigradu', *Pomorski Zbornik*, Vol. 6, Zadar (1968), pp. 455–474.

Modestin, J., 'Kritička potraživanja i pokušaj pragmatizovanja u području povjesti dubrovačke od 1205 do 1331 godine', *Izvješće kr. velike gimnazije u Zagrebu koncem školske godine* 1890/91, Zagreb (1891), pp. 3–102.

Muljačić, Ž., 'Istraga protiv Jakobinaca 1797 god. u Dubrovniku', *Anali Historijskog Instituta JA u Dubrovniku*, Vol. II (1953).

Muljačić, Ž., 'O dubrovačkoj proizvodnji tekstila u XVIII stoljeću', *Istoriski Glasnik*, No. 1, Belgrade (1956), pp. 61–70.

Muljačić, Ž., 'Američka revolucija i dubrovačka pomorska trgovina', *Pomorski Zbornik*, Vol. 6, (1968), pp. 521–530.

Nagy, J., 'Prva utanačenja između bosanskih banova i Dubrovnika', *Rešetarov Zbornik*, Dubrovnik (1931).

Накић, М. Д., Изградња Дубровника у другој половини XIII века,' *Историски Гласник*, год. (1954), бр. 3, pp. 3–38.

Накић, М. Д., 'Трипе Бућић, которски властелин и дипломата средњевековне Српдује,' *Историски Гласник*, гол. (1954), бр. 4.

Nedeljković, B., 'Polažaj Dubrovnika prema Ugarskoj 1358–1460', *Godišnjak Pravnog Fak. u Sarajevu*, Vol. XV, Sarajevo (1967), pp. 448–464.

Nikodim M., *Episkop, Ston u Srednjim Vijekovima*, Dubrovnik (1914).

Nikolić, E., 'La Contesa del Sale Fra Venezia e Ragusa 1645–1679', *Scintille*, No. 6, Zadar (1890), pp. 8–21.

Nodilo, N., 'Privi ljetopisci i davna historiografija dubrovačka', *RAD JA*, Vol. 65, (1883), pp. 92–128.

Nodilo, N., 'Annales Ragusini anonymi', *Monumenta Spectantia Historiam Slavorum Meridionalium JA*, Vol. 14, (1883).

Nodilo, N., 'Chronica Ragusina Junii Restii . . . ,' *Monumenta Spectantia Historiam Slavorum Meridionalium JA*, Vol. 25 (1893).

Novak, G., 'Dubrovaćka diplomacija na mirovnom kongresu u Požarevcu', *Šišićev Zbornik*, Zagreb (1930).

Novak, G., 'Vunena Industrija u Dubrovniku do Sredine XVI stoljeća', *Rešetarov Zbornik iz Dubrovačke Proslosti*, Dubrovnik (1931), pp. 99–107.

Novak, G., 'Borba Dubrovnika za slobodu 1683–1699', *RAD JA*, Vol. 253 (1935).

Novak, G., 'Dubrovačko pomorstvo od svojih početaka do propasti republike', *Dubrovački Festival 1950*, Zagreb (1950), pp. 52–64.

Novak, V., 'Učešće dubrovačke flote u španskoj Nepobedivoj armadi', *Zgodovinski Časopis*, Vols. VI–VII (1953).

Novaković, S., 'Brskovo, Danj i carina sv. Spasa i putovi s Jadranskoga primorja u stare srpske zemlje', *RAD JA*, Vol. 37 (1876).

Novaković, S., 'Srpske oblasti X i XII veka', *Glasnik Srpskog Učenog Društva* Vol. XLVIII, Belgrade (1880).

Palmotić-Gjonović, J., 'Dubrovnik ponovljen, epos u 22 pjevanja', *Izdanje Stj. Škurla*, gl. 3, Dubrovnik (1878).

Pappafava, V., *Étude sur le Colonage Partiaire Particulièrement en Dalmatie et sur les Rapports du Colonage et du Contadinat dans le Territoire de l'Ancienne Republique de Raguse*, (translated by F. Arnaud), Pichon, Paris (1885).

Pappafava, V., *O kmetstvu s osobitim obzirom na Dalmaciju i o kmetskih i težačkih odnošajih u području bivše dubrovačke republike preveo s francuskoga Antun Simonić*, Zagreb (1886).

Partsch, P., *Bericht Über das Detonationsphänomen auf der Insel Meleda by Ragusa*, Wien (1826).

Павловић, Д., Нови подаци за биографију Марина Држића, *Зборник Радова*, књ. X, Институт за проучавање књижевности, књ. 1, Belgrade (1951), pp. 97–107.

Павловић, Д., О кризи властеоског сталежа у Дубровнику XVII века, *Зборник Радова*, књ. XVII, Институт за проучавање књижевности, књ. 2, Belgrade (1952), pp. 27–38.

Peričić, S., 'Reagovanje austrijskih vlast na političko djelovanje ruskog konzulata u Dubrovniku od 1815', Dubrovnik, No. 3, Dubrovnik (1966), pp. 63–83.

Poković, A'. *Rad Dubrovačkih Konzula na Rijeci 1690–1805*, (unpublished dissertation) Dubrovnik (1931).

Popović-Radenković, M., 'Dubrovački konzulat u Aleksandriji od šesdesetih do osamdesetih godina XVIII veka', *Istoriski Glasnik*, Vol. 4, Belgrade (1954).

Popović-Radenković, M., 'O trgovačkim odnosima Dubrovnika sa Bosnom i Hercegovinom (1480–1500)', *Istoriski Glasnik*, Vol. 4, Belgrade (1954).

Fra Andelko Posinković, O. P., 'Velika trešnja u Dubrovniku 1667', *Hrvatska Prosveta*, god. V, br. VII–X, Zagreb (1918).

Pudić, I., 'Ignjat Djurdjević (Ignatio Giorgi), 18th century scholar from Dubrovnik', Balkan Studies, Vol. VII, No. 1, Thessaloniki (1966), pp. 123–134.

Puhan, I., ' "Aptagi" dubrovačkog prava', *Ist. Prav. Zbornik* 2, Vols 3–4, Sarajevo (1950).

Rački, F., 'Rukopisi tičući se južno-slovinske povjesti u arkivih srednje i dolnje Italije', *Rad*, XVIII, (1872), pp. 205–258.

Rački, F., 'Iz djela E. L. Crievića, Dubrovčanina', *Starine*, IV, (1872), pp. 155–200.

Rački, F., 'Prilozi za povjest humanizma i renesanse u Dubrovniku, Dalmaciji i Hrvatskoj'. Ivan Ravenjanin, učenik Petrarkin, dubrovački kancelar (1384–1387), kano predteča humanizma u Dubrovniku, *Rad*, LXXIV (1885), pp. 135–191

Rački, F., Gelcich, G., Torbar, J., Dvorak, V., i Marković, F., 'Život i ocjena djela Rugjera Josipa Boškovića', *Rad JA*, (1887–1888, 1890), pp. 1–716.

Радоњић, Др. Јован., 'Дневник Никодице Бунића, писан непосредно после великог потреса земље 1667', *Acta et Diplomata Ragusina*, III, 2, CCLXXXII, Belgrade (1938).

Razzi, S., *La Storia di Raugia*, Lucca, 18/III/1588, Dubrovnik (1903).

Rešetar, M., 'Die Čakavština und deren einstige und jetzige Grenzen', *Archiv für Slavische Philologie*, XIII, (1891), pp. 93–109; 161–195; 361–388.

Rešetar, M., 'Zur Aussprache und Schreibung des e im Serbokroatischen', *Archiv für Slavische Philologie*, XIII, (1891), pp. 591–597.

Rešetar, M., 'Pismo nadbiscupova tajnika Dum Vlaha Squadro, o potresu', *Starine* Knjiga 25, Zagreb (1892).

Rešetar, M., 'Breve ragguaglio delle rovine cagionate dal terremoto a Ragusa il 6 aprile 1667 per raconto di alcuni Signori Ragusei pervenuti in Ancona il 23 di detto etc., – In Ancona nella Stamperia Com. le 1667', *Starine*, Knjiga 26 – R. Lopašić; Starine, Knjiga 25, Zagreb (1893).

Rešetar, M., 'Die ragusanischen Urkunden des 13–15. Jahrhunderts', *Archiv für Slavische Philologie*, XVI, (1894), pp. 321–368; XVII (1895), pp. 1–47.

Rešetar, M., 'Dubrovačka numizmatika', I–II, *Posebna Izdanja SA*, XLVII, Sremski Karlovci, Belgrade-Zemun (1924–1925).

Rešetar, M., 'Dubrovačko veliko vijeće', *Dubrovnik*, I, Dubrovnik (1929), pp. 3–10; 60–68.

Rešetar, M., 'Popisi dubrovačkijeh vlasteoskijeh porodica', *Glasnik Dubrovačkog Učenog Društva "Sveti Vlaho"*, Knj. I, Dubrovnik (1929), pp. 1–11.

Rešetar, M., ' "Drugovi" Mletačkih knezova u Dubrovniku', *Narodna Starina*, XII, Zagreb (1933), pp. 126–130.

Rešetar, M., 'Никша Зеијездић дубровачки српски канцелар XV вијека', *Глас САН CLXIX, Други разред* LXXXVII, Belgrade (1936), pp. 167–210.

Rešetar, M., 'Нове дубровачке повеље Стојановићева Зборника', *Глас САН CLXIX, Други разред* LXXXVII, Belgrade (1936), pp. 121–166.

Rešetar, M., 'Početak kovanja dubrovačkoga novca', *Rad*, *JA*, no. 1266, (1939), pp. 149–170.

Rešetar, M., 'Најстарији дубровалки говор', *Гдас САН, ССI, Одељ.* лит. и језика, Нова серија, књ. 1, Belgrade (1951), pp. 1–47.

Rešetar, M., 'Најстарија дубровачка проза', *Посебна издања САН, CXCII,* Одељ. пит. и језика, књ. 4, Belgrade (1952).

Rešetar, P., 'La zecca della repubblica di Ragusa', pos. ostisak iz *Bulletino di Archeologia e Storia Dalmata.* Split (1891–1892).

Reutz, A., *Verfassungs-und Rechtszustand der Dalmatinischen Küsten-Städte und Inseln im Mittelalter aus Ihren Munizipalstatuten Entwickelt*, Dorpat (1841).

Rogacić (Rogacci) B. S. J., 'De terrae motu quo Epidaurus in Dalmatija an. 1667 prostata est', *Proseuction ad Cosimum III Magnum Hetruriae Ducem*, Romae (1690).

Roglić, J. C., 'The geographical setting of Medieval Dubrovnik', *Geographical Essays on Eastern Europe*, (N. J. G. Pounds, ed.), The Hague (1961), pp. 141–159.

Roller, D., 'Naša prva manufaktura sukna u XV stoljeću u Dubrovniku', *Ekonomski Pregled*, br. 2, Zagreb (1950), pp. 192–202.

Roler, D., 'Dubrovački zanati u XV i XVI stoljeću', *Građa za Gospodarsku Povijest Hrvatske JA*, Vol. 2, Zagreb (1951).

Roler, D., 'Agrarno-proizvodni odnosi na području Dubrovačke Republike od XIII do XV stoljéca', *Građa za Gospodarsku Povijest Hrvatske JA*, Vol. 5, Zagreb (1955).

Rubić, I., 'Utjecaj pomorskih i kopnenih faktora na razvoj grada Dubrovnika', *Dubrovačko Pomorstvo*, Dubrovnik (1952), pp. 309–322.

Rusko, I., 'Stanje Dubrovačke trgovačke mornarice pred samu propast Durovačke republike početkom XIX st.', *Dubrovačko Pomorstvo*, Dubrovnik (1952), pp. 205-222.

Sakazov, I., 'Obšestveno i Stopansko Razvitie na Bulgarija pri Asenevcit', *Bulgarija Istoričeska Biblioteka*, Vol. III, Sofia (1930), pp. 112–148.

Sakazov, I., 'Stopanskite vrzki mezdu Dubrovnik i Blgarskit zemi prez 16 i 17 stolitija', *Državna Pečatnica*, Sofia (1930), 192 pp.

Serra, G., *La Tradizione Latina e Greco-Latina nell' Onomastica Medioevale Italiana*, Goteborg (1950).

Синдик, И., 'Дубровник и околина', *Српски Етнографски Зборник* књ. XXXVIII, I одељ. Насеља и порекло становништва књ. XXIII, Belgrade (1926), pp. 1–249.

Синдик, И. 'Комунално уређење Котора од друге половине XII до почетка XV столећа', *Посебна издања САН, CLXV,* Историски институт, књ. 1, Belgrade (1950).

Skok, P., 'O simbiozi i nestanku starih Romana u Dalmaciji i na Primorju u svijetlu onomastike', *Razprave*, izdaje Znanstveno društvo za humanističke vede v Ljubljani, IV, Ljubljana (1928), pp. 1–41.

Skok, P., 'L'Importance de Dubrovnik dans l'histoire des slaves', *Le Monde Slave*, v. VIII (2), Paris (1931), pp. 161.

Skok, P., 'Les origines de Raguse', *Slavia*, X, Prag (1931), pp. 449–500.

Skok, P., 'Slovenstvo i romanstvo na jadranskim otocima', *Toponomastička Ispitvanja*, I. II, Zagreb (1950). 271pp., 67pp.

Slade (Dolci) S. O. M., *Monumenta Historica Provinciae Rhacusinae Ordinis Minorum Napoli* (1746).

Solovjev, A., 'Le patriciat de Raguse au XV-e siècle', *Zbornik iz Dubrovačke Prošlosti Milanu Rešetaru o 70-oj Godišnjici Života*, Dubrovnik (1931), pp. 59–66.

Sorgo, Compte Duc de, *Fragments sur l'Histoire de Ragusa* Paris (1839).

Stoianovich, T., *A Study in Balkan Civilization*, New York (1967), 215 pp.

Strohal, I., 'O starosti i redakcijama dubrovačkoga statuta', *Rad CCVII*, (1915), pp. 94–100.

Stulli, B., 'Iz historije pomorskog sudstva u starom Dubrovniku', *Dubrovačko Pomorstvo*, Dubrovnik (1952), pp. 33-350.

Stulli, B., 'Ordines artis nauticae secundum consuetudinem civitatis Ragusii', *Anali Historijskog Instituta JA u Dubrovniku* Vol. I, Dubrovnik (1952).

Stulli, B., 'Prilozi pitanja o redakcijama knjige statuta grada Dubrovnika', *Anali Historijskog Instituta JA u Dubrovniku*, Vol. III, (1954), pp. 85–118.

Stulli, B., *pregled državnopravne historije dubrovačke republike*, Dubrovnik (1956), 23pp.

Stulli, B., 'Pregled povijesti pomorstva do početka XIX stoljeća', *Pomorska Enciklopedija*, Vol. IV, Zagreb (1957), pp. 33–56.

Stulli, L., *Le Tre Descrizioni del Terremoto di Ragusa 1667*, Venezia (1826).

Šišević, I., 'Računanje obujma broda u Dubrovniku XVI st.', *Anali Historijskog Instituta JA u Dubrovniku*, Vol. I, (1952).

Шишић, Ф., Екскурс о локрумским фалсификатима, у: Летопис попа Дукљанина, *Посебна издања* САН LXVII, Београд—Загреб (1928), тамо стр. 184–255.

Šišić, F., 'O hrvatskoj kraljici Margareti', *'Dubrovnik'* I, Dubrovnik (1929) pp. 124–137; 230–248; 251–268.

Škurla, S., *Sv. Vlaho*, Dubrovnik (1871).

Škurla, S., *Ragusa – Cenni Storici* Zagrabia (1876).

Šufflay, M. von, 'Die dalmatinische Privaturkunde', *Sitzungsberichte der Kaiserlichen Akademie der Wissenschaften in Wien, Phil.-Hist Klasse*, Bd. 147, 1903, Wien (1904).

Šufflay, M. von, 'Die Kirchenzustände im vortürkischen Albanien', *Illyrisch-albanische Forschungen* Bd. I, München-Leipzig (1916), pp. 183–281.

Šufflay, M. von, 'Stadte und Burgen Albaniens während des Mittelalters', *Denkschriften der Kaiserlichen Akademie der Wissenschaften in Wien*, Bd. 63, Wien (1924).

Šundrica, Z., 'Popis stanovništva Dubrovačke republike iz 1673/74 godine', *Arhivski Vjesnik*, Vol. II, No. 2, Zagreb (1959), pp. 14–24.

Švrljuga, L., 'Prinosi k diplomatskim odnošajem Dubrovnika s Francezkom', *Starine JA*, Vol. 14, (1881).

Tadić, J., 'Pomorska trgovina Dubrovnika svršetkom srednjega vijeka', *Glasnik Dubrovačkog Učenog Društva* '*Sveti Vlaho*', Vol. I, Dubrovnik (1929), pp. 117–121.

Tadić, J., 'Pomorsko Osiguranje u Dubrovniku IV stolječa', *Zbornik iz Dubrovačke Proslošti*, Dubrovnik (1913), pp. 109–112.

Tadić, J., 'Španija i Dubrovnik u XVI v.', *Posebna Izdanja SA*, No. XCIII, (1932).

Tadić, J., *Miho Pracatović-Pracat*, Dubrovnik (1935).

Tadić, J., *Jevreji u Dubrovniku do polovice XVII Stoljéca*, Dubrovnik (1937).

Tadić, J., *Dubrovčanin Serafin Gučetić, Francuski Diplomat, (1496–1547)*, Split (1938).

Tadić, J., *Promet Putnika u Starom Dubrovniku*, Dubrovnik (1939).

Tadić, J., *Dubrovački Portreti*, Belgrade (1948).

Tadić, J., 'Organizacija dubrovačkog pomorstva u XVI veku', *Istoriski Časopis*, Vol. 1., *SAN* Belgrade (1949), pp. 54–104.

Tadić, J., 'O pomorstvu Dubrovnika u XVI i XVII veku', *Dubrovačko Pomorstvo*, Dubrovnik (1952), pp. 165–188.

Tadić, J., 'O društvenoj strukturi Dalmacije i Dubrovnika u vreme renesanse', *Zgodovinski Časopsis*, VI–VII, (*Kosov Zbornik*), Ljubljana (1952–1953), pp. 552–565.

Tadić, J., 'Le Port de Raguse et sa flotte au XVIᵉ siècle. Le navire et l'économie maritime du Moyen Age au XVIIIᵉ siècle'. *Travaux du Second Colloque International d'Histoire Maritime*, Paris (1959), pp. 1–21.

Tadić, J., 'Iz istorije Jevreja u jugoistočnoj Evropi', *Jevrejski Almanah*, Belgrade (1959–1960).

Tadić, J., 'Privreda Dubrovnika i srpske zemlje u prvoj polovini XV veka', *Zbornik Filozofskog Fakulteta*, Vol. 10, No. 1, Belgrade (1968), pp. 519–539.

Tadić, J., and Jeremić, R., *Prilozi za istoriju zdravstvene kulture starog Dubrovnika I–III*, Belgrade (1938–1940).

Taljeraii, V., *Zruča za Povijest Stona*, Dubrovnik (1935).

Tartalja, H., 'Kulturna uloga ljekarne "Male braće" u Dubrovniku', *Dubrovnik*, Vol. 11, No. 1, (1968), pp. 63–72.

Temperley, H. W. V., *A History of Serbia*, London (1919).

Traljić, S., 'Trgovina Bosne i Hercegovine s lukama Dalmacije Dubrovnik u XVII i XVIII stoljeca', *Pomorski Zbornik*, Vol. II, Zagreb (1962), pp. 341–372.

Thalloczy, L., 'Konstantin Jireček, Zwei Urkunden aus Nordalbanien', *Illyrish-Albanische Forschungen*, I, München-Leipzig (1916), pp. 125–151.

Truhelka, Ć., 'Konavoski rat 1430–1433', *Glasnik Zemaljskog Muzeja*, (1917).

Убичини, А., Уговор о савезу и пријатељству међу Карлом од Валоа и посланицима српског краља Уроша потписан 27 марта 1308 год. у абатији код Мелина, *Гласник Српског ученог друштва*, XXVII, Belgrade (1870), pp. 309–341.

Vekarić, S., 'Podaci o dubrovačkim brodovima za vrijeme i nakon francuske okupacije', *Anali Historijskog Instituta JA u Dubrovniku*, Vol. II, (1953).

Vekarić, S., 'Prilozi za povijest pelješkog pomorstva u XVII i XVIII stoljeću', *Anali Historijskog Instituta JA u Dubrovniku*, Vol. III, (1954).

Vekarić, S., 'Dubrovačka trgovačka flota 1599 godine', *Anali Historijskog Instituta JA u Dubrovniku*, Vol. III, (1954).

Villari, L., *The Republic of Ragusa*, London (1904), 424 pp.

Vinaver, V., 'Dubrovacko-Albanski ekonomski odnosi krajem XVI veka', *Anali Historiskog Instituta u Dubrovniku*, god. I, Vol. I, Dubrovnik (1952), pp. 207–232.

Vinaver, V., 'Trgovina bosanskim robljem tokom XIV veka u Dubrovniku', *Anali Historijskog Institua u Dubrovniku* II, Dubrovnik (1953), pp. 125–147.

Vinaver, S., 'Sarajevski trgovci u Dubrovniku sredinom XVIII, veka', *Godišnjak Istorijskog Društva BiH*, Sarajevo (1954).

Vinaver, V., 'Ropstvo u starom Dubrovniku (1250–1650)', *Istoriski Pregled*, I, Belgrade (1954).

Vinaver, V., 'Hercegovačka Trgovina sa Dubrovnikom Početkom 18 veka', *Istoriskog Instituta Narodne Republike*, god, VIII, knjiga XI, No. 1–2, Cetinje (1955), pp. 65–94, *Istoriski Zapisi*.

Vinaver, V., 'Crno roblje u starom Dubrovniku (1400–1600)', *Istoriski Časopis SAN*, V (1955).

Vinaver, V., 'Dubrovnik i Turska u XVIII veku', SAN *Seperat*, No. CCCXXXI, Historiski Institut, knj. II, Belgrade (1960), 316 pp.

Vinaver, V., 'O Jevrejima u Dubrovniku u XVIII veku', *Jevrejski Almanah*, Belgrade (1959–1960).

Vinaver, V., 'Bosnia i Dubrovnik 1595–1645', *Godišnajak Društva Istoričara Bosne i Hercegovine*, Godina XIII, Sarajevo (1962), pp. 199–232.

Vinaver, V., 'Dubrovačka Trgovina u Srbiji i Bugarskoj Krajem XVII veka (1660–1700)', *Istoriski Časopsis* Nos. XII–XIII Belgrade (1963), pp. 18–30.

Vojnović, K., 'O državnom ustrojstvu republike dubrovačke', *Rad JA*, Vol. 103, (1891), pp. 24–67.

Vojnović, K., 'Sudbeno ustrojstvo republike dubrovačke', *Rad CV*, Zagreb (1891–(1893), pp. 1–48; CVIII, pp. 99–181; CXIV, pp. 159–220; CXV, pp. 1–36; 191–210.

Vojnović, K., 'Crkva i država u dubrovačkoj republici', *Rad*, CXIX (1894), pp. 32–142; CXXI (1894), pp. 1–91.

Vojnović, K., 'Carinski sustav dubrovačke republike', *Rad JA*, Vol. 129, (1896), pp. 90–171.

Vojnović, K., 'Državni rizničari republike dubrovačke', *Rad JA*, Vol. 127 (1896); *Starine JA*, Vol. 28, (1896).

Vojnović, L., 'Della natura, origine ed estensione dei diritti ed obblighi fra proprietari e contadini del circolo di Ragusa, e quindi sulla questione se il nuovo acquirente di una casa di contadini possa farsi presare dall'abitante di essa la servitù sulle proprie terre; con alcuni cenni sulla natura, proprietà e qualità delle terre coloniche a Ragusa', *L'Avvenire*, suppl. al No. 4, Sabbato 26, agosto Ragusa (1848).

Vojnović, L., *Dubrovnik i Osmansko carstvo* Prva knijga: od prvoga ugovora s Portom do usvojenja Hercegovine (1365-1482), S. kr. A. Belgrade (1898).

Vojnović, L., 'Bratovštine i obrtne korporacije u republici dubrovačkoj od XIII do konca XVIII vijeka', *Monumenta Historico-Juridica Slavorum Meridionalium JA*, Vol. 7, I, (1899); Vol. 7, II, (1900).

Vojnović, L., *Louis XIV et Raguse*, Paris (1907).

Vojnović, L., *Pad Dubrovnika*, I–II, Zagreb (1908).

Vojnović, L., 'Prva smrt Dubrovnika', Летопис Матице Српске; књ. 287/8. Нови Сад, (1912).

Vojnović, L., 'Les "Angevins" à Raguse (1384–1385)', *Revue des Questions Historiques*, Année 47, pp. 361–388; Année 48, pp. 5–37, Paris (1913).

Vojnović, L., 'Dubrovačko-gruške prodaje kuča i ulice staroga Dubrovnika', *Rad JA Znanosti i Umjetnosti* knjiga 196, Zagreb (1913).

Vojnović, L., *La Monarchie Française dans l'Adriatique* Paris (1918).

Vojnović, L., *Dubrovnik Jedna Istorijska Šetnja*, Dubrovnik (1922).

Vučetić, A., *Dubrovnik za Kandijskog Rata*, II dio, Č. K. Velikoga Državnoga Gimnazija, Dubrovnik (1896), 40pp.

Vučetić, A., 'Ukidanje Dubrovačke Republike 31.I. 1808', *Spomenica o Padu Dubrovačke Republike*, Dubrovnik (1908).

Vučičević-Bunića, N. G., *Grad Dubrovnik vlastelom u trešnji*, Ancona (1667).

Vujić, M., 'Prvo naučno delo o trgovini Dubrovčanina Benka Kotruljevića', *Glas SA*, Vol. LXXX, (1909).

Vukasović, V. V., 'Imena i prizimena zlatara u Dubrovniku XV v., *Zbornik iz Dubrovačke Prošlosti Milanu Rešetaru o 70-oj Godošnjici Života*, Dubrovnik (1931), pp. 67–72.

Vukasović-Vuletić, V., 'Bilješke o strankama u Dubrovniku početkom XIX vijeka', Spomenica o padu Dubrovačke Republike, Dubrovnik (1908).

Зечевић, М., *Ратовање Војислава Војиновића са Дубровником*, Belgrade (1908).

Numismatics

Adamović, V., *Della Monetazione Ragusea*, Dubrovnik (1874).

Codrington, O., *A Manual of Musulman Numismatics*, London (1904).

Colich, J., 'Coins of Dubrovnik', *Journal of Croatian Studies*, Vols. IX–X, New York (1968–1969), pp. 160–173.

Kopač, V., 'Pregled dubrovačkog novca', *Bilten Numizmatičkog Društva u Zagrebu*, Vol. 3, Zagreb (1963).

Metcalf, D. M., *Coinage in the Balkans, 830–1355*, Institute of Balkan Studies, No. 80, Thessaloniki (1965), 286 pp.

Nagy, J., 'Prva Utanačenja izmedju Bosanskih Banovca i Dubrovnika', *Zbornik iz Dubrovačke Prošlosti Milanu Rešetaru o 70-oj Godišnjici Života Prijatelji i Učenici*, Dubrovnik (1931), pp. 25–32.

Rešetar, M., *Dubrovačka Numizmatika*, Vol. I, Sremski Karlovci, Vol. II, Belgrade (1925).

Rešetar, M., 'Najstarije Dubrovačke Mince', *Numizmatika* ii–iv, Belgrade (1934–1936), pp. 65–69.

Rešetar, M., 'Početak Kovanja Dubrovačkoga Novca', *Rad JA Znanosti i Umjetnosti*, Vol. CCLXVI, Zagreb (1939), pp. 149–170.

Rešetar, P., *La Zecca della Repubblica di Ragusa*, Split (1892).

Saria, B., 'O Težini Najstarijih Dubrovačkih Dinara', *Zbornik iz Dubrovačke Prošlosti Milan Rešetar*, Dubrovnik (1931), pp. 39–42.

Vinaver, V., 'Monetarna kriza u Turskoj (1575–1650)', *Istoriski Glasnik Srbije*, 3–4, Belgrade (1958).

Vinaver, V., 'Cene i Nadnice u Dubrovniku XVIII veka', *Istoriski Časopis* SAN, knijiga IX–X, Belgrade (1959), pp. 315–335.

Architecture and Sculpture

Beretić, L., *Dubrovački Graditelj Paskoje Miličevic*, Split (1948).

Beretić, L., *Utvrđenja Grada Dubrovnika*, J.A.Z.U. Zagreb (1955). 247 pp.

Dobrović, N., *Dubrovački Dvorci*, Belgrade (1946).

Eitelberger von Edelberg, R. von, 'Kunstdenkmale Dalmatiens', Vol. IV, *Gesammelte Kunsthistorische Schriften*, Wien (1884).

Fisković, C., *Naši graditelji i kipari u XV i XVI stoljeću u Dubrovniku*, Zagreb (1947).

Fisković, C., *Prvi poznati dubrovački graditelji u Dubrovniku*, Dubrovnik (1956).

Zravković, I., *Dubrovački Dvorci*, Belgrade (1951).

Literature

Albrecht, E., 'Das Türkenbild in der ragusanisch-dalmatinischen Literatur des XVI Jahrhunderts', *Slavistische Beiträge*, Band 15, München (1965).

Deanović, M., 'Les influences italiennes sur l'ancienne littérature yougoslave', *Revue de Littérature Comparée* XIV, Paris (1934).

Medini, M., 'Damjan Juda', *Dubrovnik*, I, Dubrovnik (1929), pp. 138–143,

Medini, M., 'Dubrovnik Gučetica', *Posebna Izdanja SAN*, Vol. XXX, Belgrade (1953).

Petrovskij, N., 'O genealogiji Držića', *Rad*, CXLVIII, (1902), pp. 227–230.

Puipin, A. N., and Spasowicz, W., *Geschichte der Slavischen Literatur*, Leipzig (1880).

Rešetar, M., 'Jezik Marina Držića', *Rad*, CCXLVIII (1933), pp. 92–128.

Vaillant, A., 'Les origines de la langue littéraire ragusaine', *Revue des Études Slaves* IV, Paris (1924), pp. 222–251.

Painting

Freeman, E., *Sketches from the Subject and Neighbour Lands of Venice*, London (1881).

    Galleria di Ragusei Illustri, Ragusa (1841).

Karaman, L., 'O staroj slikarskoj školi u Dubrovniku', *Anali Historijskog Instituta u Dubrovniku JA*, Vol. 2. (1953).

Karaman, L., 'Stari dubrovački slikari', *Hrvatska Revija*, Vol. XVI, No. 3, (1955).

Kovać, K., 'Nikolasu Ragusinus und sine Zeit', *Jahrbuch der Zentralkommission*, Beiblatt Wien (1917), pp. 1–94.

Prijatelj, K., 'Slikari XVII i XVIII stoljeća u Dubrovniku', *Starohrvatska Prosvjeta* III series, No. I, (1949).

Prijatelj, K., 'Prilozi slikarstvu XV–XVII st. u Dubrovniku', *Historijski Zbornik*, Vol. IV, (1951).

Prijatelj, K., *Dalmatinska slikarska škola mogućnosti* (1955).

Prijatelj, K., *Umjetnost 17 i 18 stoljeća u Dalmaciji*, Zagreb (1956).

Tadić, J., *Graeca o slikarskoj školi u Dubrovniku XIII–XVI vek*, Belgrade (1952).

This Bibliography does not claim to be a complete list, nor does it include all the books, pamphlets, and articles that have been consulted in compiling this work, but it should be sufficient as a guide for those who wish to go deeper into the subject.

Index of Persons

Subject Index